Lab Worksheet for the Waveform Decoding Exercise

This sheet offers waveform representation of a single small Ethernet frame as captured from a 10BASE2 network segment using a digital storage oscilloscope. The actual frame captured is available for download from the resources section of the book's website, and is used for lab module 4 when the results of the hand decode are compared with the protocol analyzer d

The source MAC address in this frame begins with 00000Cxxxxxx.

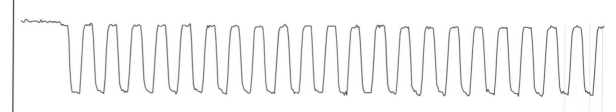

Part 1

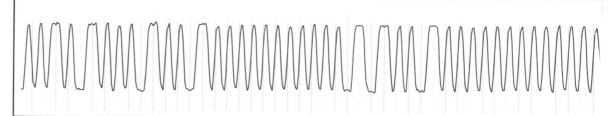

Part 2

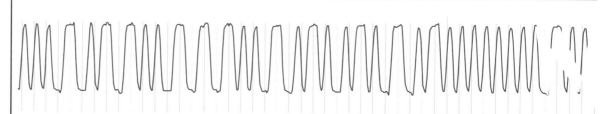

Part 3

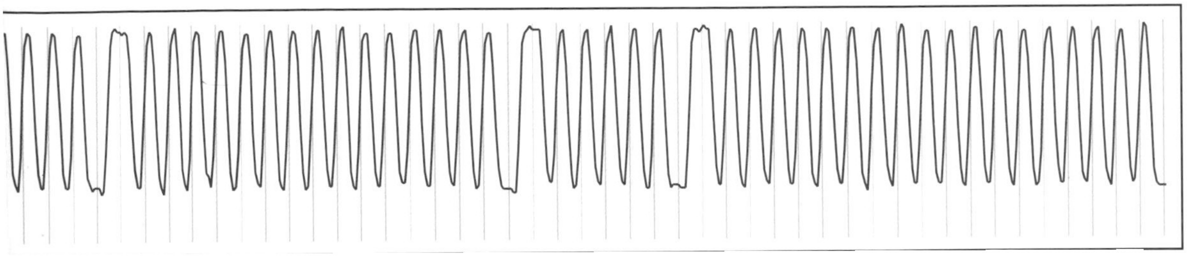

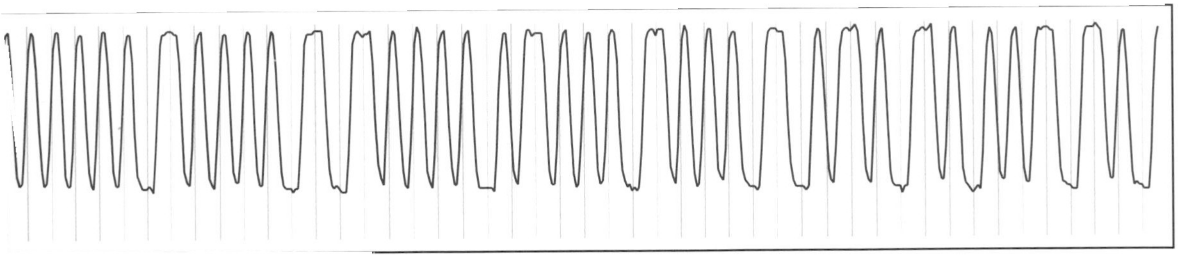

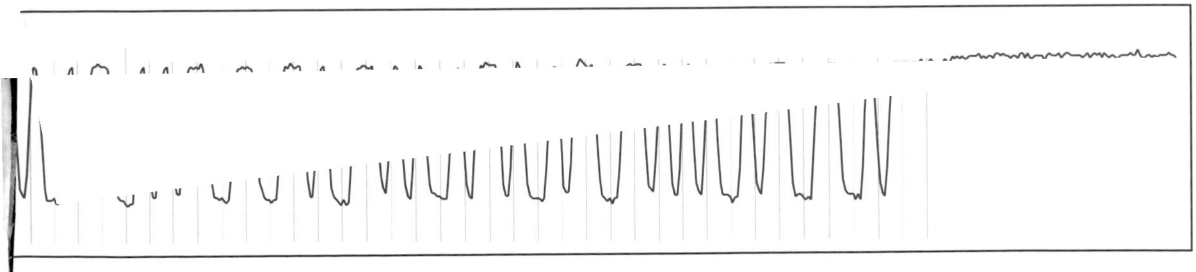

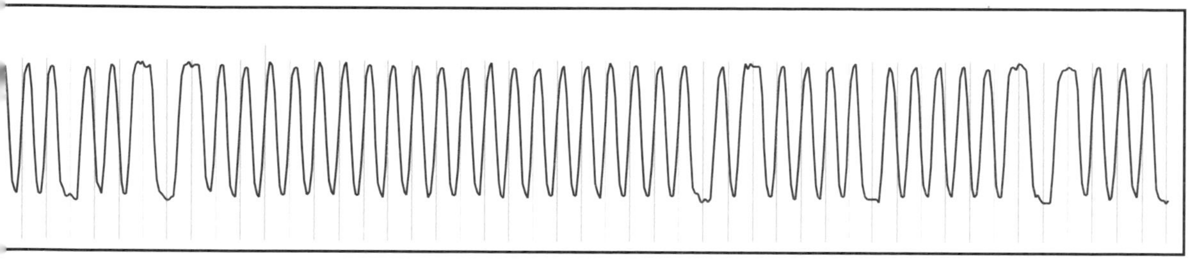

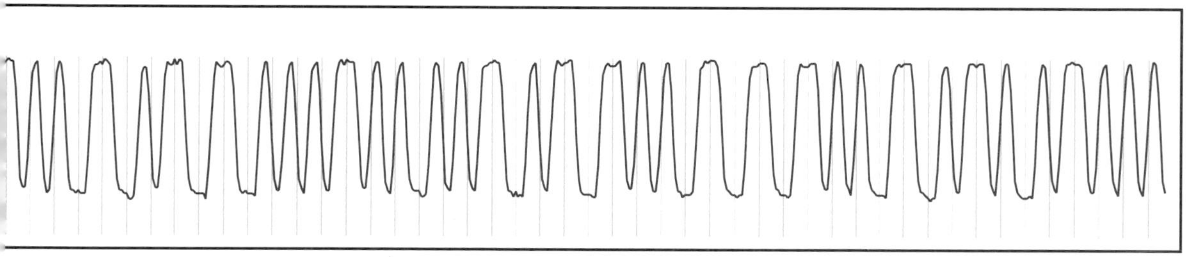

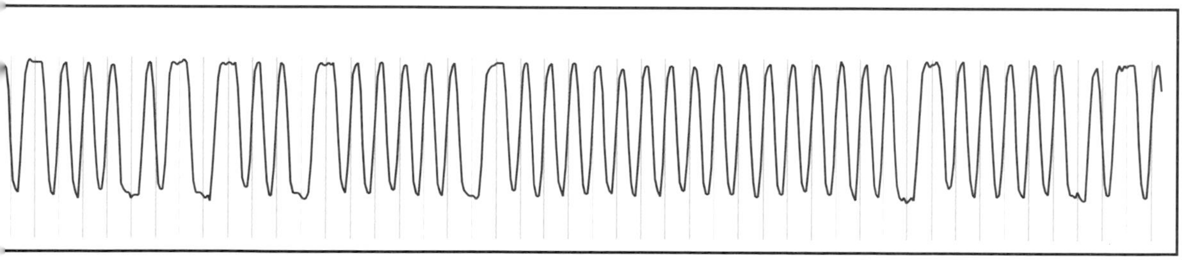

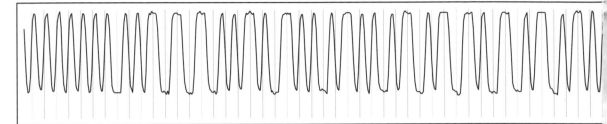

Part 4

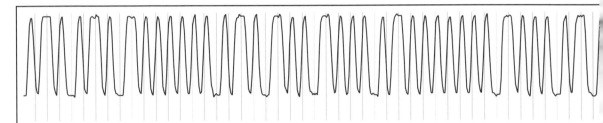

Part 5

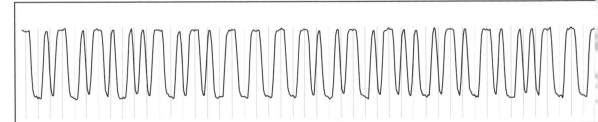

Part 6

code.

Praise for Neal Allen's *Network Maintenance and Troubleshooting Guide*

"This is one of the most informative and easy to learn books on networking basics and troubleshooting techniques. A must read for all new associates to the field of Networking."

—Javier Garcia, CCNA

"I can best summarize this book by quoting Arnold Glascow: 'Success is simple. Do what's right, the right way, at the right time.'"

—Heriberto Rebollo, Network Analyst

"The new version of the *Guide* brings hard-to-gather theory to bear on issues of practical importance."

—Dennis C. Frezzo, Ph.D.

Network Maintenance and Troubleshooting Guide

Network Maintenance and Troubleshooting Guide

Field-Tested Solutions for Everyday Problems

Second Editon

Neal Allen

✦ Addison-Wesley

Upper Saddle River, NJ • Boston • Indianapolis • San Francisco
New York • Toronto • Montreal • London • Munich • Paris • Madrid
Cape Town • Sydney • Tokyo • Singapore • Mexico City

U.S. Corporate and Government Sales
(800) 382-3419
corpsales@pearsontechgroup.com

For sales outside the United States please contact

International Sales
international@pearson.com

Visit us on the Web: informit.com/aw

Library of Congress Cataloging-in-Publication Data is on file.

Copyright © 2010 Pearson Education, Inc.

Pearson Education, Inc
Rights and Contracts Department
501 Boylston Street, Suite 900
Boston, MA 02116
Fax (617) 671 3447

ISBN-13: 978-0-321-64741-2
ISBN-10: 0-321-64741-6
Text printed in the United States on recycled paper at RR Donnelley, Crawfordsville, IN.

Editor-in-Chief
Karen Gettman

Acquisitions Editor
Jessica Goldstein

Development Editor
Sheri Cain

Managing Editor
Patrick Kanouse

Senior Project Editor
Tonya Simpson

Copy Editor
Mike Henry

Indexer
Tim Wright

Proofreader
Kathy Ruiz

Publishing Coordinator
Romny French

Book Designer
Louisa Adair

Compositor
Bronkella Publishing

Contents at a Glance

Contents

Acknowledgments

Many people won't be mentioned here, mostly because this book has grown and evolved from hundreds of comments, corrections, short training sessions (given and received), opportunities to help troubleshoot something, and many other sources over many years. I could not possibly remember them all. If you taught me some of that information, thank you. Some of the significant contributors (knowingly or otherwise) I remember specifically include

- The volunteer NOC team at the Interop trade show—thank you for regularly scheduling network emergencies! Too many to name specifically.
- Coworkers at Fluke Networks, especially Hugo Draye, Tami Settergren, Dan Klimke, and Pat Donahoo (each for different types of contribution).
- The University of New Hampshire Interoperability lab, especially Bob Noseworthy and Ben Shultz.
- My reviewers, especially Nolan Fretz, who took a lot of extra time to point out where some really obscure details were wrong.

About the Author

Neal Allen is a senior staff engineer in the Technical Assistance Center (TAC) at Fluke Networks in Everett, Washington focusing on escalated issues related to Fluke Networks' server-based monitoring solutions. His responsibilities in TAC are the particularly difficult or obscure problems, both phoned in and at various customer sites around the world. He also works closely with the design engineers on new product or feature specifications and later on alpha and beta testing of the same. Previously he was a product manager for handheld network analyzers. His responsibilities in marketing were "anything the engineers don't do," including market research, writing manuals and literature, helping to specify and beta test new products and product features, attending and delivering papers at trade shows, and providing both training and sales support worldwide. Allen has been involved in network design, installation, and troubleshooting for nearly 20 years. Although his focus has been primarily OSI Layer 3 and below, he has also designed and taught a number of short seminars and a three-quarter introductory networking course at local community colleges. Allen has been a member of the Interop trade show NOC (Network Operations Center) team since 1993 and, in addition to other responsibilities, is responsible for troubleshooting show-floor problems at the Las Vegas and New York Interop trade shows. Allen was chosen to help support and troubleshoot the network for the 1996 Atlanta Olympic Games.

How would you troubleshoot your network if denied the console password?

Introduction

Network Maintenance and Troubleshooting Guide: Field-Tested Solutions for Everyday Problems is not about routers or operating systems. Fluke Networks specializes in network diagnostic and monitoring tools, so the focus this book provides is on those areas, which have not been as well served by other industry publications and training. Although I have noticed that many networking professionals have either forgotten or never knew much of the material, the book presents some of the knowledge and skills that are most needed by a network technician.

Here's an example: I was fortunate enough to be allowed to help support the 1996 Olympics in Atlanta. The network engineers who deployed the network were very knowledgeable about architecture, design, and equipment configuration, but seemed oddly unaware of some of the basics. The following incident marked the beginning of my suspicion that this was a common situation.

Several of the competition venues were experiencing exceptionally high levels of MAC Layer errors. Walking onto the grounds for one of the venues I observed that network cabling around the site was carefully placed up against walls and fences to protect it from being walked on. We went into the local wiring closet and looked at the errors being reported by the network infrastructure equipment. I left the network engineer checking the configuration of the routers and other gear, looking for clues to the problem.

I walked around the venue following the cables. For at least half of the cable path, I found the network cable lying on top of a considerable sprawl of 208-volt power lines that also followed the walls and fences to where they were needed. As I walked around the field I moved the network cables as far from the power lines as I could without placing them at risk for damage. When I returned from my walk, the engineer commented something about how the error level was pretty bad when we got there, but sort of faded away while he was troubleshooting. I related how the errors pointed to AC power or other noise source as a likely cause of the errors, and what I had done.

To my great surprise, I had to explain the characteristics of each of the reported errors, and how the errors suggested the power lines as a likely cause of the problem. I since came to realize that even when people I met had vastly more knowledge about many networking topics than I, it was still possible they had little or no knowledge about the basics presented in this book. Or just as likely, they learned this information a long time ago but have since forgotten it.

In order of appearance, this book is written for the following three purposes:

- Basic networking skills training textbook
- "Triage" guide for new network technicians or managers of a small network
- Reference for networking professionals

This book is an introductory-level text, which means "make it simple." This concept of "simple" has been challenged almost every time it was made. The most difficult job in writing the book was to decide what to condense to a few often overly simplistic statements or exclude altogether. Still, many readers will find the level of complexity to be a challenge with even what little was retained as "the simple version." Reading passages multiple times has been reported as an effective method for eventually grasping most of, if not all, the content. Still, be warned that although every effort was made to ensure accuracy, it is sadly true that anything printed undoubtedly has inadvertent errors, important omissions, and superseded facts. Your challenge is to learn enough to be capable of identifying them.

Knowing where to obtain accurate information about networking topics is a critical skill. References are provided for many details within this book as a starting point for further reading because it was so hard to locate them in the first place.

Boundaries

The majority of the information about troubleshooting OSI Layers 1–3 can be generic in nature. After you cross certain boundaries, the discussion requires that a problem be fully defined before the discussion can continue. For example, application troubleshooting requires a detailed description of the exact application, installation, configuration, and usage patterns before a troubleshooting discussion can commence. Troubleshooting data flow from a PC to a server on the same broadcast domain does not. Troubleshooting data flow between a PC and a server separated by a router might require some additional details, depending on whether advanced functions are enabled (such as access control lists [ACLs], firewalls, or load balancing).

Similarly, as soon as you depart from how data traverses a routed network and enter a discussion about how the routers should be configured, you must provide a detailed description of the routing protocols used, vendor router models and versions involved, and so on before you can effectively discuss the configuration or troubleshooting of the configuration.

The topics in this book tend to stop at those boundaries. This is for the reason stated (you have to define the problem first), and also because once you reach those boundaries there are existing vendor training courses and vendor or industry certifications that cover the topics more effectively. The lack of extensive details on 802.11 wireless is perhaps the most noteworthy example of what is omitted, but very good wireless certification courses are available.

Media Standards Development

This is a politically sensitive topic because the whole issue of cabling standards development is as much driven by politics as technology, but still bears mention. Analysis of the general evolution of cabling standards suggests that the following may be true:

- The research into emerging new cable technologies is arguably pushed forward more by the Telecommunications Industry Association (TIA) than the International Organization for Standardization (ISO) because the TIA working groups meet more frequently. The Institute of Electrical and Electronics Engineers (IEEE) plays an important role, too, because the new networking implementations often drive some of the changes to cabling standards.

- Other national standards appear to leverage the information found in the TIA and ISO standards bodies' results, and then apply additional research in specific areas or apply modifications suitable for the local in-country electrical codes and requirements.

As a result of this nonscientific determination, the cabling references in this book will be largely made using TIA cabling standard references. Also, Fluke Networks is more closely involved with the TIA standards and working group documents, and subject matter experts are readily available.

Terms

One of the more confusing things about learning networking is the way terms are always changing. Compound this with the common practice of incorrectly using terms for the topic of discussion, or using correct terms to describe related areas where the term is imprecise or inaccurate. Finally, acronyms have an amazing capability to look the same, despite having completely different meanings if the entire terms are given. There are many examples of a single networking acronym having multiple uses depending on the context.

If care is taken to stay with proper terminology use, the movement of data through the OSI Model is accompanied by changes in terms as the data passes between layers. In common speech, this would be somewhat confusing, especially to someone new to networking. Understanding that terms are used very casually will greatly assist your ability to follow the conversation without becoming confused. In general discussion, try to focus on the conversation topic and less on the terms. If the situation relates to training, hold the instructor accountable to present new information using the correct terminology and ask for clarification often.

As an example, the words *frame* and *packet* are perhaps the most common terms used to describe a unit of data sent over the network. The following are listed terms taken from the standards documents used to define networking, and are thus the "correct" term used at each stage at which the unit of data travels. In a discussion, *frame* and *packet* may be used loosely to describe a unit of data, and might not be being used specifically to identify the OSI layer at which the transfer is being discussed. It is easy to imagine that changing terms during a short discussion to maintain strict accuracy would likely prove more confusing than enlightening.

Physical Layer

The term *packet* describes an 802.3 Ethernet transmission event that includes all Ethernet fields from the Preamble to the Frame Check Sequence (FCS). The Preamble and Start of Frame Delimiter (SFD) fields are timing information and are discarded later, but are included in a *packet*.

Media Access Control (MAC) Layer Within the Data Link Layer

The term *frame* describes the portion of an 802.3 Ethernet transmission event after the timing information has been discarded. The fields from the destination address to the FCS are counted, and tested for errors and against minimum and maximum size limits at the MAC Layer, and are described as a *frame*.

Logical Link Control (LLC) Layer Within the Data Link Layer

The 802.2 standard uses *protocol data unit* (PDU) to describe a transmission handled by the LLC Layer.

Network Layer

Internet Protocol (IP) (see RFC 791 for more information) uses *datagram* to describe a transmission unit handled by the Network Layer.

Transport Layer

User Datagram Protocol (UDP) (see RFC 768) uses *datagram*, whereas Transmission Control Protocol (TCP) (see RFC 793) uses *segment* to describe a transmission unit handled by the Transport Layer.

A level of imprecision also appears in relation to terminology used to describe a device connecting to the network. It is not uncommon to have more than one term used in the same sentence and intended to apply to the same device.

At the Network Layer it is common to use *host* to describe any device participating in the IP protocol. At almost any layer it is just as likely to hear *device, station,* or a specific functional term such as *PC, router,* or *switch* to describe a device participating on the network. Again, understand that it is common to use these terms somewhat interchangeably in discussion, and that unless great precision is being used, any one of these terms (or others not mentioned) simply refers to a device connected to the network.

Another set of terms used in this book relates to the job performed. Job titles carry enormous significance in some organizations and little at others. The job descriptions that follow are used in this text and are based on routine tasks and network access. Adapt them to your organization as appropriate. (See the "What Tool to Start With" section at the beginning of Appendix H for more detailed descriptions.)

Help Desk

Daily routine involves helping users with the installed applications on their computer. A small amount of basic connectivity troubleshooting may be involved but is typically limited to obtaining link state from the network. Most activities are handled by telephone and by remote access sessions. If onsite support is appropriate, it is typically limited to the user's workspace and does not carry beyond the first switch port.

Network Technician

Daily routine involves interacting with Help Desk staff to carry problem resolution beyond the first switch port. The job responsibility of a technician is the network and not the user. Technicians may have the password to switches, but typically do not have router passwords. Responsibilities are typically restricted to a site.

Network Engineer

Daily routine involves configuration and maintenance of the routed infrastructure for a region or entire enterprise network. Some assistance is provided to technicians as problem escalation support. Network engineers are also involved in architecture design and planning for network expansion.

Network Manager

Daily routine involves liaison activities with the company management, collaboration with the network engineer at conceptual level, and policy development for all network support activities. Depending on personal technical qualifications, a network manager may or may not have switch and router passwords, but does not routinely change configurations even if passwords are available.

Organization

Other than the obvious adherence to how the OSI Model is organized, it might seem odd that the first eight chapters appear as a networking tutorial and the *good stuff* about troubleshooting and observed network behavior does not appear until close to the end of this book. There is a simple reason for this: The troubleshooting information will not be as effective unless the theory is understood first.

As a simple example, the Fluke Networks support line often receives calls that go something like this:

Caller: I have one of your (insert product name), and I would like some help finding the source of a broadcast storm.

Support: Would you start by describing the symptoms your (product) is displaying that indicate a broadcast storm?

Caller: (Product) is showing 100% broadcasts on my network.

Support: And what is the network utilization?

Caller: <pause> ... That's odd. There is only 0.02% utilization.

Support: Are you connected to a switch?

Caller: Yes, but why do you ask?

The next few minutes are spent explaining how bridges operate. After reading this book, it is hoped that you will see humor in that support call. There are several common networking scenarios that appear in support calls and are similar in nature to the incident described—all of which are resolved by explaining basic networking principles to the caller. They tend to fall into two categories: a lack of understanding of the basic principles, which leads to incorrect conclusions; and a lack of understanding of the normal causes of observed symptoms, which prevents formulation of a troubleshooting plan. One follows the other.

The OSI Model presents a common framework for how similar or dissimilar networks may be described and interconnected. The model further provides boundaries where certain types of information is handed off under specific conditions. This model is a critical part of learning networking, although most beginning students see it as a boring waste of time. Because the OSI Model is the roadmap for all of networking, it is presented first. Without the OSI Model, it is particularly difficult to integrate networking theory and specific product information into an internally understood flow or process that will help you do your job.

Following the OSI Model you will find what amounts to the theory of operation for cabling, Ethernet, bridging and related protocols, and so on, up to OSI Layer 4. As mentioned earlier, it is not possible to cover everything. Look on this book as an introduction to networking, which uses TCP/IP and Ethernet operating over either twisted-pair or fiber optic cable systems as the example.

The troubleshooting section (Chapters 9–11) attempts to follow the same OSI Model order, although the material in Chapter 11 is separated into several different approaches or views. Troubleshooting is largely limited to ensuring that there was end-to-end delivery across the network infrastructure. Troubleshooting of higher-layer problems (OSI Layer 5 and higher), and modifications to end-to-end delivery, such as quality of service and security, are all outside the scope of this book.

At one time or another, most experts comment that "the more I learn, the more I realize I don't know." It is hoped that when you reach the end of a section or chapter you will realize that there is a lot which was not covered. When you reach the end of a chapter you should be full of unanswered questions. Enough references are cited that you should have an idea of where begin looking for answers.

Technical Details

There is a strong presence of protocol and frame detail in this book. There are two reasons for this substantial addition to the book: Most of the protocols listed in this book are unknown to the average user, and only a few fields are known to many technicians. Having a simplified summary makes reading the standards easier.

One of the ways to learn how things work and behave is to learn how various categories of devices talk to other categories of devices on the network. If you know how the conversation or negotiation is supposed to go, and which conversations are expected between like and unlike device categories, it is a lot easier to discover what is wrong when the conversation or negotiation is not producing the desired results.

Success with protocol analysis often comes down to knowing a lot about each specific protocol, and protocol analyzers are one of the four fundamental tool groups used to support networks. As a result, a lot of basic protocol and field details are presented in this text to serve as a reference for networking professionals, as well as a source of instruction for novices. These details are carefully presented in context and by the correct OSI Layer where they appear.

In at least one place in this text the level of detail far exceeds that which an average network technician or engineer would use in the course of supporting a network. The level of detail in the Ethernet implementations section was provided because it is not commonly described anywhere else (except the hard-to-read 802.3 standard), and it helps the reader to understand why the media test standards are as stringent as they are. There is a statement immediately prior to the excessively detailed section advising the casual reader to skip much of it.

Conventions Used in This Book

This book is straightforward, with just a few conventions to watch for:

- **See references.** Throughout many sections within each chapter, you'll see cross-references to other documentation, which look like this: [See 802.1D]. If the topic is of special interest, if ambiguity remains after reading the section (much was summarized or skipped), or if detailed questions remain, the cited standard or other document represents a good place for further reading about that topic. In most cases the cited reference provides either the most appropriate starting place or the most complete description for the topic located during my research.

- Each chapter closes with the section, "Chapter Review Questions," which give you hands-on practice with the chapter's content. Here is a general legend that indicates the anticipated difficulty of each question:

 Concept reinforcement. This is supposed to be extremely easy.

 The concepts were presented, but you must apply them to answer this question.

 Challenge question. If you understood the information presented, it *is* possible to answer this question.

Supplemental Materials

Visit this book's website at www.informit.com/title/9780321647412 for supporting materials, including supplemental charts and graphs.

CHAPTER 1
Using the OSI Model

This book, and most other things related to networking, is best understood when aligned with or compared to the Open Systems Interconnection (OSI) Model for network communications.

In fact, it is exceptionally frustrating to troubleshoot today's networks without understanding exactly which layer(s) each of the network infrastructure devices operate at and how that affects the flow of traffic and errors.

Quick Tour of the OSI Model

The OSI seven-layer basic reference model (see Figure 1-1) was created by the International Organization for Standardization (ISO) as standard ISO/IEC 7498. At the time of its creation the various networking protocols available were proprietary and offered little or no interoperability. The OSI seven-layer model has since become the most common reference point used when discussing network protocols, features, and hardware.

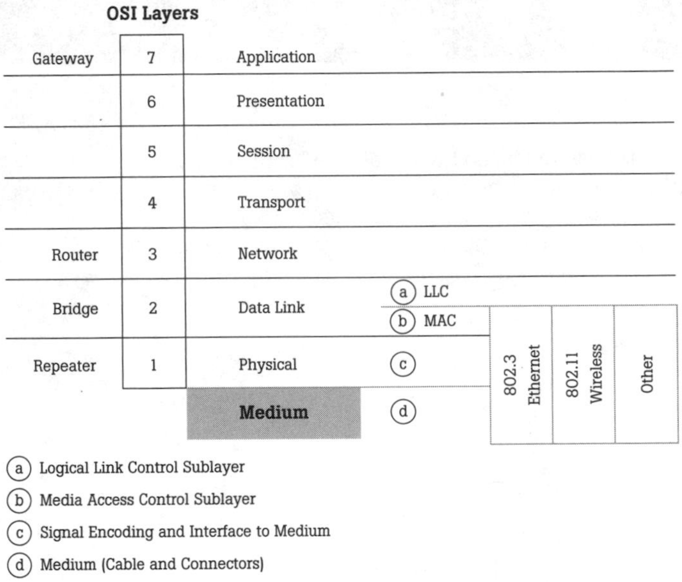

OSI Layers

Gateway	7	Application					
	6	Presentation					
	5	Session					
	4	Transport					
Router	3	Network					
Bridge	2	Data Link	(a) LLC				
			(b) MAC				
Repeater	1	Physical	(c)	802.3 Ethernet	802.11 Wireless	Other	
		Medium	(d)				

(a) Logical Link Control Sublayer

(b) Media Access Control Sublayer

(c) Signal Encoding and Interface to Medium

(d) Medium (Cable and Connectors)

Figure 1-1. *OSI seven-layer model compared to various interconnect device functions and media access protocols*

In Figure 1-1, the term *gateway* is used in this text at Layer 7, despite the terms *router* and *gateway* being used interchangeably to mean a Layer 3 device today. The use of *router* as the correct term for a Layer 3 device is supported by 802.2 Clause 6.3. These terms are used as shown to be able to draw a distinction between a device operating at Layer 3 and one operating at Layer 7 (such as where gateways have been deployed to translate between dissimilar systems, such as a gateway between DEC [ASCII codes] and IBM [EBCDIC codes] mainframe environments).

Note: *The layers depicted in Figure 1-1 explicitly separate the physical medium from OSI Layer 1, which is in accordance with ISO/IEC 7498 Clause 5.2.2. Descriptions of OSI Layer 1 within ISO/IEC 7498 cover all aspects of converting binary to signaling for the network, right to the connector on the host, but do not describe the medium. This separation of the physical medium from the seven OSI layers is different from most popular press renditions of the OSI Model.*

Other models are also referenced in relation to networking. The additional model, which is perhaps most often referenced, originated as part of the U.S. Department of Defense (DoD) Defense Advanced Research Projects Agency (DARPA) research into time-sharing computers across a national system, which later became the Internet. The DoD Model evolved in parallel with the OSI Model and shows its focus on Internet connectivity in how the lower and higher layers are not as well defined as the two required to route packets and establish host-to-host connections (see Figure 1-2). The additional detail provided by the OSI Model greatly helped multivendor networks to become interoperable.

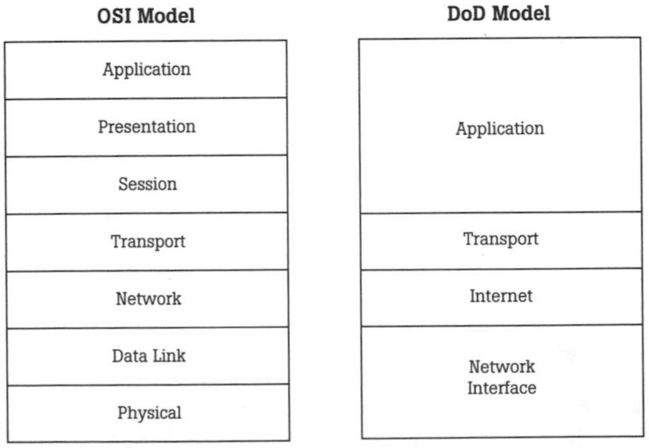

OSI Model	DoD Model
Application	
Presentation	Application
Session	
Transport	Transport
Network	Internet
Data Link	Network Interface
Physical	

Figure 1-2. *OSI seven-layer model compared to the DoD four-layer model*

Seven Layers of the OSI Model

Each layer of the OSI Model (except the Physical Layer) relies on the next lower layer to provide services as specified, but to perform these services in a manner that is transparent to the higher layer. For example, picture a higher layer opening a trap door and dropping a request in the form of a package with a note attached into a dark hole. The higher layer neither knows nor cares how the needed services are accomplished, as long as a response is received. Another analogy might be that of the relationship between a concierge at an exclusive hotel and a guest. The guest describes a desired want to the concierge and the request is granted. The process or actions used to procure the end result is unseen.

The definition for each layer that follows is only a simplified summary for that layer. For a more complete description of each layer in the OSI seven-layer model, see ISO/IEC 7498-1 or ITU-T X.200. Even summarized, the information is theoretical. To help demonstrate how the OSI Model can be used day to day, the text after the layer definitions offers a practical interpretation of how to use the model for day-to-day operations.

The important concept to learn from this section is that every layer interacts with the layer above and below it. If multiple vendors' products are integrated (software or hardware), the separation from one layer to another holds great importance. There are specific expectations at the boundary between layers, but anything happening inside a single layer or multiple layers that are implemented exclusively by that vendor is largely open to the interpretation of the vendor. As long as the boundary expectations are met at the hand-off point, the vendor is free to structure its product implementation any way it chooses. As a direct result of this boundary expectation, it became practical to assemble and operate multi-vendor networks. For the same reason, the OSI Model is commonly referenced for describing various networking products and how they operate.

Layer 7: Application Layer

Provides interface with network user

The Application Layer provides the means for an application to access network services. Generally, the application that the Application Layer assists would mean everything present in a standalone station (which has no network adapter), including the operating system and any software that is traditionally considered an application, such as a word processor or spreadsheet program. In this loose definition the word processor would reside at, say, Layer 9, and the operating system at, say, Layer 8. In practice, both software applications and the operating systems themselves have adopted services that would normally be considered part of the OSI Model into their basic structure. Other services that are not considered applications include file transfer and email, which have separately defined Layer 5–7 protocols. Of course, the user interface for those services is generally an application in this sense.

Services provided by the Application Layer include

- Quality of service
- Error recovery
- Synchronization
- Access control or authentication

This is accomplished by establishing communications with the Application Layer at the distant network resource.

Layer 6: Presentation Layer

Performs format and code conversion

The Presentation Layer provides services to the Application Layer. The Presentation Layer provides translation services as necessary to communicate requests to and from the Application Layer by establishing communication with the peer Presentation Layer in a distant network resource and reaching agreement on a common syntax and any data compression for transfers. The two Application Layers involved may use the same syntax, or they may each use a different syntax. For example, one station may be using the EBCDIC command and character set that was native for an IBM mainframe computer, and the other might be a PC using ASCII as the command and character set. The Presentation Layers involved would translate commands and character sets contained within the Application Layer's request or response as a routine function of passing traffic. The standard even allows the Presentation Layers to use a third command and character set between them if they choose to.

Layer 5: Session Layer

Manages connections for application programs

The Session Layer provides services to the Presentation Layer. The Session Layer contacts the peer Session Layer at the distant network resource to establish a communication session, determine whether both Presentation Layer entities can communicate simultaneously in full duplex or only in half duplex, to establish dialog synchronization and reset rules, and to identify how to release a connection. Session Layer activities are required for connection-oriented services, but very little is needed for connectionless services. The Session Layer performs segmentation and reassembly of data in connection-oriented mode. In connectionless mode, each transmission is passed directly through.

Layer 4: Transport Layer

Ensures error-free, end-to-end delivery

The Transport Layer provides services to the Session Layer. The Transport Layer contacts the Transport Layer at the distant network resource to establish, maintain, and release an end-to-end communication session with error recovery and flow control features for connection-oriented operation. The Session Layer may specify acceptable error rates, maximum delay, priority, and security as part of a quality of service request. Multiple independent and simultaneous connections are supported. For connectionless operation, the Transport Layer does not offer segmentation and reassembly of data, although it still provides error detection and monitoring of the quality of service.

Layer 3: Network Layer

Handles internetwork addressing and routing

The Network Layer provides the Transport Layer the functional and procedural means for one or more simultaneous connectionless or connection-oriented services. The Network Layer transfers information units of up to a maximum size between end systems in the same or different subnetworks for the Transport Layer.

The Network Layer operates independently of, and transparently to, the Transport Layer in all aspects except for providing the quality of service negotiated at the time communication to another end station is established.

A transfer may require hop-by-hop relay or routing service that is independent of the underlying communications media, although it may be necessary to mask differences between different transmission and subnetwork technologies to accomplish this.

The Network Layer establishes, maintains, and releases a logical communications link based on the Network Layer address of the destination through one or more point-to-point network connections. It provides flow control, error detection, recovery, and notification while implementing the delay, priority, and security as part of a quality of service negotiated by the Transport and Session Layers. The error detection may include any error notification provided by the Data Link Layer.

Network Layer addresses may be independent of the Data Link Layer addressing. Routing and relaying functions are provided by Network Layer entities that may span a variety of technologies in reaching the destination Network Layer address. The routing or relaying Network Layer entity determines an appropriate route between source and destination network addresses, and uses the services of the Data Link Layer to convey traffic as necessary. The relay or routing function may use parallel subnetwork connections. The Network Layer may segment, sequence, and block data to transfer it across subnetwork links.

Layer 2: Data Link Layer

Performs local addressing and error detection

The Data Link Layer provides services to the Network Layer. The Data Link Layer frames units of data up to a maximum size for transfer in a sequential order over one or more physical links using Data Link Layer addressing. The size of data units may be limited by the physical connection error rate. Data Link Layer connections are established, maintained, and released dynamically, and may be established for point-to-multipoint service such as multicasting. It may be necessary for an intermediate Data Link Layer entity to perform relay and routing services (bridging) to convey data through intermediate local area networks or across a circuit-switched network to the destination Data Link Layer address. The Data Link Layer performs error detection, recovery where possible, and reporting for transmission, format, and operational errors that may result from physical problems or problems within another Data Link Layer entity. Quality of service offered by the Data Link Layer includes throughput, delay, flow control, and service availability parameters.

Layer 1: Physical Layer

Includes physical signaling and interfaces

The Physical Layer provides services to the Data Link Layer. The Physical Layer takes bits from the Data Link Layer and transmits them in the same order received in serial or parallel to other Physical Layer entities synchronously or asynchronously, in half or full duplex. The transmission is made over the medium specified for that link, and using an encoding scheme suitable for producing a very low error rate. Each Physical Layer implementation includes specifications for such characteristics as link activation and deactivation, voltage levels, timing, data rates, maximum transmission distances, quality of medium, and connectors. It may be necessary for an intermediate Physical Layer entity (repeater) to perform relay services to reach another Physical Layer entity within a local area

or circuit switched network. Quality of service offered by the Physical Layer includes service availability, transmission rate, and transit delay.

Networking Devices and the OSI Model

For a network support person, a basic understanding of the implications of the OSI Model makes the difference between frustration and smooth operations. It is very difficult to maintain and troubleshoot a network without understanding the boundaries created by repeaters, bridges, routers, and switches.

Not separately described here, Layer 7 gateways used to be fairly common, but due to the prevalence of TCP they are not often seen now. A Layer 7 gateway completely reinterprets traffic at Layer 7 to allow communications between dissimilar network operating systems.

Repeaters

For a quick catch phrase, it could be said that *a repeater always forwards* a signal.

A hub is a multiport repeater for shared media (half duplex). Repeaters may also operate in full duplex (called a buffered distributor). Repeaters indiscriminately retransmit everything observed on one port to all other ports at the appropriate signal levels for the medium, regardless of any deterioration in the condition of the received signal. The signal is not retransmitted back out the port on which it was received. Repeaters attempt to forward everything, even if it does not remotely resemble the expected signal for that media access protocol. Part of the job of the repeater is to recondition the signal, which results in noise or other nondata signals being forwarded as meaningless groupings of proper signaling. Figure 1-3 shows where a repeater operates in the OSI Model.

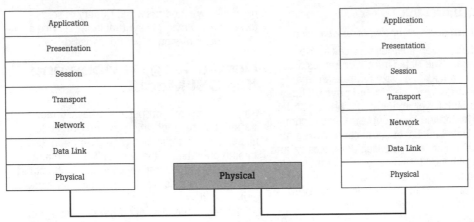

Figure 1-3. *Repeaters operate at the Physical Layer of the OSI Model*

It is not uncommon for one port of an Ethernet hub to detect noise from any number of sources (fluorescent lights, electrical power lines, radio transmitters, fans, vacuum cleaners, and so on). and to fabricate a signal to send to all other ports. This sounds like the description of a failed device, but it is the correct thing for a repeater to do. Because Ethernet implements CSMA/CD as a media access scheme, all stations connected within a collision domain must be informed when there is a signal present anywhere within the collision domain. By forwarding all signals to all parts of the collision domain, a repeater allows a transmitting station to become aware of problems during the transmission. This either causes a collision or occupies the available bandwidth with a manufactured signal (jam) for a time and thus prevents any other station from attempting to transmit. If a transmitting station becomes aware that a problem has occurred during its transmission, the Ethernet protocol can usually handle retransmission attempts. Retransmission attempts usually continue until the frame gets through, without incurring the delay associated with waiting for higher layers of the protocol stack to time-out and discover that the frame was not successfully transmitted.

Bridges

The catch phrase is *a bridge forwards unless there is a reason not to.*

A switch may be described as a multiport bridge, but assuming that your switch is acting as a full bridge is a bad idea from a troubleshooting perspective. Bridges act as boundaries for collision domains. Bridges are often used to block traffic that is local to one collision domain (both stations involved in the conversation are attached to the same physical network segment or port) from being sent to another collision domain or port. If the source and destination stations are not on the same collision domain or port, a bridge forwards traffic but prevents MAC Layer errors from being forwarded to other physical network segments. A bridge does not block broadcast traffic. Figure 1-4 shows where a bridge operates in the OSI Model.

By monitoring which MAC addresses are detected in the source address field of received traffic, bridges build and maintain a bridge forwarding table in accordance with IEEE 802.1D and are accessed by network management in accordance with RFC 1493. When a frame is received on one port a transparent bridge does two things. The bridge makes sure that the MAC address found in the Ethernet source address field is recorded in the bridge forwarding table as residing on that port. The bridge also checks the table to see whether the destination MAC address is known.

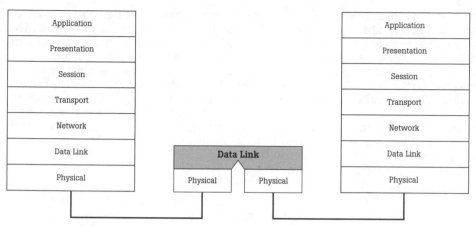

Figure 1–4. *Bridges operate at the Data Link Layer of the OSI Model*

Bridges forward all properly formed traffic if any one of the following three conditions is met:

- The destination is unknown.
- The destination address resides on a different port than the source address.
- The frame is a form of broadcast (under some circumstances multicast won't be forwarded).

If the destination MAC address is found on the same port as the source MAC address, the bridge or switch assumes that the frame has already been delivered and drops it. If the destination MAC address is found to reside on a different port, the bridge forwards the frame to the port where the address is known to reside. If the destination MAC address is unknown, the bridge forwards to all ports except the port on which it was received. A bridge also forwards all broadcast traffic to all ports except the port on which the traffic was received. Multicast is handled like broadcast unless IGMP snooping is on, and then only ports with subscribing stations receive the multicast stream. Because a bridge always forwards broadcasts, all bridges connected together are said to be part of a common broadcast domain. There is no limit to the number of bridges that may be connected together, although the level of broadcast traffic usually becomes the unofficial limiting factor. If Spanning Tree Protocol (STP) is used, the maxAge timer value may act as a limiting factor in how large the bridged topology may become. There are three common types of bridge: transparent, translating, and source-routed. Transparent bridging is usually used with Ethernet and has become the predominant bridging technique, although translating bridges are used between Ethernet and wireless segments (appearing as wireless access points).

Routers

The catch phrase is *a router will only forward if conditions require it.*

Unlike bridges, routers make forwarding decisions based on the OSI Layer 3 address (for example, IP or IPX) instead of the MAC address. A traditional router examines only traffic that the MAC Layer has found to be free of errors. Because the MAC Layer validates the traffic first, the Layer 3 routing software does not see a frame that is errored, is not addressed to the router's MAC address, or is not sent as a broadcast. If the frame was received in good condition, the router exercises a set of instructions in software (or in the hardware on recent routers) to make a forwarding decision. In some cases the frame may be forwarded back out the port on which it was received. Any number of configurations or network situations may cause the router to not forward the frame. One of the simplest causes for dropped frames is that the router does not know how to reach the destination. Another reason might be that the router has some security features enabled, such as an access list, and is administratively prohibited from forwarding the frame. Routers act as boundaries for broadcast domains. Figure 1-5 shows where a router operates in the OSI Model.

Using routers to segment networks solves one problem but creates others. Most notably, on older routers the routing decision took a lot of processor time and slowed traffic considerably (introduces latency). The latest generation of routers now makes most routing forwarding decisions in silicon at the ingress port at line rate, so this problem has diminished significantly. Routers may usually be configured to become fine general-purpose internetwork firewalls. They are very useful where the division of networks into logical groups must occur. Because routers operate at OSI Layer 3 they can effectively distinguish between, and separate traffic from, different logical networks. For example, Internet Protocol (IP) traffic can be separated from IPX, NetBEUI, and other kinds of traffic. When a protocol allows addressing divisions, such as IP subnets, they are handled similarly. Although this is considered a very poor design and a poor practice, for simple security, you could even use a router to isolate two departments from each other on the same broadcast domain by assigning each to a different subnet, and use

the router to permit data to pass from one logical network to the other on the same router port. The network administrator needs to take into account that routers are more expensive than bridges on a per-port basis. Furthermore, they are often unnecessary in situations where complex logical subnetting and exotic wide-area communications are not required. Use of VLANs may provide sufficient separation that use of routing is only needed for special circumstances.

Switches

Most people assume that a switch is not a bridge simply because it has more than two ports, but at the same time they describe a switch as being a Layer 2 device. A potentially more accurate view would be that a switch may be operating as a multiport bridge. However, because the term *switch* originated in the marketing department and has been used rather loosely there is no simple definition of a switch. A switch is not necessarily just a multiport bridge. Depending on available features and current configuration, a switch can operate at virtually any OSI layer from Layers 2 to 7. Furthermore, now that much of the forwarding decision logic is incorporated into the front-end silicon for each port instead of in software, the higher-layer functions are about as fast as the lower-layer functions. Functionality is often configurable on a per-port basis, so the

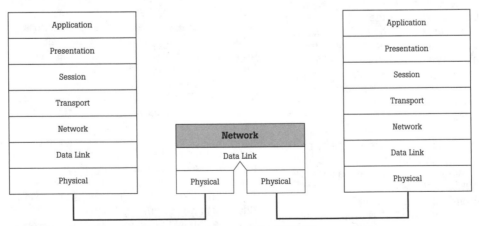

Figure 1-5. *Routers operate at the Network Layer of the OSI Model*

answer may change depending on which path is taken through a switch. If that were not enough, the type of traffic can affect the answer as well. Switches are available that allow different rules (such as a maximum bandwidth cap) for different protocols or users. An FTP file transfer might pass at 100Mbps from one port to another, but an HTTP exchange may only reach a configured limit of 5Mbps between the same two ports.

A simple description for what a Layer 2 switch does (in this case a multiport bridge), is that it creates private paths (direct bridged connections) to the requested server or service on the network, without having to share bandwidth with other devices. Although it may seem simplistic, this description is relatively close to the truth. Figure 1-6 shows a simple representation of this description.

Each station in Figure 1-6 is having a conversation with only one other station. In practice, however, instead of connecting with another single device on the network, most stations connect to one or more common servers or services. These connections are often made through a single port acting as an uplink to a router or to another switch. In this first bridge-like description of switch behavior, the forwarding decision is based on the MAC address.

Most recent switches have the capability to support Virtual LANs (VLANs). VLANs are nothing more than broadcast domains configured on a per-port or per-port-group basis. The only difference between this and a bridge is that all ports on the entire switch do not have to be in only one broadcast domain. You could go to the extreme of configuring a separate broadcast domain for each port, and use 802.1Q VLAN tagging on the uplink port to properly service them.

Traffic cannot pass from one VLAN (broadcast domain) to another without being redirected there by a router. Thus, there must be a router connected to both VLANs in order for traffic to be exchanged between them, even if both the source and destination stations in different VLANs are attached to the same switch but in different VLANs.

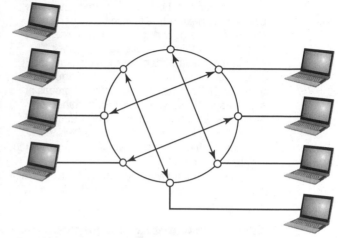

Figure 1-6. *Simple depiction of a switch creating private bridged connections between specific network devices*

Switches may offer full routing functionality. Older chassis-based switches offer optional router "blades" or cards that are actually a complete router. This type of switch typically has integrated functionality whereby after evaluating the first frame the router card can tell switch cards in the same chassis how to handle further frames in that transaction between the same two stations. This behavior avoids forcing each frame to be processed by the comparatively slow router software. Recent high-end switches have full and complex routing capabilities in the silicon that services each port.

Forwarding is also available based on Layer 4 protocols, or even Layer 5 to 7 protocols. Just like the Layer 3 forwarding description earlier in the chapter, these switches sometimes read just far enough into the frame to make the forwarding decision before actually starting to send the frame.

More advanced examples of these switches are often customized for specific applications, such as Internet service provider (ISP) data centers where a query to a popular web site is load balanced by the switch. The request is distributed by some sort of priority scheme between multiple servers performing the same function, transparently to the user. The switch may keep track of which server has the fewest active connections or is simply next in line to receive a query, and then sends the new request and all subsequent traffic related to that request to that server. The switch may even buffer frames to evaluate the content of the request and distribute requests to the least-busy server from different groups of service-specific servers based on whether the request was for text, graphics, video, audio, and so on, during the same session. Needless to say, troubleshooting this type of very advanced switch can be challenging.

However the forwarding decision is made, the switch still has to actually forward the frame.

Switch Forwarding Techniques

Operationally, there are two basic forwarding techniques used in switches (store-and-forward and cut-through), and two variations of the basic techniques (modified cut-through and adaptive or error-sensing). The names used to describe each of the techniques may vary.

Recent trends indicate that the popularity of low-latency forwarding is waning, and many vendors are now producing only store-and-forward type switches. This is very good news for troubleshooting. Each of the techniques are described in more detail in the sections that follow, as represented by Figure 1-7.

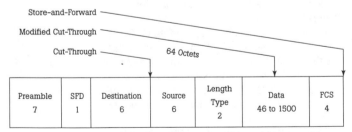

Figure 1-7. *Switch forwarding technique decision points for an Ethernet frame. Ethernet details are provided in Chapter 4.*

Store-and-Forward

A switch using store-and-forward reads the entire frame into a buffer and checks it for errors before forwarding the frame to the destination

port. This has an advantage of isolating collision domains because errored frames are not forwarded. The drawback, however, is that the latency is proportional to the length of the frame. A typical user will not notice this delay, which becomes more pronounced with each additional store-and-forward switch connected in series.

This is the technique used by a traditional OSI Layer 2 bridge for forwarding. Most vendors appear to have returned to offering only store-and-forward switches. This is presumed to be the result of marketing research that revealed that the average user does not notice the benefit provided by low-latency forwarding due to other network or server limitations, and the unwary person troubleshooting accuses the switch of misbehavior when they do not understand the implications of low-latency forwarding.

Cut-Through

A switch using cut-through makes the forwarding decision immediately after the destination MAC address has been read into the buffer. Because a cut-through switch starts forwarding before the complete frame is received, the frame may be forwarded with errors. The advantage is a low latency time because the frame is forwarded almost as soon as it arrives at the switch.

From a troubleshooting perspective, a cut-through switch behaves like a slow repeater. The effects of errors in the collision domain did not stop at the switch port. Monitoring the destination segment shows errored frames, and it can be challenging to properly identify its source. If a switch is being used to replace a shared-media hub, the number of errors is reduced from the level forwarded by the shared media hub for two reasons: Collisions appearing before or during the destination address will cause the frame to be discarded, and most forwarded errors are sent to only one other port instead of to all other ports. The attached network segment typically experiences a gain in performance even though some errors are still forwarded.

Modified Cut-Through

A switch using modified cut-through or *fragment free* offers a compromise between the store-and-forward and cut-through techniques. This switch buffers the incoming frame until the first 64 octets are received. Because contention for the Ethernet medium must be concluded within this time limit, this means that the switch effectively filters out collision fragments and the majority of errored frames.

From a troubleshooting perspective, this technique behaves as a slow repeater for legal sized frames, and again the effects of errors in the collision domain did not stop at the switch port. As with cut-through, some errors may cross into a different collision domain.

Error-Sensing or Adaptive

An error-sensing or adaptive switch represents another compromise and is available from some of the more expensive switches. This combination of techniques uses a low-latency technique while network conditions are good and store-and-forward when network conditions deteriorate. At some threshold level of detected errors the switch port dynamically changes techniques from a low-latency technique, usually cut-through, to store-and-forward. When local conditions improve and errors drop back below the threshold level, the port will resume using the low-latency technique. This configuration offers what is perhaps the best compromise of performance versus speed.

From a troubleshooting perspective, this type of switch causes an apparently intermittent problem to appear on the destination port or collision domain, and is thus a significant and frustrating troubleshooting challenge for anyone who is not familiar with this behavior. You cannot assume that errors from within a collision domain are blocked by a switch, as the switch is sometimes behaving like a very slow repeater.

Fortunately, new switches are almost always store-and-forward and the low-latency techniques are fading away.

Common Networking Tools

Choosing the right tool for the job is in part driven by where the tool fits the OSI Model the best. Some tools are a perfect fit for certain problems at specific OSI layers. Some tools are simply unsuited for some problems. Other tools may be used together to obtain multiple views of the apparent

problem. This section describes how the various tool categories may be applied to the OSI Model.

There are four major categories of networking tools: cable tester; protocol analyzer; network management; and flow protocols. Figure 1-8 shows the four major categories, plus the hybrid category of handheld network analyzer, which is also discussed in detail. Figure 1-8 shows where each type of tool is typically used and the relative frequency of problems at each layer. Notice that the majority of problems occur in areas where the user is able to easily interact with the network.

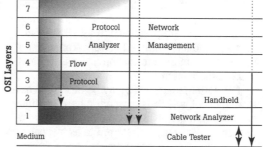

Figure 1-8. *Where common network tools fit "best" in the OSI seven-layer model, together with an estimate of where the majority of network problems occur*

A short description of each of the identified tool categories is provided.

Network Management Tools

Network management products may have functionality from Layer 1 up through Layer 7, but that depends on what is available to the network management console from each unique network. The software console typically has no view of the network itself, and usually relies on what agents around the network tell it. The accuracy of the information from a network management platform is therefore only as good as the agent providing the information, or as good as the message sent. A distinction is drawn because you may obtain different answers about a specific port or event depending on which question is asked (which Management Information Base [MIB] is used), and depending on whether the software or hardware in the reporting agent is operating correctly or is flawed or out of date. A network management console is a nice user interface sitting on top of a database of responses from a variety of network resources (agents). The capabilities of the network resource correlate directly to what information is available to network management, and in fact the information available to network management may be less than what the network resource is capable of. The specific features vary widely, although usually in direct relation to the cost of the product. Functionality is available from very low (free) for a simple fixed-feature set, to very high ($1,000,000 and more) for the flexible module-based Enterprise Applications. Network management concepts are presented in ISO/IEC 7498-4. (See Appendix F, "Simple Network Management Protocol," for more information about SNMP network management.)

Network management may be described as a strategic tool, which is most often used continuously for trend analysis. Most of the tool categories that follow may be referred to as tactical, and are usually used on an as-needed basis. Tactical tools are very mobile, whereas strategic tools tend to be permanently located.

Protocol Analyzers

Protocol analyzers are used to view the contents of individual frames taken from the medium and offer functionality from Layer 1 or Layer 2 up through Layer 7. They typically have a variety of built-in summary features that allow the user to see who is talking to whom, using which protocol, and how much. A key feature of a protocol analyzer is that exactly what is said may be viewed.

Protocol analyzers come in two general configurations:

- Software-based
- Hardware-based

The software-based protocol analyzer is usually unable to detect or report on MAC Layer errors because it is relying on a standard network adapter. For the same reason, software protocol analyzers tend to be somewhat limited in the amount

of traffic that can be captured. A typical network adapter is not well suited to capturing traffic at line rates because the operating system overhead and other activities the computer may be engaged in restrict its ability to process traffic at those rates. Furthermore, the internal bus may not be able to pass that much traffic from the NIC to the CPU. Because dropped frames are not reported, users do not often suspect that frames might have been dropped. Even when the user concludes that frame loss may have taken place, the user is left to guess where frames may be missing.

Conversely, hardware-based protocol analyzers usually have some level of integration with the front-end electronics and are able to see some or all of the errors on a link. The level of error detection is often related to the price. Because of this, hardware-based protocol analyzers are much more likely to be able to capture at line rates without dropping frames.

Both categories of protocol analyzer typically have several software modules that may be added at an extra cost. These range from support for multiple network access protocols and speeds (Ethernet, wireless, and so on), to specialized support for a protocol such as VoIP, or an integrated expert system that compares the contents of a captured trace file against libraries of common symptoms related to specific faults or causes. Once beyond the built-in or automated test summary functions, the ability to obtain useful information from a protocol analyzer is directly related to the user's knowledge about the inner workings of the protocol in question. For this reason, protocol analysis is usually the domain of the senior network support staff. Protocol analyzers are available to network management consoles in the form of remote network monitoring (RMON) agents.

Handheld Network Analyzers

Handheld network analyzers were created to bridge the skills gap between the senior network support staff and the Help Desk staff. They generally include the most commonly used features from the other three categories. The focus is to validate or troubleshoot end-to-end connectivity up through Layer 3. Additional functionality may be available at a higher cost from the other three categories, including models with broader feature sets.

The user interface is very simple and is designed for the lesser skilled technician, although senior staff will obtain more benefit from the information presented. At the low end of the category, the functionality tends to be fixed with few if any user adjustments possible. At the high end of the category, the user has considerable flexibility in modifying the testing process.

The ability to take advantage of customizing a given test is directly related to the skill level of the user. Cable test functionality is usually limited to nonfrequency-based testing. Protocol analysis is usually limited to activities performed internally by the tester but not exposed to the user, in a manner similar to the test summaries described for protocol analyzers. Network management is usually limited to basic information about a targeted device using standard MIBs with no ability to add private MIB support.

Cable Testers

Two groups of users generally use cable test products:

- The installer who is expected to certify the cable plant

- The network owner who is trying to restore network service or adding a few new runs

The cable installer needs a very high-performance product, with a simple pass/fail test result and the ability to store multiple test results.

The network owner is often attempting to resolve a failure involving a cable plant that was certified at the time of installation. This user is most interested in cable faults related to abuse and in solving problems such as opens, shorts, and miswires. For this sort of fault a lower functionality tester is adequate. However, the network owner is also often expected to install small numbers of additional cable runs, and needs the same level of certification tester as the installer for this job. Depending on the size of the network owner organization, one certification tester and several simple testers may be appropriate. Cable test

features of a hybrid handheld tester may satisfy the simple cable test needs.

Cable testers range from inexpensive and simple continuity testing that verifies a connection from one end of the cable to the other, to high-performance cable analyzers that use frequency-based testing to ensure compliance with the latest cable standards. Cable testers are only suitable for testing the media that network protocols run over, and are not suitable for testing network performance.

Flow Protocols

A recent addition to the list of available tools for network support is the category of flow protocols. When switches became common in the network infrastructure they greatly reduced the number of people affected by the typical network outage, but at the same time they made it very hard to troubleshoot because the data flowing on the network became isolated from monitoring tools.

The emerging solution to this problem is to ask the switch to provide summary reports on the traffic forwarded over all ports. The typical volume of summary traffic versus actual traffic monitored is about 3–5 percent. That is, if 100Mbps of traffic was being forwarded through a given switch port, the typical or average amount of summary information generated would be approximately 3–5Mbps. The summary information volume is dependent on the nature of the traffic forwarded by the port in question.

By having the switch infrastructure report on the activity related to some or all ports and send that activity summary information to a centralized monitoring station, the ability to "see" what a switch is doing became a routine part of network support. The level of visibility is in many ways equal to or better than RMON statistical data, but not as good as full protocol analysis. The significant advantage is that this data is available from the entire enterprise network at all times without having to solicit regular updates.

Flow protocols have varying levels of impact on the CPU of the switch providing the information, depending on which flow protocol is used and whether all data is reported or only a statistical sample is. The most common flow protocols report on any IP traffic and can break the summary down by Layer 3 and 4 protocols seen. Reporting at Layer 2 is available from at least one flow protocol.

Summary

Why was this information presented as the first chapter of this book?

The answer is simple. To understand how a network operates, you need a framework or outline into which you can store all subsequent information. To troubleshoot a network effectively, you must truly understand the boundaries where a particular symptom or error can or cannot pass. Failure to understand where those boundaries are or how to use them to your advantage greatly reduces your ability to work with networks. You would be unable to intelligently plan a new network or a network expansion, and you would be unable to effectively troubleshoot an ailing network.

A firm grasp of the boundaries created by the OSI Model, and the implications that those boundaries represent, makes the difference between frustration and success.

This book presents information in the same order that network troubleshooting should conceptually take place: from the cable upward. Note that the actual troubleshooting steps do not always start at the cable, only the conceptual thought process behind choosing which steps to take. In some instances your understanding of the boundaries created by the OSI Model enables you to perform one or two simple tests, and the results of those tests immediately rule out some layers as being suspects in a troubleshooting scenario. In other situations, a problem at a lower layer creates misleading symptoms at higher layers.

Your understanding of which OSI layers various categories of networking tools operate, their general features, and especially the limits of those tools is just as necessary. For example, even if you were a protocol genius, you probably would not be able to identify a Physical Layer problem with a typical software protocol analyzer because MAC Layer errors are almost always rejected by a standard network adapter. You would not see them.

Although the various tools may be employed in areas for which they were not optimized, there is a place where they fit best. There is no single tool that solves all your problems. Network management performs long-term trend analysis, and through that trend analysis can offer early warning for impending problems. Protocol analyzers show you exactly what the software is doing, regardless of what it said it did. Cable testers allow you to find the most obscure and mystifying cable fault because that is what they were designed to do. Handheld network analyzers bring the ability and knowledge of experienced network engineers into the hands of the front-line support staff, and allow front-line staff to solve many of the most common problems on their own—or at least permits them to intelligently describe the problem detected to senior support staff.

The greatest challenge a test tool faces is the person using it. A diagnostic or error message can be completely clear and precise, but if the technician does not understand the implications suggested by that diagnosis or error report then the tool is useless.

This chapter reviewed the following information:

- The OSI Model appears as a sequence of seven layers, each of which relies on the services of lower layers and provides service to higher layers. The tasks performed at each layer are not duplicated within other parts of the model. The lowest layers (up to the Network Layer) provide various services required for end-to-end delivery of data from one host to another, either across the local link or across the routed network. Layers above the Network Layer coordinate services with their peer services in the destination host. An understanding of the boundaries imposed by each layer is vitally important for someone supporting the network, as this knowledge imparts important clues about performance problems and also provides guidance in planning changes to the network.

- Network infrastructure devices operate in accordance with the OSI layer(s) where they participate. That is, there are exact expectations for behavior that relate directly to the OSI layer for which the infrastructure device is designed to operate. Switches break this expectation in part because they may have features that touch on multiple OSI layers. This in turn places greater requirements for support staff to understand the impact of features configured within their switched infrastructure or the observed network behavior will not make sense.

- Tools used to monitor and troubleshoot networks are also bound by the rules imposed on the OSI layers on which the tool has visibility, or from which the tool is obtaining data from the network infrastructure. Successful tool use is therefore dependent on the behavior of the infrastructure, and then further dependent on the capabilities of the tool. Failure to understand the implications of behavior from the OSI Model perspective, and failure to understand the configuration of the network infrastructure in accordance with the OSI Model boundaries and limitations, may lead to improperly applying various tool capabilities. You might not observe a network problem simply because the approach is incorrect—even when you have the best vantage point for seeing the problem.

The OSI Model is not considered an exciting aspect of networking, but understanding it is critical.

Chapter Review Questions

To aid in your comprehension of important concepts, the following questions are provided. Refer to this book's Introduction for a general legend that indicates the anticipated difficulty of each question. For answers to these review questions, see Appendix I, "Answers to Chapter Review Questions."

 1. Which standards define the much-referenced OSI Model? List both an OSI standard and an ITU standard.

 2. What is one of the benefits provided by the OSI Model, a benefit that has long outlived the actual OSI protocol?

 3. Where does a patch cable fit in Figure 1-1, and what OSI layer is its performance governed by?

 4. Provide a simple sentence that summarizes the function of OSI Layer 7.

 5. Provide a simple sentence that summarizes the function of OSI Layer 6.

 6. Provide a simple sentence that summarizes the function of OSI Layer 5.

 7. Provide a simple sentence that summarizes the function of OSI Layer 4.

 8. Provide a simple sentence that summarizes the function of OSI Layer 3.

 9. Provide a simple sentence that summarizes the function of OSI Layer 2.

 10. What simple phrase might summarize the function of OSI Layer 1?

 11. What simple phrase describes repeater operation?

 12. Under what conditions does an OSI Layer 1 repeater forward traffic? Include in your answer any conditions, and what happens if an error is received.

 13. What simple phrase describes bridge operation?

 14. Under what conditions does an OSI Layer 2 bridge forward traffic? Include in your answer any conditions, and what will happen if an error is received.

 15. What simple phrase describes router operation?

 16. Under what conditions does an OSI Layer 3 router forward traffic? Include in your answer any conditions and what happens if an error is received.

17. Define what a switch is in networking terms.

 18. List the four most common switch forwarding techniques, along with a description of the characteristic(s) that differentiate each technique from the others.

 19. Does a switch isolate collision domains? Explain your answer.

 20. Which switch forwarding technique offers the lowest latency, and what is that latency?

 21. Which switch forwarding technique offers the greatest latency, and what is that latency?

 22. What characteristic is common to the three areas of increased failures in the graphic for Figure 1-8? Hint: Why would more failures occur at just those layers in the OSI Model?

 23. How would you best describe the functionality of a network management tool as a general category?

 24. How would you best describe the functionality of a protocol analyzer as a general tool category?

 25. List several important differences between the capabilities of software and hardware protocol analyzers.

 26. How would you best describe the functionality of a handheld network tester as a general tool category?

 27. How would you best describe the functionality of a cable tester as a general tool category?

 28. What problem is solved by the introduction of flow protocols?

 29. Because problems at lower layers in the OSI Model may cause misleading symptoms at higher layers, is it always necessary to begin troubleshooting at the cable?

CHAPTER 2
Copper Media

This chapter describes issues related to installing and testing copper physical media for use in local area networks, primarily twisted-pair cabling. The OSI Model places the medium as being below the Physical Layer (see Figure 2-1). Each individual implementation of Ethernet specifies parameters for the intended medium, but usually references other cable related standards as part of that description. This chapter and Chapter 3, "Fiber Optic Media," are about the medium itself (copper and fiber, respectively).

Application
Presentation
Session
Transport
Network
Data Link
Physical
Medium

Figure 2-1. *Copper and fiber optic media in relation to the OSI Model*

Standards

Until the release of ANSI/TIA/EIA's Telecommunications Systems Bulletin 67 (TSB67), there were no standards for field testing the performance of in-stalled twisted-pair LAN cable. All the older standards (prior to TIA/EIA-568-A TSB67, which was approved in October 1995) were designed to verify either raw cable or connecting hardware components—but did not apply to a cable assembly or an installed cable link.

Information about links in general, and information specific to twisted-pair LAN cables, is provided in the text that follows. Note that the term *link* is used to describe installed assemblies of cabling components; that is, connectors and cable.

As the networking industry matures, it is interesting to note which technologies emerge as dominant and to track which specifications and technologies are omitted. For example, one of the earlier documents that defined cable requirements for networking applications was the Underwriters Laboratories document "UL's LAN Cable Certification Program" (see Table 2-1). This document reviewed IBM's Cabling System Technical Interface Specification (GA27-3773-1) for 150 ohm cables, such as Type 1 and Type 3 cable. It also provided detailed performance requirements for the following cable types that have evolved into the current Category 3 and Category 5 cables referenced by TIA/EIA-568-A.

Table 2-1. *Early 1980s Underwriters Laboratories LAN cable grades (historical reference only)*

Cable Grade	Operating Frequency	Use
Level I	(No performance criteria found)	Telephone and power-limited circuits
Level II	Up to 1MHz	Similar to IBM Type 3
Level III	150kHz to 16MHz	Approximately the same as Category 3
Level IV	772kHz to 20MHz	Slightly better than Category 3, never widely adopted
Level V	772kHz to 100MHz	Approximately the same as Category 5

Category 3 and Category 5e are the only ones described by the 2001 release of TIA/EIA-568-B (see Table 2-2). Category 5 is explicitly described as a legacy cable specification. Depending on how cheap Category 5e becomes, and on how tenacious the low-speed protocols are (such as 10BASE-T), Category 3 is likely to disappear entirely, or may be used for technologies such as telephone and xDSL. TIA/EIA-568-B includes a statement to the effect that although 150 ohm (STP-A) cable is still mentioned, it is not recommended and is very likely to be removed from the next full release of the TIA standards entirely. An example of how cabling standards evolve is provided in Table 2-3.

Table 2-2. *ISO/IEC 11801 and TIA/EIA-568 cable grades for balanced cable as of March 2008*

ISO/IEC Cable Grade	Operating Frequency	TIA/EIA Cable Grade	Operating Frequency
Class A	Up to 100KHz	—	—
Class B	Up to 1MHz	—	—
Class C	Up to 16MHz	Category 3	Up to 16MHz
Class D	Up to 100MHz	Category 5e	Up to 100MHz
Class E	Up to 250MHz	Category 6	Up to 250MHz
Class E_A	Up to 500MHz is proposed	Category 6A	Up to 500MHz
Class F	Up to 600MHz	—	—
Class F_A	Up to 1000MHz is proposed	—	—

Table 2-3. *Evolution of high-speed twisted-pair link specifications as extracted from the obsolete TIA/EIA-568-A standard, the current TIA/EIA-568-B.2 and TIA/EIA-568-C.2 standards*

	TIA/EIA-568-A TSB67 "Old" Cat 5	TSB95 "New" Cat 5	Addendum 5 Cat 5e	TIA/EIA-568-B TIA/EIA-568-B.2-1 Cat 6	TIA/EIA-568-C TIA/EIA-568-C.2 Cat 6A
Frequency Range	1–100MHz	1–100MHz	1–100MHz	1–250MHz	1–500MHz
Propagation Delay	Not Specified	Specified	Same as TSB95	Same as TSB95	Same as TSB95
Delay Skew	Not Specified	Specified	Same as TSB95	Same as TSB95	Same as TSB95
Attenuation	Specified	Same as Cat 5	Same as Cat 5	43 percent better	43 percent better
NEXT	Specified	Same as Cat 5	41 percent better	337 percent better	337 percent better
PS NEXT	Not Specified	Not Specified	Specified	216 percent better	216 percent better
ELFEXT	Not Specified	Specified	5 percent better	104 percent better	104 percent better
PS ELFEXT	Not Specified	Specified	Same as TSB95	95 percent better	95 percent better
Return Loss	Not Specified	Specified	26 percent better	58 percent better	58 percent better

The following list of standards is only a small part of what is available, but it represents some of the most likely standards of interest for a network support staff library.

International Standards

ISO/IEC 11801: IT—Cabling for customer premises

ISO/IEC 18010: Information technology—Pathways and spaces for customer premises cabling

ISO/IEC 14763-1: Information technology—Implementation and operation of customer premises cabling—Part 1: Administration, documentation, records

ISO/IEC 14763-2: Information technology—Implementation and operation of customer premises cabling—Part 2: Planning and Installation practices

ISO/IEC 61935-1: Testing of balanced communication cabling in accordance with ISO/IEC 11801—Part 1: Installed cabling

ISO/IEC 61935-2: Testing of balanced communication cabling in accordance with ISO/IEC 11801—Part 2: Patch cords and work area cords

United States Standards

ANSI/TIA/EIA-568-B.1: Commercial Building Telecommunications Cabling Standard

ANSI/TIA/EIA-568-B.2: 100 Ohm Twisted Pair Cabling Standard

ANSI/TIA/EIA-569-A: Commercial Building Standard for Telecommunications Pathways and Spaces

ANSI/EIA/TIA-570-A: Residential Telecommunications Cabling Standard

ANSI/TIA/EIA-606-B: Administration Standard for the Telecommunications Infrastructure of Commercial Buildings

ANSI/TIA/EIA-607-A: Commercial Building Grounding and Bonding Requirements for Telecommunications

ANSI/TIA-758-A: Customer-Owned Outside Plant Telecommunications Infrastructure

ANSI/TIA/EIA-862-A: Building Automation Systems Cabling Standard for Commercial Buildings

ANSI/TIA/EIA-942: Telecommunications Infrastructure Standard for Data Centers

ANSI/TIA-1005: Telecommunications Infrastructure Standard for Industrial Premises

ANSI/TIA/EIA-568-B, an update/replacement for ANSI/TIA/EIA-568-A (the Commercial Building Telecommunications Cabling Standard) requires better link performance by specifying much more stringent tests to support ever-faster networking demands, such as Gigabit and 10 Gigabit Ethernet (see Table 2-4). Unlike the earlier version, TIA/EIA-568-B was published in three sections. TIA/EIA-568-B was updated regularly following release.

- Part 1 (TIA/EIA-568-B.1, General Requirements) covers general requirements for planning and installing a structured cabling system. That is, everything from the configuration and requirements for the rooms that house the cable and equipment (see also ANSI/EIA/TIA-569-A), up through the electrical safety requirements (see also ANSI/TIA/EIA-607 and ANSI/TIA/EIA-758) and the actual network cable selection, installation, and testing requirements for both twisted-pair copper and fiber optic cables.

- Part 2 (TIA/EIA-568-B.2, Balanced Twisted-Pair Cabling Components) is mostly concerned with the connecting hardware and cable components used in 100 ohm twisted-pair copper cable networking applications. Several appendixes define the testing requirements for those components and for testing cable assemblies (patch cables and horizontal cabling). Updates have been released regularly, such as TIA/EIA-568-B.2-1, which was approved in June 2002 as Addendum 1 to the basic standard, and defines the performance specifications and test requirements for Category 6 cable and components. Addendum 10 defines Augmented Category 6 (Cat 6A) link performance requirements (approved February 2008).

- The TIA published Technical System Bulletin 155 (TSB-155) to define the cabling performance and field test requirements for the 10GBASE-T application as defined in IEEE standard 802.3an. Note that Category 6A demands a higher level of performance than TSB-155 in the frequency range from 250 to 500MHz and especially for "Alien Crosstalk."

The TIA/EIA-568-C standard update should be completely approved and published by Q3 2009. As with TIA/EIA-568-B, the document structure was reorganized. This text utilizes primarily TIA/EIA-568-B references and final test requirements because full approval for TIA/EIA-568-C had not occurred before the book went to press, and the requirements could still change.

- Part 0 (TIA/EIA-568-C.0) covers generic requirements for planning and installing a structured cabling system. Included are general requirements for architecture, length, grounding, bend radius, pulling tension, pinout, and polarity. Also included are general testing requirements.

- Part 1 (TIA/EIA-568-C.1) covers requirements for cable systems in a commercial building, or between commercial buildings in a campus environment. Provides the configuration and requirements for the rooms that house the cable and equipment (see also ANSI/EIA/TIA-569-A), up through the electrical safety requirements (see also ANSI/TIA/EIA-607 and ANSI/TIA/EIA-758) and the actual network cable selection and installation requirements for both twisted-pair copper and fiber optic cables.

- Part 2 (TIA/EIA-568-C.2) covers the connecting hardware and cable components used in balanced twisted-pair cable networking applications. Provides the requirements and test specifications for components used to create an installed link, as well as the testing requirements for installed links.

- Part 3 (TIA/EIA-568-C.3) covers optical fiber topics. (See Chapter 3.)

Table 2-4. *Required test parameters for 10GBASE-T support for TIA and ISO cabling standards*

	TIA/EIA-568-B and TSB-155	ISO/IEC 11801 and TR -24750
Wiremap	M	M
DC Loop Resistance	I	M
Length	M	I
Propagation delay	M	M
Delay skew	M	M
Insertion loss	M	M
Return loss measured from both ends	M (1)	M (1)
Near-end crosstalk (NEXT) loss pair-to-pair measured from both ends	M	M (2)
Power sum near-end crosstalk loss (TIA) PSNEXT (ISO) PS NEXT calculated for both ends	MC	MC (2)
Attenuation to Crosstalk loss Ratio Near-end (TIA) ACRN, (ISO) ACR-N	NR	MC
Power Sum Attenuation to Crosstalk Loss Ratio Near-end (TIA) PS ACRN (ISO) PSACR-N	NR	MC
Attenuation to Crosstalk Loss Ratio Far-End (TIA) ACRF, (ISO) ACR-F (formerly ELFEXT) pair-to-pair	M	MC
Power Sum Attenuation to Crosstalk Loss Ratio Far-End (TIA) PSACRF (ISO) PS ACR-F (formerly PSELFEXT)	MC	MC
Alien Near-end Crosstalk (ANEXT) Loss	M	M
Power-Sum Alien Near-End Crosstalk Loss (TIA) PSANEXT (ISO) PS ANEXT	MC	MC
AFEXT loss	M	–
Power Sum Attenuation to Alien Crosstalk Ratio Far-End (TIA) PSAACRF (ISO) PS AACR-F	M	M
Average PSANEXT Loss	M	NR
Average PSAACRF	M	NR

I = Informational, M = Mandatory, MC = Mandatory (Calculated), NR = Not required by this standard

M (1) = If measured insertion loss value at the same frequency is less than 3dB, the value is not used for Pass/Fail criteria

M (2) = If measured insertion loss value at the same frequency is less than 4dB, the value is not used for Pass/Fail criteria

Note: Informational parameters are measured but not used for Pass/Fail criteria

Basic Cable Uses

It is important to know the fundamental differences between power, telephone, and LAN links. Power cables carry low-frequency signals (typically 50 or 60Hz) and are designed to minimize power loss. Standard telephone cables do not carry much power but use up to 4kHz of bandwidth. LAN cables carry high-bandwidth, low-power signals (the most widely adopted LAN protocols use bandwidths of 4MHz and higher) and are designed to allow correct decoding of signals that are transmitted over the cabling. The industry references for this type of cable are low-voltage, telco, or data communications cable, as opposed to the normal or high-voltage electrical power cables.

The actual bandwidth required by the media access standard being installed (Ethernet, Fiber Channel, and so on) determines the minimum parameters for selecting, installing, testing, and operating twisted-pair links for networking—not the raw throughput bit-rate. The existing LAN standards that carry raw throughput data rates of between 10Mbps and 1000Mbps across two or four pairs of copper conductors typically use bandwidths between 10MHz and 100MHz. Higher speed implementations may require components and workmanship that place their costs about equal to a fiber optic cable system. Although fiber has its own set of issues, it can also avoid some distance limitations, various forms of electrical interference, and other problems associated with higher speeds on copper.

Recent efforts to define ways to deliver DC power (Power over Ethernet [PoE]) across a point-to-point network cable link for operating an end station such as a wireless access point have added complexity to an already difficult topic. The cabling standards working groups are cooperating with the IEEE to discover what effect this will have in the workplace.

The primary concerns for PoE fall into two areas:

- Ensure that the power is supplied in an electrically safe way, both for the users and for the equipment.

- Monitor the installation to ensure that pushing current through closely grouped cables (loose, in cable trays, or in conduit) does not cause the temperature to rise above the working range of the cable plant (60°C or 140°F) and create a fire hazard. See TIA-TSB 184 for more details.

A single 48-port Ethernet switch with all ports supplying 15 watts would need a big UPS and would deliver a combined 720 watts to the cable plant. The cable, the switch, and the UPS will become warmer. In addition to fire hazard concerns about the cable raceways as the amount of PoE-delivered power increases, it may be necessary to install extra power circuits and air conditioning in the wiring closet.

Test Parameters

Many of the measurements are reported in decibels (dB) and are calculated by using the following formulas:

$$dB = 20 \log\left(\frac{Voltage\_Out}{Voltage\_In}\right) \text{ or } dB = 10 \log\left(\frac{Power\_Out}{Power\_In}\right)$$

The standard unit for the gain or loss of signals is the decibel (dB). When measuring cables, the voltage out is always less than the voltage in at the other end, so the results in dB for the preceding equations are negative, although the minus sign is generally left off in discussion.

Note: The practice of using a mix of negative and unsigned numbers creates confusion but has become widespread.

The following paragraphs provide a basic introduction to a number of important copper LAN link characteristics. Understanding this information can help ensure the proper operation of your LAN installation. Note also that some of the test parameters apply only to testing twisted-pair cable, such as Near-end Crosstalk (NEXT).

Recent cabling standards describe two groups of tests: in-channel and between-channel. The in-channel tests are all related to what takes place within a single cable jacket. The external tests relate to influences from outside that cable-under-test. The following list of test parameters is grouped along those lines, but starts with a simple grouping where frequency-based analysis is not a critical factor.

Basic Tests and Parameters Required for In-Channel Testing

These basic measurement parameters are available from a range of diagnostic and monitoring tools, primarily because they do not require much circuitry to implement.

Before qualitative frequency-based testing is possible, a link must be verified for simple pin-to-pin continuity and pairing of the wires according to a specific wiring standard. A wiremap test is used for this purpose. The specific requirements of the wiremap test are to evaluate all eight conductors (wires) in the four-pair cable for the following installation and connectivity errors. Each of the following is discussed in detail in this chapter:

- Continuity to the remote end
- Shorts between any two or more conductors
- Reversed pairs
- Split pairs

- Transposed pairs
- Any other miswiring

Wiremap

A wiremap test begins with a simple continuity test to ensure that each connector pin from one end of the link is connected to the corresponding pin at the far end, and is not connected to any other conductor or the shield. If the test signal does not reach the other end, the wire is open. If the DC voltage test signal crosses onto another wire because they are touching, it is shorted. Although this is enough for telephone and other low-frequency applications, simple continuity between pins from one end of the link to the other is not sufficient for typical networking applications.

Correct Pairing

A number of vendors and organizations have supplied their own pairing diagrams over the years,

most of which are quickly fading into obscurity. The TIA/EIA-568-B standard describes two pairing diagrams intended for use with standard networking protocols T568A and T568B. The pairing schemes are electrically identical and differentiate only which pair is connected to specific pins in the 8-pin modular connections (see Figure 2-2 and Figure 2-3). Although the T568B arrangement is somewhat more widely installed, the standard identifies T568A as the preferred arrangement.

Installers are quick to learn to pair according to the wire colors marked on the jacks and punchdown blocks. Thus, mixed use of T568A and T568B components is likely to cause link faults. If a mix of components from both standard pinout arrangements is used in the same building, it is fairly certain that wiring faults will result through inattention to detail. Be sure to use the same wiring plan throughout the network.

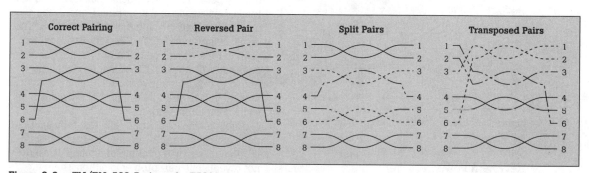

Figure 2-2. *TIA/EIA-568-B pinout for T568A*

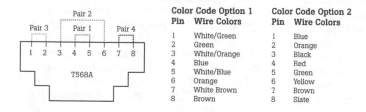

Figure 2-3. *TIA/EIA-568-B pinout for T568B*

Figure 2-4 shows how to count pin numbers on the 8-pin modular plug (RJ45).

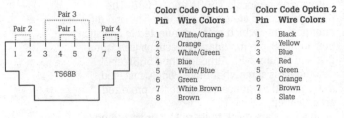

Color Code Option 1		Color Code Option 2	
Pin	Wire Colors	Pin	Wire Colors
1	White/Orange	1	Black
2	Orange	2	Yellow
3	White/Green	3	Blue
4	Blue	4	Red
5	White/Blue	5	Green
6	Green	6	Orange
7	White Brown	7	Brown
8	Brown	8	Slate

Figure 2-4 *Position of pins in the 8-pin modular RJ45 plug*

The most common wiring faults are shown in Figure 2-5.

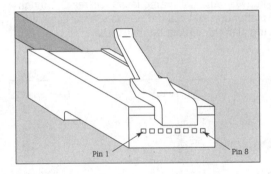

Figure 2-5 *Correct pairing and common link wiring faults*

Reversed Pairs

The reversed-pair cable fault is perhaps the simplest wiring fault. A pair reversal occurs when a twisted pair is not connected with straight-through pin-to-pin continuity. For example, if one wire of a twisted pair was connected to pin 1 at one end and pin 2 at the other, and from pin 2 to pin 1 for the second wire (see the example in Figure 2-2), then the pair is said to be reversed. As a carry-over from telephony, this is also sometimes called a *tip/ring reversal*.

Pair reversals can occur at any cable connection point, although they are most common at the RJ45 plug or jack.

Split Pairs

Using individual wires from two different twisted pairs to form a transmit or receive pair is called a *split pair*. Because the two wires are not twisted together as intended, the crosstalk cancellation effects are lost, and the two wire pairs usually begin acting as antennas to improperly hear the transmitted signal as noise on the receive pair. The effect is like a telephone circuit that is echoing whatever you say into the mouthpiece directly to the earpiece. If it is not very loud, you can sometimes continue, but if the echo gets too loud it disrupts the conversation. Although a link constructed this way exhibits correct pin-to-pin continuity, it causes errors in data transmission.

Split pairs occur most frequently from two causes: at punchdown blocks or at cable connectors, where not enough care was taken during cable installation or assembly; and from technicians not understanding the importance of the twisting of the wire pairs. The second problem is usually because the technician has taken the first twisted pair and used it for pins 1 and 2, the second twisted pair for pins 3 and 4, and so on. The result is shown in Figure 2-2, where the wires used to form a wire pair (3 and 6) come from two different twisted pairs. To someone not accustomed to building network cables, splitting apart a twisted pair to straddle the middle two pins might seem completely wrong.

Cable testers cannot literally test for a split pair using standard AC frequency-based tests. DC ohms tests by digital multimeters (DMMs) do not reveal split-pair problems either. There are several methods that cable testers use to infer that a split pair is present. One of the most common methods is to infer the presence of a split pair when the NEXT measurement fails badly. If a wire pair is split, or if a link is assembled with wire that is untwisted (such as ribbon cable or untwisted telephone cable), it will have a large NEXT problem. As a result, whenever a NEXT test fails with a significant margin, it is assumed that a split pair may exist.

Transposed Pairs

Transposed pairs occur when a twisted pair is connected to completely different pin pairs at both ends. Contrast this with a reversed pair, where the same pair of pins is used at both ends. This issue appears when color-coded punchdown blocks (for T568A and T568B) are mixed, and two different color codes are used at different locations in a single link.

Transposed pairs also commonly occur as the result of counting pin numbers from different sides of the connector or punchdown block at either end of the cable. This results in pin 1 connecting to pin 8, pin 2 to pin 7, and so on.

The cable shown in Figure 2-2 is transposed, but in a special way. When two Ethernet hubs or switches are connected together in series (cascading them), the transmit and receive pairs must be transposed; otherwise, receive is listening to receive and transmit is talking to transmit. This special cable is often called a *crossover cable*, and in this specific instance, the transposition is done on purpose. Note: Gigabit Ethernet requires that the interface be capable of correcting for transposed pairs, so use of this cable type might not be evident.

Propagation Delay

An electrical signal travels at uniform speed along a wire. The parameter used to describe this property is called the Nominal Velocity of Propagation (NVP). NVP expresses the speed at which a signal travels through a cable relative to the speed of light, and is expressed as a percentage. The actual speed of the electrical signal in a LAN cable is between 60 percent and 80 percent of the speed of light in a vacuum, or roughly 20cm (eight inches) per nanosecond. Signal speed is mainly affected by the composition of the cable insulation material (its relative permittivity).

Propagation delay is a simple measurement of how long it takes for the signal to travel down the cable being tested. This is measured on a per-pair basis on twisted-pair cable because of the physical difference in pair lengths caused by the different twist rates per pair in the cable.

Length (TDR)

Propagation delay measurements are the basis of the length measurement. TIA/EIA-568-B.1 specifies in paragraph 11.2.4.3.1 that the physical length of the link shall be calculated using the pair with the shortest electrical delay. Although the cable jacket may have length markings, testers usually measure the length of the wire based on the electrical delay as measured by the TDR function. The length of individual wire pairs inside a link may all be different, and may appear to be slightly longer than the measured length of the link being tested. This apparent discrepancy results primarily from different twist rates applied to the wire pairs within the cable, which changes the overall physical length of each pair, and thus the amount of delay measured. Another reason is that wire pairs may have different insulation material, which affects the velocity of the signal on that wire pair.

The Time Domain Reflectometry (TDR) test is used not only to determine length, but also to identify the distance to link faults such as shorts and opens. Other techniques for cable length measurement, such as capacitance and DC resistance, are unable to report the distance to a short or open.

When a cable tester makes a TDR measurement, it sends a pulse signal into a wire pair and measures the amount of time required for the pulse to return on the same wire pair. When the pulse encounters a variation in impedance, such as an open, short, or poor connection, some portion of the pulse energy is reflected back to the tester. The tester measures the elapsed time between when the pulse was sent and when the reflection was received. In addition to the comparatively large echo or reflection from the end of the cable (open circuit), smaller echoes may be detected that represent impedance changes in the link due to other forms of poor connections or defects in the cable.

The size of the reflected pulse is proportional to the change in impedance. Thus, a large change in impedance, such as a short, causes a large reflection; a small impedance change, such as a poor connection, creates a smaller reflection.

If a returning echo is larger than a threshold setting (the default is typically about 15 percent of the transmitted pulse), it displays the calculated distance to the echo source. These small echoes are called *anomalies* and are caused by cable faults of varying severity. Most testers display more than one distance: the distance to the end of the link as well as one or two anomalies along the way. Some of the faults that cause an echo reflection include poor connections, mixed-impedance cable segments, cable stubs, crushed cable, and severe kinks or over-tight tie-wraps. Cable test tools with high sensitivity are able to show a TDR plot that allows the user to see all anomalies along the length of the link.

Length measurements depend directly on knowing the NVP of the link under test. Most cable tester configuration screens enable users to choose from a range of cable types. For the length measurement, the primary purpose of choosing the cable type is to tell the tester what the approximate NVP value is for the cable being tested. For maintenance testing, you could leave the selection set at any cable type of the same impedance value as the cables you were testing all the time—providing you understood that the length measurement was not going to be precise. It is usually sufficient to learn that the problem is "a third of the way back from the end." With that information, you then look for a connection point (punch-down block, wall jack, etc.) in that general area. Almost all problems are found either at known connection points or in the user's workspace.

The choices for cable types are prepared using NVP values obtained from published specifications for each cable manufacturer and from worst-case values published in the standards. The variation in NVP from lot-to-lot of the same cable type from a specific manufacturer can be 5 percent or more, and may reach 10 percent between different manufacturers. Therefore, if length accuracy is critical to your situation, you must determine the true NVP of each cable batch installed in your network. Verify the tester's length measurement by testing a known-length sample of the same cable you will be installing or testing that is longer than 15 meters (50 feet). All cable analysis tools have a "calibrate" function that allows you to adjust the NVP value to match this cable sample. Very simple testers with a "length" function may not.

Delay Skew

Delay skew is calculated as the difference between the propagation delay for each of the four wire pairs. The fastest propagation delay among the four measurements is used as one extreme, and the slowest propagation delay measured is

the other extreme. The difference between the two measurements becomes the delay skew. EIA/TIA-568-B permits no more than 44ns of delay skew between the fastest and slowest pairs in the cable for the Permanent Link configuration, and 50ns for the Channel Link. The high-throughput network applications such as 1000BASE-T and 10GBASE-T are most sensitive to delay skew; they also permit no more than 50ns of delay skew.

Some newer high-speed network implementations, such as 1000BASE-T, achieve very high data rates by simultaneously transmitting data on all the wire pairs of a four-pair cabling link. The encoded signal is sent simultaneously in four parts, one part on each wire pair, and all four parts must be received very close to the same time to be interpreted correctly.

One of the reasons delay skew was first included in several testing standards is because some Category 5 cables were constructed with different insulating materials around the copper conductors. This construction is referred to as *heterogeneous*. Homogeneous cable construction requires that all wire pairs be constructed with one and the same kind of insulating material. The insulating material has a significant influence on the NVP of the cable. There are two (then) relatively common instances of heterogeneous cables: the 2+2 cable and the 3+1 cable. In these cables the wires in two or three pairs are insulated using Teflon FEP, whereas the wires in the other pairs are insulated using a polyethylene compound. This heterogeneous construction method was used to meet the demand for category cable in view of a Teflon shortage that plagued the industry for a few years following a fire in a Teflon plant in 1995. The Teflon FEP insulated wire pairs exhibit the typical Category 5 NVP value of 69 percent, whereas the other pairs transmit the signals somewhat slower and have an NVP value that is several points lower (65 percent or 66 percent). Those 2+2 or 3+1 cables are unable to support technologies such as 1000BASE-T due to very poor delay skew performance.

Delay skew is a critical measure for 1000BASE-T, 10GBASE-T, and any other implementation where multiple pairs are used to transmit simultaneously in the same direction. The receiver

PHY must realign the received bits so that despite receiving the first data from one data unit transmission on one wire pair several time-slots away from the last data from the same data transmission on another wire pair, the whole transmission is reassembled and delivered to the next higher layer as if it were received at the same time.

Basic Frequency-Based Test Parameters Related to In-Channel Testing

The following test parameters depend largely on the frequencies used to perform the measurement. As a direct consequence of this dependence, the appropriate standards specify the maximum allowed frequency step rate or separation between tested frequencies. These tests require a substantial amount of very sensitive circuitry, and are thus rarely found in network diagnostic and monitoring equipment because of the additional bulk that would be required. Advanced cable analysis tools are usually separate testers, and are used only to test cable. Most such cable analysis tools consist of two identical test units—one bearing a display and the other nearly faceless. Both units offer the same full test and measurement capabilities and are placed at either end of the link being tested.

Attenuation

Attenuation is signal loss or the decrease in signal amplitude over the length of a link (see Figure 2-6). The longer the cable and the higher the signal's frequency, the greater the attenuation or loss is. Therefore, be sure to measure attenuation using the highest frequencies that the cable is rated to support.

Attenuation needs to be measured only from one direction on the link (on all pairs) because attenuation of a specific wire pair is the same when measured in opposite directions.

In Figure 2-7, the signal amplitude decreases with distance to represent signal loss through attenuation and the related measurement of insertion loss.

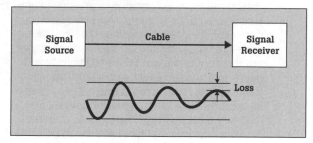

Figure 2-6. *Attenuation loss*

Attenuation is caused by a loss of electrical energy due to the resistance of the wire (converting the energy to heat), and when energy leaks through the cable's insulating material. This loss of energy (attenuation or insertion loss) is expressed in decibels (dB). Lower attenuation values are an indication of better link performance. For example, when comparing the performance of two links at a particular frequency, a link with an attenuation of 10dB (a factor of 3.16) performs better than a link with an attenuation of 20dB (a factor of 10). Link attenuation is determined by the cable's construction, length, and the frequencies of the signals sent through the link. In the 1 to 100MHz frequency range, the attenuation is dominated by the skin effect and is proportional to the square root of frequency. That is, the higher the frequency, the greater the attenuation.

Insertion Loss

The preceding discussion about attenuation assumes that the connection to the test instrument or end-user equipment and all intermediate connections in the link have a perfect impedance match. Because there is no such thing as a

Figure 2-7. *Attenuation (and the related measurement of insertion loss) results from the resistance of the transmission medium to the transmitted signal*

perfect connection, it is necessary to look at the severity of impedance discontinuities as they relate to the frequency ranges used in a local area network. Simple attenuation tends to be linear along the cable. The more cable you have, the greater the expected attenuation and that attenuation can be fairly accurately predicted because it is linear. At speeds covered by Category 5e cable (1 to 100MHz), the impedance discontinuities that result from good cable junctions have a nearly insignificant effect, and can be included in a simple attenuation measurement that ignores their contribution. At the speeds supported by Category 6 cable (1 to 250MHz), clear evidence emerges showing that these effects can be much more pronounced, and that their effect can easily reduce the performance of the link by 4 to 6dB (see Figure 2-8). Thus, TIA/EIA-568-B has changed the test parameter name from attenuation to insertion loss to include the effect of these reflections, which are separately measured as *return loss*.

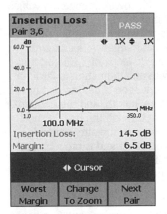

In Figure 2-8, the top curved line is the test limit for Category 5e, and does not extend beyond 100MHz because that is the highest frequency specified for Category 5e. The wavy line below it is the current test result. The vertical line at 100MHz is the cursor, which shows the current measurement result of 14.5dB at 100MHz (a margin of 6.5 dB better performance than the test limit

Figure 2-8. *DTX-1800 insertion loss test results example. The top line that extends only to 100MHz is the test results limit line for this Category 5e test. The irregular line below the limit line is the measured test result.*

at that frequency). Test results for frequencies above 100MHz begin showing the echo effects of impedance discontinuities in the form of varying (nonlinear) test results—the wave in the line.

An impedance discontinuity on a link causes a reduction in the signal strength due to part of the energy being reflected. At the first discontinuity, a portion of the signal is reflected back toward the transmitter. The effect is compounded at the second (and each subsequent) discontinuity where an additional portion of the remaining signal is reflected backward, but part of the reflection is also reflected forward again by the first discontinuity. Multiple echo effects are created. By the time a signal has passed through several discontinuities, there is a clear drop in signal strength, and there is a growing set of echoes that both follow the original outbound signal and return to the transmission source.

The effects of the echoes are twofold. First, the effective cable length of the link is reduced because some percentage of the signal did not reach the end. The signal is not loud enough to be heard as far away as before. Second, because of echoes the receiver begins having difficulties properly sampling and decoding the signal, which results in corrupted data, and in turn results in more errors occurring on the network. This sampling or misclocking problem is called *jitter*. If you are curious about how much signal is reflected at a single impedance discontinuity try the following formula. Z is the symbol for impedance. The example shows the effect of connecting a 50 ohm and 75 ohm coaxial cable together, in that order (signal source, 50 ohm cable, 75 ohm cable). Twenty percent of the signal is reflected back toward the signal source at the junction of the two cables in the example. This is obviously an extreme example of an impedance discontinuity, but the problem is the same with large or small reflections on coax and twisted pair.

$$\left(\frac{Z_2 - Z_1}{Z_2 + Z_1} \right) = \left(\frac{75 - 50}{75 + 50} \right) = \left(\frac{25}{125} \right) = 20\%$$

As mentioned, this conspicuous behavior change at higher frequencies caused TIA/EIA-568-B to stop describing this as an attenuation test and is now calling it an insertion loss test. The only real difference between the two measurements is that insertion loss acknowledges the presence of jitter and its causes.

TIA/EIA-568-B defines the formulas to calculate the allowable insertion loss for an installed twisted-pair link for both link configurations the *permanent link* (formerly the basic link) and the *channel*. In addition, TIA/EIA-568-B shows a table of allowable values for these links. The allowable values of attenuation apply to an environment at 20°C. Attenuation increases as temperature increases: typically 1.5 percent per degree Celsius for Category 3 links, 0.4 percent per degree Celsius for Category 5e links, 0.4 percent per degree Celsius from 20°C to 40°C, and 0.6 percent from 40°C to 60°C for solid conductor Category 6 links, and so on. The network technician should remember to take temperature into consideration for both installation and testing purposes. TIA/EIA-568-B specifically permits adjustment of allowable attenuation for temperature. If the intended use environment is likely to be hotter than 60°C (140°F), another type of cable should be considered.

Cable analyzers may report the worst case attenuation test result value and the frequency at which it was measured. The testers are required to use attenuation results greater than 3dB only for Pass/Fail purposes.

Return Loss

Return loss is a measure of reflections caused by the impedance changes at all locations along the link and is measured in decibels (dB). Mismatches predominantly occur at locations where connectors are present, but they can also occur in cable where variations in characteristic impedance along the length of the cable are present.

The main impact of return loss is not on loss of signal strength (there is some, but generally it is not that much of a problem), but rather the introduction of signal jitter. An example of jitter was shown in Figure 2-8, where these reflections caused a visible impact on the attenuation measurement at higher frequencies. Attenuation tends to be linear (smooth line) along a cable. The measurement in Figure 2-8 shows how the echoes arrived at the receiver of the tester in phase with some frequencies and out of phase with others, resulting in a wavy line. Figure 2-9 shows possible sources of return loss along a cable link.

A simplified description of this type of jitter is that the edge of a signal representing a data bit is shifted slightly in time, such that when the receiver circuit samples the signal it incorrectly classifies the signal as either a binary 1 or 0 when it should have been the other value (see Figure 2-10). This jitter can vary the leading edge of the signal presented to the decoder in the receiver, or add to or subtract from the signal amplitude, and thereby cause decoding errors. The closer to a perfect match of characteristic impedance of the cabling to the output impedance of the transmitter, and to the input impedance of the receiver, the better the return loss measurement will be. A lab test called the "eye-pattern" is typically used to evaluate the degree of jitter present in a network, and the corresponding loss of signal strength (the amount of energy that fails to transfer from the signal source to the receiver due to impedance mismatches).

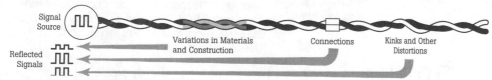

Figure 2-9. *Sources of return loss*

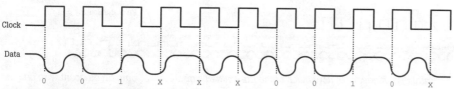

Figure 2-10. *Simplified illustration of sampling problems due to signal jitter*

Figure 2-10 assumes that the encoding scheme is edge sensitive. When the data signal becomes misaligned with reference to the clock, sampling errors take place. In the example, probable sampling errors are shown with an X in place of the binary value.

The return loss measurement varies significantly with frequency. Any variation in characteristic impedance of the cabling is one source of return loss. Another source is reflections from inside the link, mainly from connectors.

Figure 2-11 shows a typical return loss test result from a cable analyzer where the bottom curve is the limit for return loss, ending at 250MHz because Category 6 was selected for the test, and the irregular top line is the measured result for this test. The cursor is positioned at the frequency where the worst-case margin was detected. When a reported margin is positive, it indicates that the worst-case return loss is better than the limit (passed), whereas a negative margin indicates that the result exceeds the limit (failed). The cable analyzer also shows the wire pair and frequency where the worst-case return loss margin was measured.

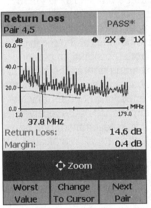

Figure 2-11. *Fluke Networks DTX-1800 return loss test results. The flat line below the irregular test result is the limit line for passing this test.*

Near-End Crosstalk (NEXT)

When it comes to overall twisted-pair link operation, crosstalk has the greatest effect on link performance. Crosstalk is the undesirable signal transmission from one wire pair to another nearby pair (see Figure 2-12). Unwanted crosstalk signals generally result from capacitive and inductive coupling between adjacent pairs. Crosstalk increases at higher frequencies and is very destructive to data signaling. Most low-speed LAN protocols need two pairs of twisted-pair cable, one pair for each direction of traffic. Higher-speed LAN protocols typically need multiple pairs, and typically operate simultaneously in both directions on each twisted pair.

Test devices measure crosstalk by applying a test signal to one wire pair and measuring the amplitude of the crosstalk signals received by other wire pairs. Near-end crosstalk (NEXT) is computed as the ratio in amplitude (in volts) between the test signal transmitted and the crosstalk signal received when measured from the same end of the link. This ratio is generally expressed in decibels (dB). Higher NEXT values (smaller received crosstalk signals) correspond to less crosstalk and better link performance. The NEXT test is also the most common method used to infer the presence of split pairs in twisted-pair links.

Although crosstalk is a critical performance factor for twisted-pair links, it is also difficult to measure accurately, especially at lower frequencies where many of the common LAN protocols operate. TIA/EIA-568-B specifies that NEXT must be measured at increments or intervals not greater than the maximum frequency step size increments shown in Table 2-5. For improved accuracy, a smaller step size is better, although this may take longer to measure. A Category 3 link needs to be tested to 16 MHz and a Category 5e link to 100MHz, because those are their maximum frequency ratings.

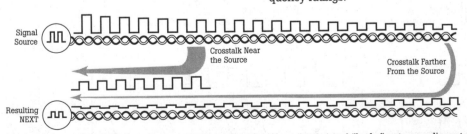

Figure 2-12. *Crosstalk is a measure of how much of the transmitted signal "leaks" onto an adjacent wire pair*

NEXT loss must be measured from every pair to every other pair in a twisted-pair link, and from both ends of the link. This equates to 12 pair combinations for the typical four-pair cabling link. To shorten test times, some older field testers allowed the user to test the NEXT performance of a link by using larger frequency step sizes. The resulting distance between measurements does not comply with TIA/EIA-568-B, and may overlook link crosstalk faults.

Table 2-5. *Maximum frequency step sizes allowed for compliance with TIA/EIA-568-B*

Frequency Range	Maximum Allowed Step Size
1 to 31.25MHz	150kHz (or 0.15MHz)
31.25 to 100MHz	250kHz (or 0.25MHz)
100 to 250MHz	500kHz (or 0.5MHz)
250 to 500MHz	1MHz

All signals transmitted through a link are affected by attenuation. The farther the signal travels, the smaller it becomes. Because of attenuation, crosstalk occurring farther down the link contributes less to NEXT than crosstalk occurring at the near end of the link (refer to Figure 2-12). If the signal that is crossing to another pair is smaller, the amount that is available to cross is correspondingly smaller too. Furthermore, the coupled signal still has to travel back to the source end and is further attenuated as it returns. Thus, near-end crosstalk is worse closest to a transmission source where the signal is the largest (greatest amplitude) and the attenuation in the return path is the shortest. To verify proper link performance, you should measure NEXT from both ends of the link; this is also a requirement for complete compliance with all the high-speed cable specifications.

Crosstalk can be minimized by twisting wire pairs more, so that the signal coupling is "evened out." Twisted-pair wiring for LANs have more twists per unit length than telephone wiring. LANs use TIA/EIA Category 3 or better cable. Telephone wiring is typically comparable to the old UL Level 1 (see Table 2-1), and might not seem to be twisted at all. The higher the category, the more twists per unit length in the cable are necessary, and the higher the frequency rating will be. To ensure reliable LAN communications, cable pairs must

not be left untwisted even for short distances. For this same reason, cables with parallel conductors (ribbon type or "silver satin" type cables) should never be used in LAN applications.

Signals from twisted-pair wiring may "leak" to the outside world and to other adjacent cables. The principle behind balanced twisted-pair cables is that, at every location along the cable, the voltage in one wire of a wire pair is equal in amplitude but opposite in phase to the voltage in the other wire of the wire pair. In addition to some other undesirable side effects, imbalance creates the effect of an antenna and receives external signals—thereby disrupting data with electromagnetic interference (EMI) and radio frequency interference (RFI). Substantial improvements have recently been made to cabling components— connectors in particular—which has had a positive impact because the majority of link problems occur at connectors, and the new connectors reduce these effects. To minimize the antenna effect, shielding the cable is a possible solution. When shielded cabling is used, however, a new set of potential problems is introduced, such as ground loops due to differences in the ground (earth) potential at opposite ends of the link. The ground-loop problem is often more serious than the EMI/RFI problem.

Generally, the problem of NEXT is worse in shielded cabling. The reason for this is that crimping the plugs to the shield of the cable enhances capacitive imbalance, one of the sources of NEXT. Also, shielded twisted-pair wiring is harder to install correctly, making it more prone to this sort of problem. Shielded twisted-pair cable comes in two basic types: 1) shielded twisted pair (STP), which has a foil shield around each individual pair and another shield around the four pairs, and 2) foil-screened twisted pair (FTP) or screened twisted pair (ScTP), which has a shield around the outside of the group of four pairs only, and is usually 100 ohm cabling. Some legacy cables could be either 120 ohm or 150 ohm cabling. With the advent of the 10GBASE-T application and the concerns over alien crosstalk, many manufacturers are promoting shielded or screened cable types. New terminology has been introduced to emphasize the cabling construction. The name F/UTP has been introduced to designate the foil around the four unshielded wire pairs. Proper grounding procedures must be followed when using these cable types. Screened cable types have been widely used in Europe because of strict laws intended to limit EMI/RFI emissions. As a side effect, they reduce external noise from interfering with the signals on the link. If proper balance is maintained, however, UTP cabling can provide EMI/RFI performance levels that also satisfy the European requirements.

Figure 2-13 shows typical NEXT test results. In both figures, the bottom curve is the TSB67 limit for NEXT and the top lines are the results for this test. When a reported margin is positive, this indicates that the worst-case NEXT is better than the limit, whereas a negative margin indicates that the results are worse than the limit. The cursor is positioned at the frequency where the worst-case margin was detected. The irregular shape of the top curve demonstrates that unless NEXT is measured at many points along the frequency range, low points (points of worse NEXT loss) could easily go undetected. Therefore, TIA/EIA-568-B defines a maximum frequency step size for NEXT measurements, as shown in Table 2-5.

If a NEXT failure is detected, it is possible to use other tests to pinpoint where along the length of the link the failure is occurring. One such test is called Time Domain Crosstalk (TDX), which is displayed in the same graphic format as a Time-Domain Reflectometry (TDR) test. The difference between TDR and TDX is that, in the case of a TDR, the signal is applied at one wire pair and the reflections are measured on the same wire pair. TDR reflections occur because of impedance anomalies. TDX applies a signal to one wire pair and measures the coupled signal on an adjacent wire pair.

Figure 2-14 shows two typical high-definition TDX test results. The vertical measurement spikes represent sources and magnitude of crosstalk. The vertical red lines are positioned at locations where the tester has determined the cable-under-test ends to be, and distance is shown at the bottom

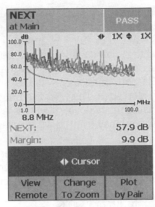
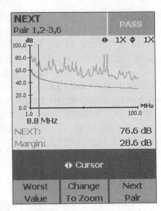

Figure 2-13. *Fluke DTX-1800 Near-end Crosstalk (NEXT) test results example. The left example shows the results for all pair combinations together. The right example shows only one pair combination. Each pair combination may be viewed separately. The cursor is at 8.8MHz, where the worst NEXT test result (smallest margin) was found.*

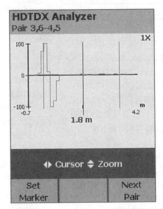
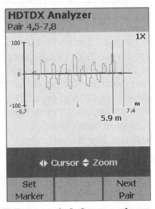

Figure 2-14. *Fluke DTX-1800 HDTDX test result. Left screen shows connector problem, right screen shows poor quality cable. The test was made with the Permanent Link test adapter, so the cable under test begins 0.7m from the tester as indicated by the vertical red lines.*

of the graph accordingly. The black vertical line is the user moveable cursor used to determine distance from the local tester end. The left graphic shows the point-source impact of a bad connection, either due to poor workmanship or poor connecting hardware. The right graphic shows crosstalk all along the cable-under test, which indicates that the cable itself is not good quality.

Attenuation-to-Crosstalk Ratio (ACR or ACRN)

ACR is calculated in an attempt to answer the question: While a transmission is taking place,

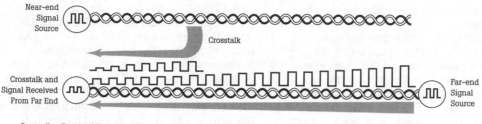

Crosstalk − Received Signal = ACR

Figure 2-15. *ACR is calculated from attenuation and NEXT measurements*

how much does the noise from crosstalk disrupt the (attenuated) signal I am listening to? (See Figure 2-15.) ACR has been renamed ACRN (to indicate near-end crosstalk) in TIA/EIA-568-B.2-10 (the Augmented Category 6 standard), and is named ACR-N in the ISO 11801 standard.

The attenuation-to-crosstalk ratio affects the bit-error rate (BER) directly and thereby the need for retransmissions. The noise consists of both externally induced noise and self-induced noise (which is NEXT). Self-induced noise usually dominates externally induced noise. The ACR is the same as the signal-to-noise ratio measurement when you deem that external noise is insignificant. The two factors considered in the calculation are NEXT and attenuation, as indicated in the name of the parameter. When insertion loss and NEXT loss measurements are expressed in dB, you can subtract the NEXT loss measurement from the insertion loss measurement to obtain the ratio. The closer the ACR result comes to zero dB, the less likely your link is going to work (see Figure 2-16).

In Figure 2-16, the top graph is based on limit value calculations for a 100-meter Category 5e "channel" configuration specified in TIA/EIA-568-B.2, and the bottom graph shows the same calculation for Category 6 as specified in TIA/EIA-568-B.2-1. Category 5e and Category 6 only offer verified performance calculation formulas out to 100MHz and 250MHz, respectively. The formulas in the standard should not be extended beyond the specified frequency values. However, for the purpose of illustration the graph for Category 5e in Figure 2-18 has been extended beyond 100MHz using the Category 5e formulas. The graphs show calculated worst-case limits and plot three values: NEXT Loss, Insertion Loss (attenuation) and the derived ACR.

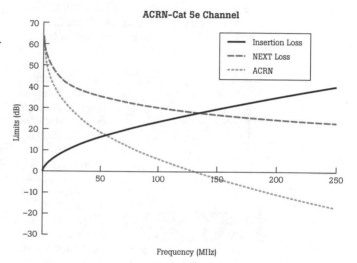

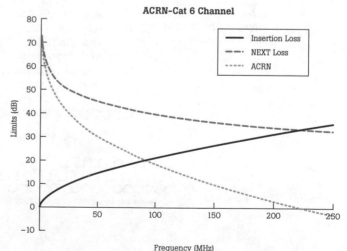

Figure 2-16. *ACRN Category 5e (TIA-568-B.2) and Category 6 (TIA-568-B.2-1) conformance*

The limit for the ACRN value can also be viewed as the difference between the Insertion Loss and NEXT Loss limit lines in Figure 2-18.

In Figure 2-16, at the point where the plot lines for Insertion Loss and NEXT Loss intersect, the desired data signal will be exactly equal to the amount of noise contributed by NEXT at this frequency and the ACR limit value crosses the zero mark. Notice that the crosstalk will begin to be louder than the data signal at around 132MHz for Category 5e, and 226MHz for Category 6. To transfer data reliably, links used in LAN applications typically must perform at least 6dB better than the noise floor. For Category 6, the IEEE asked the TIA to extend the specification beyond the point where ACRN = 0 because of noise cancellation and error correction techniques it intended to apply to the appropriate Ethernet implementation.

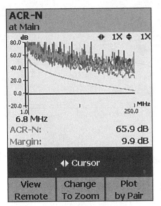

Figure 2-17. *DTX-1800 Category 6 ACRN test results example. The curve below the test results is the limit line for ACRN and extends to 250MHz as specified for Category 6.*

This test is important for technologies such as 10BASE-T and 100BASE-TX, where only one pair is used in each direction. It does not mean as much for technologies that operate in parallel, such as 1000BASE-T, where power sum measurements are far more important.

In Figure 2-17, the bottom curved line is the Category 6 limit for NEXT, and the irregular stacked test results lines above are the per-pair results for this test. The cursor is positioned at the frequency where the worst-case margin was detected. When a reported margin is positive, this indicates that the worst-case ACRN is better than the limit, whereas a negative margin indicates that the result falls below the limit and the test fails. The cable analyzer permits results to be viewed for each cable pair combination separately.

Signal-to-Noise Ratio (SNR)

The signal-to-noise ratio is the combination of all disturbances generated within a cabling link plus the noise that penetrates the cable from external sources compared to the attenuated signal that transmits the information (see Figure 2-18). The internal disturbances that affect a wire pair within a cabling link consist of PSNEXT and PSACRF (both described later) contributed from the other three wire pairs in the cabling and return loss on the pair of interest. PSACRN and PSACRF calculate only a portion of the combined disturbance. No single test parameter has been defined that represents the true internal portion of the signal-to-noise ratio. With the advent of 10GBASE-T, the noise coupling from adjacent cabling links must be added to the SNR budget of every cabling link.

An example of external noise might include the residual noise floor of the measuring instrument itself (for example, when you turn the volume on your music player equipment up very loud but don't press play—the hissing, crackly noise you hear is noise from the circuits themselves). The only problem with this measurement is being certain that you have included all the possible noise sources.

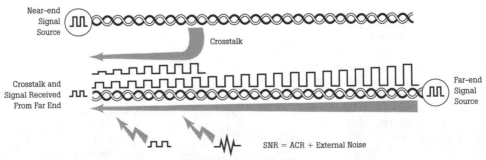

Figure 2-18. *SNR is the same as ACRN plus external noise influences*

Advanced Frequency-Based Test Parameters Related to In-Channel and External Testing

The preceding test parameters were satisfactory for Ethernet implementations up through Fast Ethernet, as they were largely limited to low speed signaling (comparatively speaking) and the use of a single pair for transmit in each direction.

The parameters shown in Table 2-6 became necessary with the introduction of Gigabit Ethernet and higher signaling implementations. In these schemes, there are multiple pairs transmitting simultaneously in each direction, and therefore the effects of signals crossing over from adjacent wire pairs or from adjacent cables becomes significant.

More of the complex measurements are calculated rather than measured, unlike most of the simpler measurements previously described.

Table 2-6. *Measured and calculated test parameters*

Measured Test Parameter	Calculated Test Parameter
Propagation Delay, Length	Delay Skew
Insertion Loss	
NEXT (pair-to-pair)	PSNEXT, ACRN, PSACRN
ANEXT, AFEXT (pair-to-pair)	
FEXT (pair-to-pair)	ACRF (ELFEXT), PSACRF
Return Loss	

Far-End Crosstalk (FEXT)

The other kind of crosstalk is *Far-End Crosstalk* (FEXT). In this case, the signal coupled into the disturbed wire pair travels to the end of the link opposite the transmission source. In Figure 2-19, observe that any FEXT travels the same distance on an adjacent pair as the transmitted signal on the original pair. All crosstalk occurring as FEXT is subject to an amount of attenuation equal to the attenuation of the link, because it always travels the full distance of the link.

Compare this with NEXT, which as discussed previously is attenuated in direct relation to the distance traveled to the point of coupling. The transmitted signal is attenuated on its way to the far end, and at any point that a portion of the signal crosses to an adjacent pair it must travel (and be attenuated) an equal distance before it arrives back at the source end.

The FEXT measurement compares the original signal to the signal coupled in an adjacent wire pair and arriving at the far end. NEXT is mostly a result of capacitive coupling along the cable, while FEXT is mostly the result of inductive coupling at connectors. For implementations that transmit on one pair in each direction, such as 10BASE-T and 100BASE-TX, FEXT is largely irrelevant. However, for technologies such as 1000BASE-T that transmit on multiple pairs in the same direction, FEXT is a very important property to test. FEXT represents another disturbance for a receiver. Consider the receiver at the right side of the bottom wire pair in Figure 2-19. This receiver is also affected by the NEXT from transmissions on the adjacent wire pair from right to left.

Because of attenuation, FEXT on longer cables is less than FEXT on shorter cables of the same type.

Attenuation to Crosstalk Ratio Far-End (ACRF)

Attenuation to Crosstalk Ratio Far-End (ACRF) is the ratio of FEXT to the attenuated signal over the affected wire pair (see Figure 2-20). Compare the

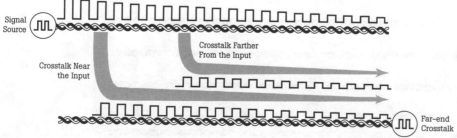

Figure 2-19. *Far-end Crosstalk (FEXT)*

FEXT disturbance to the attenuated signal arriving from the sender at the opposite end of the wire pair to assess the impact of the FEXT crosstalk on the signal transmission.

This test parameter used to be called ELFEXT, or equal level far-end crosstalk, but is renamed as the test parameter ACRF (TIA) or ACR-F (ISO) in the new versions of the standards.

Like ACRN, ACRF represents a signal-to-noise ratio for the cabling. Higher ACRF values (in dB) mean that data signals received at the far end of the cabling are much larger than the far end crosstalk signals received. Higher ACRF values correspond to better cabling performance.

NEXT and FEXT coupling mechanisms tend to be similar in cable but can differ greatly in connecting hardware. Some connectors achieve good NEXT performance by balancing the inductive and capacitive currents that cause crosstalk. Because these currents are 180° out of phase at the near end of the cabling, they cancel out, which eliminates crosstalk at the near end. However, currents that cancel at the near end add up at the far end, causing far-end crosstalk and poor ACRF performance.

In Figure 2-20, a signal is transmitted on one wire pair. A signal transmitted on an adjacent pair crosses to the first wire pair, traveling in the same direction as the "good" signal. The FEXT electrons accompany the good signal electrons to the remote receive inputs of the LAN equipment. To properly decode the desired signal the amount of FEXT crosstalk must be smaller than the desired signal.

Power Sum Near-End Crosstalk (PSNEXT)

Power Sum NEXT loss is concerned with the combined effect of NEXT from all other pairs in the cable simultaneously. TIA/EIA standards use PSNEXT, whereas ISO standards use PS NEXT. Compare this with NEXT, where the amount of a transmitted signal from one pair is measured as crosstalk on one adjacent pair.

For each wire pair in the four-pair cable, PSNEXT loss is computed from three pair-to-pair NEXT loss test results (see Figure 2-21). Statistical theory indicates that a good assumption for the intensity of the total crosstalk in a link is a power sum. The value is calculated by taking the square root of the sum of the square of each crosstalk amplitude.

For implementations that receive from only one pair in each direction, such as 10BASE-T and 100BASE-TX, PSNEXT is not relevant. However, for technologies such as 1000BASE-T that receive simultaneously from multiple pairs in the same

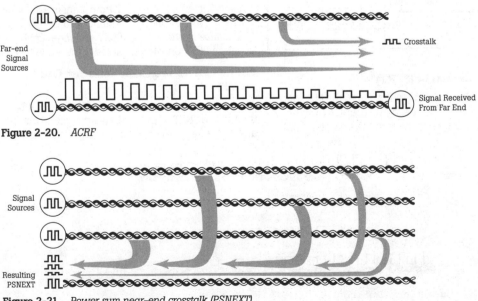

Figure 2-20. *ACRF*

Figure 2-21. *Power sum near-end crosstalk (PSNEXT)*

direction, power sum measurements can be very important tests. The cumulative effect of crosstalk from multiple simultaneous transmission sources can be very detrimental to the signal you are trying to receive. In the case of 1000BASE-T, the requirements for pair-to-pair NEXT loss as specified are such that PSNEXT loss is always satisfied if the pair-to-pair NEXT loss requirements are satisfied, so PSNEXT calculations were not required. TIA/EIA-568-B certification requires this test.

Power Sum Attenuation to Crosstalk Ratio, Near-End (PSACRN)

Power Sum Attenuation to Crosstalk Ratio, Near-End (PSACRN) was previously called PSACR. The addition of *Near-End* was recently made to distinguish it from PSACRF for the far-end measurement. PSACRN values indicate how the amplitude of signals received from a far-end transmitter compares to the combined amplitudes of crosstalk produced by near-end transmissions on the other cable pairs. TIA/EIA standards use PSACRN, while ISO standards use PS ACR-N.

PSACRN is the difference (in dB) between each wire pair's attenuation (insertion loss) and the combined crosstalk received from the other pairs. Measured PSNEXT and Insertion Loss test results are used to calculate PSACRN values. Higher PSACRN values mean received signals are much larger than the crosstalk from all the other cable pairs. Higher PSACRN values correspond to better cabling performance.

Power Sum Attenuation to Crosstalk Ratio, Far-End (PSACRF)

Power Sum Attenuation to Crosstalk loss Ratio, Far-End (PSACRF) was previously defined as Power Sum Equal Level Far-End Crosstalk (PSELFEXT). PSACRF takes into account the combined crosstalk on a receive pair at the far end from signals transmitted simultaneously on the three adjacent pairs at the near end (see Figure 2-22). PSNEXT and PSACRN are for the near end; PSACRF is for the far end. TIA/EIA standards use PSACRF, whereas ISO standards use PS ACR-F.

The affect of attenuation, measured as insertion loss, is taken into account when the FEXT for the other three pairs in the link is calculated as a sum affecting the wire pair being measured. PSACRF results show how much the far end of each cable pair is affected by the combined far-end crosstalk from the other pairs.

PSACRF is the difference (in dB) between the test signal and the crosstalk from the other pairs received at the far end of the link. PSACRF results are typically a few dB lower than worst-case FEXT results.

Alien Crosstalk

All the electronic influences thus far described have occurred within a single cable sheath. Alien crosstalk is any external influence, typically NEXT and FEXT, that is measured between adjacent cables. The influence does not project very far, and separation of between 1cm and 2cm reduces the influence to insignificant levels. Cable bundles and cable piled in conduit or cable trays is easily close enough together to suffer from this effect

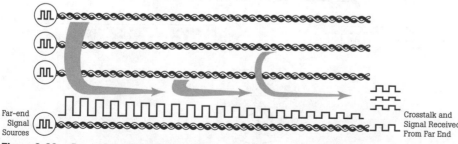

Far-end Signal Sources

Crosstalk and Signal Received From Far End

Figure 2-22. *Power Sum Attenuation to Crosstalk Ratio, Far-End (PSACRF)*

(see Figure 2-23). The effect is mitigated if the cable is placed loosely together so that no section of one cable is touching another cable for a significant distance. "Dressing" the cables for neatness by aligning them using cable ties and otherwise joining long runs together for extended distances causes alien crosstalk to increase.

This crosstalk is worst between wire pairs with the same twist rate. The effect is greater for pairs with a lower twist rate. Impact increases with the distance over which the cables run in parallel, and with the frequency of the transmitted signals.

Alien crosstalk is also affected by "ambient noise" caused by RF signals (various radio communications or noise sources) and electromechanical disturbances. Noise from these other uncorrelated sources cannot be canceled out, and is included in alien crosstalk measurements.

Virtually all the previous frequency-based measurements are repeated for alien crosstalk, with the addition of some average values. A full suite of alien crosstalk measurements is made after all the in-channel measurements have been made (and pass). Then a cable in a given bundle is selected as the *victim link* (officially it is the *disturbed link*), and signals are transmitted on all adjacent links in the bundle called the *disturber links*. A complete test suite for a 48-cable bundle could take many hours because each cable must be the victim link in turn, and all disturber links must be used for each victim link. Because this extensive testing is simply too time-consuming, a process for sampling the most likely worst-case victim and disturber links has been laboratory validated. This process is a resource available

from the Fluke Networks web site at www.flukenetworks.com/10gig in support of TIA TSB-155 testing.

Alien Near-End Crosstalk (ANEXT)

Alien Near-End Crosstalk loss (ANEXT) is the amount of unwanted signal coupling from a disturber pair in an adjacent cable measured on a victim pair in the measured cable. ANEXT is measured at the near end—the same end as the transmission source. In the same manner that NEXT is worst closest to the transmission source, ANEXT is worst nearest the adjacent transmission source.

Average Alien Near-End Crosstalk (Average ANEXT)

Average Alien Near-End Crosstalk (Average ANEXT) is the average amount of unwanted signal coupling at the near end measured for each of the four victim pairs in one victim cable at the near end.

Alien Far-End Crosstalk (AFEXT)

Alien Far-end Crosstalk loss (AFEXT) is the amount of unwanted signal coupling from a disturber pair in an adjacent cable measured on a victim pair in the disturbed (victim) cable. AFEXT is measured at the far end, the end away from the transmission source.

Attenuation to Alien Crosstalk Ratio Far-End (AACRF)

Attenuation to Alien Crosstalk Ratio Far-end (AACRF) is the difference (in dB) between the Alien FEXT from a disturber pair in an adjacent cable and the insertion loss of the victim pair in the disturbed cable at the far end.

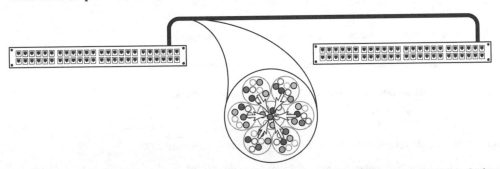

Figure 2-23. *Alien crosstalk is mostly a problem related to adjacent cables. This problem is exhibited whenever cables are in close proximity for any distance, such as a cable bundle between patch panels.*

Power Sum Alien Near-End Crosstalk (PSANEXT)

Power Sum Alien Near-End Crosstalk loss (PSANEXT) is the power sum of the unwanted crosstalk loss from adjacent disturber pairs in one or more adjacent disturber cables measured on a victim pair at the near end—the same end as the transmission source.

Power Sum Alien Far-End Crosstalk (PSAFEXT)

Power Sum Alien Far-End Crosstalk loss (PSAFEXT) is the power sum of the unwanted signal coupling from adjacent disturber pairs in one or more adjacent disturber cables measured on a victim pair at the far end—the end away from the transmission source.

Power Sum Attenuation to Alien Crosstalk Ratio Far-End (PSAACRF)

Power Sum Attenuation to Alien Crosstalk Ratio Far-End (PSAACRF) is the difference (in dB) between the Power Sum Alien Far End Crosstalk from multiple disturber pairs in one or more adjacent cables and the insertion loss of the victim pair in the measured cable at the far end.

Average Power Sum Attenuation to Alien Crosstalk Ratio Far-End (Average PSAACRF)

Average Power Sum Attenuation to Alien Crosstalk Ratio Far-End is the average of the Power Sum Attenuation to Alien Crosstalk Ratio Far End (Average PSAACRF) measurements for the four pairs in the victim cable.

The alien crosstalk evaluation of a disturbed or victim link requires that the PSANEXT and PSAACRF test parameters pass for all its wire pairs and the average of these four pairs after including the contribution by all disturber links. The disturber links must include all links bundled in the same bundle as the victim link, and links terminated in adjacent jacks in the panel if not already included because they are also part of the bundle.

Other Commonly Referenced Test Parameters

These next four test parameters are interesting, but are not usually part of a cable certification test. The problems related to these parameters are easily detected by other tests.

Capacitance

The TIA/EIA-568-B standard does not list capacitance as a required test for an installed link. To further support this, section 4 of TIA/EIA-568-B-2 states, "Mutual capacitance recommendations are provided for engineering design purposes" in several locations. If mutual capacitance is out of specification, characteristic impedance, return loss, and/or NEXT are directly affected, and field testing detects the problem accordingly with these tests.

From a troubleshooting perspective (not an engineering perspective), the goal of testing for capacitance problems is to identify the location of a link or installation fault. Rather than actually testing capacitance, it is far simpler and more accurate to use a TDR test to find the location of this sort of problem. Capacitance is also one of the test technologies used to infer the presence of split pairs in a twisted-pair cable.

Characteristic Impedance

When a high-frequency electrical signal is applied to a cable, the signal source experiences impedance. Impedance is a type of resistance that opposes the flow of alternating current (AC)—and network data is a type of high-frequency AC. A cable's characteristic impedance is a complex property, resulting from the combined effects of the cable's inductive, capacitive, and resistive values. These values are determined by physical parameters such as the size of the conductors, the distance between conductors, and the properties of the cable's insulation material.

Proper network operation depends on a constant characteristic impedance throughout the system's cables and connectors. Abrupt changes in characteristic impedance (called *impedance discontinuities* or *impedance anomalies*) cause signal reflections. Such changes in characteristic impedance can cause a high incidence of bit errors, as discussed previously.

The impact of characteristic impedance problems are more practically represented by the effect called return loss (see the description of return loss). Return loss tells you directly how bad the total effect of all reflections is.

Termination impedance present at the link ends must be equal to the characteristic impedance. Frequently, this termination impedance is included in the interface of equipment to be connected to the LAN. A good match between characteristic impedance and termination impedance provides for a good transfer of power to and from the link and minimizes reflections.

Complex high-speed LAN encoding methods, such as the 4D-PAM5 scheme used with 1000BASE-T, are even more sensitive to changes in characteristic impedance. The faster and more complex the signaling, the more sensitive the scheme is to this sort of problem. Lengths of untwisted wires must be kept to the absolute minimum, and lengths of cable with different characteristic impedance should never be mixed. If the characteristic impedance suddenly changes as a signal travels along a link, a reflection occurs that causes the signal (or a portion thereof) to bounce back toward the source. Such a reflected signal may again bounce back at another impedance anomaly and continue along the path of the originally transmitted signal. This combination of possible reflections may cause problems for the receiver (it creates signal jitter).

The characteristic impedance is almost always disturbed at connections or terminations. A LAN can tolerate some disturbance. However, it is critically important for the installer to untwist a twisted-pair cable to the minimum extent possible, particularly when installing links for high-speed LANs. In fact, for Category 5e cable, a link is permitted to have a *maximum* of 13 millimeters (0.5 inches) of untwisted wire at each termination point (TIA/EIA-568-B-1, paragraph 10.2.3). Installing an older or unrated RJ45 coupler to connect two cables normally exceeds this limit. Older RJ45 couplers often have particularly bad NEXT performance, and unless they are clearly marked with Category 5e or better ratings they should never be used in a Category 5e or better installation (the effect of poor quality couplers is shown in Figure 2-24). Rated couplers are typically larger than older poor quality couplers, and are much more expensive.

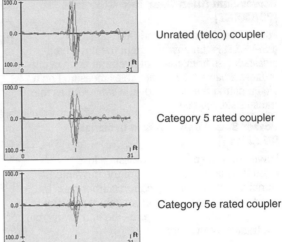

Unrated (telco) coupler

Category 5 rated coupler

Category 5e rated coupler

Figure 2-24. *DTX 1800 HDTDX test results for two 5-meter (15 ft) Category 6 patch cables joined with an RJ45 coupler. The top graphic depicts the link with an older (unrated) RJ45 coupler, the middle has a Category 5 coupler, and the bottom has a Category 5e coupler.*

Reflected signals are attenuated as they travel back, so the effect of reflections is reduced as the distance from the receiver increases. Sharp bends or kinks in LAN cable can also alter the cable's characteristic impedance. Poor electrical contacts, improper cable terminations, improper cable pairing, mismatched cable types (cables with different characteristic impedance values), and manufacturing defects in the cable all cause impedance discontinuities, resulting in degraded link performance.

An impedance measurement is sometimes used to infer the presence of split pairs in twisted-pair cable. When there is a split pair, the characteristic impedance measurement usually exhibits significantly different impedances for the pairs that were split.

Noise

Noise problems on a LAN link include impulse noise and continuous wideband noise. Noise does not include signals from other wire pairs, which are measured as forms of crosstalk.

Impulse noise is measured by counting the number of voltage spikes that exceed a certain threshold. A low impulse count is desirable for good network performance. However, an impulse noise test is not always sensitive enough for LANs that use higher levels of encoding than the common 10BASE-T networks. Wideband noise is a continuous presence of noise over a wide frequency band; it is not a part of the data transmission signal but potentially corrupts this signal. The lower the wideband noise voltage, the better the LAN performance will be. To resolve problems related to noise, it might be necessary to use other categories of tools, such as high-speed digitizing sampling oscilloscopes and spectrum analyzers with variable measurement bandwidths.

As mentioned during the discussion of NEXT, due to imbalance, LAN links also act as antennas. They can pick up noise signals from fluorescent lights, electric motors, photocopiers, and other similar devices that are located in proximity to the LAN cable. Also, when a transmitter of a radio or TV station is in the vicinity, significant noise can be picked up by the cable. Remember that the lower FM and TV bands are within the 1MHz to 100MHz range at which nearly all LAN protocols operate. Be sure to consider these external noise signal influences when you are planning your installation and route links as far away as possible or use shielded cable.

The LAN is a wideband system, meaning that all frequencies between 1MHz and 100MHz for Category 5e, or up to as high as 500MHz for Category 6A, make up the signal that is to be transmitted.

Resistance

The DC loop resistance test is a basic resistance test used to detect the presence of termination resistor(s) on coax cable and to detect poor-quality connections on twisted-pair links.

A simple coax resistance test should show one of three expected results for Ethernet: open (no termination present), 50 ohms (one terminator present), or 25 ohms (two terminators present, one at each end of the cable). For RG-59 used with WAN links and wireless the measurements would reveal 75 ohms, or 37.5 ohms. If the test result deviates much from one of those three options, a cable fault is likely. 802.3 Ethernet specifies that termination resistors shall be 50 ohms with variations of only ±1 percent. However,

the network *usually* continues to operate with variations of up to several ohms, although this introduces reflections of the data and reduces the effective maximum link length accordingly.

If the center conductor is shorted to the shield at the far end, thick coax should measure around 5 ohms at 500 meters, and thin coax should measure around 2 ohms at 185 meters (maximum lengths for Ethernet). If there are poor-quality connections along the path, each additional poor connection adds some amount of resistance. Similar tests may be made for RG-59.

For UTP, the DC loop resistance test is more significantly affected by link length. A typical DC loop resistance test on a 100-meter cable should provide results in the range of 9 ohms to 12 ohms. The TIA/EIA-568-B maximum limit is 9.38 ohms of resistance per 100 meters of UTP (at 20°C). The test on twisted pair is performed by shorting the two wires from a twisted pair together at the far end, and then measuring the resistance of the entire wire path. The quickest way to tell whether there is a problem is to compare the results from all four pairs. If one pair shows 25 ohms, and the other three are between 11 ohms and 14 ohms, it is highly probable that the 25 ohms pair has a link fault. The TIA/EIA-568-B limit for ScTP is 14 ohms per 100 meters (at 20°C).

Any problems with DC resistance show up as attenuation problems as well; therefore, DC resistance is not very important for field testing. Note that the TIA/EIA standards do not include the DC resistance test, whereas the ISO 11801 standard includes this as a pass/fail test. When deploying Power over Ethernet (PoE), it might be advisable to take note of the DC measurement results. An excessive resistance gives rise to heat and a greater than expected voltage drop.

Test Configurations

A horizontal cable run consists of up to 90 meters of solid conductor cable, plus not more than 10 meters of stranded conductor patch cables in the equipment room, the user's work area, and any intermediate cross-connect or consolidation points.

Basic Link

The basic link was obsoleted by TIA/EIA-568-B when it superseded the TIA/EIA-568-A edition of that standard. The basic link was used by installers for testing the cable "in the wall" before the network was deployed, and often before power was available in new construction. The test required better performance than the channel link because there would be additional patch cables added later.

The basic link configuration does not permit any extra connectors in the tested link, but the point of measurement starts near the field tester and ends near the field tester remote unit at the other end of the link (see Figure 2-25). Therefore, the cable that is part of the basic link adapter is included in the test results each time.

Permanent Link

The permanent link replaces the basic link in TIA/EIA-568-B. The test is still used primarily by installers for testing the cable "in the wall," before the network is deployed.

The permanent link excludes the cable portions of the test adapters but includes the mated connection at each end (see Figure 2-26). The permanent link also allows for a consolidation point, which is desirable for open office cabling installations, and therefore more practical.

The significant difference between the basic and permanent link configurations is that the reference point for the measurements was moved from the tester interface to the plug end of the test adapter cable. This new test definition requires field testers to remove or subtract all measured effects of the test cord from each test result, but the mated connection with the link jacks is still included in the test results. From an installer's perspective, the change from basic to permanent link also means a loss of approximately 2dB of NEXT margin at 250MHz, which can lead to more failures and marginal results on Category 6/Class E links.

Channel Link

The channel link test is intended for the complete end-to-end or point-to-point cable path between two network devices, including the actual patch cables that will be used (see Figure 2-27). If a single common set of patch cables is used with the tester for each successive link tested instead of the end user's patch cables, the test does not comply with the requirements.

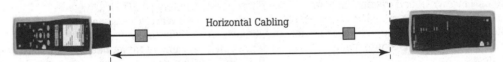

Horizontal Cabling

Figure 2-25. *Obsolete basic link test configuration*

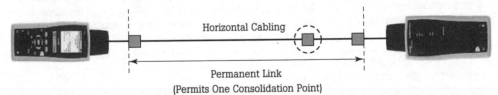

Horizontal Cabling

Permanent Link
(Permits One Consolidation Point)

Figure 2-26. *Permanent link test configuration*

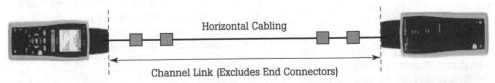

Horizontal Cabling

Channel Link (Excludes End Connectors)

Figure 2-27. *Channel link test configuration*

Patch cords can make a significant difference, particularly because of a different mating of plugs and jacks (the cable of a patch cord rarely has much of an impact unless it is severely damaged, and that is usually quite evident and detectable by a visual inspection). The end user wants the performance of the complete cabling link verified, which must include the end user's patch cables and not the instrumentation patch cables. The tested patch cable used in the channel test must be left as part of the tested link. Changing patch cables invalidates the test results, and would require a retest to recertify.

The channel configuration may include the optional consolidation point as well as a cross-connect. Often there is just a patch panel in the equipment room. The connection at the tester end is not included in the test results.

The permanent link test offers an important advantage to the network owner. Patch cords may be changed a number of times during the life of the cabling installation. A passing permanent link test ensures that adding "good" patch cords automatically provides a passing channel. This advantage can be claimed only if two important conditions are met:

- The RJ45 plug at the end of the tester permanent link adapter is a test reference plug—a plug that operates in the very center of the plug specification range for all frequency-dependent parameters. The performance requirements of the centered test (reference) plug are defined in the TIA Category 6 and Category 6A standards. Typical commercial patch cords seldom if ever meet this stringent requirement and should not be used to perform the permanent link test. The test reference plug at the end of the permanent link test adapter guarantees that the jack meets the category specification.

- The patch cords you use to complete the channel must meet the category rating of the permanent link or better. You should either purchase patch cords for the high-performance links (Category 5e/Class D or above) from reputable manufacturers, or test patch cords with the proper adapters and

against the appropriate standard to confirm their performance. Some manufacturers include the test results data with their patch cords to confirm their compliance with the standards. Be sure that a patch cord test was performed (for short cables), and not a channel test for up to 100 meters.

What Should Be Tested?

TIA/EIA-568-B contains specifications for the testing of installed twisted-pair cabling links. The primary field test parameters for such a link include

- Wiremap
- Length
- Insertion loss
- Near-End Crosstalk (NEXT) loss
- Power Sum Near-End Crosstalk (PSNEXT) loss
- Attenuation to Crosstalk Ratio at the Far-End (ACRF)
- Power Sum Attenuation to Crosstalk Ratio at the Far-End (PSACRF)
- Return loss
- Propagation delay
- Delay skew

Table 2-4 listed the test requirements for certification of Augmented Category 6 (Category 6A), as described in TIA/EIA-568-B Addendum 10. The ISO standard will publish the performance requirements for Augmented Class E (Class E_A) in a future edition of standard 11801.

You should always test to the maximum rating for the grade of cable you are installing. If you are specifying an installation that will be contracted out, require the contractor to submit electronic test results showing certification to the maximum rating for that grade of cable. A draft template for contracting a cable installation is available from the Fluke Networks web site. Look for "Field Test Specification" in the Knowledge Base. The template is kept current per the evolving standards requirements, and should help you avoid most of the typical installation problems. There are templates for both twisted-pair copper and for fiber.

Grounding and Shielding Cable

Although the primary purpose of requiring Screened Twisted Pair (ScTP) or Shielded Twisted Pair (STP) throughout most of Europe is to prevent network signals from leaking *out* of the cable, most people think of shielding as a way to prevent signals from leaking *into* the cable. Although the use of shielding is a good way to meet both requirements, there are some potential problems.

Figure 2-28 shows one style of shielded metallic connection box. Part A shows the parts of an ScTP cable. Part B shows one type of wall jack where the shielding fully encloses the end of the cable, with an arrow indicating the point where the cable shield connects to the jack shield. Part C shows a cutaway of a correctly terminated fully enclosed ScTP 8-pin modular plug (RJ45), with an arrow indicating the point that the cable shield connects to the plug shield over 360 degrees (full circle). Below that is an incorrectly terminated ScTP cable, where the cable shield does not enclose the wire pairs completely into the shield of the plug.

The fundamental purpose of a shield is to *fully enclose* a signal so that no radiated field can enter the cable and disturb the signal lines, and

equally important, so that no field is radiated out of the cable, where it could interfere with other electronic devices. Note that it is absolutely essential that shields fully enclose the signals in every regard. Extending a drain wire even a short distance past the shield of a cable to make a connection defeats the quality of the shield significantly (see part C in Figure 2-28). Proper installation requires mounting clamps that are located inside enclosed metal spaces, so that openings are absolutely minimal. Coaxial cabling systems and connecting hardware lend themselves well toward this goal.

Generally speaking, a connection to ground is made for personal safety reasons. To meet current safety requirements, almost all powered equipment must have a third wire safety connection to ground. The issue then becomes where (at what locations) connections have to be made between the earth ground (chassis) and the shield.

All earth ground connections eventually lead to a building ground location. Voltage potentials in the earth ground lead are caused by leakage currents in the various pieces of electrical equipment. The leakage current times the resistance of the ground wires cause voltage potentials, which easily can exceed several volts. Voltage potentials between buildings are generally very significant.

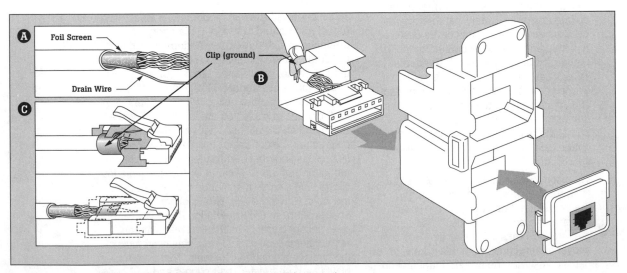

Figure 2-28. *One style of Screened (ScTP) connection*

Lightning is another important consideration when connecting buildings. For data communication between buildings, fiber optic connections are the only practical and safe solution.

You do not want to have a cable shield become a ground return path. This can be avoided in one of two ways:

- Permit only a single connection between earth ground and the shield. The recommended end for grounding an ScTP or STP permanent link is at the wiring closet end, where the ground should be bonded to the building earth ground.

- Make certain that there is no substantial voltage potential between the earth ground connections of the equipment and any connection to data communications systems. If there is no voltage, there will be no current, and therefore no problem. This is the solution that is followed for shielded twisted-pair cabling systems (STP and ScTP).

In coaxial cable systems (10BASE2 and 10BASE5), the connection between earth ground and the shield is made at one location in the cable system. This is typically done at one end of the coax run. At all other locations there is isolation between tap connections and any earth ground source. For 10BASE2, protective plastic caps are often used

to prevent accidental contact between the BNC "Tee" connector and the PC chassis. Most WAN and wireless coax use is point-to-point with little opportunity for shorts, unlike coaxial Ethernet.

Coax may be tested by measuring the current flow between the shield of the cable and the shield mating connection on the end equipment. Disconnect the cable and measure between the shield connections with a digital multimeter. Less than 20mA is unlikely to disrupt data.

When using shields with twisted-pair cabling systems (ScTP, STP), you can verify the absence of ground loop potentials by testing for them after all non-LAN electrical equipment has been installed and is operational. Then activate the LAN equipment and measure the voltage potential between the shield of the other end and the chassis of the equipment to be connected (see Figure 2-29). If the voltage is less than 1 volt AC, you may be reasonably assured that there will be no ground loop effect.

If the voltage is substantially higher, you must locate the source of the leakage. This normally involves working with a qualified electrician to correct the problem that is creating the voltage potential. This is not always easy to do, and if not possible, you should convert the connection from copper to fiber optic cable.

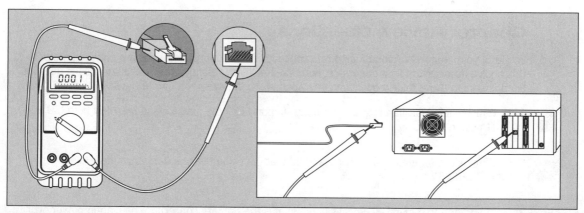

Figure 2-29. *Measuring a cable shield for AC voltage with a digital multimeter*

Summary

This chapter described copper cabling test standards, the test parameters required for compliance with those standards, and test configurations.

- Cabling standards continue to evolve. To be certain that the test results obtained certifying a new cable installation are reliable, it is important to keep the cable tester updated with the latest performance specifications.

- Testing cable to the requirements of the technology you are deploying is acceptable, but a better practice would be to test to the performance specifications of the installed cable type.

  If testing is performed to ensure that a specific technology operates, it is likely to be a less stringent test than if the performance specifications of the installed cable type were tested. Also, knowing that the installed cable performed according to the labeling of the cable instead of a lesser standard would allow a different technology to be used on the same cable plant without requiring a full retest of the cable plant. For example, if a Category 5e cable plant had been tested for use with 100BASE-TX, which requires testing to 80MHz and uses only two pairs, the entire cable plant would have to be retested before 1000BASE-T is deployed. 1000BASE-T requires all four pairs to be tested to 100MHz, plus some additional tests required by Category 5e but not for 100BASE-TX. If the cable plant is certified for Category 5e performance specifications at the time of installation, either Ethernet implementation could be deployed over the cable plant without further testing.

- Understanding what is tested will help you with both installation and testing. Knowing the operational characteristics of cable test parameters is particularly helpful in understanding the purpose for the installation guidelines (such as not untwisting pairs more than absolutely necessary), and also in understanding what to look for when troubleshooting a failed cable performance test.

- Selecting the correct test configuration is an important part of certifying a cable, but abiding by the requirements of the test configuration is just as important. If the channel test configuration is used, but the same patch cables are used to test the entire installation instead of leaving the tested patch cables in place after each test, the testing performed is invalidated. It is important to understand what is required for each test configuration.

Chapter Review Questions

To aid in your comprehension of important concepts, the following questions are provided. Refer to this book's Introduction for a general legend that indicates the anticipated difficulty of each question. For answers to these review questions, see Appendix I, "Answers to Chapter Review Questions."

 1. Which cable classifications are currently supported by the media standards? List both ISO and TIA cable types.

 2. What is the minimum cable test standard that the cable test standard must meet to support 10GBASE-T?

 3. In addition to general electrical safety, what is the primary concern for delivering power over twisted-pair cabling?

4. What types of cable fault does a wiremap test reveal?

 5. What is the difference between a reversed pair and a transposed pair?

 6. What is the difference between TIA/EIA-568-B and T568B?

 7. What is the difference between T568A and T568B?

 8. In addition to comparing wire insulation colors used for each pair at both ends of a cable, what test infers the presence a split pair? Name three test techniques.

 9. What special type of Ethernet cable is created when T568A and T568B are used on the same cable?

 10. Approximately how far does an Ethernet signal travel in 10 nanoseconds on a typical Ethernet cable?

 11. Describe the principle or process behind a TDR measurement.

 12. What is delay skew?

 13. What does the attenuation test measure?

 14. Up to approximately what frequency does insertion loss generally appear to be linear?

 15. At what location along a typical cable is return loss most frequently introduced?

 16. How is the influence of crosstalk typically reduced by the cable manufacturer?

 17. What is the measurement difference between ACR and SNR?

 18. How is NEXT different from FEXT?

 19. If ACRF fails, where is the problem most likely to be found?

 20. How is a power sum measurement different from the nonpower sum equivalent (such as NEXT and PSNEXT)?

 21. What characteristic identifies Ethernet implementations where power sum measurements could be important?

22. How is alien crosstalk different from other forms of crosstalk, such as NEXT versus ANEXT?

 23. What typically results from a change of impedance along a cable link?

 24. How is impulse noise measured?

 25. What measurement, other than DC resistance, would likely detect a DC resistance fault in a cable?

 26. What is the difference between a *permanent* link and a *channel* link?

 27. How low must current flowing over a cable shield be to avoid disrupting data communications?

CHAPTER 3
Fiber Optic Media

This chapter describes issues related to installing and testing fiber optic physical media for use in local area networks. The principles are the same for longer distance usage (usually telco or ISP), but the unique characteristics of that application of fiber optic media is not addressed by this text.

Two aspects of working around fiber optic media merit special emphasis:

- **Safety.** The wavelengths used by networking gear are outside what the human eye can detect, and therefore significant eye damage is possible if care is not taken. Some LAN uses, and most WAN uses, involve rather powerful nonvisible lasers.

- **Cleanliness.** A large percentage of field media problems are related to dirty connections. So much time can be saved if both sides of any connection are always cleaned whenever they are disturbed, even if you cleaned the connection moments ago when you last disconnected. Form a habit of cleaning all fiber before attaching it anywhere.

Fiber optic media may be preferred over copper media. The most common reasons for this preference include immunity from electrical interference and greater operating distances.

This text implies that all fiber optic cable has a glass core, but some plastic core fiber is available. The most significant plastic core performance differences are much higher attenuation per meter and poor modal bandwidth performance. Plastic core is not used in a typical LAN environment because it is an effective option only for very short distances.

Safety

Safety is not something that's forgiving enough to let you "do again" to get it right. Safety around LANs, and especially WANs or telco fiber optics, is primarily translated to avoiding permanent eye damage.

Light

The visible light spectrum that the human eye is adapted to see ranges from about 400nm (blues) to 700nm (reds). Typical networking equipment uses the following three common wavelengths: 850nm, 1300/1310nm, and 1550nm. Note that none of these wavelengths falls within the spectrum that the human eye can detect, although

the 850nm range is close enough that some red light is often seen. This is because the light source output often includes other wavelengths, not because the network equipment can use it.

Because the red light that is observed on many 850nm links is actually outside the spectrum the equipment uses, there is no reason to expect to see any visible light on an 850nm (or any other) networking link. On the longer wavelength links, there is even less likelihood that visible light will be seen, including high-powered laser links.

Permanent damage may be caused by looking into the end of a fiber. If a magnifying device is used, the likelihood of nearly instant permanent damage to your retina is high.

- Disconnect the fiber at both ends.

- Wear safety glasses rated for the wavelength of light you are working around.

- Use an optical power meter on each fiber to verify that there is no non-invisible light present before examining it.

Not infrequently has optical power metering equipment been attached to a presumably safe fiber only to see readings measured in positive dB numbers. This indicates that powerful active equipment is at the other end of the link.

Although it is a commonly used technique, using a flashlight or other visible light source to locate a particular fiber is unsafe. Specifically, staring into the fiber end while waiting for visible light to appear is very dangerous. The candidate fiber should be directed at a piece of paper, where the visible light will illuminate a small spot when the correct fiber has been found.

Glass

Fiber termination experience is a valuable skill; however, be very careful with the fiber shards created during the termination process. The tiny pieces of glass are very difficult to see under most circumstances, and if one gets under your skin it is all but impossible to see. Removal is mostly accomplished by touch, if at all. There are plenty of stories about someone who had to wait for the shard to work its way back out on its own—very slowly and painfully. Always wear safety glasses when terminating fiber. If a glass shard is believed to have landed in your eye, it is recommended that it be rinsed away instead of wiping it away. Wiping may push it into the eye tissue.

It is best to treat the fiber shards as a type of hazardous waste. Always store and transport them in a sealed container. Put cut ends on tape to prevent them from escaping the work surface. The tape may then be folded over to contain the fiber shards before placing them in the fiber shards storage bottle that has been clearly marked for such duty.

Standards

In addition to the general building requirements listed with the standards for copper cable, the following are some of the standards that apply to fiber optic media.

International Standards

ISO/IEC 11801: Information technology—Generic cabling for customer premises

ISO/IEC 14763-3: Information technology—Implementation and operation of customer premises cabling—Part 3: Testing of optical fibre cabling

ISO/IEC 60793: Optical fibres—Measurement methods and test procedures

ISO/IEC 61280: Fibre optic communication subsystem basic test procedures

ISO/IEC 61300: Fibre optic interconnecting devices and passive components

United States Standards

EIA/TIA-526-7: Measurement of Optical Power Loss of Installed Single-Mode Fiber Cable Plant

EIA/TIA-526-14: Optical Power Loss Measurements of Installed Multimode Fiber Cable Plant

EIA/TIA TSB140: Additional Guidelines for Field-Testing Length, Loss and Polarity of Optical Fiber Cabling Systems

ANSI/TIA/EIA-568-C.3: Optical Fiber Cabling Components Standard
Part 3 (TIA/EIA-568-C.3) Covers the connecting hardware and cable components used in premises optical fiber network applications. Provides the requirements and test specifications for components used to create an installed link, as well as testing requirements for installed links.

Fiber Optic Cable Design

The following is an abbreviated summary of fiber optic theories. Many aspects of fiber optic technology were left out in an attempt to keep this summary understandable and relevant to testing. If this information is of particular interest, there is a wealth of existing and emerging information available for further reading.

Two general types of fiber optic cable are found in a networking environment: singlemode and multimode.

For older LAN cables (before color was a cosmetic choice), you were usually right in assuming that a yellow cable jacket meant singlemode, whereas orange meant multimode. The availability of designer colors has minimized the certainty of fiber type based on the color of the jacket. TIA/EIA-568-C.3 and TIA/EIA-598-C specify colors as shown in Table 3-1, however, and permit other colors as long as there is printed labeling that clearly identifies the cable type.

Table 3-1. *Standard fiber cable jacket and connector colors*

Fiber Type	Jacket Color	Connectors and Adapters	Labeling
Multimode (50/125)	Orange	Black	50/125
Multimode 850nm Laser-Optimized (50/125)	Aqua	Aqua	850 LO 50/125
Multimode (62.5/125)	Orange	Beige	62.5/125
Singlemode	Yellow	Blue	SM / NZDS SM
Polarization Maintaining Singlemode	Blue	—	—
Angled Contact Ferrule Singlemode Connectors	—	Green	—

The names for singlemode and multimode origi-nate from the light conducting property of the glass strand that represents the core. In a single-mode cable, the glass strand is so narrow that the wavelength of light used is able to travel in only one specific direction or mode (see Figure 3-1).

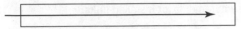

Figure 3-1. *Singlemode light transmission path*

A multimode cable has a much larger diameter, and the light can travel in more than one direc-tion or mode (see Figure 3-2).

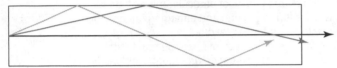

Figure 3-2. *Multimode light transmission paths*

Fiber Cable Construction

Each fiber consists of four elements: the primary coating and buffer that surrounds the outer glass cladding, the cladding, and the light conductive core (see Figure 3-3).

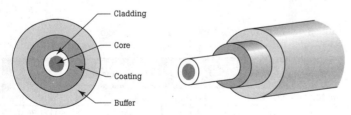

Figure 3-3. *Basic fiber optic cable elements*

There are two general configurations: loose tube buffer and tight buffer. Tight buffer, as shown to the left in Figure 3-4, is manufactured with the buffer applied directly to the fiber strand, and is typically 250 μm (microns) in diameter. This buffer significantly improves the strength of the fiber, protecting it against abrasion and im-pact shock. A loose tube buffer is where the buf-fer forms a tube around the strand of bare fiber, permitting the fiber to move independently of the buffer. Loose tube buffer often contains more than one strand of bare fiber and has a larger diameter than tight buffer. Loose tube buffer is not as com-mon in LAN applications but is used for longer telco distances, where changes in temperature cause the buffer to expand and contract, and would otherwise strain the fiber and shorten its useful life.

The cladding is made from pure silica glass with a different refractive index than the inner core. The cladding, or outer shell, is there to re-flect light back toward the center. The cladding is 125 μm in diameter for both singlemode and multimode.

The central core of the fiber comes in three sizes common to LAN environments, though other sizes are available. Singlemode fiber is approxi-mately 9 μm, whereas multimode comes in 50 μm and 62.5 μm diameter sizes (see Figure 3-5).

Cable Construction

An assembled fiber optic cable consists of the fol-lowing (see Figure 3-6):

* The bare fiber (the core, cladding, and primary coating)

* A connector plug with a ceramic ferrule to hold the bare fiber, a connector body, and a strain relief that connects to the cable buffer or outer jacket

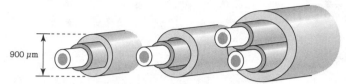

Figure 3-4. *Tight buffer (left) and loose tube buffer cables*

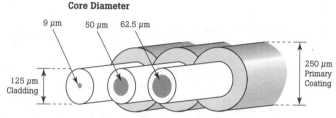

Figure 3-5. *Fiber core diameter*

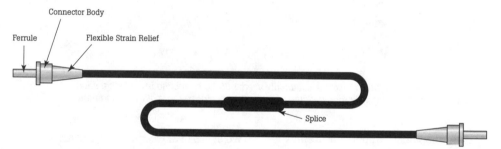

Figure 3-6. *Typical fiber optic cable elements, although splices are not usually found in a patch cable*

Many types of outer jackets are applied to the basic fiber optic cable, depending on the application. For most LAN use, a relatively thick outer jacket contains the fiber buffer and some sort of strength member. An aramid yarn is commonly used for this strength member. Depending on the intended application, there may be further additions or layers to the cable appearing between the primary coating and the outer jacket.

Splicing factory-terminated ends onto horizontal cable is becoming more and more common. The loss incurred by a splice is very small, whereas the performance in hand-terminated ends is quite variable. This creates a situation where purchasing preterminated ends and splicing them onto an installed cable results in con-

sistently better overall performance. Splicing is also much faster than terminating, which makes it more cost-effective: Labor is the largest cost item in a typical termination.

Connector Types

Manufacturing processes are becoming more reliable and accurate, and improvements in circuitry are permitting manufacturers to have increasingly higher densities of interfaces presented to the user. This results in a need for smaller connectors with tighter tolerances for movement once inserted. Common older connectors for fiber optic cables include, but are not limited to, those shown in Figure 3-7 and Figure 3-8.

Figure 3-7. *Older technology MIC connector common with FDDI installations*

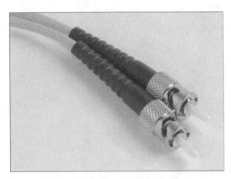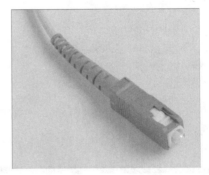

Figure 3-8. *ST (left) and SC (right) connectors, commonly used with both multimode and singlemode. SC connectors are often clipped together to form a single two–fiber connector so that polarity is maintained.*

A flurry of development by fiber optic technology vendors has produced a wide range of small form factor (SFF) connectors. SFF connectors are optical fiber duplex connectors with a size approximating that of an RJ45, which permits much greater port density in switches than the older and larger connectors. This development effort coincided with the standards body work on 10 Gigabit versions of Ethernet, which carefully avoided specifying a connector type. Instead, the standards body chose to specify the link performance requirements, and left the actual physical connector design up to the marketplace.

Two styles of SFF connector types are shown in Figure 3-9.

Test Parameters

The nature of copper media described in the previous chapter allowed for a considerable number of field performance tests. Fiber optic media does not permit field validation of many of the parameters tested by the manufacturers.

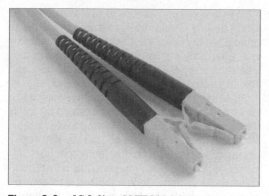 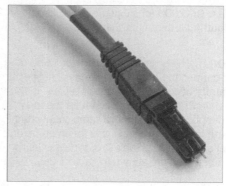

Figure 3-9. *LC (left) and MTRJ (right) connectors are examples of small form factor (SFF) connectors. SFF connectors are almost always paired and clipped together to form a single two-fiber connector so that polarity is maintained.*

Field Testing Parameters

Tests performed in the field are usually limited to attenuation (loss), length, and cable polarity. Many of the problems, which result from the topics listed in the next section on light behavior, are revealed in severity and location through testing performed with an optical time domain reflectometer (OTDR) test set.

Initial testing is almost always conducted for loss using a fiber power meter and a suitable light source. If adequate light is present, you begin a manual inspection of the link or use an OTDR to learn what is affecting passage of the light. Troubleshooting is significantly enhanced with an OTDR.

Attenuation (Loss)

Attenuation testing is accomplished by launching a referenced or calibrated amount of light into one end of the fiber, and measuring how much of that light reached the other end.

The attenuation test results should always be less than the total loss allowed by the physical layer implementation, such as Gigabit Ethernet. This is to allow for aging of the link over time and for the inclusion of a splice or two as needed for an emergency repair.

Loss is caused by almost everything, including

- Bends in the cable (singlemode is more sensitive to bends than multimode)
- Connection alignment problems
- Bad or damaged terminations
- Dirt, dust, and other contamination in fiber connections
- Finger oil on fiber end faces
- Cable manufacturing flaws
  - Impurities in the core
  - Density changes in the core
  - Bubbles in the core

ISO/IEC 11801 defines three fiber optic channel link types:

- Class OF-300 for support of applications requiring a minimum channel length of 300 meters
- Class OF-500 for support of applications requiring a minimum channel length of 500 meters

- Class OF-2000 for support of applications requiring a minimum channel length of 2000 meters

The ISO/IEC 11801 standard allows for 1.5dB of loss for connecting hardware but does not specify the quantity of connections and/or splices. It also makes note that the power budget for the intended application may permit more connecting hardware loss. Attenuation limits for an entire link channel are shown in Table 3-2, whereas limits for the fiber itself are shown in Table 3-3.

Table 3-2. *ISO 11801 (2002) limits for channel attenuation*

ISO 11801 Channel Attenuation Limit by Class	Multimode		Singlemode	
	850nm	1300nm	1310nm	1550nm
OF-300	2.55dB	1.95dB	1.80dB	1.80dB
OF-500	3.25dB	2.25dB	2.00dB	2.00dB
OF-2000	8.50dB	4.50dB	3.50dB	3.50dB

Table 3-3. *ISO 11801 (2002) limits for fiber optic cable attenuation (cable only)*

ISO 11801 Attenuation Limit for Cable	Multimode		Singlemode	
	850nm	1300nm	1310nm	1550nm
Max Attenuation	3.5dB/km	1.5dB/km	1.0dB/km	1.0dB/km

Although the TIA/EIA-568-B provided generic attenuation requirements for fiber optic channel testing (see Table 3-4), TIA/EIA-568-C.0 chose not to specify this. Instead, it indicates that a published standard should be referenced to identify the wavelength(s) and direction(s) required for the channel test. It then goes on to provide a list of implementation standards requirements in Annex D, such as Gigabit Ethernet.

Table 3-4. *TIA/EIA-568-B limits for cable attenuation (cable only, no connector loss)*

TIA/EIA-568-B Attenuation Limit by Fiber Type	Multimode		Singlemode	
	850nm	1300nm	1310nm	1550nm
50μm, 50μm laser optimized, 62.5μm	3.5dB/km	1.5dB/km	—	—
Singlemode (inside)	—	—	1.0dB/km	1.0dB/km
Singlemode (indoor/outdoor), (outside)	—	—	0.5dB/km	0.5dB/km

A cable tester acting as an optical loss test set (OLTS) usually permits users to store test results for cable plant documentation. It must be configured with the number of connectors and splices in the link under test. Without that information, it is unable to present Pass/Fail test results accurately.

To obtain reliable and repeatable results, it is important that the light source be turned on for a long enough period before testing to allow the electronic circuitry to arrive at a steady-state operating temperature such that the output level has stabilized. This stabilization period usually requires about 5–10 minutes. Once stabilized, a reference reading may be made. After calibrating the light source, don't turn the light source off or disconnect the fiber patch cable from the light source until testing is complete. If you do, recalibrate the measurement.

Length

TIA/EIA-568-C.1 defers to the application specification for length limits. A sample table of application requirements listed by fiber type is found in TIA/EIA-568-C.0, Annex D (such as Gigabit Ethernet).

Length may be measured by reading the markings on the cable jacket or by measuring length as a function of propagation delay or delay between a test pulse and the return of reflections.

Polarity

Nearly all LAN networking implementations are bidirectional systems that use separate optical fibers in each direction. The net effect of polarity testing is to ensure that TX at one end is connected to RX at the other. TIA/EIA-568-C.0 Annex B provides several examples of how this may be accomplished. The general theme is that the paired connectors are reversed at each cable junction (TX to RX). ISO/IEC 11801 Clause 10 requires similar polarity testing.

The actual testing for polarity may be accomplished with tools as simple as a flashlight or Visual Fault Locator (VFL), or as complex as an OTDR.

Light Behavior

A singlemode cable core is narrow enough that the wavelength of light used (1300nm or longer) cannot bounce within the core, and travels straight from one end to the other (see Figure 3-10).

Figure 3-10. *Singlemode light behavior*

However, when light travels through a multimode cable, not all its rays travel straight through the core. The multimode cable has a large enough core diameter that the light wavelengths used can bounce around as it progresses through the cable. Light rays that bounce more than other rays take longer to reach the end of the cable (see Figure 3-11). This behavior is measured as dispersion. Light entering the cable at too great of an angle is lost into the cladding.

Figure 3-11. *Multimode light behavior*

Dispersion

Light that takes alternate (bouncing) paths down the cable travels a longer distance than light that travels straight down the center. Although not to scale, this concept is illustrated by how far the three light rays in Figure 3-11 were able to travel after departing from the same location at the same time. This is an important concept that forms the basis for why multimode cables cannot be used for the longer distances that singlemode cables support.

If two pulses of light are sent into a multimode cable at a close interval, this minor difference in travel distance becomes more pronounced as the cable gets longer. In Figure 3-12, the pulses are shown at three unspecified distance intervals along the fiber.

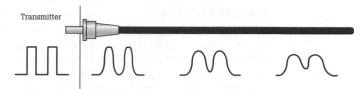

Figure 3-12. *Modal dispersion spreads light pulses in relation to distance*

Because the group of photons or light rays in each pulse has different distances to travel depending on the path taken through the fiber, they have different arrival times at the other end. Although most of the photons arrive approximately centered, a significant number of them arrive earlier or later, causing closely spaced pulses to begin to merge. This effect is called *modal dispersion*.

The photons from closely spaced pulses of light arrive at the other end, but beyond a certain distance it is not possible to accurately distinguish one pulse from the next. If the pulses are transmitted very close together in an attempt to achieve a higher throughput data rate, the effective cable length is very short.

After connector cleanliness, dispersion is perhaps the single most important transmission impediment in a fiber optic cable. Distance limits are based on the effect of dispersion.

Modal Bandwidth

Because dispersion is the controlling factor for the distance over which a particular multimode fiber optic cable can support an application, the cables are tested and labeled with a parameter called modal bandwidth.

At a given wavelength, the manufacturer transmits pulses into the cable at progressively higher frequencies until dispersion renders the signal indecipherable. From this testing the cable is then labeled according to the test results at some frequency in megahertz per kilometer for a given wavelength. For example, for a 62.5 μm cable the Ethernet standard requires a minimum modal bandwidth of 200 MHz/km to support 1000BASE-SX up to 275 meters with an 850nm light source. Beyond this distance, the capability of the receiver to faithfully recover the transmitted signal becomes questionable.

Critical Angle

One important factor associated with the bouncing effect represented by different modes or paths is the angle at which the light strikes the edge of the fiber core. If the light strikes the edge at equal to or greater than the critical angle, it continues toward the other end. If the light strikes the edge of the fiber at less than the critical angle, it leaves the core of the fiber and can be counted as increased loss.

Critical angle is measured from perpendicular to the two surfaces. When light passes at an angle from a medium that allows light to travel more slowly into the second medium where it travels faster, it tends to bend the light, as shown in Figure 3-13.

Figure 3-13. *Light bends as the angle away from perpendicular increases.*

An interesting and useful phenomenon takes place at one particular angle. The light is not allowed to escape from the first medium, even if both are transparent. It travels exactly along the edge of it (see example 2 in Figure 3-14). This is called the *critical angle*. The critical angle is calculated using the refractive index of the core and the cladding. The refractive index is a measure of how fast light travels through this medium. It is defined as the ratio between the speed of light in a vacuum divided by the speed of light in the subject material. The refractive index of the two materials is used in equation 1 to determine the critical angle.

A common refractive index for cladding is 1.45, and a common refractive index for the core is 1.47. Fiber with a uniform refractive index throughout the core is called *step index* because there is a change or step at the boundary of the core and the cladding. The following calculation produces the critical angle of 80.54° for the boundary between these two refractive indices.

$$\sin^{-1}\left(\frac{1.45}{1.47}\right) = 80.54°$$

80.54° then indicates the angle that light must approach the boundary between the core and the cladding to bounce exactly along the edge of it (at a 90° angle off perpendicular) without leaving the core (see example 2 in Figure 3-14). Light traveling at any angle that is smaller than this angle crosses the boundary into the cladding (example 1 in Figure 3-14). Light traveling at any angle that is equal to or greater than this angle remains in the core (see examples 2 and 3 in Figure 3-14).

Figure 3-14. *Critical angle*

Most light remains in the core because it strikes the boundary between the core and the cladding at greater angles than the critical angle. Because none of the light is leaving the core at this angle or greater, it is referred to as *total internal reflection.*

Bending Fiber

If the fiber were perfectly straight, the cladding would reflect all the light that entered the cable at suitable angles, and it would reach the other end. However, there are small and large bends in all fiber optic cables. As light passes through these bends, a certain amount of the light strikes cladding at an angle steep enough that it escapes (see Figure 3-15).

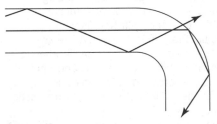

Figure 3-15. *Critical angle exceeded by excessive bend*

If bends are numerous or severe, enough light may be lost that the link fails. If the fiber is bent still further, it is placed at risk for breaking.

The wavelength of the light in the fiber determines how much effect a particular bend has. For the longer wavelengths usually associated with singlemode (1550nm and 1625nm), tiny microbends have a measurable effect. At shorter wavelengths, the microbend becomes less and less noticeable. The same microbend in a multimode cable at 850nm, or maybe even 1300nm, might not be noticed at all.

This issue forms the basis for bend radius limits. Far before the fiber is at risk of breaking, there is a significant loss in the amount of light reaching the end. Associated with bending is the amount of pulling tension. Table 3-5 details the official bend radius limits from the TIA/EIA-568-C.0 standard for situations where the manufacturer recommended limits are not known.

Graded Index

The effect of having the signal arrival times spreading out as dispersion in step index multimode fiber was a serious bandwidth limiting problem. To compensate for this, the fiber optic cable design engineers came up with a way to manufacture the fiber so that the light was pushed back toward the center. This was accomplished by varying the refractive index of the glass from the center to the edge of the core, and is called graded index. At the center of the core, the refractive index is greater (light travels at a slower speed) than at the edge.

In a graded index fiber, light traveling away from the center of the core (because of a bend or having entered the fiber at an odd angle) speeds up. As it returns toward the center, it slows back down. By manufacturing the cable very carefully, the engineers were able to cause light traveling different distances to arrive at the far end at much closer to the same time (see Figure 3-16). The modal dispersion is therefore greatly reduced.

Figure 3-16. *Light traveling through graded index fiber*

Singlemode fiber has long been optimized for low dispersion, simply because of the diameter. However, there are still some dispersion effects present. In fact, when 1550nm is used over the traditional singlemode fiber (referred to as nondispersion shifted fiber (NDSF)) to increase distance and take advantage of the lower attenuation, a fair amount of dispersion exists. To control the dispersion at 1550nm, the fiber optic design engineers tinkered some more and managed to reduce the dispersion at 1550nm to levels not unlike the older cable performance at 1300nm. These new variants were called *dispersion shifted fiber* (DSF).

Table 3-5. *TIA/EIA-568-C.3 minimum bend radius and maximum load limits for fiber*

Description	Minimum Bend Radius	Maximum Tensile load
Intra-building 2- or 4-fiber horizontal fiber (Cabling Subsystem 1)	Not less than 25mm (1 inch)	No load
	Not less than 50mm (2 inches)	222 Newtons (50 pound force)
Intra-building backbone fiber (Cabling Subsystem 2 and Cabling Subsystem 3)	Not less than 10 times the cable outside diameter	No load
	Not less than 20 times the cable's outside diameter	Under a tensile load up to the rating of the cable
Indoor/outdoor cable, and outside plant cable	Not less than 10 times the cable's outside diameter	No load
	Not less than 20 times the cable's outside diameter	Under a tensile load up to the rating of the cable

Unfortunately, it was later discovered that when dense wavelength division multiplexing (DWDM) was transmitted over DSF fiber, it simply did not work because of a nonlinearity problem. However, the older NDSF fiber worked pretty well for DWDM transmissions. The fiber optic cable design engineers then came up with non-zero-dispersion shifted fiber (NZ-DSF or NZDS) to compensate for the discovered problems. Many new engineering efforts are underway, including some radical new designs where thin hollow tubes are manufactured into the length of the fiber core. The hollow tubes prevent the light rays from dispersing even further, and suggest that remarkable fiber optic cable performance might not be far away.

Singlemode exhibits a problem related to signal polarization: polarization mode dispersion. Although singlemode propagates light in only one mode, there are two polarities (perpendicular to each other). If the fiber were perfect, the two polarities would travel at exactly the same speed. Because it is not perfect, irregularities permit one mode to get ahead of the other. As distance increases, the two polarizations begin to disperse, and arrive at different times. This problem is usually seen only on long runs, especially in the telco environment where distances are measured in kilometers. The NZDS fiber type compensates pretty well for this problem. This condition may be tested for in an installed link using specialized equipment; however, it is affected by temperature. Thus, the test must be repeated under several climate conditions to obtain a more accurate idea of the fiber performance for this parameter.

The last form of dispersion discussed here is chromatic dispersion. Each wavelength travels at a slightly different speed through the medium. Depending on which light source is used to generate the transmitted signal, it includes some amount of light in other wavelengths. DWDM and other similar communications implementations are designed to transmit multiple wavelengths. If the chromatic dispersion is positive then shorter wavelengths travel faster than longer wavelengths. If chromatic dispersion is negative then the reverse is true. To complicate matters, chromatic dispersion tends to be different for each wavelength in a given fiber. Choice of light sources has a big effect on how narrow the output signal is. Other forms of dispersion, including waveguide dispersion, material dispersion, and profile dispersion, typically affect chromatic dispersion.

Light Sources

The industry counts three basic light sources for fiber network interfaces at present: LED, VCSEL, or one of the other forms of laser, such as FP and DFB. The light emitting diode (LED) is the cheapest to manufacture but has the widest spectral width. A relatively new light source in the laser group is the vertical cavity surface emitting laser (VCSEL), which is comparatively inexpensive to manufacture but also focuses the light much better than an LED. Two other forms of laser, both of which have been available for a long time, are Fabry-Perot (FP) and distributive feedback (DFB) laser. Other types are used in networking applications but are not as common.

Light sources used with multimode cable, usually LED and VCSEL, operate at one of two wavelengths, 850nm and 1300nm. Laser light sources used with singlemode cable operate at two different wavelengths, 1310nm and 1550nm. Lasers output a very narrow range of wavelengths compared to LED sources, as shown in Figure 3-17 and Table 3-6.

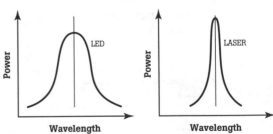

Figure 3-17. *Spectral width of LED versus laser light sources. Notice that the energy or power from a laser is output at wavelengths very close to the target light wavelength indicated by the vertical line (i.e., 1310nm), whereas the LED energy is output over a wider range of wavelengths (i.e., 1300nm). Wider spectral width increases chromatic dispersion and limits distance for high-speed data transmission.*

Spectral width is indicated with the term *full-width, half maximum* (FWHM). This measure indicates the output spectrum at the 50 percent power level.

Table 3-6. *Spectral width of various example light sources*

Light Source Type	Spectral Width (FWHM)
Surface-emitting 850nm LED	60nm
Surface-emitting 1300nm LED	110nm
Edge-emitting 1300nm LED	50nm
FP 1310nm laser	4nm
DFB 1310nm laser	0.2nm

The light output pattern for each of the primary light sources for fiber optic cable use are progressively narrower (see Figure 3-18). The surface-emitting LED light source commonly used with 850nm multimode has the broadest output pattern. An edge-emitting LED light source is necessarily more focused, and all the laser light sources have extremely narrow output patterns.

Launch Conditions

The type of output light source leads directly to whether the launch condition is overfilled or underfilled. Overfilled launch is used when the light source is not very powerful, and you want to ensure that every bit of the exposed core of the fiber is filled with output light. Underfilled launch is when output power is focused right into the fiber core without illuminating the entire face of the core. That part of the core not illuminated with the laser output is not important because all the light emitted from the laser entered the core.

The critical angle plays a role in the launch conditions too. The only emitted light that is of importance is that light which enters the fiber core and travels to the other end. We have already determined that light striking the boundary between the core and the cladding at an angle less than the critical angle leaves the core. Now we are concerned with light entering the core at greater than the critical angle.

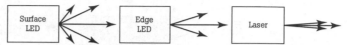

Figure 3-18. *Light source output focus*

There are two more calculations using the refractive index. One is for the numerical aperture, a measure of the light-gathering ability of a particular fiber. The other is for the angle of acceptance, which is calculated from the numerical aperture. Here is a sample numerical aperture and angle of acceptance calculations:

$$NA = \sqrt{1.47^2 - 1.45^2} = 0.24166 \qquad \alpha = \sin^{-1}\left(\sqrt{1.47^2 - 1.45^2}\right) = 13.984$$

This calculation indicates that any light entering the core from an angle of 14° or greater off perpendicular to the face of the core exceeds the critical angle and is lost into the cladding. Any light striking the core from outside the cone of acceptance is not useful (see Figure 3-19).

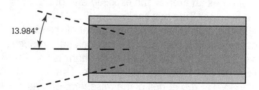

Figure 3-19. *Cone of acceptance*

Because this cone of acceptance is so narrow (the entire cone being less than 28° in Figure 3-19), the light source must be carefully aligned with the fiber to effectively transfer light. This is true in two instances: the launch conditions where the light first enters the fiber optic link and in any cable junction along the link. The launch condition has the greatest impact, however. A very slight misalignment prevents much of the light from entering the core, as shown in the top diagram in Figure 3-20.

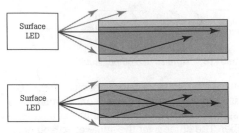

Figure 3-20. *Misalignment between the light source and the fiber core. The top diagram is only slightly misaligned, but it is clear that less light enters the core.*

Figure 3-20 also illustrates an overfilled launch. The LED is illuminating more than just the fiber core. In an underfilled launch, the light source transmits a focused beam, which illuminates only part of the exposed end of the core. An underfilled launch very efficiently transfers power into the fiber. The overfilled launch is seen with LED sources, which are not as powerful as laser sources. In an attempt to pass as much power as possible into the fiber, the focus of the light source illuminates an area of the exposed end of the fiber that is wider than just the core.

In the core, a slight misalignment of the core between two consecutive fibers does not produce as great an impact because all the light is traveling at greater than the critical angle. There is some loss at the edges of the misalignment, as shown in Figure 3-21, but the majority of the light transfers to the next cable.

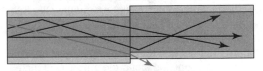

Figure 3-21. *Fiber-to-fiber misalignment*

Because of this alignment issue, it is important that the fiber patch cable attached to the light source be left undisturbed after the reference has been set when testing for loss. Removing and reattaching the fiber changes the mechanical alignment between the fiber and the light source enough to bring into question the accuracy of the measurement. The testing methodology required by the standards for loss testing incorporate this requirement.

Mandrels

Because of the launch conditions surrounding LED light sources, standards mandate the use of a mandrel wrap to quickly eliminate light that is not traveling at desirable angles. On a longer run, these modes of light eliminate themselves; however, on shorter cables, they may still be present. For multimode cables, loss testing is done with a five-wrap mandrel (see Figure 3-22). The diameter of the mandrel serves to force light into the cladding that was already traveling in the highest-order modes (a higher-order mode is any path that did not go straight down the center of the core). The net effect of the mandrel is to slightly lower the power readings on short cables, but to make them reliable and repeatable.

Table 3-7 shows the updated mandrel size information found in TIA/EIA-568-C.0. TIA/EIA-568-B provided mandrel size data only for 250 μm buffered fiber and 3.0mm jacketed fiber.

Table 3-7. *TIA/EIA-568-C.0 mandrel sizes for testing multimode*

Multimode				
Fiber Core Size	900μm Buffered Fiber	2.0mm Jacketed Fiber	2.4mm Jacketed Fiber	3.0mm Jacketed Fiber
50μm	25mm	23mm	23mm	22mm
62.5μm	20mm	18mm	18mm	17mm

If a mandrel is used to set the reference power level, it is *not* subsequently removed for testing; instead, it remains in place for testing. If the mandrel is removed, a new reference must be set.

Mandrels are not used with singlemode cable, although it is common to include a single 30mm (1.2 inch) loop in place of the mandrel to ensure that only one mode is transmitted for measurement.

Mode Conditioning

The last issue related to launching a signal into the fiber covered here is the need for mode conditioning. If a laser source is used with multimode cable, the focus of the beam is at the center of the fiber core. Due to the manufacturing process used for older fiber optic cable, this center location is not the best launch location.

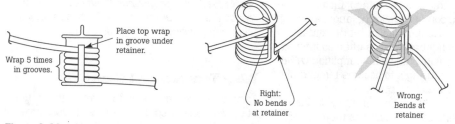

Figure 3-22. *Mandrel use. The mandrel should be wrapped with five nonoverlapping turns.*

A common process used for manufacturing fiber optic cable is to layer it from the outside inward, although another process for building from the center out is used, too. (One simple description is at www.thefoa.org/tech/fibr-mfg.htm, and the Corning company web site has a long description of several processes at www.corning.com/opticalfiber/index.aspx.) The core is built up slowly using a vapor deposition process. The resulting tube is then heated and collapsed into a rod called a *preform*. The preform is again heated and the fiber is drawn off under very carefully controlled conditions. Early implementations of this process resulted in a slight build-up of imperfect material at the center of the final fiber core, a result of the manufacturing process.

Because laser output is focused and narrow, if a laser light source were used with an older multimode cable, the light would be entering the core at the exact location of the manufacturing imperfections. To avoid this location in the fiber core, a mode-conditioning launch cable is used to launch the light off center, part way from the center to the edge of the core. In doing so, the light is transferred at full power into the fiber, although the special launch cables are fairly expensive.

Absorption

When the transmitted light energy is at or near the energy level of the molecules in the glass, it is sometimes absorbed. When light is absorbed, the energy is released as heat. The amount of absorption that occurs is so slight that it has very little effect on link attenuation measurements. This is one form of intrinsic attenuation.

Fluctuations in the density of the fiber core from the manufacturing process causes minor changes in the index of refraction, which results in scattering. This form of scattering is called *Rayleigh scattering* or *backscatter*, and is the source of the tiny amount of light that an OTDR picks up from along the length of the fiber core. This form of intrinsic attenuation contributes noticeably to attenuation.

Impurities in the fiber, most commonly in the form of water (hydroxyl), represent a form of extrinsic attenuation. Impurities such as this are more common in older fiber. There are new manufacturing processes that result in very low levels of hydroxyl contamination and are used for a type of fiber called zero–water-peak fiber (ZWPF). The worst extrinsic attenuation due to hydroxyl appears centered at about 1380nm.

Extrinsic absorption is also manifested by bending the fiber (macrobends or microbends) or placing it under other strain or stress. Bending and stress change the refractive index and critical angle of the fiber, which in turn result in extrinsic attenuation.

Fresnel Reflections

Whenever light traveling down the fiber core reaches a connection, there is a change in the index of refraction as the light crosses from one fiber to the next through the small amount of air that separates the two fiber cores. Consider the surface of each of the two fiber cores to have mirror-like characteristics. Some amount of light is reflected back toward the source. The amount of this reflection, which is called a Fresnel reflection, can be quite substantial. The amount of light reflected depends on many things; including the surface polish, condition, and the angle at which the light was traveling when it hit the surface. The amount of light reflected is often so intense that it overstimulates the highly amplified OTDR photoreceptor, causing it to become temporarily blinded (called the *dead zone*).

Because the photoreceptor in the OTDR is temporarily oversaturated, that means there is a short period following the location of the event where it is unable to "see" minor or major events. It is unable to report the condition of the fiber core until the photo receiver recovers from the flash. This blinding effect is then the source of dead zones along the link being tested by an OTDR. There could be several blind spots along the link being tested, each following an event. With older or less expensive copper cable test tools, the TDR blind spot was found at only the signal source end of the cable, and was the result of the transmitter and receiver sharing the same wire. While the transmitter was active, the receiver was unable to see smaller events. As soon as the transmitter stopped sending the test pulse, the receiver could begin observing and reporting on small events discovered along the cable.

The length or size of the OTDR dead zone is substantially affected by the power of the transmitted test pulse. On long cables (kilometers), a very high-power signal and long pulse width is necessary to "see" all the way to the end. The dead zone for this test is quite long.

Note: *Fresnel is pronounced without the "s" because the term references the French mathematician and physicist Augustin Jean Fresnel.*

Fiber Termination Polish

To minimize reflections and improve the amount of power transferred between two consecutive fibers, there are several end polish options. The closer that two fiber cores can get to each other, the smaller the disturbance will be.

There are several variations of a flat contact surface, ranging from fully flat to slightly rounded (see Figure 3-23). Flat end surfaces tend to have air gaps, and therefore suffer from greater Fresnel reflections. A slightly rounded end is called a physical contact (PC), followed by super physical contact (SPC) and ultra physical contact (UPC), with successively better finishing polish. Better polishing reduces back reflections. Back reflections on a typical hand polished PC endface measure around −30dB. A similar endface that is machine polished to SPC should provide a minimum back reflection measurement of −40dB, or −50dB for UPC. If even less back reflection is required, an APC (angled physical contact) polish might be necessary.

Angled contact surfaces were introduced to reduce the amount of return loss or reflection back toward the source (see Figure 3-24). Angled contact connections are used with singlemode fiber.

Figure 3-23. *Flat end/physical contact finishes*

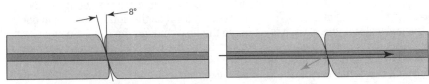

Figure 3-24. *Angled physical contact finish*

Fiber Alignment Errors and Manufacturing Flaws

Although many things can go wrong on a fiber optic cable, two categories of fault are more common than others. Coupling losses represent the most significant source of failures, with fiber manufacturing irregularities trailing far behind it but still important.

Coupling Losses

Coupling losses are observed in four common events, and one other event that is somewhat rare but still worth mentioning.

Area or Core Mismatch

Area mismatches are present when the core size between two fiber optic cables is not the same (see Figure 3-25). This form of fault is becoming much more common as more 50µm and 62.5µm cable is installed in the same building. Unless you are careful, it is quite easy to mistakenly install the wrong patch cable.

Spacing or End Gap Loss

If a connector is not fully seated, if dirt or other obstructions prevent the cores from touching, or any other source of blockage results in a gap between fiber cores, loss results. Air gaps result in differences in the index of refraction between air and the core, and serious Fresnel reflections are likely. Connecting an angle polished and a flat-end cable creates a similar reflection problem (see Figure 3-26).

Axis Misalignment

If the fiber cores are the same size but they are not properly aligned, problems result that are similar to an area mismatch (see Figure 3-27). The most common source of this fault is perhaps the use of multimode couplers, which have much more relaxed tolerances, with singlemode cables. This is also referred to as *lateral misalignment*.

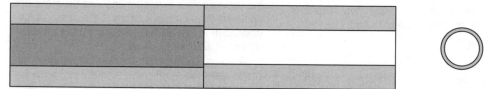

Figure 3-25. *Area mismatch, where the size of the core is different*

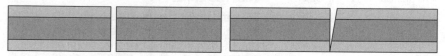

Figure 3-26. *Spacing problem where an air gap is formed, which causes Fresnel reflections to become worse*

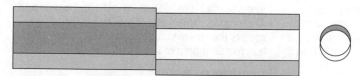

Figure 3-27. *Axis misalignment, where the same size cores do not fully overlap*

Angular Misalignment

Angular misalignment causes some portion of the light to exceed the critical angle and leave the core. Accompanying this sort of misalignment is usually an air gap, which further contributes to loss with Fresnel reflections (see Figure 3-28).

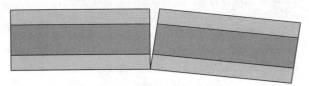

Figure 3-28. *Angular misalignment, where the axis of one fiber core is at a different angle than the other fiber core*

Numeric Aperture Mismatch

Two fibers may have their cores perfectly aligned and still exhibit loss because of differences in the numeric aperture (light-gathering ability) of the two cores (see Figure 3-29). Light traveling at some angles in the first fiber core exceed the critical angle in the second fiber core. This is a particularly difficult problem to find.

Figure 3-29. *Numeric aperture, where the light gathering properties of one fiber are wider or narrower than the other*

Fiber Irregularities

The manufacturing processes used to make fiber optic cable for networking are becoming exceptionally good. However, an occasional legacy cable or manufacturing aberration appears from time to time. Following are two such irregularities that are detectable by the network support staff.

Elliptical

The core of an optical fiber should be perfectly round to avoid introducing dispersion and to align properly with other fiber cores. The manufacturing process for some low-cost fiber might not be as accurate in detecting problems with variations in the cylindrical shape of the fiber as it is drawn (see Figure 3-30).

Off-Center

To properly align with another fiber, it is important that the core be centered within the cladding. Centricity problems may result from inaccuracies in the manufacturing process for some low cost-fiber (see Figure 3-31). Mode conditioning launch cables are manufactured to be off-center.

Figure 3-30. *Elliptical core, when the core is not perfectly round*

Figure 3-31. *Nonconcentric core, where the core is round but not in the center of the cladding*

Testing Practices and Tools

Several test configurations or methods are commonly used to test fiber optic cabling. Each has two elements in common: The launch cable (connected to the light source) is never disconnected during testing, and part of the configuration setup cabling sets the reference and tests the unknown cable. If the exact cables (shown in the following section) are not used as indicated, the test is invalidated.

Also, just as there are fewer performance metrics to test a fiber optic link versus a copper link, there are fewer tools categories to do the testing.

Test Methods

The various test standards (including ISO and TIA) all require that loss testing be performed only after the tester has been referenced or calibrated. EIA/TIA-568-C.3 Clause 5.4.3.1 prefers the one-jumper method because testing suggests this method provides the highest repeatable accuracy in measuring attenuation on both multimode and singlemode cable. ISO/IEC-14763-3 Clause 9.1.1.2 prefers the three-jumper method for satisfying the test requirements of ISO 11801.

One-Jumper Method

The one-jumper method for link loss certification assures that the measured loss of the cable under test includes the losses contributed by the connections in the end panels. All connectors, including those in the end panels, represent a major component of the link loss for shorter cabling links (less than 2km), which are common in building or campus wiring.

Fluke Networks recommends the one-jumper method for premise and campus wiring when using test equipment that allows the connection on the optical meter to be exchanged to match the connector type in the end connections (panels) of the link under test. The one-jumper method, given those conditions, provides a more accurate test result. It accurately includes the loss in the two end connections of the link under test. As stated earlier, the loss in these connections represents a significant portion of the link loss.

This method cannot be implemented for some connector types. For links such as MT-RJ, Fluke Networks developed a modified two-jumper test method that includes the full evaluation of the two end connectors.

Use the following process to perform testing with the one-jumper method:

1. Turn the light source on long enough for it to stabilize (5–10 minutes).

2. Connect the light source to the power meter with a test reference cord (high–quality patch cord). This will be called patch cable 1 (or jumper cable 1). When testing multimode cable, a mandrel should be included at the light source end.

3. Use the test meter to measure the amount of light reaching it from the light source. Store or record this value as the reference power level.

4. Disconnect the patch cable from the power meter in Figure 3-32 (not the light source!). You are ready to test. In Figure 3-33, there are two light sources, one at each end. Disconnect only the light meter end of each fiber (shown as connector number 2).

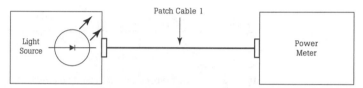

Figure 3-32. *One-jumper reference method concept used in TIA/EIA-526-14A Method B, TIA/EIA-526-7 Method A.1, IEC 61280-4-1 Method 2, and EN 61280-4.2 Method 1*

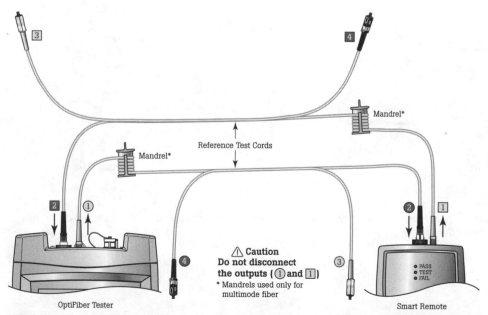

Figure 3-33. *Set Reference example using test equipment capable of testing two fibers at once. The light source is connection 1; the light meter is connection 2. Connection 1 is never disturbed once reference has been set. The other fiber in each test reference cord (with ends 3 and 4) is not used during the reference measurements.*

5. To perform actual testing, connect patch cable 1 to one end of the link to be tested, and the power meter to the other using patch cable 2 (see Figure 3-34).

6. Perform the measurement. The configuration shown in Figure 3-34 and Figure 3-35 is used after any of the three reference methods. Never disconnect the light source from patch cable 1.

Two-Jumper Method

The two-jumper reference method for link loss certification does not include the end connector in one of the two end panels (end connectors at test interface) in the loss assessment. The two end connectors in a simple two-connector fiber link segment may represent 60 percent or more of the link loss limit. Not properly measuring the contribution made by both end connectors introduces very significant errors in the measurement method.

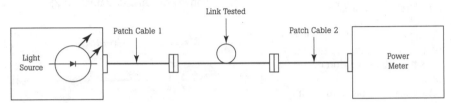

Figure 3-34. *Test procedure after setting the reference power level*

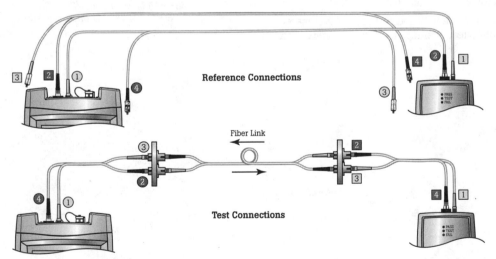

Figure 3-35. *Test procedure connections using sample test equipment configuration from Figure 3-33 for the one-jumper method*

Figures 3-36 and 3-37 illustrate how the two-jumper method is configured.

Do not remove either patch cable from the test equipment after setting the reference. This method tests the installed cable plus the loss in one end connection.

Three-Jumper Method

The three-jumper reference method for link loss certification does not include the measured loss of either of the end connectors. The IEC 14763-3 standard that promotes this method inserts assumptions in the loss limit formula. Fluke Networks does not recommend this method except for the exclusive use of the true channel model, in which the end connectors are not to be counted. Fluke Networks prefers and recommends the one-jumper method because the loss calculation for the end connectors in the three-jumper method creates a systematic measurement error. It underestimates the link loss of a multimode optical fiber link by 0.2dB or more, and it underestimates the link loss of a singlemode optical fiber

link by 0.4dB. This systematic error is furthermore influenced by the condition of the three reference cords shown in Figure 3-38 and Figure 3-39. When the condition of these cords is better than defined in the standard, the calculated test loss limit becomes lower (tighter requirement) and, vice versa, when the condition of these cords is worse than defined or assumed in the standard loss formula calculation, the test limit for the link increases (becomes more lenient).

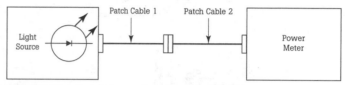

Figure 3-36. *Two-jumper reference method used in TIA/EIA-526-14A Method A, TIA/EIA-526-7 Method A.2, IEC 61280-4-1 Method 1, and EN 61280-4.2 Method 1*

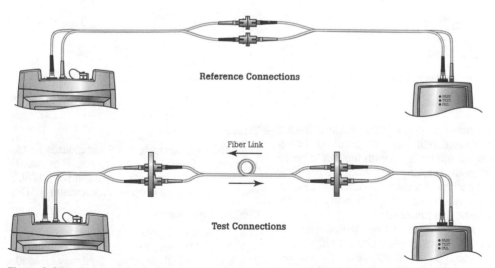

Figure 3-37. *Test procedure connections using example test equipment from Figure 3-33 for the two-jumper method*

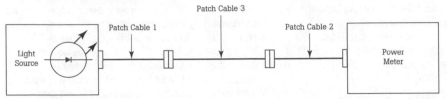

Figure 3-38. *Three-jumper reference method used in TIA/EIA–526–14A Method C, TIA/EIA–526–7 Method A.3, IEC 61280–4–1 Method 3, and EN 61280–4.2 Method 3*

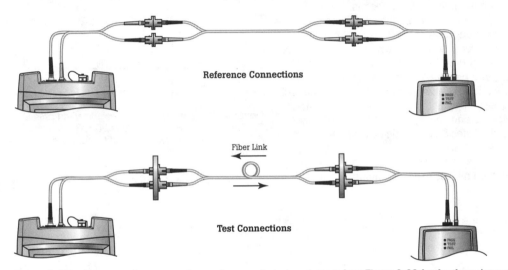

Figure 3-39. *Test procedure connections using sample test equipment from Figure 3-33 for the three-jumper method*

Do not remove patch cable 1 or 2 from the test equipment after setting the reference. Patch cable 3 is removed and replaced with the link to be tested without removing the two connectors. This method measures the installed cable and makes a calculated adjustment for the loss in the end connectors of the link under test.

Loss measurements are executed with a constant wave light source. All multimode fiber optical links should be tested with LED light sources operating at the desired wavelength(s) with the use of the appropriate mandrel. All singlemode fiber optical links should be tested with laser light sources at the desired wavelength(s).

Tools

Three tools are suggested in the standards for testing installed fiber. A visible light source or visual fault locator (VFL), an optical loss test set (OLTS), and the optical time domain reflectometer (OTDR).

Visible Light Source

Visible light sources include incandescent lights and LED and laser light sources. Anything from a flashlight to an LED "keychain" light may be used for continuity and polarity testing. A visual fault locator (VFL) makes the job easier but is simply a very powerful light source. It typically uses a Class 2 laser device—a device that emits light in the visible (red) spectrum. Note that it is very dangerous to look directly into the output, either at the source itself or at the end of a short or long fiber optic cable.

If a fiber optic strand has been broken, it is sometimes possible to see the light emitting through the buffer that surrounds the cable jacket at the location of the break. The most common use for this tool is probably in locating or verifying the correct fiber out of many at a patch panel or other distribution center, and in identifying polarity of a fiber pair.

Optical Loss Test Set (OLTS)

Used for testing power loss over a fiber optic link, the optical loss test set (OLTS) consists of a fiber optic light source and a fiber optic power meter. Light sources usually come in two configurations: 850nm and 1300nm LED sources for testing multimode, and 1310 and 1550 laser sources for testing singlemode. Gigabit and higher data rate systems use vertical cavity surface emitting laser diodes (VCSEL) sources at 850nm because these devices are much faster than LEDs, and much cheaper than the laser sources—usually between half and one fourth the cost. Even though they will be used in the production deployment, VCSEL light sources are not recommended to test and certify the link loss of installed cabling systems because the launch conditions of these devices are not uniform from device to device. For this reason, a test instrument using an LED light source is recommended. The importance of carefully controlling the launch conditions of the test to obtain repeatable and accurate test results has already been mentioned.

Power meters are almost always suitable for measuring 850nm, 1300/1310nm, and 1550nm wavelengths. The power meter is configured for the correct input wavelength before the reference level is measured and saved.

The pair (the exact light source to be used with a specific power meter) must be referenced before use. Because it takes 5–10 minutes for the output power to stabilize, allow the light source to operate for awhile before testing. If the light source is transported into a warmer or colder working environment, it is necessary to re-reference it with the power meter after the instrument has warmed or cooled to a steady-state operating temperature in the ambient environment. The power meter is nowhere near as sensitive to temperature changes as the light source.

The standards for testing installed fiber optic links require loss testing. If the light signal arriving at the end of the link—input to the receiver—has insufficient power, the receiver will not properly detect and decode the signal, which is usually the cause of the failures for an installed link. Note that dirty connections are the most prevalent reason for links to fail. Always keep the end terminations of unused links protected; clean and inspect new patch cords before plugging them in.

A flashlight is probably the most used field verification tool, but it has limitations. The fact that you can see some light at the other end of the link does not provide an adequate measure of link loss. This is even more true for the newer high-speed network technologies (Gigabit data rates and higher). These network technologies impose a maximum length and a tight insertion loss budget that can be verified only by executing accurate loss measurements. Furthermore, as more powerful nonvisible light sources are deployed, the flashlight choice is becoming correspondingly less safe for the technician to use.

Example: Even when you feel certain that you have both ends of a fiber optic cable disconnected, it is still a very bad idea to look directly into the fiber to discoverer whether white light from a flashlight can be seen. Shine the end of the fiber onto a white surface and look for reflected light. A 96-strand fiber backbone cable was installed between two halls at a convention center for use by the Interop trade show. The deal included permission for the convention center to use the fiber when Interop was not present in the facility. In preparation for the next show, the physical installation team was at the ceiling on lifts preparing to map which fiber was on which patch panel connection at both ends of the cable. By coincidence, although most mapping was going to be done by flashlight, one team was using a power meter test set (meter and light source). The first cable connection was about to be tested when the power meter technician got on the radio and announced that the reading he was seeing was +2 dB (very powerful laser). Following the cable run it was discovered that some of the fibers had been cut and spliced into a telco equipment rack. Had anyone on the team looked directly into the fiber, there would have been some eye damage.

OTDR

To permit an optical time domain reflectometer (OTDR) to see events at the beginning of a link to be tested properly, a 100-meter launch cable is often used as patch cord 1 to connect the OTDR to the link. The launch cable gives the OTDR's detector time to recover from the strong reflection at the OTDR connector. The launch cable also permits the OTDR to measure the loss of the first connector in the link. The launch cable provides a level of backscatter before the first connector to compare to the backscatter after the connector, thus allowing the OTDR to determine the loss across the connector. Without the launch cable, the backscatter before the first connector in the link is lost in the dead zone from the OTDR's connector. A receive cable, which is connected to the far end of the link, may also be used to permit the OTDR to measure the loss of the last connector in the link. To keep the physical size of this cable small, it is often constructed with unjacketed fiber in a spool that is spliced to jacketed ends.

From traces, such as shown in Figure 3-40, it is possible to identify the presence and location of splices, connections, bends, and other disruptions to the passage of light. Note: Details on how to read an OTDR trace are provided in Chapter 10, "Troubleshooting Media."

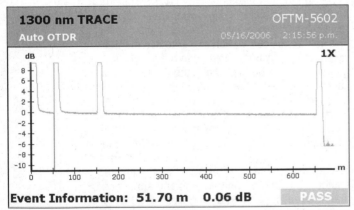

Figure 3-40. *Sample OTDR test result showing a very good quality link*

End-Face Inspection

Whenever there is a problem with a fiber optic cable link, one of the first places to check is the cleanliness of connections. Part of checking connections should be an automatic cleaning of all cable end faces. Cleaning should be performed *every time* a connection is made, even if you just disconnected the fiber for a quick glance at the end-face.

There are two common types of fiber microscope in use for testing networking cable: traditional optical lens microscopes and the more recent video camera–based tools. Some traditional microscopes offer no protection to the user from ambient light in the fiber, and cause serious eye damage if the fiber being inspected is powered. Other traditional microscopes include protective optic designs to limit dangerous light from reaching the eyepiece. Video camera systems offer full user protection from light in the fiber being tested. End-face inspection is best performed with a video fiber microscope, for safety and to be able to store the results.

End-face inspection reveals termination flaws, scratches, and dirt that may be present. The video camera systems also permit different end connectors that allow inspection of the connector jacks, not just the plugs. Even new cables should be cleaned and inspected.

Levels of Testing

TIA/EIA TSB140, "Additional Guidelines for Field-Testing Length, Loss and Polarity of Optical Fiber Cabling Systems," defines the testing parameters and procedures for testing an installed fiber optic link, as a clarification of TIA/EIA-526-7 and TIA/EIA-526-14A but not a replacement. The test is defined in two parts or levels. Testing installed optical fiber cabling for attenuation with an optical loss test set (OLTS), as described in cabling standards, and verifying the cabling length and polarity constitutes Tier 1 testing. Tier 1 testing is required; Tier 2 is optional and includes the tests from Tier 1 with the addition of an optical time domain reflectometer (OTDR) trace. An OTDR trace characterizes the installed fiber link by providing an indication of the uniformity of cable attenuation and connector insertion loss.

Tier 1

The link attenuation of optical fiber cabling, whether multimode or singlemode, should be measured with an OLTS to ensure acceptable overall quality and performance of the installed components. The use of an OLTS requires the use of quality test jumpers, referencing the light source output to an optical power meter, and access to both ends of the link under test. The power delivered at the end of the link under test is compared to the reference for calculating the resulting link attenuation, so it is important to properly set and maintain the reference measurement as discussed earlier.

This level of test requires each fiber to be measured and tested for its insertion loss (attenuation) with an OLTS. Fiber length verification may be obtained from cable sheath markings or via the OLTS (if the OLTS has length measurement capability). Polarity may be verified with the OLTS while performing attenuation tests. A visible light source, such as a visual fault locator, can also be use to verify polarity. The optical lengths of certain cables (e.g., stranded loose tube) may be longer than the cable sheath due to the fiber lay within the cable sheath.

Individual standards may call out the specific wavelengths and whether the link should be tested in both directions. Annex D of TIA standard 568-C.0 lists a number of the network application standards the distances supported and the maximum channel loss limit for different types of fiber optic cabling, depending on cable type and bandwidth rating. This standard warns that network application standards may require shorter distances and lower loss limits than the premise wiring general standards. This is the case for network standards that support transmission speeds of 1Gbps or higher.

Also note that the launch conditions of the light source into the link under test have a significant impact on the link loss. Existing standards refer to a Coupled Power Ratio (CPR) rating to characterize and standardize the launch conditions of the light for the loss test of multimode links. Some standards refer to an MPD rating (Mode Power Distribution). In upcoming standards, a new concept will supersede the CPR or MPD rating; the specifications of this new concept called *Encircled Flux* is expected to be finalized and released during the calendar year 2009. IEC standard 61280-4-1 will define the Encircled Flux requirements for launch conditions of link insertion loss testing.

Tier 2

If performed, this level adds characterization of the internal components of the link. An OTDR test locates events such as connectors, splices, and bends expressed in distance from the measurement end. An OTDR furthermore measures the loss at each connection or splice and assures attenuation uniformity the length of the link.

Using an OTDR permits the technician to locate exactly where each event is, and the relative impact that event has on the link performance. If the link loss measured in Tier 1 exceeds the limits, an OTDR identifies the location and nature of the events, causing excessive loss.

Precautions for Measurement and Testing

When measuring the performance of fiber optic cabling, take several precautions:

- Use appropriate mating adapters to interface test jumpers (used with OLTSs) or launch fibers (used with OTDRs) with the cabling system and instrumentation.
- Ensure that all connectors, mating adapters, and test jumpers or launch fibers are clean prior to and during the test measurement.
- Use test jumpers that are of acceptable quality—they are subject to heavy use. Use only test jumpers or test reference cords recommended by the manufacturer of the test equipment.
- Keep end-face inspection equipment nearby to help ascertain connector quality.
- Ensure that the power meter and light source are set to the same wavelength.
- Ensure that optical sources are turned on for sufficient time prior to testing to stabilize per manufacturer recommendations.
- Ensure that test jumpers and launch fibers are of recommended length for the OLTS and the OTDR, and are of the same fiber core size as the cable under test (e.g., use 50/125 μm test jumpers with 50/125 μm cable).

Note: *When an overfilled light launch is transmitted from a 62.5/125 μm fiber into a 50/125μm fiber, a coupling loss increase of about 4.7 decibels (dB) is possible.*

Summary

This chapter described fiber optic cabling test standards, the test parameters required for compliance with those standards, and test configurations.

- Personal safety is a serious topic when working with fiber optic cabling. The light emitted from networking gear designed to operate over multimode and singlemode cabling does not fall within the visible light spectrum. Permanent eye damage is easily possible. If hand termination of fiber optic cabling is taking place, the fiber shards that result should be handled in a manner consistent with hazardous waste.

- Cabling standards continue to evolve. Although fiber optic standards are not changing as fast as copper cabling standards, it is still important to keep the cable tester updated with the latest performance specifications to ensure that test results obtained certifying a new cable installation are reliable.

- Unlike copper cabling, there are very few parameters suited to field testing of fiber optic links Many of the parameters important to fiber optic cabling are not field testable with the currently available generation of test equipment; instead, these parameters are measured in the manufacturer's lab and made available to customers. Some of the critical parameters, such as modal bandwidth, may or may not be printed on the cable jacket. It might be necessary to research your cable type to obtain the best understanding of the performance limitations of installed fiber optic cable. The field testable performance parameters are related to power loss and the location of loss along the cable length. Because an adequate amount of light may reach the end of the link, but the link might not operate properly, it is important to be aware of the other parameters that can cause link performance problems.

- One of the most important steps for preparing to perform loss testing is to correctly set the reference level and not disturb the launch fiber thereafter. There are several common test configurations for performing loss testing. The most important aspect common to all test configurations is that the light source must be temperature stabilized, and the launch cable connection to the light source must not be disturbed until testing is complete. If these two conditions are not correctly handled then the test results are invalid.

Chapter Review Questions

To aid in your comprehension of important concepts, the following questions are provided. Refer to this book's Introduction for a general legend that indicates the anticipated difficulty of each question. For answers to these review questions, see Appendix I, "Answers to Chapter Review Questions."

 1. Which of the following networking wavelengths can be seen with the unaided human eye? Which are likely to be harmful to the human eye?

See	Harmful	
___	___	850nm (Multimode)
___	___	1300nm (Multimode)
___	___	1310nm (Singlemode)
___	___	1550nm (Singlemode)

2. Explain how easy fiber shards resulting from cable termination activities are to remove if they happen to penetrate flesh.

 3. What is the prescribed or common color for the following fiber optic cable jackets? (Note that other colors are permitted if the cable jacket is clearly marked.)

62.5 μm multimode _____

50 μm multimode _____

9 μm singlemode _____

 4. Why are the terms singlemode and multimode used? (Hint: What behavior of light is described by these terms?)

 5. What causes dispersion?

 6. What problem does dispersion create?

 7. What measurement is reported on a cable jacket or in the manufacturer's specifications that is based on dispersion test results?

 8. How is the critical angle involved in determining the maximum bend radius for a fiber installation?

 9. What significant difference exists in the manufacturing of step index versus graded index fiber?

 10. Which three types of laser are commonly used in networking applications?

 11. What is the purpose of overfilling a fiber core?

 12. Why are mandrels used when testing multimode fiber?

 13. What condition was created by some older fiber optic cable manufacturing processes that is avoided by use of a special launch cable?

 14. What is Rayleigh scattering or backscatter?

 15. What is the most obvious difference between UPC and APC finished connections?

16. Match the misalignment term with the correct problems. One term has two problems.

1	Area or Core mismatch	A	Mixed use of UPC and APC cable
2	Spacing or End Gap loss	B	Use of less precisely engineered multimode couplers with singlemode cable
3	Axis misalignment	C	Mixed use of 50µm and 62.5µm cable
		D	Mixed use of multimode and singlemode

 17. To ensure that an accurate power measurement is made, what should be done with the testers prior to setting a reference value?

 18. What actions would invalidate the reference power reading after a reference setting was made?

 19. Name several examples of a visible light source that might be used to test fiber optic cable continuity.

 20. Name a key difference between an optical loss test set and an OTDR.

 21. What is the single most common problem found in relation to a faulty or marginal fiber optic cable link?

 22. What is the primary difference between Tier 1 and Tier 2 testing as defined by TSB 140?

CHAPTER 4
Media Access Control Layer

This chapter provides a working description of Ethernet as defined by the IEEE 802.3 and ISO/IEC 8802.3 standards. Correctly speaking, Ethernet is not limited to the Media Access Control (MAC) sub-layer, but instead encompasses the medium up through the MAC Control Layer (see Figure 4-1). This chapter summarizes Ethernet from the medium up through the MAC Layer—despite the chapter title being MAC Layer only. The chapter does not attempt to describe all the available technical details.

Free Standards

An industry sponsorship project now permits interested individuals to download a PDF copy of the actual 802.3 standard from the IEEE web site to obtain the exact and complete details (http://standards.ieee.org/getieee802/). There are working groups constantly engaged in updating existing definitions and creating new definitions for Ethernet (http://grouper.ieee.org/groups/802/3/). The official "includes everything" version is updated every two or three years to include the approved updates produced by the working groups. The free download data is posted one year after it is approved. This means that there are likely to be approved updates to 802.3 that are not reflected by the free downloads. Whenever precise details are required, you are strongly advised to obtain them directly from the latest released version of the standard. Use the popular press to obtain a general understanding only, and then read the standards for complete and accurate details.

There are two fundamental ways in which stations are able to access a network: through token passing and contention.

In token-passing networks, each station is constrained from sending a message until it comes into possession of the electronic "token." By controlling the token, the station wanting to transmit a message is assured that no other station will attempt to transmit a message at the same time. This control avoids situations where data would be lost or destroyed because two or more stations transmitted at the same time. Token Ring and FDDI are examples of token-passing protocols.

In contention networks, stations wanting to transmit are not required to wait their turn; instead, they may transmit at any time they want—providing the medium appears to be idle at that instant. This creates a situation where two or more stations may transmit simultaneously, causing corruption of data. The sending stations routinely compensate for these events, and as long as the collision is detected prior to the expiration of a specified time limit no data is lost. Ethernet is an example of a contention protocol.

This chapter summarizes only the most commonly deployed implementations of Ethernet and not all defined implementations found in the 802.3 standard.

Ethernet and the OSI Model

Although Ethernet is often referred to as being a MAC Layer protocol, it touches four areas of the OSI Model (three appear in Figure 4-1). The fourth area is the MAC Control Layer, which is described in the next chapter. This chapter covers the lower half of the Data Link Layer (the MAC Layer), the Physical Layer, and it explicitly defines the medium required.

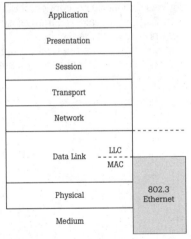

Figure 4-1. *802.3 Ethernet in relation to the OSI Model*

To move data between one Ethernet station and another on the same collision domain, the data usually passes through a repeater (see Figure 4-2). Data moving from one station to another in a collision domain is carried either on a coaxial bus or through a repeater. Both the bus and the repeater allow all other stations in the collision domain to see all traffic.

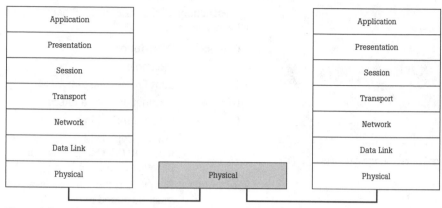

Figure 4-2. *A repeater as seen by the OSI Model*

A repeater is responsible for forwarding all traffic to all other ports. A hub could be described as a multiport repeater. Traffic received by a repeater is never forwarded back out the port it came in on. Any signal detected by a repeater is forwarded or, if the signal is not quite recognizable (such as noise), an Ethernet signal is created and substituted for any detected but unrecognizable signal. A collision domain is then a shared resource. Problems originating in one part of the collision domain almost always affect the entire collision domain.

The standard specifies maximum numbers of stations per segment, maximum segment lengths, maximum numbers of repeaters between stations, and so on. As mentioned earlier, stations separated by repeaters are within the same collision domain. Stations separated by bridges, switches, or routers are in different collision domains.

At the end of each technology description (10Mbps, 100Mbps, 1Gbps, and 10Gbps) is a section that describes the architecture rules governing legal configurations for a collision domain at that speed. Chapter 5, "Data Link Layer," describes broadcast domains, which operate in the upper half of the Data Link Layer (the Logical Link Control sublayer).

Frame Structure

When a protocol analyzer examines Ethernet data, the frame formats and data structures below are observed as described. However, if the signal is directly examined with an oscilloscope, binary values must be manually decoded and reordered for each octet according to the specific rules for that implementation as described for each Ethernet speed and implementation description within the "Ethernet Implementation Details" half of this chapter.

Bits to Bytes

At the MAC Layer, Ethernet transmits each octet (byte) in consecutive order from the Preamble to the Frame Check Sequence (FCS). However, the bit order is reversed so that the least significant bit (LSB) of each octet is transmitted first (canonical order)—except for the FCS field, which is sent most significant bit (MSB) first.

In Figure 4-3, the word "The" has been converted from the appropriate ASCII hexadecimal codes into binary.

Letter		Hexadecimal		Binary
T	=	54	=	0101 0100
h	=	68	=	0110 1000
e	=	65	=	0110 0101

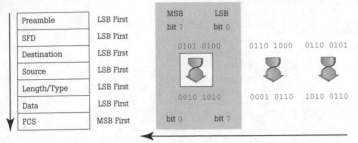

Preamble	LSB First
SFD	LSB First
Destination	LSB First
Source	LSB First
Length/Type	LSB First
Data	LSB First
FCS	MSB First

Figure 4-3. *Canonical reordering example (LSB first)*

Bytes to Field Groupings

The binary is then LSB reordered before passing the binary data from the Media Access Control Layer to the Physical Layer Ethernet implementation for line encoding and transmission. Note that each octet is reversed individually, with bit 7 becoming the last bit transmitted after reordering.

At the MAC Layer, the frame structure is nearly identical for all speeds of Ethernet (10/100/1,000/10,000 Mbps). Half duplex 1000BASE-T and the "W" versions of 10 Gigabit Ethernet have certain timing issues that require minor differences in how the interframe spacing is handled by the MAC Layer, but are otherwise the same as the other speeds. At the Physical Layer, almost all versions of Ethernet are substantially different from one another, and each speed has its own set of architecture design rules.

The basic Ethernet frame format is shown in Figure 4-4.

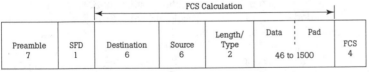

				Length/ Type	Data	Pad	
Preamble	SFD	Destination	Source	Type	Data	Pad	FCS
7	1	6	6	2		46 to 1500	4

FCS Calculation

Figure 4-4. *IEEE 802.3 Ethernet frame structure*

| Preamble | Destination | Source | Type | Data | Pad | FCS |
| 8 | 6 | 6 | 2 | | 46 to 1500 | 4 |

Figure 4-5. *The early DIX Ethernet frame format, also known as Ethernet Version 2 or Ethernet II*

Descriptions of the IEEE 802.3 Ethernet frame fields are shown:

Octets	Description
7	Preamble
1	Start Frame Delimiter (SFD)
6	Destination MAC address
6	Source MAC address
2	Length/Type field (Length if less than 0600 in hexadecimal, otherwise protocol Type)
46 to 1500	Data (if less than 46 octets, a pad must be added to the end)
4	Frame Check Sequence (CRC Checksum)

In the version of Ethernet developed by the companies Digital, Intel, and Xerox (DIX) prior to the adoption of the IEEE 802.3 version of Ethernet, the Preamble and Start Frame Delimiter (SFD) were combined into a single field, although the binary pattern was identical. The field labeled Length/Type was listed only as Length in the early IEEE versions, and only as Type in the DIX version. These two uses of the field were officially combined in a later IEEE version because both uses of the field were common throughout the industry. Figure 4-5 shows the original DIX Ethernet fields.

Descriptions of the DIX Ethernet frame fields are shown here as a historical reference:

Octets	Description
8	Preamble (ending in pattern 10101011, the 802.3 SFD)
6	Destination MAC address
6	Source MAC address
2	Type field
46 to 1500	Data (if less than 46 octets, a pad must be added to the end)
4	Frame Check Sequence (CRC Checksum)

The use of the Ethernet II Type field is incorporated into the current 802.3 frame definition. Upon receipt, a station must determine which higher-layer protocol is present in an incoming frame. This is first attempted by examining the Length/

Type field. If the two-octet value is equal to or greater than 600 in hexadecimal, the frame is interpreted according to the Ethernet II Type code indicated. If it is less than 600 in hexadecimal, the frame is interpreted as an 802.3 frame and the Length field of the frame is indicated. Further investigation is required to determine how to proceed. The first four octets of the 802.3 data field are examined. The value found in those first four octets is usually checked for two unique values, and if they are not present, the frame is assumed to be an 802.2 Logical Link Control (LLC) Layer encapsulation and decoded according to the 802.2 LLC encapsulation indicated. One of the two values tested for is AAAA in hexadecimal, which indicates an 802.2/802 SNAP encapsulation. The other value tested for is FFFF in hexadecimal, which might indicate an old Novell IPX "Raw" encapsulation.

Numerous "extra" fields may appear in Ethernet frames. In some instances, more than one of these extras may be present at the same time. Often these additional frame formats only appear on point-to-point links, and many times only between switches.

The third frame definition appears when 1000 Mbps Ethernet is used in a half-duplex transmission. The transmission must be a minimum of 512 octets in length to meet the timing requirements for collision detection, unlike the minimum of 512 bits (64 octets) required for slower speeds of Ethernet. If the actual frame transmitted is less than 512 octets, special extension symbols are appended following the actual frame to stretch the transmission out long enough to equal a minimum of 512 octets. These extension symbols are counted as part of the frame to meet the timing requirements for collision detection, but are not counted against the minimum frame size because they are discarded just like the Preamble and SFD. The extension is inserted after the FCS field and is not included in the FCS calculations.

In Figure 4–6, an extension has been added to an Ethernet frame. The extension is found only in half-duplex Gigabit Ethernet, and is not present if the frame is equal to or greater than 512 octets in length.

Preamble 7	SFD 1	Destination 6	Source 6	Length/ Type 2	Data ┊ Pad 46 to 1500	FCS 4	Extension

Figure 4-6. *A frame with 1000BASE-T extension added*

The fourth frame definition is found when Ethernet traffic is used with 802.1Q VLAN Tagging, where the frame format is modified to include an additional four octets of information (see Figure 4–7). The VLAN tag information is inserted immediately following the Source Address and prior to the original MAC Client Length/Type field. The presence of a tag may cause the frame to be up to 1522 octets in length, which is considered illegally large by very old bridges, and may be discarded unless the recipient is participating in the VLAN. The newest bridges forward frames as large as 2000 octets.

Other proprietary frame formats exist, such as the Cisco Inter-Switch Link (ISL) protocol, which was introduced prior to 802.1Q tagging (see Figure 4–8). In this encapsulation, the entire original Ethernet frame is contained within proprietary VLAN tag formatting. Twenty-six octets appear prior to the original Ethernet frame and a four-octet checksum follows it. Details about the specific fields involved are readily available from the Cisco web site. This format does not follow the standard 802.3 framing, and would be discarded by any receiving device not configured to participate in the proprietary VLAN.

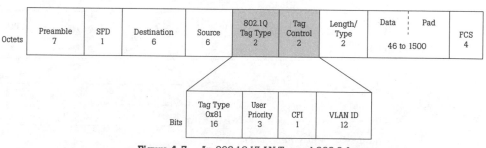

Figure 4-7. *An 802.1Q VLAN Tagged 802.3 frame*

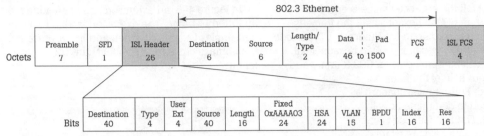

Figure 4-8. *Cisco-proprietary ISL frame format*

Another frame format introduced as a proprietary option is the jumbo frame. At this time, IEEE 802.3 does not support jumbo frames. A draft proposal was submitted to the IETF suggesting that an 802.2 EtherType code of 8870 be used to denote jumbo frames. Observed instances of jumbo frame use, however, simply enlarge the Data field. A maximum frame size of 9018 octets appeared to be the most common supported size, although one reference for existing support of up to 64000 octets has been observed. There is a general industry agreement that this proprietary frame is not intended for any implementation below Gigabit speeds, and should never be seen on 100Mbps and slower Ethernet links.

Note: *Remember that unless the IEEE adopts a proposal, it is vendor proprietary and not supported by 802.3 Ethernet. That does not mean that it is bad—merely that only one vendor supports it, and may not be interoperable with other vendors' products.*

A more recent addition to Ethernet is the MPLS labeled frame, which is moving from the WAN environment back into the LAN environment. Unlike the previous frame definitions, an MPLS frame may have more than one label (see Figure 4-9). Stacked labels are used by reading the leftmost (first) label as the significant label for "this" link. MPLS labels may be used with 802.1Q VLAN tags, which are moved over so that the MPLS label(s) appear first in the frame.

The 802.3as Frame Expansion working group was created to determine an official method of accommodating these existing and any future extra fields added to the basic Ethernet frame. The 802.3as working group was charged with modifying the 802.3 specification to extend "the size of the IEEE 802.3 frame format with an envelope frame to accommodate IEEE 802.1ad Provider Bridging, IEEE 802.1ah Provider Backbone Bridging, IEEE 802.1AE MACSec and other applications requiring encapsulation information in addition to the traditional (basic) Ethernet frame." This change provided a formal and consistent way of adding special-purpose fields to Ethernet, and at the same time adopting existing special-purpose modifications found in common use.

These envelope frame additions are typically used on interswitch links to provide additional forwarding or security information (see Figure 4-10). Some of the additions are added by the

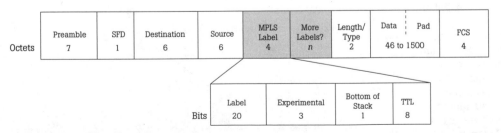

Figure 4-9. *MPLS frame format*

Octets	Preamble 7	SFD 1	Destination 6	Source 6	Length/ Type	Envelope Prefix *2 to 482*	Length/ Type 2	Data ¦ Pad 46 to 1500	Envelope Suffix *0 to (482 - Prefix)*	FCS 4

Figure 4-10. *802.3as envelope packet format*

client PC for security purposes. An envelope frame may be as large as 2000 octets. The envelope prefix is required in an envelope frame, but the envelope suffix is optional. An important feature of the envelope frame is that it may contain multiple prefixes and suffixes that are added (stacked) and removed as required, so the size could change as the frame transits the network.

A VLAN tagged frame is considered a type of envelope frame.

Basic Ethernet Frame Fields

Most of the fields permitted or required in an 802.3 Ethernet frame follow:

- **Preamble.** An alternating pattern of one and zero that is used for timing synchronization in the asynchronous 10Mbps and slower implementations of Ethernet. Except for 100BASE-T4, faster versions of Ethernet are synchronous, and this timing information is redundant but retained for compatibility. The Preamble is seven octets in length and represented by this binary pattern:

  10101010 10101010 10101010 10101010
  10101010 10101010 10101010

- **Start Frame Delimiter.** A one-octet field following the timing information that marks the octet boundary and is represented by the binary pattern that follows. The timing information represented by the Preamble and SFD is discarded, and is not counted toward the minimum and maximum frame sizes.

  10101011

  In the early DIX form of Ethernet, this octet was the last octet in the eight-octet Preamble. Although the old DIX Ethernet described the first eight octets differently than IEEE Ethernet, the pattern and usage is identical.

- **Destination Address.** This field contains the six-octet MAC destination address. The destination address may be a unicast, multicast, or broadcast address.

- **Source Address.** This field contains the six-octet MAC source address. The source address is supposed to be only the unique (unicast) address of the transmitting Ethernet station.

  An increasing number of virtual protocols use and sometimes share a specific MAC address to identify the virtual entity. One example is the Virtual Router Redundancy Protocol (VRRP) described in RFC 2338.

  In the early Ethernet specifications, MAC addresses were optionally two or six octets as long as the size was constant throughout the broadcast domain. Two-octet addressing was explicitly excluded in subclause 3.2.3 of the 1998 update of the standard, and is no longer supported in 802.3 Ethernet.

  MAC addresses are available from the IEEE, which manages their issuance. Address blocks are provided where the first three octets are assigned and the remaining three octets allow for 16 million unique addresses. If a company manufacturing Ethernet products consumes an entire block of addresses, it may request additional blocks. Some companies have numerous address blocks assigned to them. Mergers and acquisitions over the years have caused the published owner of an address block to become inaccurate. Thus, between the continuing issuance of new blocks of addresses and shifting ownership, there is no complete and accurate list of address assignments publicly available.

- **802.1Q Tag Type.** The value of the Tag Type is fixed at 8100 in hexadecimal per 802.3 subclause 3.5.4. This value conflicts with a historical EtherType assignment in

RFC 1700, but because both ends of a tagged link need to be configured to participate in a VLAN it should not be a problem.

- **802.1Q Tag Control.** This two-octet field is divided into three subfields: a three-bit User Priority field, a Canonical Format Indicator, and a 12-bit VLAN Identifier. The structure and use of the fields are defined in IEEE 802.1Q, subclause 9.3.

- **Envelope Prefix.** If present, the original Length/Type field is moved to make room, and is counted against the size of the Data field, as well as any amount of envelope prefix that exceeds two octets. The envelope (prefix and any suffix together) may represent up to 482 octets. The envelope is counted as part of the Data field.

- **Length/Type.** If the value is equal to or less than 05DC hexadecimal (1500 decimal), the value indicates Length. The Length interpretation is used where the LLC Layer provides the protocol identification. The Length field informs the receiving station how large the Data field is. The value 05DC hexadecimal also then sets the maximum client data size for Ethernet.

  If the value is equal to or greater than 0600 hexadecimal (1536 decimal), the value indicates Type, and the contents of the Data field are decoded per the protocol indicated. A list of common EtherType protocols is found in RFC 1700, beginning around page 168. The list in RFC 1700 is years out of date, and a current list is now maintained online at the Internet Assigned Numbers Authority web site (www.iana.org/protocols/).

- **Data and Pad.** The client data for this field may be of any length between 46 and 1500 octets. The content of the Data field is unspecified. An unspecified pad is inserted immediately after the user data when there is not enough user data for the frame to meet the minimum frame length.

- **Envelope Suffix.** This field is optional and depends on the type of envelope frame encapsulation(s) used. The envelope suffix may not be larger than (482 octets minus the envelope prefix).

- **Frame Check Sequence (FCS).** The mathematical result of a cyclic redundancy check (CRC) algorithm is placed in this four-octet field. The sending station calculates the checksum for the transmitted frame, and the resulting four-octet value is appended following the Data/Pad or the Envelope Suffix, if present. Receiving station(s) perform the same calculation and compare the new checksum against the checksum found at the end of the transmitted frame. If the two match, the frame is considered to be without error. The fields used in the calculation include everything from the beginning of the Destination Address to the end of the Data/Pad or Envelope Suffix as shown in Figure 4-4. The Preamble, SFD, and Extension fields are not included in the calculation. The FCS is the only Ethernet field transmitted in noncanonical order (MSB first).

  Because the corruption of a single bit anywhere from the beginning of the Destination Address through the end of the FCS field causes the checksum to be different, the coverage of the FCS includes itself. It is not possible to distinguish between corruption of the FCS field itself and corruption of any preceding field used in the calculation.

- **Extension.** This field is used exclusively with 1000Mbps Ethernet when operating in half duplex. If the frame being transmitted is not long enough to meet slotTime requirements (4096 bits or 512 octets), the transmission is extended with this field until it meets the minimum transmission duration requirement. The extension is discarded and is not counted toward minimum or maximum frame length requirements.

Theory of Operation

The 802.3 standard permits up to 1024 stations within a single Ethernet collision domain. That number may have been practical in the late 1970s or early 1980s, but it is unworkable with current technology. At the time 1024 stations was specified, the typical network was supporting a mainframe or mini computer and some terminals.

Taking into account the increases in desktop computing power and the rise in graphical and/or streaming content on the network, a more reasonable number per collision domain is probably fewer than 20. Users who regularly consume large amounts of bandwidth should not be on shared media at all.

Ethernet was designed to operate on a *bus* structure, which is a technical way to say that every station always hears all messages at almost the exact same time. The official designation is Carrier Sense Multiple Access with Collision Detection (CSMA/CD). CSMA/CD can be simplistically interpreted to mean that when two or more stations realize they are talking at the same time, they are supposed to stop and wait a polite amount of time before trying again.

The basic rules and specifications for proper operation of Ethernet are not particularly complicated. Despite the basic simplicity, when a problem occurs within a collision domain it is often quite difficult to isolate the source of the problem. Because of the common bus architecture of Ethernet (which could be described as a distributed single point of failure), the scope of the problem is usually all stations within the collision domain. In situations where repeaters are used, this could legally include stations up to four segments away—and farther if the architecture rules have been violated.

According to the rules of CSMA/CD, any station on an Ethernet network wanting to transmit a message first "listens" to ensure that no other station is currently transmitting (Carrier Sense). If the cable is idle, the station begins transmitting immediately. But the signal takes a small amount of time to travel down the cable (called *propagation delay*) and each subsequent repeater encountered introduces a small amount of latency in forwarding the frame from one port to the next. As a result, it is possible for more than one station to begin transmitting at or near the same time (Multiple Access), and a collision results (requiring Collision Detection).

In half duplex, assuming that a collision would not occur, the sending station transmits 64 bits of timing synchronization information, often known

collectively as the Preamble. After the timing information, the following is transmitted:

- Destination and source MAC addressing information
- Certain other header information
- Actual data payload
- Checksum (FCS) to ensure that the message was not corrupted along the way

Stations receiving the frame recalculate the FCS to determine whether the incoming message is valid, and hand good messages to the next higher layer in the protocol stack.

If the attached station is operating in full duplex, the station may send and receive simultaneously and collisions should not be recorded. Full duplex operation also changes the timing considerations and eliminates the need for slotTime. Full duplex operation allows for larger network architecture designs because the timing restriction for collision detection is removed, though bending the rules in this way would not be prudent. Note: Switches (multiport bridges) are generally used in place of repeaters for new installations. It has become very difficult to purchase a hub acting as a true repeater.

For 10Mbps versions of Ethernet, which are asynchronous, each receiving station uses the eight octets of timing information to synchronize its receive circuit to the incoming data, but discards it. 100Mbps and higher speed implementations of Ethernet are synchronous, so the timing information is not actually required at all. For compatibility reasons, however, the Preamble and SFD are present. All information *following* the SFD at the end of the timing information is passed to the next higher layer. A new checksum is calculated and compared with the checksum found at the end of the received frame. If the frame is intact, it must be interpreted according to the rules for whichever protocol is indicated by the Length/Type field or the LLC Layer protocol indicated by the first few octets of the data.

Almost everyone is familiar with the minimum-sized Ethernet frame being specified as 64 octets, but the actual size on the wire has always been 72 octets (64 octets plus 8 octets of Preamble and

SFD). The Preamble and SFD represent timing information discarded by the Ethernet chipset and thus not included in the frame size. Extension octets after the end of the frame are discarded in the same manner. Similarly, the largest basic Ethernet size has also been 1526 octets instead of 1518 octets, if the discarded timing information is included. When the discarded timing information is included, the unit of measure is a packet instead of a frame.

IEEE 802.1Q specifies how bridges may insert two fields into the basic Ethernet frame to identify a virtual network (broadcast domain). If 802.1Q VLAN tags are present, the frame size (again ignoring the discarded timing information) grows to 1522 octets through the addition of 4 octets of tag (refer to Figure 4-7). There are other protocol extensions that have similar effects, and were formalized in the 802.3as working group update to the Ethernet standard as envelope frames. If a VLAN tag is present but an intervening switch or bridge is not configured to participate in the VLAN, depending on the age of the hub, bridge, or switch, the frame may be considered an illegal frame and be discarded for being larger than 1518 octets. Some later-model hub designs permit a variety of oversized frame sizes through without discarding them. Frame sizes from 1522 to as much as 1536 octets have been found to pass undisturbed through newer hubs and switches, even if those infrastructure devices have no special configurations for recognizing the additional fields or participating and using those extra fields. Very recent infrastructure devices are aware of the envelope packet sizes and should pass 2000 octet frames, even if they cannot interpret the envelope.

For all speeds of Ethernet transmission at or below 1000Mbps, the standard describes how the parameter slotTime is used to manage transmissions within a collision domain. slotTime for 10 and 100Mbps Ethernet is 512 bit times (64 octets). slotTime for 1000Mbps Ethernet is 4096 bit times (512 octets, including any extension). slotTime is not defined for 10Gbps Ethernet because it does not permit half duplex operation. slotTime allows for the longest possible round-trip delay time when maximum cable lengths are used on the largest legal network architecture when all hardware latency and propagation delay times are at the legal maximum, plus the 32-bit jam signal used when collisions are detected. In other words, slotTime is just longer than the time it can theoretically take to go from one end of the largest legal Ethernet collision domain to the other end, collide with another transmission at the last possible instant, and then have the collision fragments return to the sending station and be detected. For the system to work, the first station must learn about the collision before it finishes sending the smallest legal frame size. To allow 1000Mbps Ethernet to operate in half duplex, the Extension field was added when sending small frames purely to keep the transmitter busy long enough for a collision fragment to make it back (refer to Figure 4-6). This field is present only on 1000Mbps half duplex links, and allows minimum-sized 64 octet frames to be stretched long enough to meet slotTime requirements.

As stated before, for CSMA/CD Ethernet to operate, the sending station must become aware of a collision before it completes transmission of a minimum-sized frame. This is the basis of slotTime. slotTime is approximately equal to the longest amount of time it can take for a signal to be sent from one station, travel through the entire collision domain and reach the most distant station, and return. The diameter of a collision domain is controlled by the slotTime parameter. slotTime is determined by three major factors:

- Delay within the sending/receiving stations
- Propagation delay down the cables
- Latency through repeaters

Maximum station delay and repeater latency are specified parameters. Propagation delay is determined by the cable. As an over-simplified statement: on a 10Mbps Ethernet, one bit at the MAC Layer requires 100 nanoseconds (ns) to transmit. At 100Mbps, that same bit requires 10ns to transmit, and at 1000 Mbps it takes only 1 ns. Eight inches (20.3 centimeters) per nanosecond is often used as a rough estimate for calculating propagation delay down a twisted-pair cable. For 100 meters of twisted pair this means that it takes just under 5 bit times for a 10BASE-T signal to travel the length of a 100 meter cable (~ 4.92 bit times).

Simply moving the decimal point over results in 49.2 bit times at 100Mbps, and 492 bit times at 1000Mbps for the signal to travel down the same 100m cable.

At 100Mbps the system timing is barely able to accommodate 100-meter cables. At 1000Mbps special (very inefficient) adjustments were required because nearly an entire minimum-sized frame has been transmitted before the first bit reaches the end of the first 100 meters of twisted-pair cable. It is easy to see why half duplex was not permitted in 10 Gigabit Ethernet.

Interpacket Spacing

The minimum spacing between two noncolliding packets, from the last bit of the FCS field of the first packet to the first bit of the preamble of the second packet, is shown in Table 4-1. This table ignores the special circumstance described earlier for half duplex Gigabit Ethernet, which is covered later in this chapter in the section "Frame Bursting."

After a packet has been sent, all stations on a 10Mbps Ethernet are required to wait a minimum of 96 bit times (9.6 microseconds) before any station may legally transmit the next packet. On faster versions of Ethernet, the spacing remains the same 96 bit times, but the time required for that interval grows correspondingly shorter, as shown in Table 4-1. This interval is called the interpacket spacing, the interpacket gap, or the interframe gap, and is intended to allow slow stations time to process the previous packet and prepare for the next frame.

Table 4-1. *Interframe spacing*

Speed	Interframe Spacing	Time Required
10Mbps	96 bit times	9.6 μsec
100Mbps	96 bit times	0.96 μsec
1Gbps	96 bit times	0.096 μsec
10Gbps	96 bit times	0.0096 μsec

A repeater is expected to regenerate the full 64 bits of timing information (Preamble and SFD) at the start of any frame, despite the potential loss of some of the beginning Preamble bits to slow synchronization. Thus, because of this forced reintroduction of timing bits, some minor reduction of the inter-frame gap is not only possible but expected. Some Ethernet chipsets are sensitive to a shortening of the interpacket spacing, and begin failing to "see" frames as the gap is reduced. With the increase in processing power at the desktop, it would be very easy for a personal computer to saturate an Ethernet segment with traffic and to begin transmitting again before the interpacket spacing delay time is satisfied. In past years, some vendors were suspected of deliberately violating the interpacket gap a little to improve throughput testing results in competitive product comparisons for 10Mbps products. For the most part this cheating on the interpacket spacing has not caused problems, but it has the potential to do so. With migration to Fast and Gigabit Ethernet at the desktop, this has ceased to be an issue.

When operating over 10GBASE-W implementations, the MAC Layer must provide for an additional interpacket spacing requirement. The 10GBASE-W implementations are designed to fit into an OC-192 SONET payload, which runs at slightly less than 10Gbps. For the system to operate as transparently as possible, the MAC Layer uses the variable ifsStretchSize to determine how much extra interpacket spacing is required to accommodate the slightly lower throughput rate. The simple description is that for every 104 octets transmitted, the MAC Layer decreases the interpacket spacing that follows that transmission by one octet. The receiving MAC Layer uses the same algorithm to restore the extra spacing at the other end. Other than this slight decrease in interpacket spacing, the MAC Layer is able to treat the 10GBASE-W implementations the same as any other Physical Layer implementation.

Retransmission

After a collision occurs and all stations allow the cable to become idle (each waits the full interframe spacing), the stations that collided must wait an additional—and potentially progressively longer—period of time before attempting to retransmit the collided frame. The waiting period is intentionally designed to be semi-random so that two stations do not delay for the same amount of time before retransmitting; otherwise, the result would be more collisions. This is accomplished in part by expanding the interval from which the random retransmission time is selected on each retransmission attempt. The waiting period is measured in increments of the parameter slotTime as shown in Table 4-2. slotTime applies only to half duplex Ethernet links.

Table 4-2. *slotTime parameter table*

Speed	slotTime	Time Interval
10Mbps	512 bit times	51.2 μsec
100Mbps	512 bit times	5.12 μsec
1Gbps	4096 bit times	4.096 μsec
10Gbps	Not applicable	Not applicable

Retransmission is controlled by the formula: $0 \leq r < 2^k$, where r is some random number of slot-Times and k is the number of backoff attempts (up to a maximum of 10 for the backoff value). The total maximum number of retransmission attempts is 15 (the total number of transmission attempts is 16), although the backoff value remains at 10 for the last few attempts. The formula specifies the minimum waiting period for a retransmission attempt. It is acceptable for a station to introduce extra delays that degrades its own throughput.

As an example, after the fifth consecutive collision without being able to transmit the current 10BASE-T frame, the waiting time would be a random delay interval between zero and thirty one slotTimes ($0 \leq r < 2^5$). Restated, the delay would be a random number of 51.2 microsecond time units ranging from an immediate retry attempt up to 1587.2 microseconds later.

If the MAC Layer is still unable to send the frame after 16 attempts, it gives up and generates an error to the next layer up. Such an occurrence is rare, and would happen only under extremely heavy network loads or when a physical problem exists on the network.

There is a special situation in which the MAC Layer experiences much more frequent failures

to send a frame despite the 16 attempts, and it is usually found on switched links. This is called the *capture effect* or the *packet starvation effect*. When two devices (switches or stations) connect in half-duplex and each is attempting to send a large block of traffic, a collision will almost certainly occur. Whichever station "wins" the first retransmission (usually either the switch or the PC, although the error is often reported only by the switch) has a progressively greater chance to transmit with each subsequent collision. Assume that a second collision has taken place. The first station, which succeeded in retransmitting its first frame, is again selecting a random delay between 0 and 1 time intervals, whereas the second station is now selecting among 0, 1, 2, and 3 time intervals. It is highly likely that the first station will again select a shorter delay time and be able to transmit. The first station will probably win the retransmission for 16 consecutive attempts by the second station. The second station will give up and discard the frame. Under these conditions, the switch records an excessive collisions error on that interface. This type of error is usually revealed using SNMP to query a switch port, and is often found even where there is only a single device attached to the affected port. Because Ethernet is inherently bursty, this may be reported on ports with relatively low average utilization.

Error Handling

The most common (and usually benign) fault condition on an Ethernet is the collision. Properly speaking, most collisions are not actually errors; instead, they are the mechanism for resolving contention for network access. A few collisions provide a smooth, simple, low-overhead way for network nodes to arbitrate contention for the network resource.

A variety of other fault conditions can represent errors. To help understand the often subtle distinctions between many Ethernet fault conditions (and some conditions that are not defined in the Ethernet standard), the more common errors and fault conditions have been listed here in groupings by event size:

Early Events

Preamble collision

Local collision

Remote collision

Short frame

Runt

Ghost

Midframe Events

Late collision

Late remote collision

FCS error

Alignment or Range error

Late Events

Oversize frame

VLAN tagged frame

MPLS shimmed frame

Jabber

Jumbo frame

Although some of the errors described here are not defined in the 802.3 standard, knowing one type error from another makes it possible to troubleshoot more effectively because the nature of the error helps you determine how far it is able to propagate through a network and what may have caused it. A troubleshooting discussion appears in Chapter 11, "Network Troubleshooting." It should also be noted that many troubleshooting tools are either unable to detect some types of errors or they report the observed errors with different names. In most cases, the difference in naming results from how the information was obtained. In addition to the 802.3 standard, SNMP queries based on several RFCs are frequently involved. Perhaps the two most common are RFC 1643 (Ethernet-like devices), and RFC 2819 (RMON).

The presence of errors on an Ethernet always suggests that further investigation is warranted. The severity of the problem indicates the troubleshooting urgency related to the detected error(s).

A handful of errors detected over many hours would be a low priority. Thousands detected over a few minutes suggest that more urgent attention is warranted. Frames associated with error conditions are routinely—but not always—discarded.

Collisions

Because collisions are expected events used to arbitrate access to the medium, they are discussed before the three groupings of fault conditions and errors are examined. Remember that a collision itself is usually not an error. The quantity of collisions may indicate a fault condition, however. A high collision level can prevent productive network traffic from being sent.

Collisions typically take place when two or more Ethernet stations transmit simultaneously within a collision domain. Collisions are reported as event counts by most diagnostic tools, but may be reported separately as single collisions or multiple collisions. Single collisions are just that: A collision was detected while trying to transmit a frame, but the frame was transmitted successfully on the next attempt. Multiple collisions indicate that the same frame was collided more than once before being successfully transmitted. This is different from frames with deferred transmissions because the deferred transmission frame was not collided. The medium was busy when the station or switch sought to transmit, and it was required to wait its turn to transmit. Switches may report these events as deferred transmissions through SNMP queries. Sufficient repeated collisions of the same frame cause the frame to be discarded, which is reported as being aborted due to excessive collisions. The results of collisions (partial and corrupted frames that are less than 64 octets and have an invalid FCS) are often called *collision fragments*.

Each time a collision takes place on the collision domain, an amount of time and available bandwidth are consumed. This is not usually a problem because most networks operate at substantially less than line rate. Collisions waste time in two ways. First, network bandwidth loss is equal to the initial transmission and the collision jam signal. This might be called *consumption delay*, and it affects all stations on the collision domain. Consumption delay has the potential to significantly reduce network throughput. Following each successful or failed transmission attempt is an enforced idle time for all stations (called the interpacket spacing or interpacket gap), which further impacts throughput. The second type of delay results from colliding stations implementing the collision backoff algorithm. Backoff delays are not usually significant.

The considerable majority of all collisions occur very early in the frame, often before the SFD. As soon as a collision is detected, the sending stations are to transmit a 32-bit jam signal that enforces the collision. This is done so that data being transmitted is thoroughly corrupted and all stations have a chance to detect the collision.

In Figure 4–11, two stations listened to ensure that the cable was idle, and then transmitted. Station 1 was the first station transmitting, so that station sent the most data before a collision was detected. Station 2 was able to send only a few bits before the collision was detected.

Note: *Figure 4–11 is conceptual and should not be evaluated for exact latency characteristics relative to each component of the example scenario. See 802.3, Annex B subclauses B.1.2 and B.1.3, for precise examples of latency through all components of a sample collision domain during a collision event and during a normal uncollided transmission.*

Examine Figure 4–11 closely. Station 1 was able to transmit a significant percentage of the frame before the signal even reached the last cable segment. Station 2 had not received the first bit of the transmission prior to beginning its own transmission. Station 2 was able to send only several bits before the NIC sensed the collision. Station 2 immediately deferred the current transmission and substituted the 32-bit jam signal in place of what was left to be sent. Then Station 2 ceased all transmissions. During the collision and jam event that Station 2 was experiencing, the collision fragments were working their way back through the repeated collision domain toward Station 1. Station 2 completed transmission of the 32-bit jam signal and became silent before the collision could propagate back to Station 1. Station 1, still unaware of the collision, continued to transmit. When the collision fragments finally reached Station 1, it also deferred the current transmission and substituted a 32-bit jam signal in place of the remainder of the frame it was transmitting. Upon sending the 32-bit jam signal, Station 1 ceased all transmissions. Both stations then began counting the randomly selected time interval from the backoff algorithm before attempting to retransmit the deferred frame. Stations not participating in the collision event simply wait the interpacket gap period and are able to attempt a transmission.

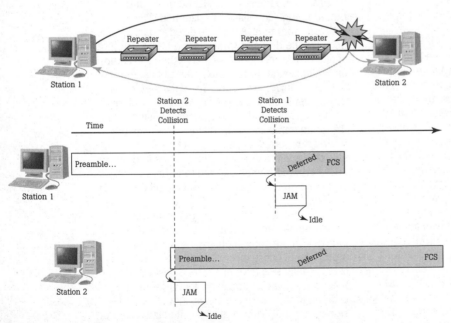

Figure 4–11. *Routine collision handling in a 10Mbps collision domain*

A jam signal may be composed of any binary data as long as it does not form a proper checksum for the portion of the frame already transmitted. The most commonly observed data pattern for a jam signal is simply a repeating one, zero, one, zero pattern, the same as Preamble. When viewed by a protocol analyzer, this pattern appears as either a repeating hexadecimal 5 or A sequence. The corrupted, partially transmitted messages are often referred to as *collision fragments*. Normal collisions (not late collisions) are less than 64 octets in length (see Figure 4–12), and therefore fail both the minimum length test and the FCS checksum test.

Early Events

Early events take place prior to the determination that a transmission event has met the minFrameSize requirement of 64 octets and appears to be properly formed. The minFrameSize parameter does not include the Preamble and SFD.

Some number of events take place due to environmental conditions, software driver problems, and other hard-to-quantify origins. If noise is detected on one port of a repeater, the repeater interprets that noise as well as it is able and forwards a signal to all other ports. There are minimum size requirements for what a repeater must transmit, too, so the noise event may be much shorter than the signal forwarded by the repeater. These events appear on the collision domain as the beginning of a frame that was deferred and no SFD is observed (see Figure 4–13).

Preamble Collision

Preamble collisions are the most common form of collision (see Figure 4–14), mostly because collision domain diameters are much smaller now than in years past. In a switched environment, the collision domain is typically represented by a single cable.

The 802.3 standard distinguishes only between the collision used for medium access arbitration (called a normal collision here) and a late collision. The closest event to a Preamble collision that the standard references is the much more narrowly defined *shortEvent* in Clauses 19 and 30.

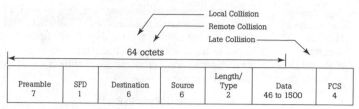

Figure 4–12. *Collision types*

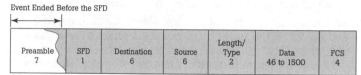

Figure 4–13. *Noncolliding Preamble event*

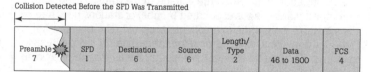

Figure 4–14. *Preamble collision*

Local Collision

A local collision exhibits the symptom of either an overvoltage state on coax, or simultaneous activity on both the RX and TX pairs when operating in half duplex.

To create a local collision on coax cable (10BASE2 and 10BASE5), the signal travels down the cable until it encounters a signal from the other station. The waveforms then overlap, canceling out some parts of the signal and reinforcing (doubling) other parts. The doubling of the signal pushes the voltage level of the signal beyond the allowed maximum. This overvoltage condition is then sensed by all the stations on the local cable segment as a collision. There is a special circuit in the NIC that monitors for this overvoltage condition. The overvoltage threshold is around −1.5 volts as measured on the coax cable.

Unexpected Collision Sources Are Possible

The overvoltage state does not require the overlap of two or more transmissions to meet the requirements of a collision. One troubleshooting even saw the following characteristics, which were opposite the expected symptoms:

- Stations near the server were unable to log in

- Stations progressively farther away from the server had a higher likelihood of being able to log in

- All stations on the far side of a repeater could log in

After a prolonged period of troubleshooting, it was discovered that the NIC in the server had become marginal and was transmitting too "hot" of a signal. The frame was properly formed, but the voltage used to transmit exceeded −1.5 volts. All stations close to the server could see that the checksum on the frame was fine; but because the voltage exceeded the collision detect threshold, the frame was counted as a collision and discarded. As attenuation diminished the voltage in the transmission with greater distance, a corresponding number of stations began to see a signal below the overvoltage threshold. The repeater forwarded the signal to another segment despite the overvoltage state, and on the far side of the repeater it was transmitted using normal voltages, so all stations were able to log in.

Understanding the required characteristics of a collision permitted the network support staff to find the root cause of the problem using a voltage meter.

In Figure 4-15, the beginning of the waveform represents normal Manchester encoded data. The amplitude of the wave doubles a few cycles into the sample—at the beginning of the collision, where the two waveforms are overlapping. Just prior to the end of the sample, the amplitude returns to normal when the first station to detect the collision stops transmitting its jam signal, and jam from the second colliding station is still observed.

On twisted pair or fiber optic cable, a collision is detected on the local segment only when a station detects a signal on the RX (receive) pair at the same time it is sending on the TX (transmit) pair. Because the two signals are on different wire pairs, there is no characteristic change in the signal as shown in Figure 4-15. Collisions are recognized on twisted pair only when the station is operating in half duplex. The only functional difference between half and full duplex operation in this regard is whether both transmit and receive circuits are permitted to be used simultaneously. If the station is not engaged in transmitting, it cannot detect a local collision. Conversely, a cable fault such as excessive crosstalk can cause a station to perceive its own transmission as a local collision.

Although grouped in the early events category, this definition is true no matter what the duration of the transmission event—no minimum or maximum size. To be counted as a local collision instead of a late collision (for this list), the event must occur before the timer for slotTime has expired.

It is possible for a local collision event to have a valid FCS checksum but, due to the local collision symptom, the frame is discarded anyway.

The 802.3 standard does not specify a local collision. For coax, the voltage level is described in Clauses 8 and 10. For twisted pair, the standard describes this condition "…shall detect as a collision the simultaneous occurrence of activity on the DO circuit and the RD circuit…," where DO is the transmit function and RD is the receive function.

Remote Collision

The characteristics of a remote collision are as follows: a frame that is less than the minimum length, has an invalid FCS checksum, and does *not* exhibit the local collision symptom of overvoltage or simultaneous RX/TX activity (see Figure 4-16).

Figure 4-15. *Midframe 10BASE2 collision captured by a digital storage oscilloscope*

This sort of collision usually results from collisions occurring on the far side of a repeated connection. A repeater does not forward an overvoltage state, and cannot cause a station to have both the TX and RX pairs active at the same time. The station would have to be transmitting to have both pairs active, and that would constitute a local collision. On twisted-pair networks, this is the most common sort of collision observed. The 802.3 standard makes reference to this type of collision as a "fragment," but does not explicitly define it. Nearly all monitoring tools that report collisions on twisted pair, such as software protocol analyzers and RMON probes, are able to report only collision fragments (what this text describes as *remote collisions*) because they are passive listening devices and see only transmissions shorter than the legal minimum size with an invalid FCS checksum. In these situations, it is sometimes possible to infer the presence of a collision by checking the last few octets of the event for the characteristic hexadecimal "A"s or "5"s pattern often seen when a colliding station jams.

This event is referred to as a *collision fragment* in the 802.3 standard but is not otherwise described.

Short Frame

A short frame is a frame smaller than the minFrameSize requirement of 64 octets and has a valid FCS checksum (see Figure 4–17). In general, you should not see short frames, although their presence is not a guarantee that the network is failing.

For troubleshooting purposes, a short frame is any data (even one octet) after the SFD, which is followed by a valid FCS checksum for the data transmitted.

The 802.3 standard specifies that a frame must be at least minFrameSize in length (64 octets). The only direct references to a short frame error described in the standard relate to shortEvents and runts. RFC 2819 describes an error called UndersizePkts that meets the troubleshooting definition for a short frame.

Runt

The term *runt* is generally used as an imprecise slang term that means something less than a

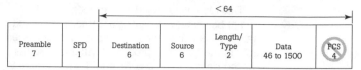

Figure 4–16. *Remote collision*

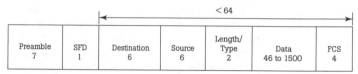

Figure 4–17. *Short frames are properly formed in all but one aspect: They are less than the minimum frame size of 64 octets*

legal frame size. It may refer to short frames with a valid FCS checksums. The typical use of *runt* usually refers to collision fragments. The Ethernet standard describes an SNMP management attribute called a runt that is subject to several possible definitions. Paraphrasing, it is greater than 74 bit times but less than the minimum frame size (64 octets at 10/100Mbps speeds, or the minimum half duplex transmission event of 517 octets at 1000Mbps), and is *not* a local collision.

Ghost

Fluke Networks has coined the term *ghost* to mean energy (noise) detected on the cable that appears to be a frame, but is lacking a valid SFD (see Figure 4–18). To qualify as a ghost, an event must be at least 72 octets long; otherwise, it is classified as a remote collision. Because of the peculiar nature of ghosts, it is important to note that test results largely depend on where on the segment the measurement is made.

Event Was Longer than 72 Octets, No SFD Was Detected, and No Collision

Figure 4–18. *Ghost event*

This type of event causes the receiving station to believe it is receiving a frame. The sensed frame never comes, however, so no data is passed up into the NIC to be processed. After awhile the sensed transmission ceases, and the NIC is able to resume sending its own messages. Each network interface may react differently, and there are no standards defining how or when an NIC should react to a noisy segment. Because no collision accompanies this error, the receiving station does not report any errors. Very few Ethernet devices even report this event as utilization. Repeaters propagate these noise signals into other segments of the collision domain.

The characteristic of this error that caused creation of the new error definition was the discovery that on some networks the various monitoring tools reported no utilization or errors, but throughput on the segment was poor or non-existent. Investigation with a digital storage oscilloscope revealed the presence of traffic bearing this characteristic.

Midframe Events

In this list, midframe events are those that occur when the transmission duration falls between the minFrameSize and maxUntaggedFrameSize limits (between 64 and 1518 octets).

Late Collision

There is no possibility remaining for a normal or legal collision after slotTime expires—usually representing the first 512 bits of a transmission. (Refer to Figure 4-12.) The specified maximums for legal network propagation times are exceeded at that point. Collisions occurring after the slotTime are called *late collisions*. The most significant difference between late collisions and collisions occurring within slotTime is that the Ethernet NIC retransmits a normally collided frame automatically, but is not expected to automatically retransmit a frame that was collided late. As far as the NIC is concerned, the upper layers of the protocol stack must deduce that the frame was lost and then initiate a new transmission with the apparently lost data. Other than retransmission, a station detecting a late collision handles it in exactly the same way as a normal collision.

In all but one case, the 802.3 standard permits a station to attempt to retransmit a frame that was collided late but does not require it. Gigabit Ethernet explicitly forbids retransmission of late collided frames.

Late Remote Collision

A late remote collision is one that takes place after slotTime has elapsed *and* on the far side of a repeater. The NIC in the reporting station on the local segment is assumed to be silent during this event because otherwise a collision would be detected. However, because the repeater would prevent observation of the local collision symptoms, monitoring hardware would have to be present on the distant segment to detect a late collision and report that information back to your reporting station. It is also possible to infer that a late remote collision took place somewhere on the other side of a repeater by analyzing the last few octets of a bad frame for the presence of the pattern normally associated with a jam signal. That is, the characteristic hexadecimal "A"s or "5"s pattern often seen when a colliding station jams. This type of collision would be detected on the local segment simply as an FCS error.

This situation meets the definition of an FCS error as defined by the 802.3 standard.

FCS Error

An FCS error is a received frame having a bad Frame Check Sequence (also referred to as a *checksum* or *CRC* error). The checksum calculated by a receiving station does not match the checksum appended to the end of the frame by the sending station (see Figure 4-19).

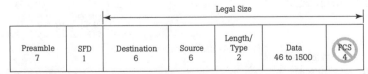

Legal Size

Preamble 7	SFD 1	Destination 6	Source 6	Length/ Type 2	Data 46 to 1500	FCS 4

Figure 4-19. *FCS errors are reported when the cyclic redundancy checksum algorithm calculated by the receiving station produces a different FCS value than what is found at the end of the received frame*

The 802.3 standard describes this error in several places. To qualify for the 802.3 definition, the received frame must meet both minimum and maximum frame size limits and not be collided. RFC 1643 relies on the 802.3 definition for this error, whereas RFC 2819 combines the FCS error with the alignment error.

Legal size can vary depending on where in the network it is observed. The original maximum size was 1518 octets, but a VLAN tagged frame increased the maximum size to 1522 octets and, with the approval of 802.3as, the maximum envelope size may reach 2000 octets.

Alignment

A message that does not end on an octet boundary is known as an *alignment error*. That is, instead of the correct number of binary bits to form complete octet groupings, there are some additional bits left over (fewer than 8).

Such a frame is truncated to the nearest octet boundary and, if the FCS checksum fails, an alignment error is reported. This is often caused by bad software drivers or a remote collision, and is frequently accompanied by a failure of the FCS checksum. If a local collision is detected, it cannot be an alignment error. The extra bits are sometimes referred to as *dribble bits*.

Range

A frame that had a legal-sized value in the Length field but that did not match the actual number of octets counted in the Data field of the received frame is known as a Range or InRangeLengthError. This error also appears when the Length field value is less than the minimum legal unpadded size of the data field.

A similar error, Out of Range, used to be reported when the value in the Length field indicated a data size that was too large to be legal. However, when the EtherType use of the Length field was adopted, this interpretation was excluded from the 802.3 standard.

Late Events

The grouping of late events in this text begins when maxUntaggedFrameSize of 1518 octets has been exceeded.

The legal field additions in an envelope frame that may extend a frame beyond 1518 octets are

configured as special handling rules for a given point-to-point link. Note that only frames already near or at the maximum frame size are affected by the addition of fields such as VLAN tags. Smaller frames become larger, but do not exceed the maximum frame size. The extra fields may still cause some stations to discard the frame.

Oversize or Long Frame

A long frame is longer than the maximum legal size. The 802.3 standard takes into consideration whether the frame was an envelope frame. It does not consider whether the frame had a valid FCS checksum. This error is usually meant when someone says that jabber was detected on the network. If the long event was classified according to the RFC 2819 (RMON) definition, anything larger than 1518 octets is either a long frame (the FCS is good) or an oversized frame (the FCS is bad) (see Figure 4–20).

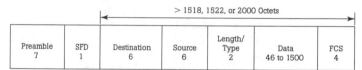

Figure 4-20. *A long frame is greater than one of the following: 1518 octets, 1522 octets in the presence of an 802.1Q tag, or 2000 octets in the presence of an envelope frame*

The 802.3 standard requires that a long frame may be counted only if it is *not* going to be counted as an alignment error or FCS error. Those errors take precedence over the long frame error, and a frame may be counted for only one category.

The proprietary use of so-called jumbo frames would be counted as an oversize or long frame error.

VLAN Tagged Frame

The 802.1Q standard defines a four-octet field that is inserted into an 802.3 frame between the source MAC address and the Length/Type field. This tag should never be seen by the average Ethernet station and is used only between Ethernet devices such as switches configured to participate in the VLAN trunk. Servers are sometimes configured to participate in a VLAN trunk. If a tagged frame is received by a station not participating in the VLAN, it is discarded as an error.

Due to the provisions for 802.1Q VLAN tagging in the 802.3 standard, when the frame is tagged, it is not counted toward being illegally large by newer hardware, including bridges or switches not participating in the VLAN. Legacy bridges or switches may discard a tagged frame instead of forwarding it when the legacy bridge or switch is not participating in the VLAN.

A VLAN tagged frame should not be counted as an error. If an older receiving station (typically a switch) is not participating in the VLAN, however, it may decide that such a frame is illegally long and discard it. If this occurs, the discard would be counted as an oversize or long frame error.

MPLS Labeled Frame

The usage of MPLS in the local area network is growing as more Ethernet switches offer MPLS functionality. MPLS is defined in RFC 3032 to use a four-octet label (often called a *shim*), inserted into the 802.3 frame in the same place as a VLAN tag (refer to Figure 4-9).

It is not unusual for MPLS shims to be stacked. This creates a situation where the extra fields added to the original 802.3 frame do not have a fixed length. MPLS shimmed frames are counted as envelope frames.

An MPLS labeled frame should not be counted as an error. If an older receiving station (typically a switch) is not participating in the MPLS configuration, however, it may decide that such a frame is illegally long and discard it. If this occurs, the discard would be counted as an oversize or long frame error.

Jabber

Jabber is defined several places in the 802.3 standard as being a transmission that is too long. Each speed has different ranges (10Mbps = between 20,000 and 150,000 bit times; 100Mbps = between 40,000 and 75,000 bit times; 1000Mbps = between 80,000 to 150,000 bit times). The Jabber timer is used by a repeater to determine when a port should be isolated. However, most diagnostic tools report jabber whenever a detected transmission exceeds the maximum legal frame size.

This presents a rather fuzzy definition because the reporting device may or may not consider a 1518-octet frame with VLAN tagging added to be larger than the legal limit. Also, there is no indication as to whether jabber has a good or bad FCS. The same event is also referred to as a veryLongEvent by the 802.3 standard.

Most references to jabber are more properly called oversized frames, drawing from the terminology described in the RMON specification in RFC 2819.

Jumbo Frame

802.3 Ethernet does not support jumbo frames. Industry has introduced support for Ethernet-like frames as large as 9018 octets. Actually, products have shipped with support for frames at least as large as 65,536 octets, but the most commonly discussed maximum size is 9018 octets. These proprietary jumbo frames are typically supported on Gigabit and faster links only.

Allowances for very large protocol data units (PDUs) exist in higher-layer protocols, but the frame sizes are limited by the MAC Layer links each packet traverses. Chapter 6, "Network Layer," mentions this large data unit support for IPv4 and IPv6.

Existing 802.3 Ethernet would classify a 9018-octet frame as an oversize or long frame error. The largest supported Ethernet frame definition is when the Envelope fields are included, creating a frame of up to 2000 octets.

Duplex

There are two duplex modes: half and full. For coaxial media, the half duplex mode is mandatory. The 10Mbps coaxial implementations are inherently half duplex in nature and cannot operate in full duplex. Twisted pair and fiber implementations may be operated in half duplex, but that mode is only an administrative imposition because there are separate paths for transmit and for receive. 100BASE-T4 is capable of only half duplex because three of the four twisted pairs are used to transmit. 1000BASE-T and 10GBASE-T are designed to transmit simultaneously (bidirectionally) on all pairs as part of normal operation. For 1000BASE-T, use of half duplex is again simply an administrative imposition, although for 10GBASE-T half duplex is not permitted at all.

In half duplex, only one station may transmit at a time. For 10Mbps coaxial implementations, a second station transmitting causes the signals to overlap and become corrupted. Fiber implementations transmit on separate pairs and the signals have no opportunity to overlap and become corrupted. Twisted pair implementations either transmit on separate pairs or are designed for simultaneous use.

Ethernet has established arbitration rules for resolving conflicts arising from instances when more than one station attempts to transmit at the same time in a half-duplex environment. Both stations in a point-to-point full-duplex link are permitted to transmit at any time, regardless of whether the other station is already transmitting.

Auto-Negotiation avoids most situations where one station in a point-to-point link is transmitting under half-duplex rules and the other is transmitting under full-duplex rules. There are only two methods of achieving a full-duplex connection at speeds below 10 Gigabit: by using Auto-Negotiation or by administratively forcing the duplex mode at both ends of the link. If one station in a point-to-point link is Auto-Negotiating and the

other is not, the Auto-Negotiating station is required to select half duplex. Thus, if one end of a link is forced to full duplex it is then incumbent upon the network support staff to force the other end to do so as well.

Failure to force both ends results in an artificially elevated error level and poor performance on the link. However, the link still operates.

Duplex mismatches are perhaps the most common problem found on switched networks.

Frame Bursting

Gigabit Ethernet presents a special problem in half duplex. It takes so long for the frame to reach the other end of the collision domain and return that a minimum-sized frame wastes vast amounts of bandwidth. slotTime for half-duplex Gigabit Ethernet is 4096 bits (512 octets). If the station sent a minimum-sized frame, almost the entire slotTime period would be spent transmitting extension symbols to stretch out the transmission long enough to meet the slotTime requirement.

To improve efficiencies somewhat, Gigabit Ethernet permits frame bursting. In a frame burst, the initial frame transmitted must meet slotTime requirements (at least 512 octets or be stretched that long with extension bits), but after that the station may continue transmitting consecutive frames until a timer expires (see Figure 4-21).

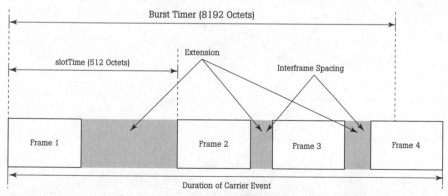

Figure 4-21. *Frame burst concept diagram and timing*

The burst limit timer is 65,536 bits (8192 octets) in duration, and a station may begin transmitting new frames separated by proper interpacket spacing until the timer expires. The initial frame extension (if required because the first frame was less than 512 octets) and the interframe spacing are formed with extension symbols to differentiate them from an idle period where another station is allowed to transmit. When the timer expires, the station may not start transmitting another new frame but may finish transmitting a frame started before the timer expired. This extreme effort to make Gigabit Ethernet operate in half duplex was largely wasted because there are no Gigabit repeaters (hubs) available. As long as Auto–Negotiation is not disabled and manual configurations used instead, virtually all deployed Gigabit Ethernet operates in full duplex.

Auto-Negotiation

[See 802.3, Clause 28]
At the time Fast Ethernet was introduced, the standard added a method of automatically configuring a given interface to match the best speed and capabilities of the link partner. This process defines how two link partners may automatically negotiate a configuration offering the best common performance level. It has the additional advantage of involving only the lowest sublayers of the Physical Layer.

10BASE-T required each station to transmit a link pulse about every 16 milliseconds whenever the station was not engaged in transmitting a frame. Auto–Negotiation adopted this signal and renamed it a Normal Link Pulse (NLP). When a series of NLPs are sent in a group for the purpose of Auto–Negotiation, the group is called a Fast Link Pulse (FLP) burst. If extended Next Page (XNP) capability is offered by both link partners, an even longer group of NLPs is transmitted. Each FLP or XNP burst is sent at a timing interval compatible with NLP link pulses, and is intended to allow older 10BASE-T devices to operate normally if they should receive an FLP burst.

In Figure 4–22, the top waveform shows NLPs occurring at the default 10BASE-T interval. The middle waveform shows FLP bursts occurring at the same intervals. The bottom waveform shows XNP bursts at more precise, but still compatible timing intervals.

10BASE-T transmits using signaling between +1 and −1 volts, for a 2-volt peak-to-peak differential signal. NLP (as well as FLP and XNP) signaling only uses the range from 0 to +1 volts. (See Figure 4–23.)

FLPs are not transmitted in synchronization, although the exchange of information must follow a specified sequence. It is easily possible for one link partner to be transmitting FLPs at different interval spacing than the other link partner as long as the interval meets the required minimum and maximum timing interval requirements. FLP bursts may be started at intervals from 8ms to 24ms. Optimized FLP bursts (using extended Next Pages) may be started at intervals from 8ms to 8.5ms.

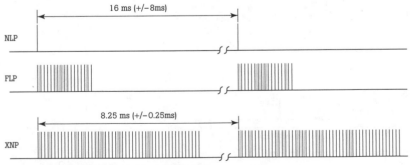

Figure 4-22. *NLP versus FLP and XNP timing*

Auto-Negotiation is accomplished by transmitting a burst of 10BASE-T link pulses from each of the two link partners. The burst communicates the capabilities of the transmitting station to its link partner. After both stations have interpreted what the other partner is offering, both switch to the highest performance common configuration and establish a link at that speed. If anything interrupts communications and the link is lost, the Auto-Negotiation process starts over. The link may be lost due to external influences such as a cable fault, power loss, cable disconnection, or due to one of the partners issuing a reset.

An FLP burst consists of 33 pulse positions (see Figure 4–24). The 33 pulse positions represent a 16-bit link code word framed by 17 clocking pulses. Clocking pulses within a burst are separated by 125 µs (+/- 14 µs). Data pulse positions are found between each clocking pulse (see Figure 4–25). If a data pulse is present, it is interpreted as a binary 1. The absence of a data pulse in the window between two clocking pulses it is interpreted as a binary 0.

When Auto-Negotiation is implemented there is always a *base page*, referring to the 16-bit link codeword exchanged. At the discretion of the two link partners, additional pages may be exchanged by setting the Next Page bit in the Base Page. The additional pages are called *Message Pages* and *Unformatted Pages*. If either link partner does

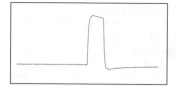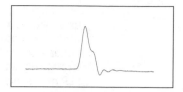

Figure 4–23. *Two sample NLP pulses. Without (left) and with (right) pre-emphasis. Pre-emphasis helps the pulse be recognized over greater cable distances.*

not set the Next Page bit, Auto-Negotiation concludes with the information found in the base link codeword alone. Message Pages have predefined 11 bit words, and Unformatted Pages are used to offer additional or clarifying details related to the link being negotiated. There is no limit to the number of next pages that may be sent, and it is possible that one link partner may have more Next Page information to send than the other. As soon as either partner sets the Next Page bit and all the message bits to zero, the other link partner recognizes that as the end of the link partner's information but may continue sending its own Next Pages. The link partner that has finished sending information sends Message Pages with a Null Message code and the Next Page bit set to 0. To end an Auto-Negotiation session, both link partners set their Next Page bit to zero.

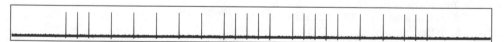

Figure 4–24. *Actual FLP Auto-Negotiation burst captured with a digital storage oscilloscope. The FLP burst is made up of multiple NLP link pulses.*

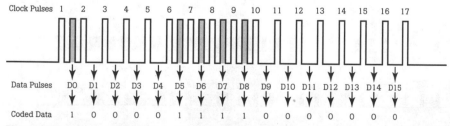

Figure 4–25. *Interpretation of Auto-Negotiation pulses. The 17 clocking pulses are always present. The 16 data pulses are present only if they represent binary 1, and are absent if they represent binary 0 in the encoded 16-bit data word. The pulses interpreted as binary 1s for data have been highlighted in gray.*

If both link partners offer the capability to send extended Next Pages (XNP), only extended FLPs (XNPs) are used after the Base Page. In this case either extended message pages or extended unformatted pages follow. An optimized or extended FLP represents three 16-bit link codewords sent at once, for a total of 48 bits in one extended Next Page exchange.

After a device has decoded the link code word offered by its link partner, it acknowledges receipt of the current word by sending at least three FLP bursts with the Acknowledge bit set. After both link partners acknowledge the current FLP link code word exchange in that manner, the link partners either move on to the next page or enable the agreed configuration and attempt to link accordingly. Link partners may send any number of Next Pages following the initial configuration Base Page and any necessary Next Pages that are associated with the Base Page.

Link partners are allowed to omit configurations that they are capable of, but are not allowed to include configurations that they cannot support. This allows the network administrator to force ports to a selected speed and duplex setting without disabling Auto-Negotiation.

In Figure 4-26, Device 2 is transmitting FLP bursts for some time before Device 1 begins transmitting. To identify different messages, a grey background was applied to the first set of each group, and a blank background for the acknowledgments of that group. Both devices transmit the base page FLP until at least three identical FLPs are received from the link partner. After receipt of at least three identical FLPs, the local device begins sending FLPs with the Acknowledge bit set but no other change is made. Each device transmits at least six FLPs with Acknowledge

set. If the Base Page for both devices included Next Page offer, or an extended Next Page and a Next Page offer, they switch to either a Message Page, extended Message Page, Unformatted Page, or extended Unformatted Page as appropriate. 10GBASE-T uses extended Next Pages, so that is sent next in this example. Again, both devices transmit extended Next Page (XNP) bursts until each receives at least three identical XNPs. Then an additional six to eight XNPs are transmitted with the Acknowledge bit set. Following a successful Auto-Negotiation, both devices attempt to link using the agreed technology and settings.

Decoding Auto-Negotiation messages from Device 2 in Figure 4-26 reveals the following process:

- The base page FLP value is converted to binary as shown.

1001000000000001

- The binary data is transmitted LSB first, just like nearly all the Ethernet frame. The binary value is reordered before it is decoded, producing 9001 in hexadecimal if converted.

1001 0000 0000 0001

1000 0000 0000 1001

- The 16-bit FLP may then be grouped into the appropriate fields.

1 0 0 1 000000 00001

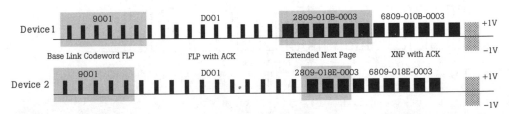

Figure 4-26. *Auto-Negotiation is not a symmetric or synchronous activity, although it follows a prescribed order. This example illustrates an Auto-Negotiation process resulting in link at 10GBASE-T.*

- Interpretation of the fields reveals the following encoding:

  00001 = Selector for Ethernet

  000000 = Technology Abilities (no low speeds offered]

  1 = Extended Next Page (Yes]

  0 = Remote Fault (No]

  0 = Acknowledge (No)

  1 = Next Page (Yes]

- The extended Next Page (XNP) is converted to binary as shown.

100100000010100110100001000000011000000000000000

- Each group of 16 bits from the XNP is sent LSB first, so the XNP is reordered in 16-bit groups. This produces in 2809010B0003 in hexadecimal if converted.

1001 0000 0001 0100   1101 0000 1000 0000   1100 0000 0000 0000

0010 1000 0000 1001   0000 0001 0000 1011   0000 0000 0000 0011

- The 48-bit XNP may then be grouped into the appropriate fields.

  0 0 1 0 1 00000001001 0 0 0 0 0
  00100001011 00000000000 0 0 0 1 1

- Interpretation of the fields reveals the following encoding:

  00000001001 = Technology Message Code for 10GBASE-T/1000BASE-T

  1 = Toggle

  0 = Ack2

  1 = Page Type (Message Page)

  0 = Acknowledge (No)

  0 = Next Page (No)

  00100001011 = Master/Slave Seed Bits

  0 = 10GBASE-T Master/Slave Manual Configuration (Disabled)

  0 = 10GBASE-T Master/Slave (Slave)

  0 = Port Type (Single Port Device)

  0 = 1000BASE-T FDX (Not Offered)

  0 = 1000BASE-T HDX (Not Offered]

  1 = 10GBASE-T (Offered)

  1 = LD Loop Timing (Offered/Capable)

  0 = PHY Short Reach Mode (Operating in Normal Mode)

  0 = Reserved

  0 = LD PMA Training Reset Request (Requests Link Partner to Train Continuously)

  00000000000 = Reserved

Auto-Negotiation is optional for most Ethernet implementations; however, Gigabit and 10 Gigabit Ethernet both require support capability for Auto-Negotiation. Auto-Negotiation was originally defined for twisted-pair implementations of Ethernet, but is also now defined for some non-Ethernet protocols.

Parallel Detection

When an Auto-Negotiating station first attempts to link, it is supposed to enable 100BASE-TX and/or 100BASE-T4 receive circuits of the front-end chipset (if supported) to attempt to immediately establish a link. If 100BASE-TX signaling is received and the station supports 100BASE-TX, it attempts to establish a link without negotiating. The same is true for 100BASE-T4. If either signaling produces a link or if FLP bursts are received, the station proceeds with that technology. If a link partner does not offer an FLP burst, but instead offers NLPs, that device is automatically assumed to be a 10BASE-T station. During this initial interval of testing for other technologies, the transmit path is sending FLP bursts. The standard does not permit parallel detection of any other Ethernet implementations.

If a link is established through parallel detection, it is required to be half duplex. There are only two methods of achieving a full-duplex link: through a completed cycle of Auto-Negotiation or by administratively forcing both link partners to full duplex. If one link partner is forced to full duplex, but the other partner parallel detects while attempting to Auto-Negotiate, there is certain to be a duplex mismatch resulting in collisions and errors on that link. If you force one end, you must force the other. The exception to this is that 10 Gigabit Ethernet does not support half duplex at all.

Many vendors implement their hardware in such a way that it cycles through the various possible states. It transmits FLP bursts to Auto-Negotiate for awhile, it configures itself for Fast Ethernet and attempts to link for awhile, and finally it simply listens for awhile. Some vendors do not offer any transmitted attempt to link until the interface first hears an NLP, an FLP burst, or a specific implementation such as 100Mbps signaling. In the silent listening state, a portable computer is able to conserve enough battery power to be quite worthwhile, although this mode is not supported by the standard.

Priority Resolution

In the anticipated event that link partners share more than one common technology capability, the following list is used to determine which technology should be chosen from the offered configurations. The list is priority ranked, with the most desirable link configuration at the top.

- 10GBASE-T
- 1000BASE-T full duplex
- 1000BASE-T half duplex
- 100BASE-T2 full duplex
- 100BASE-TX full duplex
- 100BASE-T2 half duplex
- 100BASE-T4
- 100BASE-TX half duplex
- 10BASE-T full duplex
- 10BASE-T half duplex

Fiber optic Ethernet implementations are not included in this priority resolution list because the interface electronics and optics do not permit easy reconfiguration between implementations. It is assumed that the interface configuration is fixed. If the two interfaces are able to Auto-Negotiate, they are already using the same Ethernet implementation, although there remain a number of configuration choices such as the duplex setting or flow control settings that must be determined.

Additional detailed information about Auto-Negotiation may be found in IEEE 802.3 Clauses 28, 37, and 55, and Annexes 28A, 28B, and 28C. Some additional detailed information about Auto-Negotiation is presented in Appendix C, "Auto-Negotiation," later in this book.

Power over Ethernet (PoE)

[802.3 Clause 33]

Power over Ethernet (PoE) allows a device connecting to the network to also receive power from the network. Support was specified in 802.3af and updated in 802.3at for 10BASE-T, 100BASE-TX, and/or 1000BASE-T links.

The device that draws power through the network connection is called a *powered device* (PD). The power sourcing equipment (PSE) is typically the switch, but could also be a midspan power insertion source. The PSE tests for the presence of a PD. If a PD is detected, it provides power according to the results of the classification algorithm. Some midspan power injectors provide similar voltage on the pins specified, but they do not negotiate according to the PoE rules and instead provide constant power regardless of what is connected. Some non-PoE-compliant constant power injectors provide significantly more current than the PoE standard specifies, so some care must be taken when deploying them.

Power is supplied by the PSE over two general arrangements: the Ethernet 10/100 "active pairs" (called *Alternative A*) or the 10/100 "unused pairs" (called *Alternative B*). Because 10/100 had specific expectations for where TX and RX would be found depending on whether the PSE interface was acting as a normal hub/switch, or if it was in a crossover configuration that looked like a station interface (MDI-X for hub/switch, MDI for station), there are two configurations for the 10/100 Alternative A usage (see Figure 4-27).

Note: *Only one of the three possible choices is ever energized at one time. The standard explicitly excludes the possibility of two or more choices being energized simultaneously.*

To classify a PD, the PSE checks for opens and shorts and reads the resistance of the PD. If the resistance is within a specific range, the PSE measures the current drawn by the PD to make the initial classification. This is referred to as a *Physical Layer classification*. Physical Layer classification identifies Type 1 devices as Class 0–3, and possible Type 2 devices as Class 4.

Power is applied according to the Physical Layer classification, with possible Type 2 devices receiving Class 0 power. After a Type 2 device has been powered, a second classification process called the Data Link Layer classification begins. For Type 2 devices, both the PD and the PSE attempt mutual classification with the link partner.

Data Link Layer classification is implemented using a special Data Link Layer LLDP frame employing the following TLV. Note: 802.3at was not fully approved at the time of this writing, so the information in Figure 4-28 could change. (Data Link Layer LLDP frames are described in Chapter 5, "Data Link Layer.")

Using the LLDPDU TLV, the PD requests specific power levels from the PSE. The maximum power levels are shown in Table 4-3. The PSE and PD may dynamically reallocate power at any time during PD operation.

Alternative A MDI–X	Alternative A MDI		Alternative B (all)
1 V–	1 V+		1
2 V–	2 V+		2
3 V+	3 V–		3
4	4		4 V+
5	5		5 V+
6 V+	6 V–		6
7	7		7 V–
8	8		8 V–

Figure 4-27. *PoE power is provided on two pairs according to Alternative A (MDI-X), Alternative A (MDI), or Alternative B*

Table 4-3. *PoE power levels provided to a powered device (PD)*

PD Class	Power*
Class 0	13.0
Class 1	3.84
Class 2	6.49
Class 3	13.0
Class 4	25.5

* Powered Device (PD) power supply average input limits measured in watts at the PD input per 802.3at.

Even after the entire classification process has completed, including mutual Type 2 classification, the PSE has the option of not providing power. If the PSE is not able to provide the maximum power level requested by the PD, it should not provide power to the link.

If the classification process does not produce the level of power that the PD is seeking, either through an incomplete classification process or because the PSE does not support Type 2 power, the PD is to indicate to the user that insufficient power is present.

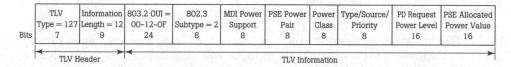

	TLV Type = 127	Information Length = 12	803.2 OUI = 00-12-0F	802.3 Subtype = 2	MDI Power Support	PSE Power Pair	Power Class	Type/Source/ Priority	PD Request Power Level	PSE Allocated Power Value
Bits	7	9	24	8	8	8	8	8	16	16

TLV Header — TLV Information

Figure 4-28. *TLV field format found within a Data Link Layer LLDPDU classification frame*

There is at least one other proprietary technology for providing power over Ethernet, which was in use at the time 802.3af was ratified. As with other older technologies, non-802.3 PoE use is diminishing.

Ethernet Implementation Details

The remainder of the chapter provides a basic description of the operation of many common Ethernet implementations. It is difficult to adequately describe how much technical detail was summarized, paraphrased, or entirely omitted to create the following highly simplified descriptions. If there is any reason to reference the following descriptions for a technical purpose, you are strongly urged to review the actual standard to acquire a feeling for the level of detail omitted. Any time that a detailed technical description is summarized in this way, an inevitable degree of inaccuracy is introduced.

Note: *The casual reader should review only the architecture rules section for each speed that follows. Other than the architecture information, the remainder of this chapter contains far more detail than would be useful for ordinary networking activities.*

The encoding schemes change from very simple to very complex as the speed increases. This is partly due to sending more information in smaller time intervals and over more than one pair simultaneously, and partly because the protocol is expected to perform error correction as a routine part of normal operation at Gigabit and 10 Gigabit speeds over twisted pair.

10Mbps Versions of Ethernet

Not covered in this section are the broadband definitions of 10BROAD36, the fiber optic 10Mbps versions of 10BASE-FL, 10BASE-FB, 10BASE-FP, and FOIRL, and the low speed implementation of 1BASE5. Due to their growing scarcity, 10BASE5 and 10BASE2 were also nearly cut from this text. They were kept primarily because the locations

where they are still found tend to be fairly important low utilization legacy installations. Almost all new installations are fiber or high-speed twisted pair-based.

Note: *Additional special rules apply for installations where fiber optic connections such as Fiber Optic Inter-Repeater Links (FOIRL) are used. For example, when five segments are present, FOIRL segments should be limited to 500 meters; when only four segments are present, FOIRL segments may be 1000 meters.*

10Mbps Ethernet has several key parameters that govern its normal operation (see Table 4–4). These parameters manage access to the medium and specify allowed transmission characteristics.

Table 4-4. *Parameters for 10Mbps Ethernet operation*

Parameter	Value
Maximum Station Count	1024 *
slotTime	512 bit times
Interframe Spacing	96 bits **
Transmission Attempt Limit	16
Collision Backoff Limit	10
Collision Jam Size	32 bits
Maximum Untagged Frame Size	1518 octets
Minimum Frame Size	512 bits (64 octets)

* Repeaters do not count toward the maximum of 1024 stations on an Ethernet collision domain.

** The value listed is the official interframe spacing. Shrinkage of the interframe spacing is expected and is caused by variable network delays, added preamble bits, and clock skew, but must never be less than 47 bit times as measured at the AUI receive line of the DTE. Burst Limit and Interframe Spacing Stretch Ratio do not apply to 10Mbps Ethernet.

10Mbps Transmission Process

A sample frame is taken through the encoding and transmission process for each speed of Ethernet, and in each of the commonly deployed technologies. Each begins with the same fully formed Ethernet frame as shown in Figure 4-29.

Figure 4-29. *Sample Ethernet frame as observed at the MAC Layer*

Figure 4-30. *Partial hexadecimal representation of the sample Ethernet frame*

The first few fields of the sample frame shown in Figure 4-29 are represented in hexadecimal in Figure 4-30.

The initial two fields of the sample frame are converted from hexadecimal to binary to permit illustration of the Physical Layer manipulations (see Figure 4-31).

Each octet is transferred least-significant bit (LSB) first from the MAC Layer to the Physical Layer, so the bits are reordered on a per-octet basis. The FCS field is not reordered. Conceptually, this is easiest to grasp as simply turning each octet over as shown in Figures 4-32 and 4-33.

Following the LSB reordering of each octet by the MAC Layer, the octets are transferred to the Physical Layer Signaling (PLS) sublayer. The PLS is responsible for notifying the MAC Layer about carrier activity on the medium and any received Signal Quality Error (SQE) messages from the Access Unit Interface (AUI).

When the PLS has a frame to transmit, it uses a set of control lines on the AUI interface to notify the Media Access Unit that it is coming, as well as sending the serialized data stream. The AUI interface is somewhat similar to RS-232 in its operation implementation, using control lines and data

Figure 4-31. *Binary representation of the first two fields in the sample Ethernet frame*

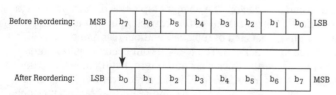

Figure 4-32. *LSB reordering of an octet*

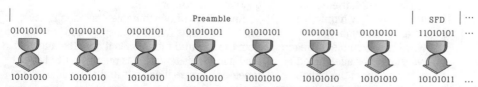

Figure 4-33. *LSB reordering of the first two fields in the sample Ethernet frame*

lines in serial communications. The AUI interface is exposed for 10BASE5, and typically contained within the network interface card for 10BASE2 and 10BASE-T.

For the purposes of this discussion, the most important control line on the AUI interface is the SQE signal. SQE is always used in half duplex, and permitted but not required in full duplex operation. SQE is active when any one of the following four conditions is true:

- Within 4 to 8 microseconds following a normal transmission to notify the PLS that the outbound frame was successfully transmitted.

- Whenever the medium attachment unit (MAU) believes that there is a collision on the medium.

- Whenever the MAU believes that there is an *improper* signal on the medium. Improper signals might include detected jabber or the reflections that result from a cable fault, such as a short. (There are separate conditions depending on which medium is attached.)

- Whenever the MAU has interrupted a transmission because it believes it to qualify as jabber; that is, it has transmitted longer than is allowed.

Octets received from the MAC Layer are serialized from left to right utilizing the Manchester encoding rules and transmitted across the AUI interface to the MAU. Manchester encoding relies on the direction of the edge transition in the middle of the timing window to determine the binary value for that bit period.

In the encoding example in Figure 4–34, there is one timing window highlighted vertically through all four waveform examples. The top waveform has a falling edge in the center of the timing window, so it is interpreted as a binary 0.

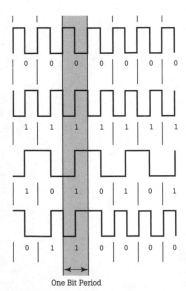

One Bit Period

Figure 4–34. *Manchester encoding example*

Depending on how you view it, the second waveform in Figure 4–34 is either 180 degrees out of phase or it is shifted half of one bit period to the side. It is otherwise identical. The result is that in the center of the timing window for the second waveform is a rising edge that is interpreted as a binary 1.

Instead of a repeating sequence of the same binary value, there is an alternating binary sequence in the third waveform example. In the first two examples, the signal must transition back between each bit period so that it can make the same-direction transition each time in the center of the timing window. With alternating binary data, there is no need to return to the previous voltage level in preparation for the next edge in the center of the timing window. Thus, any time there is a long separation between one edge and the next, you can be certain that both edges represent the middle of a timing window.

The fourth waveform example is random data that allows us to verify that whenever there is a wide separation between two transitions, both edges are in the center of a timing window and represent the binary value for that timing window.

At the Physical Medium Attachment (PMA) sublayer are two distinctly different MAUs. 10BASE5 implements a detached MAU that may be up to 50 meters away and is attached to the medium via an N-style screw-on connection or a *vampire tap*, which is clamped over the cable and pierces the cable shield to reach the center conductor. The vampire tap holds distinct advantages over the N-style connection in that it can be installed or removed without disrupting the collision domain. The N-style connection requires cutting the thick coax and reterminating the ends. The 10BASE5 MAU is powered over the AUI interface.

The 10BASE2 and 10BASE-T MAU is internal to the network adapter, and the AUI interface is not exposed. The 10BASE-T MAU may also engage in Auto-Negotiation.

Regardless of which implementation is used, the MAU accepts the Manchester-encoded signal from the AUI and retransmits it onto the attached medium. In this regard, it is nearly an OSI Layer 1 repeater because it accepts and retransmits data in either direction.

In 10BASE5 (see Figure 4-35) and 10BASE2 (see Figure 4-36), the encoded signal is transmitted at approximately zero to −1 volts. The waveform samples in Figure 4-36 and Figure 4-37 represent the end of the FCS field. Notice that the signal returns to zero volts after the end of the transmissions in both waveforms.

On 10BASE-T, the Manchester-encoded signal is transmitted at approximately +1 to −1 volts and appears on the wire as shown in Figure 4-37.

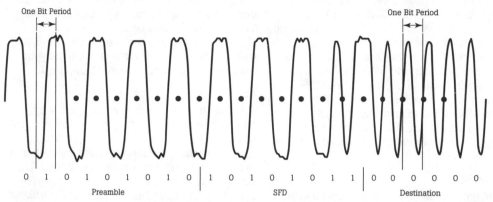

Figure 4-35. *10BASE5 signal decoded. Dots have been added as timing marks to aid in recognizing the timing windows from which the binary data was decoded.*

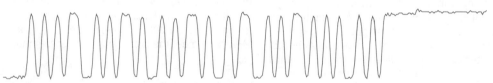

Figure 4-36. *10BASE2 signal example*

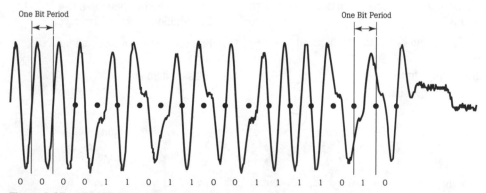

Figure 4-37. *10BASE-T signal sample decoded*

10Mbps Ethernet is asynchronous and the cable is often completely idle (zero volts) for long periods between transmissions. 10BASE-T links have a link pulse present about every 16ms, but can otherwise be idle. A link pulse uses only the positive half of the wave (+1 volt) and then returns to zero volts, as shown in Figure 4-23 through Figure 4-26. 10BASE5 and 10BASE2 could potentially be idle (zero volts) for days if no station wanted to transmit.

At reception, the signal is read according to the Manchester rules and converted back into binary, again grouped into octets. The LSB-ordered octets are reversed again, back to the original MSB order. To complete the cycle from hexadecimal to Manchester and back, the octets are converted to hexadecimal as a final operation in Figure 4-38.

Architecture

It is not only allowed, but it is expected that an Ethernet network could contain multiple types of media (that is, 10BASE5, 10BASE2, 10BASE-T, etc.). The standard goes out of its way to ensure that interoperability and backward compatibility are maintained. However, when implementing a mixed-media network, it is important to pay particular attention to the overall architecture design. It becomes easier to violate maximum delay limits as the network grows and becomes more complex. The timing limits are based on parameters such as the following:

- Cable length and its propagation delay
- Delay of repeaters
- Delay of transceivers (including NICs and hubs)
- Interframe gap shrinkage
- Delays within the station

A simple description of architecture limits follows. Annex B of the 802.3 standard provides a detailed discussion about architecture and timing considerations for 10Mbps implementations.

If your network is implemented using new high-performance hardware, it is possible that some of these limits can be exceeded, although doing so is not a recommended practice. Refer to the technical timing descriptions detailed in Clause 13 and Annex B of the current 802.3 standard and the technical information about your hardware performance before attempting it.

5-4-3 Rule

10Mbps Ethernet operates within the timing limits offered by a series of not more than five segments separated by no more than four repeaters. That is, no more than four repeaters may be connected in series between any two distant stations. The coaxial implementations have a further requirement that there be no more than three populated segments between any two distant stations. The other two allowed coaxial segments are used to extend the diameter of the collision domain and are called *link segments*. The primary characteristic of a link segment is that it has exactly two devices attached. All twisted-pair links, such as 10BASE-T, meet the definition of a link segment.

- Five segments
- Four repeaters
- Three segments with stations (coax rule only)

This concept could be extended to a 5-4-3-2-1 rule with the addition of two more items:

- Two link segments without stations (coax rule only)
- One collision domain

| 10101010 | 10101010 | 10101010 | 10101010 | 10101010 | 10101010 | 10101010 | 10101011 ... |

| 01010101 | 01010101 | 01010101 | 01010101 | 01010101 | 01010101 | 01010101 | 11010101 ... |
| 55 | 55 | 55 | 55 | 55 | 55 | 55 | D5 |

Figure 4-38. *Conversion of sample binary data back to the MSB format used at the MAC Layer*

10BASE5

A 10BASE5 "thick" coax cable has a solid central conductor, a minimum nominal velocity of propagation (NVP) of 0.77c, 50 ohms of impedance/termination resistance, and uses N-style screw-on connections. Each of the maximum five segments of thick coax may be up to 500 meters long (1,640 feet), and each station is connected to a transceiver on the coax via an AUI cable that may be up to 50 meters long (164 feet). Two types of transceiver connections are used: The most common is a clamp-on style, where a small hole is drilled into the cable through which the transceiver connects to the center conductor (often called a vampire tap). The other style requires the cable to be cut and terminated to screw the transceiver onto the two new ends.

There may be up to 100 stations on any individual 10BASE5 segment, including repeaters. Out of five consecutive segments in series between any two distant stations (see Figure 4-39), only three may have stations attached. As shown in Figure 4-39, station connections to the coax should be separated by not less than 2.5 meters (8.2 feet) to avoid creating electrical "echoes" on the cable because of alignment with fractional wavelengths. Thick coax manufactured for Ethernet is marked every 2.5 meters to aid placement of taps, and to avoid this problem. For the same reason, if a segment cannot be constructed from a single piece of thick coax, each cable used on the segment should be made from lengths equal to 23.4, 70.2, or 117 meters. These lengths may be mixed as needed to form the required overall

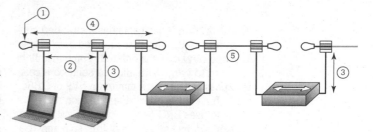

(1) Termination of each end of the coax should be 50 Ohms.
(2) Minimum distance between taps is 2.5 meters.
(3) Maximum AUI cable length is 50 meters.
(4) Maximum segment length is 500 meters.
(5) Link segments between repeaters should have a total of only two attachments; the repeaters themselves.

Figure 4-39. *10BASE5 network design limits*

length. As a last option, if these lengths are not possible, the segment should be constructed from shorter cables built of cable from the same manufacturer and lot.

Figure 4-40 illustrates one possible configuration for a maximum end-to-end 10BASE5 collision domain. Between any two distant stations only three repeated segments are permitted to have stations connected to them, with the other two repeated segments used exclusively as link segments to extend the network. To achieve the permitted 1024 stations on this design, the connections to the center segment *with stations* could be populated with 100 repeater connections, leading to other populated segments.

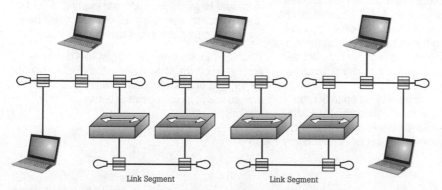

Link Segment   Link Segment

Figure 4-40. *10BASE5 architecture example—maximum end-to-end link between two distant devices*

10BASE2

A 10BASE2 "thin" coax cable has a stranded central conductor. (Be sure that stranded coax is specified when new cable is ordered—some installers find it hard to work with and use solid-core coax where possible.) It has a minimum NVP of 0.65c, has 50 ohms of impedance/termination resistance, and uses BNC T-style connections. Each of the maximum five segments of thin coax may be up to 185 meters long (600 feet), and each station is connected directly to the BNC T connector on the coax (see Figure 4-41).

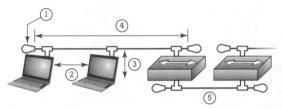

① Termination of each end of the coax should be 50 Ohms.

② Minimum distance between taps is 0.5 meters.

③ Each station must connect within four centimeters of the thin coax.

④ Maximum segment length is 185 meters.

⑤ Link segments between repeaters should have a total of only two attachments; the repeaters themselves.

Figure 4-41. *10BASE2 network design limits*

The maximum length of a *stub* (the connection that attaches a 10BASE2 station to the primary thin coax center conductor) is 4 centimeters, or about 1.5 inches. Effectively, no stubs are allowed (see Figure 4-42). Stubs of any significant length cause echoes on the cable and exhibit themselves as a variety of problems— all of which are very difficult to isolate.

There may be up to 30 stations on any individual 10BASE2 segment. Out of five consecutive segments in series between any

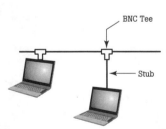
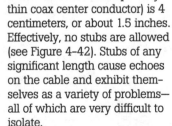

Figure 4-42. *10BASE2 stub example*

two distant stations, only three may have stations attached (just like Figure 4-40). As shown in Figure 4-41, station connections to the coax should be separated by not less than 0.5 meters (~ 1.5 feet).

10BASE-T

A 10BASE-T twisted-pair cable has a solid conductor for each wire in the maximum 90-meter horizontal cable, which should be 0.4 to 0.6mm (26 to 22 AWG) in diameter. The 10 meters of allowed patch cables use similar dimension stranded cable for durability because it is expected to experience repeated flexing. Suitable twisted-pair cable has a minimum NVP of 0.585c, has a nominal 100 ohms of impedance, and uses eight-pin RJ45 modular connectors as specified in ISO/IEC 8877. Cables between a station and a hub are generally described as between 0 and 100 meters long (0–328 feet). The precise maximum length is determined by propagation delay through the link segment (any length that does not exceed 1000ns of delay is acceptable for 10BASE-T, although it probably will not work with other twisted-pair implementations, so cable lengths in excess of 100 meters are discouraged). Usually, 0.5 millimeter (24 AWG) diameter twisted wire in a multipair cable meets the requirements at 100 meters.

Note: *Although Category 3 cable is adequate for use on 10BASE-T networks, it is strongly recommended that any new cable installations be made with Category 5e or better materials and wiring practices. Use all four pairs, and use either the T568A or T568B cable pin-out arrangement. With this type of cable installation, it should be possible to operate many different media access protocols (including 1000BASE-T) over the same cable plant without rewiring.*

10BASE-T links generally consist of a connection between the station and a hub. Hubs should be thought of as multiport repeaters and count toward the limit on repeaters between distant stations.

Although hubs may be linked in series (sometimes called *daisy chaining* or *cascading*), it is best to avoid this arrangement where possible to keep from violating the limit for maximum delay between distant stations. The physical size of a 10BASE-T network is subject to the same rules as 10BASE5 and 10BASE2 concerning number of repeaters. As shown in Figure 4-43, when multiple hubs are required, it is best to arrange them in hierarchical order to create a tree structure instead of a chain. Also, performance is improved if fewer repeaters separate stations. "Stackable" hubs, or concentrators with common backplanes that support several multiport adapter cards, permit large numbers of stations to be connected to a device that counts as a single hub (repeater).

An architectural example is shown in Figure 4-44. All distances between stations are acceptable, although in one direction the architecture is at its limit. The most important aspect to consider is how to keep the delay between distant stations to a minimum—regardless of the architecture and media types involved. A shorter maximum delay provides better overall performance.

Figure 4-44 can be redrawn to show the logical path between stations (see Figure 4-45). There are five segments and four repeaters from station 5 to any other station in these paths. For 10BASE-T connections, the maximum of three segments with stations does not apply because no other stations are on the same cable. Each connection is described as a link segment.

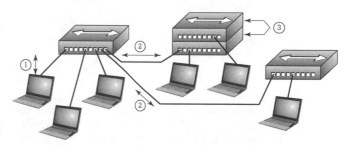

① UTP Link Segment cable length is 0 to 100 meters nominal (see description) between the station and the repeater, and between repeaters.

② Each hub is a multi-port repeater, so links between hubs count toward the repeater limit 5.

③ These two "stackable" hubs with interconnected backplanes count as only one repeater.

Figure 4-43. *10BASE-T network design limits*

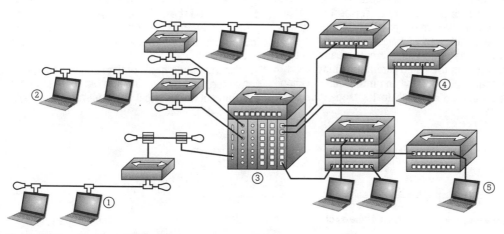

Figure 4-44. *Sample 10 Mbps mixed architecture*

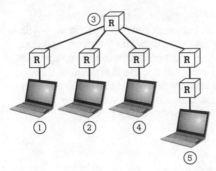

Figure 4-45. *Figure 4-43 drawn as a logical diagram (R is used to represent a repeater)*

From any station except station 5 to any other station in the diagram, the path is only three repeaters. Because these alternative paths include 10BASE5 and 10BASE2 links, the other requirements still apply there (such as only three segments with stations).

100Mbps Versions of Ethernet

Because they were never widely adopted and have largely disappeared, the Fast Ethernet versions of 100BASE-T4 and 100BASE-T2 are not covered.

100Mbps Ethernet has several key parameters that govern its normal operation (see Table 4-5). These parameters manage access to the medium and specify allowed transmission characteristics. The 802.3 standard states unequivocally that any deviation from the listed parameters may affect performance. Burst Limit and Interframe Spacing Stretch Ratio do not apply to 100Mbps Ethernet.

Table 4-5. *Parameters for 100Mbps Ethernet operation*

Parameter	Value
Maximum Station Count	1024 *
slotTime	512 bit times
Interframe Spacing	96 bits
Transmission Attempt Limit	16
Collision Backoff Limit	10
Collision Jam Size	32 bits
Maximum Untagged Frame Size	1518 octets
Minimum Frame Size	512 bits (64 octets)

* Repeaters do not count toward the maximum of 1024 stations on an Ethernet collision domain.

10Mbps Transmission Process

The same sample frame from the 10Mbps example will be taken through the encoding and transmission process for 100Mbps Ethernet, as shown in the following text. Unlike 10Mbps Ethernet, where the process was the same for all technologies until the signal was applied to the medium, the encoding process is different for each 100Mbps technology. The first difference appears immediately after the LSB reordering of each octet, and later there are distinctly different paths depending on the 100Mbps implementation.

The first few fields of the sample frame shown in Figure 4-46 are represented in hexadecimal in Figure 4-47.

The initial two fields of the sample frame are converted from hexadecimal to binary to permit illustration of the Physical Layer manipulations (see Figure 4-48).

Preamble 8	Destination 6	Source 6	Type 2	Data : Pad 46 to 1500	FCS 4

Figure 4-46. *Sample Ethernet frame as observed at the MAC Layer*

Preamble	SFD	Destination	Source	Length/Type	...
55 55 55 55 55 55 55	D5	00 C0 17 A0 02 35	00 80 20 56 33 D4	08 00	...

Figure 4-47. *Partial hexadecimal representation of the sample Ethernet frame*

Figure 4-48. *Binary representation of the first two fields in the sample Ethernet frame*

Each octet is transferred least significant bit (LSB) first from the MAC Layer to the Physical Layer, so the bits are reordered on a per-octet basis. The FCS field is not reordered. Conceptually, this is easiest to grasp as simply turning each octet over as shown in Figure 4-49 and Figure 4-50.

Following the LSB reordering of the octets by the MAC Layer, the Physical Layer separates each octet into two 4-bit nibbles as shown in Figure 4-51. (See 802.3, Clause 22—The Reconciliation Sublayer [RS] and Media Independent Interface [MII].)

It is interesting to note that the net effect of the reordering in Figure 4-51 is that the least significant 4 bits traded places with the most significant

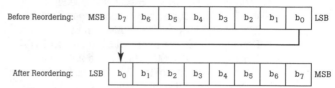

Figure 4-49. *LSB reordering of an octet*

4 bits. The data is then converted from a 4-bit data nibble to a 5-bit code group through a table look-up. This conversion is called 4B/5B encoding and is accomplished by the Physical Coding Sublayer (PCS) as shown in Figure 4-52. The code group representing the least significant nibble is transmitted first. (See 802.3, Clause 24.)

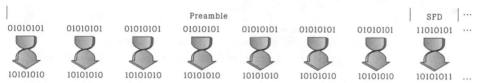

Figure 4-50. *LSB reordering of the first two fields in the sample Ethernet frame*

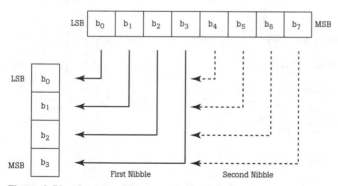

Figure 4-51. *Octet-to-nibble transmission ordering*

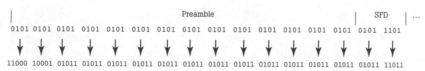

Figure 4-52. *4B/5B bit pattern following conversion*

Before the code group bit stream is passed to the next lower sublayer, the first octet of the original preamble—the first two code groups—are exchanged for the Start of Stream Delimiter (SSD) code groups by the PCS sublayer (see Figure 4-53). The SSD consists of code groups J (J = 11000) and K (K = 10001). Also, an End of Stream Delimiter (ESD) consisting of code groups T (T = 01101) and R (R = 00111) is placed immediately following the end of the FCS field as the first two code groups of the interframe spacing (see Figure 4-53 and Figure 4-54). All subsequent code groups between frames are idles. The SSD and ESD are used by the PCS sublayer to indicate the start and end of a normal data transmission only. The SSD converts back into Preamble when received, and reception of the ESD signifies the beginning of an idle state.

The conversion from 4 bits to 5 bits also means that there is now 125Mb to be transmitted instead of 100Mb during the same time interval.

Four bits at the MAC Layer require 40ns to transmit; dividing 40ns by 5 bits results in 8ns per bit. By decreasing the time permitted for each bit at the Physical Layer, the MAC Layer timing of 10ns per bit is not affected. Anytime there is no data to be sent, the PCS sublayer inserts idle code groups to fill the empty periods and maintain synchronization.

The code groups are serialized and passed to the Physical Medium Attachment (PMA) sublayer, which monitors the control lines, clocking, and synchronization (see Figure 4-55). The PMA is responsible for finding the SSD and ESD in incoming data streams. The PMA also detects far-end faults and transmits a special error code to inform the link partner that it is no longer synchronized with the incoming data stream or that there is no signal detected. A far-end fault condition results in loss of link status at both ends of the link, and the receiving partner begins sending idles until synchronization is reestablished. (See 802.3, Clause 24.)

| J | K | Preamble | | SFD | |

11000 10001 01011 01011 01011 01011 01011 01011 01011 01011 01011 01011 01011 01011 01011 11011 ...

Figure 4-53. *4B/5B bit pattern following the SSD substitution of the first two symbols*

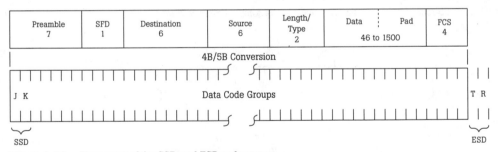

Figure 4-54. *Placement of the SSD and ESD code groups*

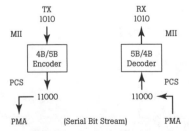

Figure 4-55. *Logical signal flow from the MII to the PMA sublayers*

At this point, the data path diverges depending on whether you are using copper (100BASE-TX) or fiber (100BASE-FX) media.

100BASE-FX

(See 802.3, Clause 26, and ISO/IEC 9314-3:1990.) This section is specific to the 100BASE-FX implementation only. For the 100BASE-FX Physical Medium Dependent (PMD) sublayer, the serialized bit stream is now prepared for transmission using NRZI (Non-Return to Zero, Inverting on ones) encoding rules.

NRZI encoding relies on the presence or absence of a transition in the middle of the timing window to determine the binary value for that bit period.

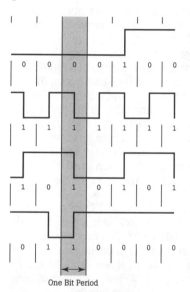

One Bit Period

Figure 4-56. *NRZI encoding example*

In the encoding example in Figure 4-56, there is one timing window highlighted vertically through all four waveform examples. The top waveform has no transition in the center of the timing window, so it is interpreted as a binary 0. No transition indicates that a binary 0 is present. If the sample waveform was all 0s on that line, the signal level represented would either be low or high across the waveform. A single 1 was introduced to indicate that 0s could be either level.

The second waveform has a transition in the center of the timing window. A binary 1 is represented by a transition. It does not matter whether the transition is rising or falling.

In the third waveform is an alternating binary sequence instead of a repeating sequence of the same binary value. In this example it is more obvious that no transition indicates a binary 0 and the presence of a transition indicates a binary 1.

The fourth waveform example is random data. Again, the presence of a transition indicates a binary 1. The first and fourth waveforms are good examples of why this encoding scheme has the potential for creating problems on copper media at higher frequencies. It is very easy to have a string of binary 0s cause a DC voltage bias on the cable, which has the potential of causing clocking errors.

The NRZI-encoded serialized bit stream is ready for transmission using pulsed light. Due to cycle time problems related to turning the transmitter completely on and off each time, the light is pulsed using low and high power. A logic 0 is represented by low power and a logic 1 by high power.

100BASE-TX

(See 802.3, Clause 25, and ANSI X3.263-1995.) This section is specific to the 100BASE-TX implementation only. After the 4B/5B substitution is made, the first octet of the Preamble—the first two symbol groups—is exchanged for the Start Stream Delimiter (SSD) symbols. The SSD consists of symbol groups J (J = 11000) and K (K = 10001).

After the substitution is made, the binary data stream is scrambled using a special 2K recursive key stream. The purpose of the scrambler is to ensure that transitions occur regularly. The 4B/5B code group selection process produced a pretty good transition density. However, the idle code group is five 1s and is sent as filler anytime there is no user data to send. This creates a constant frequency on the cable, which radiates noise. Thus, the scrambler ensures that transitions are irregularly spaced, creating multiple frequencies on the cable and dispersing the radiated energy across multiple frequencies.

This process requires a descrambler to recover the symbols from the waveform at the other end. Because the transmitter and receiver are in different hosts, it is first necessary to synchronize communications over the point-to-point link. If synchronization is lost, communication fails until synchronization can be reestablished.

The scrambler is described as "the periodic sequence of 2047 bits generated by the recursive linear function $X^{n-11} + X^{n-9}$ (modulo 2)." The key stream sequence can be generated by an 11-bit Linear Feedback Shift Register (LFSR) whose input bit is the exclusive-OR of its 11th and 9th previous bits (see Figure 4-57). As long as the LFSR is not loaded with all zeros, the output is the desired key sequence because an LFSR of n elements repeats its output every 2^{n-1} outputs.

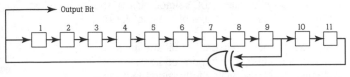

Figure 4-57. *Linear feedback shift register scrambler logical diagram*

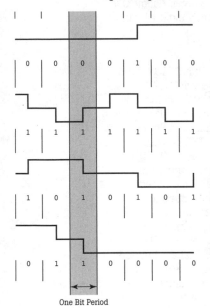

One Bit Period

Figure 4-58. *MLT-3 encoding example*

waveform examples. The top waveform has no transition in the center of the timing window. No transition indicates that a binary 0 is present. If the sample waveform was all 0s on that line, the signal level represented would either be a constant high, zero, or low across the waveform. A single 1 was introduced to move the remaining 0s to a different voltage level, and show that 0s may appear at more than one voltage level. The level is dependent on what the previous (high or low) voltage level was, and moves in the opposite direction. In this first waveform, it is thus evident that the previous voltage level (not shown) was a low level.

The second waveform has a transition in the center of the timing window. A binary 1 is represented by a transition. It does not matter whether the transition is rising or falling or whether the new level reached is high, zero, or low.

In the third waveform example, there is an alternating binary sequence instead of a repeating sequence of the same binary value. Again, this pattern helps demonstrate that the absence of a transition indicates a binary 0 and the presence of a transition indicates a binary 1.

The fourth waveform example is random data. The presence of a transition indicates a binary 1. As with NRZI, care must be taken to avoid creating a DC voltage bias on the cable. This is accomplished with the scrambler for 100BASE-TX. Figure 4-59 shows a 100BASE-TX signal sample captured from a live network connection. Rising or falling edges indicate 1s. The very steep signal changes from one extreme to the other, with a slight decrease in gradient at zero, indicate consecutive 1s. Any noticeable horizontal line in the signal indicates a 0 or consecutive 0s.

Once scrambled, the data is transmitted from left to right utilizing the MLT-3 (multilevel transmit-3 levels) encoding. The MLT-3 encoding converts the binary data stream to an electrical waveform using a continuous signaling system. MLT-3 is different from NRZI in that the signal level alternates between above and below the zero level instead of using only two levels.

In the encoding example in Figure 4-58 is one timing window highlighted vertically through all four

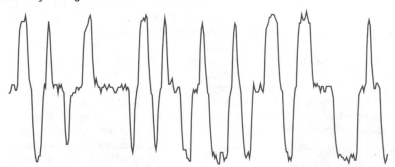

Figure 4-59. *Actual 100BASE-TX signal captured with a digital storage oscilloscope*

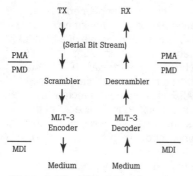

Figure 4-60. *Signal flow through the 100BASE-TX Physical Layer*

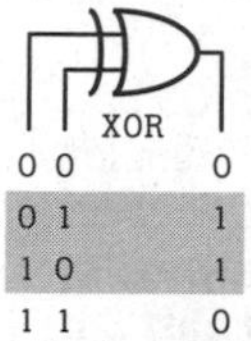

Clearly, the PMD sublayer has a lot more to do for 100BASE-TX (see Figure 4-60) than it does for 100BASE-FX (refer to Figure 4-55). On receipt at the other end of the link, the process is reversed.

During the initial process of establishing synchronization with the link partner to establish a link, the receiver circuit expects to see only idle code groups. Synchronization is established by applying the descrambler key sequence against the incoming signal. The decoded binary receive data is mathematically Exclusive ORed (XOR), with the descrambler key at the receiver to produce the original transmitted symbols (see Figure 4-61). Because the receive data stream is known to contain idle code groups, the receiving station simply shifts the descrambler key until idle code groups are produced from the binary stream.

Figure 4-61. *XOR logic gate decoding table*

In the sequence shown in Figure 4-62, the top binary string is obtained by decoding the MLT-3 signal. Below that is the correct (properly aligned) descrambler sequence for that binary string. The two are XORed to produce the resulting symbol below them.

When the 5B code groups are descrambled, the original data nibbles are recovered via a symbol-to-data table lookup as shown in Figure 4-63.

The nibbles are then grouped back into octets and reordered. To complete the cycle from hexadecimal to MLT-3 waveform and back, the octets are converted to hexadecimal in 4 as a final operation. Due to the repetitive nature of the sample data, the only visible change in 4 is in the last (right-most) octet in the example, which represents the SFD.

J	K	Preamble												SFD	
00110	10000	11000	01000	10100	11101	01011	11100	01010	01110	11001	10010	10111	10100	01100	01010
11110	00001	10011	00011	11111	10110	00000	10111	00001	00101	10010	11001	11100	11111	00111	10001
11000	10001	01011	01011	01011	01011	01011	01011	01011	01011	01011	01011	01011	01011	01011	11011

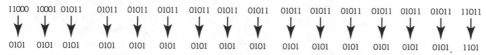

Figure 4-62. *XOR descrambling results. The top row of binary is the received data, the middle row is the properly aligned descrambler key, and the bottom row is the descrambled 5-bit code groups.*

Figure 4-63. *Data nibbles recovered by 5B/4B decoding*

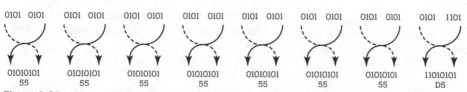

Figure 4-64. *Data nibbles reordered to restore data to the original MAC layer Preamble and SFD octets*

Architecture

The architecture rules governing older 10Mbps Ethernet as described before are more complex than the higher-speed implementations because of the cable systems. The higher-speed implementations are all point-to-point links. Fast Ethernet and Gigabit Ethernet permit progressively fewer repeaters in a half-duplex link than 10Mbps implementations.

Fast Ethernet links generally consist of a connection between the station and a hub. Hubs should be thought of as multiport repeaters, and count toward the limit on repeaters between distant stations.

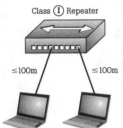

Repeaters must be labeled with the word *Class* followed by a Roman numeral I or II inside a circle, indicating Class 1 or Class 2. A Class I repeater may introduce up to 140 bit times of latency (delay). Assume that any repeater that changes between one Ethernet implementation and another (for example, 100BASE-TX and 100BASE-FX) is a Class I repeater. Also assume that any unlabeled repeater is a Class I repeater (see Figure 4-65).

Figure 4-65. *Maximum collision domain diameter for a Class 1 repeater. (The graphic depicts cable lengths for 100BASE-TX.)*

A Class II repeater may introduce a maximum of 92 bit times of latency. Because of the reduced latency, it is possible to have two Class II repeaters in series, but only if the cable between them is very short (see Figure 4-66).

As with 10Mbps versions it is possible to modify some of the architecture rules for 100Mbps versions. Unlike 10Mbps there is virtually no allowance for additional delay, and at 100 meters 100BASE-TX

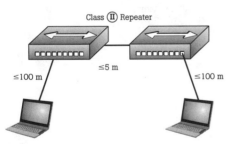

Figure 4-66. *Maximum collision domain diameter for a Class II repeater. (The graphic depicts cable lengths for 100BASE-TX.)*

is operating uncomfortably close to the edge of the hardware's capability to recover the transmit-

ted signal. If your network is implemented using recent hardware, it is possible that some of these limits can be exceeded. For example, if a longer cable is used between repeaters, shorter cables would have to be used to each station. Modification of the architecture rules is *strongly* discouraged for 100BASE-TX. Refer to the technical timing descriptions detailed in Clause 29 of the current 802.3 standard and the technical information about your hardware performance before attempting it.

Any device that adapts between different Ethernet speeds, such as between 10Mbps and 100Mbps, is operating as an OSI Layer 2 bridge. It is not possible to adapt between speeds and still be a repeater. However, the same device may repeat between ports linked at the same speed.

100BASE-FX is specified for multimode fiber. A 100BASE-TX twisted-pair cable is about the same as a 10BASE-T cable, except that link performance must meet the higher performance Category 5 or ISO Class D requirements. The 100BASE-TX cable between Class II repeaters may not exceed 5 meters.

Links operating in full duplex may be longer that what Table 4-6 shows because they are limited only by the capability of the medium to deliver a robust enough signal for proper decoding, and not the round-trip delay. Bending the 100m rule to take advantage of a longer link for full duplex is not recommended. It is not uncommon to find Fast Ethernet operating in half duplex. However, half duplex is undesirable because the signaling scheme is inherently full duplex, and forcing half-duplex communications rules onto a synchronous (full-duplex) signaling system is not a wise use of resources.

It is recommended that all links between a station and a hub or switch be configured for Auto-Negotiation to permit the highest common performance configuration to be established without risking misconfiguration of the link. Disable Auto-Negotiation and force connection configurations only if Auto-Negotiation fails, or on certain selected connections. The average station connection should be established by Auto-Negotiation.

Table 4-6. *Sample architecture configuration cable distances for half duplex operation*

Architecture	TX	FX	FX and TX
Station to Station	100m	412m	N/A
One Class I repeater	200m	272m	100m TX 160.8m FX
One Class II repeater	200m	320m	100m TX 208m FX
Two Class II repeaters	205m	228m	105m TX 211.2m FX

Table 4-7. *Parameters for 1 Gigabit Ethernet operation*

Parameter	Value
Maximum Station Count	1024 *
slotTime	4096 bit times
Interframe Spacing	96 bits **
Collision Attempt Limit	16
Collision Backoff Limit	10
Collision Jam Size	32 bits
Maximum Untagged Frame Size	1518 octets
Minimum Frame Size	512 bits (64 octets)
Burst Limit	65,536 bits

* Repeaters do not count toward the maximum of 1024 stations on an Ethernet collision domain.

** The value listed is the official interframe spacing. Shrinkage of the interframe spacing is expected and is caused by variable network delays, added preamble bits, and clock tolerances, but must never be less than 64 bit times as measured at the GMII receive signals at the DTE.

1000Mbps Versions of Ethernet

There was an attempt to produce a 1000BASE-TX version of Gigabit over Category 6 copper cable that the IEEE declined to adopt. The proposal was then taken to the TIA, which published details in ANSI/TIA/EIA-854-2001. This proposal used PAM5 encoding to transmit 500Mbps across each wire pair, two pairs in each direction, and always in full duplex. This proposal would have required users to replace the entire cable plant.

The official IEEE-approved 1000BASE-T was designed to operate on slightly better than Category 5 cable (Category 5e is even better than required by 1000BASE-T, which only required cable meeting TSB-95 requirements).

1Gbps Ethernet has several key parameters that govern its normal operation (see Table 4-7). These parameters manage access to the medium and specify allowed transmission characteristics.

1Gbps Transmission Process

The same sample frame from the 10Mbps example will be taken through the encoding and transmission process for 1Gbps (or 1000Mbps) Ethernet. 1000Mbps Ethernet also has different paths for the process, depending on which implementation is used. The first divergence in the path happens almost as soon as the data leaves the MAC Layer.

The first few fields of the sample frame shown in Figure 4-67 are represented in hexadecimal in Figure 4-68.

Preamble 8	Destination 6	Source 6	Type 2	Data ┊ Pad 46 to 1500	FCS 4

Figure 4-67. *Sample Ethernet frame as observed at the MAC Layer*

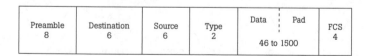

Preamble	SFD	Destination	Source	Length/Type	...
55 55 55 55 55 55 55	D5	00 C0 17 A0 02 35	00 80 20 56 33 D4	08 00	...

Figure 4-68. *Partial hexadecimal representation of the sample Ethernet frame*

The initial two fields of the sample frame are converted from hexadecimal to binary to permit illustration of the Physical Layer manipulations (see Figure 4-69).

Each octet is transferred least significant bit (LSB) first from the MAC Layer to the Physical Layer, so the bits are reordered on a per-octet basis. The FCS field is not reordered. Conceptually, this is easiest to grasp as simply turning each octet over as shown in Figure 4-70 and Figure 4-71.

Following the LSB reordering of the bytes by the MAC Layer, the Reconciliation sublayer and Gigabit Media Independent Interface (GMII) of the Physical Layer have an 8-bit wide data path so each octet is accepted without further manipulation. (See 802.3, Clause 35.)

The Reconciliation Sublayer sources the 125MHz clock that controls the flow of data through the Physical Layer sublayers. 125MHz represents 1/8 of the 1000Mbps data rate, suitable for handling an entire octet at once. The

Reconciliation sublayer also indicates when Idle or Carrier Extend should be transmitted, and ensures that the data is sufficiently corrupted to ensure an FCS error at the MAC Layer if there are transmit or receive problems.

For Gigabit implementations of 1000BASE-SX or LX, and 1000BASE-T, the path diverges here, unlike in Fast Ethernet where the path did not diverge until the Physical Medium Dependent (PMD) sublayer.

1000BASE-SX and 1000BASE-LX

(See 802.3, Clause 38.)
The Physical Coding Sublayer (PCS) accepts data from the GMII and applies 8B/10B encoding to convert the octets received into 10-bit code groups for transmission, and the reverse on reception (see Figure 4-72). The PCS is also responsible for code group synchronization at the receiver. The process was adapted from the Fiber Channel specification defined in ANSI X3.230-1994.

Figure 4-69. *Binary representation of the first two fields in the sample Ethernet frame*

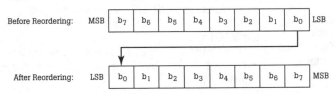

Figure 4-70. *LSB reordering of an octet*

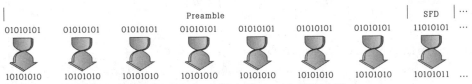

Figure 4-71. *LSB reordering of the first two fields in the sample Ethernet frame*

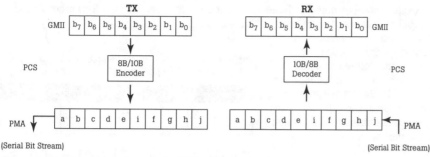

Figure 4-72. *Signal flow through the PCS*

To ensure that a DC bias does not develop in the circuit board traces and to help with clock recovery, the 8B/10B encoding selection is controlled by a running disparity calculation that directs the selection of the 10-bit code group from the positive or negative column of a table. In general, the quantity of 1s is greater than (positive) or less than (negative) the quantity of 0s. That value, or *running disparity*, determines the column from which the next code group is selected. Any given octet value has two possible 10-bit code groups associated to it (one each from the positive and negative columns). Determination of which code group to send (positive or negative) is made by evaluating the current running disparity value and following set rules to either maintain the current running disparity for the next code group to transmit or to change the running disparity for the next code to transmit. Essentially, the following rules apply:

- If the 10 bit code being sent has more zeroes than ones, the next code to transmit is negative.

- If the 10 bit code has more ones than zeroes, the next code is positive.

- If the number of ones and zeroes are equal, depending on the specific 10-bit pattern, the running disparity after the code is either the same as before or it changes.

In addition to DC balance, running disparity also allows for the detection of coding errors—which most often result from bit errors at the receiver—without having to rely on higher-layer error detection mechanisms such as the MAC Layer FCS field.

The code groups themselves are selected from the possible 10B code space of 1024 codes. The rules used to select these code groups includes a transition density between 3 and 8; no code group may include a pattern called a comma (except for special uses) or join with an adjacent code group to form a comma. A *comma* is a long run of 1s or 0s. These limits resulted in somewhat less than the required 512 valid code groups (256 each for the negative and positive columns, which represent valid 8B codes), so a few valid groups are used in both the positive and negative columns. The remaining code groups are mostly considered invalid, although 12 are used as special code groups for control purposes. Receipt of an invalid code, or a valid code from the wrong running disparity, indicates a received bit error.

Furthermore, the bits in the code group are not sequentially ordered (see Figure 4-73) and the actual calculation to determine the running disparity is performed in subgroups. The first six bits (*abcdei*) form the first subgroup and the last four bits (*fghj*) form the second subgroup of each 10-bit code being evaluated for running disparity.

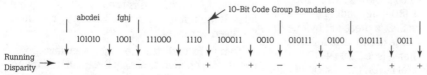

Figure 4-73. *Example running disparity calculation*

Except for the specific instances noted in Table 4–8, the running disparity of any subgroup with an equal number of 1s and 0s is neutral and assumes the running disparity of the previous subgroup. The example that follows shows how the previous running disparity is carried forward when equal numbers of 1s and 0s are present. The running disparity value at the right boundary of a 10-bit code group determines which column is used to look up the next code group. For detailed examples, see Annex 36B.

Table 4–8. *Running disparity calculation results*

Positive	Negative	Neutral
More 1s than 0s	More 0s than 1s	Same number of 1s and 0s (use previous running disparity value)
If equal to 000111	If equal to 111000	
If equal to 0011	If equal to 1100	

Code groups are handled by the PCS in pairs, and each code group is said to be either odd or even (see Table 4–9). This distinction is necessary for handling the special control codes, such as the Start of Packet Delimiter, which must always be an even code group, and because many of them are 2-byte or 4-byte ordered sets that have to stay together.

Table 4–9. *PCS designation of even and odd code groups*

Even	Odd
Code Group 1	Code Group 2
Code Group 3	Code Group 4
Code Group 5	...

Before the code groups are passed to the next layer sequentially from left to right, the first code group of the Preamble is exchanged for the Start of Packet Delimiter (SPD). See Figure 4–74. The SPD is always an even code group, the first in a pair. The SPD is shown as /S/ and consists of code group K27.7, which is either 110110 1000 (RD+) or 001001 0111 (RD–) depending on the running disparity. The SPD is preceded by Idle /I/ or Carrier Extend /R/ code groups and followed by the Data /D/ in a frame (see Table 4–10). At this level in the Physical Layer, the first bit of data

is Preamble. On reception, the SPD is converted back into a preamble octet.

Table 4–10. *Start of Packet Delimiter as it appears following an idle /I/ period or carrier extension /R*

Even	Odd		Even	Odd
I	I		R	R
S	D		S	D

Immediately following the last code group corresponding to the FCS field, an End of Packet Delimiter (EPD) is inserted into the interframe spacing. The EPD is shown as /T/ and consists of code group K29.7, which is either 101110 1000 (RD+) or 010001 0111 (RD–). The /T/ code group is always paired with either one or two Carrier Extend /R/ code groups, depending on whether the EPD began on an even or odd code group. If the /T/ code group was even, there is only one /R/ code group. If the /T/ code group was odd, there are two /R/ code groups as part of the EPD. The Carrier Extend is shown as /R/ and consists of code group K29.7, which is either 101110 1000 (RD+) or 010001 0111 (RD–) depending on the running disparity. In Table 4–11, the /D/ code represents code groups from the frame being transmitted, the last octets of the FCS field in this example.

Table 4–11. *End of Packet Delimiter*

Even	Odd		Even	Odd
D	T		D	D
R	R		T	R

Idle code groups begin immediately following the EPD code groups unless there is an additional frame to be sent in a burst. Idle is sent at all times when there is no data to be transmitted. The running disparity of Idle is intended to be neutral, so there are two defined Idle code groups: I_1 and I_2. A single I_1 is used if the running disparity is not negative at the end of the transmission event. I_2 is disparity neutral and is used for all subsequent Idles. If the running disparity is already negative, I_2 is used without I_1.

Carrier Extend stretches out a transmission event long enough to satisfy the minimum frame size requirement in half-duplex mode. Carrier Extend code groups are also used in place of idle code groups for the interframe space in a frame burst. Both usages are separate from the /R/ code groups used as part of the End of Packet Delimiter shown in Figure 4-74.

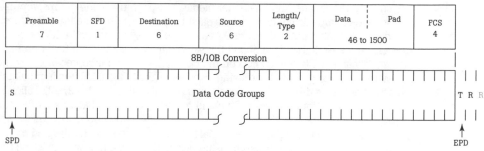

Figure 4-74. *Placement of SPD and EPD in a typical frame*

In some instances, control code groups are used in ordered sets with data code groups for special purposes such as configuration. Ordered sets consist of one, two, or four code groups. An ordered set always begins with one of the control code groups. The second code group in an ordered set is a data code group that uniquely identifies the ordered set.

The code groups are passed to the Physical Medium Attachment (PMA) sublayer, where they are serialized before sending them on to the Physical Medium Dependent (PMD) sublayer. Similarly, the PMA deserializes the code groups on reception.

To convey proper code groups to the PCS sublayer, the PMA must establish proper alignment to the incoming bit stream. Idle code groups are used as the basis for alignment. The idle code groups contain a sequence of either five 1s or five 0s (0011111 or 1100000). The idle code group is the only code group with the sequence of five 1s or 0s pattern. The pattern is known as a *comma*.

Following the 8B/10B encoding, there is now 1.25Gbps to be transmitted instead of the original 1Gbps. The original eight bits at the MAC Layer require 8 nanoseconds (ns) to transmit (1ns per bit); dividing 8.0ns by 10 bits results in 0.8ns per bit. By decreasing the time permitted for each bit at the Physical Layer, the MAC Layer timing of 1ns per bit is not affected. Consequentially, the PMA sublayer uses a 1.25GHz clock for serializing and moving the data.

The Physical Medium Dependent (PMD) sublayer now prepares the serialized bit stream for transmission using NRZI encoding rules. 1000BASE-CX is not described separately here

(see 802.3, Clause 39), but would be mapped to the appropriate copper medium at this point.

Non-Return to Zero (NRZ) encoding relies on the signal level found in the timing window to determine the binary value for that bit period. Unlike most of the other encoding schemes described, this encoding system is level driven instead of edge driven.

The encoding example in Figure 4-75 shows one timing window highlighted vertically through all four waveform examples. The top waveform is low across the timing window. A low signal level represents a binary 0. A single 1 was introduced at the end of the waveform to show the other signal level.

The second waveform is high across the timing window. A high signal level represents a binary 1. Again, a single 0 was introduced at the end of the waveform to show the other signal level.

In the third waveform, there is an alternating binary sequence instead of a repeating sequence of the same binary value. In this example, it is more obvious that a low signal level indicates a binary 0 and a high signal indicates a binary 1.

The fourth waveform example is random data. Three of these examples are good examples of why this encoding scheme has the potential for

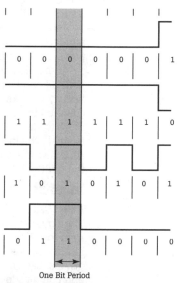

Figure 4-75. *NRZ encoding example—provided for comparison only*

causing DC voltage drift on copper media. The second example is changing levels each bit period, and would not suffer from DC voltage drift. It is very easy to have a string of the same binary signal cause a DC voltage bias on the cable, which has the potential of causing clocking errors. On fiber media this is not an issue, but may still affect the electronics used to drive and receive signals on fiber.

The NRZI (not NRZ) encoded serialized bit stream is ready for transmission using pulsed light as specified for 1000BASE-SX or 1000BASE-LX (see 802.3, Clause 38). Due to cycle time problems related to turning the transmitter completely on and off each time, the light is pulsed using low and high power. A logic 0 is represented by low power and a logic 1 by high power.

At the Medium Dependent Interface (MDI), both SX and LX specify the SC fiber optic connector, although most switch manufacturers have changed to small form factor fiber optic connectors such as SFP. The connector interface change is due to the increased port density that is possible because the SFP pluggable module is half the width of the SC pluggable module.

1000BASE-T

(See 802.3, Clause 40.)
The Physical Coding Sublayer (PCS) accepts octets from the Gigabit Medium Independent Interface (GMII) and converts them into 8B1Q4 code groups. Each code group is referred to as a vector and contains four symbols to be transmitted on four separate wire pairs.

Before the code groups are passed to the Physical Media Access (PMA) sublayer, the first two code groups, representing the first two octets of the Preamble, are exchanged for two Start of Stream Delimiter (SSD) vectors. The two SSD vectors are SSD1 and SSD2. SSD1 appears first and is represented by the vector (+2, +2, +2, +2). SSD2 follows immediately and is represented by (+2, +2, +2, −2). Following the end of the frame, immediately after the part that corresponds to the FCS field, the PCS appends two convolutional resets and the End of Stream Delimiter (ESD) as the first vectors in the interframe spacing. The presence or absence of an error dictates which of the four ESD vectors should be used. The convolutional resets are used to transition the vector code groups representing the data frame from the larger set of five possible vector voltage levels down to the limited set of three possible vector voltage levels used during idle periods.

The actual selection of which code group should be used to represent the next vector is implemented through a complex formula called a *convolutional encoder*. There was no easy way to represent or describe the convolutional encoder, except as a graphic (see Figure 4–76).

The Physical Medium Attachment (PMA) sublayer receives vectors from the PCS sublayer. Using four synchronous transmitters, the PMA continuously transmits the four-element vectors according to Four Dimensional, Five-level Pulse Amplitude Modulation (4D-PAM5) encoding rules. At the same time, and on the same four pairs of twisted-pair cabling, the link partner is also continuously transmitting. Comparing this to 10BASE2, there is a constant collision on each wire pair at all times.

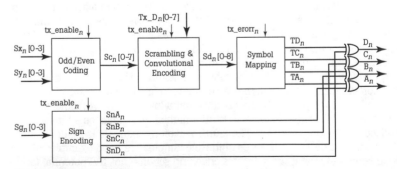

Figure 4-76. *Convolutional encoder*

Despite the constant collision of the signals, the system is able to operate through the following:

- A careful selection of voltage levels permitted for each vector (Forward Error Correction [FEC] coded symbol mapping)

- The ability to correct minor receive errors

- Hybrid isolation networks (either resistive or magnetic)

- Intersymbol interference (ISI) reduction applied to the transmitted signal via a digital partial-response filter

- Use of echo and near-end crosstalk (NEXT) cancellation applied to the received signal

The MAC Layer presents an octet of data at a rate of 1Gbps or 1ns per bit. After passing through the PCS, it is converted into a vector of four-dimensional symbols. Thus, each wire pair in the cable carries the equivalent of 250Mbps of data. Four pairs operating synchronously in parallel still add up to the original 1Gbps. Furthermore, the symbols are mapped in such a way that each signal transition on an individual wire pair represents

two bits of data. Thus, the signal is now down to the equivalent of 125Mbps of information per pair. That is the same signaling rate as Fast Ethernet, per wire pair, and each vector is 8ns in duration.

The quartet of quinary symbols are selected from the set of (+2, +1, 0, −1, −2) for data transmissions (see Figure 4-77), and from the limited subset of (+2, 0, −2) to improve synchronization for idle periods. However, to meet the requirements defined in Clause 40.6.1.1.2 of the standard, the actual voltage levels at this stage would be approximately (+1V, +0.5V, 0V, −0.5V, −1V).

To help the receiver recover the signal from the constant collision on each wire pair, the transmitter applies a partial response filter to the signal before it is transmitted (see Figure 4-78). This is accomplished by sending three quarters of the current quinary symbol voltage level combined with one quarter of the previous quinary symbol voltage level ($0.75z + 0.25z(-1)$). In effect, this introduces a controlled, known amount of intersymbol interference, which also helps to reduce the frequency content (bandwidth) of the transmitted signal (see Figure 4-79).

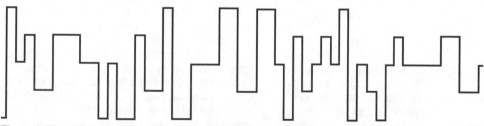

Figure 4-77. *Simulated outbound quinary symbol stream for one wire pair*

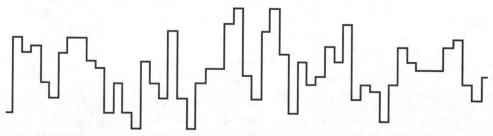

Figure 4-78. *The same simulated outbound quinary symbol stream for one wire pair as in Figure 4-77, as it would appear following application of the partial response filter*

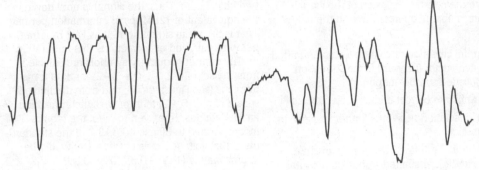

Figure 4-79. *Actual 1000BASE-T signal captured from one wire pair with a digital storage oscilloscope after several meters of cable. The signal shown occurs between +1 and −1 volts.*

It is almost surprising that the signal can be recovered at all when there are nine voltage levels on the cable during idle periods and 17 voltage levels on the cable during data transmission periods. These "extra" voltage levels result from the partial response filter.

At the receiver, the signal being transmitted must first be subtracted (cancelled) out of the inbound signal to allow only the inbound signal to be passed to the decoder and descrambler. The standard suggests that to work properly, the receiver needs to implement signal equalization, echo and crosstalk cancellation, and sequence estimation. Sequence estimation is implemented through a Viterbi error correction algorithm.

Before data communications can begin, the two link partners must determine which will source the Master PHY clock, and which will use the data stream to recover the Slave PHY clock. This is usually determined during Auto-Negotiation, although it can be manually configured. A number of other parameters are also determined in the same manner, including duplex.

Auto-Negotiation usually determines that a multiport device (a switch or hub) should become the Master PHY. There is a large table in 802.3 Clause 40.5.2 that lists the possible combinations and methods for determining which should be Master PHY if the two link partners are "equal."

After Auto-Negotiation concludes, the two link partners transmit idles until synchronization is established. As with Fast Ethernet, side-stream scrambling is implemented, so the scramblers must be synchronized. Unlike Fast Ethernet, there are several scramblers used throughout

the encoding process. Synchronization must be separately accomplished for each of the four wire pairs—a task that is made more difficult because each link partner has an auto-crossover detection function and because the twisted-pair cable specified may have up to 50ns of delay skew across the four pairs (remember that each symbol is only 8ns in duration).

Because it is not practical—and nearly impossible—to hand-decode 1000BASE-T without some pair-to-pair alignment assistance from the front-end hardware in the Gigabit Ethernet chipset, the complete final steps are not diagrammed. This is an exceptionally complex encoding scheme and the complete details are not suited for casual inquiry. The University of New Hampshire's Interoperability Lab (IOL) often posts detailed protocol descriptions, and a very good description of this scheme was posted for some time. Check the IOL site for information about various emerging technologies (www.iol.unh.edu).

Architecture

Gigabit Ethernet permits a single repeater between two stations, as shown in Figure 4-80. This configuration is appropriate for half duplex architectures, but Gigabit is rarely if ever operated in half duplex (while possible, no Gigabit Ethernet repeater is known to have been sold).

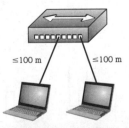

≤100 m   ≤100 m

Figure 4-80. *Maximum collision domain diameter for a Gigabit Ethernet. The graphic depicts cable lengths for 1000BASE-T.*

1000BASE-SX is specified for multimode fiber. Table 4-12 lists the maximum allowed cable lengths for 1000BASE-SX. Note that the modal bandwidth parameter is a key limiting factor in length. Modal bandwidth information is typically available from the cable vendor, and cannot be field tested with the current generation of field test technology.

Table 4-12. *Maximum 1000BASE-SX cable distances at 850nm (minimum overfilled launch)*

Medium	Modal Bandwidth	Maximum Distance
62.5μm MMF	160	220m
62.5μm MMF	200	275m
50μm MMF	400	500m
50μm MMF	500	550m

1000BASE-LX is specified for multimode and singlemode fiber.

1000BASE-LX is specified for both multimode and singlemode fiber. Table 4-13 lists the maximum allowed cable lengths for 1000BASE-LX.

Table 4-13. *Maximum 1000BASE-LX cable distances at 1300nm (minimum overfilled launch)*

Medium	Modal Bandwidth	Maximum Distance
62.5μm MMF	500	550m
50μm MMF	400	550m
50μm MMF	500	550m
10μm SMF	N/A	5000m

A 1000BASE-T twisted-pair cable is about the same as a 10BASE-T and 100BASE-TX cable, except that link performance must meet TIA/EIA TSB-95 test requirements—although use of the higher-quality Category 5e or ISO Class D (2000) or better cable is typical.

As with 10Mbps and 100Mbps versions, it is possible to modify some of the architecture rules slightly; however, there is virtually no allowance for additional delay in half duplex. Modification of the architecture rules is strongly discouraged for 1000BASE-T. Any cabling problems or environmental noise could render an otherwise compliant cable inoperable, even at distances that are within

the specification. For compatibility and performance reasons, links longer than 100 meters are discouraged. Refer to the technical timing descriptions detailed in Clause 42 of the current 802.3 standard, and the technical information about your hardware performance, before attempting any adjustments to the architecture rules.

Any device that adapts between different Ethernet speeds, such as between 100Mbps and 1000Mbps, is acting as an OSI Layer 2 bridge. It is not possible to adapt between speeds and still be a repeater.

Links operating in full-duplex links may be longer than what is shown in Table 4-14 because they are limited only by the capability of the medium and transceivers to deliver a robust enough signal to decode the signaling, and are not limited by the round-trip delay. It is extremely rare to find Gigabit Ethernet operating in half duplex. Half duplex is undesirable because the signaling scheme is inherently full duplex, and forcing half-duplex communications rules onto a synchronous (full duplex) signaling system is not a wise use of resources. Operating under half-duplex rules requires adherence to slotTime round-trip delay limitations that reduce the effective cable lengths, and there is a substantial increase in overhead introduced by the carrier extension. Furthermore, because Gigabit repeaters effectively don't exist (nobody sells them), the link is probably between a station and an OSI Layer 2 bridge (a switch) or between two bridges, so the collision domain would end at the bridge anyway.

It is recommended that all links between a station and a hub or switch be configured for Auto-Negotiation to permit the highest common performance configuration to be established without risking misconfiguration of the link, and to avoid accidental misconfiguration of the other required parameters for proper Gigabit Ethernet operation. Unlike 10/100 implementations of Ethernet, 1000BASE-T uses Auto-Negotiation to configure essential parameters for operation, such as which link partner is the clock-master and which is slaved to that clock, and for reporting whether the device is a multiport device or single-port device (used to resolve situations where both link partners want to source the clock). The other normal parameters are also negotiated, such as advertising 10/100/1000 speeds, duplex, and flow control settings.

Table 4-14. *Sample architecture configuration cable distances for half duplex operation*

Architecture	1000BASE-T	1000BASE-SX/LX	1000BASE-SX/LX and T
Station to Station	100m	316m	N/A
One Repeater	200m	220m	100m T (and) 110m SX/LX

10Gbps Versions of Ethernet

Because deployment of 10GBASE-CX4 (15m over 8 pair infiniband cable) is largely limited to the data center due to the short cable lengths permitted, it is not separately described here.

10Gbps Ethernet has several key parameters that govern its normal operation (see Table 4-15). These parameters manage access to the medium and specify allowed transmission characteristics. Note that many of the parameters necessary for operation at lower speeds do not apply to 10Gbps Ethernet simply because half duplex operation is not permitted.

Table 4-15. *Parameters for 10 Gbps Ethernet operation*

Parameter	Value
Maximum Station Count	Not applicable *
slotTime	Not applicable *
Interframe Spacing	96 bits **
Transmission Attempt Limit	Not applicable *
Collision Backoff Limit	Not applicable *
Collision Jam Size	Not applicable *
Maximum Untagged Frame Size	1518 octets
Minimum Frame Size	512 bits (64 octets)
Burst Limit	Not applicable *
Interframe Spacing Stretch Ratio	104 bits ***

* 10 Gbps Ethernet does not permit half-duplex operation, so parameters related to slot timing and collision handling do not apply.

** The value listed is the official interframe spacing. Shrinkage of the interframe spacing is expected and is caused by variable network delays and clock tolerances, but must never be less than 40 bit times as measured at the XGMII receive signals at the DTE.

*** The Interframe Spacing Stretch Ratio applies exclusively to 10GBASE-W definitions.

10Gbps Transmission Process

The same sample frame from the 10Mbps example will be taken through the encoding and transmission process for 10Gbps Ethernet. 10Gbps Ethernet also has different paths for the process, depending on which implementation is used.

The first few fields of the sample frame shown in Figure 4-81 are represented in hexadecimal in Figure 4-82.

The first few fields of the sample frame shown in Figure 4-82 are represented in hexadecimal in Figure 4-83.

The initial two fields of the sample frame are converted from hexadecimal to binary to permit illustration of the Physical Layer manipulations.

Each octet is transferred least significant bit (LSB) first from the MAC Layer to the Physical Layer, so the bits are reordered on a per-octet basis. The FCS field is not reordered. Conceptually, this is easiest to grasp as simply turning each octet over as shown in Figure 4-84 and Figure 4-85.

Following the LSB reordering of the octets by the MAC Layer, the Reconciliation sublayer of the Physical Layer assembles data from the MAC Layer into groups of four octets to fit the 32-bit wide transmit and receive data paths through the 10 Gigabit Media Independent Interface (XGMII). These four octet groups are then passed across the XGMII interface in four 1-bit wide lanes (Lane 0–3) as a single 32-bit transfer. In the absence of MAC Layer data, the Reconciliation sublayer supplies Idles to ensure a constant flow of signaling. (See 802.3, Clause 46.)

The first octet of the preamble is always aligned with lane 0 and is substituted for a Start control code by the Reconciliation sublayer. All following octets are sequentially placed into lanes as they arrive, as shown in Figure 4-86. If lane 3 of the next row of data does not contain the SFD (the binary 10101011 pattern), the frame may be discarded.

Preamble 8	Destination 6	Source 6	Type 2	Data ⋮ Pad 46 to 1500	FCS 4

Figure 4-81. *Sample Ethernet frame as observed at the MAC Layer*

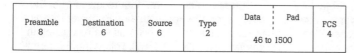

Preamble		SFD	Destination		Source	Length/Type	...
55 55 55 55 55 55 55		D5	00 C0 17 A0 02 35		00 80 20 56 33 D4	08 00	...

Figure 4-82. *Partial hexadecimal representation of the sample Ethernet frame*

Preamble	SFD	...
01010101 01010101 01010101 01010101 01010101 01010101 01010101	11010101	...

Figure 4-83. *Binary representation of the first two fields in the sample Ethernet frame*

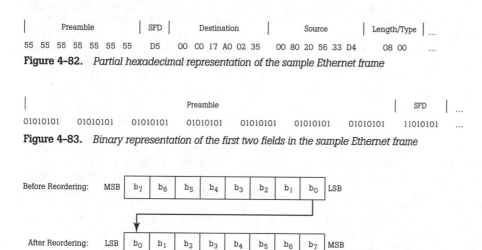

Before Reordering: MSB b_7 b_6 b_5 b_4 b_3 b_2 b_1 b_0 LSB

After Reordering: LSB b_0 b_1 b_2 b_3 b_4 b_5 b_6 b_7 MSB

Figure 4-84. *LSB reordering of an octet*

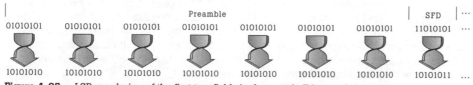

Preamble		SFD	...
01010101 01010101 01010101 01010101 01010101 01010101 01010101		11010101	...
10101010 10101010 10101010 10101010 10101010 10101010 10101010		10101011	...

Figure 4-85. *LSB reordering of the first two fields in the sample Ethernet frame*

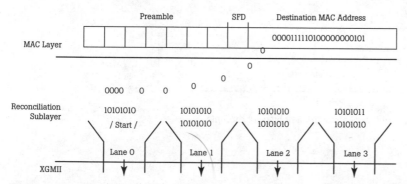

Figure 4-86. *Reconciliation sublayer grouping of octets into lanes 0–3 for the XGMII interface*

To always align the Start control character on lane 0, the Reconciliation sublayer is allowed either to (option 1) add idle control characters as necessary or (option 2) sometimes add and sometimes remove idle control characters. The first choice has the disadvantage of lowering the effective data rate slightly because you are almost always increasing the interframe spacing. The second choice requires the Reconciliation sublayer to maintain a Deficit Idle Counter but avoids continually introducing extra idles.

The Deficit Idle Counter is incremented for each idle deleted, and decremented for each idle added. The counter is supposed to stay close to zero and is not permitted to exceed +3 or −3. Thus, if the Start control character were headed toward lane 2, it would have to shift two lanes in either direction to align on lane 0. The direction it would shift depends on the current value of the counter.

The Reconciliation Sublayer also ensures that if there are transmit or receive problems, the data must be sufficiently corrupted to guarantee an FCS error at the MAC Layer. This is accomplished by substituting error control characters in the data stream. If the Physical Layer detects a remote problem with link communications, the Reconciliation Sublayer truncates any current transmission and begins sending idle control characters until the fault condition is resolved. If the Physical Layer detects a local problem, the Reconciliation Sublayer truncates any current transmission and begins sending Remote Fault sequence ordered sets. The Reconciliation Sublayer reports the Link Fault state.

After sending all the data received from the MAC Layer, the Reconciliation Sublayer inserts a terminate control character as the next octet, in any lane (see Figure 4-87). Following the terminate control character are continuous idle control characters until the next start control character or unless an error is present. The terminate control character together with a control signal constitutes an end-of-frame delimiter.

As an option, the XGMII interface may be split to accommodate a 10 Gigabit Attachment Unit Interface (XAUI). Implementation of the optional XAUI interface requires the XGMII Extender Sublayer (XGXS) on either side of it. The XAUI interface is where hot-swappable, pluggable optic modules connect (XENPAC, XPAK, X2, and so on), which may be compared to the 1 Gigabit hot-swappable GBIC modules. The XPAC and X2 modules are low profile form factors. The XGMII interface requires 74 pins and can typically only drive the signal up to 7cm (3 inches), effectively only chip to chip. XAUI signaling only requires 16 pins and can drive the signal up to 56cm (22 inches) on PCB material FR-4 or better.

The XGXS sublayer uses 8B/10B encoding to convert the data octets from each lane separately into 10-bit codes. The encoded data is then sent serially at 3.125 Gbaud across the XAUI interface, still in four separate data streams. Bit zero of the 10-bit code is sent first. On reception at the second XGXS sublayer, the data is decoded back into 8-bit octets. See Figure 4-88, which shows the first two lanes.

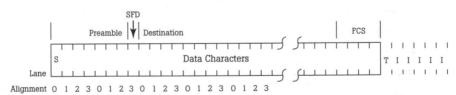

Figure 4-87. *Reconciliation sublayer lane alignment by octet example*

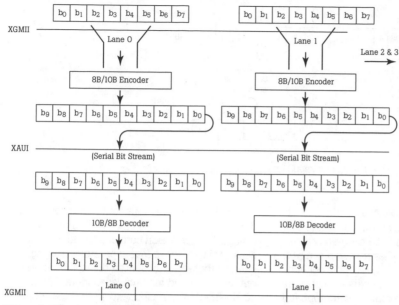

Figure 4-88. *Optional XGXS sublayers and XAUI interface*

The XAUI interface is implemented using four 100 ohm, balanced differential signal paths in each direction. This is not unlike Ethernet over twisted-pair cable, except that the extremely high-frequency 3.125 Gbaud signaling rate is specified only to a maximum of about 50cm and represents a single baud period of only 320 picoseconds each. Longer distances are not possible because of the problems inherent to higher frequencies as described in Chapter 2, "Copper Cabling." These distances are suitable for communicating between different subsystems on a single circuit board or between different subsystems across a backplane within a chassis. The maximum amplitude for the differential peak-to-peak signal shall not exceed 1600mV, and must stay within the maximum and minimum voltage limits.

For 10 Gigabit implementations, the path diverges here. The descriptions are separated into definitions for 10GBASE-X, 10GBASE-R, and 10GBASE-W in this document. The first divergence is 10GBASE-X, which does not follow the Physical Coding sublayer that both 10GBASE-R and 10GBASE-W implementations share.

10GBASE-LX4

(See 802.3, Clause 48.)

The 10GBASE-X specification, which defines 10GBASE-LX4 and 10GBASE-CX4, uses the same Reconciliation Sublayer as the other 10 Gigabit implementations but has its own Physical Coding Sublayer (PCS) and Physical Medium Attachment (PMA) sublayer. Actually, the PCS is almost the same as XAUI—using four wavelengths (LX4) instead of signal paths each way.

The PCS accepts four lanes of data from the XGMII and applies 8B/10B encoding to each lane separately (see Figure 4-89, which depicts one lane). A running disparity is maintained to ensure that a DC bias does not develop and to help with clock recovery and error detection.

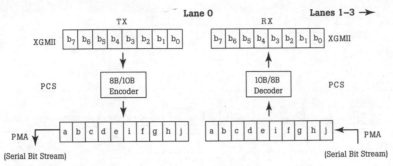

Figure 4-89. *10GBASE-LX4 (and 10GBASE-CX4) PCS lane encoding*

The PCS sublayer provides a continuous fill pattern using idles in the absence of data from the XGMII. Three different idle ordered sets may be used to substitute for idles received across the XGMII. The /A/ Align column, /R/ Skip column, and /K/ Sync column ordered sets are substituted for Reconciliation sublayer idles as appropriate, and are used primarily for synchronization and deskewing. The PCS sublayer establishes and maintains lane synchronization, performs lane-to-lane deskew and alignment, and performs PHY clock rate compensation for the four parallel lanes to the Physical Medium Attachment (PMA) sublayer.

The Start /S/ and the Terminate /T/ ordered sets are exchanged for the start and terminate control characters from the XGMII. The PCS considers the interframe spacing to have begun on receipt of the Terminate ordered set. The Error /E/ code group is signaled per lane because code violations are detected on a per-lane basis. Other codes signal link and error status.

Synchronization is achieved separately on each lane but is signaled only when all four lanes become simultaneously synchronized. This is called *code group alignment*.

The PMA sublayer takes the resulting 40-bit vector from the PCS and serializes it, still maintaining four parallel and separate lanes. The four serial data streams are passed to the Physical Medium Dependent (PMD) sublayer. The receive path recovers its clock from the serial data stream and uses that clocking to assemble 40-bit vectors to pass back up to the PCS sublayer.

The PMD receives four continuous serialized data streams in parallel at a nominal rate of 3.125 Gbaud. The PMD then converts the four electrical signal streams to four separate optical signal streams that are wavelength division multiplexed onto the attached medium (see Figure 4-90). 10GBASE-CX4 is similar, except that the serial data stream is driven through a special connector onto copper cable.

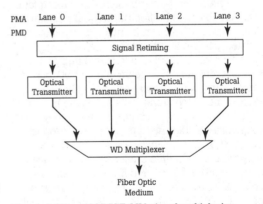

Figure 4-90. *10GBASE-LX4 signal multiplexing*

The NRZ-encoded serialized bit stream is ready for transmission using pulsed light. Due to cycle time problems related to turning the transmitter completely on and off each time, the light is pulsed using low and high power. A logic 0 is represented by low power and a logic 1 by high power.

On receipt from the medium, the optical signal stream is demultiplexed into four separate optical signal streams. The four optical signal streams are then converted back into four electronic bit streams as they travel in approximately the reverse process back up through the sublayers to the MAC Layer.

10GBASE-LX4 is specified for both multimode and singlemode fiber. Table 4–16 lists the maximum allowed cable lengths for 10GBASE-LX4.

Table 4–16. *10GBASE-LX4 transmission distances at 1300nm*

Medium	Maximum Distance
62.5μm MMF	300m
50μm MMF	240–300m *
10μm SMF	10km

* Maximum distance depends upon the modal bandwidth.

10GBASE-R and 10GBASE-W

The 10GBASE-R Physical Coding Sublayer (PCS) is common to both 10GBASE-R and 10GBASE-W implementations, although the standard describes it under the 10GBASE-R heading. (See 802.3, Clause 49.)

The PCS accepts data from the XGMII and applies 64B/66B encoding. Because the XGMII interface transfers 32 bits of data at a time, the PCS must assemble two transfers before encoding the data (see Figure 4–91). On gathering 64 bits of data, the PCS encodes it using 64B/66B encoding.

The actual 64B/66B encoding is not very spectacular for eight lanes of data. The PCS sublayer codes a block of 64 bits of data with a sync header of 01 in binary, and the data is undisturbed. If the block contains any control codes the sync header is 10 in binary. The original 64 bits plus the sync header becomes the 66-bit code block. For any 64-bit transfer not completely composed of data, the encoding becomes a bit more interesting.

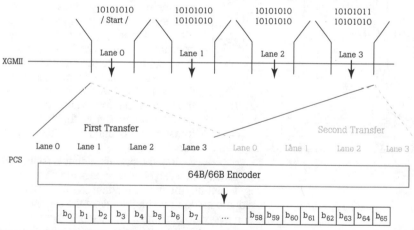

Figure 4–91. *The PCS sublayer assembles two XGMII 32-bit transfers before 64B/66B encoding the data*

Control characters are only 7 bits each, and ordered sets are composed of a 4-bit /O/ code accompanied by three data characters. This leaves room for an 8-bit Block Type field, which immediately follows the sync header and precedes the rest of the payload for that block. Examine the permissible combinations of codes and data in Table 4-17. Notice how the various groupings of data and control characters form a 66-bit block. You may notice that many of the possible block codings have a few unused bit positions left over (which are set to zero).

Table 4-17. *64B/66B block coding options*

Input Data — Data Block	Bit Position 0 1 2	2	10	18	26	34	42	50	58	65
$D_0 D_1 D_2 D_3 / D_4 D_5 D_6 D_7$	0 1	D_0	D_1	D_2	D_3	D_4	D_5	D_6	D_7	
Control Block — Sync Header / Block Type Field	↕									
$D_0 D_1 D_2 D_3 / D_4 D_5 D_6 T_7$	1 0	0xFF	D_1	D_2	D_3	D_4	D_5	D_6	D_7	
$D_0 D_1 D_2 D_3 / D_4 D_5 T_6 C_7$	1 0	0xE1	D_1	D_2	D_3	D_4	D_5	D_6	C_7	
$D_0 D_1 D_2 D_3 / D_4 T_5 C_6 C_7$	1 0	0xD2	D_1	D_2	D_3	D_4	D_5	C_6	C_7	
$D_0 D_1 D_2 D_3 / T_4 C_5 C_6 C_7$	1 0	0xCC	D_1	D_2	D_3	D_4		C_5	C_6	C_7
$D_0 D_1 D_2 T_3 / C_4 C_5 C_6 C_7$	1 0	0xB4	D_1	D_2	D_3		C_4	C_5	C_6	C_7
$D_0 D_1 T_2 C_3 / C_4 C_5 C_6 C_7$	1 0	0xAA	D_1	D_2		C_3	C_4	C_5	C_6	C_7
$D_0 T_1 C_2 C_3 / C_4 C_5 C_6 C_7$	1 0	0x99	D_1		C_2	C_3	C_4	C_5	C_6	C_7
$T_0 C_1 C_2 C_3 / C_4 C_5 C_6 C_7$	1 0	0x87		C_1	C_2	C_3	C_4	C_5	C_6	C_7
$S_0 D_1 D_2 D_3 / D_4 D_5 D_6 D_7$	1 0	0x78	D_1	D_2	D_3	D_4	D_5	D_6	D_7	
$C_0 C_1 C_2 C_3 / S_4 D_5 D_6 D_7$	1 0	0x33	C_0	C_1	C_2	C_3		D_5	D_6	D_7
$O_0 D_1 D_2 D_3 / S_4 D_5 D_6 D_7$	1 0	0x66	D_1	D_2	D_3	O_0		D_5	D_6	D_7
$O_0 D_1 D_2 D_3 / O_4 D_5 D_6 D_7$	1 0	0x55	D_1	D_2	D_3	O_0	O_4	D_5	D_6	D_7
$O_0 D_1 D_2 D_3 / C_4 C_5 C_6 C_7$	1 0	0x4B	D_1	D_2	D_3	O_0	C_4	C_5	C_6	C_7
$C_0 C_1 C_2 C_3 / O_4 D_5 D_6 D_7$	1 0	0x2D	C_0	C_1	C_2	C_3	O_4	D_5	D_6	D_7
$C_0 C_1 C_2 C_3 / C_4 C_5 C_6 C_7$	1 0	0x1E	C_0	C_1	C_2	C_3	C_4	C_5	C_6	C_7

/S/ = Start control code

/T/ = Terminate control code

/O/ = Sequence Ordered Set (which is accompanied by three data characters)

/C/ = Control character

/D/ = Data character

Start /S/ control characters may appear in only lane 0 or lane 4. (Lane 4 would be lane 0 in the second transfer—both representing the beginning of a 32-bit word.) Terminate /T/ control characters may appear in any lane because the location of the end of the FCS field is determined by the amount of preceding data. There are always a minimum of four idle /I/ control characters following a terminate control character, even if a few are due to be deleted to maintain the proper clock rate compensation. To adapt between different clock rates as required for the WAN Interface Sublayer (WIS) or 10 Gigabit Sixteen-Bit Interface (XSBI), the PCS sublayer inserts or deletes idles in groups of four. Sequence-ordered sets may also be deleted to adapt on reception. Idles may not be inserted while data is present, but must wait for the interframe spacing.

Because MAC Layer data may contain long runs of the same binary value, the block is scrambled before it is transmitted (see Figure 4-92). Scrambling is performed to ensure that there are enough transitions for the receive clock to maintain synchronization. The sync header that always appears in the first two bit positions is not submitted to the scrambler, and is reattached to the block after the scrambler. The data, starting with the leftmost bit from what would have been lane 0 from the first XGMII transfer, is submitted to the scrambler serially.

Rapid block alignment is facilitated by having the sync header bypass the scrambler. By searching the incoming data stream for a transition between two bit periods at the same location every 66 bits (the sync header), alignment may be achieved very quickly. If a candidate block boundary does not include a transition between the first two bit periods, the block boundary is shifted and the next 66 bits are tested. During initial synchronization, the comparison and shift process continues until the sync header is located.

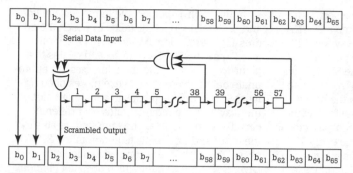

Figure 4-92. *PCS scrambler operation. The two-bit sync header bypasses the scrambler.*

The final operation that the PCS performs on the transmit data is to slice it into 16-bit vectors. Because 66 is not divided evenly by 16, alignment of the 16-bit vectors becomes skewed so that they do not have any direct relationship to the boundaries of the 66 bit blocks. This operation is performed by a process called the Gearbox, and is required whenever the WIS sublayer or XSBI interface is present (see Figure 4-93). If neither is present, the 16-bit wide data path created by the Gearbox is optional. On receipt of data, the Gearbox reassembles and realigns 66 bit blocks to the proper boundaries before passing the blocks farther up into the PCS sublayer.

10GBASE-W Only

(See 802.3, Clause 50, and ANSI T1.416-1999.) The WAN Interface Sublayer (WIS) is exclusively for 10GBASE-W support and communicates with the 10GBASE-R PCS sublayer through the WIS Service Interface. Use of WIS offers compatibility with SONET STS-192c as specified by the ANSI standards body (based on T1.416-1999), as well as the Synchronous Digital Hierarchy (SDH) VC-4-64c container specified by the ITU standards body. Implementation of WIS allows MAC Layer traffic to be transparently mapped into these two logical frame formats for existing WAN communications links. The WIS specification is not intended to be compliant with either SONET or SDH because it does not include all the fields and functions, but it seems that most manufacturers are implementing it that way. Multiplexed SONET/SDH formats are explicitly not supported.

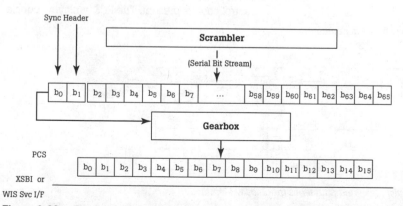

Figure 4-93. *The Gearbox creates 16-bit vectors for the XSBI interface to the PMA sublayer for 10GBASE-R, or for the WIS Service Interface to the WIS sublayer for 10GBASE-W*

The WIS sublayer receives 16-bit vectors from the PCS sublayer and maps them into a SONET-compatible WIS frame. Along the way the WIS sublayer uses the data to generate path as well as line and section overhead for the SONET Synchronous Payload Envelope (SPE). The last step for the WIS sublayer is to scramble the header and SPE data to create the WIS final form of the frame (see Figure 4-94). The WIS sublayer creates a complete SONET-compatible frame every 125 microseconds. The completed frame is passed in 16-bit data groups across the XSBI interface to the Physical Medium Attachment (PMA) sublayer.

In the SONET protocol the terms *section*, *line*, and *path* relate to the distance in which the addressing information is valid across the virtual link (see Figure 4-95). The term *section* relates to a point-to-point link, and the addresses are appropriate only between two active pieces of equipment. The term *line* relates to equipment along the way that can redirect traffic over different circuits as appropriate. The term *path* relates to the entry and exit points to and from the SONET cloud. The path is also somewhat similar to a Layer 3 IP address pair, which does not change as the request travels across an IP network.

In Figure 4-95, the Add/Drop Multiplexer places the data into the SONET cloud. The signal regenerator performs a task not unlike an Ethernet repeater, although it is more intelligent. The Digital Cross Connect is similar to an Ethernet switch in that it forwards traffic to the correct circuit and does not send it down any other circuit it is servicing.

10GBASE-T

(See 802.3, Clause 55.)
For 10GBASE-T, the Physical Coding Sublayer (PCS) accepts data from the XGMII and applies 64B/65B encoding (see Figure 4-96). Because the XGMII interface transfers 32 bits of data at a time, the PCS sublayer must assemble two transfers before encoding the data. On gathering 64 bits of data, the PCS sublayer encodes it using 64B/66B encoding.

The actual 64B/66B encoding is simply to identify whether all eight lanes held data or a control code is present. The PCS sublayer codes a

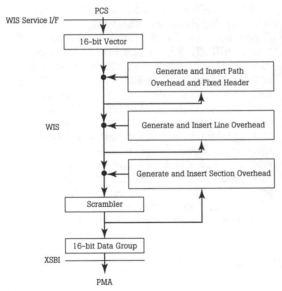

Figure 4-94. *WIS sublayer frame generation*

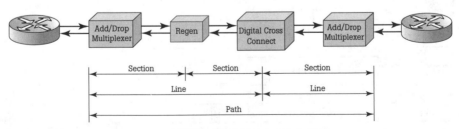

Figure 4-95. *SONET section, line, and path terms graphically identified*

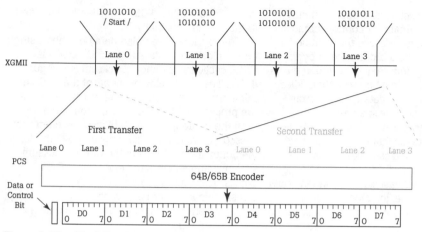

Figure 4-96. *The PCS sublayer assembles two XGMII 32-bit transfers before 64B/66B encoding the data*

block of 64 bits of data with a data/control header of 0 in binary, and the data is undisturbed. If the block contains any control codes, the data/control header is 1 in binary. The original 64 bits, plus the data/control header, becomes the 65-bit code block.

Control characters are only 7 bits each, and ordered sets are composed of a 4-bit /O/ code accompanied by three data characters. This leaves room for an 8-bit block type field, which immediately follows the data/control header and precedes the rest of the payload for that block. Examine the permissible combinations of codes and data in Table 4-18. Notice how the various groupings of data and control characters form a 65-bit block. Notice that many of the possible block codings have a few unused bit positions left over (which are set to zero).

Table 4-18. *64B/66B block coding options*

Input Data	Bit Position 0,1	|0	|8	|16	|24	|32	|40	|48	|56 |64
Data Block									
$D_0 D_1 D_2 D_3 / D_4 D_5 D_6 D_7$	0	D_0	D_1	D_2	D_3	D_4	D_5	D_6	D_7
Control Block									
$D_0 D_1 D_2 D_3 / D_4 D_5 D_6 T_7$	1	0×FF	D_0	D_1	D_2	D_3	D_4	D_5	D_6
$D_0 D_1 D_2 D_3 / D_4 D_5 T_6 C_7$	1	0×E1	D_0	D_1	D_2	D_3	D_4	D_5	C_7
$D_0 D_1 D_2 D_3 / D_4 T_5 C_6 C_7$	1	0×D2	D_0	D_1	D_2	D_3	D_4	C_6	C_7
$D_0 D_1 D_2 D_3 / T_4 C_5 C_6 C_7$	1	0×CC	D_0	D_1	D_2	D_3	C_5	C_6	C_7
$D_0 D_1 D_2 T_3 / C_4 C_5 C_6 C_7$	1	0×B4	D_0	D_1	D_2	C_4	C_5	C_6	C_7
$D_0 D_1 T_2 C_3 / C_4 C_5 C_6 C_7$	1	0×AA	D_0	D_1	C_3	C_4	C_5	C_6	C_7
$D_0 T_1 C_2 C_3 / C_4 C_5 C_6 C_7$	1	0×99	D_0	C_2	C_3	C_4	C_5	C_6	C_7
$T_0 C_1 C_2 C_3 / C_4 C_5 C_6 C_7$	1	0×87	C_1	C_2	C_3	C_4	C_5	C_6	C_7
$S_0 D_1 D_2 D_3 / D_4 D_5 D_6 D_7$	1	0×78	D_1	D_2	D_3	D_4	D_5	D_6	D_7
$O_0 D_1 D_2 D_3 / S_4 D_5 D_6 D_7$	1	0×66	D_1	D_2	D_3	O_0	D_5	D_6	D_7
$O_0 D_1 D_2 D_3 / O_4 D_5 D_6 D_7$	1	0×55	D_1	D_2	D_3	O_0 O_4	D_5	D_6	D_7
$O_0 D_1 D_2 D_3 / C_4 C_5 C_6 C_7$	1	0×4B	D_1	D_2	D_3	O_0 C_4	C_5	C_6	C_7
$C_0 C_1 C_2 C_3 / S_4 D_5 D_6 D_7$	1	0×33	C_0	C_1	C_2	C_3	D_5	D_6	D_7
$C_0 C_1 C_2 C_3 / O_4 D_5 D_6 D_7$	1	0×2D	C_0	C_1	C_2	C_3	O_4	D_5	D_6 D_7
$C_0 C_1 C_2 C_3 / C_4 C_5 C_6 C_7$	1	0×1E	C_0	C_1	C_2	C_3	C_4	C_5	C_6 C_7

(In the Control Block section, bit position 0 is the Data/Control Header and the first payload byte is the Block Type Field.)

/S/ = Start control code
/T/ = Terminate control code
/O/ = Sequence Ordered Set
/C/ = Control character
/D/ = Data character

Start /S/ control characters may appear in only lane 0 or lane 4. Terminate /T/ control characters may appear in any lane because the location of the end of the FCS field is determined by the amount of preceding data. Sequence-ordered sets may also be deleted to adapt on reception. Idles may not be inserted while data is present, but must wait for the interframe spacing.

If an error is detected, an /E/ error is substituted for the bad code so that the MAC Layer is notified of a problem and can take appropriate action.

Because MAC Layer data can contain long runs of the same binary value, the block is scrambled before it is transmitted (see Figure 4-97). Scrambling is performed to ensure that there are enough transitions for the receive clock to maintain synchronization. The data, starting with the data/control header bit and followed with the least significant bit from what would have been

lane 0 from the first XGMII transfer, is submitted to the scrambler serially.

The resulting scrambled data becomes a single 65-bit block. Fifty blocks are used to calculate CRC8 cyclic redundancy checksum (see Figure 4-98). The eight delay elements of the CRC8 are initialized to zero before the group of 50 blocks are processed. The CRC8 calculation continues until the entire group of 50 blocks has been processed, the remaining contents of the eight delay elements are used to form the CRC8 checksum, which is appended to the end of the 50 65B blocks. The contents of the delay elements are transmitted in the order suggested by the graphic, with element 7 transmitted first and element 0 transmitted last.

The group of 50 65B blocks is prepended with a leading auxiliary bit (reserved—not used at this time), and followed by the calculated CRC8 checksum. Altogether this forms a single PHY frame.

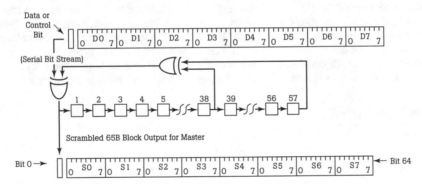

Figure 4-97. *PCS scrambler operation*

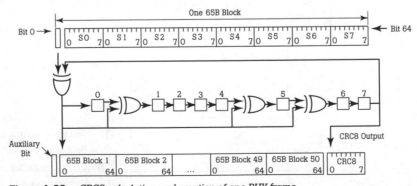

Figure 4-98. *CRC8 calculation and creation of one PHY frame*

The assembled PHY frame is passed through a low-density parity checksum (LDPC) calculation. The process for calculating the PHY frame is best represented by a graphic (see Figure 4–99). The first three bits are passed unencoded to the result frame. The next four bits are used in two ways: They are passed to the PHY frame and they are used as input bits to the LDPC encoder. This continues for a total of 430 pairs of 3-bit and 4-bit pairs. The next 7-bit grouping consists of the usual three unencoded bits. The next three bits are treated the same as the previous sets of four input bits. To finish the 7-bit grouping, the first LDPC parity bit is used. Following that, the three unencoded bits are accompanied by 4 bits of

LDPC parity bits for the remaining 81 sets of 7-bit groups. The total number of bits in the resulting PHY frame is 3584, or 512 7-bit groups.

The LDPC process accomplishes two things: The transmitted data contains enough transitions to facilitate clock recovery by the Slave loop timing circuits, and the ability to detect errors is enhanced.

The PHY frame is DSQ128 mapped from 7-bit groups into two-dimensional symbols (see Figure 4–100). The three uncoded bits and the four coded bits are used to determine the resulting DSQ128 symbol. The possible symbols are chosen from a limited set of "maximally spaced 2D symbols" so that errors are easier to detect.

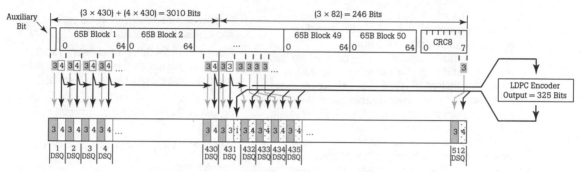

Figure 4-99. *Low density parity checksum encoder used to complete the PHY frame*

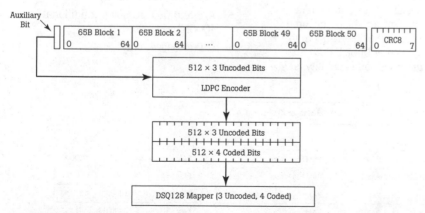

Figure 4-100. *DSQ128 mapping process*

Each 2D-DSQ128 symbol has two PAM16 components, called $PAM16_1$ and $PAM16_2$. Each PAM16 component can take any value from the set $(-15, -13, -11, -9, -7, -5, -3, -1, 1, 3, 5, 7, 9, 11, 13, 15)$. The mapping is accomplished using the 3-bit unencoded and 4-bit coded bits (see Figure 4-101).

The 512 2D-DSQ128 symbols are mapped into 256 4D-PAM16 symbols at the Physical Medium Attachment (PMA) sublayer. The two PAM16 components ($PAM16_1$ and $PAM16_2$), are mapped onto two consecutive time periods on the same wire pair. The transmission symbol period for each symbol is 1.25ns, or 800 megasymbols per second.

The 16 component values (between -15 and $+15$) are converted to voltage levels ranging between $+1$ and -1 volts for each wire pair. The signal is transmitted as a differential signal between the two wires of the pair.

Before communications can begin, the two link partners must determine a number of operating parameters, including which link partner sources the Master PHY clock and whether the Slave uses the data stream to recover the Slave PHY transmit clock. If loop timing is not possible, both transmit as a Master. This is usually determined during Auto-Negotiation, although it can be manually configured. Unlike slower versions of Ethernet, 10GBASE-T is *required* to offer support for Auto-Negotiation and extended Next Pages.

Auto-Negotiation weighs three parameters to determine which link partner should become the Master PHY. The greatest weight is given to a multiport device (a switch or hub). If both are the same, the loop timing support capability is the next determining factor; that is, can the link partner derive transmit clocking from the received signal. If only one link partner supports loop timing, that link partner becomes Slave. The third factor is to compare the value used for seed bits, where the link partner using the higher value is Master. A description in 802.3, Clause 55.6.2 describes this process and provides examples. If the two link partners are exactly equal, the Auto-Negotiation process fails and is restarted.

10GBASE-T Receive Process

After Auto-Negotiation concludes, the two link partners begin training to achieve synchronization on all four wire pairs. Training is initiated first on Pair A. During the training period the receiver must

- Perform signal equalization, as well as echo and crosstalk cancellation

- Compensate for differential delay variations of up to 50ns across the wire-pairs (measured as delay skew by cable testers)

- Detect and compensate for pair swaps (reported as Tip/Ring polarity reversal by cable testers)

- Detect and compensate for crossovers

  — No crossover

  — A/B crossover only (traditional 10/100Mbps crossover)

  — A/B and C/D crossover (traditional 1000Mbps crossover)

  — C/D crossover only

	DSQ128 Mapper (3 Uncoded, 4 Coded)						
Pair A	$PAM16_1$ <0>	$PAM16_2$ <0>	$PAM16_1$ <4>	$PAM16_2$ <4>	...	$PAM16_1$ <508>	$PAM16_2$ <508>
Pair B	$PAM16_1$ <1>	$PAM16_2$ <1>	$PAM16_1$ <5>	$PAM16_2$ <5>	...	$PAM16_1$ <509>	$PAM16_2$ <509>
Pair C	$PAM16_1$ <2>	$PAM16_2$ <2>	$PAM16_1$ <6>	$PAM16_2$ <6>	...	$PAM16_1$ <510>	$PAM16_2$ <510>
Pair D	$PAM16_1$ <3>	$PAM16_2$ <3>	$PAM16_1$ <7>	$PAM16_2$ <7>	...	$PAM16_1$ <511>	$PAM16_2$ <511>

Figure 4-101. *4D-PAM16 mapping process*

The purpose of this training is to have the receiver extract signal levels from the wire pair, find all four parts of the same 4D-PAM16 symbol, and match them back up before passing the symbol up to the next process. During training, the PHY transmits special PAM2 code groups only. The code groups transmitted during training have PAM16 component values of [−9, 9] only to permit the descrambler in the link partner to identify the correct starting point.

After the descramblers synchronize, each link partner sends PHY control information, at regular intervals, which contains transmitter power settings and other information for startup operation. The InfoField is 16 octets (see Figure 4-102), which is XORed with the last 128 bits of the PMA 16384 PAM2 frame on wire Pair A. The InfoField is also sent at intervals of 16384 "bits" throughout normal operation.

Part of the process includes having each link partner set its output power level to 4, which equates to a power backoff (PBO) setting of 8dB. Then each reports on the link partner's detected power level and requests changes if necessary (in the next transmitted InfoField). PBO levels are set in increments of 2dB between 0dB and 14dB. Signal to noise ratio (SNR) is also communicated the same way to help the receivers extract the 4D-PAM16 symbols from the incoming signal.

There are four different frame formats for the InfoField used to communicate link partner PMA PHY control information. Refer to 802.3, Clause 55.4 for a lengthy discussion of the parameters used and the process for establishing synchronization during the training phase of link startup.

Start of Frame Delimiter 0xBBA70000	3 Transmitter Settings	Message Field	SNR Margin	Message Field Dependent	Message Field Dependent	CRC16
4 Octets	3 Octets	1 Octet	4 Bits	1.5 Octets	4 Octets	2 Octets

InfoField Format

Start of Frame Delimiter 0xBBA70000	3 Transmitter Settings	Message Field	SNR Margin	Reserved	Transition Counter	Reserved	Vendor Specific	CRC16
4 Octets	3 Octets	1 Octet	4 Bits	2 Bits	10 Bits	2 Octets	2 Octets	2 Octets

InfoField Transition Counter Format

Start of Frame Delimiter 0xBBA70000	3 Transmitter Settings	Message Field	SNR Margin	Coefficient Exchange	Coefficient Field	CRC16
4 Octets	3 Octets	1 Octet	4 Bits	1.5 Octets	4 Octets	2 Octets

InfoField Coefficient Exchange Format

Start of Frame Delimiter 0xBBA70000	3 Transmitter Settings	Message Field	SNR Margin	Reserved	Reserved	Vendor Specific	CRC16
4 Octets	3 Octets	1 Octet	4 Bits	1.5 Octets	2 Octets	2 Octets	2 Octets

InfoField (not transition counter and not coefficient exchange) Format

Figure 4-102. *PMA PHY Control InfoField frame formats*

Training proceeds until descrambler synchronization alignment is achieved across all four wire pairs (see Figure 4-103). The training process also synchronizes the PMA to the PCS such that there is alignment with the PCS PHY frame boundary for the 65B LDPC frames.

The PMA receives 4D-PAM16 symbols and collects 256 (which are aligned with the start of the PHY frame) and transfers them back up to the PCS.

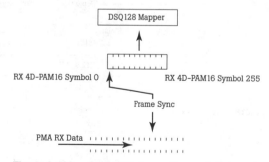

Figure 4-103. *PMA symbol reception and alignment*

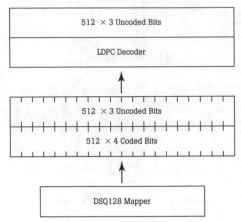

Figure 1-104. *DSQ128 unencoded on reception*

The group of 256 4D-PAM16 symbols are mapped back into 512 2D-DSQ128 symbols, and then the DSQ128 symbols and passed to the LDPC decoder (see Figure 4–104).

The PCS LDPC decoding process validates the received checksum and results in 50 65B blocks. Then each 65B block is descrambled (see Figure 4–105).

The Data/Control bit is removed, and the 8-octet block is passed back through the XGMII in two 4-octet transfers (see Figure 4–106).

As the Reconciliation sublayer handles the two 32-bit transfers it restores the first octet of Preamble in place of the /Start/ control code (see Figure 4–107). The data is restored to MSB order and represented in the hexadecimal from which it started in this example.

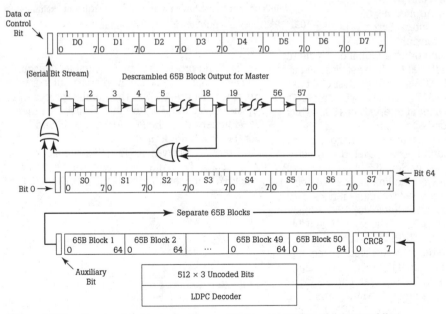

Figure 4-105. *Receive data block checksum validation, separation, and descrambling*

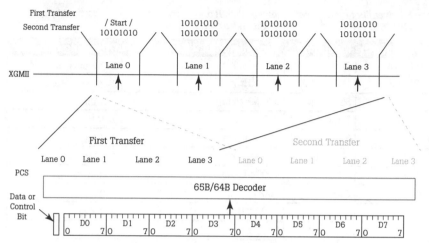

Figure 4-106. *65B/64B decoding and transfer back to the MAC Layer as octets*

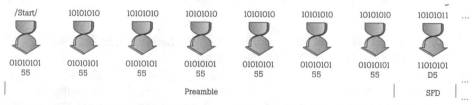

Figure 4-107. *Symbol substitution, reordering, and reconversion back to hexadecimal of the first two fields in the sample Ethernet frame at the receiver*

Architecture

No repeater is defined for 10 Gigabit Ethernet because half duplex is explicitly not supported.

As with 10Mbps, 100Mbps, and 1000Mbps versions, it is possible to modify some of the architecture rules slightly. Possible architecture adjustments are related to signal loss and distortion along the medium. Due to dispersion of the signal and other issues, the light pulse becomes undecipherable beyond certain distances. Refer to the technical timing and spectral requirements detailed in Clause 52 and Clause 53 of the current 802.3 standard, and the technical informa-

tion about your hardware performance before attempting any adjustments to the architecture rules.

10Gbps Ethernet is specified for both multimode and singlemode fiber. Table 4-19 lists the maximum allowed cable lengths for each combination of R and W specifications, as well as the LX4 specification. Note that the modal bandwidth parameter is a key limiting factor in length. Modal bandwidth information is typically available from the cable vendor and cannot be field tested with the current generation of field test technology.

Table 4-19. *10 Gigabit Ethernet fiber optic implementations. Both R and W specifications are covered by each appropriate entry (i.e., 10GBASE-E covers both 10GBASE-ER and 10GBASE-EW).*

Implementation	Wavelength	Medium	Minimum Modal Bandwidth	Operating Distance
10GBASE-LX4	1310 nm	62.5μm MMF	500 MHz/km	2–300m
10GBASE-LX4	1310 nm	50μm MMF	400 MHz/km	2–240m
10GBASE-LX4	1310nm	50μm MMF	500 MHz/km	2–300m
10GBASE-LX4	1310nm	10μm SMF	N/A	2–10km
10GBASE-S	850nm	62.5μm MMF	160 MHz/km	2–26m
10GBASE-S	850nm	62.5μm MMF	200 MHz/km	2–33m
10GBASE-S	850nm	50μm MMF	400 MHz/km	2–66m
10GBASE-S	850nm	50μm MMF	500 MHz/km	2–82m
10GBASE-S	850nm	50μm MMF	2000 MHz/km	2–300m
10GBASE-L	1310nm	10μm SMF	N/A	2–10km
10GBASE-E	1550nm	10μm SMF	N/A	2–30km*

*The standard permits 40km lengths if link attenuation is low enough.

10GBASE-T and 10GBASE-CX4 maximum allowed cable lengths are specified in Table 4-20.

Table 4-20. *10 Gigabit Ethernet copper implementations*

Implementation	Cable Type	Operating Distance	Reference Standard
10GBASE-T	ISO Class E / TIA Category 6	55m to 100m*	ISO/IEC TR-24750
10GBASE-T	ISO Class E / TIA Category 6 (unscreened)	55m	TIA/EIA TSB-155
10GBASE-T	ISO Class E / TIA Category 6 (screened)	100m	
10GBASE-T	ISO Class E$_A$ / TIA Augmented Category 6	100m	ISO/IEC 11801 Ed 2.1 TIA/EIA 568-B.2-10
10GBASE-T	ISO Class F	100m	ISO/IEC TR-24750
10GBASE-CX4	Twinaxial cable assembly (or other cable type if test parameters are met)	Up to 15m	

* Up to 100 meters if the alien crosstalk to insertion loss requirements from 802.3, Clause 55.7.3.1.2 and Clause 55.7.3.2.2 are met.

Ethernet for Subscriber Access Networks

Subscriber access network versions of Ethernet, sometimes referred to as *Ethernet in the first mile* (EFM), are not described here because they fall outside the LAN environment scope that this text is intended to support. EFM includes the implementations of: 2BASE-TL, 10PASS-TS, 100BASE-BX10, 100BASE-LX10, 1000BASE-BX10, and 1000BASE-LX10 at this time. These implementations are used by an Internet service provider (ISP) to provision an Internet connection to the home in place of older modem technology or more recent DSL technologies. The connection is typically between the home and the Telco central office (CO). A comparative analogy for the CO would be the switch closet nearest the user's desk in an office building.

Several aspects of EFM should be noted. First, only full duplex is supported. This full-duplex support comes in two operating modes: the normal full duplex and a simplified full duplex. Simplified full duplex is used with point-to-multipoint optical topologies where passive optical splitters may be used. Despite the requirement for full duplex, there is an allowance for copper links to use a version of half duplex defined in 802.3, Clause 61.

Other significant differences include support for copper at low speeds only (2 and 10Mbps), and only fiber optic media for 100 and 1000Mbps. The transmission distances supported on copper media are substantially affected by cable quality and performance.

The various EFM implementation maximum allowed cable lengths are specified in Table 4-21.

Table 4-21. *Maximum cabling distances for Ethernet in the first mile*

Architecture	Data Rate*	Maximum Distance*	Media
2BASE-TL	2Mbps	2,700m	One or more pairs of voice grade copper cable
10PASS-TS	10Mbps	750m	One or more pairs of voice grade copper cable
100BASE-LX10	100Mbps	10,000m	One pair of singlemode fiber
100BASE-BX10	100Mbps	10,000m	One singlemode fiber
1000BASE-LX10	1000Mbps	550m	One pair of multimode fiber
1000BASE-LX10	1000Mbps	10,000m	One pair of singlemode fiber
1000BASE-BX10	1000Mbps	10,000m	One singlemode fiber
1000BASE-PX10	1000Mbps	10,00 m	One singlemode fiber
1000BASE-PX20	1000Mbps	20,000m	One singlemode fiber

* Maximum defined distance or rate, depending on local conditions.

Summary

This chapter described Ethernet. The popular press, various expert opinions, and word of mouth contain bits and pieces of information about how Ethernet works. Some are mostly correct, most are somewhat correct. However, there are also a lot of misconceptions about how the rules and mechanics of transmitting data over Ethernet are implemented. Furthermore, as Ethernet evolves into ever-faster implementations, the built-in allowance for poor-quality installations diminishes. The Ethernet protocol can only compensate so much, and after that things break.

- The frame structure and field organization and definitions for various Ethernet frame types are provided.

  The basic framing remains constant for all implementations of Ethernet; however, there are differences found below the MAC Layer depending on the implementation. There are also different field additions depending on where within a broadcast domain the frame is found. Between bridges (switches) there are several frame modifications, such as VLAN tagging and MPLS, and although it is rare to see these additions on a station connection, it is possible for them to exist there.

- Ethernet uses CSMA/CD to handle routine signaling. The specific rules that govern access to the medium and error handling are provided.

  For half duplex collision domain operation, the sending station must learn about problems within the collision domain before a timeout value has expired. If a problem is discovered within this time limit, Ethernet manages error recovery and retransmission automatically and upper layers are not aware of the problem. If a problem is discovered after that time limit, Ethernet recovers from the error condition but abandons the current transmission. If the transmission is abandoned, upper layers must discover the loss and take action to retransmit. At higher layers, the recovery takes considerably longer to recover than if the error occurred within the time limit where Ethernet recovers and retransmits.

  For full duplex operation, the concept of a collision does not exist, although other types of error may still disrupt communications. Because collisions do not exist for full duplex, there are no error recovery and retransmission techniques employed. Any errored frame is lost, and upper layers must discover the loss and recover from the problem.

- A listing of the characteristics that identify the specific type and probable location for many Ethernet errors is provided.

  The specific characteristics for many types of Ethernet error conditions are described. Additional information is provided indicating differences which may be reported, depending on which definition for an error condition is used to describe the error condition.

- The mechanism and rules for Auto-Negotiation are described.

  Auto-Negotiation is a means for achieving the highest performance link from among the various capabilities that two link partners have in common. Full understanding of the operation of Auto-Negotiation helps prevent or detect situations where links may be operating suboptimally.

- The mechanism and power levels for Power over Ethernet are described.

  Power over Ethernet (PoE) provides a means for the network link to provide adequate power to sustain the operation of low-power network devices that may be deployed to locations far from the nearest AC power source. An understanding of the operation of PoE helps prevent or detect situations where links may experience problems obtaining adequate power from the network link.

- The process and encoding techniques for many common Ethernet implementations are described, including architecture design rules.

  At the MAC Layer, Ethernet is almost exactly the same regardless of implementation. At the Physical Layer, each implementation of Ethernet abides by slightly to greatly different rules and encoding procedures. Understanding the media limitations and the architecture limitations helps avoid, prevent, or detect situations where links may experience operational problems.

Chapter Review Questions

To aid in your comprehension of important concepts, the following questions are provided. Refer to this book's Introduction for a general legend that indicates the anticipated difficulty of each question. For answers to these review questions, see Appendix I, "Answers to Chapter Review Questions."

1. Where can an interested party obtain copies of current IEEE standards, which standards are available, and what is the cost for those standards? Include any other significant information which you feel is relevant in your answer.

2. What are the characteristics of the two most common methods employed by stations seeking media access on a network?

3. Under what conditions would a frame be sent back out the same port of a repeater on which it was received?

4. What behavior is exhibited by a repeater when noise is detected on a port?

5. When is a station considered to be on the same collision domain as another station, and when is it considered to be on a different collision domain? Specifically, what separation is required in order to make that determination?

6. Ethernet MAC Layer frame field definitions are the same at all speeds, true or false?

7. Ethernet signal encoding is the same at all speeds, true or false?

8. Define LSB and MSB and how that affects Ethernet.

9. List the order in which the defined fields in 802.3 Ethernet appear in a frame. Include the size (in octets) for each field.

10. What is the difference between 802.3 Ethernet framing and its predecessor, DIX Ethernet?

11. What other common names did the DIX Ethernet definition go by?

12. What distinction is drawn by 802.3 Ethernet in deciding whether the field is Length or Type?

13. If the frame contains an 802.3 Ethernet Length field, is there any way for the protocol stack in the receiving station to determine what protocol is encapsulated?

14. Under what condition is the standard 802.3 Ethernet framing modified due to the Ethernet implementation that is used to transmit it, and what is that change?

15. How is an Ethernet frame modified when 802.1Q VLAN tagging is applied?

16. Do the frame changes described in your answer for VLAN tagging in question 15 meet the length limits for 802.3 Ethernet?

17. Name two noncompliant frame definitions that may be seen on an 802.3 Ethernet collision domain. List the differences in those frame definitions that make them fail to comply with the 802.3 standard.

18. What is the maximum legal size for an Ethernet frame?

19. What is the maximum number of stations that can legally be attached to a single collision domain? What is a more reasonable number? Why?

20. What is implied by the phrase "a *distributed single point of failure*"?

21. What are the significant differences between half and full duplex operation?

22. What is the Preamble field used for in 10Mbps versions of Ethernet? What is it used for in faster versions of Ethernet?

23. What is the size of the minimum Ethernet frame?

24. What two possible outcomes result when an infrastructure device (repeater, bridge, or switch) receives a legal Ethernet frame that is longer than 1518 octets?

25. What is slotTime used for?

26. How was slotTime modified to accommodate Gigabit Ethernet?

27. What compensation technique is applied by the MAC Layer to accommodate 10GBASEW implementations of 10 Gigabit Ethernet (which run at slightly less than 10 Gigabit at the Physical Layer)?

28. Use the retransmission algorithm to calculate how long the maximum backoff time interval would be for a seventh consecutive collision at 10 Mbps.

 29. Is a collision an error?

 30. Because Ethernet is a common bus technology, it is said that each station sees exactly the same thing as all other stations. Is that actually true?

 31. List the characteristics of a collision fragment.

 32. Explain the difference between a local and remote collision.

 33. How can a late collision be distinguished from a local or remote collision?

 34. Can a late remote collision be detected, and if so, how?

 35. What definition of jabber is most common within the networking industry, and where is that definition taken from?

 36. Is a large VLAN tagged frame considered to be jabber?

 37. What is the difference between jabber and a long frame?

 38. Is a jumbo frame considered jabber or is it a long frame?

 39. What error or errors could a Runt be classified as if the general usage were applied? How is general usage different from what the standard defines?

 40. How much of a frame has to be different for it to qualify as an FCS error?

 41. How would you describe an alignment error?

 42. How would you describe a range error?

 43. What is a ghost?

 44. What is Auto-Negotiation?

 45. What is the difference between a single pulse used as part of an FLP burst and the Link Pulse used by older 10BASE-T stations?

46. If two interfaces indicate support for 100BASE-TX and 100BASE-T2 in the FLP burst, which would be chosen as the operating speed?

 47. To achieve the highest speed possible at all times, the network administrator configured the server interface to 100BASE-TX full duplex. The switch port is AutoNegotiating. What is the result?

 48. In what ways can a full duplex link be established?

 49. If a 1000BASE-T interface was operating in half duplex and sent a minimum-sized frame (64 octets), what percentage of the transmission would be represented by extension bits? Don't forget that slotTime starts at the beginning of the Preamble.

 50. If 100BASE-T is a synchronous protocol, what does that imply about using it in half duplex?

 51. How does frame bursting help in half duplex Gigabit Ethernet?

 52. What encoding system is used for 10Mbps Ethernet, and how is a binary one value distinguished from a binary zero value?

 53. Is it possible to have no Ethernet signal transitions on the wire for as long as an hour using 10Mbps Ethernet? If your answer is no, explain why not. If your answer is yes, explain how.

 54. Explain the 5-4-3 rule.

 55. If maximum cable lengths are used, what is the maximum physical distance that could separate two 10BASE5 stations?

 56. Although the standard says that it is legal to have 1024 stations on a collision domain, is it possible to attach that many stations that a legal architecture is assembled using 10BASE2 exclusively? Show your math.

 57. How many hubs can be placed in series between any two distant 10BASE-T stations?

 58. Do stackable hubs count as one repeater or as the number of hubs that were stacked? How about hub "blades" in a hub chassis?

 59. Are 10Mbps Ethernet timing requirements loose enough to tolerate a little cheating on the architecture limits? Explain your answer.

 60. Are 100Mbps Ethernet timing requirements loose enough to tolerate a little cheating on the architecture limits? Explain your answer.

61. What encoding systems are used for 100Mbps Ethernet, and how is a binary one value distinguished from a binary zero value?

 62. How do you apply the 5-4-3 rule to 100Mbps Ethernet?

 63. What distinguishes a Class I repeater from a Class II repeater?

 64. If maximum cable lengths are used, what is the maximum physical distance that could separate two 100BASE-TX stations?

 65. What encoding systems are used for 1Gbps Ethernet, and how is a binary one value distinguished from a binary zero value "on the wire"?

 66. How do you apply the 5-4-3 rule to 1Gbps Ethernet?

67. What encoding systems are used for 10Gbps Ethernet, and how is a binary one value distinguished from a binary zero value?

For questions 68 to 73, see Figure 4-108.

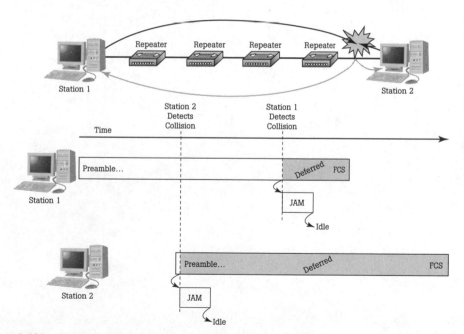

Figure 4-108. *Routine collision handling in a 10Mbps collision domain*

68. Which station should be repaired or replaced for causing collision problems on the local collision domain?

___Station 1

___Station 2

___Both

___Neither

69. If you have a software protocol analyzer loaded on Station 1, how much of the original frame sent from Station 2 do you capture?

70. If you have a software protocol analyzer loaded on Station 2 instead, how much of the original frame sent from Station 1 do you capture?

71. Will you ever be able to detect the identity of the distant station that is party to the collision (from the perspective of whichever station you are monitoring from)?

72. Is the destination address of a collided frame of any value?

73. What is the likelihood that the frame was destined for the station that collided with it?

CHAPTER 5
Data Link Layer

The Data Link Layer is usually depicted as having two sublayers: Media Access Control (MAC) and Logical Link Control (LLC), though additional sublayers are becoming more common (see Figure 5-1). The Media Access Control sublayer was described in the preceding chapter on Ethernet, and is the lowest sublayer. Above the MAC Layer is an increasingly more common (optional) MAC Control sublayer. If the MAC Layer for the interface is capable, then another optional sublayer called Operations, Administration, and Maintenance (OAM) may be used. OAM was added to Ethernet in conjunction with Ethernet in the First Mile (EFM) implementations in 802.3 Clauses 56–67. The MAC, MAC Control, and OAM sublayers apply to a single interface. Also optionally, a link aggregation may be created that spans multiple interfaces and appears as a single logical interface to higher layers. Above that, as the highest sublayer in the Data Link Layer, is where the MAC Control Client resides.

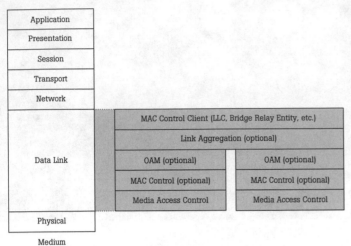

Figure 5-1. *Sublayers within the Data Link Layer*

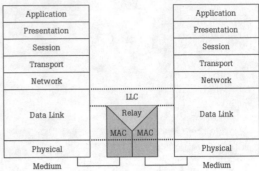

Figure 5-2. *Bridge (relay agent) placement in the OSI Model*

Bridges

Bridges are thought of as Data Link Layer devices because they separate collision domains. According to 802.1D, the standards document that describes the operation of a bridge (relay agent), bridges actually operate at the MAC Layer as shown in Figure 5-2. Bridge management and other aspects of a bridge may operate at higher layers, such as the LLC Layer, but the relay agent operates at the MAC Layer. Because the job of an Ethernet bridge is to forward traffic between collision domains, they are discussed here instead of in the previous chapter that described activities within a collision domain. A switch may be described as a multiport bridge. The term *bridge* is used instead of *switch* because switches are not always OSI Layer 2 devices but bridges are.

Bridges are able to evaluate traffic at the MAC Layer and forward traffic without involvement from upper-layer entities. Traffic may be forwarded between like protocols, such as between two Ethernet segments, and between unlike protocols, such as 802.5 Token Ring and ISO 9314–2 FDDI.

Transparent bridges evaluate the passing frames and forward when appropriate but do not modify the frame. Translating bridges will change the MAC Layer protocol as a frame is forwarded. Both of these bridge types are able to forward traffic without requiring the transmitting station to care where the destination station is located within the bridged topology. Wireless was leveraged from the same 802.3 frame format as Ethernet, and though differences exist there is no need to do heavy-duty MAC Layer protocol translation.

A third type of bridging (called source route bridging) requires the transmitting station to discover the location of the destination station via broadcasts and then include bridge routing information in subsequent unicast traffic, so that the bridges are able to operate in ignorance and the transmitting station does all the work. As each source route bridge forwards a broadcast, it appends its identity into the Routing Information Field (RIF). The receiving station reads this field and responds to the broadcast by copying this routing information into the response frame as instructions for how to return to the first station.

An encapsulating bridge has the ability to transfer communications between two homogeneous networks that are connected by a heterogeneous network. The bridge does this by inserting the data that is to be transferred between the homogeneous networks into the data frames of the heterogeneous network. Because the data frames of the homogeneous networks are encapsulated into the data frames of the heterogeneous network, this type of bridge is called an encapsulating bridge.

The use of an encapsulating bridge is probably best illustrated by example. Assume that you want to connect two legacy Token Ring networks separated by an Ethernet network. You can place encapsulating bridges on either side of the Ethernet network to allow the two Token Ring networks to communicate with one another.

Other variations of bridging techniques exist too, such as source route transparent. However, just as Ethernet and TCP/IP are becoming the de facto network protocols, the transparent bridging common to Ethernet is becoming the de facto bridging technique.

Bridge Forwarding Table

A bridge forwards traffic in accordance with a static or dynamic list (bridge forwarding table, also known by other names depending on the switch vendor) showing which devices have been observed on each port. As the bridge receives each frame, it evaluates the source address. If the source address is not already in the dynamic list, it is added to the list and associated with the port it came in on. If a station is moved and appears as a source attached to a different port, the dynamic list entry is corrected. Any single entry in the dynamic list is considered valid for a configured aging period. The recommended default time period is five minutes, after which the entry is deemed no longer trustworthy and is deleted. Depending on the bridge, network support staff can often modify the aging period from 10 seconds to 1,000,000 seconds. There is also a permanent or static table. Network support staff may configure specific devices, such as servers and routers, into the forwarding table list as permanent entries to limit unnecessary forwarding to other ports, and to ensure that traffic is always immediately forwarded to the right port.

If the bridge is unable to find a destination MAC address in the bridge forwarding table, the frame is forwarded (*flooded*) to all other ports. Just like a repeater, a bridge never retransmits a frame out the port from which it was received. This behavior will continue until the destination

MAC address responds. This behavior is the basis for transparent operation within the broadcast domain. A frame addressed to an unknown destination will be forwarded to all ports within the broadcast domain. Once the destination port is known, any subsequent frames will only be forwarded to that port. When using network diagnostic tools that generate traffic it is very important to remember this behavior. Network support staff can accidentally flood an entire broadcast domain with the configured level of traffic if the destination MAC address is not carefully chosen. Using a protocol analyzer to replay a captured trace file may have a similar effect.

If Layer 3 forwarding is in use, there probably isn't an active bridge forwarding table at all, as all forwarding is instead controlled by the routing table. In this state it is more accurate to think of the switch as a router for troubleshooting purposes.

Effect of Forwarding

A frame forwarded by a transparent bridge is passed through with virtually no modifications. If the bridge is forwarding between two instances of the same protocol and speed, it will emerge from the other side of the bridge in a cleaned-up state similar to having passed through a repeater. The deteriorated signal that arrived at one port will be refreshed as it is retransmitted by the bridge onto the next collision domain. Changing speeds will cause the physical layer signaling to change but will not affect the MAC Layer data.

A translating bridge will have an effect on the MAC Layer fields of the frame, but should not alter the higher-layer contents. For example, an Ethernet to Token Ring bridge will extract the addressing and data payload and use that to construct an entirely new MAC Layer frame. There are some dangers involved with this sort of bridge. Ethernet permits the data field to reach 1500 octets in a single frame. FDDI and 4Mbps Token Ring permit more than 4000 octet frames, and if Token Ring is operating at 16Mbps it can reach approximately 18,000 octets in a single frame. Within a single broadcast domain it is critical that the data field size does not exceed the smallest size permitted by any technology used in that broadcast domain.

Failure to match all data field sizes to the lowest common denominator will result in larger frames being discarded in parts of the broadcast domain while smaller frames pass through undisturbed.

Ethernet supports three different maximum frame sizes: 1518, 1522, and 2000 octets, though the data field size remains limited to 1500 octets for all. A bridge is supposed to choose (or be configured for) a single frame size and use only that size as the limit for discarding illegally large frames. For example, if the bridge is set for the older 1518 octet frame size, and a large frame bearing a VLAN tag is received, the 1522 octet frame should be discarded. The MAC Layer is not supposed to change behavior depending on what is in the frame. That is for the next higher layer to handle. The standard recommends setting the MAC Layer to 2000 octet frames to permit VLAN tags and envelope frames to be used. This is usually not a user-configured value.

If the frame is forwarded between two bridges participating in a VLAN, the VLAN tag will be added to the frame as it passes between bridges. The VLAN tag will be removed when it arrives at the destination port, restoring the frame to exactly the same contents as when it was transmitted. VLAN tags should never appear at destination ports except in special circumstances where the destination station itself (such as a file server) is configured to support VLAN tags.

Similarly, if an envelope frame is used, a bridge configured to use the special feature will add the appropriate envelope prefix and possibly an envelope suffix. Subsequent bridges in the path may add or remove prefixes (and suffixes) along the way. By the time the frame is forwarded to the destination port, all the envelope prefix and suffix fields should have been removed and the frame should again appear as it was transmitted.

Priority

Bridges permit the establishment of priorities when forwarding traffic. The priority queuing system is used to deliver a certain Quality of Service (QoS). See 802.1D Appendix G for a discussion of priorities and traffic classes.

Expediting or priority queuing is very important for applications that require a regular arrival of consecutive frames. Two examples of such protocols are videoconferencing, where low to medium resolution video is streamed across the network, and telephone calls placed through the network infrastructure instead of the public telephone system, such as Voice over IP (VoIP). Irregular spacing in the delivery of this sort of traffic causes poor signal quality. The overall delay in the delivery (latency) is usually less important than ensuring regular spacing of frames (jitter) and packet loss as long as the delay is within limits. According to ITU G-114, the one-way latency should not exceed 150ms, which is perhaps a little high for good voice communications. A formula for measuring jitter is provided in RFC 3550.

Spanning Tree Protocol

(See 802.1D and 802.1Q.)
Bridged (switched) networks may operate with or without a protocol such as the Spanning Tree Protocol (STP). The primary reason for using Spanning Tree is to prevent bridging loops. If no parallel paths are anticipated due to network design, Spanning Tree is not needed and is often considered undesirable. The reason for disfavor is probably that it is being used in a network to provide for path redundancy rather than to prevent bridge loops. The original protocol was not designed with redundancy/failover performance in mind and will not quickly recover from a path failure. Failover of STP could take more than 30 seconds. Note: Improvements found in 802.1W Rapid Spanning Tree Protocol (RSTP) reduce failover time to between single-digit seconds and subsecond times.

An additional area of trouble is that Spanning Tree will use its own logic to close a path, separate from the logic used at OSI Layer 3 to close a redundant routed path. Sometimes this interaction isolates a portion of the network from any path "out." Understanding how both OSI Layers 2 and 3 operate will permit the network design to take advantage of both to produce a reliable design, though it requires some thought.

One of the desirable use models for deploying bridges (switches) is to allow for redundant paths from the user to various network resources. This is accomplished by placing two or more bridges logically in parallel to offer multiple paths within a broadcast domain. Because all broadcasts are always forwarded to all ports on a bridge (except the port it was received upon), a parallel path places the network at risk of having a single broadcast frame suddenly occupy all available bandwidth within the broadcast domain (broadcast storm). It would loop endlessly between ports in the parallel path, and would proceed away from the parallel path in all directions each time the frame looped, like ripples on a pond.

The location of such a bridge loop is exceedingly difficult to find, and the resulting broadcast storm will often continue unabated until the parallel path is blocked or disconnected. One method for preventing parallel path problems is to use Spanning Tree, because that is what it was originally designed to do. In Spanning Tree, one bridge is elected as the root of a hierarchy. All the bridges use Bridge Protocol Data Unit (BPDU) broadcasts to discover where parallel paths exist and which is the lowest-cost path back to the root bridge. Once this data has been exchanged, only one bridged connection from any number of parallel paths is left in a forwarding state, and all others are blocked administratively. Spanning Tree BPDUs continue to be received on blocked ports.

The Spanning Tree protocol specifies regular communications between bridges to ensure that the port that is supposed to be forwarding traffic is still open and available. If Spanning Tree believes that the forwarding port in a parallel path has become unavailable, a previously blocked path will be opened. One drawback to using Spanning Tree is that it may take 30 seconds for the protocol to decide that a forwarding port is no longer in service and for a bridge with a port in parallel to unblock that path and begin forwarding.

Many vendors have a configuration option that allows the network support staff to configure the bridge to begin forwarding traffic from a newly activated port immediately, even though Spanning Tree is in use. This configuration relies on an act of faith by the network support staff. They are assuming that no new bridges will be connected that could create a parallel path. If this special "trust me" mode is not used, it can take more than 30 seconds before the port begins forwarding traffic for a just activated port.

Rapid Spanning Tree Protocol (RSTP) is an update to the 802.1D standard and supersedes the original Spanning Tree Protocol. Either or both may be used within a broadcast domain, as RSTP will compensate for the differences. RSTP will recover from a failed path considerably faster than STP.

When Spanning Tree shares information between participating bridges using BPDU frames, BPDUs are sent to the fixed destination MAC address of 01:80:C2:00:00:00 using the LLC 802.2 protocol type of 0x42. BPDUs are typically sent every 2 seconds from the root bridge within a Spanning Tree topology. The root bridge BPDUs are forwarded by all the participating bridges, and some of the information is modified by each Spanning Tree bridge within the hierarchy as it forwards the BPDU.

The election of a root bridge within the hierarchy is made via the highest priority Bridge Identifier (smallest value). The first part of the Bridge Identifier, the priority number, is first used to determine the root bridge. If there is a tie for which bridge has the lowest bridge priority, the bridge MAC address (the other field in the Bridge Identifier) is used. Because the priority number may be changed via the bridge configuration, it is possible to select which bridge should be chosen as root.

All ports on the root bridge are called designated ports, and they will all forward traffic. All other bridges have to determine which port has the least cost path to the root bridge. This selection is done using the root path cost. If more than one port has an equal (lowest) root path cost, the Bridge Identifier and Port Identifier fields (respectively) are used as tie-breakers. Once the root port is selected, the other ports on the bridge are evaluated using a similar selection process to determine which port will be the designated port that forwards traffic from all other network segments which the bridge services. All other ports on all other bridges leading from that bridged segment will enter a discarding state after one port is chosen as the designated port.

When a path fails, any bridge may send a topology change notification BPDU. This causes a cascading series of BPDUs to be sent, which in turn cause formerly blocking ports to transition to forwarding, and some formerly forwarding ports to transition to discarding such that one path is opened for data to pass through in reaching all other parts of the broadcast domain.

The functional diagram in Figure 5-3 shows a bridge hierarchy after the Spanning Tree protocol has stabilized a topology. Note that all segments of the network are reachable by one path only. All other paths are temporarily in a blocking state.

The 1998 version of the standard placed an arbitrary limit on the diameter of an STP controlled bridged hierarchy of seven bridges between any two distant stations (802.1D Clause 8.10.2). This limit was imposed because of the delays involved in propagating BPDUs throughout the broadcast domain in order to properly maintain forwarding from all segments. The 2004 version of the standard did not provide an explicit value for the maximum diameter of an RSTP hierarchy, but indicated that the Message Age timer would limit the diameter (802.1D Clause 17.9).

Spanning Tree Protocol Frame Fields

The basic Spanning Tree frame formats are shown for Configuration BPDUs (see Figure 5-4), Topology Change BPDUs (see Figure 5-5), and Rapid Spanning Tree (see Figure 5-6).

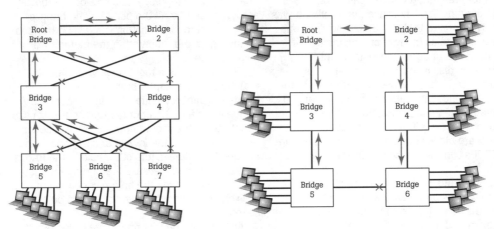

Figure 5-3. *Spanning Tree forwarding hierarchy examples. In both examples, if a forwarding link fails, a blocked link will begin forwarding.*

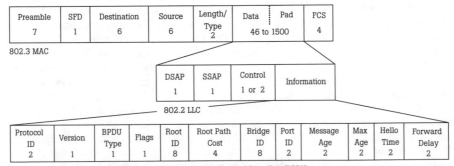

Preamble	SFD	Destination	Source	Length/ Type	Data	Pad	FCS
7	1	6	6	2	46 to 1500		4

802.3 MAC

DSAP	SSAP	Control	Information
1	1	1 or 2	

802.2 LLC

Protocol ID	Version	BPDU Type	Flags	Root ID	Root Path Cost	Bridge ID	Port ID	Message Age	Max Age	Hello Time	Forward Delay
2	1	1	1	8	4	8	2	2	2	2	2

802.1D Spanning Tree Protocol (STP) Configuration Bridge Protocol Data Unit (BPDU)

Figure 5-4. *Spanning Tree Configuration BPDU frame fields*

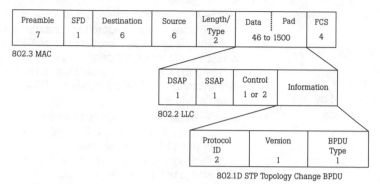

Figure 5-5. *Spanning Tree Topology Change Notification BPDU frame fields*

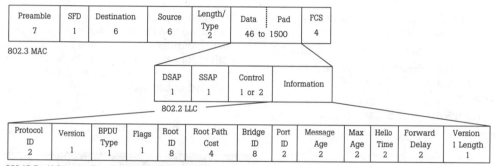

Figure 5-6. *Rapid Spanning Tree BPDU frame fields*

Descriptions of the 802.1D Spanning Tree Configuration, Topology Change, and Rapid Spanning Tree frame fields (combined) are provided:

Octets	Description
7	Preamble
1	Start Frame Delimiter
6	Destination MAC Address
6	Source MAC Address
2	Length/Type Field [data = 8808]
46	Data
1	802.2 LLC Destination Service Access Point (DSAP)
1	802.2 LLC Source Service Access Point (SSAP)
1	802.2 LLC Control Field
2	Protocol Identifier Field

Octets	Description
1	Protocol Version
1	Type
1	Flags
8	Root Identifier
4	Root Path Cost
8	Bridge Identifier
2	Port Identifier
2	Message Age Timer
2	Max Age Timer
2	Hello Time Timer
2	Forward Delay Timer
1	Version 1 Length
0 to 44	Reserved (data = all zeros)
4	Frame Check Sequence (CRC Checksum)

Descriptions for Spanning Tree Protocol frame field definitions are provided:

- **Protocol Identifier Field.** A value of 0x0000 is used to identify all bridge management protocol BPDU uses.

- **Protocol Version.** STP is identified by 0x00, RSTP is identified by 0x02.

- **BPDU Type.** There are presently three BPDU types defined.
  - STP Configuration BPDUs are 0x00
  - RSTP BPDUs are 0x02
  - STP Topology Change BPDUs are 0x80

- **Flags.** STP uses the following flag values:

  STP uses only two bits, with the remaining six bits held in reserve:
  - Bit 1 = Topology Change if set to binary 1
  - Bits 2–7 = Reserved, should be set to binary 0
  - Bit 8 = Topology Change Acknowledgement if set to binary 1

  RSTP uses the following flag values:
  - Bit 1 = Topology Change if set to binary 1
  - Bit 2 = Proposal if set to binary 1
  - Bits 3–4 = Port Role (Unknown = 0, Alternate = 1, Root = 2, Designated = 3)
  - Bit 5 = Learning if set to binary 1
  - Bit 6 = Forwarding if set to binary 1
  - Bit 7 = Agreement if set to binary 1
  - Bit 8 = Topology Change Acknowledgement if set to binary 1

  Example: Topology Change would be encoded as 10000000 in binary.

- **Root Identifier.** The Root Identifier indicates the current root bridge in the STP topology. The value in this field is composed the same as the Bridge Identifier for all bridges. The most significant two octets are broken down by bit groupings. The most significant four bits represent an assignable priority value that may be used to manage the relative priority of bridges. The next 12 bits represent a locally assigned system ID. The remaining six octets are the MAC address. This is a change from prior versions of the standard to better support Multiple Spanning Tree Protocol (MSTP), where the old two-octet priority was split to create the system ID that now facilitates identification of individual instances of Spanning Tree.

- **Root Path Cost.** Some arbitrary value for path cost that represents the Root Path Cost in a received BPDU plus the cost of the local port. Each successive bridge further from the Root Bridge will have a larger value for the Root Path Cost. The Root Bridge uses a Root Path Cost of zero because it is the root.

  There is a recommended list of port values based on the link speed ranging from 1 to 200 million, as shown in Table 5-1. A larger value indicates a less preferred path. The path cost may be modified in the bridge configuration to force a particular path to be preferred or avoided.

Table 5-1. *Recommended Root Path Cost parameter values from 802.1D (2004)*

Link Speed	Path Cost
Less than 100Kbps	200,000,000
1Mbps	20,000,000
10Mbps	2,000,000
100Mbps	200,000
1Gbps	20,000
10Gbps	2,000
100Gbps	200
1Tbps	20
10Tbps	2

These recommendations are substantially different from the 1998 version of the standard. The 1998 recommended values (shown in Table 5-2) are for historical reference. If a bridge that supports the old values for path cost is used with a new bridge supporting the new values, it should set its path cost to 65,535.

Table 5-2. *Obsolete recommended Root Path Cost parameter values from 802.1D (1998) (shown for historical purposes only)*

Link Speed	Path Cost
10Mbps	100
16Mbps	62
100Mbps	19
1Gbps	4
10Gbps	2

The Root Path Cost value is represented by the total cost of the path between the port leading to the root bridge. When the root bridge BPDU is forwarded out through the hierarchy, each receiving bridge will take the value received and add to it the value associated with its port leading to the root bridge. That will be the new Root Path Cost in the BPDU that is forwarded outward away from the root bridge.

- **Bridge Identifier.** The most significant two octets are broken down by bit groupings. The most significant four bits represent an assignable priority value that may be used to manage the relative priority of bridges. The next 12 bits represent a locally assigned system ID. The recommended default bridge priority value is 32,768, from within the range of 0 to 61,444 (in steps of 4096 so that the system ID value is not disturbed). The remaining six octets are the bridge MAC address.

  The number of bits used for the priority value was reduced and a system ID created from those bits in the 2004 version of the standard to better support Multiple Spanning Tree Protocol (MSTP). The system ID facilitates identification of individual instances of Spanning Tree.

- **Port Identifier.** The most significant octet of the Port Identifier is an arbitrary value used for a port priority. The recommended default port priority value is 128, from within the range of 0 to 240 (in steps of 16). The least significant octet represents the port on the bridge. All zeros is not a legal value for the Port Identifier.

- **Message Age timer.** The value is represented in units of 1/256th of a second. This timer measures the duration of time since the last protocol update was received. The current information is discarded if this timer reaches Max Age.

- **Max Age timer.** The value is represented in units of 1/256th of a second. The maximum amount of time before the protocol information is discarded. The recommended default value is 20 seconds, from within the range of 6 to 40 seconds.

- **Hello Time timer.** The value is represented in units of 1/256th of a second. The duration of time between periodic transmissions of Configuration BPDUs by designated ports on the root bridge. The recommended default value is 2 seconds, from a possible value of 1 to 10 seconds.

- **Forward Delay timer.** The value is represented in units of 1/256th of a second. This timer represents the delay used when transitioning ports to the Forwarding state. Typically this time is spent learning addresses so that fewer frames are flooded when the port begins forwarding. The recommended default value is 15 seconds, from within the range of 4 to 30 seconds.

- **Version 1 Length.** This value indicates how much Version 1 information is present. This parameter is used in RSTP with the value set to 0x00. This field was added to facilitate creation of newer versions of Spanning Tree.

VLANs

When VLANs are configured on a multiport bridge (such as a switch), the ports configured to be part of a particular VLAN form a separate broadcast domain. There may be multiple bridges participating in the same VLAN, and there may be multiple VLANs configured on a single bridge. Every port configured for a specific VLAN is part of a single broadcast domain, even if the broadcast domain spans multiple bridges. If multiple bridges are involved, at least one port will be used as a trunk port to share VLAN tagged traffic with other participating bridges. The trunk port will carry traffic for all VLANs that extend to other bridges in "that direction."

Spanning Tree is required to treat each VLAN as a separate broadcast domain, and to create a Spanning Tree topology that services that broadcast domain. There may then be multiple instances of Spanning Tree on a single bridge if multiple VLANs are configured for that bridge. The standards also allow for one instance of Spanning Tree that can support multiple VLANs within a bridge, as long as each VLAN is treated as a separate broadcast domain.

The bridge may determine which VLAN a particular port belongs to by fixed configuration or by dynamic assignment based on such variables as MAC address, IP address, or even protocol. A particularly complex process might determine the VLAN for a given port based on assigned DHCP address. If the bridge makes a dynamic assignment and multiple stations are resident upon a given port, the assignment will be made based on the first frame transmitted after the port becomes active. Most configurations are fixed or static, which are also the easiest to troubleshoot.

MAC Control Sublayer

The MAC Control sublayer is optional (see Figure 5-7). If this sublayer is not implemented, the MAC entity will communicate directly with the MAC Control client, such as the Logical Link Control (LLC) entity. The purpose of this sublayer is to allow the local MAC Client entity to exchange LLC data with peer LLC entities. One

such use is to communicate flow control requests, such as the Pause operation described in Appendix C, "Auto-Negotiation."

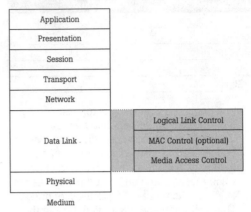

Figure 5-7. *MAC Control sublayer location within the OSI Model*

Frame Structure

The MAC Control frame is specified as using the reserved EtherType code of 0x8808 in the Length/Type field. The contents of a MAC Control frame are specified below (see Figure 5-8). Each MAC Control frame may contain only one instruction (Opcode). The frame is described as being exactly the minimum frame size. Because the frame is destined for the MAC Control sublayer, it is not passed to a higher layer.

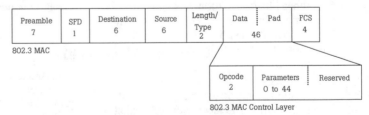

Figure 5-8. *MAC Control frame fields*

A listing of the MAC Control frame fields is provided:

Octets	Description
7	Preamble
1	Start Frame Delimiter
6	Destination MAC Address
6	Source MAC Address
2	Length/Type Field [data = 8808]
46	Data (Always equal to the minimum frame size)
	2 MAC Control Opcode Field
	0 to 44 MAC Control Parameters Field (frame must not exceed minimum frame size)
	0 to 44 Reserved [data = all zeros]
4	Frame Check Sequence (CRC Checksum)

Descriptions for the MAC Control frame fields are provided:

- **Opcode Field.** The MAC Control Opcode field is two octets. A list of codes is provided in 802.3, Annex 31A, though only the Pause code of 0x0001 is currently defined.

- **Parameters Field.** This field will contain any parameters defined for the Opcode specified in the frame. The field length may be anywhere from zero octets to the remaining portion of the data field for a minimum sized frame.

- **Reserved Field.** This field is used in the same manner as the 802.3 Pad. A MAC Control frame is a fixed length of (minimum frame size). If the Parameters field does not require all the space allowed in a minimum sized frame, the remainder of the frame is completed as the Reserved Field. The Reserved Field is always filled with only zeros.

Slow Protocols

The Operations, Administration, and Maintenance (OAM), and Link Aggregation sublayers are optional. If implemented, there are specific slow protocols associated with each. The OAM sublayer has one protocol, and the Link Aggregation sublayer has two protocols.

The Slow Protocols frame is specified as using the reserved EtherType code of 0x8809 in the Length/Type field. Although there are allowances for point-to-multipoint multicasting, the OAM and link aggregation slow protocols are used specifically between two link partners, and should never be forwarded by a bridge. These slow protocols use a reserved multicast destination MAC address of 01:80:C2:00:00:02.

To avoid adversely impacting a link, no more than 10 slow protocols may be used in any 1-second period, and no more than 10 frames within a slow protocol may be transmitted during the same period on that link (not more than 100 frames per second total). Also to limit the impact of slow protocols, the standard recommends that the size of a transmitted slow protocol frame should not exceed 128 octets, though the current implementation of OAM may exceed that recommendation today.

Link Aggregation Sublayer

(802.3 Clause 43 moved to 802.1AX in 2008.)
Link aggregation represents the use of two or more physical links as a single logical link. Data is distributed across all the physical links in the logical link, and the MAC Control Client treats the aggregation as a single link. Prior to the adoption of link aggregation as part of the Ethernet standard, this technology was dependent upon using the same brand of equipment at both ends of the connection. Terms for pre-standard deployments and some current implementations include Ethernet trunking or port trunking, various forms of multi-link trunking, NIC or port teaming or trunking, and EtherChannel.

The most common use of link aggregation is to increase bandwidth across backbone or other critical link segments where unused ports are available, or where higher speed ports are prohibitively expensive. For example, aggregating four Gigabit Ethernet links provided a logical link supporting 4 Gbps throughput. Aggregation may be applied between any two devices, including stations, servers, and switches. So-called "quad" NICs in servers provide four Ethernet ports and may be connected to the same switch in an aggregation, thus boosting the server's potential throughput to a single broadcast domain.

Link aggregation supports adding or removing individual links dynamically. When this is done there are specific restrictions applied to prevent frame duplication and to maintain frame ordering so that a given conversation does not receive frames out of order.

The requirement that frames be received in the correct order is most easily accomplished by sending all the frames in a single conversation through only one physical port within the aggregation. This would be noticeable if only a single conversation (such as a backup) were taking place, but if multiple conversations were present the benefits of multiple physical ports used in aggregation would produce throughput similar to a higher speed port. Similarly, if the load balancing method were based on MAC address, it is possible that all the server traffic to all destinations could be assigned to a single port from the aggregation, and again, performance would be the same as when only a single physical link were used.

When removing a link from the aggregation, or when redistributing the traffic load across the aggregation, it is important to ensure that all queued frames have been received first. This may be accomplished by one of two means: wait a sufficiently long period of time that any buffered frames would have been transmitted (time value depends on link speed), or transmit a marker frame. A marker frame is queued exactly the same as all other traffic. Upon receipt of a marker frame, the receiving port in an aggregation is required to transmit a response marker back on the same port. When the response marker is received, and as long as no further frames have been sent over that port, it is certain that all queued frames have been received at the far end and that specific port may be removed the link aggregation, the traffic formerly destined for that port may be redistributed, or load balancing can be redistributed.

As long as the configuration is not set manually, a link aggregation will configure itself using the available parallel links once an aggregation group is defined. Failure of a link in the aggregation is compensated for automatically, typically in less than one second. The terminology used for describing the configuration process involves the Actor (local) and the Actor's Protocol Partner. There are two modes in which the Actor and Protocol Partner operate: active and passive. In passive mode no attempt to aggregate is taken unless a LACPDU is received.

Two protocols are used with link aggregation: Link Aggregation Control Protocol (LACP) and Link Aggregation Marker Protocol (LAMP). Both are slow protocols.

Forming an Aggregation

The links are not actually negotiated because there is no negotiation; instead, the various parameters are exchanged and compared. If a set of links have the same partner system identifier and operational key, and there are no configuration or capability reasons why they should not aggregate, they will form an aggregation.

- **System Identifier**, composed of the system priority and part of the MAC address.
  - The first two octets of the system identifier are the two system priority octets.
  - Beginning with the third octet of the system identifier are the first six octets of the MAC address.
- **Port Identifier**, composed of port priority and port number.
  - The first two octets of the port MAC address are used as the first two octets of the port priority. A MAC address of 00:C0:17:12:23:45 would yield 00C0 as the first two octets of the port priority.

— The third and fourth octets of the port MAC address are used as the port number (zero is not permitted). A MAC address of 00:CO:17:12:23:45 would yield 1712 as the port number.

- **Keys.** Two capabilities keys are used: the *operational key*, which reflects what is actively in use; and the *administrative key*, which may include modifications configured by the system operator. The keys include information such as

  — The physical characteristics of the port (such as speed and duplex)

  — Any administratively configured limitations

  — Higher-layer protocols (such as an IP address)

  — Any limitations or special characteristics of the port itself

The ports that form an aggregation must have essentially the same configuration. Some of the reasons why an aggregation will not form include

- Different speed (10M/100M/1G/10G)
- Not Full Duplex
- Protocol filtering does not match

- Different QoS settings
- Different VLAN assignments

All links in the aggregation are monitored constantly for any changes that would affect the aggregation. A change could include an administrative change to the configuration. If any change is detected internally or via the Partner's Link Aggregation Control Protocol Data Units (LACPDUs), then it is evaluated to see whether any of the links in the aggregation should be disabled, an existing link removed, a new link added, or the traffic redistributed.

Each logical aggregated link will be represented by a unique MAC address. To the MAC Client above it in the system the aggregated link appears as a single logical link. The aggregator identifier used by the logical link aggregator function is chosen from one of the unique MACs from the ports forming the aggregation. Or, if none of the MACs for the physical ports are used, an additional globally unique MAC or a locally administered MAC will be used by the aggregation logical link.

Link Aggregation Control Protocol Frame Structure

The format for a Link Aggregation Control Protocol PDU is shown in Figure 5-9.

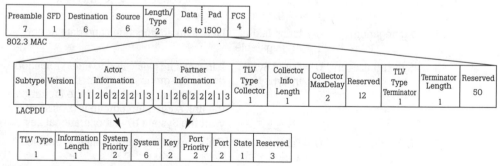

Figure 5-9. *Link Aggregation Control Protocol frame fields*

Link Aggregation Control Protocol (LACP) Frame Fields

A listing of the Link Aggregation Control Protocol frame fields is provided:

Octets	Description
7	Preamble
1	Start Frame Delimiter
6	Destination MAC Address (Slow protocols use a destination MAC address of 01–80–C2–00–00–02)
6	Source MAC Address
2	Length/Type Field [data = 0x8809]
110	Data (LACP uses a fixed frame size of 128, which equates to a data field size of 110 octets)

Octets	Description
1	Link Aggregation Protocol Subtype (LACP uses subtype 0x01)
1	LACP Version Number (the current version is 0x01)
1	TLV type (the first TLV type is Actor Information—Actor Information uses a value of 0x01)
1	Actor Information Length (the length is a fixed value of 0x14)
2	Actor System Priority (set manually or by policy)
6	Actor System (System ID = Actor MAC address)
2	Actor Key
2	Actor Port Priority
2	Actor Port
1	Actor State

Bit	Description	Value	Notes
0	LACP Activity	0 = Passive 1 = Active	Waits for or seeks aggregation
1	LACP Timeout	0 = Short 1 = Long	Timeout control value for this link
2	Aggregation	0 = Individual 1 = Aggregatable	Link is an aggregation candidate or not
3	Synchronization	0 = Out of Sync 1 = In Sync	If in sync, it is allocated to an aggregation group, the group is associated with a compatible aggregator, and the identity of the link aggregation group is consistent with the System ID and operational key
4	Collecting	0 = False 1 = True	Collection of incoming frames is enabled
5	Distributing	0 = False 1 = True	Distribution of outgoing frames is enabled

Bit	Description	Value	Notes (Continued)
6	Defaulted	0 = False 1 = True	Partner values are from received LACPDUs (False), or using defaults for Partner (True)
7	Expired	0 = False 1 = True	Actor's Receive machine state is expired

3   (Reserved)

1   TLV type (the second TLV type is Partner Information—Partner Information uses a value of 0x02)

1   Partner Information Length (the length is a fixed value of 0x14)

2   Partner System Priority

6   Partner System (the Partner's System ID, which is the MAC address)

2   Partner Key (provided by the partner)

2   Partner Port Priority (provided by the partner)

2   Partner Port (provided by the partner)

1   Partner State (provided by the partner and decoded the same as Actor State)

3   (Reserved)

1   TLV type (the third TLV type is Collector Information—Collector Information uses a value of 0x03)

1   Collector Information Length (the length is a fixed value of 0x10)

2   Collector Maximum Delay

12   (Reserved)

1   TLV Type (the fourth TLV type is the terminator, 0x00, which used to indicate that no further TLVs are present in the message)

1   Terminator Length (the length for termination is a fixed value of 0x00)

50   (Reserved)

4   Frame Check Sequence (CRC Checksum)

Link Aggregation Marker Protocol (LAMP)

The Link Aggregation Marker Protocol (LAMP) is used to indicate when all traffic queued for a specific port has been sent. The marker PDU is placed in the port queue with no special handing or priority so that it will be processed when the queue reaches it. Use of the LAMP protocol is optional, but if a LAMP PDU is received by a port it is mandatory that it respond on the same port.

When a bridge wishes to reallocate traffic or ports within a link aggregation it may send a marker PDU on the appropriate port and either wait until a corresponding marker response PDU is received or a timer expires. In either case, it can be reasonably sure that all frames in the queue for that port have been sent.

Link Aggregation Marker Protocol frames are the simplest form of 802.3 frame and are never tagged. They should only appear on the aggregation ports, and are not forwarded. In fact, a marker PDU is only sent on a single port, and the response must be received on the same port.

Link Aggregation Marker Protocol Frame Structure

The format for a Link Aggregation Marker Protocol frame is shown in Figure 5-10.

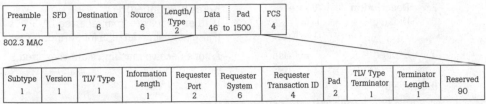

Preamble	SFD	Destination	Source	Length/ Type	Data	Pad	FCS
7	1	6	6	2	46	to 1500	4

802.3 MAC

Subtype	Version	TLV Type	Information Length	Requester Port	Requester System	Requester Transaction ID	Pad	TLV Type Terminator	Terminator Length	Reserved
1	1	1	1	2	6	4	2	1	1	90

802.3 Marker PDU and Marker Response PDU

Figure 5-10. *Link Aggregation Marker Protocol frame fields*

A listing of the Link Aggregation Marker Protocol frame fields is provided:

Octets	Description
7	Preamble
1	Start Frame Delimiter
6	Destination MAC address (slow protocols use a destination MAC address of 01-80-C2-00-00-02)
6	Source MAC address
2	Length/Type field (data = 0x8809)
110	Data (LAMP uses a fixed frame size of 128, which equates to a data field size of 110 octets)
1	Link Aggregation Marker Subtype (LAMP uses subtype 0x02)
1	LAMP Version Number (the current version is 0x01)
1	TLV type (Marker Information = 0x01, Marker Response Information = 0x02)
1	Marker Length = 16 (0x10)
2	Requester Port (as assigned by the requester)
6	Requester System (the system ID uses the appropriate MAC address)
4	Requester Transaction ID (as assigned by the requester)
2	Pad = all zeros (this is only used to force alignment with 16-octet memory boundaries)
1	TLV Type (Terminator) = 0x00
1	Terminator Length = 0x00
90	Reserved = all zeros (This field is used to force all PDUs to be the same size and facilitate future protocol changes. The standard permits the Marker Response PDU to include the Marker PDU contents in this reserved field instead of all zeros.)
4	Frame Check Sequence (CRC Checksum)

Note: *The Requester Port, Requester System, and Requester Transaction ID field contents are copied from the Marker PDU and used in the Marker Response PDU. The values in these fields reflect the bridge sending the Marker PDU always, and not the responding bridge that sent the Marker Response PDU.*

Operations, Administration, and Maintenance (OAM) Sublayer

(See 802.3 Clause 57.)

The Operations, Administration, and Maintenance (OAM) sublayer is optional, and may even be implemented for some ports but not others. OAM is a subset of ITU-T Y.1730.

OAM provides for a remote loopback capability that will cause the OAM peer to stop forwarding frames and instead copy all received frames from the attached link back onto the attached link as a loopback function. While in loopback state the link partner will still receive and evaluate any OAMPDUs, so it is possible to terminate the loopback or query the OAM sublayer entity during loopback. While in loopback, all received good traffic (except OAMPDUs) are looped back without any modification. Errored traffic is discarded.

During loopback both OAM peers must send information OAMPDUs to maintain communications.

Because OAM may be used to diagnose a potential fault condition, it is possible that the OAMPDU commands may be lost. OAMPDUs may therefore be sent multiple times to increase the likelihood that one will be received by the link partner. OAMPDUs that are repeated can be discarded upon receipt. Also, if the MAC Control Pause command is used it will affect all traffic, including OAMPDUs.

A given OAM device may be in active or passive mode. In active mode the OAM sublayer is able to perform OAM discovery, send and respond to information OAMPDUs, send and respond to event notification OAMPDUs, send and respond to variable request OAMPDUs, send and respond to loopback control OAMPDUs, and send organization-specific OAMPDUs. In passive mode the OAM sublayer may do all the same actions except perform discovery or send queries for variable request or loopback.

OAMPDU Frame Structure

The format for an Operations, Administration, and Maintenance PDU frame is shown in Figure 5-11.

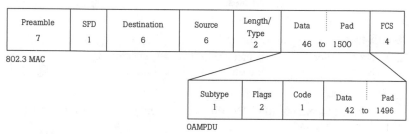

Figure 5-11. *OAMPDU frame fields*

A listing of the OAMPDU frame fields is provided:

Octets	Description
7	Preamble
1	Start Frame Delimiter
6	Destination MAC address (slow protocols use a destination MAC address of 01-80-C2-00-00-02)
6	Source MAC address for the port that sent the OAMPDU
2	Length/Type Field (data = 0x8809)
46–1500	Data

	Octets	Description
	1	Subtype (OAM uses subtype 0x03)
	2	Flags

Bit	Flag Name	Description
0	Link Fault	1 = The receive path has detected a fault
1	Dying Gasp	1 = An unrecoverable fault was detected
2	Critical Event	1 = A critical event was detected
3	Local Evaluating	0x0 = Local discovery failed
4	Local Stable	0x1 = Local discovery process has not completed
		0x2 = Local discovery process complete
		0x3 = Reserved.

Bit	Flag Name	Description
5	Remote Evaluating	Both bits are set to zero unless remote_state_valid is
6	Remote Stable	set to TRUE; then the values are set to match the last valid received Local Stable and Local Evaluating values from the remote OAM peer.
7–15	Reserved	Reserved

1 Code

Code	OAMPDU Name	Description
00	Information	Sends local and remote OAM information.
01	Event Notification	Provides alerting for remote DTE of link event(s).
02	Variable Request	Query for one or more specific MIB variables.
03	Variable Response	Query response for one or more specific MIB variables.
04	Loopback Control	Enables/disables remote loopback.
05–FD	Reserved	Reserved
FE	Organization Specific	Used for organizationally specific extensions, which are identified by the unique OUI.
FF	Reserved	Reserved

42–1496 Data/Pad (contains the OAMPDU data and any pad necessary to reach minimum frame size)

4 Frame Check Sequence (CRC Checksum)

Logical Link Control Sublayer

(See 802.2.)
The Logical Link Control (LLC) sublayer is common to all of the IEEE 802 media access protocol specifications (see Figure 5-12). The LLC sublayer performs services for the Network Layer and relies on the services of the MAC sublayer without regard for which medium access method is employed or the type of media used.

There are three modes of operation for communications at the LLC sublayer:

- **Type 1.** Unacknowledged connectionless
- **Type 2.** Connection-oriented
- **Type 3.** Acknowledged connectionless

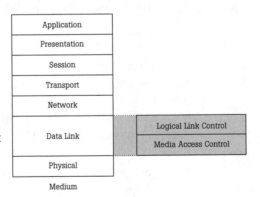

Figure 5-12. *Logical Link Control sublayer location within the OSI Model*

The LLC sublayer provides for a fairly complex set of commands for connectionless and connection-oriented communications. Two frame formats are available: the 802.2 LLC format and the 802 LLC Sub-Network Access Protocol (SNAP) format, which is an extension of the first format.

802.2 LLC

The DSAP, SSAP, and Control fields are collectively known as a Protocol Data Unit (PDU). A valid PDU is at least three octets in length. A PDU may or may not include an Information field.

The format for a Logical Link Control PDU frame is shown in Figure 5-13.

A listing of the LLC PDU frame fields is provided:

Octets	Description
7	Preamble
1	Start Frame Delimiter
6	Destination MAC address
6	Source MAC address
2	Length/Type Field (interpreted as length for an 802.2 frame)
46–1500	Data (if less than 46 octets—including DSAP, SSAP, and Control—a pad must be added to the end)
	1 802.2 LLC Destination Service Access Point (DSAP)
	1 802.2 LLC Source Service Access Point (SSAP)
	1 or 2 802.2 LLC Control Field (2 octets if sequencing is used)
	43–1497 802.2 LLC Information
4	Frame Check Sequence (CRC Checksum)

802.2 LLC Field Definitions

Descriptions for the LLC PDU frame fields are provided:

- **DSAP Field.** The Destination Service Access Point (DSAP) address field identifies one or more service access points. The address is separated into two parts (see Figure 5-14). The left-most bit (the LSB) identifies whether

the address is an individual or group address. If the first bit is a 1, the address is a group address. If the first bit is a 0, the address is an individual DSAP address. The remaining seven bits identify the actual address. If the address is all 1s, it represents a global or broadcast address. Specific values for the Link Service Access Point fields are available from the IANA web site (www.iana.org/assignments/ieee-802-numbers).

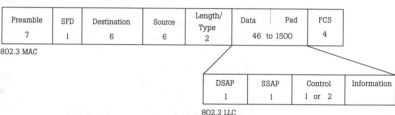

Figure 5-13. *802.2 LLC Encapsulation*

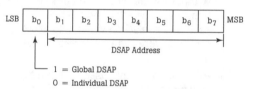

Figure 5-14. *DSAP address field interpretation.*

- **SSAP Field.** The Source Service Access Point (SSAP) address field identifies the service access point that originated the frame. The address is separated into two parts (see Figure 5-15). The leftmost bit (the LSB) identifies whether the address is a command or response. If the first bit is a 1 then the frame is an LLC response. If the first bit is a 0, the frame is an LLC command. The remaining seven bits identify the service access point that originated the frame.

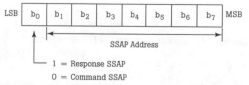

Figure 5-15. *SSAP address field interpretation*

- **Control Field.** The Control field may be either one or two octets in length, depending on whether the communication is sequenced and whether it is supervisory in nature.

    — Type 1 operation permits LLC entities to exchange information without first establishing communications. These LLC frames have no flow control, are not acknowledged, and have no error recovery procedures. Data transfers may be point-to-point, multicast, or broadcast.

    — Type 2 operation requires that a logical link be established before any information is passed. A means for establishing, using, resetting, and terminating point-to-point connections is provided. PDUs are sequenced to allow for error recovery and flow control.

    — Type 3 operation provides a means for exchanging acknowledged point-to-point Link Service Data Units (LSDUs) without establishing a data link connection. Unlike type 1, in type 3 operation each frame is acknowledged to allow for error recovery and proper frame ordering.

    The Poll/Final bit is only used with the XID and Test functions with type 1 operation,

with the bit set to 1 for a command (Poll) or response (Final) function. In type 2 operation, the Poll/Final bit is also set to 1 to solicit (Poll) a response or respond (Final) to a query, and provides a distinct command/response linkage during both normal operation and recovery situations. In type 3 operations, a command is sent with the Poll bit set to 0 to solicit a response having only a status subfield, and a 1 to solicit a response having both a status subfield and Link layer Service Data Unit (LSDU) subfield in the Information field.

The Information transfer format (I-format) is used in a Type 2 operation to perform a sequenced exchange (see Figure 5-16).

The Supervisory control format (S-format) is used in a Type 2 operation. This format is used to manage certain data link operations, such as to request a retransmission or to request a temporary pause in transmissions (see Figure 5-17).

The Unnumbered format (U-format) is used with any of the three Type operations to provide additional data link control functions and to provide unsequenced information transfer (see Figure 5-18). Typical usage of the 802.2 LLC frame is with this format.

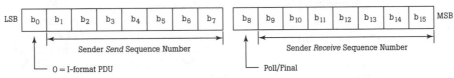

Figure 5-16. *I-format control field interpretation*

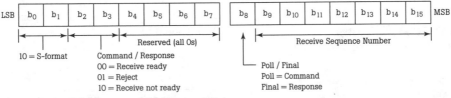

Figure 5-17. *S-format control field interpretation*

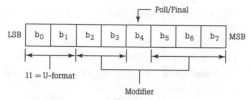

Figure 5-18. *U-format control field interpretation*

- **Information Field.** This field supplies parameters for LLC peer-to-peer commands, or is the data field containing the next-higher layer protocol for the typical non-LLC protocol usage.

802 SNAP

The 802 Subnetwork Access Protocol (SNAP) is available as an extension of the 802.2 LLC frame format. By setting the 802.2 DSAP and SSAP fields to 0xAA, the SNAP LLC extension is indicated.

The OUI and Type fields are collectively known as the SNAP Protocol Identifier field. The Protocol Identifier and Protocol Data fields are collectively known as a Protocol Data Unit (PDU).

The format for an 802 SNAP frame is shown in Figure 5-19.

The SNAP is an extension of the 802.2 LLC, offering support for more than the 127 unique protocols allowed by the two Link Service Access Point (LSAP) fields (the DSAP and SSAP), and allowing vendors to create their own protocol subtypes. Because SNAP is itself a defined protocol code within the protocol types supported by the

802.2 standard, the DSAP and SSAP are always set to the hexadecimal value of 0xAA, designating this to be a SNAP frame.

A listing of the 802 SNAP frame fields is provided:

Octets	Description
7	Preamble
1	Start Frame Delimiter
6	Destination MAC address
6	Source MAC address
2	Length/Type Field (interpreted as Length for an 802.2 frame)
46–1500	Data (if less than 46 octets—including DSAP, SSAP, Control, OUI, and Type—a pad must be added to the end)

	Octets	Description
	1	802.2 LLC Destination Service Access Point (DSAP) (data = AA)
	1	802.2 LLC Source Service Access Point (SSAP) (data = AA)
	1 or 2	802.2 LLC Control Field (2 octets if sequencing is used)
	3	802 SNAP Organizationally Unique Identifier (OUI)
	2	802 SNAP Type Field
	38 to 1492	802 SNAP Protocol Data
4		Frame Check Sequence (CRC Checksum)

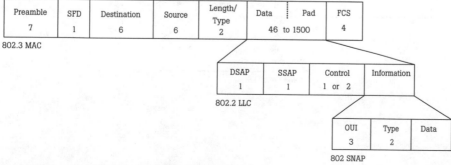

Figure 5-19. *802.2 Ethernet SNAP encapsulation*

802 SNAP Field Definitions

Descriptions for the 802 SNAP fields are provided:

- **OUI Field.** The Organizationally Unique Identifier (OUI) field is loaded with the first 24 bits of an IEEE-assigned number representing a single organization. The first bit (the LSB) in the first octet of the OUI may be changed to indicate an individual (0) or group address (1). The second bit in the first octet may be changed to indicate that the protocol is assigned globally or locally. If this bit is changed, the first 24 bits then become a locally administered protocol. For a protocol that is used publicly, both of these bits should be set to 0 so that the OUI is recognizable by all other stations.

  The OUI field is identical to the OUI assignments made to organizations for use as MAC addressing. For Ethernet the order of bits in the address field in the MAC frame is the same as the order used for the OUI field in the SNAP header (canonical order). If the protocol used in the frame is identified by a registered EtherType, the SNAP header uses 00:00:00 as the OUI, and the EtherType in the SNAP Type field. The Internet Assigned Numbers Authority (IANA) and the IEEE web sites maintain lists of assigned addresses, as well as links to other lists. Not all OUI assignments are public; however, the most recent public OUI assignments are available from a searchable database on the IEEE web site (http://standards.ieee.org/regauth/oui/index.shtml).

- **Type Field.** The Type field is locally administered by the organization. By changing the value in this field, an organization may specify individual protocols for specific uses.

- **Protocol Data.** The next-higher layer protocol data.

Novell Raw

Novell IPX Raw, or Novell Raw, is actually a Network Layer protocol, but because 802.1Q Clause 8.9.1 treats it as an LLC encapsulation, the description fits best here. The 802.3 Length/Type field is used as Length. Immediately following the 802.3 Length/Type field is the two octet Novell IPX checksum field. This checksum field is filled with the default (unused) checksum value of all ones, or FFFF in hexadecimal. This default value is treated like a protocol identifier. The remainder of the 802.3 data field would be filled with other IPX header and data. Interestingly, the default checksum value gives the appearance of a global broadcast for an 802.2 encapsulation. This frame type pre-dates the adoption of the 802.3 standard. Some printers still announce print services using Novell encapsulations, so this is included simply because it still appears on networks, though it is rarely actually used as an active protocol. The format for a Novell IPX Raw frame is shown in Figure 5-20.

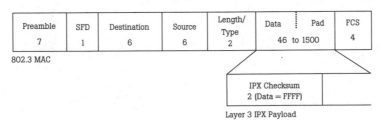

Figure 5-20. *Novell Raw encapsulation*

Summary

This chapter described the normal operation, operating rules, and protocols used by bridging devices, including switches operating as Layer 2 multiport bridges. The chapter also described the sublayers found within the Data Link Layer, except for the MAC Layer, which was described as part of Chapter 4, "Media Access Control Layer."

- Although there are several different styles or modes of bridge operation, the transparent bridge found with Ethernet has become the most common. A short description of several bridging modes was given. The rules for deciding when to forward, as well as forwarding limitations, were described. Included in the discussion were details about several configurations related to bridging, such as prioritization and VLANs.

- The frame structure, field organization, and definitions for various Data Link Layer protocols were provided.

Common usage refers to some of these Data Link Layer protocols as encapsulations. Protocols such as 802.2 LLC or 802 SNAP provide a means to define multiple private or reserved protocols. Other Layer 2 protocols are used for specific link management tasks, such as link aggregation.

Chapter Review Questions

To aid in your comprehension of important concepts, the following questions are provided. Refer to this book's Introduction for a general legend that indicates the anticipated difficulty of each question. For answers to these review questions, see Appendix I, "Answers to Chapter Review Questions."

1. In transparent bridging, which does all the work in locating the destination station in a transmitted frame: the station or the OSI Layer 2 bridge (switch)?

2. In source route bridging, which does all the work in locating the destination station in a transmitted frame: the station or the OSI Layer 2 bridge (switch)?

3. When a frame is received by a bridge, the bridge places which of the following fields in temporary tables for use in making forwarding decisions? Mark all that apply.

___ Destination MAC Address

___ Source MAC Address

___ Destination IP Address

___ Source IP Address

4. If the bridge does not yet know where the destination Ethernet MAC address in a received frame resides, it will

___ ARP for that host

___ Ping that host

___ Forward to all ports

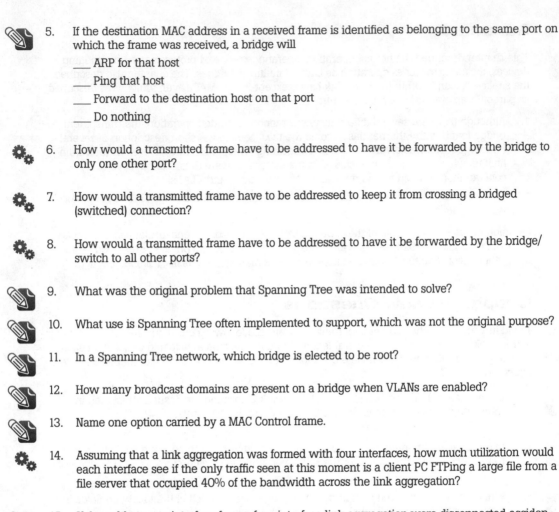

5. If the destination MAC address in a received frame is identified as belonging to the same port on which the frame was received, a bridge will

___ ARP for that host

___ Ping that host

___ Forward to the destination host on that port

___ Do nothing

6. How would a transmitted frame have to be addressed to have it be forwarded by the bridge to only one other port?

7. How would a transmitted frame have to be addressed to keep it from crossing a bridged (switched) connection?

8. How would a transmitted frame have to be addressed to have it be forwarded by the bridge/switch to all other ports?

9. What was the original problem that Spanning Tree was intended to solve?

10. What use is Spanning Tree often implemented to support, which was not the original purpose?

11. In a Spanning Tree network, which bridge is elected to be root?

12. How many broadcast domains are present on a bridge when VLANs are enabled?

13. Name one option carried by a MAC Control frame.

14. Assuming that a link aggregation was formed with four interfaces, how much utilization would each interface see if the only traffic seen at this moment is a client PC FTPing a large file from a file server that occupied 40% of the bandwidth across the link aggregation?

15. If the cable to one interface from a four-interface link aggregation were disconnected accidentally, would that cause the logical interface formed by the aggregation to fail?

16. If a link aggregation group was defined on two bridges, would an aggregation form itself if a second cable were connected between the two bridges, or would it require that the bridges be further configured and the newly active interfaces explicitly specified?

17. If an eligible interface received an OAM loopback command on a given interface, what would happen to any subsequent traffic received on that interface?

18. What was the major limiting factor of the LLC encapsulation that was addressed by creating the SNAP encapsulation?

19. What four protocols are referred to as the encapsulation choices for Ethernet?

CHAPTER 6
Network Layer

The Network Layer relies upon the services of the Data Link Layer to move messages along individual network segments, such as across an Ethernet collision domain or a WAN link. The Network Layer is responsible for end-to-end delivery of the message, where the Data Link Layer was only responsible for moving the message across one point-to-point link or across one collision domain or broadcast domain. (See Figure 6-1.)

Application
Presentation
Session
Transport
Network
Data Link
Physical

Medium

Figure 6-1. *The Network Layer in relation to the other OSI layers*

Because the Network Layer and Data Link Layer are operating more or less independently of each other, each has its own addressing scheme and error detection and reporting mechanisms. IP networks use the Internet Control Message Protocol (ICMP) to notify other Network Layer devices about detected problems. The Network Layer relies on the Address Resolution Protocol (ARP) to create a temporary association between a Network Layer and Data Link Layer address.

Although this chapter describes the now-dominant IP protocol, many other Layer 3 legacy protocols are still in use (such as NetBEUI and IPX).

Routers

Routers operate at the Network Layer (see Figure 6-2) and are used to separate logical networks (which may be called networks, subnetworks, or subnets). The customary configuration is to use a single broadcast domain to support a single logical network. However poor the practice may be, it is easily possible for two or more logical networks (subnets) to exist within a single broadcast domain.

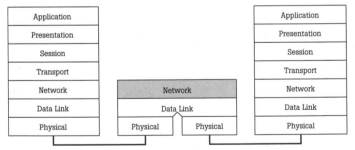

Figure 6-2. *Where a router fits in the OSI Model*

There are two common uses for the term *gateway*. It is frequently used interchangeably with the term *router* when discussing IP configurations and concepts. This usage is supported by the RFC documents. It is also used less commonly

to describe the OSI Layer 7 function of translating between completely dissimilar networks, such as between an IBM mainframe environment using the EBCDIC character and command set, and the more common UNIX-based or Windows environments using ASCII character and command set. This text uses the term *router* for OSI Layer 3 forwarding references, and *gateway* for OSI Layer 7 conversion references in order to provide specific and precise descriptions.

Note: *For specific information about routers and routing protocols, consider one of the router-based certification programs that are available. This text defers to those focused training programs for most router and all routing protocol information.*

OSI Model Implications: Effect of Forwarding

This topic is in two parts: The first part is about how routing tables change depending on where in the network they are seen. The second part is about how addresses are handled by a router as it forwards a datagram.

If a network is connected to the Internet, it has routers in it. Within a private network, each router port connects a logical subnetwork to the larger network, and each router port requires a unique address from within the address range serviced by that router interface. If it is not connected to the Internet, it is entirely possible that the IP addresses in use in that network are arbitrarily chosen, and therefore follow few of the normal conventions, except the requirement that a unique address range be used for each logical network.

It is worthwhile to note that routers closer to the core of the network or Internet use different subnet masks than local hosts use because they need to know only enough to forward a message to the next router along the way.

Inside a private network, the network manager will have further divided the address range, and will assign more restrictive subnet masks (fewer host bits) to have each router port support a unique block of addresses.

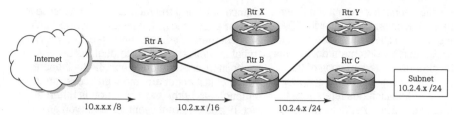

Figure 6-3. *Sample multiple router network connected to the Internet*

Example: In Figure 6-3, the example network is connected to the Internet and has a Class A (/8 CIDR) address space to use. Notice that to the Internet, the entire example network is summarized into the 10.x.x.x /8 routing entry. Any traffic bound for a 10.x.x.x address is sent to Router A. Router A consults its route tables and learns that any traffic bound for 10.2.x.x /16 should be sent to Router B. Router B consults its route tables and learns that any traffic bound for 10.2.4.x /24 should be sent to Router C. Router C has that subnet directly attached and forwards traffic to specific hosts on the subnet.

Within any given broadcast domain or collision domain, for a router to receive a frame the frame must be addressed specifically to the MAC address of the router's network interface or be a MAC Layer broadcast address. Other MAC addresses are not recognized by the network interface in the router. If the MAC address is recognized the interface accepts the frame, strips off the Layer 2 information, and hands the remainder of the message up to Layer 3. Because the Layer 2 framing is removed before the Layer

3 routing engine receives the request, the outbound network interface in the router must create new Layer 2 framing to forward the request. On the destination interface of the router the Layer 2 addressing is altered to reflect the proper source and destination MAC addressing for the next segment. The Layer 3 fields of the request are usually undisturbed.

In Figure 6-4, the Layer 2 information is discarded before Layer 3 receives a request. If forwarding is appropriate, the router creates new Layer 2 framing on the outbound interface.

Internet Protocol (IP)

The TCP/IP protocol originated from research funded by the Defense Advanced Research Projects Agency (DARPA) and continues to evolve through the efforts of a large number of organizations. The protocol is commonly referred to as TCP/IP, although this is only one combination of the basic protocol, Internet Protocol (IP), together with one of the OSI Layer 4 protocols, Transport Control Protocol (TCP).

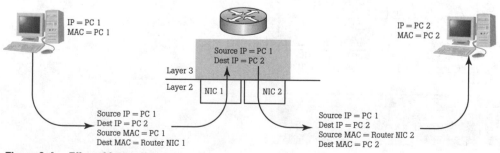

Figure 6-4. *Effect of forwarding*

To obtain specific information about the different clarifications and additions to the basic TCP/IP protocol suites, you are advised to obtain copies of the published Request for Comment documents (RFCs). Begin by obtaining a recent copy of the rfc-index.txt file, which offers a short description about each document and includes references to other RFCs that may obsolete or supercede each entry. The process that a draft RFC undergoes is becoming much more rigorous, and is substantially different than when the process began. RFCs are now published first as informational, and for certain proposals they also follow a standards track. If they pass through the rigorous standards track they are assigned a second number in the format STD xxxx that indicates that they are also an Internet Official Protocol Standard. RFCs may be obtained from many sources, perhaps the best of which is www.rfc-editor.org. Most of the RFCs are text documents ending in .TXT, although some are PostScript (.PS) or .PDF files.

Figure 6-5 shows several of the common protocols that operate on top of the IP protocol, and their dependencies. One of the first reference RFCs is included for each protocol in Figure 6-5. Although a specific RFC is listed for each protocol, there are usually several RFCs that apply. IP itself is a connectionless protocol that relies on higher layers to guarantee delivery of data. As a general description, the IP protocol provides "best effort" or "connectionless" delivery of data. User Datagram Protocol (UDP) provides a slightly better chance of having the data delivered because it is a Layer 4, but because it is also a connectionless protocol there is still no guarantee. TCP provides "reliable" delivery of data through its Layer 4 connection-oriented operation. IP itself operates on top of just about any medium access protocol, although easily the most common is Ethernet. In fact, IP and Ethernet seem to have won as the protocols of choice for local area networks (LANs).

Note that the dependencies implied by Figure 6-5 are somewhat indistinct. For instance, an Address Resolution Protocol (ARP) frame contains some of the fields required by IP, but not all. DNS services generally run over UDP, but may also run over TCP if a more reliable connection is appropriate for the application. IP is usually transmitted over local area network connections such as Ethernet and 802.11 wireless, but may also be sent over telecommunications links such as Point-to-Point Protocol (PPP).

Each protocol layer places additional overhead that measurably reduces network throughput. The amount of overhead depends on each specific protocol. If the datagram represented by Figure 6-6 were a minimum sized frame, there would be room for 6 octets of higher-layer data (9 percent of the frame). Almost the entire frame is overhead. A maximum-sized frame would have room for 1460 octets of higher-layer data (96 percent of the frame). This illustrates how larger frame sizes utilize the network more efficiently. It is best to configure all equipment to utilize the largest frame size that crosses all interconnected LAN segments. Doing so optimizes the bandwidth usage. Probably the most common maximum transmission unit (MTU—indicating the size of the data field at Layer 2) is 1500 octets.

OSI Layers					
7	TELNET RFC 854	FTP File Transfer Protocol RFC 959	SMTP Simple Mail Transfer Protocol RFC 821	SNMP Simple Network Management Protocol RFC 1098	DNS Domain Name System RFC 1034
6					
5					
4		TCP RFC 793		UDP RFC 768	
3	ARP RFC 826	RARP RFC 903	ICMP RFC 792	BOOTP RFC 951	DHCP RFC 2131
	IP RFC 791				
2	802.2				
1	802.3 / 802.5 / 802.11 / Other		Media Access Protocols		

Figure 6-5. *IP and the OSI Model*

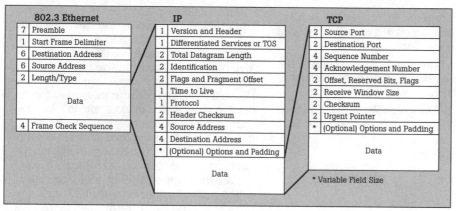

Figure 6-6. *TCP datagram example. A minimum-sized TCP datagram allows for 6 octets of data field.*

In Figure 6-6, a minimum-sized Ethernet frame allows room for 6 octets of TCP data. A minimum-sized Ethernet frame is 64 octets, of which 18 octets are Ethernet fields (64 − 18 = 46). IP adds at least another 20 octets of header (46 − 20 = 26). TCP adds at least another 20 octets of header (26 − 20 = 6).

IPv4 Addressing

IP version 4 (IPv4) addresses are globally controlled and issued in fixed address blocks. Because the purpose of the Internet is to interconnect many networks into a single worldwide virtual network, there must be a single entity managing the address assignments, the Internet Assigned Numbers Authority (IANA). If there are no plans for your network to be connected to the Internet, it is not necessary to obtain an official address range, and one of the reserved private network ranges from RFC 1918 may be used instead.

Table 6-1 shows three address blocks that are reserved for private network use. These three blocks are arbitrarily selected ranges that are no different from any other address range; however, they are not routed through the Internet by Internet service providers (ISPs). Private networks often use one of these address ranges for internal use, and then use Network Address Translation

(NAT) to link to the Internet. In Table 6-1, Classless Inter-Domain Routing (CIDR) notation shows the network portion of the IP address followed by the number of network bits in the address in the format *network address/number of bits in network address.*

Table 6-1. *IANA reserved three address ranges for private networks in RFC 1918*

Private Address Space	CIDR Notation
10.0.0.0–10.255.255.255	10.0.0.0/8
172.16.0.0–172.31.255.255	172.16.0.0/12
192.168.0.0–192.168.255.255	192.168.0.0/16

To obtain a unique IP network address range most private networks should contact their local ISP. Addresses are also available from local Internet registries (LIR), national Internet registries (NIR), or the appropriate regional Internet registry. The IANA web site and each organization below maintains a list of countries and the responsible registry. There are presently only five such regional registries (see Figure 6-7):

- African Network Information Center (AfriNIC). The continent of Africa.

- Asia Pacific Network Information Centre (AP-NIC). The entire Asia Pacific region (Asia and Oceania).

- American Registry for Internet Numbers (ARIN). North America, a portion of the Caribbean and North Atlantic islands.
- Latin American and Caribbean Internet Addresses Registry (LACNIC). Latin America and the Caribbean.
- Réseaux IP Européens Network Coordination Centre (RIPE NCC). Europe, the Middle East, and parts of Asia.

An IPv4 address is four octets, or 32 binary bits, in length. To improve readability, the thirty-two 1s and 0s in an IPv4 address are separated into four groups of eight bits (four octets), and then converted by octet into decimal. A period is used to separate the decimal number representing each octet. The period is inserted to ensure that the separation is obvious, and to make the address format immediately evident. The resulting number is in a format known as *dotted-decimal*.

If you are viewing an IP address with a protocol analyzer or other network diagnostic tool, you see the address in either hexadecimal or dotted-decimal notation. Using an example address of 192.168.5.130, the different formats are shown in Table 6-2. If you will be dealing with IP addresses regularly, it would be beneficial to practice making these conversions.

Initially, the 32-bit IPv4 address range was divided into five classes of addresses. Class A offered the largest number of available hosts, Class B offered a smaller number, and Class C offered the smallest user range. It is very difficult to obtain a new IPv4 address block assignment at this time. Class D was reserved for a special user-definable and limited form of broadcasting, and Class E was reserved.

In Table 6-3, the Address Range column specifies part of the first octet of the address and is commonly used as a quick check of the legacy address class.

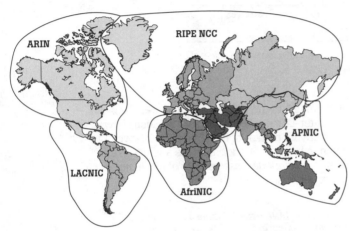

Figure 6-7. *Geographic responsibilities for the five regional Internet registries presently active*

Note: *There are actually fewer hosts than suggested by Table 6-3 for each class of address. Use of all 1s or all 0s in the host identifier field is not permitted.*

Figure 6-8 shows how the first bits determined the class of an IPv4 address. Each IPv4 address is divided into two logical fields: a network identifier field and a host identifier field.

By locating the first binary zero value (reading left to right), you can determine which legacy class of address was being used. Because binary numbering is not user friendly, most people quickly learn the decimal number ranges that correspond to each class shown in Table 6-3. The remaining binary digits represent the host address within the specified network.

Table 6-2. *Sample IP address numbering system conversion table*

Binary	1100 0000	1010 1000	0000 0101	1000 0010
Hexadecimal	C 0	A 8	0 5	8 2
Dotted-Decimal	192	168	5	130

Table 6-3. *Formal (legacy) IPv4 address class ranges*

IP Address Class	Address Range (First Octet)	Default Subnet Mask	Unique Addresses
Class A	0–127	255.0.0.0	16,777,216
Class B	128–191	255.255.0.0	65,536
Class C	192–223	255.255.255.0	256

It is sometimes thought that you can learn the network address by simply identifying the address class. This is far from true. The address classes were originally used to administratively manage the issuance of address blocks. Once issued, these blocks may be combined with other blocks or split into smaller blocks. RFC 1338 was published in 1992, and was even then proposing issuance of combined blocks of Class C addresses instead of the dwindling supply of Class A and B address ranges. RFC 4632 officially obsoleted the concept of classful addressing, and offered a best practices strategy for CIDR addressing.

The process of combining two or more contiguous address blocks into a single logical and larger network address block is called *supernetting*. Splitting an address block into smaller ranges is called *subnetting*.

Broadcast domains with large numbers of hosts are not desired for a variety of operational and security reasons. Routers are used to separate broadcast domains (such as VLANs). It has become common practice for network managers to take several bits from the host field to create smaller address blocks with fewer host addresses. This process of subnetting serves to subpartition a network address block.

The term *subnet* can be confusing because it has been commonly used in at least three different ways (see Figure 6-9). Common practice uses *subnet* to describe 1) the network identifier indicated by the legacy address class; 2) the complete network identifier—including any subnet; and 3) the binary bits taken from what the class code suggests is part of the host field. Using the third definition for subnet, RFC 950 explicitly states that all zeros or all ones in the subnet field should not be used. RFC 1878 updated this by including all zeros and all ones in the subnet field as valid subnets.

Each port on a router requires a unique network address range, and this is a simple method of obtaining the necessary addresses—just cut pieces off your assigned address space. In Figure 6-9, bits were taken from the host field of an address and included as part of the network address using the process of subnetting.

Combining the address from Table 6-2 and using the same subnetting as Figure 6-9, the

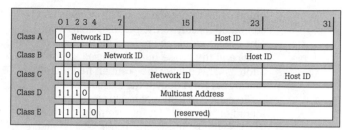

Figure 6-8. *IPv4 address class range identification*

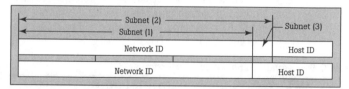

Figure 6-9. *IP subnet definitions*

network identifier for the example address would be as shown in Table 6-4. The resulting host bits in the example are nulled out with "x" characters in the binary representation, and zeros are substituted when converting to hexadecimal and dotted-decimal notation.

Table 6-4. *Example IP address conversi*

Binary	1100 0000	1010 1000	0000 0101	10xx xxxx
Hexadecimal	C 0	A 8	0 5	8 0
Dotted-Decimal	192	168	5	128

Subnet Mask

These examples highlight the need for some way to tell all network devices how to read the 32-bit address. The mechanism used to describe how to split the address into network identifier and host identifier is called the *subnet mask*. It is precisely because of this process that address classes became meaningless in an operating network environment. All that matters is the full 32-bit address and the subnet mask.

The configured subnet mask allows each host to determine how much of the 32-bit address is used to identify which IP network or subnet the host belongs to, and how much is used to uniquely identify each host. This scheme can be compared loosely to the postal system, where a city and street name are used for the network address and the house number is used for the host address. This allows the postman (the router) to quickly sort and deliver the messages.

To calculate a subnet mask, set all network identifier bits to "1" (in this example, use the first 26 bits—the leftmost three octets plus two more bits from the rightmost octet) and the host identifier bits to "0" (the rightmost six bits). The string of 1s and 0s is then converted to dotted-decimal, and the resulting number becomes the subnet mask. This example is the correct subnet mask for the address in Table 6-5.

Table 6-5. *Example subnet mask conversion*

Binary	1111 1111	1111 1111	1111 1111	1100 0000
Hexadecimal	F F	F F	F F	C 0
Dotted-decimal	255	255	255	192

Most configurations use CIDR notation, but some legacy systems still require the dotted-decimal or hexadecimal format for a subnet mask. However, as long as you can convert between the three types of addressing formats, you should be able to satisfy any requirement.

Be careful when creating and configuring the subnet mask. The block of 1s and 0s should be contiguous—no mixing of 1s and 0s. It is easily possible to accidentally create and use a noncontiguous mask where some bits are skipped over, such as

11111111 11111111 11111111 01000000

This is not only a bad idea, but you will find that most software does not support noncontiguous masks. You would also be constantly troubleshooting the resulting addressing problems—not to mention what would be required to administer the addresses themselves and explain them to anyone else. Noncontiguous masks most often result from changing the mask by subtracting or adding to the decimal number instead of converting to binary first. CIDR notation avoids this problem entirely.

Host Identifier

Nearly any combination of the host identifier bits in an address may be used for any device connecting to the subnet. There are two exceptions. The host identifier bits should never be set to all "1" or all "0." These two addresses are reserved as current and historical broadcast addresses, respectively. This means that all subnet address blocks have two fewer usable addresses than the total possible for that block, which may be expressed as $(n - 2)$. For example, a CIDR /24 address block has only 254 available host addresses out of the 256 unique addresses.

Other Special Addresses

The IANA web site (www.iana.org/assignments/ipv4-address-space/) is the official, maintained document and lists the appropriate RFC references for each of the special addresses:

- **0.0.0.0/8**

  The address of all 0s is sometimes used by a host as a source address during initialization as it joins the network, usually when soliciting a DHCP address. It is never permitted to form a valid destination address.

  An address of all 0s was used as the broadcast address, but this has since fallen into disuse.

  This address also appears often in routing tables as 0.0.0.0 and means the "default route" (see RFC 1519).

  If in a source address the network identifier field of an IPv4 address is set to all 0s, the message is from or for a specified host on only the local broadcast domain.

  0.0.0.*<host identifier>*

- **10.0.0.0/8**. This address block is reserved for private network use (not routed to the Internet) in RFC 1918.

- **127.0.0.0/8**. This address block is called the local loopback address and is reserved for testing. If a host uses this address to send data, the IP protocol stack is to return the data to the sending application without actually having transmitted it out on the network.

If a frame is somehow observed on a network bearing a 127.x.x.x network address, it should never be forwarded. The value found in the host identifier portion of the address does not matter.

- **169.254.0.0/16**. This is described as the "link local" address block. An address in this range may be auto-configured by a host if no other IP address is available, and may then be used for communications between hosts on the local broadcast domain. For example, a Windows PC picks an address in this range if a static address is not configured and no DHCP response is obtained. See RFC 3927 for details.

- **172.16.0.0/12**. This address block is reserved for private network use (not routed to the Internet) in RFC 1918.

- **192.0.2.0/24**. This small address block is reserved for use in documentation and example code. Addresses within this block should never be routed to the Internet.

- **192.88.99.0/24**. This block is reserved for use in situations where IPv4 and IPv6 are both in use, and are referred to as 6to4 relay anycast addresses. See RFC 3068 for details.

- **192.168.0.0/16**. This address block is reserved for private network use (not routed to the Internet) in RFC 1918.

- **224.0.0.0/4**. This address block is reserved for use as IPv4 multicast addresses.

- **255.255.255.255/32**. The address of all 1s is used as a broadcast address for the local broadcast domain. This form of broadcast is received by all hosts in all subnets if multiple logical networks are present in the broadcast domain. It is never permitted to form a valid source address. Broadcasts addressed this way should not be forwarded beyond the local subnet.

- **x.x.x.(address)**. If the *host identifier* field of an IPv4 address is set to all 1s, the message is intended for all hosts within the local logical subnet (refer to Figure 6-7). Another form of this directed broadcast or subnet broadcast is to distinguish the subnetted portion of the address from the network identifier, and set all subnet and host identifier bits to 1 for an "all subnets" broadcast. An older form of the subnet broadcast that is no longer used was to fill the host identifier field with all 0s. A subnet broadcast address is never permitted as a valid source address.

<network identifier> <subnet identifier><host identifier>

Note: *Most networks are configured with the routers at either the lowest or highest addresses in the subnet range, the lowest being perhaps more common.*

Host Configuration

Host configurations are critical to proper IP network operation. Depending on the network and which parameters are improperly set, incorrect configurations may function properly for a time. If the network design is changed slightly the host may stop operating, or will operate intermittently for no apparent reason.

The basic configuration parameters are

- **IP address.** A unique IP address that is within the attached IP network's subnet address range.

  Example shown in dotted-decimal: 192.168.202.25

- **Subnet mask.** The bit mask that is used to identify the separation point between the network identifier and the host identifier in the host's 32-bit IP address. If not specified in the host's configuration, the IP configuration software often prompts with the default subnet mask for the legacy IP address class.

  Example: /24 or 255.255.255.0

- **Default router.** IP implementations rely upon being told the IP address of a local router. This router is where the host sends traffic destined for any nonlocal address (as determined by the address mask). If this router fails or becomes inaccessible, communication off the host's local IP segment is not possible. Many hosts now also permit configuration of a secondary router address. This configuration may be called the default *gateway* in the host configuration.

- **DNS Server(s).** Hosts use Domain Name System (DNS) servers primarily to resolve ASCII names into IP network addresses. Where possible, hosts should have more than one DNS server in their configuration to increase the chances of reaching one. Also, use of a DNS name instead of an IP address permits the server or service to be relocated to different addresses without causing connectivity problems.

  Example: www.flukenetworks.com resolves to address 129.196.231.98 today, but might not resolve to that address in the future; however, use of the DNS name works anyway.

The incidence of dynamic host configuration has risen rapidly. The Dynamic Host Configuration Protocol (DHCP; see RFC 2131) is an adaptation of the original Bootstrap Protocol (BOOTP; see RFC 951 and 1542). BOOTP required each host MAC address to be manually entered into the server tables and associated with an available IP address prior to when the host needed to connect. This was undesirable in two ways: the requirement for manual entry of each host, and the permanent allocation of an IP address for each host in the table. DHCP improved upon this method in both areas. The association of IP address to host is performed dynamically at the time the host requests an address, and the IP address is released for re-use as soon as the address lease period expires. DHCP still allows for static IP address assignments, if desired. For security purposes this may be a consideration, because it may prevent unknown hosts from automatically obtaining a valid configuration for the attached network.

IPv4 Datagram Structure

Unlike previous field descriptions in this text, the Internet Protocol fields are specified in variable bit lengths that do not always align with octet boundaries. These descriptions are therefore provided in bits instead of octets.

Internet Protocol (IPv4) Datagram Fields

Bits	Description
4	Version
4	Internet Header Length
8	Differentiated Services—formerly Type of Service
16	Total Length
16	Identification
3	Flags
13	Fragment Offset
8	Time to Live
8	Protocol
16	Header Checksum
32	Source Address
32	Destination Address
Variable	(optional) Options
Variable	Pad—used only if the Options do not end on a 32-bit boundary
	*Data

* The size of the Data field is calculated by deducting the header from the size of the Layer 2 data field.

IPv4 Field Descriptions

(See RFC 791 for the basic IPv4 fields.)

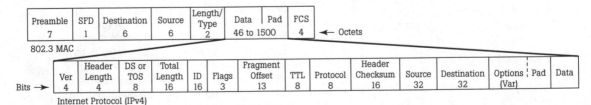

Preamble	SFD	Destination	Source	Length/Type	Data	Pad	FCS	
7	1	6	6	2	46 to 1500		4	← Octets

802.3 MAC

Ver	Header Length	DS or TOS	Total Length	ID	Flags	Fragment Offset	TTL	Protocol	Header Checksum	Source	Destination	Options (Var)	Pad	Data
4	4	8	16	16	3	13	8	8	16	32	32			

Bits →

Internet Protocol (IPv4)

Figure 6-10. *Internet Protocol version 4 (IPv4) fields*

Descriptions for the IP datagram fields are provided:

- **Version.** The protocol version field is four bits in length. It directs the protocol stack in the receiving host on what fields to expect and how to interpret those fields. The following protocol codes were early efforts at developing IPv6, and have been superseded by the release of IPv6. Current usage will be 4 or 6.

  5—Stream Transport (ST)

  7—The Next Internet (TP/IX), or more recently Common Architecture for the Internet (CATNIP)

  8—The P Internet Protocol (PIP)

  9—TCP and UDP with Bigger Addresses (TUBA)

The following field descriptions are only valid for IPv4 as indicated by the value 4 in the Version field:

- **Internet Header Length.** The Internet Header Length field is four bits and indicates the number of 32-bit words used to form the header. The minimum valid header length is five (5×32-bit words = 20 octets).

- **Differentiated Services.** The Differentiated Services (DS) field is eight bits in length and is used to define the policies used to determine the per-hop behavior (PHB) to be applied to packets received within a differentiated services domain (see Figure 6-11). Two bits within the field are currently unused, and any value found there should be ignored. The other six bits represent the Differentiated Services Codepoint (DSCP) and are used to describe a single per-hop behavior policy. In RFC 2474 Differentiated Services supersedes Type of Service from RFC 791 entirely, but offers limited backward compatibility with Precedence when used as per-hop best-effort forwarding as described in RFC 1812.

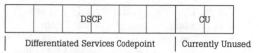

Figure 6-11. *Differentiated Services (DS) fields*

For historical reference, the Type of Service field identified the level of urgency with which the sender would like the network to forward the packet (see Figure 6-12). The network may or may not give preference according to this requested status. RFC 1349 clarified the use of these parameters and permitted only one type of service to be selected, instead of the individual bits in RFC 791, which could be specified individually or in groups.

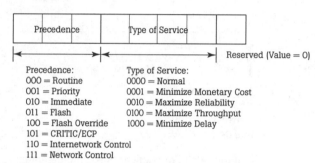

Figure 6-12. *Precedence and Type of Service (ToS) fields*

- **Total Length.** The Total Length parameter is 16 bits in length and describes the total number of octets of the datagram, including the header. Hosts are required to accept a minimum of 576 octets as a single datagram or as a fragmented datagram. The maximum value for this field is 65,535 octets. The maximum size is substantially larger than typical MTU sizes allow.

- **Identification.** The Identification field is 16 bits in length and contains an unspecified but unique value selected by the transmitting host to identify the fragments of one datagram from another, used to aid the reassembly of fragmented datagrams. The value must be unique for that source destination pair and protocol for the duration of time the datagram might be transiting the network or Internet.

- **Flags.** The Flags field is three bits in length and is used for control flags (see Figure 6-13). The first bit is reserved, and should always be set to zero. The second bit is the Don't Fragment (DF) bit, and is set to 1 when fragmentation should not occur. Setting the DF bit to 0 indicates that fragmentation of this datagram is permitted. The third bit is the More Fragments (MF) bit, and is set to 1 when the current datagram is not the last part of a fragmented datagram. Setting the MF bit to 0 indicates that this is either an entire and complete datagram, or that it is the last part of a fragmented datagram.

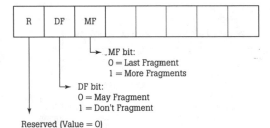

Figure 6-13. *Control flags*

If the Don't Fragment bit is set, the datagram may not be fragmented as it passes through the network. It may be discarded though, and this is the usual result if the datagram is too large for the MTU of any part of the path the DF datagram must transit.

- **Fragment Offset.** The Fragment Offset field is 13 bits in length and is used to indicate the relative position in the original datagram where this fragment begins (see Figure 6-14). The value in this field represents blocks of eight octets. For example, if the first fragment had 1480 octets of data (octet positions 0 through 1479 correspond to block positions 0 through 184), the second

fragment would have a Fragment Offset of 0000010111001, which is 185 in decimal. 185 blocks corresponds to 1480 octets (185 × 8), which is where the second fragment begins in the original datagram.

- **Time to Live.** The Time to Live (TTL) field is eight bits in length and represents values from zero to a maximum of 255. Routers reduce the count in this field before forwarding a datagram. The field was originally intended to indicate the maximum number of seconds that a message was permitted to exist on the network. Any datagram still in transit after this length of time is probably in a routing loop and should be discarded.

Increases in network speed and processing power have extended the meaning to either physical "hops" (being forwarded by a router counts as one hop, and one is deducted from the TTL field); an administratively adjusted cost that would be greater than one hop (the router deducts some value greater than one from the remaining TTL value when it forwards the datagram); or time (if a router holds a datagram for longer than one second it typically decrements the TTL by one for every additional second). If after deducting the cost for forwarding the datagram the remaining value is equal to or less than zero, the datagram is discarded. Discarding a datagram for this reason usually, but not always, causes an ICMP message to be returned to the original sending host.

- **Protocol.** The Protocol field is eight bits in length and identifies the OSI Layer 4 protocol encapsulated in the Data field of the datagram. The protocol is decoded into decimal rather than hexadecimal. The currently maintained list of registered protocols is found on the IANA web site (www.iana.org/assignments/protocol-numbers/). There are approximately 143 registered protocols,

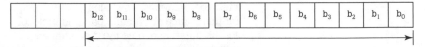

Figure 6-14. *Fragment offset field*

although the list continues to grow. The original list was updated by RFC. The last list update by RFC (now long out of date) is found in RFC 1700.

- **Header Checksum.** The IP Header Checksum is 16 bits in length and represents a simple checksum for only the header and any options. It does not validate the integrity of the Data field of the datagram. The checksum is computed by calculating the one's complement of the complement sum of all 16-bit words in the header and options. Because the checksum itself is part of the header, the checksum field is substituted with zeros for the calculation. Because some header fields are modified during transit, the checksum is recalculated each time the IP header is processed.

- **Source Address.** The Source Address is 32 bits in length. See previous sections of this chapter for further information on valid IP Source addresses.

- **Destination Address.** The Destination Address is 32 bits in length. The pool of valid Destination addresses is slightly larger than that of Source addresses because addresses reserved for specific uses, such as multicasting, may also be used.

- **Options.** Options are of different field lengths, but the options field(s) must end on a 32-bit boundary. Options may or may not be present in any given datagram, but all hosts are required to support all options. Multiple options may be present in any datagram.

There are two kinds of option: single octet options, and options formed of three parts. The second format for an option begins with an Option-Type octet (see Figure 6-15), followed by an Option-Length octet, and finally the appropriate Option-Data octets for the specified Option-Type.

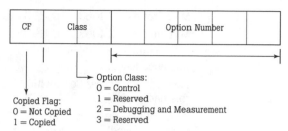

Figure 6-15. *Option-Type fields*

- **Copied Flag.** The Copied Flag (CF) field is used to indicate whether the option should be included in the header of all fragments that result from IP datagram fragmentation in transit. If the flag is set to 0, the option only appears in the first fragment. If the flag is set to 1, the option is copied into all fragments.

- **Option Class.** There are two classes of options in use: Control, or Debugging and Measurement. The option class field is set to 0 for Control and 2 for Debugging and Measurement.

- **Option Number.** There appear to be approximately 26 options that have been defined, and may or may not be in use. Specific details about each may be found in the reference document but are not provided here.

Option Number	Description (Reference)
0	End of Options List (RFC 791)
1	No Operation (RFC 791)
2	Security, DoD Basic Security (RFC 791, RFC 1108)
3	Loose Source Route (RFC 791)
4	Time Stamp (RFC 781, RFC 791)
5	DoD Extended Security (RFC 1108)
6	Commercial Security (option number might be being used as US MIL STD instead)
7	Record Route (RFC 791)
8	Stream ID (RFC 791, RFC 1122)
9	Strict Source Route (RFC 791)
10	Experimental Measurement (No reference found)

11	MTU Probe (RFC 1063, RFC 1191)
12	MTU Reply (RFC 1063, RFC 1191)
13	Experimental Flow Control (No reference found)
14	Experimental Access Control (No reference found)
15	[ENCODE] (No description or reference found)
16	IMI Traffic Descriptor (No reference found)
17	Extended Internet protocol (RFC 1385, RFC 1883, IPv6)
18	Traceroute (RFC 1393)
19	Address Extension (IPv7, believed abandoned)
20	Router Alert (RFC 2113)
21	Selective Directed Broadcast (RFC 1770)
22	(unassigned)
23	Dynamic Packet State (No reference found)
24	Upstream Multicast Packet (No reference found)
25	Quick-Start (RFC 4782)
30	Experimental (RFC 4727)

If the option is not a single octet of Option-Type, there is an Option-Type octet, an Option-Length octet, and some number of Option-Data octets. The Option-Type octet is defined above. The currently maintained list of registered option numbers is found on the IANA web site (www.iana.org/assignments/ip-parameters).

- **Option-Length.** The Option-Length octet reports the number of octets that represent the option. The length count includes the Option-Type and Option-Length octets in the count, in addition to the Option-Data octets.

- **Option-Data.** The Option-Data field is variable in size and is determined by each option separately. Some Option-Data fields change size as the datagram transits the network.

- **Padding.** Padding is added to any datagram where the header does not end on a 32-bit boundary. This is probably going to happen only when options are used. The remainder of a partially completed 32-bit word in the header is padded out to the next 32-bit boundary with zeros. All options are implemented in octets, so padding is present as one, two, or three octets of zeros.

Internet Control Message Protocol (ICMP)

The ICMP (RFC 792) is an integral part of IP. Technically, ICMP is a protocol based on IP but many ICMP functions are required in IP implementation. ICMP datagrams can be used to solicit a response (such as ping) or are generated due to an error condition detected by a host or a router. ICMP datagrams may contain more information than just their own source and destination. Those ICMP datagrams created due to an error also contain the IP header of the offending IP datagram. Analysis of these datagrams and of the original IP header offers a wealth of information in a troubleshooting scenario.

Most Useful ICMP Messages

Some of the ICMP messages are interesting, but not as useful for general network troubleshooting as others. A Timestamp ICMP datagram is interesting, but if several of these datagrams were detected on the network they would not have the same troubleshooting importance as, say, several Unreachable datagrams. The following ICMP message types are routinely used in the troubleshooting process.

PING (Echo Request/Echo Reply)

Probably the most used diagnostic tool is the *ping*, indicating a simple query and response process. The actual IP ping test is formed from ICMP Echo Request and Echo Reply datagrams. Ping is able to test connectivity and, to some extent, response times to a destination host. A simple ping test requires only a destination IP address. Note that the first ping may fail. This seems to be common when the destination host needs to perform an address resolution using ARP before replying.

Advanced ping analysis includes continuous testing to monitor for intermittent failures. For the most part, each ping request should get one response back from the target host. All IP hosts should support ICMP Echo datagrams. If more than one TCP/IP stack is running on the target, an equal number of replies may be expected. Duplicate IP addresses on a network also result in multiple replies.

Time Exceeded

For other than datagrams addressed to the router itself, when a router receives an IP datagram for forwarding it decrements the Time-to-Live (TTL) field as appropriate (see RFC 1812). If after decrementing the TTL field it discovers the TTL field equal to zero (0), it does not forward the datagram to the destination, and instead may return an ICMP Time Exceeded datagram to the original sender. Each router decrements the TTL field so that routing loops eventually clear of data. Time Exceeded datagrams are integral to the function of Trace Route.

Destination Unreachable

The Destination Unreachable message is subcategorized to include specifically what was unreachable:

- **Network Unreachable** datagrams are returned when a router is unable to deliver a datagram to the destination network. The Network Unreachable datagram indicates that a host or router did not know a path to the destination IP network. Network or routing problems are a common cause of this message type. Incorrect IP addresses are another common cause.

- **Host Unreachable** datagram is sent by a router when it is unable to forward the IP datagram to the destination host, although the correct logical network was reached. Usually the host is either turned off or not reachable due to some broadcast domain or collision domain problem. Host unreachable messages are also caused by incorrect IP addresses.

- **Port Unreachable.** After an IP datagram arrives at the destination host the IP protocol stack forwards the data payload to higher layers. If there is no process

listening to the indicated TCP or UDP port, the Port Unreachable datagram is sent back. Attempting to connect to an unsupported service is a common cause for these messages to appear spontaneously on a network. For example, trying to open an FTP session with a host that does not have an FTP server service running.

Source Quench

Hosts and routers may send a Source Quench datagram back to a sending host when the offered traffic load exceeds either the current capacity of an intermediate link or the processing capacity of the destination host. Receipt of a Source Quench should cause the recipient host to reduce its output of transmitted traffic until Source Quench messages are no longer received.

Redirect

Routers send Redirect datagrams back to the host originating a datagram when it finds that the next hop router is on the same network as the host. The host is then supposed to begin sending any additional datagrams via the router identified in the Redirect datagram. The first router still forwards the datagram that caused the Redirect.

Redirects are intended to shorten the path datagrams take while traveling to their destination. Passing a datagram across the same subnet twice is inefficient. Redirect datagrams may also be sent if there is a more efficient path for a requested Type of Service.

Parameter Problem

A router or destination host may reply with a Parameter Problem datagram when there is some problem with the header or optional parameters in the header of a datagram. The Parameter Problem response is sent only if the original datagram was discarded because of the problem. The response includes the first eight octets of the discarded datagrams data. If a higher-layer protocol uses port numbers, those port numbers are expected to appear in the returned portion of the datagrams data.

Trace Route

Trace Route is a more advanced tool that takes advantage of the ICMP error messages sent by routers and hosts. Trace Route is used to discover the one–way path that an IP datagram takes through a network destination. It does not discover the return path, which may be asymmetrical. Purists may argue that the return path is easily discovered by adding other parameters such as loose source routing, but those features are rarely or unreliably enabled nowadays.

Most IP protocol stacks support some form of the trace route command, including traceroute, tracert, and tracepath for IPv4, and traceroute6 for IPv6.

ICMP Echo Request datagrams are sent to the destination using hopefully unsupported Layer 4 port numbers. If the datagram reaches the target, a Destination Unreachable:Port Unreachable message is sent back to the source. The datagrams are sent with progressively larger TTL values, starting with a value of 1. When the first router encounters the datagram, it discards the datagram and sends an ICMP Time Exceeded message. The Trace Route application gradually increments the TTL value so that after several retries the next datagram passes through the first router (which decrements the TTL value) and the second router sends back a Time Exceeded message. This process continues until the destination is reached, or a Network Unreachable or Host Unreachable message is returned (see Figure 6-16).

This methodology allows the entire path to be discovered, providing all the following assumptions are true:

- All the routers in the datagram path support sending back ICMP "Time Exceeded" messages. Network managers sometimes disable ICMP responses on routers and firewalls for security purposes.

- There is a currently valid path through the network to the target host. If not, traceroute indicates where the path fails.

- The target host supports UDP and ICMP. If UDP or ICMP are not supported, the host does not send back a Port Unreachable message when it receives the test datagrams.

- The target host really is not running the assumed "unused" UDP port. If the host is actually using that port, no reply is given when the message finally reaches that host.

ICMP Field Definitions

ICMP traffic is sent using a specific IP datagram format, and using a value of 0x01 as the IP protocol field value in Figure 6-17.

Descriptions for the ICMP datagram fields are provided:

- **Type.** The Type field is 8 bits in length and indicates the ICMP message type. This Type field is roughly analogous to a protocol code and specifies the specific ICMP message and format of the fields that follow.

- **Code.** The Code field is 8 bits in length and specifies which, if any, clarification or additional level of detail is added to the ICMP message type. Not all ICMP messages have defined codes that accompany them. If no code is specified, the field is set to 0.

- **Checksum.** The Checksum field is 16 bits in length and covers the ICMP fields only, starting with the Type code.

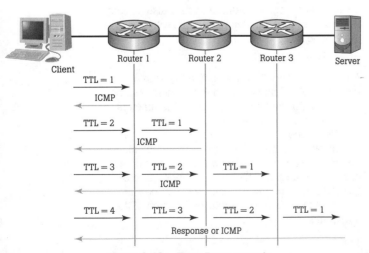

Figure 6-16. *Trace Route example*

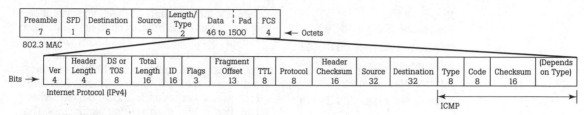

Figure 6-17. *ICMP datagram format*

ICMP Message Types

RFC 792 defines a total of 11 messages. Additions have been made by various RFCs and IETF working groups. Each type is preceded by the type value, and any assigned codes are shown immediately. Additional fields specified by many of the messages are not listed. The following ICMP messages are defined at the time of this writing.

Depending on the type of ICMP message, there are a variable number of additional fields defined. Research the ICMP message type to learn specific additional field details. The original specifying RFC is shown below, although additions may have been made within other documents. If no RFC reference was provided below, the type was specified in an IETF working group document.

Type	Name
0	Echo Reply (RFC 792)
3	Destination Unreachable (RFC 792)
	0 Network unreachable
	1 Host unreachable
	2 Protocol unreachable
	3 Port unreachable
	4 Fragmentation needed but Don't Fragment bit set
	5 Source Route failed
	6 Destination network unknown
	7 Destination host unknown
	8 Source host isolated
	9 Communication with destination network is administratively prohibited
	10 Communication with destination host is administratively prohibited

Type	Name
	11 Destination network unreachable for Type of Service
	12 Destination host unreachable for Type of Service
	13 Communication administratively prohibited
	14 Host precedence violation
	15 Precedence cutoff in effect
4	Source Quench (RFC 792)
5	Redirect (RFC 792)
	0 Redirect for the network
	1 Redirect for the host
	2 Redirect for the Type of Service and network
	3 Redirect for the Type of Service and host
6	Alternate Host Address
	0 Alternate address for host
8	Echo (Request) (RFC 792)
9	Router Advertisement (RFC 1256)
	0 Normal router advertisement
	16 Does not route common traffic
10	Router Selection (RFC 1256)
11	Time Exceeded (RFC 792)
	0 Time to live exceeded in transit
	1 Fragment reassembly time exceeded
12	Parameter Problem (RFC 792)
	0 Pointer indicates the error
	1 Missing a required option
	2 Bad Length
13	Timestamp (Request) (RFC 792)

Type	Name
14	Timestamp Reply (RFC 792)
15	Information Request (RFC 792)
16	Information Reply (RFC 792)
17	Address Mask Request (RFC 950)
18	Address Mask Reply (RFC 950)
19–29	Reserved
30	Traceroute (RFC 1393)
31	Datagram Conversion Error (RFC 1475)
32	Mobile Host Redirect
33	IPv6 Where-Are-You
34	IPv6 I-Am-Here
35	Mobile Registration Request
36	Mobile Registration Reply
37	Domain Name Request (RFC 1788)
38	Domain Name Reply (RFC 1788)
39	SKIP
40	Photuris (RFC 2521)
	0 Bad SPI
	1 Authentication failed
	2 Decompression failed
	3 Decryption failed
	4 Need authentication
5	Need authorization
41	Experimental Mobility Protocols (RFC 4065)
42–252	Unassigned
253	RFC 3892-style Experiment 1 (RFC 4727)
254	RFC 3892-style Experiment 2 (RFC 4727)

IPv6 Addressing

An IPv6 address is 16 octets, or 128 bits in length. Countless software applications, routers, gateways, DNS servers, and many other parts of a network's infrastructure have to be upgraded to support this addressing scheme. Upgrading to accommodate the larger address may be possible by simply updating the operating code and adding memory. Most recently released versions of operating systems and infrastructure hardware now support IPv6, but not all. If you have not already deployed IPv6, as a network professional you should begin planning to add IPv6 or convert your network to the IPv6 address scheme. RFC 3484 discusses which address should be used when both IPv4 and IPv6 are operating together. The transitional or co-existence schemes fall into three general techniques:

- Dual-stack (perhaps the most favored)
- Tunneling
- Translation

Available Address Space

There was a scare at the end of the 1990s that suggested that all the IPv4 Internet addresses would be consumed imminently. Although not exactly an inaccurate concern, a concurrent upsurge in malicious attacks across the Internet had the unexpected side effect of removing much of the short-term pressure for solving the shortage of addresses problem. With the rise in hacking and the availability of only relatively small blocks of IPv4 addressing, more companies implemented firewalls and other methods of security. One of those other methods of making it harder for a hacker to gain access to an internal network was to use the private address space identified in RFC 1918 through an intermediate device that performed Network Address Translation (NAT). RFC 1918 allows a company to utilize up to /8 private address space internally. A simple description of NAT is that it takes an Internet request from a station on the inside and records the pertinent identification of the station. Then it acts as that station's proxy and makes the request out into the Internet for that station but using the IP address held by the NAT server. Replies are cross-referenced in the table collected earlier and readdressed back to the original sending station on the inside. Thus, the real identity of the requesting station is unknown to the Internet. By having the first router or the firewall perform NAT services in addition to its other duties, the corporation provided one more layer of insulation from a hacker and at the same time reduced its requirement for valid Internet addresses to a handful or to even a single IP address.

This is not to say that the current IP version 4 (IPv4) address space satisfies all needs now, only that widespread conversion to the next addressing scheme, IPv6, has been delayed a few years. As the Internet reaches deeper into our culture, and almost every conceivable electronic device becomes Internet accessible, desire for unique public IP addresses grows. Most users will experience little or no inconvenience from a change to IPv6, but most network managers will find this change requires an upgrade to part or the entire network infrastructure. The longer conversion is delayed, the more likely it is that IPv6 support is available in the feature set of the equipment or software deployed in your network. Because the standards organizations are always very careful to ensure backward compatibility wherever possible, there are several efforts underway to ensure that there are well-defined methods for IPv4 and IPv6 to coexist in the same network.

Whenever the standards organizations are required to expand a specification because the older specification became bound by a limit inherent to the architecture, they ensure that the previous limit will not be an issue for a long, long time. They usually add a few new concepts to the updated standard in the process. IPv6 is no exception. Over time, numerous limiting factors were discovered in IPv4, such as the following:

- **Insufficient addresses for the burgeoning use of the Internet.** As everything from a cell phone or pager to a refrigerator becomes Internet capable there are simply not enough available addresses to support the projected demand.

- **Poor allocation of the existing address space.** Many organizations holding Class A and Class B address blocks do not actually need anywhere near that number of addresses, but they were understandably unwilling to surrender the block and readdress their entire network.

- **Fragmented address blocks.** As larger organizations changed Internet service providers without changing the address

block they are using, it caused the routing tables of the core Internet routers to grow to enormous proportions. Any block or subblock of addresses may appear anywhere in the Internet, and the core routers had to support that. As a result, the Internet community started requiring route aggregation to limit this address sprawl. It has become progressively more difficult to move an address block.

The solution to these and other problems, as well as adding more flexibility, was determined to be a 128-bit address (16 octets). 2^{128} calculates out to a decimal number with 39 digits (340,282,366,920 ,938,463,463,374,607,431,768,211,456). According to RFC 3513 only 15 percent of the possible addresses have so far been made available for assignment by the regional authorities. The new address space that IPv6 represents is so large that it has been humorously said that Earth got a pretty big block of the available addresses.

Other reasons for switching to the larger address ranges offered by IPv6 include having fixed addressing for always-on access (such as xDSL and cable to the home), for applications that are difficult, expensive, or impossible to operate through NATs (such as IP telephony, peer-to-peer gaming, and home servers), and to phase out NATs to improve the robustness, security, performance, and manageability of the Internet. Enhancements offered include serverless plug-and-play automatic configurations, end-to-end IP-layer authentication and encryption. At the same time the quality of service (QoS) features and routing protocols were carried forward from IPv4.

The major changes between IPv4 and IPv6 include

- The Source and Destination address size changed from 32 bits to 128 bits.

- The Time to Live (TTL) field became the Hop Limit field, serving the same purpose.

- The Protocol field became the Next Header field, serving the same purpose.

- The Type of Service field became the Traffic Class field, serving the same purpose but enhanced.

- The Fragmentation flags were moved out of the base header.

- The Options were moved out of the base header and became part of the data payload.

- The Header Length field was eliminated because the base header was now a fixed size.

- The Length field specifies the data payload only, because the base header size is now fixed.

- A new Flow Label field was added to facilitate routing.

The following information should be considered a simplified and incomplete summary of IPv6. A great deal of development is underway surrounding adjustments, enhancements, and additions to IPv6, and it would be impossible to provide a completely up-to-date description of everything about IPv6.

Address Notation

The format of an IPv6 address is described in RFC 4291 and is composed of eight blocks of 16 bits each (written in hexadecimal notation), separated by colons.

    FEDC:BA98:7654:3210:FEDC:BA98:7654:3210

To provide a means for all existing IPv4 addresses to continue to be supported after a conversion to IPv6 there are two formats. In both formats all leading bits are set to zeros. The first format is used as a temporary measure to tunnel IPv4 traffic through an IPv6 environment and is called an IPv4-compatible IPv6 address. In this format, bits 81 to 96 are set to all zeros, followed by a globally unique IPv4 address. This first method has been deprecated, and currently IPv6 transition mechanisms do not support it. The second format sets bits 81 to 96 to all ones, followed by a globally unique IPv4 address. This second format allows IPv4 addresses to be used in IPv6 networks and is called an IPv4-mapped IPv6 address. In both cases, the IPv4 portion of the address is usually shown in the traditional dotted-decimal notation, although it too may be shown in hexadecimal. Note that the IPv6 portion is separated by colons, and the dotted-decimal portion is separated by periods.

    0000:0000:0000:0000:0000:0000:123.234.12.34
    0000:0000:0000:0000:0000:FFFF:123.234.12.34

The format may be compressed to eliminate long strings of contiguous zeros by placing two colons together, only once in any address. The same two examples are shown again in this compressed form, where all the leading zeros were replaced by the double-colon compression notation.

    ::123.234.12.34
    ::FFFF:123.234.12.34

The shortest possible form of this zero compression format is seen with the loopback address and the unspecified address. (Datagrams bearing the loopback address are never supposed to be actually sent on the network or forwarded by any router. The unspecified address may not be configured as a source address for an interface. It is usually used temporarily by a host that does not yet have an address and is seeking one from an address server such as DHCP.)

    0:0:0:0:0:0:0:1 becomes ::1 (loopback)
    0:0:0:0:0:0:0:0 becomes :: (unspecified)

Individual blocks of 16 bits that have leading hexadecimal zeros may be shown without leading zeros, and blocks of 16 zeros may be reduced to a single zero. Both formats are shown in the following example:

    1080:0:0:0:8:800:200C:417A

This address may be further compressed using the double-colon notation that can be used *once* in an address to eliminate strings of zeros.

    1080::8:800:200C:417A

To use a literal IPv6 address as part of a URL it is necessary to place the address (in any of the acceptable formats) between square-bracket characters because the colon is itself a reserved character for URLs (RFC 2732).

    http://[1080:0:0:0:8:800:200C:417A]/index.
    html

The current system (above) requires up to 39 characters to represent a full IPv6 address (32 hexadecimal digits and seven colons). To reduce the typical address length, RFC 1924 proposed converting the address to base 85, which would result in constant address lengths of only 20 characters. The character set for base 85 was selected from the ASCII character set, and uses 0–9, A–Z, a–z, and most punctuation characters. The sample IPv6 address of *1080:0:0:0:8:800:200C:417A* would appear as *4)+k&C#VzJ4br>0wv%Yp* using this format. This proposal was not adopted.

Network Address Prefix

An IPv6 address is separated into two fields: the network identifier called the prefix, and the interface identifier. The prefix designation that accompanies an address performs the same task as the subnet mask in IPv4: It identifies which part of the full address represents the network identifier and which represents the interface identifier. This is written using Classless Inter-Domain Routing (CIDR) notation as described in RFC 1519. The use of subnet masks was discontinued in favor of CIDR.

In the address below the IPv6 address example is accompanied by a CIDR prefix length designation that indicates that the leftmost 64 bits represent the network identifier. Immediately below the example is the same address rewritten with all hexadecimal numbers represented, and "x" characters substituted for the interface identifier. Because each hexadecimal number represents four binary bits, the /64 notation means that the leftmost 16 hexadecimal numbers in the full address are the network identifier prefix.

1080:0:0:0:8:800:200C:417A/64

1080:0000:0000:0000:xxxx:xxxx:xxxx:xxxx

Interface Identifier

Each interface that is active in an IPv6 network is required to have a unique IPv6 address. Because multiple network prefixes may exist on the same broadcast domain, as seen in IPv4, more than one address may be assigned to an interface. In most cases, the address is formed from the network prefix and an interface identifier derived from the MAC address in a modified IEEE EUI-64 format.

The modified EUI-64 format is created by complementing (inverting) the universal/local bit in the first octet of a MAC address. In IEEE 802.3 Ethernet, the first two bits of the MAC address

hold special significance. The first bit indicates whether the address is an individual or group address, and the second bit indicates whether the address scope is universal or locally administered.

A fixed value of FFFE in hexadecimal is also inserted after the third octet of the Ethernet MAC address. (RFC 2464) In the following example the first octet is also modified as directed by inverting the universal or local bit:

00C017A00145   Ethernet MAC Address

0**2**C017**FFFE**A00145   Modified EUI-64 interface identifier

Locally administered Ethernet addresses should not be used to derive the modified EUI-64 interface identifier. If a locally administered address is used anyway, it should properly reflect the correct IPv6 local or global status as shown in Figure 6-18.

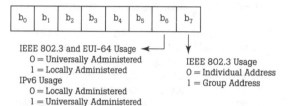

Figure 6-18. *IPv6 Universal/Local address bit in a modified EUI-64 interface identifier*

If a host already has an actual EUI-64 address, it is only required to invert the universal/local bit. The address is then fully compliant with the requirements for the interface identifier field.

If the Data Link Layer protocol is something other than Ethernet, there are definitions available for forming the interface identifier from the addressing format that is common on that type of link. If the Data Link Layer protocol does not utilize a MAC address, such as with a serial link, manual configuration or use of the global interface identifier from another interface is necessary. If another interface is referenced as a way of creating the interface identifier, the interface identifier must not change if the host is rebooted or if interfaces are added or deleted.

Address Types

There are three types of addresses defined for use in IPv6 networks: unicast, anycast, and multicast. The broadcast address found in IPv4 is replaced with expanded multicast capabilities.

Interfaces configured to use IPv6 are required to have a link-local address. They may also have site-local and global addresses. Figure 6-19 shows most of the special or reserved addresses that have been set aside for use in IPv6. From within the reserved 0:0:x:x:x:x:x:x range there are two special addresses assigned for use as Loopback and the unspecified address.

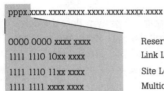

Figure 6-19. *Partial IPv6 address allocation list*

In Figure 6-19, the "p" characters represent hexadecimal address prefix. The "x" characters are used here as unspecified hexadecimal or binary placeholders. In Figure 6-19, under the hexadecimal representation of the 128-bit address is a binary representation of certain special address prefixes. All other address space is either allocated or unassigned global unicast address space.

Unicast

Unicast addresses are different from multicast and anycast addresses, in that they specify a single interface. There are at least three methods for obtaining a unicast address: manual configuration, stateful manual configuration from a server (such as DHCP), and stateless autoconfiguration.

In addition, within IPv6 there are three forms of unicast address: link-local addresses, site-local addresses (deprecated), unique-local addresses (replacement for site-local), and global addresses.

Link-Local

A link-local address is only to be used within a subnet, and should not be forwarded (routed) within a site (see Figure 6-20). The link-local ad-dress is primarily used when no routers are present, for neighbor discovery, or during automatic address configuration. The network prefix for a link-local address is FE80::/64, and the interface identifier is the modified EUI-64 address. RFC 2462 suggests that the interface identifier may be as large as 118 bits before manual address configuration is required; however, larger interface identifiers would not be compatible with the network prefix size.

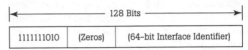

Figure 6-20. *Link-local address format*

Link-local addresses are exactly that, they are only valid on the local subnet prefix. Routers are not to forward any datagram with a source or destination link-local address.

Special addresses:

* The reserved address of 0:0:0:0:0:0:0:1 is called the local loopback address and is considered a link-local address. It is generally used for testing. If a host uses this address to send data, the IP protocol stack is to return the data to the sending application without actually having transmitted it out on the network. If a frame is somehow observed on a network bearing a local loopback address it should never be forwarded. Compare with the IPv4 address of 127.0.0.1.

* The reserved address of 0:0:0:0:0:0:0:0 is called the unspecified address and is considered a link-local address. It is sometimes used temporarily by a host as a source address during initialization (as it attempts to join the network). Use of this address as a source indicates that the sending host has no address. It is never permitted to form a valid destination address.

Site-Local

Site-local addresses are used within a single site (see Figure 6-21). The network prefix for a site-lo-cal address is FEC0::/64, again with the modified EUI-64 interface identifier. Unlike the link-local address, the site-local address supports subnet-ting. Although not required, it is expected that the same subnet identifier is used for both local and global prefixes if the site is Internet accessible.

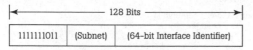

Figure 6-21. *Site-local address format*

Datagrams bearing site-local addressing may be forwarded within the site, but routers are not to forward any site-local datagram beyond that site. Site-local addressing has been deprecated in favor of unique local addressing (see the rational presented in RFC 3879).

Unique-Local

Instead of the deprecated site-local addressing, the alternative of unique-local addressing was defined in RFC 4193 (see Figure 6-22).

Selecting the value for the global ID is de-scribed in RFC 4193 and represents a pseudo-random number. To avoid contention, you must not choose sequential values.

Site-local and unique-local addressing is used as routable address space within a site but is not globally routable on the Internet, much like the three private address blocks from RFC 1918 (the 10.x.x.x, 172.16.x.x, and 192.168.x.x prefixes).

The advantages for using unique-local ad-dressing instead of site-local addressing is that they are compatible with both DNS and routing because they do not create the ambiguities that were possible with site-local addresses. Global DNS should never resolve unique-local address-ing, as these addresses only have meaning within a specific site.

Aggregatable Global

The aggregatable global unicast address was defined in RFC 2073 and 2374 (see Figure 6-23). The address is specified in three different levels: public topology, site topology, and interface iden-tifier.

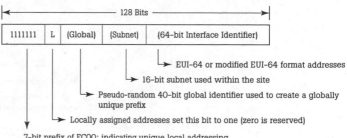

Figure 6-22. *Unique-local address format*

Figure 6-23. *Aggregatable global address format*

Two prefixes were referenced: 010 and 001. These represent global IPv6 prefixes. The next field represented the appropriate regional Internet registry. The third field typically represented the service provider you pay for Internet access. The fourth field was for local site use.

This format was deprecated in favor of the global unicast address format in RFC 3587.

Global

Global unicast addresses are formatted almost the same as the site-local address, except they are preceded with a global routing prefix (see Figure 6-24 and Figure 6-25). The global routing prefix is hierarchically administered to limit the size of routing tables on the backbone Internet routers. Route aggregation was a cornerstone consider-ation during the initial development of IPv6.

Figure 6-24. *Global address format*

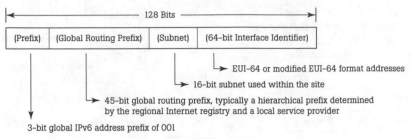

Figure 6-25. *Typical global format breakdown as used in the field*

At present, only addresses from within the global routing prefix of 001 (the leftmost three binary digits) has been made available from a local Internet registry (LIR), national Internet registry (NIR), or from the appropriate regional Internet registry (RIR). Given the relative number of addresses that this represents compared to the entire number of IPv4 addresses possible, it will be some time before the next prefix is needed.

Special addresses:

- The *IPv4-compatible IPv6* address of 0:0:0:0:0:0:x.x.x.x is considered to be a global unicast address and must use a globally unique IPv4 address within it. Bits 81 to 96, immediately left of the IPv4 address, are set to all zeros. This address was deprecated.

- The *IPv4-mapped IPv6* address of 0:0:0:0:0:FFFF:x.x.x.x is considered to be a global unicast address and must use a globally unique IPv4 address within it. Bits 81 to 96, immediately left of the IPv4 address, are set to all ones.

- The *ISATAP* (Intra-Site Automatic Tunnel Addressing Protocol) scheme address is represented by concatenating the IPv6 address of FE80:0000:0000:0000:0000:5EFE: (also written as FE80::5EFE) with the hexadecimal IPv4 address of the host. Thus, the format appears as FE80::5EFE:xxxx:xxxx (where the "x" characters are substituted with the hexadecimal IPv4 address). An example IPv4 address of 192.168.23.165 (0xC0A817A5 in hexadecimal) would be FE80::5EFE:C0A8:17A5. ISATAP requires

the configuration of a potential routers list to operate, as there is no broadcast-based discovery. See RFC 4214.

- The *Teredo* tunneling scheme address block of 2001:0000:/32 represents one of the transition technologies for migrating to IPv6. Teredo offers a means for an IPv6 client to traverse a NAT. IPv4 UDP is used as the encapsulating transport protocol and communicates via Teredo servers and Teredo relays. Teredo uses an IPv4 multicast address of 224.0.0.253 to locate other Teredo clients on the same subnet. See RFC 4380.

- The *6to4* tunneling scheme address block of 2002::/16 represents one of the transition technologies for migrating to IPv6. 6to4 permits IPv6 traffic to cross an IPv4 network without having to establish explicit tunnels first. Implementation of 6to4 relies on routers and relays using IPv4 protocol 41 to encapsulate/decapsulate the IPv6 traffic. See RFC 3056.

Anycast

Anycast addresses look the same as unicast addresses (see Figure 6-26 and Figure 6-27). To become an anycast address the unicast address must be assigned to multiple interfaces and the host(s) bearing those interfaces must be configured to recognize that address as an anycast. Typically these interfaces are in different hosts, but they may appear on different interfaces of the same host. This usage bears similarity to both a duplicate address and a virtual address used by some redundant path protocols such as Virtual Router Redundancy Protocol (VRRP).

Figure 6-26. *Reserved anycast address formed with EUI-64 or modified EUI-64 format addresses. Interface identifier is 64 bits long and begins with all ones except for the universal/local bit, which is set to zero.*

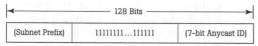

Figure 6-27. *Reserved anycast address formed with non-EUI-64 format address. The subnet prefix is at least 3 bits long (usually much longer), and the interface identifier is not longer than 118 bits.*

A datagram bearing an anycast destination is forwarded to the closest interface having the destination anycast address, as calculated by routing protocols. The anycast address may never appear as a source address and must be assigned to routers only (no end-destination hosts). Anycast destinations are to be maintained as separate "host route" entries in routing tables, and in an extreme case may be assigned a global routing prefix that is recognized as a unique routing destination by the entire Internet.

It should be noted that anycast definitions are still somewhat immature, and a variety of procedural issues must be resolved before anycast usage is more reliable when multiple possible recipients are present. Because of the way anycast is defined it is inherently nondeterministic, a second or subsequent frame in a conversation might be delivered to a destination different from the previous anycast recipient. This would result in the new destination not having the earlier datagram(s) transmitted, and thus is unable to respond to the query. Fragmented frames could likewise be impossible to reassemble.

Special addresses:

• The subnet router anycast of (subnet prefix)::0 is a unicast address where the interface identifier is set to all zeros. It is typically used by any host or application that needs to communicate with the routers on that subnet. The subnet router anycast is to be delivered to one router on the

subnet, although all routers attached to the subnet are required to support subnet router anycasts for all subnets where they have an interface configured in that subnet.

• Reserved anycast addresses are described in RFC 2526. There are two types of reserved anycast address: those formed from EUI-64 formats and those formed from non-EUI-64 formats. The rightmost seven bits are reserved as follows:

— 1111111 Reserved

— 1111110 Mobile IPv6 Home-Agents

— 0 to 1111101 Reserved

Multicast

No broadcast addresses were defined in IPv6. That function of IPv4 has been replaced with more flexible multicast services (see Figure 6-28).

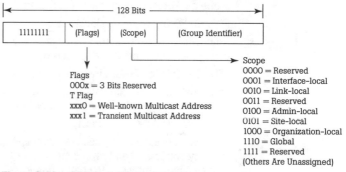

Figure 6-28. *Multicast address format*

As with IPv4 multicasting, a host must request to join a multicast group to have the traffic for that group delivered to it. If no host is requesting participation in a given multicast group, the infrastructure network that supports that host may prune distribution of the multicast traffic so that it does not enter the host's subnet at all.

Technically, the multicast address is assigned as an additional interface address. Traffic for the multicast group is then delivered to all interfaces bearing that address.

The T-flag is used to specify whether a multicast group ID is permanent or temporary within the scope. Nonpermanently assigned multicast addresses are only valid within a scope. That is, a nonpermanent multicast would not have the same meaning at a different site even if the group ID was the same. Similarly, routers should never forward a multicast beyond the scope where it is valid.

Multicast addresses should never appear as a source address.

Well-known or permanent multicast addresses within IPv6 may be further specified as node-local, link-local, site-local, and global. All multicast addresses with prefixes of FF00:0:0:0:0:0:0:0 to FF0F:0:0:0:0:0:0:0 are reserved.

Multicast addresses have scope. The scope defines how far the address is valid.

- Interface-local addresses are valid for only a single interface on a host. Typically this scope is used for loopback purposes.

  FF01:0:0:0:0:0:0:0—Interface-local prefix

- Link-local addresses are valid for the same scope as corresponding unicast addresses.

  FF02:0:0:0:0:0:0:0—Link-local prefix

- Admin-local addresses are administratively configured and represent a small scope.

  FF04:0:0:0:0:0:0:0—Admin-local prefix

- Site-local addresses are valid for the same scope as corresponding unicast addresses.

  FF05:0:0:0:0:0:0:0—Site-local prefix

- Organization-local addresses are administratively configured and represent a larger scope—usually intended to span multiple sites within one organization.

  FF08:0:0:0:0:0:0:0—Organization-local prefix

- Global addresses are valid for the entire IPv6 Internet.

  FF0E:0:0:0:0:0:0:0—Global prefix

- Unassigned address scopes are available to define additional multicast regions.

In addition to specific prefix meanings, there are a number of assignments for suffix meanings. For example, the suffix of FF0x:x:x:x:x:x:101 indicates Network Time Protocol and would be used to communicate between all the NTP servers within the scope identified by the multicast prefix.

IPv6 Datagram Structure

The Internet Protocol version 6 fields are specified in variable bit lengths that do not always align with octet boundaries. These descriptions are therefore provided in bits instead of octets in Figure 6-29.

Internet Protocol (IPv6) Fields

A listing of the IPv6 frame fields is provided:

Bits	Description
4	Version
8	Traffic Class
20	Flow Label
16	Payload Length
8	Next Header
3	Hop Limit
128	Destination Address
128	Source Address
*	Data Payload **

* The size of the Data field is calculated by deducting the header from the size of the Layer 2 data field.

** The beginning of the Data Payload field may be occupied by optional extension headers.

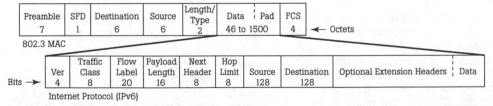

Figure 6-29. *Internet Protocol version 6 fields*

IPv6 Field Descriptions

Some IPv4 header fields have been made optional or have been dropped altogether to reduce the size of the most common header. See RFC 2460 for the basic IPv6 fields.

Descriptions for the IPv6 frame fields are provided:

- **Version.** The Version field is 4 bits in length and directs the protocol stack in the receiving host on what fields to expect, and how to interpret those fields. For IPv6 the version number is 6.

- **Traffic Class.** The Traffic Class field is 8 bits in length and is used to define various forms of Differentiated Service. This field is used to identify different classes or priorities for IPv6 datagrams, such as those defined in RFC 2474, RFC 2475, RFC 2597, and RFC 3246.

- **Flow Label.** The Flow Label field is 20 bits in length and is used to identify a particular flow. Usage of flows requires both a flow label that is not zero *and* the same source and destination address to provide a unique flow identification.

  The source station assigns the flow label and is expected to ensure that the same flow label is not reused within 60 seconds, even if the source station is rebooted. Datagrams received 60 seconds or more after the last datagram containing the same flow label may not be assumed to be part of the same flow, unless the upper-layer protocol has defined a longer time interval or has otherwise refreshed the state of the flow in some way. Any flow label set to all zeros is not labeled. Nonzero flow labels are considered labeled. The flow label assigned by the source must arrive at the destination unchanged.

- **Payload Length.** The Payload Length field is 16 bits in length and specifies the size of the data payload. This field explicitly excludes the header; however, *extension* headers are considered part of the data payload and are included in the length. The Payload Length is specified in octets. The largest number possible for this 16-bit field is 65,535 octets.

IPv6 requires that hosts be capable of processing a minimum MTU of 1280, and set a default MTU size of 1500 on Ethernet. If the source host is trying to send a datagram larger than the path MTU (RFC 1981), it may pre-fragment the frame before sending, but that is strongly discouraged. Hosts are expected to perform path MTU discovery before transmitting data, or to use the minimum MTU size. Although provisions are defined, fragmentation is not supposed to be commonplace as it is with IPv4. IPv6 routers are even encouraged to discard datagrams that exceed the MTU and return ICMP "datagram too big" messages instead.

For desired payloads that exceed the 65,535 octet limit, RFC 2675 defines a method of specifying payloads of up to 4,294,967,295 octets, and refers to this usage as creating jumbograms. The Payload Length field is set to all zero when jumbograms are present. Jumbograms are only appropriate for links with an MTU larger than 65,575. It should be noted that typical MTU sizes at this time are a small percentage of the size allowed by the 16-bit field.

- **Next Header.** The Next Header field is 8 bits in length and identifies the header that follows immediately after the IPv6 header. If extension headers are used, this code identifies the header type. Each subsequent Next Header field is used in the same manner. The protocol type codes used after any extension headers are the same as those used for IPv4.

- **Hop Limit.** The Hop Limit field is 8 bits in length and indicates the remaining number of hops that this datagram is permitted before being discarded. Usage is essentially the same as with the Time to Live (TTL) field in IPv4; however, no expectation of time is associated with the count as it originally was in IPv4. Each router forwarding the datagram decrements the count, and discards any datagram where the resulting count is not greater than zero.

- **Source Address.** The Source Address field is 128 bits in length and identifies the address of the originator of the datagram.

- **Destination Address.** The Destination Address field is 128 bits in length and identifies the address of the intended recipient of the datagram. Unlike the IPv4 destination address, it is possible that if a routing header is present in an extension header, this destination address may not be the ultimate recipient.

- **Data Payload.** The beginning part of the Data Payload field is occupied by any optional IPv6 extension headers. Following any optional extension headers is the upper-layer data, such as TCP.

Optional IPv6 Extension Headers

In IPv4 any desired options were included in the header, but in IPv6 the optional headers are included as separate headers placed between the fixed-size base header and any upper-layer information that may be in the data payload. The optional extension headers are actually part of the data payload.

Extension headers must be processed in the exact order they appear. Consequently, there is a recommended order for the appearance of these optional extension headers:

Code	Description (Listed in Recommended Order)
00	Hop-by-Hop Options header (must be first per RFC 2460)
43	Routing header
44	Fragment header
50	Encapsulating Security Payload header (see RFC 2406 for more information on order)
51	Authentication header (see RFC 2406 for more information on order)
60	Destination Options header (final destination)
xx	(Upper-layer payload—see RFC 1700 or IANA web site)

Other Headers

58	Internet Control Message Protocol (ICMP)
59	No next header

Defining a new extension header has been made much easier in IPv6 than it was in IPv4. The original set of registered extension headers is shown above. Below are many of the additional extension headers that have been defined.

ICMPv6

The Internet Control Message Protocol messages for IPv4 were adapted for use with IPv6 and are called ICMPv6 (ICMP for IPv6) (see Figure 6–30). An important administrative change was the grouping of messages where all error messages appear in message types 0 to 127, and all informational messages appear in message types 128 to 255. The initial set of messages is defined in RFC 2463, but at the same time additional messages were added as part of RFC 2461. Further messages have since been defined in RFC 3122 and several IETF working documents.

ICMPv6 Field Definitions

ICMPv6 messages may be preceded by other extension headers, something that is not suggested in the graphic for Figure 6–30. The IPv6 Next Header code for ICMPv6 is 0x58 in hexadecimal, and would appear in either the IPv6 Next Header field or the Next Header field in the last extension header prior to the ICMPv6 message.

Descriptions for the ICMPv6 frame fields are provided:

- **Type.** The Type field is 8 bits in length and indicates the ICMPv6 message type. This Type field is roughly analogous to a protocol code, and specifies the specific ICMPv6 message and format of the fields that follow.

- **Code.** The Code field is 8 bits in length and specifies which, if any, clarification or additional level of detail is added to the ICMPv6 message type. Not all ICMPv6 messages have defined codes that accompany them. If no code is specified, the field is set to.

- **Checksum.** The checksum field is 16 bits in length and includes a pseudo-header in the calculation. The checksum allows for detection of corruption of the ICMPv6 message.

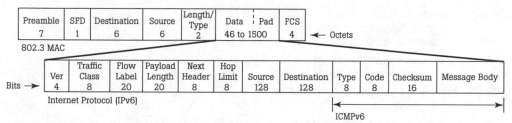

Figure 6-30. *ICMP for IPv6 (ICMPv6) frame format. Although this graphic does not show it, other extension headers may precede the ICMPv6 message.*

ICMPv6 Message Types

The list of ICMPv6 messages specified at the time of this writing includes the ones shown here. Each is preceded by the type value, and any assigned codes are shown immediately after.

Type	Name
1	Destination Unreachable (RFC 4443)
	0 = No route to destination
	1 = Communication with destination administratively prohibited
	3 = Address unreachable
	4 = Port unreachable
2	Packet Too Big (RFC 4443)
3	Time Exceeded (RFC 4443)
	0 = Hop limit exceeded in transit
	1= Fragment reassembly time exceeded
4	Parameter Problem (RFC 4443)
	0 = Erroneous header field encountered
	1 = Unrecognized Next Header type encountered
	2 = Unrecognized IPv6 option encountered
100	Private Experimentation (RFC 4443)
101	Private Experimentation (RFC 4443)
103–126	Unassigned
127	Reserved for expansion of IPv6 ICMP messages (RFC 4443)

Type	Name
128	Echo Request (RFC 4443)
129	Echo Reply (RFC 4443)
130	Multicast Listener Query (RFC2710)
131	Multicast Listener Report (RFC2710)
132	Multicast Listener Done (RFC2710)
133	Router Solicitation (RFC 4861)
134	Router Advertisement (RFC 4861)
135	Neighbor Solicitation (RFC 4861)
136	Neighbor Advertisement (RFC 4861)
137	Redirect Message (RFC 4861)
138	Router Renumbering (No reference found)
	0 = Router renumbering command
	1 = Router renumbering result
	255 = Sequence number reset
139	ICMP Node Information Query (RFC 4620)
	0 = Data Field contains query subject as IPv6 address
	1 = Data Field contains query subject as name
	2 = Data Field contains query subject as IPv4 address
140	ICMP Node Information Response (RFC 4620)
	0 = Successful reply
	1 = Responder refused to answer, Reply data field empty
	2 = Qtype is unknown, Reply data field empty

Type	Name
141	Inverse Neighbor Discovery Solicitation (RFC 3122)
142	Inverse Neighbor Discovery Advertisement (RFC 3122)
143	Version 2 Multicast Listener Report (RFC 3810)
144	Home Agent Address Discovery Request Message (RFC 3775)
145	Home Agent Address Discovery Reply Message (RFC 3775)
146	Mobile Prefix Solicitation (RFC 3775)
147	Mobile Prefix Advertisement (RFC 3775)
148	Certification Path Solicitation Message (RFC 3971)
149	Certification Path Advertisement Message (RFC 3971)
150	ICMP Messages for Experimental Mobility Protocols (RFC 4065)
151	Multicast Router Advertisement (RFC 4286)
152	Multicast Router Solicitation (RFC 4286)
153	Multicast Router Termination (RFC 4286)
154	FMIPv6 Messages (RFC 5268)

0 = Reserved

1 = Reserved

2 = RtSolPr

3 = PrRtAdv

4 = HI

5 = HAck

6–255 = Unassigned

Type	Name
155–199	Unassigned
200	Private Experimentation (RFC 4443)
201	Private Experimentation (RFC 4443)
202–254	Unassigned
255	Reserved for expansion of ICMPv6 (RFC 4443)

Summary

This chapter described the general operation of routing devices, including switches operating as Layer 3 routers. The chapter also described frame structure and field definitions for IPv4 and IPv6. The chapter did not cover routing protocols, which are better described by other reading and training resources that focus on that topic.

- The general operation, frame structure, and field definitions for IPv4 are provided. The ICMP error reporting protocol for IPv4 is also described.

  IPv4 addressing, address notation, subnetting, and special reserved addressing, as well as the meaning and use for the protocol fields, are defined. The ICMP protocol is used to offer Layer 3 error notification and to allow for exchange of information relevant to managing Layer 3 operations.

- The general operation, frame structure, and field definitions for IPv6 are provided. The ICMP error reporting protocol for IPv6 is also described.

  The IPv6 protocol has been around for some time now but is far from a mature protocol. Some parts of the world have limited deployment of IPv6, whereas other parts have fairly extensive deployment. The IPv6 addressing and address notation, as well as the meaning and use for the protocol fields, are defined. The ICMPv6 protocol is used to offer Layer 3 error notification and to allow for exchange of information relevant to managing Layer 3 operations.

Chapter Review Questions

To aid in your comprehension of important concepts, the following questions are provided. Refer to this book's Introduction for a general legend that indicates the anticipated difficulty of each question. For answers to these review questions, see Appendix I, "Answers to Chapter Review Questions."

 1. What link is there between a MAC Layer address and a Network Layer address?

 2. Is a subnet equivalent to a broadcast domain? Explain your answer.

 3. Where is one resource for obtaining current copies of RFCs?

 4. How can you tell if the RFC you are reading is the current one, or if it has been updated or superceded by another more recent RFC?

 5. Do routers change any of the addressing when a datagram is forwarded? Explain your answer.

 6. What percentage of a minimum sized TCP/IP datagram (a TCP segment with no options) is actually data, versus protocol overhead?

 7. The Internet Assigned Numbers Authority (IANA) has reserved three address ranges for private address space (not routable through the Internet). There is one Class A address subnet, one Class B address subnet, and one Class C address subnet. True or false? Explain your answer.

8. Explain how dotted–decimal works. Include an example of how to convert from hexadecimal using the address of your workstation (not the example in the book).

 9. What is the purpose of subnetting?

 10. What is the difference between subnetting and supernetting?

 11. Define what the term *subnet* refers to.

 12. Analyze the following address. Describe what you find. Include the range of available host addresses for the subnet.

    0.0.0.157

    255.255.253.0

 13. Take the following address block and subnet mask and find two details that fail to follow the "default" standards. Then calculate the range of host addresses that can be assigned using this information.

    IPv4 Address: 197.78.165.0

    Subnet Mask: 255.255.253.0

 14. What elements of an IP address configuration represent the bare minimum for a typical PC operating on an Internet-connected subnet?

 15. Here is the hexadecimal excerpt from a protocol trace file showing the header for Layer 3. This figure begins with the MAC Layer Length/Type field showing 0800 (IP) as the protocol. Use the IP frame format descriptions to locate, identify, and look-up the Layer 4 protocol carried by Layer 3.

Hex	00 01 02 03	04 05 06 07	08 09 0A 0B	0C 0D 0E 0F
0000:				08 00 45 00
0010:	00 24 A3 82	00 00 01 11	16 08 81 C4	91 74 EA 02
0020:	03 04			

 16. What problem is suggested by an ICMP Port Unreachable message? Include what worked and what didn't in your answer.

 17. How many possible individual addresses are represented by IPv4? How many for IPv6?

 18. Provide an example of the different ways that an IPv6 address may be shortened to eliminate strings of zeros.

 19. Use the MAC address of your workstation and convert it to a Link-Local IPv6 address in EUI-64 format.

20. What is an Anycast?

21. What is the IPv6 broadcast address? Explain your answer.

22. What is the size of an IPv6 header?

23. What is the maximum size of the IPv6 data payload? Provide an explanation for your answer.

24. Where do IPv6 Extension Headers appear in the packet?

25. How would you know if the frame you were looking at was an IPv6 ICMP message?

CHAPTER 7
Transport Layer

Transport Layer protocols are used by the client or server host systems, and operate above and independently of the protocols and processes used at the Physical, Data Link, and Network Layers to move data between the source and destination host(s). (See Figure 7-1.)

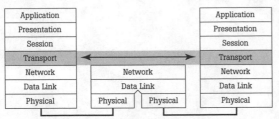

Figure 7-1. *The Transport Layer in relation to the other OSI Layers*

The infrastructure network may manipulate, evaluate, or modify Transport Layer data in transit (referred to as being *in flight*), but this is due to reasons such as performance, load balancing, and security. Per the OSI Model, the Network Layer is responsible for end-to-end delivery and should not be tinkering with the Transport Layer at all, unless the datagram was too large and had to be fragmented to fit through a smaller link.

In the same manner that ARP dynamically (temporarily) links an OSI Layer 2 MAC address to an OSI Layer 3 IP address, Layer 4 protocols such as Transport Control Protocol (TCP) or User Datagram Protocol (UDP) create dynamic links that include the OSI Layer 3 IP address and a protocol code called a port number identifying the next-layer application.

The Transport Layer offers support for OSI Layer 5–7 protocols (see Figure 7-2). The most common Transport Layer protocols are UDP and TCP. There are more than 5,000 published RFCs,

and many apply to or rely upon UDP or TCP. This chapter touches on only a small part of the information significant to the Transport Layer, and only that portion of the information which is most important for understanding certain common performance problems. Examples of other Layer 4 protocols include Stream Control Transmission Protocol (SCTP) described in RFC 4690, and Datagram Congestion Control Protocol (DCCP) described in RFC 4340.

OSI Layer 4 is used in two ways: for connectionless and connection-oriented data transfer. This is significant in one important troubleshooting perspective. A connectionless protocol, such as UDP, doesn't care whether anyone actually received a given datagram, but a connection-oriented protocol such as TCP won't proceed unless it is sure the specified destination host has acknowledged receipt of the previous data segment. To provide for this guaranteed delivery, connection-oriented protocols have a lot more overhead than connectionless protocols. For this reason, UDP is associated with what might be termed "housekeeping" protocols like DNS, DHCP, and router and server advertisements.

For example, using TCP instead of UDP for a simple DNS or DHCP request would require the overhead of setting up, maintaining, and shutting down a connection—directly increasing the bandwidth used and the time it takes for these processes to work. Similarly, UDP is used for streaming protocols such as voice and video, where a lost datagram is far less important than delayed or out-of-order datagrams. Multicast and broadcast-based (one-to-many) applications also use UDP because it would otherwise require a lot of overhead to establish and monitor a connection with each of an unknown number of multicast subscribers or all hosts. With connectionless protocols, the upper-layer application is responsible for tracking lost packets and retransmission requests, if the developers deemed this necessary. TCP is used when the reliable transfer of data is critical to the application. For example, if you were copying a file across the network you care greatly if segments are received (and stored) in the right order without missing any segments or having any duplicate segments. Failure to do so would result in a corrupted file.

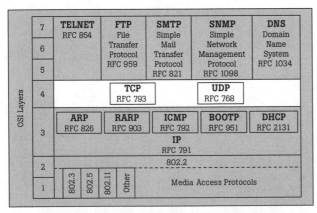

Figure 7-2. *The Transport Layer offers support for the multitude of OSI Layer 5–7 applications, and relies upon OSI Layer 3 for delivery*

TCP and UDP Ports

Both TCP and UDP use numeric identifiers called *ports* to identify the next layer application to which to pass their data and are effectively the protocol codes for a Layer 5–7 application, such as TELNET, FTP, or HTTP. These ports are numbered from 1 to 65535 (zero is reserved). Ports are determined independently by both the client and the server, with each application choosing the port it wants to listen on. A list of TCP port assignments is available from the Internet Assigned Numbers Authority (IANA), at www.iana.org/assignments/port-numbers.

There are three general groupings of ports:

- Ports 0 through 1023 (0x0 to 0x3ff in hexadecimal). These *well-known ports* represent well published services.

- Ports 1024 through 49151 (0x400 to 0xbfff in hexadecimal). These *registered ports* are reserved under IANA authority.

- Ports 49152 through 65535 (0xc000 to 0xffff in hexadecimal). These are *dynamic* or *private* ports.

For example, a client host using a web browser wanting to contact a web server would first choose the source port it plans to listen on for this conversation because this is not a port that it expects other people to be using. The client host chooses what is often known as an ephemeral port, typically in the dynamic port range. In this example, let's say port 51,234 is selected for the client host to listen on. For the destination port the *well known* port for web servers (HTTP = port 80) is selected. This request is then passed to OSI Layer 3 (normally IP), where it is sent on its way. When the server receives the request and passes it up through IP to TCP, the TCP process uses the destination port number (port 80) to determine what application this should be sent to (the web server). When the web server application wants to respond to the client host, it passes the data back to TCP, which then uses the client host's original ephemeral port of 51,234 as the destination port and its own port of 80 as the source. This way, the client host knows which of the possibly multiple active web browser windows this

traffic is destined for. This process works the same for TCP and UDP; although in a connectionless protocol like UDP the receiving host does not have to respond to the sender's port number (although many do). Instead, the job of tracking and maintaining any connections between the two hosts is left up to the applications themselves, hence the term *connectionless*.

Be aware that use of these port assignments or port ranges is not absolute. Due to security reasons, many network administrators have chosen to relocate important services defined by the well-known port range to higher port numbers. This makes it more difficult for a hacker to detect and disrupt services. Although it is most common for the server to use a lower-numbered port than the client, it is easily possible for the server to have a higher-numbered port. Also, Layer 5–7 applications may require more than one TCP port to operate. It is not unusual for a single large application, such as a big database application, to use multiple port ranges for different services, and all are required to make the overall application operate. Some applications use a single port per connection, but that port is selected from a port range (such as 1433 to 5000), and each client connection randomly picks a destination port from within that range for connecting to the server.

Some applications use control ports and data ports. FTP is a good example, where TCP port 21 sets up the file transfer (control) and TCP port 20 sends the file (data). Other applications use a combination of TCP and UDP for their data transfer. Still others, like DNS, may actually choose to use either TCP or UDP dynamically based on the amount of data to send.

Transmission Control Protocol (TCP)

TCP is a connection-oriented protocol that requires acknowledgment for each transmitted segment of data. Because of the acknowledgments, TCP is considered a reliable data transfer protocol. TCP ensures that no data is sent to the upper-layer application that is out of order, duplicated, or has missing pieces. It can even manage transmissions to attempt to reduce detected congestion.

TCP Segments and Maximum Segment Size (MSS)

A TCP *segment* is the OSI Layer 4 block or unit of data transmitted at OSI Layer 3 in a single outbound transmission. A TCP segment may be split into smaller parts along the way to the destination by OSI Layer 3 if the segment passes through a link with a smaller frame size. If this happens, it is said to be fragmented.

The maximum segment size (MSS) option announces the maximum receive segment size that the sender of that option is expecting. This announcement is made during the initial connection setup only. For most Ethernet implementations the MSS is 1460 bytes, which is the maximum Ethernet frame size of 1518 minus all the OSI Layers 2, 3, and 4 header information. If OSI Layer 3 or 4 options are used, this will be a number smaller than 1460. If an intermediate link between two distant hosts has a still smaller maximum transmission unit (MTU) than that which will pass the segment, it may be appropriate for an administrator to manually reduce the MSS to a size that fits through the entire path without fragmentation. If tunneling is used, there may be additional header information that must be accommodated. It is not unusual for the MSS to be reduced when VPN encrypted tunnels are used. In fact, one of the first troubleshooting steps to take when having difficulties establishing and maintaining a TCP connection when no errors are present might

be to reduce the MSS. Various VPN applications have utilities to help the user change this value in the host PC, and may describe this operation as changing the MTU. There is an MTU discovery process that is described by several RFCs, which can automatically set the MTU size to the smallest MTU for the data path (called the path MTU).

When TCP is given a transmission job from an OSI Layer 5–7 application, it splits the job into segments. The job could be sending a single keystroke (TELNET), or it could be sending a multi-gigabyte file transfer (FTP). TCP divides up the job as required to fit into the MSS and sends as many segments as are required to complete the job. The transmission may therefore require a single segment containing only one octet of data, or the transmission could be multiple 1460 octet segments sent in succession. Some TCP segments carry no data at all because the header is all that is required.

TCP Sockets and Connections

A TCP socket consists of an IP address, such as 192.168.1.100, and port number, such as 80. The socket would then be noted as 192.168.1.100:80. A TCP connection between two hosts consists of a pair of TCP sockets. In Figure 7-3, the socket identifying the client PC is circled (IP address 192.168.145.26 and TCP port 1065). The server socket is not circled but is part of the connection. The TCP connection in Figure 7-3 is then <209.85.173.147:80,192.168.145.26:1065>.

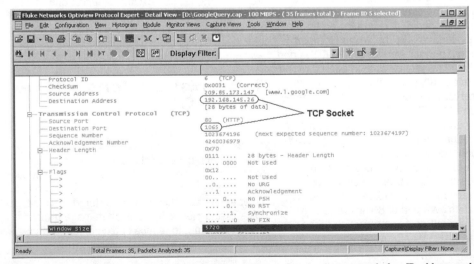

Figure 7-3. *TCP socket viewed in OptiView Protocol Expert. A socket is composed of an IP address and TCP port number.*

Opening and Closing Connections

TCP uses a sequence of steps to open and close connections so that both parties to the connection have formally agreed to open the connection and have exchanged some configuration information, and later both are certain the connection is closed. Connections are opened using a three-way handshake and closed using one of several means ranging from a four-way closing handshake to an abrupt termination. If watchdog timers are employed by the OSI Layer 5–7 application involved in this connection, the connection may also be timed-out and terminated as a result of inactivity.

TCP Three-Way Handshake

The three-way handshake creates a reliable OSI Layer 4 connection between two hosts (identified via TCP sockets). The handshake process includes the TCP port numbers that will be used by each host, respectively.

TCP operations are often described using a bounce chart. Figure 7-4 is an example of a bounce chart, and depicts the logical flow of the TCP connection. The further down a bounce chart, the later in time as measured from the top of the chart. Most protocol analyzer software offers bounce chart analysis of a selected conversation.

The first segment transmitted in Figure 7-4 is the client request to open a connection, and includes the synchronization (SYN) flag and a sequence number (sequence numbers are covered later in this section). The second segment transmitted is an acknowledgment (ACK) from the server for the sequence number from the client, and the server's synchronization request (SYN) with its own sequence number. The third segment transmitted is the acknowledgment (ACK) from the client for the sequence number from the server. A connection is now open.

Four-Way Closing Handshake

The four-way handshake used to close a connection is initiated by either of the hosts involved. Each sends a segment with the FIN flag set, and then ACK the other's FIN, creating four segments (see Figure 7–5).

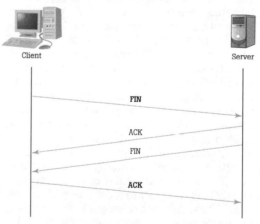

Figure 7-5. *Four-way full closing handshake bounce-chart diagram*

It is also possible to have a half-closed connection, where only one host receives the FIN flag segment. This can be the case when the responding host's FIN is lost or deleted but has already closed the connection and does not retransmit the lost segment.

The last method provided by TCP for closing a connection is for either host to send a reset (RST) flag segment. This is not unlike simply hanging up a telephone in the middle of a conversation.

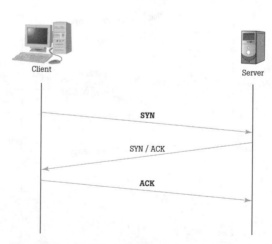

Figure 7-4. *Simplified TCP three-way handshake bounce-chart diagram*

Reset is usually seen when, for example, a web browser window is closed. The PC hosting the web browser window has the application close without telling TCP to issue a graceful shutdown. TCP sends the reset to inform the web server that the connection has terminated abruptly.

Some operating systems use the RST flag to close all connections, which can cause problems such as a half-closed connection if the segment with the RST flag is lost.

Sequence and Acknowledgment Numbers

TCP uses an acknowledgment function to explicitly notify the TCP peer that all data transferred up to a certain point has been received properly. This is described as a *cumulative* acknowledgment scheme. If there are any gaps in the data, TCP cannot acknowledge that all data up to this point has been properly received. For example; if TCP sent ten segments from a client PC to a server but only nine arrived (one through five, and then seven through ten), TCP could only cumulatively acknowledge proper receipt of the first five. Segments six through ten would have to be retransmitted. Multiple segment retransmissions like this were problematic, and several innovative schemes for correcting for an out-of-order or missing frame were later introduced, such as the Selective Acknowledgment (SACK) method described later.

The cumulative acknowledgment system used by TCP is based on the ability of TCP to know exactly how many octets of data have been sent, as well as which data octets are in *this* segment. During the initial connection setup the two TCP peers exchange sequence numbers. This first sequence number represents the zero point for all sequence numbers for that conversation. Each time a segment is transmitted, the sequence number is incremented by the number of octets of data that are contained in that segment. The presence of certain control flags (usually in data-less packets) also causes the sequence number to increment by one.

The sequence numbers are chosen using various means but for the purposes of troubleshooting they are essentially random. (Some utilities can use the initial sequence numbers selected by a host to determine the operating system of

the host; this process is called host fingerprinting.) The acknowledgment (ACK) for any given segment is that segment's SYN number, plus the number of data octets in the segment, or looking at it another way, this would be the next expected sequence number that the host is expecting.

In the first segment of Figure 7-6, the client PC selected a random sequence number of 100 to start, and did not include an acknowledgment number (it has not received any sequence numbers from the server). In the second segment the server acknowledged the client SYN request's sequence number by incrementing it by one and using that value as the acknowledgment number. The server also supplied its own random sequence number of 2000. The client acknowledged that sequence number and incremented it by one to account for the server's SYN request.

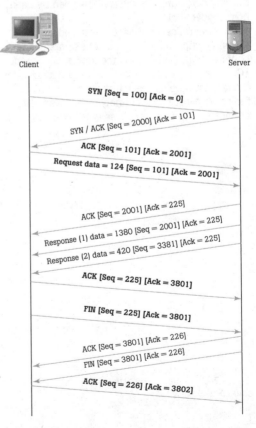

Figure 7-6. *Simplified example of how sequence numbers keep track of data transmitted*

The third segment completed the three-way handshake. Following that, the client sent a 124-octet sized request for data from the server. The server acknowledged the request, incrementing the acknowledgment number by 124 accordingly. Then the server began sending the requested data. In the server's second response segment, notice that it has changed the sequence number to reflect the 1380 octets of data from the server's first response segment. The client PC waited for two segments before acknowledging in order to minimize acknowledgment overhead, and then acknowledged all the data received. Upon receiving all the server's data, the client ends the connection. Both sides increment sequence counters to account for the FIN flag. The connection is now considered closed.

Once the data is received by the host it is placed in a TCP buffer, and if there are no missing segments the application is notified that there is data available and that data is passed to the receiving application. If there are missing segments, whether due to out-of-order segments or the segments just getting lost, the data must remain in that buffer until all the data up to the highest received sequence number is complete.

It's important to note that both the client and the server are maintaining separate sequence numbers and acknowledgments, so a problem with lost packets in one direction might not affect traffic in the other direction.

Retransmission

In TCP, retransmission is the process of resending lost packets. Once TCP transmits a segment, it buffers that segment and waits for an acknowledgment. Acknowledgment of that segment must occur within a certain time or TCP decides that the transmission was lost and retransmits it. The amount of time that TCP waits depends on the implementation, but might be based on the RFC 1323 smoothed round-trip time (SRTT) or the RFC 2988 estimated round-trip time (RTT). When browsing web pages there are times when a particular graphic begins to download and then stops for a moment. The duration of time between when it stopped and when it resumed may be attributed to TCP recovering from a lost or misor-

dered segment. In many cases, if you refresh the page the graphic downloads faster than if you simply wait for TCP to recover.

Because TCP stops sending data or slows the transmission rate when it detects missing packets, lost packets are one of the most common reasons that applications slow down.

Selective Acknowledgment (SACK)

The selective acknowledgment (SACK) option described in RFC 1072 allows individual segments from a series of transmitted segments to be acknowledged, so that all segments following a missing segment don't have to be retransmitted. When a segment is determined to be missing, usually because the sequence number indicates some number of missing segments, the receiving host responds with a SACK that reports the following:

- The most recent acknowledged segment, showing sequence numbers for the left and right edges

- One or more additional left and right segment edges, identifying acknowledged blocks that have been received but are higher than the sequence number the receiver for which the receiver has issued a cumulative acknowledgment

The quantity of noncontiguous blocks reported is limited by the size of the TCP Options field. The sender may retransmit a missing segment after receiving the SACK information, or may simply begin again with the next expected segment and resend all. SACK prevents the sender from having to wait the entire TCP timeout value to discover that a segment was received out of order or lost.

Two examples of the use of SACK are provided. The first is illustrating a lost segment. The second is illustrating an out-of-order segment. These examples simply show the concepts involved. The server would normally wait several ACKs to see whether the problem resolved itself before retransmitting. And although the client PC would send SACKs for every received segment until the problem was resolved, it would not ACK every segment received.

Out-of-Order Segment

In Figure 7-7, the server's second segment was misordered somewhere along the way to the client PC, arriving some time later instead of when it should have arrived.

Note that upon receiving segment three and finding that segment two was missing, the client PC used SACK to notify the server that the most recently received segment boundary was segment three, and that the last cumulative acknowledgment was good up through segment one. The server re-sent segment two because the SACK boundaries indicated that was the missing segment. When segment two arrived, the client PC notified the server that the last cumulative acknowledgment boundary was good up through segment three. Because that brought the cumulative acknowledgment up to match the highest sequence number involved, the client PC no longer needed to use the SACK options, and simply ACKed segment four. When the client PC received the duplicate segment two it ignored it because the cumulative acknowledged sequence number was higher than what was found in the duplicate segment.

Lost Segment

In Figure 7-8, the server's second segment was lost somewhere along the way to the client PC.

Again, the client PC used SACK to notify the server that the most recently received segment boundary was segment three, and that the last cumulative acknowledgment was good up through segment one. When segment four arrived, the client PC would modify the SACK boundaries indicating the most recently received segment boundaries as between the beginning of segment three until the end of segment four, and again indicate that the last cumulative acknowledgment was good up through segment one.

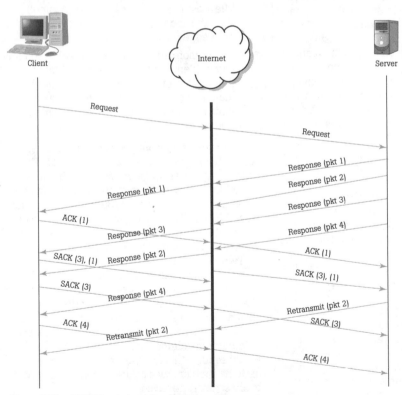

Figure 7-7. *SACK for an out-of-order segment*

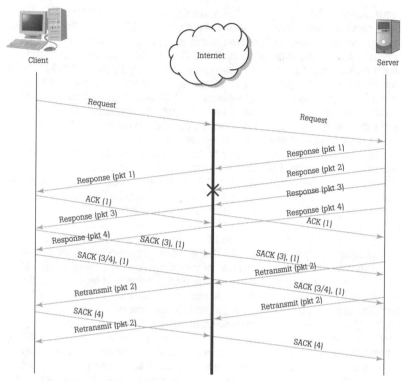

Figure 7-8. *SACK for a lost segment*

When the retransmitted segment two arrived, the client PC's SACK indicated that the last cumulative acknowledgment was now good up through segment four.

If the segment two acknowledgment had been lost instead of the actual segment, the server would have realized that nothing was wrong when the segment three cumulative acknowledgment arrived. Because segments are not usually retransmitted until enough ACKs (or SACKs) indicate that the segment is actually missing, it would have taken no action at all to recover.

Window Size, Window Scaling, and Sliding Window

TCP uses the header field for window size to specify the maximum amount of data that a sender may transmit without receiving an acknowl-

edgment for that data. This is established during initial connection setup. After the connection is open, the window size variable represents how much buffer space the receiving host has empty and is available for temporary storage of received data. Once the receiving host's application has retrieved data from this temporary buffer, it informs the sending host that there is unused buffer available, and the sending host may resume transmission.

The situation is a little like reconciling your expenditures against a bank account. You know how much money you have to start with; this is the sender's window size. The sending host may transmit (spend) any amount of data up to the window size. The sending TCP host keeps track of how much data it sent (spent). However, if the sending host believes that it has transmitted an amount of data equal to the window size, then no additional receive buffer is available (you have "spent" all the money in your account and may not spend any more until the bank acknowledges a deposit). When the receiving host processes data in this temporary buffer, it changes the window size to match how much was removed from the buffer. Because the change makes more space available in the buffer, compare it to making a deposit in the sender's account. The sender is unable to take advantage of the new space until it receives a new window size indication from the receiving host. When an acknowledgment arrives at the sending host, that acknowledgment can be compared to the bank acknowledging a deposit. The difference between the previous acknowledgment and this new acknowledgment represents the size of the deposit. The sending host is again permitted to transmit up to an amount of data equal to the newly open buffer on the receiving host, as indicated by the windows size in the latest acknowledgment.

In Figure 7-3, the server offered an initial window size of 5720 octets. The client is permitted to send up to 5720 octets of data to the server without hearing back from the server that the data was received without errors, misordering, or duplication. As the client sends data in MSS units (or smaller), the server places the data in the temporary receive buffer and acknowledges receipt of the new data. If the server does not process that received data right away, it also reduces the available window size with each acknowledgment so that the client receives a running tally of how much free buffer space the server has available. If the buffer fills up completely without the server processing any of that data, the server sends an acknowledgment indicating that the window size is set to zero—there is no available buffer space for new data. If instead the server processes all data immediately, the window size remains at the maximum value. This process of announcing how much unused buffer space is available through the window size field is referred to as the *sliding window*. Sometimes the window is open (window size > 0), and sometimes it is closed (window size = 0). How far the window is open is determined by the size of the available buffer space on the receiving host. The graphics in Figure 7-9 through Figure 7-12 illustrate this process of changing the window size to announce available buffer space.

The maximum size that the TCP window size field may be set to is 65535 octets. For today's networks this is not large enough to fully utilize the available bandwidth. A mechanism called *window scaling* was initially defined in RFC 1072. This option permits the window size field to be left-shifted up to 14 bits to enlarge the window size up to 1 gigabit. This option may only be established during the connection setup—during the three-way handshake.

The problem solved by increasing the window size is not immediately apparent but can easily be illustrated. The important factor to consider is how many MSS segments may be transmitted before an acknowledgment is received. This is a measure of how much of the receiver's window size will be filled while data is in flight (unacknowledged). If the sender and receiver were on the same local switch there would be very little delay between the transmission and reception of the frame. At most there should be one MSS in flight.

In Figure 7-9, the conveyor belt between the server and the client PC represents the entire network path between the sending and receiving hosts. The length of the conveyor belt represents delay over the path. Each segment transmitted is represented by a cup of data on the conveyor belt. Unused cups at the PC end represent unfilled server window buffer as indicated by the windows size parameter stated during connection setup and updated in each acknowledgment.

Figure 7-9. *Delay between transmission and reception while connected to the same local switch is very slight. At most, there should be one segment in flight.*

In Figure 7-10, the client PC has used all the data cups, which equates to having transmitted enough data to fill the server's available window size buffer. Due to the long delay over the path separating the server and client PC, the first cup has not arrived at the server yet, and the client is forced to stop transmitting. The link experiences idle periods before and after the data cups, and the client PC waits for an acknowledgment (an empty cup) indicating that buffer space is again available.

In Figure 7-11, the server has received and processed two of the segments from the PC, but the acknowledgments and new window size information (indicating that two new segments may be transmitted) are in flight back to the PC. The PC is idle more time than it is transmitting.

If the window size was larger, the PC could continue to transmit, filling the path to the server constantly. The window size must be large enough that acknowledgments can make the entire round trip back to the PC before the PC runs out of cups (see Figure 7-12).

There are various stories about how very large backups across large bandwidth but long latency paths have required excessive amounts of time to complete. One story has a weekly backup taking progressively longer, until it took more than 50 hours to complete and a consultant was called in to find out why because the path between sites would have permitted a much faster transfer. Changing the window size reduced the time required for the backup to just over three hours by permitting TCP to efficiently use the path.

Congestion Control

RFC 2581 describes the concepts of slow start, congestion avoidance, fast retransmit, and fast recovery. The purpose of congestion control is to ensure that data is transferred at the highest reliable rate without overwhelming the infrastructure between the two hosts, while remaining as efficient as possible in the face of errors. That is, congestion control reduces the rate of transmission if segments are lost, but otherwise increases the transmission rate in an attempt to move data at the highest possible reliable rate.

Slow Start

Slow start is used to explore how reliable the path is between the two hosts. If slow start is able to successfully transmit larger and larger blocks of data (parts of a single data transfer), it eventually reaches a point where the network is deemed

Figure 7-10. *Delay between transmission and reception when separated by a high bandwidth, high latency link, such as a cross-country or transoceanic link, would permit an entire window size to be in transit with idle before and after the transmission*

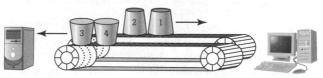

Figure 7-11. *Once the server has acknowledged a segment and cleared that segment from the buffer the PC can transmit again*

Figure 7-12. *If the window size is large enough that a continuous stream of segment transmissions and the corresponding acknowledgments can be in flight, a large bandwidth, long latency path may be fully utilized*

reliable, and the rate of increase in the amount of data *in flight* is increased until that amount is equal to the receiver's window size. Slow start is only effective on large data transfers.

The two most important parameters for slow start are

- CWND = Congestion window (sender side limit on how much may be in flight and unacknowledged)

- SSTHRESH = Slow start threshold (used to determine whether slow start or congestion avoidance is used to control TX)
  - Slow start is used when CWND <= SSTHRESH.
  - Congestion avoidance is used when CWND >= SSTHRESH.

There are several options for determining the starting CWND value, but in general it starts at double the sender MSS value (CWND = 2xMSS). The SSTHRESH value will be much higher, depending on the receiver window size. The sender transmits sufficient segments to meet CWND, then stops and waits for those segments to be acknowledged. Error-free receipt of all acknowledgments for the previous CWND worth of transmitted segments permits the sender to increase the size of CWND by one MSS.

In Figure 7-13, the server increases CWND by one MSS each time the entire CWND data block is acknowledged. The graphic is for illustration, because a typical TCP/IP stack in a host does not acknowledge each segment received. Instead,

it appears to wait for some amount of data or a timeout before acknowledging.

In Figure 7-13, notice that the client PC is very slow to clear its receive buffer. This is indicated by the announced changes in window size in each acknowledgment. It appears that if the FTP transfer went on long enough, the PC would eventually send a zero-window acknowledgment. A zero window indicates that the entire receive buffer is full. That would prevent the server from sending any additional data until the PC sent another acknowledgment showing that the receive window was again open. An example of how a PC was slow to clear the receive buffer is shown in Figure 7-14.

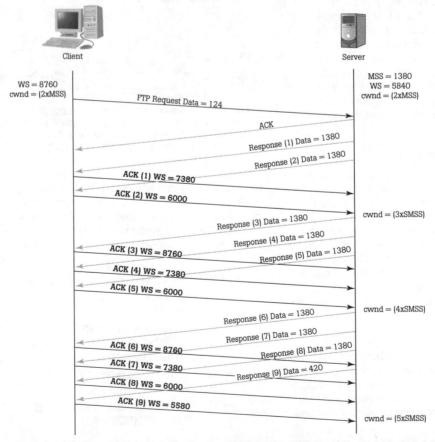

Figure 7-13. *The sender transmits segments until it reaches CWND worth of unacknowledged (in flight) data. During slow start, each time it has received acknowledgments for all that block of data (represented by the current CWND value) it is permitted to increase the value of CWND by one MSS.*

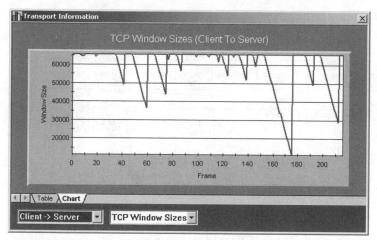

Figure 7-14. *OptiView Protocol Expert example of a PC slow to clear the receive buffer for new transmissions. The available buffer space reached zero at about frame 176 in the data transfer.*

Congestion Avoidance

The CWND value is compared against the SSTHRESH value. As long as CWND is smaller than the SSTHRESH value the host is in slow start. When the CWND value reaches or exceeds the SSTHRESH value, the host transitions to congestion avoidance. In congestion avoidance mode, the value of CWND is permitted to increase one MSS for each round-trip time (RTT). Congestion avoidance will be used thereafter until an error is detected.

Fast Retransmit

If an error is detected, such as a lost segment, fast retransmit may be used. A retransmission is sent whenever the retransmission timer expires without the sending host receiving acknowledgment for a transmitted segment, or when three duplicate acknowledgments are received, which indicates a missing segment. Duplicate acknowledgments may be caused by dropped or lost segments, segments that were reordered in transit, and segments or acknowledgments that were somehow duplicated while in transit. After receiving four identical acknowledgments, a host using fast retransmit resends the missing segment without waiting for the retransmission timer to expire.

Fast Recovery

Fast recovery identifies new segments transmitted following a fast retransmit, and before the recovered/retransmitted segment is acknowledged. The sending host simply fills in the missing segments indicated from the sequence number where the segment was lost and continues to transmit while old segments, the retransmitted segments, and new segments are all in flight and unacknowledged. During fast recovery, the sending host reduces CWND by half (the result is not less than double MSS) but otherwise continues as before. The result is a higher data transfer rate than starting slow start over, but lower than it was so as to mitigate congestion on the path to the destination.

TCP Segment Structure

Like the OSI Layer 3 Internet Protocol specification, the TCP fields are specified in variable bit lengths that do not always align with octet boundaries. These descriptions are therefore provided in bits instead of octets.

The format for a TCP segment is shown in Figure 7-15.

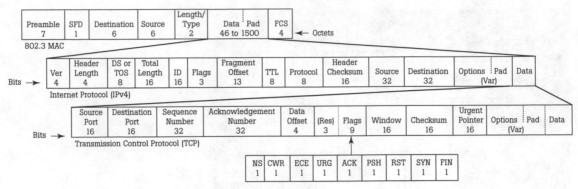

Figure 7-15. *Transmission Control Protocol (TCP) fields*

A listing of the TCP segment fields is provided:

Bits	Description
16	Source Port
16	Destination Port
32	Sequence Number
32	Acknowledgment Number
4	Data Offset
12	Flags
	3 (Reserved)
	1 ECN-Nonce (NC)
	1 Congestion Window Reduced (CWR)
	1 Explicit Congestion Notification-Echo (ECE)
	1 Urgent (URG)
	1 Acknowledge (ACK)
	1 Push (PSH)
	1 Reset (RST)
	1 Synchronize (SYN)
	1 (FIN)
16	Window
16	Checksum
16	Urgent Pointer
Variable	(optional) Options
Variable	Pad; used only if the Options do not end on a 32-bit boundary
	* Data

* The size of the Data field is calculated by deducting the header from the size of the Layer 3 data field.

TCP Field Descriptions

[See RFC 793 for the basic TCP fields, with additions as noted.]

Descriptions for the TCP segment fields are provided:

- **Source Port.** The Source Port is 16 bits in length. This port number represents the OSI Layer 5–7 application on which the host is listening. If this segment is transmitted by the client, the port will be an ephemeral (random) number that should not be chosen from the well-known port range. If this segment is transmitted by the server, this port may be a well-known port from the range up to 1023, or an assigned port utilizing a higher port number that was coded by the application programmer or chosen by the user at the time the application was installed.

- **Destination Port.** The Destination Port is 16 bits in length. This port number represents the OSI Layer 5–7 application to which the source host is connecting, or attempting to connect, on the destination host. Specific port numbers are as described under the Source Port description.

- **Sequence Number.** The Sequence Number field is 32 bits in length. Each TCP host selects a sequence number at random during the connection setup, which represents the zero value for this session. All subsequent transmissions of data cause this number to be incremented by the number of octets transmitted, plus an increment of one for some of the control flags (such as SYN). Specific starting sequence numbers are avoided, partly to prevent an attack from easily guessing the sequence number and taking over the connection.

The sequence number included in a segment represents the first data octet in the segment. Because each segment transmitted specifies exactly which block of data is being sent (indicated by the sequence number), it is easy for the receiving host to determine whether the new segment was received in order and that all prior segments have been received. This number is incremented as appropriate and used as the Acknowledgment number by the distant receiving host for this connection.

Due to the higher bandwidth links that have become available in recent years, it is possible to wrap the 16-bit value used for the sequence number, so that the same sequence number could be in flight twice. Further research will reveal how this problem is being addressed (see RFC 1323 to begin).

- **Acknowledgment Number.** The 32-bit acknowledgment number represents an explicit statement from the receiving host that it has properly received all data up to this cumulative acknowledgment number. The number represents which segments the distant sending host has been successful in transferring to this receiving host in order and without gaps. All data octets are counted, as well as certain control flags. If the local host receives a segment that contains a sequence number that does not match up with what the local host calculates as the right number for the next contiguous block of data, the local host acknowledges only the data that has been previously (cumulatively) received correctly, and does not acknowledge the newly received segment. This behavior may be modified slightly if the Selective ACK option is in use.

- **Data Offset.** The Data Offset field indicates where in this segment the header ends and the data payload begins. A simple TCP segment contains 20 octets of header. Any difference between 20 bytes and the value

indicated by the Data Offset field represents Options. The Data Offset field indicates the total number of 32-bit words in the TCP header, and the TCP data payload begins on the next octet. Thus, the smallest value seen in the data offset field is 5 (5 times 32 bits = 20 octets). The largest value is 15 (15 times 32 bits = 60 octets) and indicates the presence of 40 octets of options.

- **Flags.** There are six original 1-bit control flags, and three additional flags added later (see Figure 7-16):

  — **Reserved.** The first three bits are reserved and should be set to zero.

  — **NC.** The ECN-nonce (NC) flag was added in RFC 3540. This flag permits the receiving host to notify the TCP peer that an acknowledged segment was received unmarked. This bit detects the presence of a device between the source and destination hosts that is concealing or dropping congestion notification.

  — **CWR.** The congestion window reduced (CWR) flag was added in RFC 3168. This flag informs the TCP peer that the congestion window has been reduced in response to an ECE flag, or together with the ECE control flag in a SYN to communicate explicit congestion notification (ECN) capability.

  — **ECE.** The explicit congestion notification echo (ECE), or ECN-Echo (ECE), flag was added in RFC 3168. Use of this flag depends on additional fields used in the IP header. The ECE flag indicates congestion to the TCP peer, and during connection setup to communicate ECN capability.

  — **URG.** The urgent (URG) flag is set when urgent data is included in the segment. If the URG flag is set, the Urgent Pointer field is significant. It is exceptionally rare that this flag is used in today's networks.

  — **ACK.** The acknowledge (ACK) flag is used with the acknowledge sequence number to inform the destination host that all data up to this value is cumulatively acknowledged as having been received. The SYN and FIN flags are also acknowledged.

— **PSH.** The push (PSH) flag informs the destination host that the data in this segment should be passed up to the OSI Layer 5–7 application now, and that host should not wait for the buffer to fill first.

— **RST.** The reset (RST) flag abruptly terminates an open connection. The RST flag may be used by either host in a connection. A data segment containing a RST flag is usually not acknowledged, though recent denial of service attack profiles have caused some servers to acknowledge a segment with a RST flag. This keeps the connection open long enough for the other host in the connection to respond, and thereby keep the connection open, defeating the attack.

— **SYN.** The synchronization (SYN) flag begins a connection and is accompanied by the random sequence number that represents zero for the sending host for counting transferred octets in this connection. The SYN flag is counted as an increment of one sequence number to ensure that proper acknowledgment of this operation is performed.

— **FIN.** The FIN flag initiates the graceful closure of an open connection. The FIN flag may be used by either host in a connection to initiate closing. The FIN flag is counted as an increment of one sequence number to ensure that proper acknowledgment of this operation is performed.

- **Window.** The Window field is 16 bits in length. During connection setup, the window size field announces the amount of receive buffer that the sending host has allocated for unprocessed received segment data. During routine data communications this field announces how much buffer is empty, starting with the reference point indicated by the acknowledgment sequence number in the same segment.

- **Checksum.** The 16-bit Checksum field contains a checksum calculated for all the header and data.

- **Urgent Pointer.** The 16-bit Urgent Pointer field is significant only when the URG flag is set. When significant, this field indicates where the non-urgent data begins in this segment. Urgent data is passed separately up to OSI Layer 5–7, and then the normal data is processed routinely. Urgent data is exceptionally uncommon in today's networks.

- **Options and Padding.** The Options field is zero to 40 octets in length, appearing in words of 32 bits (4-octet groups). The actual size of the Options field is specified using the Data Offset field.

Use of the Options field indicates a willingness to participate in certain extra data-handling processes. Options are offered during connection setup, and if both sides agree to participate in the specific option or options mutually offered, additional option fields might used during routine data handling. Options are specified in octets, and the Options field must end on a 32-bit boundary. If there are insufficient options octets to fill a 32-bit block, the remaining octet(s) are padded so that the Option field reaches the 32-bit boundary.

There are two types of option. The first type is a single-octet option. Multiple-octet options are specified first with an option-kind octet, followed by an octet indicating option length, and finally by the actual option data octets.

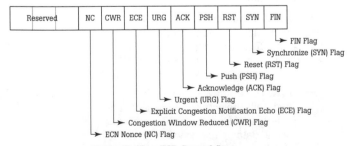

Figure 7-16. *TCP Control flags*

- **Data.** The minimum size of the Data field is zero. The maximum size of the Data field is determined by subtracting all OSI Layer 3 and Layer 4 header information from the maximum OSI Layer 2 data field size. For Ethernet, the maximum OSI Layer 2 data size is 1500 octets. Subtract from that the IP and TCP headers, and the result is a maximum of 1460 octets of TCP data if no IP or TCP options are used.

User Datagram Protocol (UDP)

User Datagram Protocol (UDP) is a very light-weight protocol defined in RFC 768. Unlike TCP, it is not connection oriented, meaning it does not require acknowledgment of each transmitted datagram. The primary uses for UDP includes service advertisements, such as routing protocol updates and server availability, one-to-many multicast applications, and streaming applications, such as voice and video, where a lost datagram is far less important than an out-of-order datagram.

User Datagram Protocol (UDP) uses the term *datagram* instead of *segment* to identify a single block of data transmitted. Because of the reduced overhead (no tracking of order, watching for duplicates or lost data, and so on), UDP is faster and more efficient than TCP. Discussion about the process used by UDP is very brief because of this

lack of internal tracking of data. Once transmitted, UDP is finished with that datagram. If any tracking is required it must be done by the OSI Layer 5–7 application.

Because UDP has no concept of congestion control or congestion avoidance, the network infrastructure usually relies on discarding excess UDP traffic to restrict data flow through a congestion point.

User Datagram Protocol (UDP) Datagram Structure

The User Datagram Protocol (UDP) fields are specified in octets because there was no need for an extensive number of different fields to maintain any connection or data transfer tracking record.

The format for a UDP datagram is shown in Figure 7-17.

A listing of the User Datagram Protocol (UDP) datagram fields is provided:

Octets	Description
2	Source Port
2	Destination Port
2	Length
2	Checksum
*	Data

* The size of the Data field is calculated by deducting the header from the size of the Layer 3 data field.

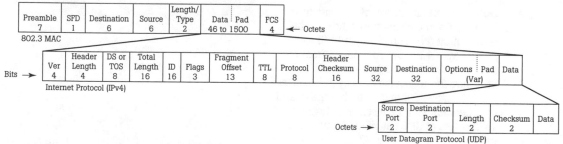

Figure 7-17. *User Datagram Protocol (UDP) fields*

UDP Field Descriptions

(See RFC 768.)

Descriptions for the UDP datagram fields are provided:

- **Source Port.** The Source Port is two octets in length. This port number represents the OSI Layer 5–7 application on which the host is listening. If this segment is transmitted by the client, the port will be an ephemeral (random) number that should not be chosen from the well-known port range. If this segment is transmitted by the server, this port may be a well-known port from the range up to 1023, or an assigned port utilizing a higher port number that was coded by the application programmer or chosen by the user at the time the application was installed.

- **Destination Port.** The Destination Port is 16 bits in length. This port number represents the OSI Layer 5–7 application that the source host is connecting to, or attempting to connect to, on the destination host. Specific port numbers are as described under the Source Port description.

- **Length.** The 16-bit Length field contains the octet count for the entire UDP header and data. This value should never be less than eight (representing the header).

- **Checksum.** The 16-bit Checksum field contains a checksum calculated for all the header and data.

- **Data.** The minimum size of the Data field is zero. The maximum size of the Data field is determined by subtracting all OSI Layer 3 and Layer 4 header information from the maximum OSI Layer 2 data field size. For Ethernet, the maximum OSI Layer 2 data size is 1500 octets. Subtract from that the IP and UDP headers and the result is a maximum of 1472 octets of UDP data if no IP options are used.

Summary

This chapter described the two most common protocols from among the Layer 4 protocols: TCP and UDP.

- The general operation, frame structure, and field definitions for TCP are provided. TCP is a connection-oriented protocol that uses a handshake process to establish a connection between two hosts. The parameters and process for creating this connection are explained. Also explained is the mechanism for determining that each transmitted segment has been received, and how recovery of a missing segment is accomplished. After reliable data delivery is assured, the parameters related to window size become important.

- The frame structure and field definitions for UDP are provided. UDP is a connectionless protocol that relies on *best effort* delivery by the attached network.

Chapter Review Questions

To aid in your comprehension of important concepts, the following questions are provided. Refer to this book's Introduction for a general legend that indicates the anticipated difficulty of each question. For answers to these review questions, see Appendix I, "Answers to Chapter Review Questions."

1. What scheme does TCP use to ensure that all data is successfully transferred in order and without duplication?

2. Compare the maximum segment size with window size. What similarities or differences exist?

3. What is special about TCP ports below 1024?

4. What is a TCP socket? Provide an example.

5. Describe each step required for a TCP three-way handshake.

6. What control flags may be used to close a TCP connection?

7. Assume that a client PC and a server use full formal TCP rules to open and immediately close a session. If the PC's initial sequence number was 350, what will it be when the session is closed?

8. If you plan to transfer a huge file across a high-bandwidth, long latency WAN link, what single TCP parameter can you change to provide the best throughput, and what change would be made?

9. How much performance increase would be provided by using TCP slow start during a Telnet session?

10. Describe the fundamental difference between TCP and UDP.

11. What mechanism does the network infrastructure usually rely upon to control excess UDP transmissions?

CHAPTER 8
Preventing Problems

To prevent network problems, you must be proactive instead of reactive, which requires you to be not only prepared but alert to changes. Network emergencies happen—the question is whether you are prepared to handle them. These emergencies range from a failed server NIC to a fire or other disaster. Disaster planning is necessary, but routine problems, rather than disasters, are the topic of this section.

Standards-based approaches to planning, installing, and maintaining a network may be found in several places, including ISO 20000 and the Information Technology Infrastructure Library (ITIL). ITIL originated in the United Kingdom's Office of Government Commerce (OGC) and predated ISO 20000.

Strategy for Network Maintenance

One approach to effectively dealing with routine problems is described by these seven strategic concepts:

1. Management involvement in network decision making
2. Preparation and planning
3. Problem prevention
4. Early problem detection
5. Quick problem isolation and resolution
6. Investing more in tools and training rather than additional staff to accommodate growth
7. Quality improvement approach to network management and maintenance

1. Management Involvement in Network Decision Making

Upper management must demonstrate that it cares about the network performance by creating a framework that facilitates problem prevention and resolution. It must also be part of a regular review process to ensure that the network is fulfilling its promise to the organization.

Additionally, management must collaborate with technical managers to ensure that network objectives match business objectives. Together, they should arrive at reasonable guidelines for establishing which portions of the network are high-priority operations. For example, in a major manufacturing company it should be clear that the network associated with the manufacturing line has higher priority than the president's PC.

2. Preparation and Planning

Having a documented plan is essential. The plan should indicate who is responsible for each area of the network, criteria for preventative maintenance and types of performance metrics that are monitored, how problems are escalated, and what tools are used to troubleshoot the network.

There should be agreed-upon and documented guidelines for problem detection, isolation, and resolution, as well as day-to-day operations such as moves, adds, and changes.

3. Problem Prevention

The earlier a problem is identified and fixed, the less expensive it is.

Educating end users on do's and don'ts qualifies as an important element of problem prevention. Examples include telling users to contact the Help Desk to move their computer or asking end users to be careful about running over cables with equipment or furniture. Network devices such as servers, routers, and switches should not be accessible to end users.

Another aspect of problem prevention is the testing and certifying of network cable during installation and after moves, adds, and changes.

Finally, the network should be documented and regularly monitored for performance.

4. Early Problem Detection

Even with the best problem prevention plan, some problems inevitably occur. To reduce the impact of the problems, the network should be monitored so that performance deviations can be identified immediately.

This means using traditional SNMP-based network management systems, the newer flow protocol monitoring solutions (IPFIX, NetFlow, sFlow, and so on), and other monitoring capabilities, such as syslog servers and syslog mining applications. Test those monitoring solutions with periodic after-hours throughput testing to ensure that the installed monitoring solutions spot the extra traffic, and that throughput testing does not reveal any latent problems in the infrastructure network.

Trouble-ticketing applications are used by Help Desks to log and track network problems. It is essential to have a single, centralized Help Desk to quickly receive and respond to problems reported by individual users.

5. Quick Problem Isolation and Resolution

The previously mentioned centralized Help Desk discusses the problem with the caller and, if needed, dispatches a front-line troubleshooter who, armed with the right tools, should be able to quickly diagnose and fix almost all single-user problems.

When the front-line staff member cannot solve the problem, he or she should escalate the problem to a more experienced staff member.

For quick problem isolation and resolution, it is important that the support staff be armed with the appropriate tools for their skill level and job function. Protocol analyzers, handheld network testers, and cable testers are used by the different levels of network staff to troubleshoot network problems in the user space, and network management (SNMP, flow protocols, and so on) from the network operations center.

6. Investing More in Tools and Training Rather Than Additional Staff to Accommodate Network Growth

The old saying, "Sometimes you have to spend a little money to save a lot of money," is also true for successful network maintenance. The industry trends toward using smaller staffing levels to accomplish more support can be accomplished only if care is taken to regularly invest in training and tools. Providing the right tools and ongoing training to fit the function and experience level of each staff member empowers him or her to maximize his or her efficiency.

7. Quality Improvement Approach to Network Management and Maintenance

A quality improvement approach means tracking metrics such as the number and nature of network failures and problems. Tracked metrics should be trended and posted where the entire support staff is kept aware of how they are doing. Network performance is measured and compared against goals (which were set in conjunction with upper-level management). Reports are regularly provided to management, which in turn helps management remain sufficiently informed to stay actively involved.

Documentation

Documentation is one of the necessary evils for a network. It is often very difficult to keep the documentation current, and yet without documentation it is very difficult to plan for growth, manage, or troubleshoot the network. Incomplete or inaccurate documentation may lead to erroneous initial conclusions, whereas an absence of documentation may significantly delay many activities.

Methodology

All backups and other documentation should be copied to a safe offsite location in case a failed server, failed storage array, improperly configured backup system, or a nasty virus or attack destroys the local backups. If the backups are not tested and kept offsite, there is no guarantee they will be available when needed.

Discovery and Baselining

Network professionals must first know what they're dealing with. Discovery means asking the following: What kind of equipment exists? What is the traffic today? Who are the users? It should include hardware inventory, applications, router configurations, switch configurations, network cabling, and protocol usage. Engineers should evaluate current network performance, including traffic patterns, bandwidth optimization, Internet connectivity, and network vulnerabilities.

Baselining means creating documentation of the current state so that there is something to work from to plan changes and measure against to validate them. An invaluable part of any documentation is a functional diagram of the network to accompany any trending information, and allow more accurate visualization of what is taking place on the network.

Design Assistance

The next step is designing the plan for making the changes using the documentation as a guide. What is the end goal and how will you get there? This is the stage at which the IT team makes decisions about redesigning physical or logical interconnections, the addressing scheme, server location changes, and so on, and then creates a design to facilitate those decisions. When creating a deployment plan, it is important to document in extreme detail (down to the config statements, cables used, port assignments, and so on) exactly what needs to be done. Lack of detail in the plan will translate directly to more time spent during the deployment, and possible inadvertent changes in the expected outcome.

Validation

The third step is validating the design after implementation. Are all the devices configured correctly? Did a user get moved? Did the switch get changed? Network professionals verify that changes were made, and then document, report, and baseline the network again for future reference. Performing this second baseline immediately allows the impact of the change to be measured before other alterations of the network design or traffic patterns dilute the measurement accuracy.

A well-documented network greatly simplifies troubleshooting. The process of creating the documentation often reveals minor problems that can be corrected before they become major problems. This is particularly important when applications running on the network are considered mission-critical or when a problem prevents numerous users from doing their jobs.

A good way to determine the completeness and accuracy of your documentation is to answer this question: "Could someone reconstruct or troubleshoot any part of the network from just this set of documents?"

When sufficient care is taken in planning and installation, future maintenance and troubleshooting jobs will be considerably easier. Documentation is most easily created during installation.

However, it may be produced for an existing network. A new member of the network support staff could be assigned to collect and build this set of documentation under the direction of more senior staff. It would teach them more about the network in a short time than any amount of instruction or reviewing someone else's notes. Aside from being a good training exercise, it is likely to reveal errors and omissions in any existing documentation. Networks evolve constantly, and documentation is almost always out of date.

The following suggestions are a starting point, and by no means represent all the documentation opportunities for avoiding problems or for being better prepared to solve problems.

Create a Server Log and Software Library

Searching for unlabeled cables and missing software, looking through vendor online help systems, and trying to find vendor support telephone numbers consumes valuable time and patience during a crisis. If the file server must be rebuilt from a fresh install, trying to remember the minor adjustments required to make it operate properly with your software and network are nearly impossible unless the changes were made quite recently.

Server Log

A server log should contain all pertinent information and software required to re-create the server following a catastrophic hardware failure, or to answer any general vendor question during a support incident.

- A list of the entire hardware configuration, including server serial number or other maintenance agreement numbers
- Copies of the setup/installation programs for all installed software, including any custom configurations for the installed software
- A list of all user accounts configured on the server, and a matrix showing their respective security and access privileges

- A list of serial numbers and version numbers, license keys, technical support phone numbers, maintenance agreement numbers, and web sites for all software and hardware vendors

- A time-stamped log of all configuration changes made to the file server, and by whom

- A log of all major problems encountered, including symptoms and what was required to resolve those problems

- If the server was "hardened" for security, a list of anything that broke installed software and had to be backed out or worked around

Software Library

Create a configuration library to store the configuration of all switches, routers, firewalls, and so on. If you set up a TFTP server just for this purpose, it is much more likely that configuration changes will be recorded as they are made. Establish a naming convention that identifies the source device as well as the change date so that locating the previous configuration is simplified. Do not overwrite the previous backup configuration

- Create a repository—accessible only by the support staff—that contains current copies of all installation/setup software, redistributable updates and patches, and other files or configurations in use anywhere on the site.

- Use an imaging software application such as Norton Ghost to capture a pristine image of each of your standard user PC platforms. Standardizing on a limited set of choices for new PCs will help. This image should be refreshed regularly as security patches and software updates are released. Pre-install all standard corporate software. Then use the image to overwrite any new PCs (with an image that matches the PC model) to match a corporate standard before delivery. Use the same image to correct problems with security, viruses, and replaced hard drives. Relying on a supported common software

image will make Help Desk activities much easier and failure recovery a simple matter. Another source of standardized PC and server image is to use a Virtual Machine (VM) image. When shut down, this typically appears as a folder on the host computer and is easy to back up and restore. Be sure to provide an easy means for users to back up critical data as a routine part of daily activities, so that a reimage is an inconvenience and not a catastrophe.

Create a Network Diagram

Some classes of problem are almost impossible to troubleshoot without a functional diagram, and almost trivial to troubleshoot if you have one.

Prepare a functional block diagram something like Figure 8-1 that shows how each major network component or segment is attached to, and functions with, the rest of the network (stations, switches, routers, etc.). If switches are present, be sure that any configured VLANs appear on the diagram as distinctly separate broadcast domains—especially if they span multiple switches. Distinguish redundant paths always, and primary paths from backup or failover paths where possible.

Cable Plant Documentation

For the "official" method of documenting a cable plant, see TIA/EIA-606.

- Compare cable lengths against maximum-length limits for your topology per IEEE 802.3, TIA/EIA-568, or other appropriate standard.

- Label each individual cable segment at both ends, especially if punchdown blocks or patch panels are used. A better practice is to label each end twice: once close to the end and again farther back, to prevent accidental label removal in the event of cable retermination.

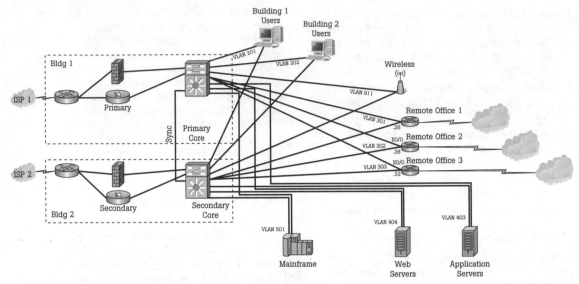

Figure 8-1. *Sample functional network diagram. This represents a simple overview. More detailed functional drawings of each subsection would normally be created also.*

- Obtain a floor plan or blueprint and draw the route, location, and name of each major cable path on each floor. For star topologies, especially note the location of all punchdown blocks and patch panels. Especially note the location of any intermediate cable junctions. A physical layout map is often helpful in identifying wireless interference sources located near access point placements.

- Users should be able to provide cable ID information to the network maintenance staff, so the ID must be clearly marked either on the cable or the wall jack in each office space. An example is provided in Figure 8-2.

- Require new cable installations to be certified to the maximum rating of the medium per TIA/EIA-568 test limits, and insist on complete test results (not summary test results) for every link installed in electronic format before the job is signed-off. Virtually all the Category 5e or better cable testers on the market today have a software database system that stores and manipulates these test results. Have the installer show you how to use this database system after it is installed on your PC. When you are comfortable that the results are all present, that all test results meet the requirements, and that you can operate the software satisfactorily, back up that database.

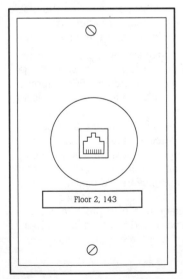

Figure 8-2. *User work area cable identification example*

- If you are specifying a new cable installation, ensure that your requirements specify the latest changes in cable technology. A draft template for contracting a copper or fiber optic cable installation is available from the Fluke Networks web site (www.flukenetworks.com/SOW). Look for a "Field Test Specification." The template is kept current per the evolving standards requirements, and should help you avoid most of the typical installation problems.

- If cables do not conform exactly to TIA/EIA-568, draw a diagram of the exact pin-out or wiremap for each cable type used, as shown in Figure 8-3. Cabling installed in the last 10 years should comply with TIA/EIA-568.

- Periodically spot-check existing links and compare against archived test results. If your existing cable plant has not been tested against at least Category 5e test limits, that could be another assignment for the new person. Add the new test results to the database and compare the old and new measurements.

- Fiber optic links should be tested for signal loss (attenuation) because the connections tend to get dirty over time. If signal loss is tested at multiple wavelengths, changes in bend radius are more likely to be detected.

- While performing retesting of existing cables as a maintenance activity or during troubleshooting, verify that all cables are properly labeled and are properly and carefully terminated, all cable runs avoid sources of electrical noise, and maximum segment lengths have not been exceeded. Retesting an entire cable plant seems excessive, but the improved diagnostic features of the recently introduced Category 5e or better cable testers, together with the gradual deterioration of a cable plant and incidental cable abuse, make retesting an excellent proactive and preventative measure.

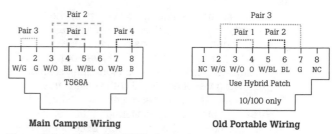

Figure 8-3. *Example of RJ45 pin-out documentation*

Depending on which source you consult, Physical Layer faults represent anywhere from a moderate percentage to a very significant percentage of all network problems. Typical numbers range from 20 to 80 percent of all problems.

Develop a Baseline

Network administrators need to know what normal behavior is for their networks; otherwise, they will be unaware of early telltale indicators and minor symptoms that warn of impending problems. The metaphor of a medical checkup is useful in understanding what is normal for a given network. Every person is different, yet there are certain norms that apply to healthy people in general. The same holds true for networks. The best way to become familiar with what normal operation looks like is to establish what *normal* is for their network.

Documenting and establishing the normal behavior of a network may be done a little at a time by collecting baseline measurements as you perform routine activities, or by planning and preparing a complete network assessment. A number of third-party service companies do not accept new contracts for maintaining large networks until they have first prepared a network assessment for the candidate network. The resulting information is used in many ways. It reveals existing fault or performance conditions that can then be factored into the contract pricing. It provides both parties a factual starting point for discussing strategies for performance improvement. It also provides protection for the third-party company so that it cannot be held accountable for existing conditions or problems.

Baseline monitoring may be established for nearly anything, and can be as simple as a binder full of graphs and reports reflecting network performance during a week of monitoring, or as complex as a fully installed monitoring solution showing trendlines for all critical paths in your network. After a reference point is established, results from regular monitoring of the network can be compared with that reference point to develop a performance trend that can then alert you to any significant deviations. This reference point establishes *normal* for your network. Normal may not be acceptable, and confusing the two is easy to do. After you have a baseline showing normal, which has been developed long enough to be representative of your network, it is time to judge that performance against the *acceptable* criteria and plan any necessary changes.

Validate the baseline before making any major change to the network, such as new hardware or software modifications. Continue monitoring throughout so that the baseline can show whether changes had the desired effect. Without before-and-after validation, it is difficult (if not impossible) to interpret test results obtained after the change. This could lead to improperly attributing performance problems to a change that had either a neutral or positive impact. Afterward, the new results serve as a reference point establishing what normal is.

Changes that should be monitored include the following:

Try it before you buy it. Just because the salesperson said it will, doesn't always mean it can.

- The addition of any new high-use software on the network.

- Structural changes, such as a new switch or router, or division of a large network segment into smaller segments.

- The addition or elimination of a new WAN pathway.

- Any moderate-to-large changes in the number of stations/users on the network. This includes moving groups of users to a new segment. (Be sure to monitor the old and new segments, you may be surprised by a change or lack of change in one or both segments.)

- Changes in work shifts for users, such as moving one group to an early shift.

- Installation of a new server or application.

This information will help guide you in exploring avenues of performance improvement, and help to quickly isolate the source of problems when they occur.

Traffic Monitoring

A lot can be learned by simply listening or, in the case of network management, asking questions regularly. Four categories of tools are usually used for this activity: SNMP-based network management, flow protocol monitoring, protocol analyzers, and handheld network analyzers. These categories of tools also permit report generation for most of the documentation suggestions listed next. For WAN links, it may be necessary to distinguish traffic patterns for each channel and direction. For example, Frame Relay should be characterized for each DLCI in use, as well as the serial link as a whole. Flow protocol monitoring would also show ongoing trends of the users and protocols used.

Frame Size Distribution

A simple frame size distribution can reveal applications that are not behaving properly on a network. Many older applications were not designed to operate with a network between the application and the data source. One such problem to watch for is an application that makes inefficient and repeated tiny queries to a remote data source instead of reading a larger amount of the data in each query. This sort of test is readily available from virtually all protocol analyzers.

Protocol Distribution

Another way to categorize traffic is by protocol (see Figure 8-4). Network management software, flow protocols, and protocol analyzers can provide some or all of this type of information, depending on their capabilities. Protocol analyzers provide information about the distribution of different protocols within the total utilization. Network management software itself knows nothing about the network but gathers information from custom hardware probes, other devices on the network (LAN or WAN), or both. The quantity and quality of information from network management software is limited only by the capabilities of the devices supplying information to it, and is usually easier to interpret than information from protocol analyzers. The new category of flow protocols also provides protocol and user address information. The flow protocols are less intrusive than SNMP-based management because flow protocols are sent routinely from configured infrastructure devices, typically as UDP traffic, rather than the query/response model SNMP uses.

- Use SNMP, flow protocols, or taps/span ports to monitor and record the typical top senders, receivers, and broadcasters, preferably as conversation pairs rather than simply senders or receivers. Knowing who uses the most network bandwidth is useful in a number of ways. Knowing the typical time of day for high usage is equally helpful. Continuous monitoring and trending of this information reveals unexpected traffic and network additions that were unannounced.

- Flow protocols provide this type of information for all monitored links. Using flow protocol monitoring on WAN links is particularly useful for containing costs by identifying unusual or inappropriate path usage. For example, one network was preparing to upgrade to a higher bandwidth international link until it was discovered that web traffic was crossing the link. Changing the router-forwarding rules to pass web traffic through the local Internet connection avoided an upgrade to the international link.

Top Talkers

Network documentation should show which specific stations are the greatest contributors to traffic on the network. Trending applications, protocol analyzers, and handheld network analyzers often offer this sort of report as a standard feature. This knowledge enables support staff to keep a close watch on the network resources that are relied on most heavily, and identify the users who place the greatest demand on the network. Reconfiguration and expansion of the network is often driven by this analysis.

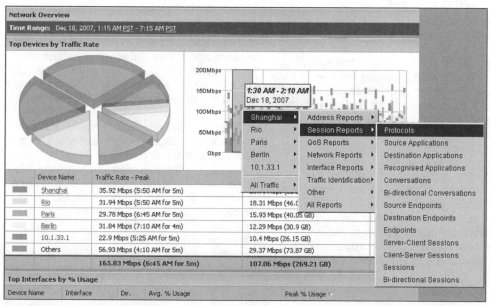

Figure 8-4. *Traffic distribution for a critical path example. A variety of data views are available from the NetFlow Tracker application for a selected time period on that critical path.*

Top Conversation Pairs

Track the amount of traffic between any two stations is another way to graph the top talkers, but in a more meaningful format than simply listing who is talking. This report quickly identifies the "power user," and significantly enhances the decision-making process for network improvements. Decisions about which segments or users should migrate to faster links first, or whether a server should move to the same switch as a group of users or be upgraded, are easier to justify with statistical evidence.

Because switches have become the primary station connection point, it is less critical to monitor at the Data Link Layer on most networks. It is still important to know which station is contributing traffic and where the traffic originates, particularly routed traffic. Again, the report is most useful when showing conversation pairs instead of simply which stations are transmitting or receiving the most traffic. The report should be separated by conversations within each protocol. More advanced monitoring solutions are able to read into the traffic and present results by application rather than protocol, even when the application utilizes more than one protocol.

Routed Traffic Analysis

Network Layer protocols include enough information in each frame to very clearly identify the logical source and destination network segment. The importance of this routing information relates to how efficiently data is moved between logical networks. The fewer routed connections a message must cross, the faster the response time.

By evaluating how much traffic is from the local network and how much is from other networks, it is relatively simple to determine whether moving one or more servers or users improves performance. In many cases, it may be simpler or more practical to replicate a server or service on the local segment, or install caching (such as content delivery networking and application acceleration technologies) than to restructure connections. This is especially true if the high-use server or service is located across a WAN connection.

- Monitor source and destination network addresses for abnormal or unusual amounts of routed traffic that indicates nonoptimal paths between stations and network resources.

- Evaluate the content of network traffic passing through WAN links. Verify that the traffic should be there, and that high-cost links are not burdened with inappropriate service advertisements or routing updates.

- Use traffic analysis data to determine whether performance and cost could both be improved by use of caching servers. Recent caching products have become quite sophisticated and provide significant benefit.

- Where WAN links are involved, evaluate the nature of the traffic crossing the connection. Most normal traffic is TCP based, which will back off in the presence of congestion. Protocols such as VoIP and Video are usually UDP based and keep coming even when a router gets congested.

- Set network management alarm thresholds based on measured peak utilization plus a small margin. Modify thresholds as experience dictates.

Trending

The best tool for developing trending is a network management system (either using traditional SNMP or using the newer flow protocols), which can also be configured to send notification if configured thresholds are exceeded, or when traffic stops.

General utilization statistics provide insight into the overall segment traffic and when usage peaks occur. Network utilization should not be confused with the utilization of any particular file server, although both numbers are good to know. In this case, utilization is a percentage of the total capacity, or bandwidth, of the network. There isn't really a "good" or "bad" amount of average utilization. This goes back to the *normal* versus *acceptable* discussion. However, high utilization can cause problems for half duplex Ethernet, other shared media networks such as 802.11 wireless, as well as traffic crossing WAN links.

Each network segment should be monitored for traffic patterns over long periods to document short-term, high-volume traffic periods that may occur first thing in the morning when all employees are getting started, or right after lunch. Because of software timers, scheduled late-night backups, and other regular maintenance activities, it is important to collect and analyze data to observe these routine activities. The minimum period for initial monitoring is 24 hours per day for seven consecutive days. Deviations from normal often represent the cause of a sudden drop in network performance. This information also enables the network administrator to determine a downtime schedule for regular maintenance

when it will have the least impact. And it provides a baseline against which suspicious off-hour activity can be evaluated for security purposes.

The easiest format in which to present this information is with daily and weekly graphs with drill-down capability to learn greater detail about an observed event. With this information, network management systems may be configured for thresholds and alarm levels. Support staff will quickly develop a feel for whether the current measurement is normal. The most common sort is for the highest traffic source, assuming that high utilization is the problem (see Figure 8-5). Some monitoring applications also store all data so that a single frame from a conversation within a selected interval may be detected, rather than keeping only the "tops."

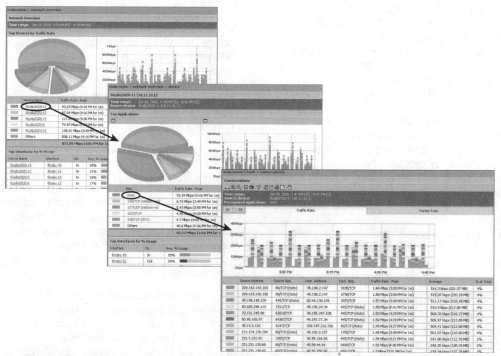

Figure 8-5. *Trend analysis drill-down example. NetFlow Tracker sorts the database for the highest utilization interface (first or rear screen), the highest utilization protocol on the selected interface (middle or second screen), and the highest utilization conversation within the selected protocol for time intervals down to one minute granularity (third or front screen). All reported traffic may be seen.*

Proactive Activity and Preparedness

A variety of actions may be taken in advance of a detected or reported problem. These tests and procedures facilitate corrective action after problems take place, but more importantly they tend to reveal latent problems before they reach the failure state. These and many other steps are part of being prepared.

Monitoring the Physical and MAC Layers

For wired networks, it is easiest to rely on MAC Layer errors to isolate the location of probable Physical Layer faults as well as marginal or failed hardware and duplex problems. For wireless networks, the MAC Layer errors do not provide enough information for locating or identifying whole classes of common problems.

Results from tests at higher layers are often misleading if the network cabling or other Physical Layer equipment is faulty. A quick check of information available from the Physical or MAC Layer can be very helpful for this purpose. The MAC Layer is directly affected by Physical Layer problems, and because it is tasked with doing its best to insulate higher layers from problems, it often masks many problems from notice. Information available from the Physical and MAC Layers is never seen by the average network user, but can be viewed by special software and/or monitoring tools.

A distinction is made between shared media versus switched media environments because troubleshooting is approached differently. The tests performed are similar, but the approach and expectations may differ.

Shared Media Architecture

Any perturbation of a shared media network affects whole groups of users. Older half duplex Ethernet segments and all 802.11 wireless segments are affected. The list of suggestions for shared media is suitable for full duplex and switched environments; it is simply harder to obtain to the same degree of visibility into what

is taking place compared to the visibility that can easily be obtained in a collision domain. Other media access protocols may be approached in the same manner.

- Check half duplex wired segments for maximum 802.3 architecture repeater count limits for your topology. The 5-4-3 rule only applies to 10Mbps. Daisy-chained hubs in a user workspace may provide convenient ports, but may also introduce errors. Users rarely inform network support staff that a hub was attached.

- Transmit background traffic into each collision domain to sensitize any latent errors that might suggest a media or duplex problem. In particular, watch for excessive collision levels, FCS errors, late collisions, and ghosting.

- Check the environment where wireless will be (or is) deployed for interference that is competing with your network (see Figure 8-6 later in this chapter). It is possible that well-distributed and channel-separated access point placement cannot overcome the background RF noise in some channel bands. This noise might not be detectable without a spectrum analyzer.

Switched Architecture

The primary difference between a shared media segment and a switched segment is the number of users affected. A switched connection typically services only one network device, and therefore a problem on that link affects only a single user. The following tests are a continuation of the tests listed for shared media, and may be applied to both environments:

- Use SNMP or console access to check switch ports for collisions, collision fragments, alignment errors, FCS errors, late collisions, and so on. The most common problem on a switched network is duplex mismatch, and these are some of the characteristic symptoms. Similarly, dirty fiber connections may result in various MAC Layer errors and warn of impending service disruptions.

- Use SNMP or console access to check switch ports for more than one MAC address. Most networks are now designed for a single station connection per port. Multiple MAC addresses suggest that either the user has attached an additional hub or switch, or that an access point was connected. On most networks, only the switch uplink ports should have more than one MAC address present, authorized access points would also constitute a switch uplink port.

- Stress test each switched path by performing bidirectional throughput testing from station connections on each switch and going back to the switch providing the uplink, leaving the VLAN or other broadcast domain toward the data center. Use your functional network diagram to ensure that all paths have been tested with traffic rates in excess of 90 percent of the path bandwidth to ensure that no duplex mismatches or other problems exist. Depending on which end is set to which duplex setting, it is possible to perform throughput testing in one direction with good results. Be sure to perform testing simultaneously in both directions.

- Use SNMP to review all active ports in the switched network for the presence of MAC Layer errors. Switch port interface statistics reveal areas to investigate for bad cables, noise sources, and other Physical Layer problems that reduce performance. Some collisions may be present if the station linked at half duplex.

- Look for excessive broadcast traffic. Extensive use of VLANs has diminished the frequency of excessive broadcast traffic generally, but fault conditions are often revealed by elevated broadcast traffic levels. Remember that all stations within a broadcast domain must stop and evaluate all broadcasts. 1 percent broadcast traffic at 10Mbps represents as many as 140 broadcasts per second. At Gigabit rates that could be 14,000 broadcasts per second, 1 percent broadcast traffic at Gigabit rates could cause your PC to appear to be locked up.

- Use the rate-limiting features available from many switches to block any broadcast traffic in excess of a configured percentage. Doing so will permit the network to continue to operate in the face of a bridging loop (which results in a broadcast storm). Choose a percentage high enough for routine network use to continue (consult your baseline), but low enough that a broadcast storm does not debilitate performance. At the same time, ensure that network management generates an alert if the broadcast level approaches the configured ceiling. This technique also allows you to access devices through the attached network despite the presence of a broadcast storm.

Top Error Reporting Stations

Every network will experience some number of errors. After observing the behavior of a network segment for a period of time, the normal level of errors will become evident. Any sudden or intermittent rise in the number of errors should be viewed as a warning that a problem is developing on the network, and should be investigated.

For shared media, consider the ratio of error frames to normal data frames. If a particular station is identified as being involved in a disproportionate number of errors, that station should be investigated for possible misconfiguration, malfunction, or failure. One exception to this would be if that station is generating a majority of the valid network traffic, and the ratio of errors to good traffic is similar to that of other stations. Investigate situations where a specific station is associated with errors regularly.

For switched media, a few errors may be present due to a variety of reasons. However, single-station connections to switch ports should not routinely have any errors. Investigate any persistent error count. Watch for duplex mismatches in particular. On even moderately recent hardware, Auto-Negotiation will avoid nearly all duplex problems, except in situations where the driver software is flawed. Download new drivers and leave Auto-Negotiation enabled on stations and workgroup switches.

Collisions

For shared media Ethernet, the number of local and remote collisions (collisions occurring within the first 64 bytes of a frame) depends on a relationship between the number of stations attempting to transmit at a given moment, the number of repeaters (including hubs) separating transmitting stations, and the size of the frames they are transmitting. A reduced traffic level conceals many problems that could be totally debilitating at higher traffic levels. Also note that some problems, such as late collisions, might not be detectable unless the measuring device is transmitting from the measurement point at the same time that monitoring is being performed.

Because collisions are considered a normal part of Ethernet operation, a relative measure indicating what impact the collisions are having is more important than a simple collision count. There is a long-standing industry reference of a 5 percent average collision rate being the point where you even *begin* to notice the collision level. Ethernet will continue to operate adequately in the presence of higher average collision levels.

Note that utilization and collisions are related. On shared media links, the average utilization should be evaluated in relation to the level of collisions and errors detected. As long as the average error or collision level remains quite low and the link is not fully saturated, the link is probably not overutilized. Concern about detected errors often depends on the type and quantity of errors. Collisions can spike quite high without seriously disrupting communications, as long as the average collision rate remains low enough. There is a generally accepted rule of thumb that anything more than an average of 40 percent utilization on shared media is cause for concern. This utilization level has been shown to be quite conservative by several studies, including *Measured Capacity of an Ethernet: Myths and Reality* by Boggs, Mogul, and Kent, although more recent research suggests that this paper presented slightly elevated throughput levels as an artifact of their very slow PCs not contending as aggressively as more recent PCs.

For switched media, it is unusual but possible for a station to link to the switch in half duplex.

If this occurs, as long as there is only one station per switch port the average half duplex utilization should be able to reach 80–90 percent without any problems. Collisions will necessarily be present because collisions are the medium arbitration method in half duplex. All the collisions should occur very early in the frame, and there should never be any late collisions or FCS errors.

If Auto-Negotiation is enabled, the station should link at full duplex. Failure to link at full duplex is almost always the result of one link partner having been administratively forced to full duplex while the other link partner was obligated to select half duplex because of the Auto-Negotiation rules. This produces collisions, late collisions, FCS errors, and so on. Watch for these errors to identify duplex mismatches.

Recent versions of switch software may assume that all links will be full duplex, so the presence of more than a *very* small number of collisions causes the switch to disable the port—even though it linked in half duplex. The configuration may be changed to prevent port disabling in the presence of collisions.

Noise

At 10Mbps it is important to measure the energy on the cable to see whether it is actually in the form of valid data frames, or if it is simply electrical noise that is causing other stations to believe that valid frames are present when they are not. The term *ghost* is used to describe this type of noise.

Network bandwidth is reduced by an amount slightly greater than the amount of ghosting present because stations are required to wait the interframe gap before transmitting. Ghosts will not be observed as errors by standard 10Mbps network adapters because the signal appears to be a transmission from another station. The presence of ghosts causes stations to back off in the same way they would if another station were transmitting. This type of error reveals a Physical Layer problem and often indicates problems such as ground loops, noise sources near the cable, or bad repeaters. Very few tools will detect ghosts. Ghosting is never acceptable, and should always be viewed as a medium- to high-priority problem, depending on the quantity detected.

At speeds above 10Mbps, the link is almost always synchronous and Physical Layer fault conditions such as noise will usually cause the link to go down. Watch for link LEDs turning on and off, and look for MAC Layer errors on a switch port.

As with other media access protocols, the 802.11 wireless MAC is supposed to deal with environmental problems like RF interference (noise) transparently to higher layers. Unfortunately, this generally results in dropped higher-layer connections, VPN tunnels dropping, and generally poor performance with no indication of the cause. It is possible to infer the presence of RF interference by monitoring the MAC Layer errors, but isolating the source of the interference almost always requires a spectrum analyzer. If your wireless is used for noncritical traffic such as web surfing, a bit of poor performance may be acceptable. However, if business-critical traffic crosses the wireless network, periodic monitoring of the RF health would be an appropriate part of regular site surveys. The location measured to provide the capture shown in Figure 8-6 was unsuitable for 802.11b/g because of the background noise, but 802.11a would work well.

In Figure 8-6, the top-left pane shows that two RF interference sources are occupying significant portions of the spectrum used by 802.11b/g. The bottom-left pane shows that channels 1 and 6 are about half occupied by something, but there is still some unused bandwidth available for data transmission. Channel 11 is almost entirely blocked by the microwave and fixed-frequency interference source. The top-right pane shows bar graphs per channel indicating the noise floor from the current measurement location. The plus symbols (+) indicate the signal strength for the access point heard best from the current measurement location out of the 35 access points detected. In the 802.11b/g band, only channel 6 has a signal clearly above the background noise floor, as well as all the access points in the 802.11a band. The bottom-right pane is a traditional spectrum analysis signal measurement graph. The 802.11b/g bands are nearly completely unusable from the measurement location this screen capture was taken from. The rogue access points operating on channel 2 and channel 8 were contributing to the problems with channels 1 and 6. The visible symptom seen by 802.11b/g users was that they

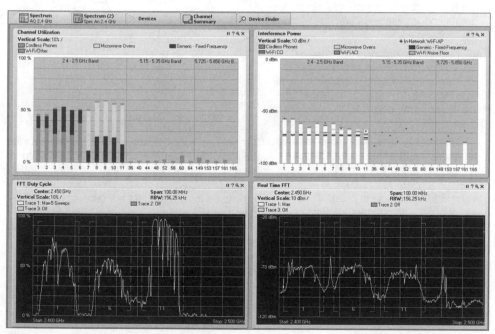

Figure 8-6. *Wireless interference shown by AnalyzeAir*

had great signal strength from the access point they were associated with, but found the network nearly totally unusable. The 802.11a users had no problems at all. An attempt was made to trace the generic noise source shown in dark blue (including a portion of the brown, which the spectrum analyzer was having trouble separating from the 802.11 traffic), and it was decided that the likely source was the mercury vapor lighting in the convention center where this screen was captured. The microwave oven appeared intermittently, but when it was on, it disabled channel 11 completely.

Until performance has been characterized for the particular access point models considered, from a practical load perspective:

- Assume that a consumer-grade access point can only support about 10–15 active users (email, web, etc.), whereas a commercial-grade access point can support perhaps 30–35 active users.

  - The limits on user support *should not* be different between consumer and commercial access points. Probably for market segmentation purposes (to justify the higher cost for commercial access points), performance differences have been observed.

- For a dense user community to have good service, you would use the nonoverlapping channel separation concepts to build your grid (see Figure 8-7), while at the same time turning the antenna power all the way down and disabling 802.11b.

  - Commercial systems offer more features related to multi-access point environments that mean you can support more users in a given space, but this will involve additional access points. Features are available from recent wireless offerings that permit same-vendor access points operating in adjacent airspace to self-adjust channel and power settings for maximum coverage.

  - Although disabling 802.11b is desirable, it is often not possible because many non-PC wireless devices do not support

the 802.11g, 802.11a, or other newer specifications. This is especially true when legacy or embedded devices are present. Having such a device present but undocumented is a common cause of poor performance (and very difficult to diagnose).

- Wireless devices will run at the fastest speed they can reliably operate. For example, 802.11b will transmit at 1, 2, 5.5, and 11Mbps depending on various operating conditions. If you discover devices operating at low speeds from within the operational selection offered by the supported technology, you have a network design problem in the local environment.

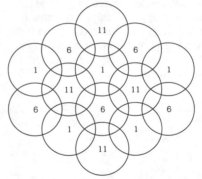

Figure 8-7. *802.11b/g use of nonoverlapping channels to build a grid coverage. A comparable grid may be created for 802.11a.*

It should be noted, though, that the arguments for the sort of nonoverlapping channel grid shown in Figure 8-7, or proposals to have less than 25MHz of separation, which would allow four channels to be used for the grid, do not take into consideration the effect of client radios. The interference present is more significant than an analysis of the access point placement and channel separation suggests. Further reading on the effect of cross-channel interference may be found by searching the web for the term "near-far effect."

Although access points permit any channel legal for your country to be selected, the manufacturers of access points seem to have optimized the code for channels 1, 6, and 11. These are the channels with the widest separation that are legal in the United States. If you are using multiple access points, try to ensure that they are grouped on nonoverlapping channels, because this permits them to listen to and interpret the management protocol between each other. Interpreting the management traffic on the same channel is far less disruptive than dealing with traffic from adjacent overlapping channels, which is ignored except as noise. Field test results show a noticeable improvement in performance with this configuration scheme. Also permit access points to adjust the output power to optimize coverage if the access point has that capability. Excess output power increases the probability of multipath interference without increasing the performance to compensate.

When deciding which channel(s) to use, be sure to do a site survey. Most access points ship with channel 6 configured, possibly because interference sources such as microwave ovens are more likely to be found near channel 1 and cordless phones near channel 11. Some locations are so rich in other wireless use that a site survey can reveal as many as 200 access points operating close enough to detect. Picking the best channel for 802.11b/g access points requires knowledge of any such existing RF environment. Use of 802.11a avoids the problem of picking nonoverlapping channels and avoids most of the common interference. Repeat the site survey periodically to adapt your installation to changes made nearby.

Note: *For specific information about wireless technology, consider one of the wireless certification programs that are available. This text defers to those focused training programs for nearly all wireless information.*

Monitoring the Network Layer

The Network Layer must provide logical station addressing services that duplicate the physical station addressing services provided by the Data Link Layer, and it must also provide for error handling and reporting. Each Network Layer protocol will issue and respond to a specific set of errors that control its operation. Many of these errors are

related to proper delivery of messages between interconnected LANs and WANs—typically across routed connections, and to avoiding data loss because a receiving station is busy and unable to accept data at that moment.

For example, ICMP messages within the IP traffic reveal problems related to misconfigured routers and hosts, and help identify congested devices. Monitor for any ICMP traffic within each broadcast domain, and look for errors that indicate problems with the delivery and routing of IP traffic. Watch for similar error indications from other protocols.

Locate Users and Addresses

Managing IP address allocation in a planned and meaningful scheme is important. There are many purchased applications for this purpose, and even some good open-source applications (such as IPplan). Establishing a means for identifying the current user and location of an IP address is critical for troubleshooting.

- When static addressing was common, it was important to maintain a list of all addresses detected on your network. With DHCP addressing, it is important to be able to identify the current user of a particular address. Establish a method for cross referencing MAC and IP addresses with the user. If your network is fairly stable, use DHCP reservations for important hosts and leave a pool of unassigned addresses for visitors and new hosts. If reservations are used, either map DNS names appropriately or consider some of the utilities for mapping login accounts to IP addresses dynamically. Another option is to dynamically write the MAC address into DNS when DHCP addresses are issued for live troubleshooting, and log the event to syslog for tracking historical troubleshooting activity. Alternatively, use NetBIOS to identify the current host using a given IP address. Windows responds to NetBIOS discovery as a default state.

- For 802.11 wireless, be sure to specifically record the identity of all authorized access points in addition to the client stations. Use this list to establish or update authentication server configurations, such as 802.1x with a RADIUS backend. Recent innovations include the ability to demark a physical perimeter and deny access from outside the building or other perimeter.

- For wireless users, establish a means for quickly identifying which access point they are presently associated with so that you can rapidly learn the general location of any address. This is useful for security purposes in addition to general network and user support.

Response Time Testing

Knowing the normal response time for a specific path, or whether a specific path is still operational, is very important to solving problems once they happen. Use whatever means of response time testing that may be available for your network.

Most response time testing is performed at the Network Layer; however, some functionality has been defined for the Data Link Layer. The IEEE 802.2 LLC defines "XID Command PDU and Response PDU" frames (referred to here as another form of ping) for the LLC sublayer. This type of ping is effective only within a broadcast domain. Unfortunately, most Ethernet products don't appear to respond to the LLC ping frame—although 802.2 requires it in Clause 6.6.

It might be more important to test response time at the Network Layer than at the Data Link Layer because Network Layer traffic crosses the end-to-end path. If a problem exists, this will be revealed quickly without taking time to test each segment separately, including WAN links. As the path between stations becomes more complex, greater variations in the response time can be expected. Knowing the normal amount of time it takes to cross a specific path, or whether a specific path is still operational, is vital to network support staff. Without this information, it is extremely difficult to locate the source of network slowdowns and failures.

- Run the appropriate Layer 3 ping test(s) to verify LAN and WAN connection paths, to learn average response times, and to ensure reliable connectivity to network resources.

The test can also run in continuous mode, which will help isolate intermittent paths and interconnect devices by showing how often packets are dropped.

- Use a similar utility to learn the response time for higher-layer protocols such as TCP for a specific port number. Servers are often still up and running on the network, even though a hosted application has failed or stopped responding for some reason. The Layer 3 ping does not show this, but using the Layer 4 port number for a connection attempt does. Traditional SNMP-based network management would show the server as being up and operating but would not indicate whether the service was operating.

- Depending on how a discovery packet is formed, it is possible to send a succession of frames out toward a specific destination. Each subsequent frame is permitted to get one hop closer to the destination address, and the response time for each frame is measured. By this means, often referred to as *traceroute*, an exact listing of the routed path leading to the destination address can be obtained (see Figure 8-8). Failure of this process identifies the IP address of the router where the delivery of messages to the specified destination station fails. Security features on many routers and firewalls disallow ICMP messages, so it is easily possible that no response from one or more hops along the path may be followed by responses later in the path. Alternatively, at that point, the router or firewall might terminate all responses.

Monitoring the Transport Layer

A considerable part of monitoring the Transport Layer is actually looking for symptoms, which suggest problems at lower layers. These symptoms often relate to retransmissions and difficulty in achieving high throughput because the TCP slow-start process is not able to reach its full potential for large transfers (see Figure 8-9).

```
Command Prompt                                                        _ □ X

C:\>tracert www.cnn.com

Tracing route to www.cnn.com [64.236.16.20]
over a maximum of 30 hops:

  1    <1 ms    <1 ms    <1 ms  10.232.124.249
  2     3 ms     1 ms     1 ms  10.232.124.18
  3     3 ms     2 ms     2 ms  500.Serial1-8.GW4.SEA4.ALTER.NET [157.130.178.49]
  4     2 ms     2 ms     2 ms  117.ATM3-0.XR1.SEA4.ALTER.NET [152.63.105.146]
  5     2 ms     2 ms     3 ms  0.so-0-0-0.XL1.SEA4.ALTER.NET [152.63.107.234]
  6    23 ms    23 ms    22 ms  0.so-5-0-0.XT1.SCL2.ALTER.NET [152.63.1.13]
  7    23 ms    23 ms    22 ms  0.so-6-0-0.BR1.SCL2.ALTER.NET [152.63.57.49]
  8    23 ms    22 ms    23 ms  pop2-sjg-P3-3.atdn.net [66.185.141.213]
  9    27 ms    27 ms    27 ms  bb2-sjg-P1-0.atdn.net [66.185.150.98]
 10    33 ms    33 ms    33 ms  bb2-las-P7-0.atdn.net [66.185.152.22]
 11    33 ms    32 ms    33 ms  bb1-las-P2-0.atdn.net [66.185.152.24]
 12    71 ms    71 ms    71 ms  bb2-hou-P6-0.atdn.net [66.185.152.27]
 13    67 ms    66 ms    66 ms  bb1-hou-P1-0.atdn.net [66.185.152.152]
 14    81 ms    83 ms    81 ms  bb1-atm-P7-0.atdn.net [66.185.152.184]
 15     *        *        *     Request timed out.
 16     *        *        *     Request timed out.
 17     *        *       ^C
C:\>_
```

Figure 8-8. *Traceroute example using a command prompt from Windows. When there is no response due to a network problem or a firewall dropping ICMP traffic, an asterisk (*) is shown for the attempt. Notice that either an IP address or name may be used because the traceroute utility will resolve the name to an IP address before starting.*

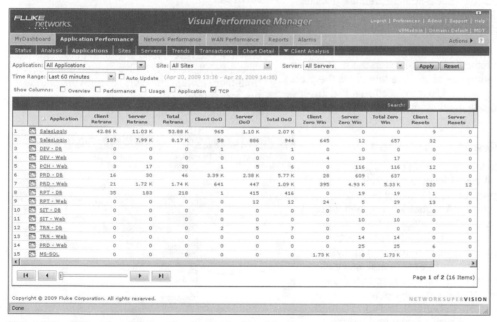

Figure 8-9. *TCP performance metrics reported by Visual Performance Manager's Application Performance Monitoring tests*

If the lower layers are operating without problems, less-than-optimum performance may sometimes be traced to Transport Layer configuration parameters. Changing the window size for hosts performing large transfers may be helpful if simple bandwidth and file size calculations suggest that a large transfer should have taken considerably less time even when zero windows are not observed. Dropped packets suggest buffering or queuing problems, flapping routes, and so on.

If monitoring suggests that further investigation is warranted, use of one or more of the following would be the next step in either isolating the source of the problem or further characterizing the problem:

- SNMP analysis of infrastructure devices along the path, checking for errors and utilization statistics

- Flow protocol analysis of utilization statistics

- Console access to infrastructure devices along the path, checking for errors and utilization statistics

If no errors or bandwidth problems are discovered, protocol analysis is often the next step in discovering the cause. In a few cases the problem is due to Layer 4, but more often it is a lower-layer problem showing as a Layer 4 symptom.

Application Monitoring

Application monitoring comes in several forms. A useful level of monitoring would be to track or trend protocol level response times. A higher level of monitoring tracks transactions made by the application, possibly across multiple protocols. The highest level of monitoring analyzes those actions and transactional activities and attempts to pass judgment on the application efficiencies. Just as with baseline development in general, most application monitoring is concerned with identifying

what normal is and presenting that as a trend or graph. Only the more expensive application-monitoring tools use the built-in rules and libraries to produce reporting on whether normal is acceptable. These advanced tools will necessarily be customized for specific programs or database types, whereas the application-monitoring tools that operate at lower levels may be applied to well-known or new and unknown applications.

Trending and monitoring solutions reveal when the monitored activity is behaving abnormally. These solutions typically ignore periods of no activity, assuming that there are no users submitting requests to the server. There are two situations that relate to zero traffic being observed for a particular service: no current requests to be satisfied, and the service being unavailable. Both situations are possible, but one should trigger an alert to the support staff. Ping and SNMP testing will reveal that the server is up, but not that the service is up.

Basic application monitoring may be used to isolate which server or application within a tiered application server farm is the source of a slow-down. It can reveal load-balancing problems (see Figure 8-10), and it can also exonerate the servers from blame when the client or network path to the server farm is the problem.

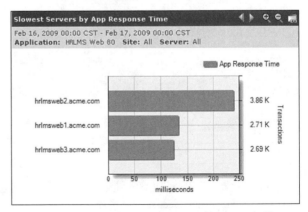

Figure 8-10. *Load-balancing problem revealed by Visual Performance Manager's Application Performance Monitoring tests*

Higher-level application analysis performs live monitoring of various applications in much the same way that post-processing has long been available using captured traffic from the network. The more recent live monitoring solutions may be highly customized to show an extensive variety of metrics in a format unique to each user's preferences. The metrics monitored may be configured with thresholds for alarm notification.

Either as part of routine monitoring or as the result of an alarm, it is possible to view the transaction details via a protocol analyzer trace file to discover the source or cause of a particular type of slowdown or failure. Unfortunately, with many applications this involves a tiered architecture with multiple servers closely interacting and depending upon each other. Obtaining synchronized captures, and having the knowledge of each part of the application required to analyze this from a trace file, would be challenging. More recent advances in application monitoring permit storage of transaction details from the entire tiered architecture for a short period as part of the monitoring process. For transactions taking place

within the last few days, it is possible to begin with the initial client request at Tier 1, and follow the transaction details back through multiple tiers looking for abnormal behavior. Storing all transactions for longer periods requires a very large storage capacity, and beyond a short duration of time the troubleshooting value of that stale information is eclipsed by the cost of storage.

In Figure 8-11 through Figure 8-13, a single Tier 1 client request is followed back into a tiered architecture to learn the cause or source of a slowdown. The first screen shows slightly more than 23 seconds for the encrypted HTTPS request to be satisfied. Despite not being able to decrypt the request, it is possible to bracket the time interval for the request and examine activity in the second tier. Figure 8-12 shows three Tier 2 transactions, one of which took about 2.5 seconds. Following that 2.5 second transaction to Tier 3 shows multiple database calls required to satisfy it. In this example, it seems that the first tier server is the source of most of the delay.

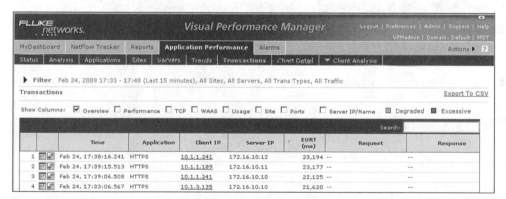

Figure 8-11. *Following requests through a tiered architecture—this screen shows the first tier HTTPS request. The first transaction will be used as the key to look at the second tier. The results are sorted to bring the slowest responses to the top of the list.*

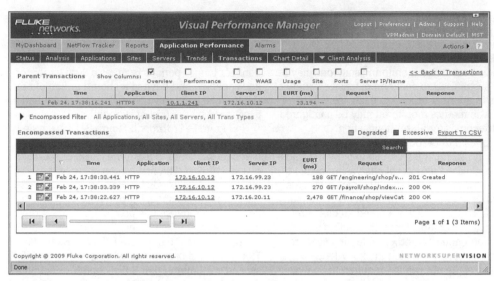

Figure 8-12. *Following requests through a tiered architecture—this screen shows the "parent" transaction, as well as Tier 2 activity most likely to relate to the Tier 1 transaction. The third transaction will be used as the key to look at the third tier.*

Figure 8-13. *Following requests through a tiered architecture—this screen shows both "parent" transactions, as well as Tier 3 activity most likely to relate to the Tier 1 transaction.*

A high-level analysis will take an application view of the traffic on the wire plus the processes within the server. An example might be an Oracle database transaction. Oracle may use several different protocols during the conduct of a single transaction. The very high-level analysis would monitor the transaction across multiple protocols, and may be tracking more than 200 metrics within the server. This sort of analysis is starting to become more common, and can be exceptionally useful for fine-tuning application configurations. Due to the highly customized nature, an application monitoring solution of this type is likely to monitor only one vendor's implementation of the single application.

Application-monitoring solutions are now considered to be basic and required tools for the support staff. Use of these tools permits the support staff to become aware of system degradation long before the users would notice, and to learn about outages at least as soon as the users. The key advantage provided by application monitoring is that even when the support staff becomes aware of the problem at the same moment as the user community, the application-monitoring solution informs them exactly what went wrong and where. Because the data is stored for a period of time, it is also possible to go back in time and see what led up to the problem. A number of monitoring solutions automatically trigger a protocol analysis capture to be taken continuously in a FIFO manner for a period of time or at the first sign of the problem onset, so that the exact cause may be identified.

Summary

This chapter described a variety of considerations for planning for support, monitoring performance, and documenting a network in a methodical way such that network down time is minimized. None of the suggestions and descriptions are expected to provide any special insight, and instead ought to be self-evident after a moment's reflection.

- Undertake planning, installing, and maintaining a network according to a process that includes all the key staff and addresses the full lifecycle of the network.

- Create full network documentation and implement a process to keep that documentation as up to date as possible.

- Ensure that critical support resources are readily available to support staff, and that all critical network resources are subject to a tested and regular backup cycle. Ensure that a copy of the backups are offsite so that an earthquake, fire, or other disaster does not destroy the originals and the backups at the same time.

- Monitor network behavior and performance. Use that information to support the network, and to plan network changes and upgrades to accommodate changing network demands in a timely and orderly manner.

The suggestions provided are only a starting point, and should be expanded on and modified according to local conditions and limitations.

Chapter Review Questions

To aid in your comprehension of important concepts, the following questions are provided. Refer to this book's Introduction for a general legend that indicates the anticipated difficulty of each question. For answers to these review questions, see Appendix I, "Answers to Chapter Review Questions."

 1. What seven strategic concepts provide a framework for dealing effectively with routine network support?

 2. What is one way you can judge whether your documentation is complete or accurate enough?

 3. During a troubleshooting incident, what value would a network functional diagram play?

 4. Does development of a baseline establish what is acceptable or what is normal? Explain your answer briefly.

 5. Over what minimum duration of time should a network be monitored for trending purposes?

 6. Name two types of information that may be learned from response time testing.

 7. Name two types of information that may be learned from application monitoring.

CHAPTER 9
Troubleshooting

Learning the art of troubleshooting is often a slow and tedious process of learning from mistakes and hours of study. The process may be accelerated by trying to follow a formula, by recording the results of prior troubleshooting episodes, and by gathering troubleshooting information from all available resources.

Best Method

As yet, there is no "best" method for troubleshooting, just as there is no single tool that solves all your networking problems. This chapter describes several different approaches to troubleshooting. Humor illustrates the problem that troubleshooting presents.

The first example is the saying, "When the only tool you have is a hammer, everything begins to look like a nail." This can be interpreted in many ways. One way to interpret this is to describe how a person who has become very proficient at a particular network diagnostic product is able to apply that product to situations it is technically unsuited for. This is not because the product is capable of detecting certain classes of problems, but because the user can interpret the test results based on experience and knowledge and arrive at a conclusion that is close to correct. Another way to interpret this is that the user was able to bludgeon the network hard and long enough that the marginal or failed element was eliminated in some way, and the user concluded that bludgeoning is a suitable substitute for troubleshooting.

Another example is the joke about how several blindfolded people were tasked with describing an elephant (see Figure 9-1). Everyone disagreed because the only information they had was what each person directly experienced. The person touching the tail described how an elephant was like an odd snake. The person touching the leg described how an elephant was like a tree. Descriptions of the trunk and the flank of the elephant produced further contradictory descriptions. Each description was accompanied by the emphatic assurances of the person providing the description that their description was correct, because that is the only first-hand experience that person had of an elephant. To add confusion, they all agreed on what the skin felt like.

If the person troubleshooting does not have a working knowledge of the technology, adequate information gathered from multiple points or information sources, or is lacking experience for a broader interpretation, incorrect assumptions and conclusions are made. The accuracy and speed of troubleshooting depends on the knowledge, skill,

and experience of each technician involved and the tools at their disposal. It sometimes requires interpretation by an uninvolved third party who is able to provide an objective opinion.

Process

The key to successful troubleshooting is for the technician to know how the network functions under normal conditions. This enables the technician to quickly recognize abnormal operation.

Unfortunately, many networking products are not delivered with adequate performance specifications, theory of operation, or condensed technical data to aid in troubleshooting. The more successful technician will thoroughly study whatever data is available and develop in-depth insight into the function of all components and how to operate them. Finally, he or she will remember that conditions appearing to be serious defects are often the result of improper usage or operator error.

The foundation of this insight is usually gained through formal training. But the true troubleshooting master learns through trial and error, comparing notes with others, and discovering tried-and-true methods not often taught in school. Following a good formula or process for troubleshooting that includes careful documentation of your actions and your hypothesis for what might be causing each problem can help flatten your learning curve and at the same time shorten the time required to solve network problems.

Two extreme approaches to troubleshooting almost always result in disappointment, delay, or failure. On one extreme is the theorist or *rocket scientist* approach. On the other is the practical or *caveman* approach. Because both approaches are extremes, the better approach is somewhere in the middle using elements of both.

- The *rocket scientist* analyzes and re-analyzes the situation until the exact cause at the root of the problem has been identified and corrected with surgical precision. This sometimes requires taking a high-end protocol analyzer and collecting a huge sample (megabytes or gigabytes) of the network traffic while the problem is present and inspecting it in minute detail. Although this process is fairly reliable if performed by a skilled protocol analyzer user, few companies can afford to have their networks down for the hours—or days—it can take for this exhaustive analysis.

- The *caveman's* first instinct is to start swapping cards, cables, hardware, and software until miraculously the network begins operating again. This does not mean it is working properly, just that it is operating. Unfortunately, the troubleshooting section in some manuals actually recommends caveman-style procedures because providing suitable technical information is too much trouble. Although this approach may achieve a change in symptoms faster, this approach is not very reliable and the root cause of the problem may still be present. In fact, the parts used for swapping may include marginal or failed parts swapped out during prior troubleshooting episodes.

For the technician in search of a better way to troubleshoot, try the approach that follows. Once learned, the art of troubleshooting can be applied with very slight changes to almost any corrective situation. The process described next could be used to fix a lawnmower, a camera, or a software program.

Analyze the network as a whole rather than in a piecemeal fashion. One technician following a logical sequence will almost always be more successful than a gang of technicians, each with their own theories and methods all troubleshooting the problem at once.

The logical technician asks the user questions, runs diagnostics, and thoroughly collects information. In a short time, he or she can analyze and evaluate the symptoms, zero in on the root source of problems, make one adjustment or change one part, and cure the problem. The key is to logically isolate the smallest failing element and replace or reconfigure it. *Complete understanding of the cause of the failure is not required at this time.* The primary goal is to rapidly restore network operation. After the network is again running, further analysis may be undertaken—preferably in a lab environment.

Figure 9-1. *Personal experience often makes it difficult to accept another perspective or opinion.*

There are many technicians with years of experience who have not yet mastered the basic concept: A few minutes spent evaluating *all* the symptoms can eliminate hours of time lost chasing the wrong problem. All information and reported symptoms must be evaluated in relation to each other, as well as how they relate to the overall operation of the network; only then can the technician gain a true understanding of what they indicate. After you have collected data about the symptoms, you will then need to conduct tests to validate or eliminate what you think the problems could be. If adequate symptoms are known, perhaps the evaluation process is mental and does not involve the network or physical testing at all. When you think you understand the problem, you must then verify it. At this stage, your efforts will be directed toward attempting to cause the problem to recur on demand.

Just as important: The logical technician always performs a checkout procedure on any repaired equipment or system, no matter how simple the repair. Far too often the obvious problem is merely a symptom of another, less obvious problem and until the source is eliminated, the situation will continue or reappear.

After the problem has been solved, document and share the identifiable symptoms and the solution to that problem so that others don't have to reinvent what you have learned.

Don't start troubleshooting the user's network problem unless the problem is still there following a cold start. Many "network" problems originate in the operating system housekeeping.

The last step is to provide feedback and training to the users. If they are informed of what action caused the problem or the nature of the problem and solution, they will either avoid doing it again in the future or will be able to provide a more specific description for the next problem.

Eight Key Steps to Successful Troubleshooting

The following list of steps provides a guideline for approaching most problems: anything from fixing a lawnmower to a network. The list also supports the troubleshooting process later proposed by the CompTIA training program.

1. Identify the exact issue.
2. Re-create the problem (if possible).
3. Localize and isolate the cause.
4. Formulate a plan for solving the problem.
5. Implement the plan.
6. Test to verify that the problem has been resolved.
7. Document the problem and solution.
8. Provide feedback to the user.

Step 1. Identify the Exact Issue

Defining the scope of the problem and deciding on the exact issue is important. Have the person who reported the problem explain how normal operation appears, and then demonstrate the perceived problem. If the reported issue is described as intermittent, instruct the user to contact you immediately if it ever happens again. It is very difficult to fix something that is clearly working just fine right now.

Don't jump to conclusions about what the users mean. Take the time to really understand the problem encountered, feeding back what you think they are saying. Don't discount what the users report simply because it sounds implausible. The users do not have your knowledge of networking and probably are describing the problem poorly. For example, if users report an error message of some sort, they most likely didn't write it down and don't actually know what it said. You

may be given error text that is either made-up or remembered from some other episode that is not relevant to this issue. *Something* annoyed the user enough to contact you.

Which Approach Is Best?

Has it ever worked? If the reported failure has never worked properly, treat the situation as a new installation and not a troubleshooting event. The process and assumptions are completely different.

Step 2. Re-create the Problem

Ask yourself if you understand the symptoms, and verify the reported problem yourself if possible. Problems are much easier to solve if they can be re-created on demand. Seeing the problem will allow you to observe error messages and various symptoms the user might not think important to relate, and may even provide the opportunity for you to collect network statistics during the event.

If the problem is intermittent, instruct the user what sort of symptoms are likely and provide a *written list* of what questions you are seeking answers to so that the user can gather some of the information if you are unable to respond quickly enough to see it yourself. When possible, leave a diagnostic tool gathering information continuously. A protocol analyzer may be left gathering all traffic from the network and overwriting the buffer as it fills. Have the user halt its operation and/or store the current test results from other testers *immediately* upon rediscovering an intermittent problem.

Step 3. Localize and Isolate the Cause

When you have defined the problem, and re-created it if necessary, you should attempt to isolate that problem to a single device, connection, or software application. Reducing the scope of the problem in this way is where *divide-and-conquer* begins; the goal is to isolate the problem to the smallest element that could cause the problem. Test for and eliminate as many variables as possible. Assuming that the initial problem report came from an individual user, a thumbnail outline of one general approach might be as follows:

- Locate the user's network connection port using a documentation database lookup, room wall plate information, or user MAC or IP address.
- Locate switch and port, and log in to the switch console.
  - Verify that the port is up and not disabled.
  - Verify that there are no port errors and that the duplex, speed, and VLAN are correct.
- Contact the user to verify MAC or IP, and NIC configuration.
- Visit the user location.
  - Connect a diagnostic tool in place of the user's station and obtain a DHCP address configuration, or assume the IP addressing of the problem station.
  - Verify connectivity to DHCP server, DNS server, and default router using ping.
- If connectivity testing fails, test patch cable and horizontal cable for possible problems.
- If cable is appears to be okay, move to wiring closet and connect a diagnostic tool directly to switch and repeat connectivity tests. Try an adjacent free port if connectivity tests fail.
- If the switch port is okay, place the diagnostic tool inline to verify or troubleshoot station connectivity.
- If the diagnostic tool connects but the station does not, verify NIC configuration.

Chapters 10, "Troubleshooting Media," and 11, "Network Troubleshooting," offer guidance in selecting appropriate tests to align with the reported symptoms, which is based on the theoretical knowledge presented in Chapters 1 through 7. It is not necessary or desirable to start all troubleshooting episodes with cable testing, though your mental checklist should start there. If you fully understand the operation of the network, performing a continuous ping test could be your starting point because the results will direct your troubleshoot-

ing higher or lower in the OSI Model. The symptoms themselves may suggest a starting point for troubleshooting. For example, if presented with an error message generated by a software application, start with the application, not the cabling. Some example considerations follow.

Is any normal function missing, or is there an abnormal response? Use the data gathered by your network-monitoring tools to aid you in this process. Particularly note the time of day the problem existed. Sometimes the problem source can be localized by correlating events to time, and then monitoring at that same time another day.

Determine whether *anything* was altered at that station or on the network just before the problem started. Often the user does not realize that changing something seemingly unrelated can cause problems on the network, such as rearranging the location of a portable heater or photocopier, or installing a new software application or adapter card. Do not discount the local environment when you are looking for change. Temperature changes (heat is often a problem), electrical use from adjacent spaces—including nearby businesses, time of day or day of the week, and influences from electronic sources. Even the passage of an elevator or use of a cordless phone should be noted.

Can the problem be duplicated from another station, or using other software applications at the same station? Identify whether the problem is limited to one station or one network resource, such as a printer. Move one segment closer (one switch or router closer) to the network resource and try again. If the problem goes away when you move closer to the network resource, test or replace the intervening infrastructure equipment.

If the problem affects an entire shared media segment, isolate the problem by reducing the variables to the fewest possible number. Try shortening the cable segment on a bus topology, or temporarily recabling a ring or star topology to create the smallest possible network for troubleshooting purposes. Try a different switch or hub. If the problem is on the same shared media segment as the network resource, try turning off or disconnecting all but two stations. Once those two are communicating, add more stations. If they are not communicating, check the Physical Layer

Never believe users...unless they confess. Verify everything yourself.

possibilities, such as the termination of the cable, the cable itself, or the specific ports used on the infrastructure equipment (hubs and switches). If the problem is on a wireless segment, try the problem station in another area of the building so that you associate with a different wireless access point (and possibly move out of range of a previously unknown interference source). If possible, try another wireless frequency because the 802.11b/g frequency range is often contending with many interference sources, whereas the 802.11a frequency range is still relatively free of competition.

If the problem can be isolated to a single station, try a different network adapter, a fresh copy of the network driver software (without using any of the network software or configuration files presently found on that station—delete them if necessary). Try accessing the network using a diagnostic tool from the existing network cable connection for that station. If the network connection seems intact, determine whether only one application exhibits the problem. Try other applications from the same drive or file system. Compare configurations with a nearby but operational workstation. Try a fresh copy of the application software (again using none of the existing software or configuration files).

If only one user experiences the problem, check the network security and permissions for that user. Find out whether any changes have been made to the network security that might affect this user. Has another user account been deleted that this user was made security equivalent to? Has this user been deleted from a security grouping within the network? Has an application been moved to a new location on the network? Have there been any changes to the system login script or the user's login script? Compare this user's account with another user's account who is able to perform the desired task. Have the affected user log in and attempt the same task from a nearby station not experiencing the problem. Have the other user log in to the problem station and try the same task.

Step 4. Formulate a Plan for Solving the Problem

After a single operation, application, or connection is localized as the source of the problem, research, and/or consider the possible solutions to the problem. Consider the possibility that some solutions to the problem at hand may introduce other problems.

Chances are good that the problem you are experiencing is not all that unique. Use the resources available on the web or from your vendors to see whether they already have published solutions.

Note 1: *To avoid unwanted repetition, and to make it possible to back out any changes made if things get worse, be sure to carefully and completely document all actions taken during the problem resolution process. Copy all configuration files to a safe place before modifying them— especially on switches, routers, firewalls, and other key network infrastructure devices.*

Note 2: *It is advantageous to open a second terminal session into the switch or router where the commands required to reverse a configuration change are typed in and ready to execute prior to actually implementing the change in the first window. This is likely the fastest way to recover from changes that adversely affect your network.*

Step 5. Implement the Plan

Your actual solution to the problem may be replacing a network device, NIC, cable, or other physical component. Some categories of wireless problem might not be solvable without substantial engineering effort, such as switching part of the building to 802.11a. If the problem is software, you might have to implement (or remove) a software patch, reinstall the application or component, or clean a virus-infected file. If the problem is the user account, the user's security settings, domain membership, or logon scripts may need to be adjusted.

For network hardware, it is most expedient to simply replace a part and attempt to repair the part later. Another option is to change the connection to a spare port and cover or otherwise mark the suspect port. Remember that the goal is to restore full operation of the network as soon as possible.

Two avenues exist for solving software problems. The first option is to reinstall the problem software, eliminating possibly corrupted files and ensuring that all required files are present. This is an excellent way to ensure that the second option—reconfiguring the software—works on the first try. Many applications allow for a software switch that tells the installation program to disregard any existing configuration files, which is a good way to avoid being misled by the error and duplicating it yet again. If this option is not evident, it is often better to remove the application before reinstalling it. Be sure to reboot the problem station *before* installing fresh software because many operating system updates and patches are installed in the background and only await the next reboot to take effect.

If the problem is isolated to a single user account, it is often faster to repeat the steps necessary to grant the user access to the problem application, operation, or domain as if the user had never been authorized before. By going through each of these steps in a logical order, you will probably locate the missing or incorrect element faster than by spot-checking. Sometimes everything is configured correctly and it still does not work due to some sort of corruption. In some situations, it might be expedient to simply delete the whole account and start over, or to remove the station from the domain and re-add it. With the increase in standardized images and virtual systems, it might be faster and more appropriate to reimage or copy a new virtual instance onto the problem station and start fresh. A fresh standard image is also likely to have the latest operating system patches and the latest virus protection already applied.

Step 6. Test to Verify That the Problem Has Been Resolved

After you have implemented the solution, ensure that the entire problem has been resolved by having the user test for the problem again. Also, have the user quickly try several other normal operations with the equipment. It is not unheard of for a solution to one problem to cause other problems, and sometimes whatever was repaired turns out to be a symptom of another underlying problem.

Step 7. Document the Problem and Solution

Documentation is useful for several reasons. First, documentation can be used for future reference to help you troubleshoot the same or similar problem. You can also use the documentation to prepare reports on common network problems for management and/or users, or to train new network users or members of the network support team.

Step 8. Provide Feedback to the User

There is often a temptation to fix the problem and leave. However, if network users reported the problem they will appreciate knowing what happened. This will encourage them to report problem situations in the future, which improves the performance of your network. Another reason for feedback is that if the user could have done something to correct or avoid the issue, it may reduce the number of future network problems.

A good working relationship between network support staff and the user community can significantly enhance your ability to keep the network running smoothly. Failure to take users seriously or making unprofessional remarks can cause adversarial relations to develop, and can undermine your ability to do your job.

There is also a saying that 75 percent of fixing a problem is "fixing the user." If the user does not agree that the problem has been taken to its conclusion (whether or not the problem has been corrected, or you have explained *to the user's satisfaction* that a fix is impossible for the following technical, financial, or political reasons…), you have not ended this support issue.

A Place to Start

Like everything else, don't assume that a short course and a book or two will make you the networking equivalent of Sherlock Holmes. Take the time to learn one or two aspects of networking very well before seeking the next topic. Feel free to ask for help or guidance with everything else in the meantime. This approach will help you avoid making many common blunders.

The first suggested step in troubleshooting is to gather information. If you don't know what normal operation is like, and you don't know the behavior of the underlying technology, it is difficult to gather information and symptoms about the current failure effectively.

A good example is a sadly too frequent comment on a technical support phone line for network diagnostic tools:

Caller: Please help me isolate this broadcast storm!

Response: What symptoms are you experiencing?

Caller: My tester is reporting 100% broadcasts, so I have a broadcast storm.

Response: What is the utilization percentage right now?

Caller: (pause) That's odd. It says 0.03% utilization, but 100% broadcasts.

Response: By chance, are you connected to a switch port?

In this example, the caller did not understand the normal behavior of a bridge. All broadcasts are always forwarded to all other ports. But only appropriate unicast traffic is forwarded to a given port. Evidently, the tester in question was not soliciting any network traffic, so the only traffic observed passively consisted entirely of broadcasts.

When starting out, try to follow up on topics of interest from the first subject(s) of study so that your knowledge expands from a central point. Hopefully, you will be working up the OSI Model as you progress. A significant number of senior networking specialists have either forgotten or never knew the basic operation of many elements of the network. Technology is changing very fast in this industry, and they have usually chosen to focus on the higher-layer aspects to the exclusion of developments in the lower layers. This causes them to make incorrect assumptions about some symptoms, and delays problem resolution accordingly. Because these people are often in positions where network architecture decisions are made, a number of expensive upgrades have been purchased unnecessarily. Nobody knows it all, so ask for help when you are unsure. Consult multiple sources when the answer sounds too good to be true or is questionable.

Similarly, each course or book offers insightful knowledge and experience in specific networking topics, but sometimes goes on to address topics that would be better left to other subject matter experts. One of the indications that you understand a topic or concept well enough is when you can identify the point where that happens, if it does.

If you are just getting started, try to arrange your course of studies in the following order. The order listed provides two benefits: the LAN topics appear in order from easiest to most challenging (the amount of knowledge required to master topics expands and diversifies as you go up the OSI Model); and mastery of topics in OSI Model order provides a sound foundation for understanding and troubleshooting problems in higher layers.

- Cabling and issues related to *physical media*.
- Media access protocols, issues related to connectivity *from the NIC to the first hub or switch*, and the OSI Model.
- Network Layer protocols and issues related to a broadcast domain (the connection *from the NIC to the first router*).
- Higher-layer functions as your needs and interest dictates. For example, *protocol behavior*. (After end-to-end dataflow is taking place, what happens?)
- WAN technologies (the end-to-end connection across the whole network).

Summary

This chapter described how troubleshooting is a skill that depends largely on the knowledge of the technician. The ability to apply that knowledge when evaluating symptoms determines how quickly additional tests may be selected that localize and isolate the problem to the smallest correctable element. After the cause of the problem is determined and a solution implemented, further steps related to documentation and user training should be taken as appropriate to the situation.

Solving the problem is often not the end of the situation. What is learned should feed back into the continuous process of planning and maintenance described in Chapter 8, "Preventing Problems."

Chapter Review Questions

To aid in your comprehension of important concepts, the following questions are provided. Refer to this book's Introduction for a general legend that indicates the anticipated difficulty of each question. For answers to these review questions, see Appendix I, "Answers to Chapter Review Questions."

 1. What is the most important aspect of a given network that must be known by a technician in order to recognize that something is amiss?

 2. What would a good approach to troubleshooting be? What should be avoided?

 3. What eight troubleshooting steps are listed in this book (and happen to be recommended by the CompTIA organization)? Use your own words to describe (briefly) what should or should not be done at each step in the process. (It is possible to succinctly summarize this information in 1–3 sentences per step.)

 4. List an important safety measure that might be prepared and ready when troubleshooting switch and router configurations during the business day.

 5. Why is "fixing the user" so important?

 6. As a generalized answer, what order is recommended for studying networking topics?

CHAPTER 10
Troubleshooting Media

This chapter is separated into two sections:

* Copper media
* Fiber optic media

Chapters 2, "Copper Media," and 3, "Fiber Optic Media," described the behavior and testing techniques for copper and fiber optic media separately, as the behavior of electrons and photons in a network cable are quite different. This chapter addresses them separately, but because networks incorporate both media types, the troubleshooting of media is combined into this single chapter.

Troubleshooting Copper Media

Troubleshooting copper media relies heavily on an understanding of what good workmanship looks like, and on knowledge of the behavior that each field diagnostic test is measuring. The tools used for certification of a new cable installation are the same as those used to isolate and locate failures. The difference is that troubleshooting relies on the expectation that the suspect cable passed a certification test in the past, and something has changed that needs to be located and corrected.

Tools

A broad range of tools can be used to troubleshoot copper cabling, although with the move to higher and higher data rates, the less complex and inexpensive tools are simply unable to detect problems that affect the high data rate technologies. On the other hand, if the cable plant was fully and properly certified at the time of installation, the less complex and less expensive tools may be adequate for locating faults caused by abuse and neglect.

Continuity Testers and Toners

Many different continuity testers are available, and some are available at very low prices. The test capabilities range from the attractive equivalent of a battery and light bulb used to ensure that there is a connection from one end to the other, up to the ability to test continuity by pair and to map pin-to-pin wiring.

The best use of this category of tester is in the Telco industry, where wire continuity is one of the more important issues. This category of tester is not well suited for network applications.

The ability to source and trace tone for finding unlabeled cables is usually available separately at a low cost. Finding unlabeled cables is a common problem, and the ability to trace cable should be available to all network support staff, particularly the help desk and network technicians.

Pair Testers

This category of tester is distinguished from a continuity tester by its ability to detect a split pair. A split pair is the simplest problem related to frequency that plagues network cable, and should be a minimum entry point for a network cable tester. If a cable passes the split pair test, it has a pretty good chance of passing a basic Category 5 certification test.

Pair testers are just adequate for troubleshooting an already certified cable plant. The certification process would have revealed any frequency related problems at the time of installation, and failures occurring later are almost always related to cable abuse.

The high end of this category of tester is well suited for most noncertification-related tasks. It still should not be considered as an alternative for proper cable plant certification because it is simply unable to certify the performance of the frequency-dependent test parameters. It is, however, a very capable troubleshooting tool at an attractive price.

Testers in this category should be considered for each technician as a standard part of their toolkit because they are smaller and far less expensive than a full certification tool. Providing this level of tester to frontline support staff would vastly improve their ability to solve problems on the first visit. A significant number of problems faced by the frontline technician are cable related, so equipping them to test for that type problem and training them to test the cable very early in the troubleshooting process saves a lot of time and frustration. The tester should be at least capable of finding opens, shorts, pairing problems (including split pairs), and the distance to a detected fault. The ability to source tone is a plus.

Some testers in this category are able to test for cable pairing, shorts, and opens from only one end. This offers a decided advantage when terminating cable because the technician is then confident that a certification tester can be left attached and ready while the technician goes to the other end to finish terminating. The certification test can be accomplished immediately then, while the technician is there and completely prepared to reterminate the cable if a problem is detected. It does not take many immediate repairs to recover the comparatively low cost of this preliminary screening tool.

Frequency-Based Field Certification Testers (Cable Analyzers)

The first generation of field certification testers usually offered selections for Category 5 cable types, but the tester performed tests only up to the frequency rating it was designed for—often a maximum of 10 or 20MHz. Many of these testers are still in use, and the users are not aware that the tester is unable to certify a 100MHz cable. This generation of tester should be considered a high-quality pair tester in this list because of its limited frequency range.

The second generation of field certification testers became available in late 1995 or early 1996 and offered 100MHz testing. Care must be taken with some of these older testers; in the interest of a faster test time, the default setting was often for testing at wider frequency intervals than the standards specified. If this fast test mode selection was used, the tester could skip over frequencies that failed the currently configured test. This generation of tester is capable of certifying Category 5 cable but not Category 5e cable (both 100MHz). There are some additional tests required for Category 5e that the hardware in this generation of tester is simply not equipped to perform. This generation of tester usually allowed the user to store summary test results for several hundred cables. Complete test results for all tests performed were rarely available for even the most recent test performed.

The third generation of field certification testers became available in late 1997 to early 1998 and offered testing to Category 6 speeds or higher. Choosing a Category 5e or Category 6 cable type almost ensured that the second- or third-generation tester would do what you expected. It is still possible to choose a test standard such as 10BASE-T that causes the tester to limit the frequency range, test suite, and number of pairs tested to something less than what cable type chosen is able to support. This generation of tester is easily distinguished from the previous testers because the accuracy required for Category 6 (250MHz) made it necessary to have different cable interfaces depending on whether the Channel Link, Permanent Link, or the now obsolete Basic Link was specified. These cable interfaces are often dubbed as noses for the tester. After the concept of different cable interfaces was accepted by the manufacturers, who were reluctant to require the user to carry around a bag of interfaces, the capability to test fiber with the same tester became easily possible. This genera-

tion of tester is capable of storing more than 1,000 test result summaries and saving a small number of complete test results. By changing the removable storage media, the user is able to save an unlimited number of either test results. Having complete test results electronically permits the network manager to reevaluate the entire cable plant at any time to see how many links support a new cable quality requirement.

The fourth generation of field certification tester became available in early 2004 and rivals the accuracy of lab-quality equipment. The tested frequency range exceeds ISO Class F (600MHz) cable. Unexpectedly, although the range of frequencies tested increased substantially between the third- and fourth-generation testers, other improvements in electronics allowed for a reduction in the overall test time despite the vastly increased number of tests performed.

The fifth generation of field certification tester became available in late 2006 and is identifiable by it capability to perform alien crosstalk testing. This feature is needed to certify 10GBASE-T and Category 6A/ISO Class F_A installations. Depending on the make, model, and age of the fourth-generation tester, it may or may not be upgradeable to perform alien crosstalk testing.

The anticipated next generation of field certification tester will have a tested frequency range of at least 1GHz.

Margin

There are two issues related to margins: the accuracy of the tester and the margin between the measured test results and the standards limits.

Measurement Accuracy

TIA/EIA-568-B.2, Annex I, paragraph I.2.2, requires that if the measured result is closer to the Pass/Fail limit than the measurement accuracy of the tester, the instrument should indicate that there is a statistical probability to doubt the Pass/Fail outcome. For example, if the accuracy of an instrument were +/- 2dB, and the measured margin is only 1dB, it is possible that the tester could either fail a good link or pass a bad link. When this situation is possible, the tester is required to qualify the Pass/Fail judgment with an asterisk (*), indicating this possible test result interpretation error (see Figure 10-1).

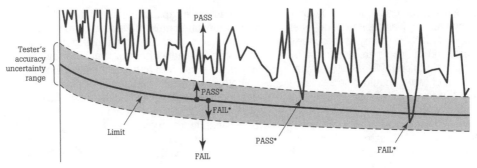

Figure 10-1. *Cable tester measurement accuracy uncertainty*

Test Results Margin

For troubleshooting and link performance purposes, a worst-case margin is far more important than a relatively useless worst-case test result. Be careful which number you rely on. Worst-case test results almost always appear around the highest frequencies measured. This compares to claims that under optimum conditions a certain model of automobile is capable of exceptionally good fuel economy, when what you really want to know is how efficient that particular vehicle is for in-city driving.

Interestingly, the worst-case margin is often measured at lower frequencies where exceptionally small amounts of crosstalk are permitted. This is also right around the frequency range where the most energy is typically transferred.

Prorating Cable Test Results

Keep in mind that field testers are told which standard to use for comparing measured test results against, and the test results simply need to be better than the worst-case limit. That means that when you test a short cable against the test standard for Category 5e, the tester does exactly that. It will compare all results against the Category 5e limits for a 100-meter link. It does not know that you intend to connect a short, barely passing cable to other cables to form a link. Each cable may have received Pass results separately, but together they fail. The tester does not prorate against the measured length before comparing test results against the limits.

During the late 1990s the infrastructure network at the Interop trade show experienced random bad links throughout the network each time the network was deployed, despite complete pretesting of all individual cables. After a few shows it became apparent that the entire copper cable plant—some 2 million feet of Category 5 cable—needed to be prorated. This was necessary because there was no way to anticipate which cable would be used for a particular link or what length that link needed to be. Sound familiar? After consulting the available standards and other resources for guidance it was determined that there was nothing published that would provide limits for prorating based on length. After a long chat with cable test design engineers some arbitrarily selected lengths and NEXT performance limits for prorating the Category 5 Basic Link test results were chosen. Those numbers were adjusted following each subsequent trade show deployment until no more performance failures were reported on the installed links. Bad links were still found, but virtually all remaining cable problems were visibly identifiable as resulting from cuts, abrasions, and other abuse. There is no math or theory to back these numbers up, but they make a nice place for someone to start from. The prorating limits for Category 5 after the third adjustment follow:

0–15 feet—At least 9dB margin better than the limit   **100–200 feet**—At least 4dB margin better than the limit

15–50 feet—At least 5.5dB margin better than the limit   **200–300 feet**—At least 3dB margin better than the limit

50–100 feet—At least 5dB margin better than the limit

These sample limits should transfer readily to Category 5e unadjusted.

General Testing and Installation Issues

Most networks have converted from coax to Category 3, to Category 5 or Category 5e, and soon to Category 6 or Category 6A twisted-pair links. However, there is still a surprising amount of coax used for WAN and wireless, and in legacy network LAN segments where low bandwidth is still satisfactory. Fiber is at or approaching a price point where it will rival Category 6A twisted pair in overall cost (material, installation, and network adapters). There are installation and maintenance issues that are different for all cable types. Following are several testing and troubleshooting issues for each cable type.

As mentioned, despite the conversion from legacy coax Ethernet to twisted-pair implementations there is still a lot of coax used for WAN and wireless links. The coax type for thin Ethernet is 50 Ohm RG-58, whereas WAN links and 802.11 wireless antenna extension cables typically use 75 Ohm RG-59 and may experience virtually the same cable problems. The 93 Ohm RG-62 cables used for ARCNET is no longer common in networking.

Types of Twisted-Pair Cable

The similarity between older standards and newer standards for a particular designation, such as Category 5, has created situations where a cable manufactured (and labeled) in compliance with an older version of a standard no longer meets the same designation in a new, similarly labeled standard. This is true for the TIA/EIA-568 standard as well as the ISO/IEC 11801 standard.

Category 5 or ISO/IEC Class D cables manufactured between 1995 and 1999 generally meet the requirements for TSB67. When TSB95 was published in 1999, most new cable was manufactured to meet those tighter test limits, but the actual cable labeling often did not change in a way that the average person would notice. The cables might have included a date too, either Category 5 (1999) or Category 5 (2000), for example. The same is true for Class D (1999) or Class D (2000). What changed was the marketing campaign from the manufacturers. The manufacturers began differentiating their cable from other

manufacturer's products with fast-sounding product names. When Addendum 5 to TIA/EIA-568-A was released, the same thing happened again. This time the cable label might have changed to Category 5e, Category 5 (2000), or Category 5 (2001). A plethora of cables have names that were selected to suggest that they are perfect for Gigabit Ethernet and beyond. In fact, 1000BASE-T runs just fine on Category 5 cable that passes TSB95 test requirements. Category 5e is a better performing cable than 1000BASE-T requires. Similarly, 10GBASE-T runs on cable that meets the test requirements for TIA/EIA TSB155 or ISO/IEC TR-24750. Category 6A and Class E_A links perform better than 10GBASE-T requires.

This labeling situation is important to the consumer in two very important ways. First, do not place too much faith in the cable labeling or cable product family names. Instead, rely on the field cable tester results for performance to a selected cable standard of performance. Sometimes a link does not pass the labeled performance level; other times the cable performs to a higher grade (when installed with excellent workmanship). Second, because the standards sometimes change without altering the name of the cable grade, it is sometimes difficult to identify which version of the standard the product actually complies with. This did not have a particularly pronounced effect on 100MHz cables (Category 5 and Class D), but on the higher-speed cable systems the effect was alarming. The initial products from different manufacturers that were promoted as meeting the first drafts for Category 6 standards were fine when used as a complete end-to-end single-vendor system, but they sometimes tested to a lower grade when mixed with Category 6 components from other vendors. You had to maintain the same vendor and product family throughout the entire link to achieve the expected performance. The early or prestandard Category 6A and Class E_A links may well have similar results.

Thus, if you are attempting to upgrade your cable plant to a higher level of performance, it is necessary to retest each link in its final configuration to ensure that the link meets your expectations. Do not trust any labeling or marketing guarantee if you do not have a completely homogenous cable system installed at the same time from the same run of manufactured cable and connecting hardware. Even then, the installation workmanship may result in substandard performance. Test everything against the expected performance rating in its final permanent link and channel link configurations. The various link configurations of channel link, permanent link, and the now obsolete basic link are explained later. For now, be aware that this largely translates to leaving the tested patch cables in place for the user; you cannot use one set of patch cables to test all the links.

Naming of cables is an interesting subject too. The official designations are Category 5 or Category 5e. Attempts to promote Category 5E (uppercase "E") as being better than Category 5e (lowercase "e") are not supported by the standards. Such distinctions in the cable or connector designation were created by marketing. The cable manufacturers also came out with cables labeled Category 6e in apparent anticipation that the standard would use that as the next designation, which it did not. The TIA/EIA cable grade above Category 6 was chosen to be Category 6A (uppercase "A"). There is no Category 7, other than cabling components for ISO/IEC 11801. Specifically, the connectors, punch-down blocks, and so on are specified up to Category 7, but an assembled ISO link is specified as Class F. TIA/EIA has not published a Category 7 designation, and probably will not.

Cable Autotest

After a cable analyzer (a frequency-based cable tester) autotest function has failed a cable link, verify the following. Note: the first four bullets should be accomplished before testing begins on each new job:

- Has the tester been appropriately configured for this autotest?

- Has the correct link type been selected (permanent link or channel)?

- Are you using the appropriate cable interface adapter for this test? Some third-generation testers required interface adapters to match the installed cable for permanent link testing.

- Are you using the most current version of tester software? As noted earlier, standards

specifications change during the development phases. Sometimes standards are amended and "fine tune" the performance specification for one or more test parameters.

- Do the cable and connectors used in the installation match the performance settings of the selected test?

- If the link is a TIA Category 6/ISO Class E, or Category 6A/Class E_A installation, are all components matched appropriately? Some Category 6/Class E and Category 6A/Class E_A links installed before the standards body voted to approve that cable standard might not operate at the specified performance level when mixed with other vendor's materials.

- Is the tester at ambient temperature and in calibration? Temperature affects test results.

- Are the tester's batteries adequately charged? Some test results become unreliable when the tester batteries fall below 20 percent of full charge on some cable testers.

- Have you carefully reviewed the installation quality of terminations and reterminated where necessary?

- Are the cables too neatly "dressed?" If tie wraps are too tight, or if high-performance cable (TIA Category 6/ISO Class E, and especially Category 6A/Class E_A) is aligned perfectly in parallel for too great of a distance, it can create problems that otherwise would not exist.

If test results pass or fail with a marginal (*) result, examine the details to see whether there is a point-source problem that could be corrected to improve the measured result in a retest. Run TDR or TDX tests and examine the graph for evidence of the fault location.

If the test failed without displaying any marginal test results (those marked with an asterisk [*]), and there were no wiremap failures, there is very little chance that tuning the cable achieves a Pass test result for Category 6/Class E. If this is the case, use the advanced diagnostic features available from your cable analyzer to attempt to isolate the connection, cable, or patch cord as the source of failure. Start by running TDR or TDX tests and examine the graph for evidence of the fault location.

If the cable itself seems to be the source of the fault, or if you have a homogeneous Category 6/Class E system (all cable and connectors are part of a system from one vendor), save complete test results and record the tester's model, serial number, and software version. Contact the appropriate cable supplier, share your test results with them, and work to resolve the problem. Category 6/Class E products were sold for about two years before the standard was approved, and sometimes were not interoperable with other vendor's Category 6/Class E products. Similar issues may exist for early Category 6A/Class E_A cable installations.

Wiremap

Wiremap failures are the easiest to locate because they involve opens, shorts, and pairing faults. Use wiremap test results and length measurements to isolate the location of termination, continuity, and pairing faults. Some split pair faults may require a distance-to-crosstalk test (such as TDX) that operates in a manner similar to a distance-to-fault test (length or TDR) and is described in the "Advanced Cable Diagnostics" section.

Most wiremap failures occur at cable terminations, either at the RJ45 (plug or jack) or at an intermediate cross-connect or patch panel. Faults at the RJ45 can usually be seen by checking the wire colors carefully against T568A or T568B pinout colors, or by checking the RJ45 plug for wires that did not seat fully to the end of the connector when it was crimped. While checking for wires that were not fully seated, also try check to see whether the correct type of RJ45 was used (stranded or solid wire pins)—although that is difficult once crimped (see Figure 10-2).

Using the wrong style of pin may cause intermittent connections after a period of time, although the cable usually works immediately after it is made.

Another source of RJ45-related problems is how well the connector was crimped. In the group of four bad crimps shown in Figure 10-3, the top-left crimp pressed the end pins down adequately but not the center pins. The top-right crimp is exactly the opposite—the crimp tool pressed firmly in the center but both edges did not press adequately. The bottom two crimps show where pressure was applied firmly on one side of the crimp, but insufficient pressure was applied to pins on the other side and they were not adequately crimped. These four problems are usually associated with a low-cost crimp tool constructed with a plastic frame, where the plastic flexes as more pressure is applied. A multitude of other bad crimps are possible, including all pins being pressed evenly, but not far enough.

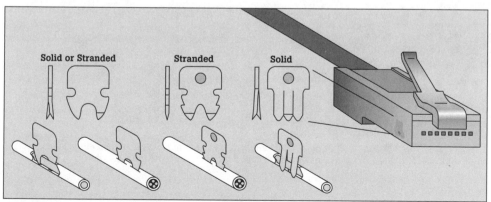

Figure 10-2. *Sample pin styles for crimping stranded and solid cable in an RJ45 plug*

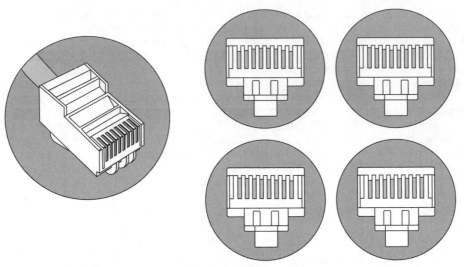

Figure 10-3. *Examples of bad RJ45 crimping*

Partial crimps are likely when the tool does not ratchet down, and permits the RJ45 to be removed from the tool before it is fully crimped. Sometimes the crimp tool is damaged and one or more pins are not crimped at all. Sometimes the crimp tool is not rigid enough, and it flexes to produce the problems shown in Figure 10-3. If a previous RJ45 plug was not crimped well, one of the wires in the jack might have been pushed flat, and might not extend out far enough to make contact with the pin in the RJ45 plug (see Figure 10-4).

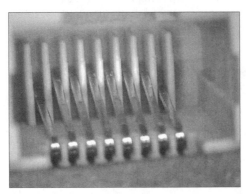 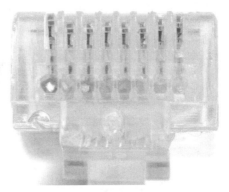

Figure 10-4. *(Left) RJ45 jack damaged by improperly crimped RJ45 plug pin. Outside pin on either side is permanently depressed. (Right) RJ45 plug that was not crimped properly (same as the top-right crimp in Figure 10-3).*

The jack problem in Figure 10-4 can often be corrected by finding a thin pointed tool and carefully rebending the pin so that its normal resting position places it in alignment with the other undamaged pins again. Take your time, and do not over-bend the damaged pin in your attempt to fix the problem. Be aware that this attempt may void some product warrantees. However, the risk in attempting this is small because the RJ45 jack is already damaged. If this problem is found in a classroom environment where students regularly make patch cables it might be appropriate to make a very short extension cable with a plug and jack, so that the extension cable is damaged by student cables instead of the equipment.

Be careful to examine the plastic separating each pin in the RJ45 plug because abuse or neglect may cause the plastic to bend over the pin and prevent the corresponding wire in the jack from making contact. This is a fairly common problem with patch cables.

In Figure 10-5, the top RJ45 plug has easy-to-see damage to the plastic separation between pin connections. Two pins will not make contact, and the third might not. The bottom RJ45 plug has bent plastic also, but without comparing the separation distance it is hard to see that the rightmost pin has too small a gap for contact with the wire in the plug.

Also examine the RJ45 jack to see whether any of the wires have been bumped out of their track and are shorting against an adjacent wire (see Figure 10-6).

Front View

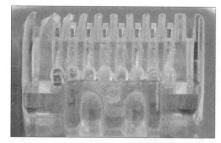

Top View

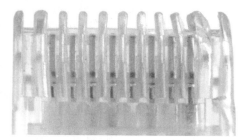

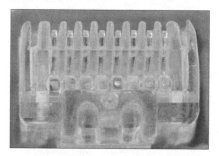

Figure 10-5. *Two examples of damaged RJ45 plugs found while troubleshooting*

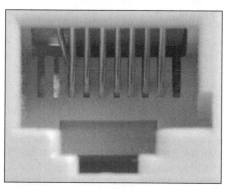

Figure 10-6. *Pin out of place inside an RJ45 jack*

Length

The problem of having network cabling installed by someone untrained in the requirements still results in cable installations in excess of the maximum allowed 100 meters. The cable may simply be too long. If the cable is too long, look for coiled service loops that the installer may have left and remove one or more. Service coils in ceilings and walls were common (and useful) at the time of Category 5 cable, but coiled cable causes various crosstalk problems with Gigabit and 10 Gigabit Ethernet.

Also check to see whether the NVP setting for the tester is incorrect, which results in inaccurate length measurements. NVP may be calculated by most cable analysis tools by simply measuring the physical length of a moderately long cable (at least 15 meters or 50 feet), and having the tester then calculate the length of the same cable. Adjust the tester's length calculation if necessary to obtain the NVP for that cable sample.

If one or more pairs of the cable are of substantially different lengths, check intermediate patch panels and interconnection points for loose wires and improper connections. Most such wiring faults are at these intermediate connecting points. Be aware that there will be minor length differences for each pair in almost all cables because the twist rate varies on each pair.

The TIA/EIA-568-B standard directs that the length of the shortest pair determines the overall length of the cable. This means that a long cable could have one or more pairs that measure longer than the standard allows, and the test still passes.

If the cable is unexpectedly short, look anywhere that facilities work or construction is underway or has recently been performed. If you have a general idea where the cable path lies, it should be relatively easy to estimate the location of the fault based on general length information. A common location for cut cables is the edge of new carpet, and doorways or other locations where the cable might have been pinched. Broken tabs on the RJ45 plug permit the plug to retract from good contact in the jack, and may cause opens over time without being immediately evident.

The electronic length of a pair is affected by the dielectric insulation used on the wire. If one or two pairs in the cable have a different insulation material than the other pairs, the NVP—and therefore the length—will be markedly different (see Figure 10-7).

Most high-performance network cable has Teflon as an insulation material on each wire. However, for about a year in the mid-1990s there was a Teflon shortage after a fire in a key Teflon manufacturing plant. Until a new Teflon supply became available, manufacturers experimented with using PVC as an insulator on the least-used wire pairs to reduce cost. The cable was generally available with either one or two pairs insulated in PVC and may be referred to as 3:1 or 2:2 cable. This mix of insulation material affects propagation delay and therefore length and delay skew. This type of cable is unlikely to perform adequately for Category 5e uses and should be replaced.

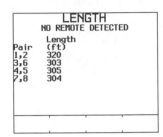

Figure 10-7. *Length measurement for a cable where three pairs use Teflon as the insulation material and one pair uses a PVC compound*

Insertion Loss

Insertion loss, more commonly known as attenuation, is usually associated with cable length. The amount of signal lost tends to grow proportionally to the length of the cable. Thus, the first place to check when trying to solve this problem is the overall length of the cable. Shortening the cable should help, if it can be done. Although the most logical cause, length is often not the source of the problem.

A far more common source of this problem is a very poor connection that often results from a loose cable, dirty or oxidized contacts, and so on. One bad patch cable can easily cause an entire link to fail. This type of problem increases return loss, which is why the attenuation test was changed to insertion loss. Run TDR or TDX tests and examine the graph for evidence of the fault location.

Another source of this fault is the wrong Category cable used, such as Category 5e cable used for a link being tested to Category 6A limits. Again, run TDR or TDX tests and examine the graph for evidence of the fault location.

Near End Crosstalk (NEXT), Alien NEXT (ANEXT), and Power Sum NEXT (PSNEXT)

Excessive crosstalk, usually reported in the NEXT test results, originates in two places: inside the link (in-channel) and outside the link. Crosstalk originating inside the link has the worst effect in the region nearest the transmission source where the transmitted signal is also the loudest. If the cable is left untwisted for more than the allowed 13mm (0.5 inch), the crosstalk will be correspondingly worse. For crosstalk, workmanship at each connection point should be examined (see Figure 10-8).

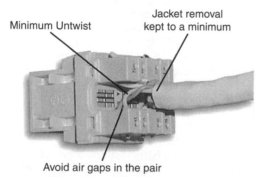

Figure 10-8. *Good workmanship example—pairs are untwisted only enough to terminate*

Reterminate any connection with visibly untwisted wire pairs. Try removing and repunching the cable at intermediate cross-connect locations if removing untwisted wire segments is not sufficient. The old Telco-style 66 blocks should not be used for network cabling because they have very poor crosstalk and other test result performance. To satisfy Category 5e, 6, and 6A requirements, the 110 style or other punchdown block should be marked for the level of performance it offers. Before spending time attempting to resolve crosstalk issues, refer to the "Advanced Cable Diagnostics" section for additional tests to help pinpoint the source of crosstalk problems.

There is a special situation in which a failing test result at a specific frequency or frequency range does not cause the overall test result to fail. The ISO standards include a so-called "4dB rule." Over the frequency range in which the link insertion loss is less than 4dB, NEXT tests pass regardless of the measured NEXT result as long as the ACR parameter passes. The TIA and ISO standards apply a similar rule for the evaluation of the measured return loss values. Over the frequency range in which insertion loss is less than 3dB the return loss test is informational only and is not used in the link Pass/Fail decision.

Noise

There are generally three types of noise:

- Impulse noise that is more commonly referred to as voltage or current spikes induced on the cabling

- Random (white) noise distributed over the frequency spectrum

- Alien crosstalk (crosstalk from one cable to another adjacent cable)

Of the three, impulse noise is most likely to cause network disruptions. Most cable analyzers have impulse noise test capabilities. The 802.3 standard set the default threshold level for the detection of impulse noise at 264 mV in Clause 14.4.4. For higher-speed network applications such as 1000BASE-T, the threshold value for impulse noise detection is 40mV in Clause 40.7.6. If there are very few pulses at this threshold level (less than 1 in 100 seconds), the cabling can deliver very good support (see Figure 10.9).

Impulse and random noise sources include nearby electric cables and devices, usually with voltage levels that are much higher than the voltage level of network signals and with high current loads. These may include large electric

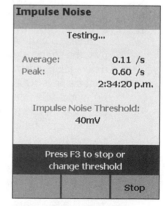

Figure 10-9. *DTX-1800 impulse noise test*

motors, elevators, photocopiers, coffeemakers, fans, heaters, welders, compressors, and so on. Another less obvious source is radiated emissions from transmitters, including: TV, radio, microwave, cell phone towers, hand-held radios, building security systems, avionics, and anything else that includes a transmitter more powerful than a cell phone. Some cable analyzers average this sort of noise out of the test results. In this case, the link test may take longer to run because many additional measurements must be taken.

A small amount of noise "riding" on top of the network signaling does not materially affect the ability of the receivers in NIC cards and other active network devices to properly detect and interpret the network signals.

If the noise is significant enough that the tester cannot average it out and the link fails test parameters such as NEXT, locate the noise source and move it or reroute the cable. If neither of these remedies are feasible, you may consider a shielded twisted-pair cable or an optical fiber cable. Finding the source can be challenging because external noise sources are often intermittent. Use of a spectrum analyzer is often required to determine the frequency and magnitude of the noise. While searching for the source, be very aware of what is occurring in the area. The sudden absence of noise can be as helpful in locating the source as its continued presence. Discover what was just used or turned off.

Alien crosstalk is a special case of noise because it is induced by other cables in the same pathway. Anytime a twisted-pair link is tested in a cabling bundling in which some links are active, the chances are very good that the tester will detect alien crosstalk—especially when the adjacent traffic is 100BASE-TX. Testers like the Fluke Networks DSP Series report an "external noise detected" message. Alien crosstalk does not often affect the reliability of network traffic operating at speeds below 10GBASE-T.

In general, detected noise does not impede or interfere with the reliable operation of the network if the following conditions are met:

- The cable analyzer completes an Autotest and the test results yields a "Pass."

- The impulse noise test executed on the affected cabling links shows less that 0.01 average pulses per second when the detection threshold is set to 40 mV.

- If a link is tested in a bundle with active links and the link passes with a NEXT headroom of 3dB or better over the required performance specification of the network application. If the cabling will be used to support 10GBASE-T, a separate set of alien crosstalk tests should be executed.

ACRF or Equal Level Far-End Crosstalk (ELFEXT)

Far-end crosstalk is generated by the same mechanisms that cause near-end crosstalk. The majority of crosstalk is the result of capacitive coupling along the cable. The far-end crosstalk signal is the result of signal coupling along the length of the entire link. All crosstalk resulting in the far-end crosstalk measurement will have traveled the total length of the link. Near-end crosstalk is much more sensitive to the location in the link where the crosstalk took place. The crosstalk generated in the region of the link closest to the transmitter (near end of the measurement) contributes much more to the measurement result (and the signal disturbance of the network signal) than a similar crosstalk signal induced on the disturbed pair at a long distance from the transmitter.

The effect of the far-end crosstalk must be evaluated in relation to the strength of the desired signal that has also traveled the length of the link. As long as the desired signal is significantly stronger than the FEXT disturbance, the reception will not be impaired. This measurement of FEXT relative to the attenuated signal used to be called Equal Level Far-End Crosstalk but has in the newer standards received the name "Attenuation-to-Crosstalk ratio, far-end" (ACRF). Installed links usually perform much better for the ACRF evaluation than they do for NEXT. Problems with FEXT would foretell problems with alien crosstalk as well. As a general rule, solving NEXT problems eliminates most FEXT problems measured as ACRF or ELFEXT. If this is not the case, check whether the cables are tied too tightly in big bundles. Loosen the bundles and allow more free flow for the cables in the pathway to reduce the effects of FEXT.

First, try replacing the RJ45 plug at the problem end of the link, and if that is not sufficient, try replacing the plug and jack with a mated pair from a cable system offered by a single vendor.

Return Loss

Return loss is a measure of all reflected energy caused by impedance mismatches or impedance changes along the link. It indicates how well the cabling's characteristic impedance matches its rated impedance over a range of frequencies. Small impedance changes may be caused by the manufacturing process of the cable. Impedance mismatches may be introduced by connecting hardware or by patch cords and equipment cords whose impedance does not match the cabling impedance very well.

The termination impedance at both ends of the link must be equal to the characteristic impedance of the link to avoid reflections. A good match between characteristic impedance and termination impedance in the end equipment provides for an efficient transfer of power to and from the link and minimizes reflections. Return loss results vary significantly with frequency.

One small source of return loss is variations in the value of the characteristic impedance along the cable. This may be due to slight untwisting or separation of wires in the pairs, or due to variations in the diameter and section of the metal conductors and the uniformity of the insulation. The parameter Structural Return Loss (SRL) measures the return loss of just cable by itself and is a function of the impedance uniformity along the length of a cable. SRL is an indication of how consistent the manufacturing process for that cable was.

Another source of return loss is reflections from inside the installed link, mainly from connectors. Mismatches predominantly occur at locations where connectors are present. The main impact of return loss is not on loss of signal strength but rather the introduction of signal jitter. For full-duplex signaling on each wire pair as used in 1000BASE-T and 10GBASE-T, return loss causes a direct noise disturbance for the signals traveling in the opposite direction. Return loss is to be measured and evaluated from both ends of the link (signal traveling in both directions). Signal reflections truly cause loss of signal strength but generally this loss due to return loss does not create a significant problem.

Because return loss causes reflections, the TDR test is used to locate the discontinuities causing the problem (see Figure 10-10). The TDR trace depicts the magnitude of the signal reflection along the length of the cabling link. The more severe the return loss problem, the greater the amplitude at the problem location on the TDR trace.

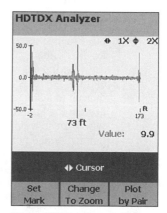

Figure 10-10. *Sample High Definition TDR test results from DTX-1800. This screen appears to have a very bad connection to the permanent link adapter, and a bad connection (maybe a consolidation point) or bad patch cable about 70 feet from the tester.*

Propagation Delay

TIA/EIA-568-B permits up to 498ns of propagation delay for the permanent link and up to 555ns of propagation delay for the channel link, for all categories. It is unlikely that this parameter could fail without other parameters failing as well. Failing propagation delay suggests inappropriate or bad cable in the link, or a cable that is simply too long.

Check the overall length of the cable. Inspect the cable closely to see whether the correct type of cable was installed. Also check whether the NVP setting in the tester matches the NVP rating of the cable. (NVP, or Nominal Velocity of Propagation, expresses the relative speed of the electrical signal over the cable. This parameter is used to convert the timing/delay of reflection into distance or length.)

Delay Skew

TIA/EIA-568-B permits up to 44ns of delay skew for the permanent link and up to 50ns of delay skew for the channel link, for all categories. Both of these numbers are quite generous. It is fairly difficult to fail delay skew if good materials were used in the link. A delay skew failure is possible if wire pairs in a single cable have different insulation material on different pairs. See the discussion under the "Length" heading earlier regarding different insulation materials. A failure is also possible if various lengths of twisted-wire pairs were used as a patch cable or jumper at a connection point.

Varying the lengths of pairs at any point along the link probably indicates bad workmanship because individual (loose) pairs should never be used for networking applications. This situation should cause other parameters to fail too.

Inspect the connection points in the link, and if the workmanship appears reasonable, you may have little choice but to replace the entire cable run. Test a sample of the new cable before installing it to be sure your materials are not causing the problem.

Interpreting Copper Cable Test Results

Before troubleshooting a failing cable link, verify the tester configuration. This step is critical to obtaining accurate test results. At a minimum, verify that the correct test specification and link type have been selected. Also, the test standards have evolved sufficiently that the requirements for a particular test might no longer be the same

as what is loaded in the software of your tester. Check the tester manufacturer's web site for new tester software regularly, perhaps two or three times per year.

Unlike network failures, cable failures are approached in approximately the same manner whether the link is newly installed or has failed during operation. There are many instances where a poor quality link has been in service but has stopped working due to the operating environment and influences. These influences include visible damage to the cable, as well as placing noise sources near the cable or moving the cable near a noise source. Another less obvious condition is that a new network physical layer implementation is now in use, such as an Auto-Negotiating network adapter that has linked at 1000Mbps instead of the 100Mbps that has been customary. This sort of condition could result from a new network adapter having been installed in the station, or from moving the connection to a different port on the hub or switch, or moving the connection to an entirely new hub or switch. Some ports monitor the link for polarity faults (pair reversals) and crossover cables (transposed pairs), and correct for them internally. The newly connected port might not be doing that, and an existing cable fault is finally exposed. Table 10-1 suggests many common sources of failure and the test that reveals them. This table is by no means the only source of these failures, nor does it portray the only test(s) that reveal the listed failures.

The following troubleshooting sequence, instructions, and interpretations assume that a cable analysis tool capable of performing frequency-based testing to the required range is used (100MHz for Category 5e/Class D, 250MHz for Category 6/Class E, 500MHz for Category 6A/Class E_A, and 600MHz for Class F). The cable testing features of many network diagnostic tools permit testing the non-frequency based parameters, but should not be confused with a proper and complete cable certification test.

Table 10-1. *Most likely cable test failures and causes*

Open	Short	Reversed Pair	Crossed Pair	Split Pair	Length problems	Delay Skew	Insertion Loss	NEXT	Return Loss	ACR-F (ELFEXT)	Alien Crosstalk	Description
•	•				•				•			Cut, broken, or otherwise abused cable
•	•											Damaged RJ45 plug or jack
			•									Mixed T56A and T568B color codes on same cable
						•						Different insulation material on some pairs
•	•	•		•	•		•	•	•			Poor workmanship at cable junction or connector
								•	•			Improper wiring at cable junction or connector
								•	•			Improper, poor quality, or Telco rated RJ45 coupler
								•	•	•	•	Poor quality or lower-rated RJ45 plugs/jacks
								•	•			Bad or poor quality patch cord(s)
									•			Mixed use of 100 ohm and non-100 ohm cable
					•		•					Cable is too long or NVP is set incorrectly
								•	•	•	•	Untwisted or poorly twisted cable (includes too low of a cable rating, such as Category 5 instead of Category 6)
								•	•			Cable ties too tightly fastened along cable
								•		•	•	External noise source near cable
											•	Cable too closely aligned for a moderate to long distance—remove bindings and/or separate slightly

See Appendix A for further causes.

Advanced Cable Diagnostics

To resolve a fault, it is necessary to know the location of the fault. Most effort is spent in locating the source of the fault. After the location is known, a physical inspection usually reveals the nature of the fault. Use either a time domain reflectometry (TDR) test or a time domain crosstalk (TDX) type test to learn the location of most faults (see Figure 10-11). Then try one or more of the following steps at the general location of the fault to resolve it:

- Repunch connections
- Replace patch cords
- Remove or loosen any tightly binding cable ties
- Replace connectors
- Remove or enlarge service loops of cable

The heading for this section is rather bold, but the processes come down to running a couple of extra tests and interpreting them carefully.

Twisted Pair Installation Issues

Category 6 and Category 6A cable is different from older cable categories. With Category 5e it is possible to leave a service loop "in the wall" for contingencies (a service loop is a coiled loop of cable that is left at the time of installation, and is intended either to allow for length lost to reterminations or to permit the end to be moved a short ways farther). With Category 6 and Category 6A the crosstalk performance requirements or the return loss performance might not be met if a tight service loop is present. A service loop places a segment of the cable in close proximity with itself long enough to induce additional crosstalk. A two-meter service loop could appear as a single (loose) loop slightly more than half a meter in diameter, which would not cause crosstalk problems, or as a tight loop only a hand-span in diameter with four loops tightly aligned in close proximity for those two meters that could cause crosstalk problems.

Twisted-pair cable used for medium to high-speed networks requires an increasingly greater number of twists per inch: the higher the speed, the greater the number of twists per inch. Flat, gray untwisted cable used for telephone systems (sometimes referred to as "silver-satin") should never be used for network applications. Although the network may continue to operate after one or more silver-satin patch cables are installed, a quick look at the MAC Layer protocol is apt to show a noticeable increase in errors. Even if the network survives a small number of these cables without a significant increase in errors, these cables might yet be what pushes the network into failure when something else becomes marginal. This type of cable is likely to cause a 100 Mbps or 1000 Mbps Ethernet link to fail immediately.

Purchase and use only high-quality crimp tools for twisted pair. Poor-quality crimp tools often fail to press the pins evenly into the RJ45. Poor crimping is due to not pressing one end side as firmly as the other, or by flexing and not pressing the middle pins or the outside pins as firmly (refer to Figure 10-3). The resulting problems tend to either damage the RJ45 of the equipment they are used with, fail to operate the first time out, or become intermittent in the future.

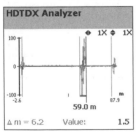
① Bad patch cord

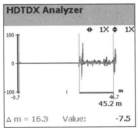
② Bad section of cable

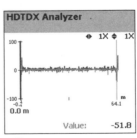
③ Bad spool of cable

Figure 10-11. *DSP 1800 HDTDX test results for several common cable faults. Left is a low-quality patch cord used in a better quality channel; center is a low-quality cable segment; right is a low-quality cable length.*

If the crimp was not adequate, you can almost always find a better crimp tool and simply recrimp the RJ45 plug. Be sure to find and discard the bad crimp tool. The intermittent problems caused by a bad crimp are quite difficult to troubleshoot because you rarely suspect a cable when data is flowing and the link light is on.

When building your own twisted-pair links, be particularly careful to purchase the correct connectors for the type of wire used (refer to Figure 10-2). Stranded wire is always used for patch cables, and is almost always the connector type offered unless you specifically request solid wire connectors. In the short term, both may function adequately, but if the wrong connector is used it usually results in intermittent connections over time. For example, if a stranded wire connector is used for solid wire, the pin simply touches one side of the wire and may stop making contact after the link is flexed or the pins oxidized during normal use.

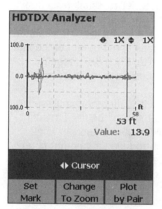

Figure 10-12. *DTX 1800 HDTDX test result showing the effect of a single Category 3 RJ45 plug on the first patch cord in a Category 6 channel. The vertical cursor is resting on the start of the second patch cord at 53 feet. The test configuration is for Category 6 channel.*

Also watch for older RJ45 plugs that are not rated for the newer higher-frequency cable systems. Newer plugs are labeled for their rated performance. Most RJ45 plugs look almost identical, and it is easy to accidentally use an older quality plug with a newer cable system (see Figure 10-12).

It is somewhere between difficult and impossible to obtain usable cable test results when testing a twisted-pair link that is still connected to a hub or NIC, switch, or other infrastructure equipment. The passive circuitry in the device interface distorts the signals used to test the cable, and causes results to become marginally to wildly inaccurate. The test signals may also (briefly) confuse the port itself, although the port almost always recovers on its own after receiving a transmission of "normal" data, without requiring a reboot.

Although it may work for slower-speed applications like telephone service, a single twisted-pair link should never be used by two network stations or two types of service unless your media access protocol has been specifically designed to be coexistent with the other service. Leave unused pairs idle if you want to avoid intermittent problems (like losing data every time the telephone rings). As the data transmission speed increases, the likelihood of problems increases (a 235kHz Apple LocalTalk connection is nearly immune to this problem, but an 80MHz 100BASE-TX connection would be highly susceptible). 1 and 10 Gigabit Ethernet both require all four pairs, so this shared-use is impossible.

No product is able to perform a complete test on a twisted-pair cable without connecting a loopback device to the other end of the run. Part of the reason for this is that to comply with the requirements of the standards that govern link testing, a pass or fail judgment might not be given unless the suite of tests includes a wiremap test, and that cannot be made without the loopback device. Another reason is that the link must be terminated with a resistance value equal to the impedance of the link for other measurements to be made accurately. Finally, the industry standards for certification require that a number of frequency dependent test parameters such as NEXT loss, FEXT, and return loss are to be tested from both ends of the cabling link. In other words, the link must be evaluated in both directions. The "remote test unit" is therefore the same size and offers the same measurement capability as the main unit. The test results data is collected, displayed, and stored in the main unit..

If twisted-pair cables must to be bound together, they should be bound loosely. There are a number of commercial fastening systems available that can be used to tidy up a wiring closet or a cable bundle. Be sure that you do not overtighten! When bundles of twisted-pair cable are too tightly bound at intervals along the length of the link, it changes the electrical characteristics and causes network errors. You should always be able to slide a single cable in the bundle forward and backward through a fastening with little effort. TIA/EIA-568-B.1 paragraph 10.1.1 states that cable ties should not even deform the cable sheath, and that you should be able to slide the cable tie loosely around the cable bundle. If you must pull firmly (TIA/EIA-568-B.1 clause 10.2.2 allows for a maximum 25 pound force (110 Newtons) of pulling tension during installation), or if the cable cannot be moved at all, your data is at risk. There have been instances where network problems *almost* disappeared when tie-wrap cable fastenings were removed to allow troubleshooting to begin.

Category 6A test requirements for alien crosstalk suggest that a carefully "dressed" cable plant experiences greater problems than one permitted to sprawl loosely but orderly. Alien crosstalk problems may be mitigated by placing cable in a free-flowing manner in trays or on ladders so that any one cable does not remain adjacent with any other cable for any significant distance. Separation of as little as one centimeter reduces or eliminates alien crosstalk problems. Conversely, if a cable bundle is aligned precisely for best aesthetic appearance it may experience moderate to failing levels of alien crosstalk.

Handle LAN cable carefully during installation and later during use. If the cable is kinked severely, walked on, caught under heavy office furniture, or driven over, it causes localized changes in the characteristic impedance, and may physically damage the insulation and wire. This abuse can result in point-source cable problems, usually NEXT and return loss problems for minor damage and shorts or opens for more significant damage. Use a TDR test to locate the fault.

Be careful when specifying interconnecting hardware for twisted pair. Make sure you use TIA/EIA-568-B pinouts for either the T568A or T568B specification throughout the entire network. If hardware such as punchdown blocks or wall jacks color coded for dissimilar pinouts is used together on the same link, the color codes for the wire positions will not match, and the links will fail wiremap testing unless custom patch cables

are used. Mixing T568A and T568B has the same effect as installing a crossover cable.

If high-speed protocols will ever be used on the twisted-pair cabling, it is vitally important to follow all the installation guidelines for Category 5e, Category 6, or Category 6A cabling. This includes no sharp bends or kinks in the cable. Also, do not untwist the pairs more than absolutely necessary for any connection, and avoid routing cables near any sources of electrical noise. High current draw equipment, electric motors, and RF signal sources are disruptive to network traffic.

Avoid installing cable near elevators. Movement of the elevator car itself is disruptive because the mostly iron car behaves much like a giant electromagnet when it travels up and down. More than one backbone cable run has later been moved away from a very handy and accessible elevator shaft to avoid frequent but intermittent network disruptions.

Be sure to test twisted-pair links for the frequency-dependent NEXT crosstalk tests from both ends of a link. There is always a transmission source at both ends, and it is not uncommon to obtain different results at either end of the link. For the same reason, TIA/EIA-568-B requires both ends to be tested using the frequency-dependent tests.

Never mix cables with different characteristic impedances. Media filters may be used to adapt between new and old cable systems for low speed use, but they introduce yet another potential failure point and should be avoided wherever possible. Replace a legacy cable plant instead of using media filters.

When untwisting wire pairs to install connectors or make connections at punch-down blocks, make the untwisted sections as short as possible, and maintain the original twist rate right to the separation point. For compliance with Category 5e and higher cabling standards, the untwisted section may not exceed 13mm (about half an inch) but a shorter untwist distance is better.

Do not make sharp bends or kinks in the cable. The radius of bends in a cable should be larger than one inch, although TIA/EIA-568-B.1 clause 10.2.1.1 permits four-pair twisted pair to have a cable bend radius only as tight as four times the diameter of the cable.

Avoid installing cable near locations that will experience wide temperature variations. The attenuation (insertion loss) will fluctuate by 1.5 percent per degree Celsius for Category 3 cable and 0.4 percent per degree Celsius factor for Category 5e cable. Category 6A may fluctuate 0.4 percent per degree Celsius between 20° and 40° C, and 0.6 percent per degree Celsius between 40° and 60° C. The following illustrates the temperature effect on network operation. A switch uplink cable from a computer room was installed in the suspended ceiling just below the roof in a desert climate (Arizona). The building air conditioning was automatically turned off right when the workday was scheduled to end. The network remained operational until spring, when the weather began to get quite warm. As summer approached, the network would become intermittent, and then fail within an hour of when the air conditioning turned off. Just after sundown, when the outside temperature dropped, the network would start working again. When the uplink cable was moved away from the roof, the network stopped failing in the evenings.

When upgrading a link from Category 5 to Category 5e, it is often possible to obtain passing results by replacing some or all the RJ45 plugs and jacks, and thus avoid the expense of pulling new cable. The additional tests for Category 5e are greatly affected by the plug/jack construction and mating. Category 5e easily supports Gigabit Ethernet, so replacing the cable plant with Category 6 or Category 6A is not necessary. Category 6 that passes Addendum 10 test requirements is sufficient for 10 Gigabit Ethernet.

Coax Installation Issues

These suggestions apply equally to legacy RG-58 Ethernet as well as RG-59 used for WAN links and 802.11 wireless antenna extension cables.

Coax requires termination at both ends of every run. The resistance value of the termination should be equal to the characteristic impedance of the cable; otherwise, electrical "reflections" of the data signal result. Sometimes the end of a coax run is attached directly to network equipment, which must then be configured or designed to supply the required termination internally.

Thin coax used for Ethernet may be grounded at only one point along the run, and thick coax is required to be grounded at only one point along the run. In either case, there should never be a second ground connection because problems often develop when a second ground connection point is present. The most common source of multiple ground points is when a thin coax "Tee" connector is rotated on the back of the PC and comes in contact with a grounded protective shield around the connector of another cable.

A coax cable may be tested with or without the termination present at the other end. If the far termination is present and is the correct value for that cable, you will not obtain a length measurement because the termination is doing its job. If the far termination is faulty or not present, a length measurement will be possible. If there is a fault along the cable, a distance-to-fault measurement is possible whether or not the end of the cable is properly terminated.

Never try to make a coax cable test from some point along the cable because you will receive signals from both directions down the cable, and the electrical characteristics will distort the results—possibly significantly. If you must test from a point along the run, disconnect the cable at that point and test each direction separately. One exception is that DC resistance may be measured from any connection point. Along the cable you should see both terminators, and from either end you should see only one.

For the same reason that you never test from the middle of a coax run, never attach an extra segment of coax—often called a stub—to any point along the run because it forms a second path for the data. All station attachments to coax should be made directly to the trunk. Adding stubs causes severe reflections, which in turn corrupts any data transmitted.

Lengths of not more than 4cm from the center of the coax trunk to the input of the network adapter are specified in 802.3, clause 10.6.3. This distance is more than adequate for a Tee connector, but not long enough for any additional cable. This suggests a good guideline for all coax cable use, including WAN and wireless.

Few products are able to perform a length measurement test on an active network link. The

TDR pulse corrupts passing data, the passing data corrupts the TDR pulse, or data is detected as TDR errors. If your tester is unable to test an active link, try the test on an idle link (with all traffic removed). If that fails, either disconnect the link from all stations, or turn off all the stations connected to the link while testing is performed.

If multiple types of coax are used for a single run, the data transmitted will be partially reflected back toward the sender at each change of cable type (change of impedance value). If the run is short enough, there will be little or no detectable effect from the user's perspective. When more cable is included to add more stations, the network either operates intermittently or stops working altogether for no apparent reason. Because the network operated prior to the new additions, the old link will not be suspect.

Never mix cables with different characteristic impedances. The various cable types (RG-58, RG-59, and RG-62) all have different characteristic impedance, and mixing them creates reflections. Joining an RG-58 and an RG-59 cable causes 20 percent of the signal to reflect at the junction. The result of this is reduced effective cable lengths, as well as jitter and other data sampling errors. The link probably will not fail outright unless it is approaching the length limit for the technology, but it will be problematic. If the run is short enough, there may be little or no detectable effect from the user's perspective. When more cable is added, the network either operates intermittently or stops working altogether for no apparent reason.

Troubleshooting Fiber Optic Media

Troubleshooting fiber optic media relies heavily on knowledge of the behavior of light, and cleanliness. Safe troubleshooting involves never looking into the fiber ends or into the connectors on the active equipment. The tools used to certify a new cable installation are the same as those used to isolate and locate failures. In a manner similar to how mixing different performance categories of copper media is likely to reduce link performance, mixing different fiber diameters, or mixing the same diameter with different modal bandwidth, causes problems. Learning to recognize the symptoms of these and other situations is critical to solving fiber optic cable plant problems.

Tools

There is a fairly narrow range of tools that may be used to troubleshoot fiber optic cabling. At the low end are effectively continuity testers. Intermediate-level testing is performed to check that optical power levels are satisfactory across the link. Advanced diagnostics require an Optical Time Domain Reflectometer (OTDR), which is fairly expensive. If power levels are unsatisfactory, or if OTDR testing reveals a point-source problem, cleaning and end-face inspection is appropriate. Cleaning should be undertaken at any time that a fiber optic connection is disturbed.

Safety

Safety should be considered at all times when working with fiber optic cable. Wavelengths used in networking are outside the visible light spectrum (the human eye begins to see violet light around 380nm and stops seeing red light around 750nm—see Figure 10-13). Many light sources used in networking are laser-based, and some are very powerful. You should never look straight into either a fiber optic cable end or any fiber optic equipment jack. Place dust covers over unused equipment jacks, both to keep the connection clean and to prevent eye damage from the non-visible light being transmitted.

Figure 10-13. *Visible light is below the wavelengths of light used in networking applications, at approximately 380nm to 750nm*

Safe viewing of a visible light source is best accomplished by pointing the end of the fiber at white paper, or holding the paper in front of the fiber connection point. Never look directly into any connection from which nonvisible light may be emitting.

Continuity Testing

One method for fiber continuity and pair polarity testing uses visible light. Popular sources for visible light include a standard white-light flashlight, as well as the many colors of very bright LED keychain lights now available. Special network flashlights are available that come with your choice of connector, including SC, ST, and so on (see Figure 10-14). The network flashlights typically offer focused bright red light, but from an incandescent source, not laser. Continuity may also be tested using visual fault locator (VFL) laser light sources, which operate in the visible light spectrum (see Figure 10-15). VFL light sources may be incandescent or laser based, but are most often Class II lasers operating at 650nm (red light).

Although not always possible due to the specific coatings used on a fiber optic cable, some cables permit the location of a fault to be seen if there is a break or other severe fault in the cable.

Attenuation or Loss Testing

The terms *loss* and *attenuation* can be used fairly interchangeably in relation to fiber optic cable, although loss can be attributed to a point-source fault. An Optical Loss Test Set (OLTS) is a special tester combining a light source and light power meter that tests for the total amount of light loss (attenuation) on a fiber link. The light source produces a continuous wave at specific wavelengths connected to one end of the fiber. A power meter with a photo detector is connected to the opposite end of the fiber link. The detector measures optical power at the same wavelengths produced by the light source. The light source may be LED or laser based, and is similar to the type of light source used for networking applications. The

measured result is then used to see whether the required power budget has been met for the technology to be used on the link. Per TIA and ISO standards, which both define testing of installed fiber, an OLTS is a Tier 1 test device.

Do not look into fiber with a remaining good eye.

Figure 10-14. *Flashlight manufactured for use with fiber optic cable*

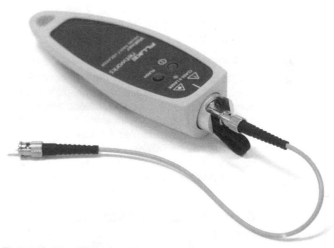

Figure 10-15. *VFL used to locate a break in a patch cable. Note that light does not penetrate all fiber jackets at a break.*

OTDR Testing

An Optical Time Domain Reflectometer (OTDR) graphs the reflections and backscatter from a high-power light pulse sent into the test fiber in much the same manner as a TDR test shows reflections in a copper link-under test. When the pulse of light meets connections, breaks, cracks, splices, sharp bends, or the end of the fiber, some amount of the light reflects back toward the OTDR, where high-gain light detectors measure the strength of the reflection. In addition, a small amount of light is reflected back from the crystalline structure of the glass itself as backscatter, and is represented by the sloping trace along the length of the OTDR test result. The backscatter slope is used to measure attenuation. Close examination of the resulting graph reveals characteristic changes in the graph plot that may be interpreted as the cable features mentioned earlier. As with a TDR, the delay between transmission of the light pulse and detection of any reflections may be interpreted as distance to the event. An OTDR trace is valuable because it makes it possible to certify that the workmanship and quality of the installation meets the design and warranty specifications, for current and future applications. With an OTDR, the performance of each splice and connector can be measured. Per TIA standards an OTDR is a Tier 2 test device; the ISO standard refers to the OTDR test as the extended test.

End-Face Inspection

Optical or video microscopes permit fiber end-face inspection, looking for dirt and contamination on fiber optic cable ends and on the end-equipment transmitters, or for problems with the end-face polish on fiber optic cables. Typical magnification is between 200x and 400x. One recent study indicated that more than 80 percent of all fiber problems were related to contamination.

General Testing and Installation Issues

Most networks have a few "spare" fibers pulled at the time of installation. The care related to dust covers and general cleanliness around unused fiber ranges from rigid requirements that all fiber is connected to active gear or capped properly, down to a very casual attitude about dust covers and not touching the fiber end-face. Casual behavior results in two problems: the fiber becomes dirty and does not pass adequate light for the link on which it is eventually used, and dirt from the fiber patch cable end-face is pushed into the connector and deposited on the transmitter or receiver, or on the fiber end-face in the connector of a patch panel. Subsequent cleaning of the fiber patch cable end-face will not solve this problem.

When fiber optic networks are upgraded, the most common concern is whether the same type of fiber will be required (singlemode or multimode). Other areas of concern should include the modal bandwidth of existing fiber, and what the maximum link length is which that fiber supports for the new technology. Many links fail to operate for these reasons, while a simple power measurement indicates that more than adequate levels of light reached the far end of the link.

Types of Fiber

The general assumption is that there is singlemode and multimode fiber, but it goes a bit deeper than that. Several examples are provided.

Some of the older multimode has been called "FDDI" fiber. This refers to a generation of fiber optic cable construction and glass quality called step-index fiber. The manufacturing process for this generation of older fiber optic cable left impurities, defects, and variations in the refractive index in the glass core. LED light sources were used with step-index fiber, and excited many modes in the fiber. Because of the core size of multimode fiber optical cable, light is allowed to travel along many different paths. Each possible path through the core is called a *mode*. Any path at greater angles away from straight down the center line is called a *higher mode*. Because distance traveled is increased as the angle away from the center increases, the light would arrive at the far end later than the light that traveled straight down the center line of the core. This difference in travel time causes a sharply transmitted pulse to arrive as a rounded bump. This is called *modal dispersion*. Firing pulses at high data rates results in the rounded bumps blurring together and becoming impossible for the receiver to distinguish one from the next. Therefore, dispersion limits the speed of transmission along a multimode fiber optical link. For instance, using FDDI grade multimode optical fiber cabling limits the distance over which 1Gbps Ethernet can be supported to 220 meters; this fiber type can only support 10Gbps transmission rates over very short distances (26 meters or less).

The next generation of cable was called graded index, which uses a different composition of glass as you progress outward from the core, causing the light rays to bend back toward the center. Instead of bouncing off the cladding, light in this type of fiber tends to flow more like a sinusoidal wave, often without quite touching the cladding. This type of fiber reduces the modal dispersion, permitting the transmitted signals to be recovered at greater distances than older step-index fiber.

Laser-optimized multimode is manufactured using an advanced version of the graded index construction, which results in less modal dispersion. The transmitted signal arrives more sharply defined at the far end, which permits higher signaling rates to be transmitted. The early laser-optimized fiber, which was first introduced in the mid 1990s, is not capable of supporting 10 Gigabit. More recent formulations of glass and better manufacturing processes that result in a more tightly controlled refractive index began appearing as early as 1999 and are rated for 10 Gigabit. At the same time, because a wider glass core allows more modes and more modal dispersion, laser-optimized fiber designed to support 10Gbps transmission rates only uses the narrower 50μm multimode fiber. Because there are fewer modes found in the 50μm cable, the signal may be reliably recovered at greater distances and at higher data rates.

Singlemode fiber has had similar changes. The concept of singlemode fiber is that the core is so narrow that only one mode can exist at the wavelengths used—straight down the center. The basic construction is nondispersion-shifted fiber (NDSF), which worked very well at 1300/1310nm. This type of fiber didn't work that well for 1550nm use. Instead, the cable was reformulated to move the optimum supported wavelength to 1550nm, and was called dispersion-shifted fiber (DSF).

When DWDM networking was introduced, it was discovered that the DSF fiber had some odd nonlinearities, so non-zero dispersion shifted fiber (NZ-DSF) was created. Other more specialized fiber compositions and constructions are being developed now, such as polarization-maintaining (PM) fiber.

Research the parameters associated with any installed fiber before repurposing it to be used for a new technology.

Cable Autotest

Field testing of installed optical fiber links amounts to testing polarity, length, and attenuation. Short of laboratory grade equipment, there is as yet no convenient way to perform field testing of many fiber properties.

Polarity may be verified using a visible light source such as a VFL or flashlight, and by testing both fibers in a pair simultaneously with an OLTS or OTDR.

Length may be obtained by examining the cable jacket markings, or from some OLTS. An OTDR provides excellent length information.

Overall channel attenuation may be measured with either an OLTS or an OTDR. OTDR test results can assist with loss budget calculations for a channel link by providing attenuation information about each detected event individually (see Figure 10-16).

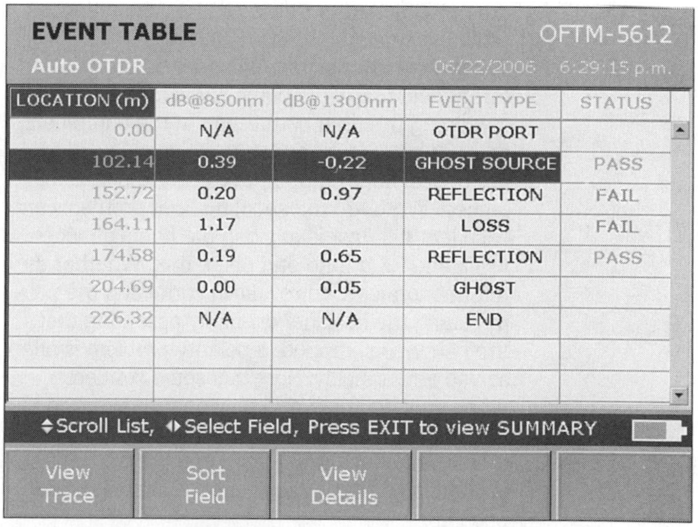

EVENT TABLE — OFTM-5612
Auto OTDR — 06/22/2006 6:29:15 p.m.

LOCATION (m)	dB@850nm	dB@1300nm	EVENT TYPE	STATUS
0.00	N/A	N/A	OTDR PORT	
102.14	0.39	-0.22	GHOST SOURCE	PASS
152.72	0.20	0.97	REFLECTION	FAIL
164.11	1.17		LOSS	FAIL
174.58	0.19	0.65	REFLECTION	PASS
204.69	0.00	0.05	GHOST	
226.32	N/A	N/A	END	

⬍Scroll List, ◄►Select Field, Press EXIT to view SUMMARY

| View Trace | Sort Field | View Details | | |

Figure 10-16. *OptiFiber OTDR screen showing event interpretation and loss measured at each event location*

Interpreting Fiber Optic Test Results

For twisted-pair copper cable, the most common problems can be traced to poor quality materials and to not maintaining the proper twisting for each connection. On fiber optic cable the most common problems relate to using the correct materials (singlemode or multimode connectors—such as barrel connectors where singlemode has far tighter alignment tolerances), maintaining the proper bend radius, and cleanliness.

Field testing fiber optic cable is considerably simpler than copper. Test for and connect according to the measured polarity, test for legal lengths, and ensure there is enough light reaching the far end. Isolating the location of a problem usually requires an OTDR. In some cases it is not possible to discover the exact cause of a detected problem, only that it is happening "here." For example, discovering that a multimode barrel connector was used on a singlemode link would only be revealed by loss at that connection, and replacing the barrel connector would solve it.

Polarity

Polarity does not actually fail—the point of the test is to learn and mark or pair cables according to the polarity pairing scheme employed within your network. Typically, polarity testing is accomplished as part of initiating the attenuation measurements. If the light source and light meter are not attached to the same fiber, they do not produce results.

Some networks pay little attention to polarity throughout the cable plant, and simply rely on swapping the fiber connection at the equipment end when the connection is not established as the optical fiber equipment cords are first attached. When troubleshooting fiber problems an excellent first test is to swap the fibers attached to TX and RX at one end of the link. Whether the information learned results in correcting the pairing along the channel or simply accepting that the pair was swapped, a polarity problem is often solved very quickly. Note that some connector types provide a key and may only be inserted one way. This style must then support the polarity requirements and ensure that the transmitter is connected to the receiver at the other end for each link.

Length

An OTDR reveals the overall channel length, which may then be compared against the implementation specifications for the networking technology used. The OTDR may also reveal a link that is shorter than expected, which may be the result of a break in the cable.

If an OTDR is not available, knowledge of the cable plant or access to the original installation certification documentation can be very beneficial. Utilizing the length markings on the cable jacket is another way to learn the length of each individual cable segment in the channel link. Again, the resulting channel length may then be compared against the implementation specifications for the networking technology used.

In either case, pay close attention to the modal bandwidth for the installed cable type. In many cases this will have to be researched based on cable jacket markings, and then cross referenced against distance limitations for the networking technology used when operating on cable with that modal bandwidth.

Attenuation Test Failure

Attenuation or loss testing is performed with a fiber optic power meter. Before measuring power loss verify the following:

- The number of adapters and/or splices is set correctly on the tester (for limits that use a calculated loss budget value). Note that this number applies to the optical fiber path when you use a tester that tests both strands in the link with one test, not the sum of all connectors from both strands.

- The correct fiber type is selected in the tester setup configuration.

- A valid power reference was set on the tester after turning it on.

- Before you set the reference, ensure that the tester has reached a steady state internal operating temperature. A good rule of thumb may be to let the instrument warm up for a minimum of 10 minutes, but for a total time that equals one minute for every degree (°F) difference between its storage location and the ambient temperature in the place where you are now using it, and without disconnecting the patch cord attached to the light source after setting the reference.

- Use VFL to ensure you are on the correct fiber. A VFL usually also isolates the location of broken or cracked fiber (refer to Figure 10-15).

Clean all fiber connections (plugs and jacks) in the problem path (including the output port on the end equipment). Visually inspect the end-face of each cable. Look for cracks, scratches, or persistent contamination. Quickly wiping the end-face with a fiber grade cleaning solvent might not be enough to dislodge some types of contamination (see Figure 10-17).

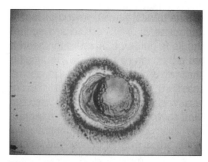

Figure 10-17. *Fiber end-face contamination in the form of a mold or fungal growth*

Test individual patch cables with the OLTS. After setting the reference with a good patch cable, another patch cable should show close to zero loss. Any discrepancy should be investigated. If the problem is intermittent, try flexing the patch cable while testing to see whether changing the alignment opens or misaligns a crack or other damage. Do not exceed the bend radius while flexing.

If an OTDR is not available, apply *divide and conquer* techniques—move closer to the other end and retest. Look for a large change in the loss results that does not correspond with how much of the link was removed by moving forward. Attenuation

of the actual fiber in a LAN environment tends to be negligible, so base your judgment on the standards limit for the installed technology (for example, a maximum of 0.5dB of loss for each connector pair in a link).

There may be one or more dirty or damaged connections in the cabling. Clean all fiber end-faces and retest, or use the OTDR to locate bad connections.

A patch cord or fiber segment has the wrong core size. If the patch cords are the correct type, use the OTDR to look for mismatched fiber in the remainder of the link.

The cabling has a bad fusion or mechanical splice or a sharp bend. Use the OTDR to locate these faults.

Inspect the cable path. Is the cable kinked or bent at an angle that exceeds the bend radius? Are cable fastenings causing microbends? (See Figure 10-18.)

Was a multimode coupler used on a single-mode cable run? The mechanical tolerances for singlemode couplers are much smaller, which prevents core misalignment and the corresponding loss of power. Also, connectors and cables are only rated for a certain number of insertions. If the cable or connector has been used a great deal, it could be becoming "sloppy" and not aligning the fiber correctly. An OTDR measurement would reveal the location of this and other related problems.

If the failure being resolved relates to a single device, it is sometimes due to the end-equipment transmitter. Either the connection inside the equipment is dirty or the transmitter is not outputting adequate power. Try connecting the OLTS to the

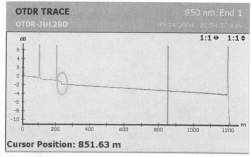

Figure 10-18. *Microbend in fiber, and the corresponding signal loss as seen by an OTDR (circled)*

suspect port to obtain a power reading, and then compare that reading against other similar ports.

Advanced Cable Diagnostics

Advanced diagnostics for fiber optic cables rely almost entirely on use of an OTDR. There are two test configurations.

- Testing from just one end of the link (see Figure 10-19)

- Testing from one end of the link while the other end is looped back onto the return fiber in the pair

A typical OTDR trace is shown in Figure 10-20. The left dotted vertical line is positioned at the end of a 100-meter launch cable (launch fiber). Distances shown on the x-axis have been zeroed at the end of the launch cable. The solid vertical line indicates the current cursor position 464.18 meters from the end of the launch cable. The end of the cable being tested is found at about 925 meters, followed by another 100 meter cable (receive fiber).

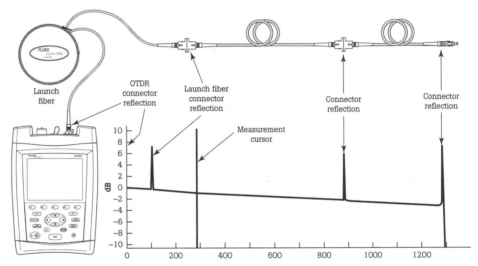

Figure 10-19. *Typical test configuration*

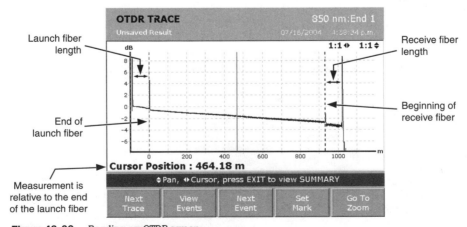

Figure 10-20. *Reading an OTDR screen*

Each of the large spikes in the trace represents significant Fresnel reflections. This type of reflection is caused by a connector. The height of the bump in the trace designates the amount of light energy reflected from that event. Smaller in this case is always better. Each such reflection also signifies the beginning of a short blind spot where the OTDR receiver is oversaturated and unable to "see" small events immediately following the large reflection.

Notice that the continuous trace slopes gradually down from left to right. The slope is the result of a form of loss called scattering, which returns a very small amount of light back to the OTDR receiver. By placing two cursors on the display (the vertical dotted lines) and measuring the amount of elevation change on the y-axis, it is possible to determine the amount of loss represented by a selected event or segment of cable. Some OTDR testers automatically report the total loss observed along the link-under-test.

To begin interpreting an OTDR trace there are a small number of basic waveform shapes to watch for; many of them are described later in this chapter. As your skill at troubleshooting with an OTDR increases, you learn to identify more subtle characteristic event signatures. In addition to the trace, your OTDR may provide an event table that lists each of the events "seen" by the OTDR, their location, the loss observed at that location, and whether this loss exceeds the limits you have specified for the type of event observed.

Large Reflective Event

When a pulse of light is reflected back to the OTDR from a potentially serious event it is shown as a spike or tall bump in the trace (see Figure 10-21).

A large reflective event with high loss or excessive tailing may be identified as an end event though it occurs before the end of the cabling. This sort of event may be caused by the following:

- A dirty, scratched, cracked, misaligned, or unseated connector. Misaligned or unseated connectors can also cause strong reflections

that produce ghosts. Bad connectors should be cleaned, repolished, or replaced.

- A good connector with a sharp bend or crack within the dead zone immediately following the event. If the cable is tightly bent the tester may indicate a break, especially at longer wavelengths. Use a visual fault locator to identify the precise location.

- A crack in the fiber. Use a visual fault locator to identify the precise location.

- A connection between mismatched fibers (different core sizes, numerical apertures, or another mismatch in parameters). The bottom example in Figure 10-21 shows a larger core (on the left) connected to a smaller core.

Small Reflective Event with High Loss

An event that produces a small reflective event but has high loss may be caused by a very sharp bend, a crack, or a mechanical splice with high loss (see Figure 10-22). If the event is a bend, it may show higher loss at a longer wavelength. Use a visual fault locator to verify the problem. Bad mechanical splices should be reworked.

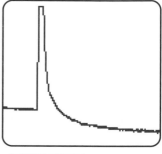
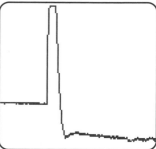

Figure 10-21. *Large reflective events*

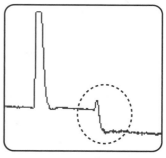

Figure 10-22. *Small reflective event with high loss*

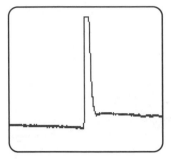

Figure 10-23. *Large reflective event with gain*

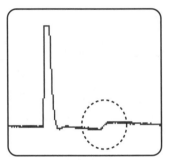

Figure 10-24. *Small gain event*

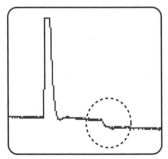

Figure 10-25. *Small loss event*

Large Reflective Event with Gain

A large reflective event accompanied by a gain is usually caused by a connection between mismatched fibers (different core sizes, numerical apertures, or other parameters). Figure 10-23 shows a smaller core size (on the left) connected to a larger core size (on the right). Testing from the other end would show a large reflective event with more loss than a connector should have, such as the bottom example in Figure 10-21.

Small Gain Event

Small gain events are typically caused by a splice between mismatched fibers (different core sizes, numerical apertures, or other parameters). See Figure 10-24. Testing from the other end would show a loss at the event's location. The difference between the gainer's value and the loss value is what the event's loss would be if the fibers were not mismatched.

Small Loss Event

Small loss events are usually caused by bad fusion splices, a splice between mismatched fibers or a bend (see Figure 10-25). A good fusion splice between matching fiber types typically shows only 0.1dB to 0.3dB of attenuation. If the event is a bend, it may show higher loss at a longer wavelength. Use an OTDR to precisely locate bends. A visual fault locator may sometimes be used to locate bends.

Ghost After the Cable End

Ghost events are duplicate reflections caused by light bouncing back and forth between connectors. When the trace falls off sharply (tails) it indicates the end of the cable, either the true end or a cut or break. Spikes in the trace after the trace tails off sharply—called *ghosts*—generally do not indicate a fault in the cabling (see Figure 10-26). You can usually determine that reflections are ghosts because they occur at multiples of distances to connectors and they show almost no loss. Multiple ghosts from the same source are spaced equally apart.

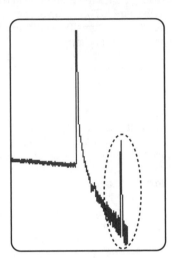

Figure 10-26. *Ghost after the cable end*

Ghosts in the Middle of the Cable

Ghosts occurring in the middle of the cabling may be caused by a highly reflective connector or a connector that is not seated properly. A poorly seated connector usually shows significant loss, as shown in Figure 10-27. A connector with the wrong type of polish can also cause strong reflections that result in ghosts.

One of the indicators of a ghost event is

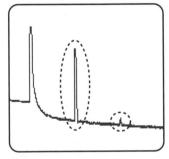

Figure 10-27. *Ghosts in the middle of the cable*

that there appears to be no associated loss related to the observed event. In Figure 10-27, there is no drop in the slope of the backscatter line following the ghost event. The backscatter continues to drop at the same rate before and after the ghost event as though it did not exist.

Hidden Event

A hidden event occurs when the event is within the shadow or "dead zone" of the previous event. The event is detected, but not enough information is available to measure its loss separately from the previous event. The hidden event may be a connection a short distance from the first one, such as the end of a patch cord, a sharp bend, or a crack within the dead zone of the previous connection. If the event is not a connection, inspect the fiber near the event's location. Use a visual fault locator to reveal faults.

The first hidden event in Figure 10-28 appears to be a cable connection, with a severe reflective event immediately following it. The second hidden event precedes what appears to be a cable connection. The third hidden event also precedes what appears to be a (dirty or damaged—note the tailing) cable connection by almost enough distance to be beyond the dead zone. The fourth and last example shows multiple problems located in close proximity, but all within the dead zone of the preceding event(s).

Manipulating OTDR Traces

OTDRs operate in the time domain. Everything displayed in an OTDR trace is represented from left to right in time according to when the OTDR learned about it. Thus, measurements along the x-axis may be correlated directly to distances. Measurements along the y-axis represent the amplitude or severity of an event.

A pulse of some amplitude and duration is sent by the OTDR, and the size and duration of all reflections are shown in the resulting trace. The

following information will aid in interpreting the OTDR trace.

Measuring the Loss of an Event

OTDRs provide the ability to select an event or cable segment and report on the change in signal strength between the beginning and end. This is accomplished by moving the vertical cursors to either side of the event of interest. The OTDR calculates the power level difference between the two cursor positions.

Measuring the Length of a Segment

Using exactly the same procedure, placing the vertical cursors on either side of the segment of cable permits the OTDR to calculate the distance represented by the space between the cursors (see Figure 10-29).

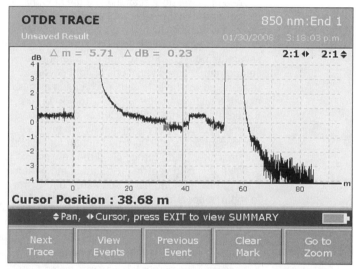

Figure 10-29. *Measuring selected events with the OTDR cursors. The dotted and solid vertical cursors are used to measure the length represented by an on-screen event; in this example there are 5.71 meters between cursors, representing a loss of 0.23dB between the cursors.*

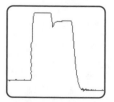 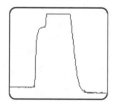 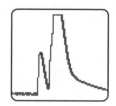 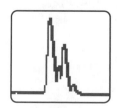

Figure 10-28. *Hidden events*

Fiber Installation Issues

A loss budget calculation takes into account the type of fiber and the number of connections in the path. Optical fiber splices must not exceed a maximum attenuation of 0.3dB, and attenuation associated with a connector should be no worse than 0.75dB.

To correctly measure the power lost on the tested fiber the light source output and light meter measured power level must be zeroed out in a process called *setting the reference*. The light source and light meter are connected with a test reference cord (very high-quality short patch cable), and the received light level is the reference level that corresponds to 0dB in loss. After setting the reference, the test reference cord attached to the light source must not be disconnected or the process must be repeated. Reseating the connector at the light source alters the amount of light entering the cable and invalidates the reference reading. Also, the light source should be temperature stabilized and left turned on for several minutes prior to setting the reference. Temperature causes variations in light power transmitted by the light source, changing as much as half a milliwatt between 25°C and 50°C. Also, the light source gradually becomes brighter for several minutes after being first turned on, just as fluorescent lights will become brighter for several minutes after being turned on. If the light source was left in a cold vehicle overnight in the winter, it should be brought inside and allowed to warm to room temperature before using. Similarly, if it was left in a hot vehicle in the summer it should be allowed to cool to room temperature before using.

Using a properly stabilized and referenced light source, the power loss across a tested fiber optic link may be measured. Once the loss reading has been taken, the measured loss is compared to a specified loss budget for the link to determine whether it passes the Basic or Tier 1 certification. TIA/EIA TSB140 describes the requirements for testing an installed fiber optic link.

When testing fiber, it is imperative that the light source has been turned on for a sufficient amount of time prior to testing that the measurement circuitry has reached a steady state. This stabilization period requires a minimum of about 10 minutes, but allow a total time that equals one minute for every degree (°F) difference between its storage location and the ambient temperature in the place where you are now using it. After the circuitry has stabilized, set the reference level and begin testing. If the ambient temperature changes significantly, this process will have to be repeated to obtain accurate results. Don't expect a tester reference level taken in a temperature controlled office to provide accurate test results in an unheated warehouse.

Singlemode cable has experienced a lot of engineering innovation over the last few years. One of the promising experiments was to tune the performance characteristics of the cable to eliminate a problem with dispersion at 1550nm. This cable became known as dispersion shifted fiber (DSF). Unfortunately, although the effect of this tuning was to improve the performance for single wavelength use, when dense wave division multiplexing (DWDM) came along it was discovered that the engineering tinkering prevented DWDM from working at all. The good news is that older and newer cable designs work with DWDM.

The type of polish applied to fiber can be a source of loss. If an angle-polished fiber (which presents a surface that is angled to 8–10 degrees off perpendicular) is coupled with a flat-ended fiber, there is a noticeable loss in transferred power. Be careful of which cable types are installed or even available in your work area. Some perfectly good cables are discarded after failing in a live link for loss problems because nobody noticed which type of end polish they had.

Mixing 50μm and 62.5μm patch cables is very easy to do. The one-time loss caused by mating a 62.5μm output horizontal cable into a 50μm patch cable is enough to cause an otherwise barely passing link to fail. It usually requires a fair bit of troubleshooting before anyone examines the printing on the cable jacket and realizes that this mixing has taken place. The reverse, where the 50μm output is mated to a 62.5μm patch cable, is all but undetectable because virtually all the output light transfers into the 62.5μm receiving cable. Using an OTDR pinpoints the location of the 62.5μm to 50μm connection. Almost the only other method of finding this sort of fault is to read the cable jackets, which implies that you already suspect the nature of the problem.

Temperature affects light sources. LED sources are sensitive to temperature increase, and may lose half a milliwatt of output light with a rise in temperature from 25°C to 50°C. If a network device was operating before being moved or exposed to a hot environment, turn on the air conditioning or cool the device by turning it off for a bit to see whether it can be made to work again. If that causes it to begin working again, consider changing the working environment or changing the interface to a VCSEL laser source, which is less sensitive.

Experience has shown that visual inspection of the connections built in to the end equipment can be very revealing. As an extreme example, this image was captured from a new, just-unpacked third-party OTDR interface connector (see Figure 10-30). The inspection was conducted after initial test results with the product were wholly unsatisfactory. On cleaning the OTDR it operated as originally expected.

Because of the connector problem earlier, it is strongly recommended that all fiber optic cables be cleaned and inspected before inserting into any connector—even if you just disconnected it. The opportunity for pushing dirt into the connector, or for moving dirt around inside the connector, is very high. Dirt obstructs the light source or the light sensor, forces the two end-faces apart, creating additional loss and dispersion, and may scratch the fiber core.

Microscopes for inspecting the end-faces on fiber optic cables have long been available. Equipment is now available for inspecting the inside of connectors, and cleaning kits are available that fit into the jack of virtually all fiber connectors. Experience has shown that cleaning the jacks, too, has a very positive effect on the performance of legacy cable and equipment. The benefit is present, but not as pronounced for new installations.

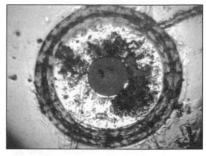

Figure 10-30. *Dirty fiber optic connection example*

Attenuators

Several interesting on-the-spot field adaptations to compensate for an oversaturated receiver include

- Pencil lead rubbed over the patch cable tip to attenuate the signal
- The patch cable loosened in the connector and taped down, creating an air gap to attenuate the signal
- A meter or more of fiber patch cable rolled into a tight circle (approximating a mandrel) to attenuate the signal
- A multimode patch cable inserted as the last cable in a singlemode run to attenuate the signal

Although none of these are recommended, they appear to have temporarily solved the problem and permitted the link to come up. Unfortunately, all these solutions were left in place and not corrected with a proper attenuator later. This resulted in a return trip later to troubleshoot why the link went down.

As output power increases, the chance of having a laser source damaged from back reflections increases. The reflections disrupt the light amplification process inside the laser cavity. At lower power the back reflections only cause the output to become unstable and perhaps unusable. The laser used in most LAN applications will not be damaged, but it may become unusable until the back reflections are resolved.

Summary

This chapter described troubleshooting installed copper and fiber optic media. Specific information about the tools, and the testing and installation issues unique to each media type, are provided.

- The available tools for performing each defined category of test are described, along with notes about the tests each is most suited for, and in some cases about testing that is unsuited to the tester. Special note should be made of which testers are capable of certification testing and which are suited only for troubleshooting. Knowledge of the capabilities and limitations of each tester used enhances your ability to successfully apply the tools to troubleshooting scenarios.

- Each of the specific tests described in Chapters 2 and 3 are revisited from a field troubleshooting perspective. Multiple tips and examples are provided to guide interpretation of test results and test failures, and to provide probable causes of a test failure. An additional and more detailed list of possible causes for copper media faults is provided in Appendix A, "Copper Test Failure Cause Tables."

The intent of this chapter is to provide sufficient troubleshooting information and guidance to allow most media related problems to be quickly isolated and solved. This is possible because media problems are relatively finite—the network is disconnected for media testing and problems are limited to the link under test.

Chapter Review Questions

To aid in your comprehension of important concepts, the following questions are provided. Refer to this book's Introduction for a general legend that indicates the anticipated difficulty of each question. For answers to these review questions, see Appendix I, "Answers to Chapter Review Questions."

Copper Media

 1. Name three copper cable tester categories, along with an identifying feature for each.

 2. What potential problem may be present if cable test results have an asterisk (*) beside some of the measurement results?

 3. Is it possible for a Category 5 cable to pass Category 5e testing? Briefly explain your answer.

 4. Is it possible for a Category 6 cable to fail Category 5e testing? Briefly explain your answer.

 5. A certain amount of organization in the wiring closet is good; however, list at least three reasons why the following statement might not be true: "Dressing" the installation with wire ties and other methods of grouping and aligning cables is not only good for the organization of the wiring closet; it can improve network performance and troubleshooting.

 6. Describe two significant ways in which RJ45 plugs are not all the same.

7. Describe at least one significant way each in which connectors (RJ45 plugs and RJ45 jacks) may be damaged by poor handling.

 8. Name three possible causes for a single-ended cable length test to reveal the following pair lengths:

Pair 1—277 feet

Pair 2—276 feet

Pair 3—279 feet

Pair 4—261 feet

 9. Name two possible causes for insertion loss to fail.

 10. What is the most probable cause for NEXT to fail?

 11. What test would be used to discover the location of a return loss fault?

 12. In general, what two time-domain tests can be used to discover the location of most faults?

Fiber Optic Media

 13. Name four fiber optic cable tester categories, along with an identifying feature for each.

14. What three general parameters are involved in field testing fiber optic cable?

15. If an OTDR is unavailable, what other means can be used to determine the length of an installed cable (assume that some length of the cable is inside a wall or is otherwise inaccessible)?

16. What effect does modal bandwidth have in relation to using an existing fiber optic cable run for a new purpose?

17. True or False: Microbends in a cable are insignificant and do little to interfere with network performance.

18. Name at least one cause for each type of advanced fiber optic cable diagnostic fault:

- Large reflective event
- Small reflective event with high loss
- Large reflective event with gain
- Small gain event
- Small loss event
- Ghost after the cable end
- Ghosts in the middle of the cable
- Hidden event

 19. If you suspect that a failing link might be due to oversaturation of the receiver, what trouble-shooting options are available to test for this?

CHAPTER 11
Network Troubleshooting

Not every tool is right for you. Tools should be selected on the basis of who will use it, and what that person is expected to do day to day. Matching skill level, test speed, and how detailed the test results are makes a big difference in how successful someone is with a new tool. See the section titled "What Tool to Start With?" in Appendix H, "Network Diagnostic Products Used in This Book."

Tools

There are four primary categories of network support products, and two more that combine features of the other three for ease of use or for specialized advanced analysis (see Figure 11-1):

Primary
Cable testers

Protocol analyzers

Network management applications

Flow protocol monitoring

Hybrid
Handheld network testers

Advanced or specialized analysis tools [not shown]

Network Tools "Best Fit"

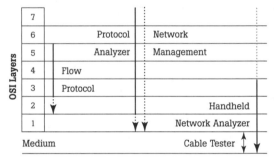

Figure 11-1. *Generalized tool functionality graph. Dotted lines indicate possible functionality.*

Cable Testers

Cable testers were described previously in Chapters 2, "Copper Media," 3, "Fiber Optic Media," and 10, "Troubleshooting Media," on media testing (copper and fiber). They are used as much for maintenance and troubleshooting as they are for new installations.

Protocol Analysis

Protocol analyzers are used to view the contents of individual frames taken from the medium, and offer functionality from Layer 2 up through Layer 7. To most broadly define the category think of a protocol analyzer as a frame viewer. You are able to collect large numbers of frames from a network connection and view the contents in exhaustive detail, frame by frame. Accompanying this fundamental purpose and ability is found a variety of built-in summary views of the stored or live traffic. These views range from ranked listings of who is talking to whom at each OSI layer, how many frames of each protocol are present on the link, who is sending each of these frames, what errors are present, and so on. More expensive protocol analyzers have libraries of symptoms indexed to common network problem summaries, and can be used to analyze trace files. These libraries are referred to as *expert systems*, and serve to automate much of the troubleshooting process. The expert systems also make it possible for a less skilled technician to use a protocol analyzer more effectively. There are also specialized test libraries and features for certain protocols, such as Voice over IP (VoIP), or database analysis as seen traversing the network.

Protocol analyzers are most effective for protocol problems—situations where the traffic is achieving end-to-end delivery across the network infrastructure but is still not performing properly, or for situations where the infrastructure protocols are not performing properly. The built-in test summaries may also be used as a vehicle for performing baseline network performance trending. However, they must be moved from location to location until the entire network has been monitored for a suitable period of time, usually a full and uninterrupted week of monitoring from a single location.

To troubleshoot in a switched network environment, protocol analyzers require assistance in the form of mirror or span port configurations, splitters and taps, or shared media hubs. Connecting a protocol analyzer to a spare switch port is not effective without setting up a mirror configuration.

Network Management

Consider All the Costs

One study indicated that as little as 10 percent of purchased network management software was fully installed and maintained at the end of the first year. Be sure that you fully understand what is required before making the purchase. For a typical system, the purchase price of the software might be less than the annual maintenance and staffing costs.

Network management products may have functionality from Layer 2 up through Layer 7, depending on what is available to the network management console on an individual network. A limited cable test is also available from some recent Ethernet chipsets, the results of which should be available to network management.

A fully installed and maintained network management platform is often the first line of defense. It alerts the network support staff of sudden network outages and impending outages slightly faster than the user community. It is also one of the more important tools for planning network growth. Without long-term trend analysis data it is very difficult to effectively plan and schedule upgrades and additions in a timely, cost effective, and nondisruptive manner.

During the process of configuring and tuning the installation of a network management system, the operators identify which network elements (switches, routers, servers, and so on) should be monitored, and for which parameters. The network management console comes with preset default thresholds for typical monitored parameters, but although they are a good place to start they are rarely perfect for the unique properties of any one network. Over the first weeks and months, thresholds will be adjusted and customized to account for the utilization levels found on each segment, and to meet the mission and priorities of the company in which it was installed.

Most network infrastructure devices support the standard MIBs, but not all. It is often necessary to compile private MIB definitions into the network management console, so that it can obtain SNMP data from all the infrastructure devices that should be monitored. Private MIBs include features and functionality that is not available from the generic standard MIBs, and are therefore a desirable addition. If private MIBs are included, it becomes mandatory that they be updated each and every time the operating code in an infrastructure device is updated, and a different private MIB is usually required for each different model of device from even the same manufacturer.

Until the network has been adequately baselined, the information available from a network management system is interesting and helpful, but not reliable. It is difficult to interpret results without knowing what the normal utilization and error levels are for each segment. Remember, a baseline simply identifies "normal"; it does not pass judgment on whether "normal" is acceptable.

Until recently, troubleshooting in a switched network was almost impossible without SNMP support. Interestingly, there is a conceptual flaw underlying the basis for claiming the network is "up" now that switches have been widely deployed. The old technique for determining up/down status, and therefore whether the network was operating, was to use SNMP or pings to "talk" to the infrastructure device. If the infrastructure device responded, it was assumed that users were also up and running because the same data paths were often used for both activities. Now that switching has provided a simple means for separating the data paths (such as VLANs), the fact that a ping or SNMP query to an infrastructure network device was successful across the management VLAN tells you nothing about whether a user can reach a server.

Flow Protocols

The problem of "seeing" into a switched network was addressed with mirror and span ports, taps, RMON in the switch, and other solutions that were suitable for a given link but unsatisfactory for monitoring a network in general. This resulted in the development of various flow reporting protocols, such as sFlow and NetFlow.

The flow technology that appears to be gaining prominence is the IETF's protocol IPFIX, which is an adaptation of Cisco's NetFlow version 9. NetFlow/IPFIX reports on OSI Layers 3 and 4 primarily.

Flow technologies have an advantage over previous traffic monitoring solutions in that the switch itself utilizes much of the information already, so gathering the information is in part an extension of normal operation. Traffic reported within flow summaries is often only the traffic crossing a routed boundary, although sFlow is able to report on OSI Layer 2. Depending on the features of the switch, NetFlow/IPFIX may be configured to report on bridged traffic. The summarized flow information is sent to a flow collector anywhere in the network. Flow monitoring may be enabled on a per-interface basis. This means that it is possible for traffic volume, protocols used, and conversation data to be gathered for every switch interface and presented at a central console without temporarily breaking links or adding extra hardware.

Because only a summary of the traffic is sent, this solution is not suitable for protocol problems. For general use, monitoring and troubleshooting flow monitoring is similar to SNMP's RMON2, but the raw data is sent continuously without requiring a request for each update. And the data tends to be more granular (greater detail) than what is found in typical SNMP responses.

Handheld Network Analyzers

Handheld network analyzers were created to bridge the skills gap between the senior network support staff and the Help Desk staff. They generally include the most commonly used features from the other three categories, but do not eliminate the need for the other three categories. The focus is to validate or troubleshoot end-to-end connectivity up through OSI Layer 3.

In the interest of restoring network service as quickly as possible, this category is best used as a first-in tool when a problem is reported. Although they are often able to help locate and eliminate the source of a network problem, they can be just as effective in quickly eliminating many possible sources of the problem so that the other tools and staff may be deployed more effectively.

Advanced Analysis Products

Virtually all the other, and often more advanced, live data or post-processing monitoring and reporting products utilize protocol analysis, SNMP network management, and flow protocol data as the source for the presented results. A few also require infrastructure device configuration dumps to provide complete analysis results.

Troubleshooting Generalized User Complaints

Users are a good barometer for the performance of your network. They are rarely reluctant to report perceived or actual substandard network performance. Unfortunately, they also rarely have the knowledge that would help you troubleshoot the problems they report. Furthermore, the problem descriptions provided by the user are sometimes imaginative, and may bear no relation to reality. Always remember that their lack of technical knowledge should not be interpreted as an indication that no problem exists. Something annoyed the user enough to contact you. Often, the source of the problem is user error, misuse, or mismatch of expectations, and a few minutes of user training will make both of you happier.

Note: *Before you begin troubleshooting in earnest, verify that the desired server or service has operated successfully in the past from the problem location. The troubleshooting process is completely different if you are trying to solve a new installation problem instead of attempting to restore service to something that has been up and running.*

Almost all user complaints fall into three general categories of user complaint:

- Can't connect
- Dropped connection
- Poor performance

Some problems relate to shared media (hubs), some to switched media, and some relate to both.

For each general problem category, a generalized troubleshooting tree is provided. Each step along the path is determined by the results of one or more tests. The following discussion does not include all possible variations, but instead forms an outline for how to troubleshoot. Conversely, the discussion provides a fairly detailed series of steps. The detail is provided as an attempt to be clear about why that test is important, and what to look for. Do not take that to mean that every test should be performed. Use common sense to choose which steps to try and which to bypass for now. Think of this list as a mental checklist. While troubleshooting, watch for all these situations, and mentally check them off. When one of the items on the list is not mentally checked off, try the test.

Note: *If you change collision domains during the testing process, be sure to start with your mental list of collision domain tests again when you connect at the next location.*

Problem: Can't Connect

The following procedures assume that this server or service has been operating properly prior to this problem, and you have already

- Cold-booted the station in question (a warm-boot does not reset all adapter cards). This also applies any loaded but unapplied patches. Experience suggests that PnP devices sometimes seem to require two or three reboots to fully install.

- Verified that the station does not have any hardware failures.

- Verified that required network cables are present and properly connected.

- Verified that the network adapter is not disabled, and has valid addressing for the subnet (static or DHCP). Check also to see what the operating system NIC status reports for frames sent and received, if either is zero then investigate.

- Verified that nothing has been changed recently on the problem station or the server that might have caused this problem, such as reconfiguring or adding software or hardware.

This problem is usually manifested when the user is unable to connect to a server or service. The user is often not able to discriminate between inability of the station to link to the network and inability to connect to a particular server or service. Compared to the other problem categories, this is the easiest to isolate. Determine whether the problem is isolated to this station or a small group of stations (collision domain problem, including a single switch port) or if it affects many stations (broadcast domain or interconnected networks problem).

Before troubleshooting the hardware, try connecting using your own login account or have the affected user attempt the exact same network operation from another nearby station that is operating correctly. This is the fastest way to isolate user-account problems from network problems. If the first user is still unable to connect, troubleshoot the first user's account. Observing the user during an alternative attempt can also reveal errors in the series of steps the user is accustomed to taking in connecting to the network. A moment of training may prevent significant future frustration by the user.

Collision domain problems affect the local medium and prevent reliable communications to the first Layer 2 or 3 infrastructure device—or the local server or service you are trying to connect to. They typically result from

- Bad cables

- Errors or excessive traffic on the local collision domain

- Blocked or misconfigured switch ports

- Failed or misconfigured station NIC

- Corrupted, unbound, or misconfigured software drivers

Virtually all these collision domain problems can be identified with an inline test while the user attempts to connect following a cold reboot. Rebooting a workstation is fairly important because many operating system problems are difficult or impossible to re-create or isolate, and reloading the operating system clears these mysterious problems for a time.

Don't assume that it has failed.
Don't assume that it works, either.
Skepticism saves you time.

Many users have both a wired and wireless NIC enabled. If the PC is trying to use a wireless NIC instead of a wired connection, the exact location or PC orientation may be preventing adequate connectivity. There are many blind spots in most wireless networks, and some are quite small. Moving the PC even a few inches or rotating it slightly has been known to reestablish a wireless link. If people are congregated near the PC, they might be blocking the signal.

Broadcast domain problems begin after a reliable MAC Layer link is established, and are typified by a failure to create a logical connection across a bridged environment. Included in this category are Network Layer addressing issues that would prevent communications to servers and routers attached to this broadcast domain.

- Marginal or failed uplink port somewhere in the path, possibly the result of a bad cable
- Broadcast storm or other excessive traffic within the broadcast domain (not necessarily traffic observed on the local port)
- ICMP errors present, IP addressing incorrect for the local subnet, or duplicate IP address
- DNS and DHCP failures
- Station or server improperly advertising routes (only devices that have somewhere to route packets to should advertise routing protocols)

Addressing and some other problems are revealed by the same inline test that may be performed during the collision domain testing. Be sure to repeat collision domain testing if you change locations within the broadcast domain. If an address is obtained and/or correct, it might be necessary to either gather a protocol analyzer trace file for analysis or use network management software to interrogate infrastructure devices within the broadcast domain.

Interconnected network problems begin after a reliable link is established to the router offering a path out of the broadcast domain. The level of complexity usually increases and the level of access often decreases if the server or service resides beyond a WAN connection instead of residing on an adjacent LAN, but the process is similar.

- Unstable routing due to marginal or failed port somewhere beyond the broadcast domain, possibly the result of a bad cable
- Incorrect routing configurations, including DHCP request forwarding configuration for when the server is not on the local subnet
- VPN problems, including MTU size
- Firewall or other security blocking, such as login account or password problems

Use of ping and traceroute almost always reveals the location where troubleshooting *can't connect* problems should begin. For faster troubleshooting once a remote location is identified as being suspect, use network management to query the suspect infrastructure device and the infrastructure device immediately prior to it. One or the other should show errors of some type or excessive utilization. Establishing a reliable end-to-end connection at the Network Layer resolves most problems. Be sure to repeat collision domain and broadcast domain tests each time you move to a new location during the troubleshooting process. If ping responses are reliable but the link is still failing, increase the size of the ping frame. This reveals MTU size problems in the routed path. VPNs add overhead to the frame, and the user MTU must be correspondingly smaller. If end-to-end Network Layer delivery appears to be reliable, protocol analysis is the next step. Capture and analyze the connection attempt. It may be necessary to repeat the capture from the server or service end of the link to ensure that requests are arriving or that responses are leaving.

If ping and traceroute are successful, try using Telnet to the required port. Successful Telnet connections establish a link but might not produce visible evidence of this (see Figure 11-2). If the Telnet connection is refused, that service is not available. A refused or failed connection is always obvious (see Figure 11-3).

Telnet sent to a particular TCP port may be thought of as a type of *port ping*. Because not all applications behave similarly, it is important to test the behavior before it is needed for troubleshooting so that you know what to expect. Various security-related tools are available that can test for open ports, too, such as the open source tool nmap.

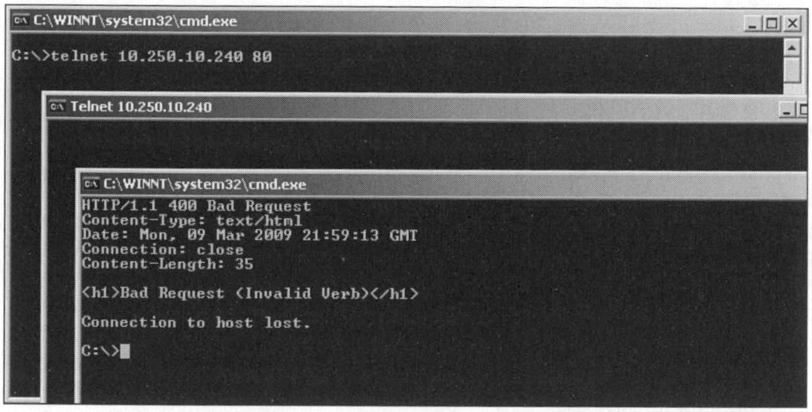

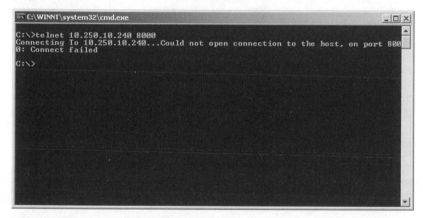

Figure 11-2. *A successful telnet to port 80, followed by <CTRL><Z> to terminate connection. A successful connection often produces a blank screen. Only after the connection terminates does anything get posted to the display.*

Figure 11-3. *A failed telnet to port 8000 shows an attempt to connect, followed by a failure message.*

Problem: Connections That Drop

Connections that drop may be caused by the same conditions that prevent a connection from being established in the first place. Consider any of the situations described under the "Problem: Can't Connect" heading.

The following procedures assume that this connection has been operating properly prior to this problem, and you have already

- Cold-booted the station in question (a warm boot does not reset all adapter cards). This also applies any loaded but not applied patches. Experience suggests that PnP devices sometimes seem to require two or three reboots to fully install.

- Verified that the station does not have any hardware failures.

- Verified that required network cables are present and properly connected.

- Verified that the network adapter is not disabled and has valid addressing for the subnet (static or DHCP). Check also to see what the operating system NIC status reports for frames sent and received—if either is zero, investigate.

- Verified that nothing has been recently changed on the problem station or on the server or service that might have caused this problem, such as reconfiguring or adding new software or hardware.

- Eliminated potential station memory allocation problems and software conflicts on the station by loading only the minimum software required to operate a test application across the network. As a last option for this test, disable any virus checking or security software, but turn it back on right after the test.

- Monitored the user's station for applications that are consuming microprocessor resources or hanging the system long enough to exceed connection timers, possibly a virus.

The reason for dropped connections is a logical or physical connectivity loss. This is manifested by cable-related problems or by difficulties getting through a switch, bridge, router, or WAN connection. Upper-layer protocols implement various timers that terminate a station's logical connection if the timer expires without having heard from that station. Thus, if frames are being dropped across a switch, bridge, router, or WAN connection, it is possible to lose your connection to the server or service while still operating perfectly on the local collision domain or broadcast domain.

Determine whether the problem is isolated to this station or a small group of stations (collision domain problem, including a single switch port) or if it affects many stations (broadcast domain or interconnected networks problem). Ask other users in the area if they have had similar problems. Ask also if the problem has been related to time of day, the type of query, or when some seemingly unrelated event or action in the vicinity takes place.

Collision domain problems affect the local medium and disrupt communications to the first Layer 2 or 3 infrastructure device—or the local server or service you are trying to connect to. They typically result from

- Bad cables
- Marginal or intermittent station NIC, or port on hub or switch

- Errors or excessive traffic on the local collision domain
- Duplex mismatches
- Electrical noise and other environmental disruptions

Many collision domain problems related to dropped connections can be identified by disconnecting the user's station and attaching a tester in its place. Through the user's normal cable, exercise the network connection and attempt to reach the problem server or service. Restore the user's connection and leave an inline tester monitoring the link or a protocol analyzer gathering traffic and statistics. Instruct the user on what information to gather from the tester immediately after the connection fails again, and how to stop and save the captured traffic for later analysis.

Many users have both a wired and wireless NIC enabled. If the PC is trying to use a wireless NIC instead of a wired connection, the exact location or PC orientation may be preventing adequate connectivity. There are many blind spots in most wireless networks, and some are small. Moving the PC even a few inches or rotating it slightly has been known to reestablish a wireless link. If people are congregated near the PC, they might be blocking the signal.

Broadcast domain problems begin after a reliable MAC Layer link is verified, and they are typified by a failure to maintain a logical connection across a bridged environment. Included in this category are Network Layer issues that can disrupt communications to servers and routers attached to this broadcast domain:

- Marginal or failed uplink port somewhere in the path, possibly the result of a bad cable
- Spanning tree problems, possibly the result of a bad cable
- Broadcast storm or other excessive traffic within the broadcast domain (not necessarily traffic observed on the local port)
- Duplex mismatches between ports somewhere in the path
- Duplicate IP addresses
- Station or server improperly advertising routes (only devices that have somewhere to route packets to should advertise routing protocols)

Continuously ping the local router to check for lost frames on the broadcast domain. Use network management to interrogate the infrastructure devices in the path between the user's connection and the router, server or service, looking for errors or high utilization that appear to correspond to times when the connection was lost. Restore the user's station and use a protocol analyzer to monitor and/or capture traffic related to the problem server or service. If the problem is intermittent, leave the protocol analyzer gathering traffic. Instruct the user on how to stop the capture immediately if the connection fails again. This sort of problem is often intermittent and difficult to troubleshoot unless the user can summon you while it is happening or capture and examine a record of the communications leading up to the failure.

Interconnected network problems begin after a reliable link is verified to the router offering a path out of the broadcast domain. Reliable access to Internet servers or services is more problematic than reliable access to servers or services on adjacent LANs because of Internet service provider (ISP) outages and denial of service attacks that are beyond the control and visibility of the local network support staff. Possible sources of unreliable access beyond the local broadcast domain include the following:

- Unstable routing caused by marginal port or link somewhere beyond the broadcast domain, possibly the result of a bad cable

- Excessive traffic across a low-speed LAN or WAN link, possibly causing traffic to be discarded or buffer capacity to be exceeded

- Overloaded server or service

Ping and traceroute testing may reveal the location where troubleshooting connections that drop problems should begin. Run tests continuously to detect the probable location of fluctuating or intermittent problems. For faster troubleshooting after a remote location is identified as being suspect, use network management to query the suspect infrastructure device and the infrastructure device immediately prior to it. One or the other should be showing errors of some type or excessive utilization. Perform a throughput test that validates the path capacity between the user connection and the server or service; monitor the path with

network management while the throughput test is performed to see whether any errors appear. Establishing a reliable end-to-end connection at the Network Layer nearly always resolves dropped connection problems. Be sure to repeat collision domain and broadcast domain tests each time you move to a new location while troubleshooting using the divide-and-conquer process. If end-to-end Network Layer delivery appears to be reliable, protocol analysis is the next step. Leave a protocol analyzer gathering traffic. Instruct the user on how to stop the capture immediately if the connection fails again. If the server or service is overloaded, or if there is something within the user's station that is consuming microprocessor resources or disrupting communications, the protocol analyzer trace file should identify which end of the connection to investigate first.

Problem: Slow or Poor Performance

Poor performance may be caused by the same conditions that prevent a connection from being established in the first place, or from the same conditions that cause connections to drop. Consider any of the situations described under the "Problem: Can't Connect" and "Problem: Connections That Drop" headings.

The following procedures assume that this connection has been operating properly prior to this problem, and you have already

- Verified that nothing has been recently changed on the problem station or the server or service that might have caused this problem, such as reconfiguring or adding new software or hardware.

- Eliminated potential station memory allocation problems and software conflicts on the station by unloading all but the minimum software required to operate a test application across the network. For this test, disable any virus checking or security software but reenable it immediately after the test.

- Tested the user's station for viruses and looked for applications that are consuming disproportionate amounts of the microprocessor resources or hanging the system long enough to exceed connection timers.

The most common reasons for slow or poor performance include overloaded or underpowered servers, unsuitable switch or router configurations, traffic congestion on a low-capacity link, and chronic frame loss. Tiered applications may suffer poor performance when any one of the servers in the tiered hierarchy suffers delays. Analyzing tiered applications can be tricky because it is often difficult to map all the dependencies.

Determine whether the problem is isolated to this station or a small group of stations (collision domain problem, including a single switch port) or if it affects many stations (broadcast domain or interconnected networks problem). Ask other users in the area if they have had similar problems, whether with the network or a particular application. Ask also if the problem has been related to time of day, the type of query, or when some seemingly unrelated event or action in the vicinity takes place.

Collision domain problems affect the local medium and disrupt communications to the first Layer 2 or 3 infrastructure device—or the local server or service you are trying to connect to. They typically result from

- Bad cables
- Marginal or intermittent station NIC, or port on hub or switch
- Errors or excessive traffic on the local collision domain
- Duplex mismatches
- Electrical noise and other environmental disruptions

Many collision domain problems related to slow or poor performance can be identified by disconnecting the user's station and attaching a tester in its place. Through the user's normal cable, exercise the network connection and attempt to reach the problem server or service. Restore the user's connection and leave an inline tester monitoring the link or a protocol analyzer gathering traffic and statistics. Instruct the user on what information to gather from the tester immediately after the connection fails again, and how to stop and save the captured traffic for later analysis.

Business-critical applications should rarely be delivered wirelessly, owing to the many possible impediments and generally lower available bandwidth. Check which NIC is being used to access the poorly performing server or service. If the circumstances dictate that wireless is appropriate, use a spectrum analyzer to check for continuous or intermittent noise sources, or any other competition for the frequency band in use for this wireless link.

Broadcast domain problems begin after a reliable MAC Layer link is verified, and they are typified by a failure to maintain a logical connection across a bridged environment. Included in this category are Network Layer issues that can disrupt communications to servers and routers attached to this broadcast domain, such as the following:

- Marginal or failed uplink port somewhere in the path, possibly the result of a bad cable
- Spanning tree problems, possibly the result of a bad cable
- Broadcast storm or other excessive traffic within the broadcast domain (not necessarily traffic observed on the local port)
- Duplex mismatches between ports somewhere in the path
- Duplicate IP addresses
- Station or server improperly advertising routes (only devices that have somewhere to route packets to should advertise routing protocols)

Continuously ping the local router to check for lost frames on the broadcast domain. Use network management to interrogate the infrastructure devices in the path between the user's connection and the router, server, or service, looking for errors or high utilization that appear to correspond to times when the connection was lost. Perform a throughput test to various points across the broadcast domain, being careful to use the same uplinks as the desired traffic travels. Watch for inconsistent throughput results that reveal duplex mismatches and other error-related problems. Restore the user's station and use a protocol analyzer to monitor and/or capture traffic related to the problem server or service. Watch especially for ICMP errors and TCP retransmissions. If the poor performance problem is intermittent, leave the protocol analyzer gathering traffic. Instruct the user on how to stop the capture immediately if the connection fails again. This sort of problem is often intermittent and difficult to troubleshoot unless the user can summon you while it is happening or capture and examine a record of the communications leading up to the failure.

Interconnected network problems begin after a reliable link is verified to the router offering a path out of the broadcast domain. If performance is unsatisfactory all the time, the problem is probably related to a poor configuration, inadequate capacity somewhere, or some other systemic problem. If performance varies and is not always unsatisfactory, the problem is probably related to an error condition or is being affected by traffic from other sources, such as the following:

- Unstable routing caused by marginal port or link somewhere beyond the broadcast domain, possibly the result of a bad cable

- Excessive traffic across a low-speed LAN or WAN link, possibly causing traffic to be discarded or buffer capacity to be exceeded

- Overloaded server or service

Ping and traceroute testing may reveal the location where troubleshooting slow or poor performance problems should begin. Run tests continuously to detect the probable location of fluctuating or intermittent problems. For faster troubleshooting once a remote location is identified as being suspect, use network management to query the suspect infrastructure device and the infrastructure device immediately prior to it. One or the other should be showing errors of some type or excessive utilization. Perform a throughput test that validates the path capacity between the user connection and the server or service; monitor the path with network management while the throughput test is performed to see whether any errors appear. Establishing a reliable end-to-end connection at the Network Layer nearly always resolves dropped connection problems. Be sure to repeat collision domain and broadcast domain tests each time you move to a new location while troubleshooting. If end-to-end Network Layer delivery appears to be reliable, protocol analysis is the next step. Capture and analyze the connection attempt. If the server or service is overloaded, or if there is something within the user's station that is consuming microprocessor resources or disrupting

communications, the protocol analyzer trace file should identify which end of the connection to investigate first.

General Troubleshooting Advice

Theory and practical experience determine which test to perform first. Consider past experience with the same or similar equipment and related symptoms, as well as the probability of what is likely to fail or what suffers from repeated failures.

Can you eliminate several possibilities with a single test? A functional diagram of the network is enormously helpful in visualizing the problem and saving valuable time. In general, it's best to subdivide or isolate a problem into a smaller functional section—removing the largest convenient section first (called the divide-and-conquer approach). Start at any convenient spot near the center of the problem collision domain or broadcast domain and divide the problem in half. Continue halving the problem until you've isolated it to the smallest possible section.

Don't assume that the user is providing complete and accurate information, or that the user even knows what counts as potentially affecting network operation. It's best to verify it yourself, or have the user show you how the problem was discovered. In the confusion and stress that accompany a network failure, small but important things are often overlooked.

Example 1: A Change Unrelated to the Network

The network failed at a small business when an additional salesman was hired. The new salesman didn't even have a computer yet, only a telephone. The addition of a new telephone line exceeded the capacity of the existing telephone switch configuration and a new card was installed. The addition of another card exceeded the capacity of the power supply for the telephone switch and a larger power supply was installed. The network fault was ultimately traced to a switch in the computer room, which was fastened to the other side of the same wall in nearly exact alignment with the telephone switch power supply. The radiated electrical noise from the new power supply was corrupting traffic as it passed from the servers to the users through that one switch. Moving the switch a very short distance solved the problem.

Example 2: Overlooking the Obvious

A reasonably competent user moved offices and declined all offers from the network support staff for assistance. Two days after the move the user finally—reluctantly—phoned the Help Desk for assistance. After a lengthy telephone diagnosis the Help Desk technician determined that the user's account was good, the PC was good, addressing was correct, and the PC's network connection showed link. The technician came out and was in the user's office less than a minute before discovering that while the user's PC had link, there was no cable connecting the hub in the user's office to the network.

Finally, if something fails a second time do not replace it until you have made absolutely certain that the source of the problem has been identified and corrected.

When troubleshooting an Ethernet collision domain be careful to avoid spending time troubleshooting symptoms instead of the real problem. Many technicians have the tendency to assume that if their understanding of the theoretical model describes a specific error resulting from a specific problem, no other problem could cause that error. Marginal or failed equipment seldom obediently reads the appropriate standard. The technician then starts trying to solve the wrong problem.

Example 3: Theory Says This Can't Happen

A network was assembled with very early versions of 10/100 Ethernet switches. The network had perhaps 20 switches from a variety of vendors and was operating very well under the test conditions. When real users were added, an odd intermittent dropped-connection problem was observed. After considerable troubleshooting it was finally determined that one model of the switch had faulty firmware. Any time the bridge forwarding table for a single port exceeded the allocated maximum number of entries the switch dropped the oldest entry entirely—as if it no longer existed—and that oldest station's traffic was immediately ignored instead of being flooded to all ports. When that station was rebooted (dropped link on the port) and again entered the network, a different station was dropped from the list but the original problem station then worked great for some time. According to theory, traffic for the new station should have been flooded to all ports if the forwarding database was full. Also, no station address should have been discarded from of the forwarding table until it had been silent for the aging period of the forwarding table.

Example 4: Theory Says This Can't Happen

A small work area was serviced by a consumer-grade wireless access point. Performance was considered good by the users, except that periodically a new connection could not be established. One day there was a meeting, and there were more than 10 people in the work area attempting to use the wireless link. It was not possible for all of them to gain access to the network, but those who connected had great performance. The odd thing was that the people who had been present longest had access but none of the recent arrivals did. After troubleshooting it was determined that the access point appeared to have a bridge forwarding table sized for only about 10 MAC addresses. Any attempts to connect beyond that number were denied. Rebooting the access point cleared the bridge forwarding table, and the first 10 PCs to try were able to connect to the network through it. This is almost exactly the opposite behavior from the previous example.

Because of the common bus topology and potentially extended physical layout of shared media Ethernet, some Physical Layer problems often display different and conflicting symptoms depending on where measurements are made, and depending on the conditions and location of the measurement.

Example 5: No Errors Detected

Two stations are located at opposite ends of an over-long collision domain (too many repeaters in the series; see Figure 11-4). Assume that both stations begin transmitting at nearly the same instant and that collisions result. If measurements were made midway between the stations, only normal local or remote collisions would be detected. However, if measurements were made near either end of the collision domain, late collisions could be detected.

In this example, late collisions are not detected from the monitoring point because the repeater count to the most distant station(s) appears to be within the limits. However, between the two most distant stations the repeater count is double the limit.

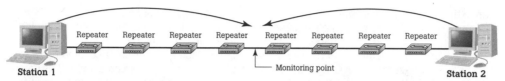

Figure 11-4. *The selected monitoring point on an Ethernet collision domain can obscure some errors*

Example 6: Symptoms Don't Seem to Match the Problem

With 15 to 20 stations on a moderately long length of thin coax, a user rearranges his office, physically moving a station away from the BNC cable tap. To reconnect the station, an additional length of coax is attached from the station to the original BNC Tee connector (the extra cable is called a "stub"—see Figure 11-5). As long as that station, or any other station in close proximity, is not transmitting then monitoring is unlikely to reveal any problems. But if any station near the stub is transmitting, monitoring is likely to reveal remote collisions or FCS errors. Theory suggests that if the voltage level does not reach the collision detect threshold on coax, collision fragments indicate a problem on the other side of a repeater. The technician is led to troubleshoot in the wrong area because the signal reflections generated by the stub are small enough that resulting problems appear to be from another segment.

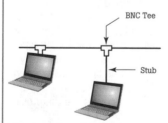

Figure 11-5. *Coax cable stub*

A related problem is possible with WAN and wireless use of coax, only it would be harder to locate because the expectation is for a single cable to be used between the two active devices.

Avoid Misleading Symptoms

If not identified, misleading symptoms can waste time and effort. Avoid them by using the following three guidelines whenever you troubleshoot an Ethernet collision domain problem:

- Make measurements from several locations within the collision domain whenever a moderate to large collision domain (on shared media) is involved in a troubleshooting scenario and *any* MAC Layer errors are detected.

- If the symptoms of the problem remain relatively constant regardless of where the measurement is made, troubleshoot according to what the detected problem suggests.

- If the symptoms are different at some or all the locations along the segment where measurements are made, direct troubleshooting toward a Physical Layer problem—no matter what the symptoms may suggest.

Use the divide-and-conquer troubleshooting approach for solving collision domain problems. Look for bad cables, bad connections, failed or marginal hardware, noise sources, and ground loops. Check to see that

- Station connections are properly fastened (RJ45 connections do not have broken or missing latch tabs)

- BNC connectors rotated far enough to "latch," and so on

- Each individual piece of cable is of the correct characteristic impedance or that multimode links are using the same fiber core diameter throughout a link (mixing 50nm and 62.5nm cable is very easy)

- All cables are firmly crimped or clamped into the connectors, and so on

To enhance the quality of measurements made, configure the test tool to transmit a small amount of background traffic from the measurement point while the measurement is being made. The addition of 100 frames-per-second of 100-byte frames to the MAC address of the tester is sufficient. Field results indicate that within a collision domain the quality of measurements made while the tester is generating traffic are moderately to greatly enhanced over a simple monitoring test. When traffic is added, many otherwise subtle and inter-mittent Physical Layer problems are revealed to the monitoring device.

If the category of error described as an Eth-ernet ghost is ever detected, there is a Physical Layer problem. Again, disregard symptoms sug-gested by any other test result and begin looking for the Physical Layer problem. Once the ghosts are eliminated, it is safe to consider the implica-tions of new test results.

Specific Error Types

Because switches have become the common con-nection point, the art of troubleshooting a collision domain and the related understanding of what detected or reported errors suggest is quickly becoming lost knowledge. This is unfortunate because the errors are still present on point-to-point links between stations and the switch, or between switches. The only significant difference is that in most cases it affects only a single user. Table 11-1 (half duplex and shared media) and Table 11-2 (full duplex) follow the text descrip-tions and summarize the information presented by the text descriptions.

Collisions

Be careful when troubleshooting collision prob-lems because the obvious answer is usually wrong. The addresses found in collision frag-ments belong to stations that transmitted legally. Stations that sent enough of the current frame to have a source address in a collision fragment usually started transmitting first, although that depends in part on your monitoring point within the collision domain. Most of the stations that col-lide with those legally transmitted frames are also operating legally (they did not "hear" anything

on the wire, so they began to transmit). If there is a station that has gone "deaf" and is stepping on other transmissions because it does not hear them, it will likely never be discovered because it transmits into another transmission and its data is always corrupted. Troubleshoot the presence of too many collisions, but don't examine the fragments closely. Using the corrupted data from collision fragments just causes frustration.

Late Collisions

A late collision is detected after the slotTime timer has expired, indicating that the collision occurred illegally late. As described in Chapter 4, "Media Access Control Layer," the slotTime timer indicates the maximum amount of time required for a signal to travel to the far end of a legally architected collision domain, collide with another transmission, and return to the transmitting sta-tion to be detected as an error.

In half-duplex Ethernet networks, late col-lisions are often detected simply as FCS errors because the reporting station was not transmit-ting, and thus was not a participant in the late collision. Because a late collision is recorded only when there is a local collision symptom (over-voltage or simultaneous receive/transmit), late collisions are usually detected as such only if they occur on the same side of the repeater as the monitoring station. On 10BASE5 and 10BASE2, this is not too difficult to arrange because many stations are typically attached on the same cable. For noncoaxial Ethernet segments, the station is directly linked to a repeater, and therefore must be transmitting to detect a late collision. It is pos-sible to infer the presence of a late collision by examining the last few octets of an FCS-errored frame to see whether there is an alternating 1, 0 pattern, but there is no guarantee the diagnosis is correct.

Late collisions result from improper installation of the network, physical damage to the network, or failed network adapter(s) somewhere within the collision domain. The old attribution that a late collision is literally the result of a too-long cable is challenged by calculating the delay in-troduced by cable only—requiring a cable around five kilometers long. Although propagation delay introduced by the cable is a factor, it is much more likely that other factors, such as cable impedance mismatches, signal attenuation along the cable, too many repeaters, and marginal interfaces result in situations where a shortened cable still has late collisions. Duplex mismatches will also produce late collisions. The station improperly connected in full duplex does not care whether there is already a signal on the collision domain.

Short Frame

Short frames appear as properly formed frames with a valid checksum, except that the frame size does not meet the minimum size requirement. This usually means that the NIC driver did not pad small frames.

The most likely cause of a short frame is a faulty card or an improperly configured or corrupt NIC driver file.

Jabber and Long Frames

This heading uses the definition of jabber where the transmission is illegally long and has a bad FCS. 802.3 Ethernet Jabber is based on a timer rather than a frame size, and is used by shared media repeaters in determining when to disable a port.

- The most likely causes of jabber are a faulty NIC and/or faulty or corrupt NIC driver files, bad cabling, or grounding problems.

- The most likely causes of long frames are a faulty NIC and/or faulty or corrupt NIC driver files, or use of a jumbo frame configuration.

- Older infrastructure equipment may assume that anything larger than either 1518 octets or 1522 octets is illegally long, even if it has a valid FCS. If so, that older infrastructure device discards the illegal frame.

- Jumbo frames (anything between 2000 octets and 65,536 octets—although normally not larger than 9018 octets) are illegal according to 802.3 Ethernet, and probably will be discarded by any infrastructure device not specifically configured to support them. Use of jumbo frames is a vendor-dependent or vendor-proprietary feature.

Ghosts

Ghosts are easily created by a variety of causes on coaxial Ethernet. They may also be caused by something as simple as installing a second crossover cable between two hubs on half duplex. The parallel path sometimes causes very strange symptoms. The hub does one of the following three things:

- Locks one port out, sometimes requiring a power cycle or SNMP management intervention to reopen the port. This is fortunately the most common result.

- Cyclically locks the port out, checks later to see whether it is okay. The standard says that after the jabber timer expires (20,000 to 50,000 bit times), the hub should close the port for a while before reopening it to see whether the attached device has stopped transmitting. If jabber is again detected, the port may be closed for another cycle. This may continue forever.

- Allow the error to continue uninterrupted. This is not permitted by the standard.

The error level often fluctuates between very little and most of the available bandwidth for no apparent reason. In addition to ghosts, this second crossover cable fault usually produces collisions, late collisions, and FCS errors.

Grounding

If shielded twisted pair is used (either ScTP or a form STP common with ISO Class F cables), it is important that both ends of the link tie the cable screen or shield to ground, and that there are no significant voltage potential differences between electrical ground at both ends of the link. Large office buildings often have ground potential differences when the electrical distribution system is created from multi-phase circuits divided into single-phase outlet strings.

The standard requires 10BASE5 to be grounded, whereas it only recommends that 10BASE2 be grounded—although it's a good idea to connect the ground to avoid problems. If problems develop after you have grounded a segment, and it worked prior to that time, the segment is probably shorted to ground somewhere already.

Table 11-1 and Table 11-2 summarize much of the description in this section as a simple table of Ethernet errors and the most probable causes. The tables portray the likely distinctions between half and full duplex links separately.

Table 11-1. *Half duplex and shared media Ethernet error*

Causes	Error Type				
	Late Collision	Short Frame	Jabber	FCS	Ghost
Bad SW Drivers		•	•	•	
Faulty/Marginal NIC	•	•	•	•	•
Repeater Fault	•		•	•	•
Too Many Repeaters	•			•	
Illegal HW Configuration	•		•	•	•
Cable Too Long	•			•	
Cable Fault	•		•	•	•
Termination	•		•	•	•
Bad Grounding	•		•	•	•
Induced Noise	•		•	•	•
Duplex Mismatch	•			•	

Table 11-2. *Full duplex Ethernet errors*

Causes	Error Type					
	Collision Fragments	Short Frame	Jabber**	FCS***	Dropped Link	Alignment
Bad SW Drivers		•	•	•		
Faulty/Marginal NIC	•	•	•	•	•	•
Duplex Mismatch*	•			•		•
Cable Too Long				•	•	
Cable Fault			•	•	•	•
Induced Noise			•	•	•	•

* Duplex Mismatch may be due to having one link partner using Auto-Negotiation and the other using a fixed full duplex setting.

** Jabber might also be reported in the presence of nonstandard jumbo frames.

*** FCS errors are likely to include late collisions.

Some Simple Guidelines

There are many simple and somewhat obvious things that may be accomplished without spending a noticeable amount of extra time or effort, but that go a long way toward having a more reliable network.

Cable

Networks depend on cables. Don't disregard them as just another commodity that can be obtained anywhere or casually created as needed. The demands placed on the cable system by higher-speed networking implementations suggest that even newly purchased cables should be subject to a certification test before use. Why risk wasting hours of troubleshooting time for something that could have been avoided with a two-minute effort? Many low-cost patch cables introduce more problems than the rest of the cable link on which they are used.

- Don't install long cables. Make all runs as short as possible, and certainly no longer than is permitted by the media access protocol you are using. For example, never install UTP runs longer than 100 meters.

- If you build your own cables or buy premade cables, be sure to test them with a reliable cable tester before you use them—especially if you are already in troubleshooting mode. Patch cables are a notable problem with high-performance cable systems, such as Category 6 or Category 6A. Patch cables should be tested using a cable analyzer configured for patch cord testing; otherwise, the test limits applied are for 100 meter cables.

- Fiber optic cable terminations are best made by splicing short factory-terminated ends onto installed horizontal fiber. Hand polishing ends usually results in a poor quality termination, whereas it is much more difficult to splice poorly. It is also a lot faster to splice, less loss is associated with a typical splice when compared to a hand-polished connector, and splicing tends to cost less overall.

Network

Just as with network cabling, there are some simple common sense actions that can be factored into a network design that either limits the effect of a fault or speeds network recovery from a fault.

- Limit the number of stations on each segment. The processing power of today's station far outstrips the power of a station at the time the limits were specified. A typical collision domain probably shouldn't have more than a few stations today, although the standard permits up to 1,024. The conversion to switched networks means that in most cases the collision domain is the switch and one station.

- Isolate high-traffic stations from the rest of the users with switches. Logically (by VLAN) or physically group stations onto broadcast domains that include the most-used server. It is better to have slower response time from seldom-used resources than to degrade response time to resources used frequently. In a switched network this might mean placing the most-used servers in the same VLAN as the user community. Installing multiple NICs in a server is not costly but can noticeably improve user response time.

- Watch for special networking situations, and be prepared to change your network architecture to accommodate them.

> **Example 7: Bending the Rules Means That You Must Understand Them**
>
> Microsoft "NLB" load balancing relies on having all clustered servers in the same broadcast domain. Clients send traffic to a virtual address, which the servers never answer, responding instead with their own physical MAC address instead of the virtual MAC address. This causes the switches servicing the cluster to keep flooding requests to all ports, because according to the bridge forwarding table no response means an unknown destination. If other servers or clients are in the same broadcast domain as the cluster, they receive every server request, which in turn diminishes their performance in direct proportion to the number of server requests. Similarly, two clusters should not be attached to the same broadcast domain.

Link State

When hubs were common the link state LED was controlled directly by the port silicon. Except for unusual hardware failures, it was safe to say that if the link LED was illuminated, the port was forwarding traffic. Now that switches are common, that is no longer true. In most cases, it appears that the link state LED is software controlled and is not always trustworthy. If the link LED is off, it is fairly safe to assume that a problem exists. If the link LED is on

- A blinking LED (which may be accompanied by clicking sounds) suggests that Auto-Negotiation has chosen a higher speed than the cable can support. The port negotiated to the higher speed, attempted to link but was unsuccessful, dropped its attempt to link, and restarted Auto-Negotiation. This cycle can continue forever or, on recent switches, the switch logic may realize that the cable is incapable of the highest speed and it offers fewer choices (lower speeds only) in subsequent Auto-Negotiation FLPs until the link is established. In this way it may drop all the way down to 10Mbps when you are expecting Gigabit.

- The LED might be illuminated but there is no link (software controlled LED). This has become most evident during troubleshooting when the patch cable for the problem link is removed from the switch entirely but the link LED remains illuminated. Reboot the switch.

- The LED may be illuminated but only one end is linked and not the other. This is most common with fiber optic connections. Check both link partners for link status.

- Possible but least likely, the link may be active but the link LED is off.

How Much Utilization Is Okay?

Shared Ethernet networks are believed to suffer from throughput problems when average traffic loads approach the generally accepted maximum average capacity level of 40 percent. Actually, the 40 percent average percentage is conservative and higher average percentages are certainly possible. See the paper, "A new binary logarithmic

arbitration method for Ethernet" by Mart Molle for more detail. The first solution to excessive traffic is to microsegment collision domains by installing switches (resulting in a collision domain on each port). This solution works well until the amount of broadcast traffic grows too large. Because bridges and switches always forward all broadcast traffic to all ports, even infrequent broadcasts from each station are eventually too many when the station count for the broadcast domain goes up.

If a single station is connected to a half duplex switch port, the amount of utilization that is acceptable can best be learned by monitoring the switch port statistics. There is some level of collisions, but because there are only two devices on that link (the switch and the station) the link should be usable even with a high average utilization. There will likely be excessive collision errors reported by the switch periodically, resulting from the Ethernet capture effect. This problem is not terribly significant overall and results in a slight reduction in performance. The port should still be capable of more than 80 percent utilization in half duplex. If the link is allowed to negotiate to full duplex instead of half, the connection should be capable of approaching theoretical limits for full line rate Ethernet; depending on the processing power of the attached station (the current generation of switches is capable of sustaining line-rate traffic at the minimum frame size for up to at least Gigabit speeds—although 10 Gigabit is still uncertain due to backplane performance and other factors).

Another problem manifests itself when all the servers or services are reached through a single switch uplink path. Unless the uplink path has more bandwidth than all the simultaneous station requests, the uplink itself becomes a bottleneck. By locating servers on the same switch as the users (and assuming that the server has a connection large enough to handle all user requests at once), the users experience the best performance. VLANs may be used to logically place the users in the same broadcast. Using a VLAN trunk to pass uplink traffic to the servers can experience periodic slowdowns because of high traffic volumes in VLANs other than the one being monitored. Check traffic statistics on the trunk port.

Even when logical grouping by VLAN is performed, it is still necessary to examine the network architecture to see whether bottlenecks exist. If too much traffic is required to pass through an inadequate aggregation path, a potentially useful architecture design is defeated. To prevent this, the network administrator should limit inter-segment traffic by carefully considering which stations should attach to each segment. The process involves an investment of time and might need to be repeated regularly on extremely dynamic networks. Monitor uplink paths as a part of routine maintenance to detect impending saturation of any one path. Use RMON or flow protocols to monitor which servers are experiencing the greatest demand.

The ubiquitous presence of switches and their evolving feature set has created a comparatively inexpensive method of controlling network congestion. Switches have not solved the congestion problem, of course. The bulk of the congestion problem has only moved from the collision domain to either the broadcast domain or the uplinks. Network congestion typically manifests itself to users with the following symptoms:

- Highly variable response times

- Network time-outs or server disconnects

- Inability to establish network connections

- Slower application loading and/or running

Also, consider that server-based applications are often divided across multiple physical servers, creating a tiered environment. If any server in the tiered architecture experiences performance problems, it affects overall application performance. A tiered architecture is often difficult to troubleshoot, unless inter-server traffic is monitored and trended. The most common problem observed with a tiered architecture has been where a particular server resource is shared between multiple applications. The server receives a request for one application that requires substantial processing, and other application queries are delayed accordingly. Because the request is busy processing had nothing to do with the other applications, the burdened server is not suspected as being the cause of the performance degradation in the other applications. Also, the staff supporting applica-

tions might not realize that additional servers are involved in processing requests for the problem application.

Tiered Applications

A few common situations apply to troubleshooting tiered applications, such as load balancing, determining which tier is the source of a slowdown, and mapping the participating servers.

Load Balancing

By monitoring all the traffic passing through a load balancer, it is possible to determine whether the current configuration or load-balancing option (which load-balancing scheme) is working as desired (see Figure 11-6).

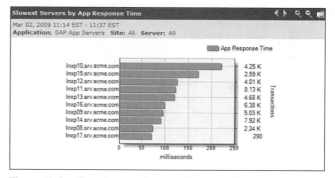

Figure 11-6. *Sample server farm performance measured by application response time and by volume of transactions as shown by Visual Performance Manager*

Problem Tier

If all traffic from within a tiered application is being monitored, it is easily possible to determine which tier is responsible for a slowdown. For example, assume that a three-tiered application is being monitored.

If performance for the sample architecture in Figure 11-7 was experiencing poor performance, the source of the slowdown could be any of the three servers shown. The web server must receive a response from the application server before it can respond. The application server must receive a response from the database server before it can respond.

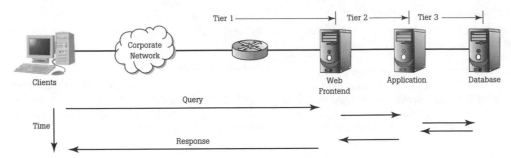

Figure 11-7. *Sample tiered application architecture*

Assume that the user community complains about poor performance, indicating that there is about 15 seconds between the client web browser requesting a screen and the beginning of the response when normally the response begins to appear in about one second. Three possible situations are equally likely where the web server is responsible for the slowdown:

- It could be waiting for a response from the application server.

- It could be busy processing something locally, and just isn't getting around to servicing the new request as rapidly as usual.

- Not shown in the drawing, and often overlooked, the web server could be waiting for a response from a server not considered part of the three-server application or not

known to be related to it. This could be a DNS lookup, client authentication, or other similar housekeeping type query.

In Figure 11-8, the client response is held up in or by the web server for some reason. The problem could just as easily be the applications server for all the same reasons (see Figure 11-9). And it could be the database server with a nearly identical graphic. To the user there is no difference, but monitoring the traffic to and from each server in the tier would reveal which became slow.

Both Figure 11-8 and Figure 11-9 depict possible situations where client response is unexpectedly slower than normal. Both situations, and Figure 11-10, show behavior that could be investigated for performance improvements if the client response time was "normal."

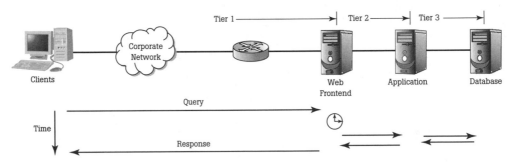

Figure 11-8. *Sample tier 1 problem*

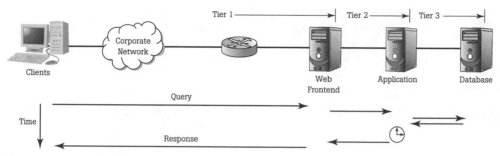

Figure 11-9. *Sample tier 2 problem*

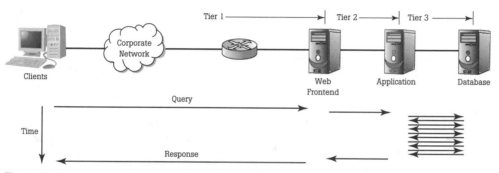

Figure 11-10. *Example of how normal behavior could be slow in a tiered application*

In Figure 11-10, it may be that the database query made by the application server could be optimized to retrieve entire records instead of individual fields per query, or the table that is being queried might not be indexed. There are many optimization actions that may be taken by the database support staff once the exact nature of the problem or routine behavior is known.

In Figure 11-11 notice that abnormal performance for the first and second tier servers is almost identical, and how the third tier server performance is almost perfectly normal. This is a nearly classic example of a problem related to the second-tier server. The next step would be to examine the problem server to learn what other applications are running on it, whether it is I/O bound in any way (such as insufficient RAM, hard drive space, single hard drive controller, and so on), as well as examining the nature of the query made to that server. It may be that the second-tier server is depending on an authentication server not thought to be involved in this application, or some other dependency that is being affected by

external influences. Even changes to antivirus scanning behavior could cause this sort of change in performance. Another clue to the situation in Figure 11-11 is that only two sites are involved. Asking the users from that site about their use of the application could quickly reveal the source of the slowdown.

Mapping a Tiered Application

You can map the actual interactions between servers in a tiered application in many ways. One method, which is effective at discovering unexpected interactions, is to simply monitor the traffic. Setting up a switch mirror or span port, or a tap that copies all the traffic passing to and from the known first server in the application, permits you to see which other hosts are involved in the application. For example, if a diagnostic tool, such as a protocol analyzer or a handheld tool such as the Fluke Networks OptiView, were used to monitor this traffic, there are built-in tests to present conversation pairs.

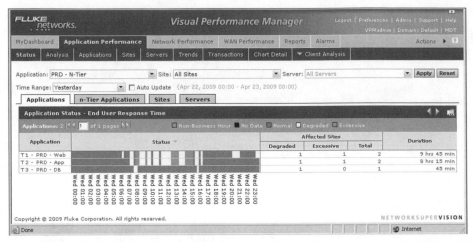

Figure 11-11. *Visual Performance Manager example of how a back-end tiered server problem could be responsible for poor user performance. This is the same as Figure 11-8, showing a Tier 2 problem in a three-tier environment.*

In Figure 11-12, the highlighted address (10.248.1.30) is known to be a web server. The OptiView has also detected this and placed a server icon beside the entry. The first appearance of this address in the left column was highlighted, and the Host Conversations tab was clicked.

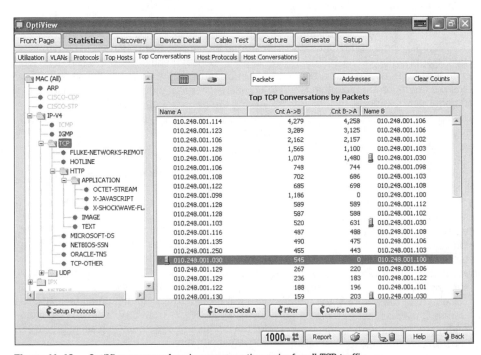

Figure 11-12. *OptiView screen showing conversation pairs for all TCP traffic*

The information in Figure 11-13 is recorded in a table. This process is repeated and recorded until either all significant packet count conversations are mapped, or all conversations are mapped. The packet capture process is repeated for servers revealed as *n*-tier data sources for the first-tier server. If adequate knowledge of the network is not available to indicate which addresses represent known servers, an additional step may be taken to discover that information.

To begin a more detailed mapping process, a protocol trace file is captured for all TCP traffic, such as shown in Figure 11-14.

Once a representative sample of traffic is captured, the file is opened and examined. In Figure 11-15 a transmission from the known 10.248.1.30 server is observed, and the destination TCP port is right-clicked to offer a choice to apply the selected destination TCP port as a display filter is selected.

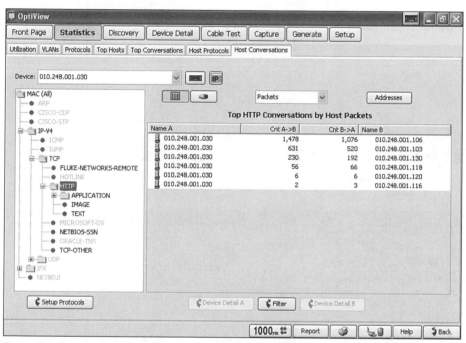

Figure 11-13. *OptiView screen showing conversations to/from the selected 10.248.1.30 address*

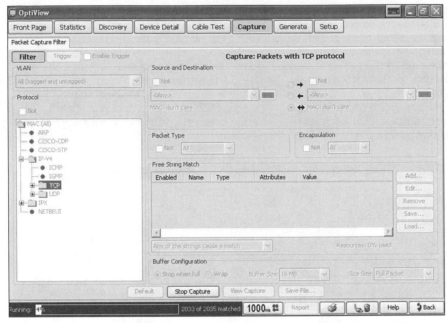

Figure 11-14. *OptiView protocol capture screen, showing all TCP traffic being captured*

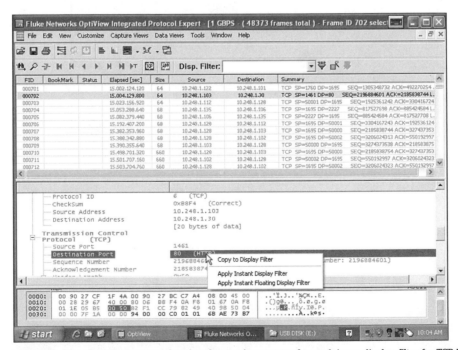

Figure 11-15. *OptiView screen showing the starting process for applying a display filter for TCP Port 80 as a destination*

The filter is applied, and all packets in the capture file with TCP Port 80 queries are presented in Figure 11-16.

Repeating this process for each IP address or protocol eventually permits you to map all the interactions between servers and clients in a tiered application. Use the data placed in a table to create a drawing showing the various interactions, by protocol (see Figure 11-17).

Unfortunately, this process can take some hours in a complex environment. After drawing the complete functional diagram, it is almost always necessary to consult with the server group

and the applications group to determine whether certain mappings are relevant to the application being drawn. It is also likely that the server and applications staff are unaware of some of the dependencies imposed by the deployment of the application. For example, it is taken for granted that the user is a member of the domain, but authentication of that status may be part of the application login process. If the domain controller is busy, it could slow down the login.

It is not unusual for the final drawing to look a bit like a plate of noodles, and to cause more than a little consternation among all the parties involved (see Figure 11-18).

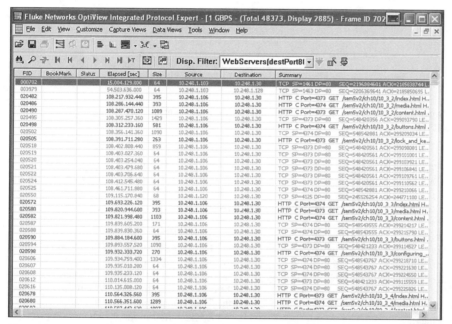

Figure 11-16. *OptiView screen showing the results of the display filter for all destination TCP port 80 traffic*

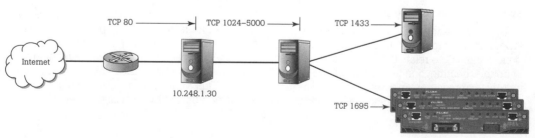

Figure 11-17. *Simple tiered application functional drawing*

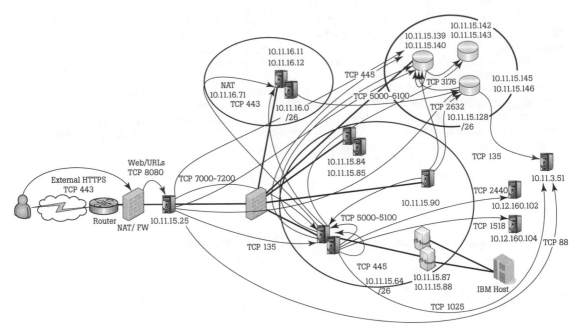

Figure 11-18. *Sample functional drawing for a complex application with multiple dependencies. Notice that two servers originally reported to be part of the application were not observed to be participating at all.*

Following the mapping process for a tiered application, it is then appropriate to establish a performance baseline. Track response time per conversation pair during low and high-use time periods.

If a problem is found or reported, examine variations in performance during periods of good user response time and poor user response time. Following the tiered dependencies look for the last tier where the performance is slow *right now* and examine the processes, CPU and memory usage, and NIC utilization and errors for the furthest back server that was slow. This is described under the "Problem Tier" heading earlier.

Switching Technology Issues

Many of the features and benefits offered by a switch are immediately evident to most people. It is more difficult to relate those same features back to troubleshooting, and to consider all the ways that this improvement in technology also makes the job of troubleshooting much more difficult

(see Appendix E, "Techniques for Troubleshooting Switches"). Here are several issues that should be kept in mind while designing or troubleshooting a switched network.

Multiple Simultaneous Connections

One important aspect of switch technology is the ability to support multiple simultaneous separate conversations (see Figure 11-19). You can never be certain where the traffic is flowing to or coming from. This is especially true because a single station may be simultaneously communicating with several other devices.

Because each port on the switch should be isolating a collision domain, some of the connections established may be operating correctly, whereas others are operating poorly. To the user, the single cable attaching a station to the switch is "the" connection to the network. Anything software does after that is "the network" and therefore "the network" has a problem, not a particular application hosted by a specific server.

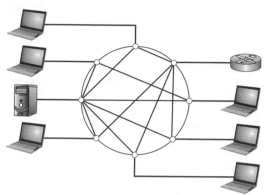

Figure 11-19. *Logical conversation matrix example. Most client PCs communicate with servers or off-subnet through routers. Peer-to-peer communications are possible but less frequent.*

Latency

Latency is the time delay measured from the point when the switch starts receiving a frame to when it begins to forward the frame out the destination port. The greatest influence on latency is the forwarding technique used by the switch. For cut-through there is a fixed latency representing slightly more than 112 bits because it is designed to forward the frame immediately after receiving the Destination MAC address.

The latency through a store-and-forward switch is dependent on the size of the frame, because it must receive the complete frame before making the forwarding decision. To illustrate, on a store-and-forward switch, a 1000-octet frame on a 100BASE-TX network has slightly more than 80 microseconds of latency (at the MAC Layer 1000 octets = 8000 bits at 10 nanoseconds per bit).

The availability of low-latency switches has diminished substantially. This may be due to people realizing that the user is unlikely to actually notice the performance enhancement provided. There are not that many situations where using a low-latency forwarding technique produces a user-noticeable difference. However, the support staff has probably noticed that it is much more difficult to troubleshoot the network when low-latency forwarding is enabled. For troubleshooting purposes, a store-and-forward switch is a wonderful thing. The errors always stop at the port.

Variations in delay (jitter) are a much more critical factor on the network. Streaming applications such as video and Voice over IP (VoIP) require fairly constant latency to operate well, although too much delay is bad. These applications are often assigned priority queuing through the switched matrix. By placing a higher priority on this traffic any other traffic is necessarily lower in priority. There is a finite amount of bandwidth through any path, and if some of the traffic is expedited, the rest is delayed.

Forwarding Table Address Support

In older switches there was a direct purchase price correlation between switches that supported as few as one MAC address per port and switches that are suitable for backbone applications where potentially thousands of addresses must be tracked. Reductions in the cost for memory have significantly reduced this situation, but the specific performance characteristics for switches designed for a workgroup versus the backbone are still quite different.

If the actual number of MAC addresses exceeds the amount of storage available in the bridge forwarding database in the switch, or for a specific port, the switch *should* forward any frame with an unrecorded destination address to all ports except the port on which the frame was received. It should flood the frame.

If a protocol analyzer (typically a monitor only tool) is attached to an available switch port, almost all the traffic observed should be broadcast traffic. Nonbroadcast frames should be few and far between. If a comparatively large amount of nonbroadcast traffic is seen, it suggests that one of several situations is present on the broadcast domain. It could be that the switch is flooding far more traffic than it ought to because it maintains very few, or only a single address per port in its forwarding database. The traffic could be being sent to a destination address that is not responding. Use of virtual addressing often looks like an unknown destination to the switch and causes flooding too.

Another related situation is when the switch is aging addresses out of the forwarding table in a very short period of time—as little as 30 seconds has been observed recently. This situation produces an increased amount of nonbroadcast traffic on all ports, as if the destination addresses are unknown. This is sometimes a configurable parameter in the switch.

Frame Buffering and Overall Capacity

Most network traffic appears in irregular bursts. The average utilization on a network is typically measured well below 10 percent, and the equipment manufacturers are aware of that. Low-cost switches are designed with lower performance components and less memory, and often don't have the backplane capacity to sustain line rate traffic on all ports for long—if at all. Even new switches might not be able to support the load if all traffic attempts to cross the backplane. However, for normal use they are more than adequate.

If a switch is presented with more traffic than it can immediately transfer and/or buffer, it simply drops the excess traffic. Dynamic buffer allocation is one of several ways to compensate for less installed memory. By shifting the available memory to support traffic bursts from different ports, switch vendors are able to keep the cost of parts down and still satisfy typical usage trends without dropping frames. Dropped frames cause slowness that appears similar to slowness caused by MAC Layer errors. In either case, the upper-layer protocols have to time-out and retransmit. The switch does not generate any errors to clue the network support staff that this problem exists.

If high bandwidth traffic flow is part of a critical business application, the entire path from the user's connection to the server(s) should be stress tested. This may be accomplished in the lab with lab-grade test tools, where all ports of a sample switch are loaded to line rate and monitored simultaneously. Or it may be accomplished in the field using various throughput or RFC 2544 capable test tools. Be aware that RFC 2544 testing assumes that no traffic is lost due to any dilution from other traffic sources, so using it outside the lab must be done with an understanding that some loss is probably okay. Load testing should be conducted with traffic having as close to the same characteristics (same protocol(s), QoS, frame size distribution—or multiple tests at different frame sizes—and so on) as the actual application. If line-rate capacity testing is appropriate, it

should be planned for after hours so that normal work is not interrupted.

Routing Versus Switching

Full routing services used to be performed in software and were therefore microprocessor intensive and slow. Virtually all OSI Layer 2 forwarding (bridging) is performed in hardware, and most OSI Layer 3 forwarding is now performed in hardware too. Hardware-based forwarding is much faster than software-based forwarding.

Using switch configurations to logically group users together in the same broadcast domain with the normally accessed services using VLANs is one way to improve network performance without having to physically locate the servers near the users.

Some advanced configurations rely upon traditional routing to establish the path for a transaction (such as an FTP transfer). After the path is determined, the routing software tells the hardware front-end what pattern to use to recognize further traffic in the transaction so that it can be forwarded by the hardware without involving the routing software. This is an advanced form of OSI Layer 3 switching. A less complex implementation of OSI Layer 3 switching is to simply read further into the frame before making the forwarding decision. By using the IP address instead of the MAC address for the forwarding decision, the switch hardware is able to rapidly forward traffic that would normally have to be evaluated by the routing software. There are other schemes for forwarding by even higher layer criteria.

Take the internal switch forwarding process into consideration when the network architecture is planned. Some switches work better than others in critical locations.

Spanning Tree

Spanning Tree was created primarily to prevent parallel paths from forming and causing bridging loops. It was also long used to automatically manage redundant paths, so that the network would failover and recover itself, although somewhat slowly. Lately, the network demands have pushed it out of favor because recovery from a failed path takes place too slowly. Still, Spanning Tree is often enabled by default on a switch.

Spanning Tree Network Diameter

There are limits to the number of repeaters that may be placed in series between any two distant stations on a collision domain. For bridges the only limit was the Max Age timer in the Spanning Tree Protocol. If Spanning Tree was disabled, you could connect as many bridges (switches) in a series as you wanted. The 1998 version of the 802.1D standard indicated that no more than seven bridges should separate any two distant stations. The 2004 version of 802.1D didn't specify a number, but instead referred to the Max Age timer. RSTP supports a greater number of bridges in series than STP, but there is still a limit.

Flapping Link

If a forwarding port in a Spanning Tree network has become marginal and is going up and down, this causes substantial disruption of the entire broadcast domain. Because Spanning Tree takes a comparatively long time to reconverge it is possible that a flapping link could prevent any forwarding of data.

Watch for any topology change BPDUs. With Spanning Tree this is a different type of BPDU, but with Rapid Spanning Tree it is a flag setting in the BPDU. In a normal network it is very unusual to see a topology change notification at all. Seeing more than one during a troubleshooting situation is highly suspicious and should be investigated immediately.

Remember that 802.11 Access Points are also bridges, and can contribute to this problem, particularly if a wireless link is used to extend a broadcast domain. It is very easy to disrupt wireless communications, particularly on a point-to-point bridge link. Anything ranging from construction equipment moving through the path, to people walking past the antenna, or movement of the Access Point itself.

Link Aggregation

Spanning Tree is supposed to treat a link aggregation as one logical port. However, not all aggregations form properly. The following three behaviors have been observed when connecting an additional parallel path between two bridges and expecting an aggregation to form or increase:

- One of the link LEDs for what would be the aggregation ports cycles to yellow, and then orange, and then off. Spanning Tree treated the additional parallel path as a parallel path instead of an additional path for the aggregation, and the link aggregation did not form. Spanning Tree either forced the port into the "discarding" state or shut it down.

- The new link comes up normally, link LEDs are green. Then when the first broadcast frame passes the link all the LEDs turn red because a broadcast storm just started and the broadcast domain is experiencing total utilization. The link came up as simply another port, and the link aggregation did not form.

- The new link comes up normally and a link aggregation formed. The traffic load between the two bridges is shared across the links in the aggregation.

Broadcast Storms

Portions of the broadcast domain connected by more than one active path result in a bridging loop unless the network detects the parallel path and compensates for it. Because switches are essentially multiport bridges, they are exposed to the same types of problems as bridged networks, including bridging loops.

Figure 11-20 shows how a bridging loop occurs when a broadcast frame is transmitted on one segment, bridged to another segment, and finally returned to the original segment via a different path. Upon returning to the first segment, the frame is forwarded through the loop again and again.

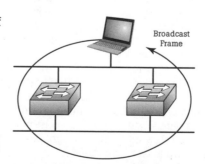

Figure 11-20. *Parallel bridged path*

This behavior is due to the expectation that a bridge forwards a broadcast to all ports except the port it was received on. Because the broadcast returned through a different path, it is again forwarded. This situation is described as a broadcast storm, where the same broadcast frame circles endlessly and consumes all available bandwidth.

802.1D Spanning Tree (STP or RSTP) allows bridging devices on the network to communicate with each other, and the Spanning Tree algorithm determines a forwarding path. All other paths are then blocked as shown in Figure 11-21, and broadcast storms are avoided.

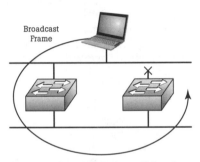

Figure 11-21. *Blocked parallel path*

Additionally, the Spanning Tree algorithm monitors for path failures and automatically opens an alternative path to recover from a path failure. Bridging loops may be inserted accidentally or through carelessness when a redundant backup path was intended. If Spanning Tree is not used, great care should be taken to avoid bridging loops because they are very difficult to troubleshoot.

A somewhat recent method of controlling the effect of a broadcast storm is to apply rate limiting to your switches. One use of this feature is to restrict a selected protocol to a configurable utilization level. Using rate limiting features, the total broadcast rate on a network could be artificially limited to perhaps 15 percent. By capping the utilization level for broadcasts, other traffic still gets through during a broadcast storm and the support staff has a better chance of locating the source of the unexpected parallel path quickly. 15 percent is far beyond the broadcast level that might be expected on a normal broadcast domain.

If you have console access to the switches, you could clear the interface counters and then ask for the MAC addresses:

```
clear counters
show mac
```

These or similar commands should reveal the source MAC address. With that information (and good documentation) you could discover the port that station is attached to and disable it. Log in to each switch and look for the source MAC address found in the broadcast storm packets.

- The MAC address that is the source of the broadcast storm appears on either an uplink port or a station port.
  - If the MAC address is found only on a known uplink port, the parallel path isn't on the current switch.
  - If the MAC address is found on a port that isn't known to be an uplink port, and there is more than one MAC address associated with that port, it is likely that you have found the parallel path. Disable the port and see whether the broadcast storm stops.
  - If the MAC address is found on a nonuplink port, and there is only this one MAC address shown for that port, this is probably the PC's normal connection and not the parallel path.
- If two ports are used as known uplink ports on a switch in a Spanning Tree–enabled network, only one should be active and the other should be blocking. If both are showing utilization through them, disable one and see whether the broadcast storm stops.

Duplex

One of the most common problems on a switched network is a duplex mismatch. Table 11-3 describes expected duplex configuration behavior.

A duplex mismatched link comes up and operates, albeit slowly. The full-duplex link partner believes that it is okay to transmit at any time it wants, including times when the half-duplex link partner is already transmitting. The half-duplex link partner aborts a transmission if the full-duplex partner transmits at the same time it is already transmitting, which may be at any time during a transmission event. On the half-duplex end, there is an administrative rule that states that simultaneous activity on both the TX and RX pairs constitutes a collision, and it must act accordingly. If the event occurred after the half-duplex end had transmitted at least 64 octets, that frame is usually lost and not retransmitted. The full-duplex side is not aware that both the half-duplex link partner's transmission and its own were discarded, and the full-duplex side frame is certainly lost. It is up to the OSI Layer 4 protocol to recover from the lost frame. A few lost frames cause the user application to become frustratingly slow. If enough frames are lost, connection-oriented OSI Layer 4 protocols such as TCP may drop the connection.

Four known troubleshooting situations exist:

- When one link partner is negotiating and the other is only using full duplex, the result is a duplex mismatch—always. This is by far the most common problem today.

- The Auto-Negotiation implementation is broken in some way and does not properly negotiate the link. This is rare, but it does happen. It used to be a problem with the earliest Fast Ethernet devices, but it seems to happen most often these days on Gigabit links (but still very rare).

- The link is negotiated to the highest matching speed and duplex, but the cable cannot support that configuration and link fails, which restarts Auto-Negotiation. The link light blinks on and off continuously.

- The link partner is applying rules to the negotiation:
  - If the highest matching speed and duplex is negotiated, but the link fails repeatedly, some devices change what is offered in the FLP for subsequent attempts to link. The noticeable symptom is that although both link partners are capable of a higher speed, the link comes up at a lower speed than what is possible. There is a slight delay before this link is established.

  - If one device is capable of only 10Mbps, half duplex, although the resulting link is appropriate, the switch port periodically shuts down. After much research the only explanation appears to be that the switch vendor has changed the switch operating system expectations such that only switched point-to-point links exist anymore, and collisions indicate a link problem. An elevated collision level causes the switch to shut down the port. There may be an obscure command that

When learning new networking skills, always study the standards in conjunction with the popular press. Standards may be hard to understand—but they have the advantage of being accurate.

Table 11-3. *Expected outcomes when Auto-Negotiation and fixed duplex configurations are used*

Duplex Configuration	Auto-Negotiating	Fixed or Forced Half Duplex	Fixed or Forced Full Duplex
Auto-Negotiating	Safe. Selects the best configuration common to both partners. Very rarely fails to produce a reliable connection unless there is a marginal port or cable.	Works because Auto defaults to half duplex if the link partner is not also Auto-Negotiating.	Duplex mismatch guaranteed.
Fixed or Forced **Half** Duplex	Works because Auto defaults to half duplex if the link partner is not also Auto-Negotiating.	Works, and is safe because Auto-Negotiation defaults to half duplex.	Duplex mismatch guaranteed.
Fixed or Forced **Full** Duplex	Duplex mismatch guaranteed.	Duplex mismatch guaranteed.	Works—if you are careful. Works well for servers and uplinks that are never disturbed.

disables this *shutdown on errors* behavior, but it is not commonly used. Insert a cheap 10/100 hub (link one device at 10Mbps and the other at 100Mbps to block the collisions), or insert another type of switch between the half-duplex device and the first switch to block the collisions and test for this situation.

- Some switches offer the highest possible speed only during the first FLP cycle. Usually this means only Gigabit is offered. If the link partner is found to offer only a lower speed, and Gigabit is not an option, it renegotiates with more options.

VLANs

VLANs should be considered separate logical networks or broadcast domains. Grouping hosts within a broadcast domain by VLAN assignment is much easier than moving cable connections. This capability simplifies moves, additions, and changes to network configurations. Ports on a switch that are assigned to the same VLAN are thereby logically grouped into broadcast domains where unicast, broadcast, and multicast frames are forwarded freely (as appropriate). For a frame to leave the broadcast domain it must pass through a routed connection. Each VLAN typically contains its own bridge MIB information and supports its own implementation of the Spanning Tree Protocol.

It is impossible to discern whether VLANs are enabled, or which port resides in which VLAN by simply examining a switch. It is necessary to consult the switch configuration to learn that information. VLAN assignments may also be configured to take place dynamically based on various criteria, including protocol, subnet, and MAC address. Although the rational for this configuration was never clearly explained, one observed network configuration based dynamic VLAN assignments upon the address the PC received from one of several DHCP servers. When asked, the network support staff admitted that a clever user could manually assign an IP address to their PC and this would cause the VLAN assignment to change accordingly.

Switch ports may be configured for host attachment or for trunking purposes. A trunk port has 802.1Q VLAN tags inserted into each frame. A tagged frame cannot be processed by a normal host unless it is specially configured to transmit tagged traffic—which is very rare. The presence of a tagged frame on a normal port usually means that it will be discarded. The user attached to that port will not be able to connect to the network either, although a link is established and the PC's NIC statistics show some traffic. On Windows XP, the NIC statistics showed outbound traffic for all queries made by the PC. Inbound traffic was only reported if the destination MAC matched the NIC. Even tagged broadcast traffic was unreported.

Specific Test Suggestions

The following test and problem suggestions and ideas are grouped by OSI layer, in collision domain issues, broadcast domain issues, and interconnected network issues. The following lists do not contain all the ideas and problems described in the individual technology sections found in other chapters, so be sure to read those sections too. The suggestions and ideas are only a starting place for troubleshooting, and certainly do not encompass all possible problems you will encounter. This list is intended to offer an example of how to approach problems related to restoring end-to-end delivery of data. The vast majority of all networking problems relate to end-to-end delivery. Once the data has been safely delivered to the destination, a whole new realm of protocol and operating system specific problems are faced. Troubleshooting beyond end-to-end delivery requires a solid understanding of each protocol or operating system involved. Protocol problems are normally the domain of senior support staff.

Collision Domain Issues

A collision domain problem relates primarily to cable faults and simple or basic MAC Layer link problems. A collision domain may be a grouping of hubs, or it may be only a single cable between a station and a switch. If your network architecture includes larger multihub or coaxial collision domains, many of the broadcast domain tests may be applied to your collision domain.

Cable Fault

Many problems can be corrected by simply re-seating cables that have become partially disconnected. As you perform your physical inspection, look for damaged cables, improper cable types, and poorly crimped RJ45s. Suspect drop cables should be subject to a simple cable test, and/or exchanged with a known-good cable. Do not assume that just because a cable is new (just out of the package), it works. Test it first. If you make your own cables, they should also be tested before you attempt to troubleshoot with them—anyone can have a bad day and miswire the termination. Also test for simple cable faults (shorts, opens, and especially for split pairs).

Determine whether a station connected by twisted pair or fiber is successfully linking to the network at the MAC Layer. Test twisted pair for voltage levels and the presence and polarity of link pulses. Test fiber for power level and link indicator LEDs. Many new switches, and some NICs, have autosensing ports that compensate for polarity faults on a twisted-pair cable. Moving a station from a newer switch that compensates for some types of cable fault to an older hub or switch may cause you to believe that the older device is at fault, when in fact the newer switch was compensating for an existing cable fault.

Twisted Pair

Twisted-pair links between hubs and switches require crossover connections at 10/100 speeds, although Gigabit Ethernet is required to compensate automatically. Stations are connected with cables that are not crossed over, often called straight cables. Check for crossover cables or hub and switch ports that are configured as a crossover with a simple button press. Many new switches, as well as all 1000BASE-T links, are also able to compensate for crossover cables used instead of straight cables. Some simple hubs use a single connection internally to service a cross-over port and an adjacent "straight" port—you may not use both RJ45 jacks. This configuration is usually indicated beside the jacks for the shared port. Newer switches use 10/100/1000 interfaces paired with SFP ports similarly.

Split pair cables operate either poorly or not at all, depending on the Ethernet speed you are us-ing, the length of the split segment, and how far it is located from either end. The farther the split is located from a transmitter, the less disruptive effect it has. If the split is short, such as a patch cable, and it is located midway between the two ends of a long run, 10BASE-T may operate mostly error free. Even a short split cable anywhere along a 1000BASE-T link will likely disrupt traffic, and may even prevent the link from coming up.

Fiber

All fiber links are crossed over. The connectors are always the same on stations and infrastructure equipment, so the TX output is connected to the RX input through careful attention to the cable polarity. Check fiber for swapped RX/TX connections when polarized or small form factor multi-fiber connectors are not used. Someone might have reconnected the cable incorrectly after disconnecting for some reason.

If a spare fiber optic cable did not have dust covers on it, it should be considered suspect even if it tested good yesterday. Clean all fiber optic cables before attaching them as routine procedure, even if you just unplugged it for a momentary test.

If a fiber optic power test fails, inspect and clean all connections on the link. While walking the cable path between ends, watch for excessively tight bends and over-tightened cable ties that cause micro bends.

Coax

Typically, if there is a physical problem on coax the result is usually a catastrophic failure of the segment. This should be easily and quickly located, and the problem corrected using the divide-and-conquer troubleshooting approach. Move the cable terminator to divide the segment into smaller parts for troubleshooting. Also, many testers offer a DC resistance test that helps to quickly locate improper, missing, or multiple terminators. For termination problems it is also easy to use a resistance test from an electrical multimeter. With one terminator present there should be 50 ohms measured, with two present there should be 25 ohms measured or RG-58 cable, and 75 ohms or 37.5 ohms on RG-59 cable, respectively. For intermittent problems, have someone watch the test tool while the cable is jiggled and flexed carefully for the entire length of the segment. Most intermittent problems are related to a poor connection, and manipulation of the cable usually reveals the location.

If you can use a moderate amount of tension to pull the connector from the cable, the cable should be reterminated—do not simply slip the loose connector back on. This is a particularly common problem on coax cables with BNC connectors.

Link Fault

Because most LED link lights are now software controlled they are no longer trustworthy. If the link light is illuminated, it may or may not mean that a valid link is present. If the port is faulty, it might be possible to disconnect the cable and still have the link light illuminated. If the link light is off, it is still a fairly good indication that no link is present, but not a certainty. It is not uncommon to see a link LED illuminated at one end of a failed link but not at the other.

If a 10BASE-T device is connected to a switch that is "hard set" or only capable of 100BASE-TX, the link LED on the 10BASE-T device often shows that the link is active but fails to communicate. The 100BASE-TX switch does not show a link, and the 100BASE-TX Ethernet segment is unaffected.

If a 100BASE-TX device is connected to a shared media 10BASE-T hub (collision domain) it does not show a link, but it causes somewhere between 33 percent and 100 percent collisions on the 10BASE-T collision domain. The 10BASE-T hub shows a link, and if it has status LEDs it usually also shows constant utilization and/or collisions with those status LEDs. But you may have to look at more than the link state LED to discover this.

If a cable fault is the cause of link failure, an Auto-Negotiating 10/100/1000 device may successfully negotiate a link to 100BASE-TX or 1000BASE-T, but might not be able to subsequently establish MLT-3 or 4D–PAM5 signaling synchronization. This results in the link light blinking on and off as the Ethernet chipset repeatedly negotiates a connection speed, and

then fails to link. If the cable fault isn't severe, the link may come up and operate very poorly for a short time before the link fails and is again renegotiated. If the affected port is a parallel uplink between switches, this fault can cause Spanning Tree problems and loss of logical connectivity across a broadcast domain.

Collisions

Collisions are normally a more significant problem on shared media than on switch ports. Both situations are described later in this text. Average collision counts on shared media should generally be below 5 percent, although that number is conservative. Be sure that you are basing judgments on the average, and not a peak or spike in collisions.

If the average utilization is high (sustained peaks in excess of 60 percent for shared media and in excess of 80–90 percent for switched links) and collision counts are acceptable (average is below 5 percent for shared media and below 1 percent for switched links), the network might simply be saturated. There might be too many stations transmitting within this collision domain, or the network architecture might need optimizing for shorter distances between distant stations.

Use a diagnostic tool to monitor the collision domain. Excessive collisions or errors may degrade communications, causing dropped connections and poor performance, or may be severe enough to prevent communications at all. There should be no ghosts at all. If there are any ghosts, use the divide-and-conquer method of troubleshooting to isolate the source before troubleshooting other symptoms. Check whether collisions are bursty, where a noticeable increase in collisions does not follow a similar increase in traffic. That is, if there is a large change in the number of collisions without a corresponding increase in the traffic level, you have a problem in the Physical Layer somewhere—usually related to when one specific station transmits. Bursty collisions and errors are most often caused by a problem with the physical media, such as missing or incorrect terminators, impedance discontinuities (bad connectors, cable "stubs," crushed cables, etc.), and marginal or failed network interface cards.

Shared Media

Excessive collisions are most often caused by a problem with the physical media, such as missing or incorrect terminators, impedance discontinuities (bad connectors, cable "stubs," crushed cables, etc.), and bad network interface cards.

There are several things to watch for in relation to collisions:

- Does the detected collision level track approximately with the utilization level?

  If changes in utilization and collision levels track together reasonably closely, there may simply be too many stations transmitting on the collision domain, assuming that there is a collision problem at all.

- Are there spikes of detected collisions that do not follow the utilization level?

  If there are spikes of detected collisions that are significantly different from the general fluctuation in utilization, the collisions may often be traced back to a single source. It might be a bad cable to a single station, a bad uplink cable on a hub or port on a hub, or a link that is exposed to external electrical noise. Over time the problem station may be isolated by monitoring the traffic sources at the same time as the collision level bursts higher. Note which station(s) are transmitting at the time when spikes of collisions are detected. If the problem seems to relate to transmissions from a single station, troubleshoot that suspect link. If the problem seems to relate to transmissions from multiple stations, compare that information against your functional network diagram to see whether there is a common path between those stations and the rest of the collision domain. The single station could be an uplink from the collision domain to a switch, and the functional diagram should reveal that all the other stations are beyond that link. One or more stations set to full duplex within a collision domain also causes this sort of collision problem, as well as other errors.

- Are there collisions when there is no apparent utilization to cause them?

If there are abnormal numbers of collisions taking place when there is little or no utilization to cause them, suspect a noise source near a cable or hub. Use divide-and-conquer troubleshooting to isolate the location of the fault, adding traffic to the network from the monitoring tool while troubleshooting. This sort of fault must usually be diagnosed after hours because portions of the collision domain will be disconnected from the network during troubleshooting.

- Are there approximately 33 percent or 100 percent collisions?

  If connected to a 10Mbps collision domain and there is either approximately 33 percent or 100 percent collisions, there might be a station attempting to insert into at 100Mbps. This collision level results from a station transmitting an MLT-3 encoded 100Mbps signal to the 10Mbps hub. The 10Mbps hub turns on the link state LED and forwards its best interpretation of the MLT-3 signal as Manchester encoded data. The 100Mbps end is not able to establish synchronization, and thus does not turn on the link state LED or forward any received traffic to the MAC Layer. The reverse situation does not result in a problem. If a 10Mbps station attempts to insert into a 100Mbps-only hub, that station will not achieve MLT-3 synchronization and the hub will not turn on the link state LED or attempt to interpret and forward the Manchester encoded signal.

To track down the source of collisions, it is often necessary to have traffic on the network. Use a traffic generator to add a small amount of traffic while you are monitoring. A safely insignificant level of traffic is 100 frames-per-second, 100-byte frames, which is still sufficient to sensitize nearby faults and allow them to be located. Be sure that the destination MAC address for generated traffic does not affect other parts of the network while you are troubleshooting. Using a destination address within the collision domain prevents the traffic from crossing bridged connections and disrupting other users. Do not make up a nonexistent destination MAC address because doing so floods it to all parts of the broadcast domain. If the generated level of traffic is very low (such as the suggested level), the destination address could be set to that of the tool or station generating the traffic without disrupting its operation.

Some media-related problems are traffic-level dependent. Try gradually raising the traffic level to more than 50 percent, and at the same time watching the error and collision levels. Many monitoring tools offer LED indicators for both, which makes it much easier to vary the traffic level while watching for resulting errors or elevated collision levels. Be careful when doing this because you can easily saturate the network. Solving collision-related problems can be very tricky because the measurements are largely dependent upon the observation point. Results can vary between two observation points separated by only a few feet on the same cable. Make tests from multiple locations and watch for changes in the nature of the problem.

If collisions get worse in direct proportion to the level of traffic, if the amount of collisions approaches 100 percent, or if there is no good traffic at all, the cable system may have failed.

- For twisted pair, test the entire original cable path between the hub and the station connection. Do not substitute a known-good patch cable before testing because patch cables are the most likely source of the problem.

- For coax, try a DC continuity test. You should see about 25 ohms if both terminators are present and you are testing from a BNC Tee connection or 50 ohms if you are testing from an end.

- For fiber, check to see whether the connections are fully seated and/or clean. A loose connection or a dirty connection can result in the receiver misinterpreting input signals as a result of poor signal quality, and usually results in other errors in addition to collisions.

If repeaters are present on the local segment, if repeaters are connected to hubs, or if hubs are cascaded, check to see that signal_quality_error (SQE, sometimes known as "heartbeat") is

set properly. SQE is found in association with AUI ports and should never be enabled between repeater devices—including hubs. A repeater misinterprets an SQE signal and generates a collision jam signal. The worst-case symptom of this problem is a reported collision rate of exactly 50 percent. Usually there is other traffic present and the percentage is reduced (diluted by the other good traffic). These events are not really collisions, though, and the network should operate without apparent problem other than some slowness at high utilization levels. This problem is somewhat unique because traffic from the "network" to the "host" side of the AUI connection does not show any of these false collisions, and traffic from the "host" side to the "network" side shows one such event for each frame passing through.

If the collision domain is very small, collision events take place very early in the frame. Nearly all devices capable of recording collision classify only whether the collision was normal (took place before a legal frame size had been transmitted), or if it was a late collision. No indication is given to how much bandwidth lost to collisions because collisions were taking place later in the frame. If such a test is available from your diagnostic tool, check for average bandwidth lost to collisions that is greater than 0.5 percent. There is no rule of thumb to accompany this measurement, but field experience indicates that less than 0.5 percent is normal, and greater amounts indicate poor architecture designs and other problems. Isolate this situation by divide-and-conquer troubleshooting until the percentage is reasonable. Then compare your test results against a functional network diagram to see whether adjusting the architecture of the collision domain helps. Shorter distances between distant stations significantly improves this situation.

Although the LANMeter test tool has been discontinued, Figure 11-22 shows the relative amount of time lost to collisions, shown by percentage. With the conversion to switches for virtually all user connections, test suites for collision related faults have all but disappeared.

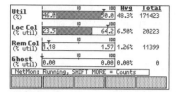

Figure 11-22. *LANMeter Collision Analysis test results*

Switched Media

Operating a switched port in half duplex is a poor use of resources unless the port connects to a shared media collision domain, or to an older device that is not capable of full duplex. Nearly all Fast Ethernet and Gigabit Ethernet implementations are synchronous, and therefore the underlying link is operating in full duplex even when the administrative rules require half-duplex data transmissions.

Half Duplex

If the average utilization is high (sustained peaks in excess of 60 percent for shared media, and in excess of 80–90 percent for switched links), and collision counts are acceptable (collision average is below 5 percent for shared media and below 1 percent for switched links), the network might be saturated. This is somewhat unlikely because an Ethernet segment normally experiences very high collision rates if there is too much utilization. As utilization approaches 100 percent on shared media, the number of collisions can grow exponentially until they far exceed the number of good frames. It might be necessary to install a switch, bridge, or router to divide the segment into small enough groups to support the traffic load.

A special situation described as the Ethernet *capture effect* or the *packet starvation* effect was discovered as switches became widely available in the mid-1990s. When two devices in half-duplex are each attempting to send a large block of traffic, a collision will certainly occur. The station that "wins" the first retransmission has a better chance of transmitting with each subsequent collision because it has a smaller range of backoff values to choose from. Even in situations where there is only one station attached to a half-duplex switch port it is not that unusual to see an excessive collisions error reported by the switch. This indicates instances where the switch has "lost"

enough collision retransmission attempts that it gave up on sending that frame, and the upper-layer software on the source station has to handle retransmission. Because Ethernet is inherently bursty, this may be reported on ports with relatively low average utilization. Problems related to this situation usually do not develop unless utilization becomes significant. Poor performance is most likely if enough retransmission attempts fail, although dropped connections and an inability to connect are possible.

Full Duplex

Full duplex connections should not have collisions on them. If collisions are recorded, check for duplex mismatches and for collision fragments that are being forwarded from other ports.

Errors

In general, there should be no errors (including late collisions, jabber, short frames, FCS errors and ghosts) on a network. If viewed from network management, the exact name of the error may change depending on the definition provided in the MIB you are using. The severity of the fault determines the urgency for troubleshooting. If the detected errors are few and infrequent, the problem can be ignored for a time. As the error level rises, it becomes progressively more urgent to troubleshoot. Your baseline network documentation should include notes on which parts of the network are routinely observed to have a few errors and the error type(s). Knowing this information prevents you from troubleshooting a minor problem that is unrelated to a new user complaint. Many consultants have consumed significant time and money solving a longstanding error condition that is unrelated to the reason the consultant was hired—simply because the network staff was unaware of the presence of those errors.

If errors are present, identify the source MAC address for errored frames. Test source stations and their cables to isolate the specific failure. Try replacing the software driver files with fresh copies from the source diskettes or by downloading the latest drivers from the manufacturer's web site, making certain to completely reconfigure them because the configuration might be the problem. Try replacing the suspect network adapter.

Some errors result from a variety of environmental or cable faults, and the source station might be operating correctly. If ghosts are detected, troubleshoot a media fault or Physical Layer problem regardless of any other symptom detected and before troubleshooting anything else. Once the Physical Layer fault is corrected, retest and troubleshoot according to any symptoms that may remain. Ghosts can result from a bad cable, a noise source near a cable, grounding problems, transients, and other noise in alternate current (AC) power feeding any station, hub, switch, router, wiring closet, and so on. Another source of ghosts and other errors is a parallel uplink path between two hubs in a collision domain, which can create an odd feedback loop between the hubs.

Any type of user-reported problem can result from high error levels on a local segment or a bad cable. At times of very high collision or error rates, some infrastructure devices may shut down a port briefly, and then reopen it, which can result in dropped sessions and poor performance. If the errors and collisions are not excessive, it's not likely to be a media-related problem unless they can be correlated to when the problem station transmits.

Connect a diagnostic tool in place of the problem station and check for high network utilization or abnormally high collisions. Rerun the test while transmitting a moderate amount of background traffic (100 frames per second, 100-byte frames is enough). If you notice the collision counts or errors increase at the same time the tool transmits, perform a cable test on the station cable connecting to the hub or switch. Watch especially for split pair faults.

If the diagnostic tool detects errors, determine the type and quantity of the errors present. A small number of errors (single digits) per second are unlikely to cause a dropped connection unless they relate to the connection servicing the problem station, the server or service, or the uplink leaving the collision domain. Identify the MAC address of the stations having errored frames and try testing from the network connection for those stations. In a collision domain the use of

divide-and-conquer troubleshooting is very effective as long as you remain aware of when you are disconnecting the path between a source and destination for traffic, and thus removing all traffic. If it is necessary to disconnect the source and destination, substitute with traffic generated by the tester while you troubleshoot. Certain collision domain problems remain hidden unless traffic is transmitted fairly close to the fault.

NIC Test

A multitude of peculiar problems can be resolved by a cold reboot of the suspect station (restart is not adequate—the power must turn off). One example is when a station with an older version of Microsoft Windows has had the network cable disconnected for a period of time. Reconnecting the cable does not reestablish network communications, although the NIC performs all required actions to establish a link. The operating system has given up on the NIC, and short of a reboot there is little that will cause it to resume speaking to the NIC. Using an inline tester reveals that no traffic is transmitted by the station. On more recent versions of Windows, it is possible to disable and reenable the NIC to "wake it up" from a variety of conditions, without resorting to a reboot.

Check for link lights at both the station and the hub or switch end, although the presence of a link light is not a guarantee that the port works. Many link lights are now software controlled, and are therefore not to be trusted during troubleshooting. The absence of a link light is still a fairly reliable indication of a problem.

Disconnect the problem station or the station identified as the source of errored frames from the network, and attach a monitoring tool in its place. Be sure to use the problem station's original cable for this test, not a known-good cable.

Test also from the network side back toward the suspect station. Use a spare cable to attach the test tool to the station and watch the power-up process. Unless you are familiar with low-level operating system commands it is often necessary to cold-start the station to get it to speak on the network. Once a station has completed the initial boot-up process it might not speak on the network again without these special commands. On more recent versions of Windows, it is possible to simply disable and reenable the NIC to accomplish this. Observe the link process and the protocols that the station is sending. Ensure that the station is even speaking, because many problems relate to station configurations not recognizing or attempting to utilize the network adapter. Look for signal strength and other physical layer parameters (see Figure 11-23). Check the NIC configuration to ensure that your protocol (usually TCP/IP) is bound to the NIC.

Not all network adapter faults are conveniently hard-down, and they might not exhibit the fault during testing. If the fault appears to be intermittent, it might be appropriate to replace the network adapter and driver software as part of the diagnostic process.

Some portable PC (notebook) NICs ship with a special power-saving feature enabled. This feature causes the NIC to listen for link pulse, but it does not transmit anything at all (including link pulse) until it hears a signal on the receive circuit. To conserve power the entire transmit circuit in the NIC is shut down until the receive circuit indicates that a transmission is warranted. This feature has been known to cause link problems with some other network devices. Try disabling this power-saving feature in the software configuration of the NIC, or use a test tool to see what signals are offered by the NIC.

Inline Test

Perform an inline test by connecting the problem station to the network in series through a diagnostic tool, and then have the tester monitor the connection process after the station reboots. Most testers with this capability also monitor the traffic for responses to network queries and report initialization problems such as failure to obtain a DHCP address, or DNS not responding (see Figure 11-24).

Auto-Negotiation is supposed to prevent mismatches between half and full duplex; however, in a switched environment this is one of the most common problems. Insert a monitoring tool inline between the station and the hub or switch, and verify that both ends of the link are operating at the same duplex setting (see Figure 11-25). If an inline tool is unavailable, test or validate each end separately for duplex setting. In some instances the port operates with a duplex configuration different than the configuration software indicates.

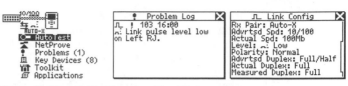

Figure 11-23. *NetTool low signal level test results example. This is sometimes due to a marginal interface, but more often it is due to a poor quality or very long cable.*

Figure 11-24. *NetTool inline test results example showing two PC boot-up problems detected*

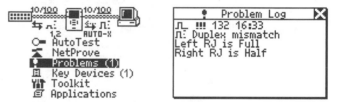

Figure 11-25. *NetTool duplex mismatch detected results. Observe the outline versus solid arrows on the left screen.*

If one end of the link is negotiating and the other end is not, the negotiating side defaults to half duplex. If the nonnegotiating side is forced to full duplex, a duplex mismatch results. At low utilization levels (sometimes "low" is as high as 80 percent), there may be little evidence of the duplex mismatch. Performance problems begin to manifest themselves as utilization through the link rises, and become apparent when the busy transmitter is in half duplex. Because most network traffic goes from the server to the PC, it often takes very high utilization before a PC in half duplex aborts enough transmissions to be noticed.

Port Test

Perform a port test by attaching a test tool in place of a problem station, and then check the polarity and signal strength from the port to ensure that it is correct and robust enough. If the voltage level for the port as measured at the station end is low, test the port again using a patch cable connected directly to it. If the voltage is still low, move the station cable to another free port on the switch to verify that the switch port has not become marginal or bad. Cable faults often reduce signal strength to a point where it is difficult for the station to decode the traffic, or disrupt the signal so that it cannot be reliably decoded. A bad cable may cause any number of symptoms or errors to appear.

Review the results of Auto-Negotiation and ensure that the port is offering a speed that the station is capable of negotiating to. A number of newer switches offer only 100/1000Mbps connections and no longer support 10Mbps. Older switches may only offer 100Mbps connections. Some switch ports and copper GBIC or SFP links are 1000Mbps only, as shown in Figure 11-26.

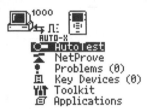

Figure 11-26. *NetTool test results showing only Gigabit Ethernet capability*

Try another port on the hub or switch. Some communications problems relate to marginal or failed hub or switch ports. The Ethernet and TCP/IP protocols are generally robust enough to compensate for many faults, but losing a few critical frames may be enough to drop the connection. Try a different hub or switch too. Some interfaces simply won't link to certain other interfaces. Although Ethernet is standardized, that does not mean that everything is fully compliant with the standard.

Try pinging a server or router through the port to ensure that traffic successfully reaches other parts of the network from this port and that replies are successfully returning. It could be that the port is linking properly but is isolated from the rest of the network due to a configuration problem.

Switches and bridges configured for Spanning Tree block just-opened ports for at least 30 seconds before allowing traffic through in an attempt to prevent a bridging loop from forming.

The longest waiting period observed has so far been two minutes. Being blocked for two minutes causes some DHCP and other login queries to fail and be abandoned. If this problem is suspected, try attaching the problem station to the switch through a shared media hub, and boot the station. The hub opens and maintains the switch port link and bypasses this timer for the station. Recent switch configuration options allow for a port to be opened for traffic almost instantly, although the port is completely disabled immediately on receipt of a Spanning Tree BPDU frame.

Try a throughput test from this port to other parts of the collision domain or broadcast domain. This exercises the port thoroughly as well as the uplink from this hub or switch. The throughput test may reveal buffering problems in a switch and duplex mismatches. Many newer switches are offering a feature that administratively limits the maximum rate at which a particular protocol is supported through a port. Throughput testing can reveal an artificially configured ceiling on some or all traffic.

Connect a monitoring tool in place of the station and sample the traffic present on the connection. Ensure that there is traffic present (see Figure 11-27). The error rate should be insignificant or nonexistent.

If there is just Spanning Tree BPDU traffic present on a switch port, the port is probably blocked, disabled, or isolated in some way. Try another port. Also check to see whether the traffic is VLAN tagged. A common misconfiguration is when a station port is accidentally tagged for a VLAN. Stations are almost always unable to read tagged traffic. In some situations a file server is configured to support multiple VLANs and attaches directly to a VLAN trunk.

Check for unusually high broadcast levels. Broadcasts should be relatively low because each station must stop what it is doing and evaluate each broadcast. The average should be well below 5–10 percent of available bandwidth at 10Mbps, which supports up to about 14,000 frames per second. The broadcast rate should be very low indeed on faster Ethernet implementations, which support far higher numbers of frames per second.

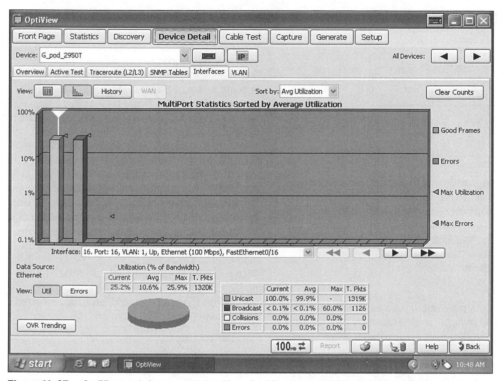

Figure 11-27. *OptiView switch port statistics. Here, OptiView is using RFC 1643 (Ethernet-like devices) as a data source, but may also use RFC 1213 (MIB II) or RFC 2819 (RMON Ethernet) if they are available.*

A 100Mbps switch port on a typical network experiences below 0.5 percent broadcast rates. If there is a very large switched broadcast domain, this number can climb up into single-digit broadcast rates. Although no industry standard for broadcasts in a switched environment has been recognized, efforts should be taken to reduce the size of the broadcast domain whenever the average broadcast rate exceeds one percent of a 100Mbps link. Because each station processes each broadcast frame, the broadcast rate measurably slows network performance.

Be careful to check the statistic that your monitoring tool is reporting, because most tools report both the total utilization and the percentage of the received traffic that is made up of broadcasts. On a typical switch port, a monitoring tool sees close to 100 percent broadcast traffic but less than 1

percent total utilization. That means that nearly all the traffic being received from the switch is broadcast traffic—which is likely because the monitoring tool is not soliciting much (if any) traffic from the network.

Check the encapsulation protocol. Most IP packets on Ethernet networks use Ethernet II MAC frames. In some cases, IP may be seen as it exists on Token Ring and FDDI networks: over 802.2 and SNAP. Problems may exist if IP hosts need to be specially configured to handle 802.2 and SNAP encapsulations (see Figure 11-28). This issue is most common when there are Ethernet-to-Token Ring source-route transparent bridges still in use.

Figure 11-28. *NetTool inline test results encapsulation mismatch example*

Utilization

Use a diagnostic tool to monitor the collision domain. Watch for high network utilization and abnormally high collisions. Run the test again with a slight amount of background traffic enabled. If you notice the collision counts or FCS errors increase at the same time you transmit, perform a cable test on the attached link.

Shared Media

Monitor the network to determine whether the network Physical Layer is currently experiencing high network utilization, excessive collisions, or unusual error conditions. Despite much popular commentary to the contrary, Ethernet sustains a much higher average utilization level than the very conservative industry rule of 40 percent. The most significant controlling factors appear to be frame size and number of stations attempting to transmit. If a lot of stations are attempting to transmit small frames, high collision rates and low utilization are possible, which does not significantly impair communications. If only a few stations are transmitting and the frame size is very large, the utilization rate may be close to the maximum but the collision rate should be very low—again, not likely to significantly impair communications. High utilization and high collision rates are generally bad and impairs communications.

If utilization is determined to be excessively high, consider installing a switch or router to reduce the amount of traffic on the collision domain or to break the collision domain into smaller sections. High utilization stations (power users, servers, and so on) should be on separate switch ports. Monitor the high utilization with a test tool to discover the source. Discover what operation is causing the elevated traffic levels and either have that operation rescheduled for an off-peak time, or isolate the user on a separate switch port.

Switched Media

A switch port with only one device attached can easily sustain close to line rate utilization for extended periods of time without problem. Thus, check for how long the port is experiencing high utilization. If the utilization is consistently exceptionally high, it might be that this link is inadequate for the load and a higher-speed link is required.

Failure to connect problems should not have high utilization present, so if there is much of any utilization present when only one device is attached to the port, this warrants further investigation. Well below one percent is expected. Use a traffic monitoring tool to discover the nature of this traffic. It may be that the port has been configured as a mirror port or the network is experiencing a broadcast storm.

In a switched environment, use SNMP to query the local switch for any reported errors on your port and on the uplink port. If errors are reported, test the cable attached to that port.

Station Problems

Corrupted NIC card drivers and software and interrupt conflicts within the station can cause the station to ignore or fail to respond to queries. Try connecting a diagnostic tool to another port in the collision domain and sending the problem station continuous pings in the appropriate protocol. You should receive one response for each ping request. Try reinstalling and reconfiguring new driver files from source diskettes, or obtain a more recent version from the manufacturer of that network adapter.

The latest drivers might not be bug free yet, so if there is no newer version then try a recent older version. Software drivers are provided in two formats: a generic format that should work for any standard PC, and ones customized for a particular brand or model of PC. Be sure to use the best driver for your application.

Similarly, some applications were written to take advantage of specific features and functions available from then-current operating systems. These optimized applications might not operate well with newer versions of the operating systems. Symptoms can include anything from long periods of apparent inactivity to sporadic network

It won't install because the instructions are wrong. When phoning for help, ask for the software patch too.

connectivity. Try other software applications, being certain to completely disable or unload suspect applications for the test.

Test the station for viruses. There is no way to predict the behavior of a station that has been infected by the latest computer virus. Also try unloading as many programs as possible, leaving only just enough to link to the network. There are many software programs that do not behave well with others or are trying to share resources improperly. If possible, try booting from floppy or CD to bypass all the software and operating system loaded on the station entirely.

Not all stations are created equally. No matter how fast the LAN speeds are and how large or fast the server is, actual performance still will not exceed the performance capabilities of a slow station. Make sure the entire link's performance is understood, including the capabilities of the stations. For example, the PCMCIA network adapter manufacturers were reluctant to make a 10/100 version of the card when 100BASE-TX first appeared because the bus servicing the PCMCIA port was unable to support 100Mbps operation. Typical performance over the bus peaked at perhaps one third of the card's capability.

Broadcast Domain Issues

A broadcast domain problem relates primarily to end-to-end connectivity problems in a bridged environment (Data Link Layer problems). If the problem station is directly connected to a single switch port, it may be difficult to distinguish a collision domain problem from a broadcast domain problem simply because the collision domain may exist on only the cable attaching that station to the switch.

Do not attempt to solve what appears to be an IP problem until you have verified that no other problems exist in lower layers of the protocol stack. Many hours of troubleshooting time have been wasted chasing symptoms, when the real problem was a bad port, a bad cable, or bad interface card. If the collision domain is functioning without evident errors, the scope of the problem moves to the broadcast domain.

Switch Port Issues

Single-user per switch port may be considered a broadcast domain issue for troubleshooting purposes, because the collision domain is limited to that single link. Whenever possible, try moving the user connection to a nearby unused switch port that is configured for the same broadcast domain early in the troubleshooting process. Static discharge and other situations can render a switch port marginal and nearly failed without exhibiting noticeable symptoms. By trying another port you can often shorten the troubleshooting cycle considerably with this very quick test. Be aware that adjacent ports may be part a port group controlled by a single chip, so a group of four ports is often affected similarly.

If the switch is reporting errors on any of the ports associated with the problem station, or the server or service that it is using, connect a diagnostic tool to the errored port in place of the attached station. Using the existing station cable, generate a small amount of traffic while analyzing the network through that link. Also run a cable test on the cable from that switch port.

If there is unexpected high utilization appearing on a port in a datacenter, check to see whether a special load-balancing feature is in use that first appeared in Microsoft Windows NT and is carried forward in Windows 2000 as Network Load Balancing (NLB). This feature satisfies the desired goal of having up to 32 servers receive all queries in parallel so that failover is all but instant. However, if it is implemented without isolating the server cluster on a separate broadcast domain, all requests to the cluster are sent to all stations in the broadcast domain. The feature is implemented by having all requests sent to a virtual MAC address, one that is never responded to. This improper use of a MAC address is not supported by the standards, and causes all switches and bridges to flood all requests to all ports in the broadcast domain. To compound matters, most servers are connected using higher speed links (100Mbps or higher), and many stations are still linking at 10Mbps. It is quite possible that the server traffic is consuming most of or all the station's switch port capacity.

Broadcast Storm

Connect a monitoring tool to the station cable in place of the problem station, and sample the traffic present on the connection. If the tool reports nearly 100 percent utilization, and virtually all the utilization consists of broadcasts, you are experiencing a broadcast storm (see Figure 11-29). Almost the only way to stop a broadcast storm is to disconnect the problem parallel link between two bridging devices (usually switches). Troubleshooting broadcast storms is nearly always a primitive process of running from switch to switch and disconnecting uplink cables. It is difficult to use any software diagnosis during the broadcast storm because the nature of the problem causes all available bandwidth to be consumed.

Because the entire broadcast domain is nonfunctional during a broadcast storm, do not be shy about pulling uplink cables from switches until the broadcast storm stops. Reconnect links that did not cause the problem to go away. Nobody is able to use the network until you stop the broadcast storm. After you locate the problem parallel link in the bridged environment, leave it disconnected until you find the other link that was forwarding traffic in parallel. Either remove one of the parallel paths or enable Spanning Tree

Protocol to prevent both paths from being active at the same time.

Spanning Tree is designed to prevent a broadcast storm, but there are situations where it can happen anyway. Many switches now allow the user to tell the switch to allow ports on the switch to join the network as quickly as possible, instead of waiting to ensure that the port does not connect to a parallel bridged path first. When this configuration is implemented, the support staff is telling the switch "trust me, I would never plug a bridge into this port." This configuration reduces the delay that a user experiences when first linking to the network from 30 seconds to two minutes (depending on the switch and the firmware level) down to a few seconds. Because a bridging loop is possible, one vendor disables forwarding for a port if this feature is enabled and a Spanning Tree BPDU frame is received on that port.

If a relatively new feature called rate limiting is implemented in switches, it is possible to administratively limit broadcasts to only a small percentage of the available bandwidth—such as 10 or 15 percent. If this is done, the network continues to function—slowly—in the presence of a broadcast storm, and troubleshooting the problem is not a crisis.

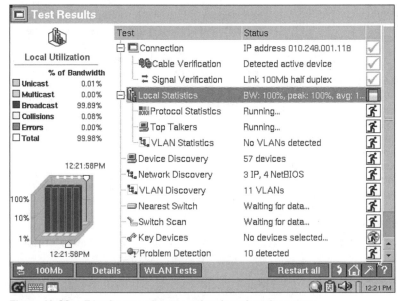

Figure 11-29. *EtherScope main screen showing a broadcast storm*

Switch Path Connectivity and Other SNMP Use

Use network management software or a diagnostic tool to check for high network utilization and abnormally high errors within the broadcast domain, especially on the path between the problem station and the desired server or service. If utilization is not consistently high (switch ports with a single station attached may exhibit average utilization exceeding 70 percent without problem), and the number of errors is very small, you might have software configuration problems with the server or service.

In a switched environment, it is difficult to troubleshoot due to the very nature of switches and bridges. Only traffic that should be received by a particular station appears on that station's port. Because visibility of all other traffic is thus blocked, it becomes necessary to ask the switch what is happening within that switch. Again, due to the very nature of the technology, one switch is unaware of what is happening in any other switch so it is necessary to query each and every switch in the broadcast domain to learn even the most rudimentary information about traffic patterns and errors. To learn the full details about those traffic patterns, it is still necessary to gain a view of the traffic itself with a protocol analyzer or diagnostic tool with similar features.

The switch only cares about delivering the data, and generally does not look beyond the simple source and destination address. Simple utilization information from switch ports is not likely to reveal that several stations are running a networked game. Discovering that a station is subscribed to an Internet radio station is not possible through simple utilization information. These and many other situations require that a detailed look at the traffic be taken, usually through a mirror port configured for an uplink, or through taps and splitters used on uplinks.

For an individual user problem, the scope of the problem is usually clear, and blind discovery is not required. Configuring a mirror port or installing a tap or splitter is far beyond the scope of normal day-to-

day troubleshooting by the Help Desk or frontline support staff. It is often much easier and faster to use a network management (SNMP or flow protocol–based) feature to examine statistics on ports appearing in the path between the user and the problem server or service. The basic utilization and error information from each port in the path either suggests that the problem is not network related or identifies which link should be investigated first. Often, there are more factors involved than a single simple failure.

Intermediate Link Bottleneck

In Figure 11-30, it can be quickly seen that both ends of the path are operating at 1000Mbps (Gigabit) in full duplex (two solid arrows). The second switch in the path, however, is operating at 100Mbps. Furthermore, one of the switches' ports is in half duplex (solid arrow and outline arrow). Troubleshooting this user's problem should begin at the link between the switch named TAC-3560G, port 24 and the switch named FastIron, port 16 because there is probably a duplex mismatch on that link. Also, if the second switch (FastIron) is only capable of 100Mbps, it should be replaced or moved out of this path.

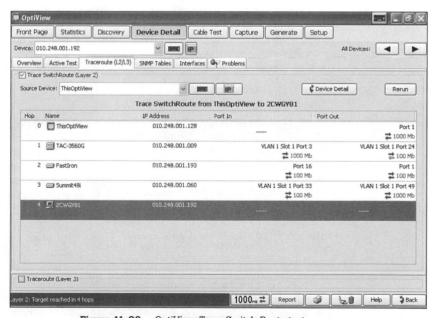

Figure 11-30. *OptiView Trace Switch Route test results. This test displays the OSI Layer 2 path between two selected hosts on the local broadcast domain.*

Although the available features vary between products, network management software can further aid the troubleshooting process before the technician departs. Many other useful bits of information can be learned that help the troubleshooting process. If the Help Desk software and any network management software are integrated, or the Help Desk has at least read access to a network management console, all this information could be provided in a troubleshooting ticket before the first visit to the user takes place.

A relatively new category self-induced partial path blockage is possible within the broadcast domain where ports may be configured individually or in groups for limited traffic levels. If one of the ports in the path between the problem host and the name server is rate limited for certain protocols or certain addresses, one type of the problem host's traffic might not be getting through rapidly, whereas other types are, such as when web traffic is very slow but FTP file transfers from the same server are rapid. The obvious conclusion is to accuse the web server of having performance problems, when it might actually be a rate limiting problem. Check the local broadcast domain to learn the path between the two hosts through the switched hierarchy, and then check the configurations of the appropriate ports for any rate limiting configuration. Using various different protocols for throughput testing can also reveal this sort of issue.

Discovery, Traffic Analysis

Use a monitoring tool such as a protocol analyzer to examine traffic patterns. In switched networks, it is necessary to either configure a mirror or span port, or to use a splitter or tap on an uplink path to view the traffic. Look for unusual traffic patterns, such as traffic between two hosts on the same subnet being sent via the router MAC address. This particular situation would normally be accompanied by ICMP errors, so watch for those too. Here are several ICMP message types that are associated with troubleshooting situations:

- **ICMP Redirects** indicate that the station is using a suboptimal router to forward traffic.
- **ICMP Source Quench** indicates that a path or destination is being overloaded.

- **ICMP Unreachable** messages indicate that a network, host, or service is not available because it is a nonexistent host, it was turned off, the route to it has failed, or that service is not loaded on the destination host.
- **ICMP Time Exceeded** indicates that either a message traveled too far and was discarded or there is a routing loop somewhere.

Other ICMP messages are defined, but these are the most likely messages to be seen when network difficulties exist.

Look for unusual network activity, such as people playing traffic-intensive network games (Doom, Quake, and newer variations). These games consume significant network bandwidth, and uplinks and routed paths may become congested as a result. Shared media segments are particularly impacted by networked games, including wireless links.

Look for more than one logical network or subnet operating over this broadcast domain. This may be an intentional configuration in some networks, configured in this manner to isolate one user group from another. A local router configured to support multiple subnets on a single port (multi-homed) provides a means for all stations to talk to each other. Multiple logical networks on a single broadcast domain is often an indicator that two usually isolated broadcast domains have been accidentally cross-connected in a wiring closet or VLANs have been misconfigured. The additional traffic might be disrupting communications. Routing protocol updates from presumably distant networks may be confusing the local routers. Traffic might be taking asymmetrical paths to distant resources due to the improper connection. SNMP tools, such as the Trace Switch Route test result shown in Figure 11-30, identify which port a selected host is attached to, and the network support staff can then determine where the improper connection was.

Many diagnostic tools inventory the local broadcast domain from any unused switch port, and then evaluate whether there are any hosts configured with dissimilar subnet mask configurations.

For problems related to a single host, use a monitoring tool in-line to see whether requests made by the host are being responded to (see

Figure 11-31). Have the user attempt several network operations during the test, such as refreshing the user's mailbox, checking a web site, and linking to a network drive.

Figure 11-31. *NetTool inline test results showing infrastructure services unavailable*

Traffic Analysis

Mirror or tap key uplinks within and leading out of the broadcast domain to learn which stations contribute the most traffic. If you observe any unusual traffic patterns or protocols, go to the station identified and discover what the user is doing on the network. It might be necessary to ask that the action be performed during off-peak times, or it might be necessary to move user(s) to another subnet or broadcast domain to improve network service for remaining users. Logically or physically relocating the most used servers or services to the same broadcast domain would permit the switch hierarchy to manage traffic more efficiently than using routed paths.

Filter for the address of the server or service and check to see which stations are making the most requests of that device. Filter on the address of users reporting problems to learn which server(s) they are connected to. Many configurations utilize multiple servers for a single service, placing security-related tasks on one server, login account tasks on another, mail on a third, and so on. A single transaction could require contributions from multiple servers, and only one of them needs to be slow or problematic to disrupt network service. Software is still being written that is not "network savvy" and may be making highly inefficient read requests from nonlocal drives across a LAN or SAN connection. It might be necessary to move an application to another server, upgrade the existing server, or add a new server.

Monitor the traffic to learn which protocols consume the most bandwidth. Many multicast services, such as VoIP and video conferencing, are sensitive to variations in latency. Video is also sensitive to variations in bandwidth. If other traffic is intermittently delaying or disrupting these services, it might be necessary to assign priority queuing. Use protocol analyzer features to monitor call quality parameters during idle and busy times on the network to set a baseline and to diagnose performance problems (see Figure 11-32).

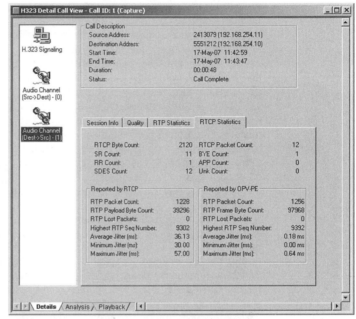

Figure 11-32. *OptiView Protocol Expert VoIP call details example. Statistics are presented that are found in the RTCP data, as well as statistics calculated from the raw frames on the wire.*

For any type of problem, a protocol analyzer trace file of the event can be invaluable. Start capturing before the action is attempted, and do not stop the capture until after the failure is evident. If possible, capture all traffic and use display filters to limit the amount of frames presented for viewing rather than capturing only traffic with specific characteristics. By capturing all traffic, it is possible to discover and correlate unexpected events and other protocols with the failure. If the problem is intermittent, having all possible information about the event enhances the likelihood of resolution.

If you are unfamiliar with normal operation of the protocol or process, try capturing another trace file showing a different user successfully completing the task. Use the good and bad captures for comparison.

ping

Run a ping test from the problem station to see whether there is basic connectivity all the way to the server or service. Also try connecting somewhere else in the broadcast domain and pinging back to the problem station. If either ping fails, begin troubleshooting the link failure in the path. Try using a diagnostic tool to move one switch closer to the destination station, server, or service, and attempt the ping again. Continue moving closer until a ping response is obtained. When you obtain a ping response, troubleshoot the last switch that was bypassed. If the ping is not responded to from a port on the same switch as the server, try moving the server to another port, or try pinging from the server to an address that other stations receive responses from. It may be the server that has the problem, not the reporting user's station.

If the reported problem is intermittent, use a diagnostic tool to run a continuous Network Layer ping from the problem station's connection to the problem server or service. Except for the first ping, which is sometimes not responded to, you should receive the same number of responses as requests sent. Discrepancies may indicate a marginal network adapter or hub or switch port, and frames are being dropped.

If the user reports an intermittent problem, and the problem is not evident at this time, try running a continuous ping in the background on that user's station.

```
C:>ping -t 192.168.38.4
```

Later, when the user determines that the problem has returned, have the user check the results in the ping window. Good ping results generally indicate that the network is operating properly but an upper-layer service on the ping destination is not. Ping is sometimes responded to by the lower layers, even when a station or server operating system or an application running there is

completely locked up. If ping responses are good, troubleshoot the source station and the destination server for operating system and application related problems.

Don't forget to test the cable at both ends (client and server ends) and on uplinks between. Many intermittent problems are related to marginal cables.

Throughput Test

When performance is poor or connections are dropped intermittently, it might save time to draw a matrix of all switches within the broadcast domain and perform a throughput test between each end-to-end combination path in the matrix.

A 5- to 10-second line-rate test transmitting simultaneously in both directions is often adequate. If the test is too short, issues related to buffering will not be revealed. Particularly long tests may be appropriate for some situations, but for most situations a test duration of less than a minute is more than sufficient. This testing should either reveal or exonerate problems with a particular path or uplink.

Links that are duplex mismatched have noticeably lower performance than properly configured links. If there is limited buffer space available on an older or less expensive switch, a longer throughput test may reveal that larger file transfers are affected and smaller transfers are not.

If possible, run the test using different packet sizes. Some end-to-end links are not able to handle all frame sizes equally.

Host IP Configuration

Connect a diagnostic tool in place of a problem station, and monitor the available traffic or discover the local broadcast domain. Check the configuration described in your network documentation to ensure that the problem station's configured address falls within the range allowed by the local subnet. Check the configuration of a nearby station in the same subnet to ensure that your documented subnet is accurate, or use a monitoring tool to see whether the majority of addresses match the subnet range you are expecting, and if the assigned address is within that range.

Restore the user connection through an inline monitoring tool to check for addressing problems and ICMP errors that may be present. These OSI Layer 3 errors are often forgotten or ignored but can quickly reveal the nature of the user's problem.

Before fixing the hardware and configurations, remember that after IP traffic arrives at the destination it is passed from the network interface up to the station or server operating system. Most operating systems require a password or some other sort of user identification and authentication before access is given. In fact, many applications offer similar password protection. This simple problem is often overlooked and is easily verified. Try logging in with another account and password before troubleshooting. The user may be confusing inability to gain access to an account with inability to reach the network.

Manual Address Assignment

It is not uncommon for a single MAC address (network interface) to have more than one IP address assigned to it—especially router or server interfaces. However, except for the very special case represented by virtual addresses, a single IP address absolutely may not be used by more than one MAC address.

Check to see what the current host IP address is and whether the network adapter bearing that address is currently active. For Windows PCs, try one of these commands:

```
C:>ipconfig /all
C:>winipcfg
```

For Linux PCs, try this command:

```
>ifconfig -a
```

If you are not logged in as root, specify the directory where the command is located:

```
/sbin/ifconfig -a
```

A given host may be assigned any IP address, provided that no other station is assigned the same address and the address is not a reserved or broadcast address. Addresses are issued in blocks by the appropriate Internet authority, but those block ranges—which are represented by address class groups—are meaningless once assigned. An ISP may subnet or supernet them in any way they want as long as routing supports the assignment. Do not assume that a Class C address, such as 192.168.x.x, is going to be using a Class C subnet mask.

The subnet mask tells a host station how much of the 32-bit IPv4 address represents the network address and how much represents the host's address. Except for the Class C address ranges, few indeed are the address ranges that are not supernetted or subnetted. If a host is using the wrong subnet mask, it might decide that it does not really exist on the same logical network segment as certain other local hosts, and the first host will not talk directly with them.

The most common subnet mask error is to configure the host with a subnet mask that matches the address class instead of the subnetted address. This causes the host to believe that more (or fewer) addresses are within the local subnet than should be. An incorrectly configured host often communicates exclusively with servers on other subnets, and because the local router address was supplied as part of the host configuration, it usually operates as though it were configured properly.

A host with too few host bits in the mask believes that some hosts on the local broadcast domain are in another network, and it tries to send requests via the router. The router, knowing that the other host is in the same subnet, may ignore the requests. The router may also forward the request within the same subnet, which is very inefficient as each request or reply is transmitted twice. A host with too many host bits in the mask believes that some hosts on another broadcast domain are actually local, and attempts to communicate directly with that other host without relying on the router to forward requests. Because Proxy ARP is often enabled in routers by default, and circumstances are in the host's favor, hosts with an incorrect mask often go undetected.

If a router has an incorrect mask, the problem manifests itself very quickly. Requests from some hosts are forwarded, and others are ignored (see also the section "Proxy ARP," which may hide this). At the same time, it is important to understand that some router configurations rely on using an apparently incorrect mask. An example is route aggregation, where a router closer to the Internet accepts all requests for a large group of subnets, and therefore uses a mask with more host bits than a router closer to the destination subnet.

The simplest solution to a single host problem is to review the configuration and compare the configured mask with another local host that is operating correctly, or compare it with the known configuration parameters for that subnet as indicated by network monitoring or by the network documentation.

If a host does not have a default router configured (sometimes shown as default gateway), all communications with hosts on other than the local subnet fail. More often, problems occur when the address in the router field is not actually a router or is a suboptimal router.

Dynamic Address Assignment

If the host is configured using DHCP, be wary when moving around. If the host was working fine only a short time earlier on a different connection, and the new connection does not work, try requerying the DHCP server. Disconnecting a PC does not always cause it to release an old IP address, and that address might not work on the new subnet.

For older Windows clients, issue the following two commands from a DOS window. Newer Windows operating systems attempt this for you when the link comes back up.

```
C:>ipconfig /release
C:>ipconfig /renew
```

For Linux hosts, the commands vary by distribution, but the commands shown usually work. Alternatively, start with "man dhcp" and see what is suggested:
  To release:

```
> dhcpcd -k
> dhcpcd -n
```

If DHCP is enabled, simply bringing the interface back up usually works:

```
> ifconfig eth0 up
> ifup eth0
```

The "up" commands shown assume the first Ethernet interface (eth0). You might need to open a different interface.

If no address is obtained, insert an inline monitoring tool or gather a trace file with a protocol analyzer to discover whether queries are actually being sent and whether responses are being returned (see Figure 11-33). If queries are being sent, it might be necessary to go to the DHCP server end to monitor whether the requests are arriving and whether a response is being sent. This identifies which end may have a problem, or whether the path between them should be investigated. If the request and response are not seen at both ends, use divide and conquer to locate the infrastructure device that dropped it. There is a special configuration for routers when the DHCP server is not located on the same subnet as the clients. This DHCP helper configuration may be in error.

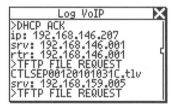

Figure 11-33. *NetTool inline test results for a successful DHCP request by a VoIP phone, followed by a TFTP configuration file request*

Duplicate IP Addresses

Two hosts with the same IP address cause either intermittent connection problems for both hosts or severe problems for one host (see Figure 11-34). If the problem host is rebooted, the functioning host becomes the problem host. To better understand this issue, consider the saying "Whomever ARPs last, wins." This saying is explained by defining the behavior of an ARP cache. Whenever an ARP is observed on the network, each router (and many other hosts) either creates a new entry or updates an existing entry for the source IP address in the ARP request. Following that, any further traffic from a prior conversation is then directed to the new MAC/IP address pair. The new host discards the traffic because it is for a conversation in which it is not a participant. Until the old host ARPs again, all traffic for its IP address is sent to the second host—which is improperly sharing its IP address.

Example 8: Duplicate IP Makes Printer Unavailable

A host accidentally configured to the same IP address as a networked printer transmitted an ARP request during its boot process. The router servicing the subnet promptly updated the ARP cache with the new MAC address information, and began forwarding all print request traffic to the new host instead of the printer. The host that caused the problem was turned off after a very brief time so that the duplicate address was no longer present on the broadcast domain. The router, however, continued to send all print request traffic to its MAC address until the ARP cache aged the improper MAC/IP address pair out of the ARP table (in this case it was four hours later). When the router ARP table finally discarded the problem MAC/IP address pair, the router then ARPed for the printer and suddenly printing resumed for no apparent reason. During the intervening four hours the network support staff tried everything imaginable to restart printing services for that printer, except rebooting the printer. Had they rebooted the printer the problem would have been solved immediately because the printer would have ARPed for the default router when it booted. The problem was blamed on the software print spooler and on the printer itself for most of the day, when in fact they were operating perfectly.

A simple method to discover stations with duplicate IP addresses is to send ARPs to the problem IP address. For each ARP request, you should usually see only a single ARP response. There are at least three situations where you might receive multiple responses, though.

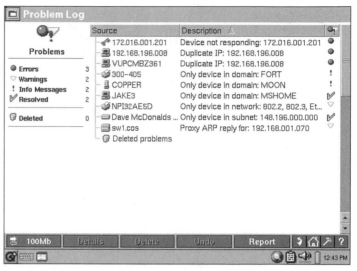

Figure 11-34. *EtherScope problem log showing a duplicate IP error*

- If a host has more than one IP protocol stack loaded, each stack responds to the ARP request. All such responses have the same MAC and IP address in the response. This is often a mysterious surprise but is not a problem situation.

- If Proxy ARP is running on a router servicing your subnet, the router may respond to local queries in addition to off-subnet queries. You might receive a response from the target address as well as the router. Routers that are acting in this manner simply forward subsequent traffic to the correct address, so this apparently duplicate response is not generally problematic.

- If two or more hosts are improperly configured to share the same IP address, each responds to the ARP. Each responding host will answer with its own unique MAC address and the duplicated IP address. This is a problem.

Diagnostic tools enable the user to ping a target IP address, and usually ARP the target address before issuing each ping request. In addition to the number of ping responses, check to see how many ARP responses were received. With the exception of the first ping, which some hosts routinely but improperly fail to respond to, there should be an equal number of requests and responses. If the numbers are different, investigate the cause.

Some diagnostic tools and software inventory the local broadcast domain and report which switch port a particular host is connected to, aiding in quickly locating the hosts involved in duplicate IP problems (see Figure 11-35).

Proxy ARP

If a host is using an invalid address for the local subnet, it can transmit, but replies do not find their way back. In some cases, enabling Proxy ARP on a local router permits these incorrect configurations to operate normally. Conversely, disabling Proxy ARP can help you locate misconfigured hosts.

Proxy ARP is often enabled by default on a router, and does not appear in the configuration unless you disable it. A router with Proxy ARP enabled forwards traffic even though the sending station does not have it configured as the default router.

If a router forwards requests sent by an improperly addressed station, replies are sent to the appropriate subnet for the source address, not back to the source station connected to the wrong subnet. A protocol analysis capture at the destination end will look correct: a request followed by a response. At the station end, only the request is seen.

VLANs and Subnets

If traffic monitoring reveals a different subnet, check to see whether other ports on the switch are in the same subnet or other subnets. There are several ways to dynamically assign a port to

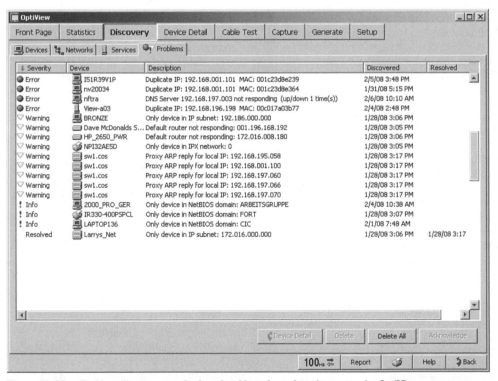

Figure 11-35. *Problem discovery results from local broadcast domain as seen by OptiView*

a VLAN in addition to a fixed manual assignment. If a station is in the wrong VLAN, it usually means that it is also in the wrong IP subnet and the station is unable to communicate. If DHCP addressing is open and unassigned (IP addresses are not tied to MAC addresses as it is with BOOTP), the station may obtain a valid address for the new subnet and operate correctly but slightly slower or faster due to traffic being routed differently.

In some cases, the switch is not properly configured and there is leakage between VLANs. Some traffic that should remain within a broadcast domain is instead being forwarded to another broadcast domain. In most cases, this is accidental and should be investigated and corrected. In some very obscure cases this was intentional, although highly unusual and not recommended.

DNS Failure

DNS is used to simplify many network activities but is not required for basic network operation. To make network and Internet use more user friendly, web browsers and most other applications that access the network permit entering the name of a desired server or service. The name is immediately converted to a network address, usually by requesting a Domain Name System (DNS) server to look up the name and provide the address. By having users access services by name, it is easy for the service provider to relocate the service to compensate for network outages or to improve service. If the service was routinely accessed by IP address, it would be somewhere between very difficult and impossible to inform users of a new address.

There are three classes of name resolution failure: one is the simple inability to reach the server, the second is when the server is reachable but no name resolution takes place, and the third is when the wrong address is given for the requested name.

Name Server Unreachable

Ping to the address of the name server as shown in your station configuration. If the ping fails, use a traceroute test to identify where the communications failure is occurring, and troubleshoot at the most distant router that responded to discover why it was unable to communicate to the next router after it (toward the destination).

If a ping to the IP address works, try the ping again using the name of the server instead of the address. Or try an nslookup for the name of the server.

```
C:\>ping 192.168.38.4
C:\>ping www.flukenetworks.com
C:\>nslookup www.flukenetworks.com
```

Watch to see whether the IP address resolved from the ping attempt is the same as the one you just pinged. If the address ping works but the name does not resolve to the same address, double-check the correct address of the name server. If no name resolution takes place, or if the resolved address is incorrect, proceed to one of the next two categories: no answer from name server or wrong address returned.

No Answer from Name Server

If the appropriate name server is reachable by ping, verify that the host is configured for that address. Verify that the station is properly configured for DNS or other name resolution services. Use the appropriate software utility, or issue one of the following commands from a DOS window as appropriate for your version of Windows, or a similar command for other operating systems:

```
C:>ipconfig /all
C:>winipcfg
```

For Linux PCs, the DNS server address is listed in the resolve.conf file. Your file location may be different:

```
> cat /etc/resolv.conf
```

If possible, hosts should have more than one DNS server configured. If a host is configured for at least two DNS servers that can be reached over different paths, the probability of applications failing due to no access to DNS is lower.

If the configured DNS domain of the host is different from the domain served by the name server you are querying, the result is usually the same as not reaching the server at all. Pings to the DNS server work fine; you simply do not receive a response to queries for domains the DNS server does not know. Check the host configuration for the correct domain and the proper spelling of the correct domain name.

Use a network diagnostic tool to determine which other DNS servers may be accessible from this location, and try configuring the problem host to a detected DNS server address. If that works, determine why the configured DNS server is unavailable.

Wrong Address Returned

A typical DNS database consists of two separate files: one containing the name-to-address lookup table, and a second containing the address-to-name lookup table. It is quite easy for these two files to be out of synchronization because of a typographical error. This may result in an erroneous entry or an entry that looks up correctly in one direction but not the other (such as name-to-address works, but address-to-name does not). Linux system tools such as nslookup, dig, and host can also be used to diagnose these problems. Recent versions of Windows also support nslookup.

```
C:\>nslookup www.google.com
   Server:  dns.fluke.com
   Address: 192.168.120.97

   Non-authoritative answer:
   Name:    www.l.google.com
   Addresses: 209.85.173.104,
209.85.173.147, 209.85.173.99,
209.85.173.103
   Aliases: www.google.com
```

Note that the response included several IP addresses for one name. This is normal for large Internet sites. Use the returned address(es) to look up the DNS name associated as the next step.

```
C:\>nslookup 209.85.173.104
   Server:  dns.fluke.com
   Address: 192.168.120.97

   Name:    mh-in-f104.google.com
   Address: 209.85.173.104
```

Nslookup also enables you to specify which DNS server should be queried. If the DNS server is unspecified, nslookup uses whichever DNS server is configured as the default for your station. The nslookup command is not available from all operating systems.

If there is a table error in the DNS server, the response may be inaccurate. Performing both a forward and a reverse lookup reveals this fault.

DNS is not the only available method of obtaining an IP address. Responses to a name query can come from a configured server or from a local cache. To speed up the lookup process, or to avoid using the

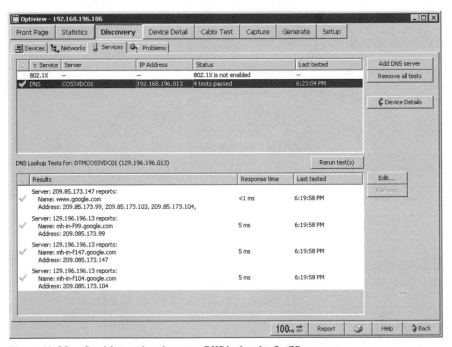

Figure 11-36. *Good forward and reverse DNS lookup by OptiView*

DNS server at all for regularly accessed resources, users may have commonly used names and addresses stored locally on their host in files or in temporary name caches. Either might be configured incorrectly or might have become inaccurate due to changes in the network.

Microsoft clients determine whether the name requested is either a host's name or a NetBIOS name and base their name resolution order on that decision. For example, when a Microsoft Client attempts to connect to another computer using the Universal Naming Convention (UNC) syntax, which is \\servername\resourcename, the servername is considered to be a NetBIOS name. However, when a ping command is issued to a computer name (such as C:>ping server1), the name pinged is considered to be a host name. The order in which a Microsoft host tries to resolve the name to an address is based on the type of name and the configuration of the system. See Table 11-4 for the resolution order based on type of name.

If the name being looked up appears with an IP address in any of the local or internal locations listed in Table 11-4, the host does not make a DNS query on the network. It also might not use DNS at all to resolve the name. Windows clients prefer to use the information found locally or from a Windows name server. If the information stored locally is incorrect, the host is unable to establish communications with the server or service desired.

Table 11-4. *Name resolution order of Microsoft Windows NT*

	Host Name	NetBIOS WINS Client	NetBIOS non-WINS Client
1	Name Cache	Name Cache	Name Cache
2	HOSTS file	WINS Server	NetBIOS Broadcast
3	DNS server	NetBIOS Broadcast	LMHOSTS file
4	WINS server	LMHOSTS file	HOSTS file
5	NetBIOS Broadcast	HOSTS file	DNS Server
6	LMHOSTS file	DNS Server	

Table 11-4 is valid for most general uses related to the older Windows NT, although as with everything else some exceptions exist for unusual configurations. For example, Windows NT clients could be configured as a B node, P node, M node, or H node, which affects the order of queries and whether some are even made. Thankfully, the name resolution process has become more simplified.

Other versions of Windows use different name resolution processes, such as the one shown in Table 11-5. If you are troubleshooting a name resolution problem related to a Windows client, it might be necessary to research the resolution order for that exact version and service pack level. It is usually enough, though, to understand that there are multiple places to look when DNS does not work as expected.

Table 11-5. *Name resolution order for Microsoft Windows XP and 2003*

1	Match local host?
2	DNS client resolver cache* (IPv4 and IPv6)
3	DNS server (IPv4 and IPv6)
4	NetBIOS Name Cache (IPv4)
5	WINS server (IPv4)
6	NetBIOS Broadcast (IPv4)
7	LMHOSTS file (IPv4)

* If hosts file exists it is loaded into the DNS client resolver cache (IPv4 and IPv6)

Operating systems, such as UNIX and Linux, resolve names according to the list configured in the hosts.conf file and DNS, although the process is far less involved than Windows. The following command lists the contents of the hosts.conf file:

```
> cat /etc/hosts.conf
```

This should not be confused with a hosts file, which contains manually entered names and addresses just like the hosts file used with Windows.

Because these local files are consulted first, use of these additional lookup files has become a common way to "black hole" certain hacking attempts and accidental redirects to dangerous or inappropriate sites. It is also a good way to stop ads from popping up in web pages. Just load the advertisement server DNS name into the list in the file and associate it with the local loopback address of 127.0.0.1.

Interconnected Networks Issues

The following procedures assume that this server or service has been operating properly prior to this problem, and you have already

- Determined that the host has been configured with the correct IP address

- Determined that the assigned address is valid for that subnet

- Determined that the default router or gateway address is correct and configured properly

When troubleshooting collision domains and broadcast domains it is fairly safe to say that if you do everything "right," it should work. When troubleshooting problems between interconnected networks you might have done everything right and it still might not work. That is largely because the adjacent network may be fundamentally different, and the interface between the two networks needs to accommodate these differences.

The majority of the internetwork faults relate to simple end-to-end connectivity, and the location to focus troubleshooting efforts on may be effectively identified with ping and traceroute. On occasion it is necessary to perform an end-to-end throughput test at the capacity of the subscribed end-to-end path. The phone number of your Internet service provider's network operation center is your best friend in these instances. It is often best to coordinate your test with them, to ensure that they are observing the link at the same time.

Intermittently dropped frames are a symptom of capacity problems such as a Frame Relay link exceeding the committed information rate, and of a cable fault such as a split pair on twisted pair or a ground loop on coax, or some other error condition in the path. If dropped frames are suspected, perform a cable test on the cables attaching any of the devices in the path between the station

and the server or service, including the station and the server.

ping and traceroute

If the server or service to which the user is connecting is on the far side of a WAN or routed connection, check for basic connectivity and response times through those segments by using a ping test. Compare the results with your baseline or audit results. If a ping test fails, try a traceroute test to learn where the path has failed. Traceroute traditionally solicits three responses from each hop along the way. If results are good up to a certain point, and nothing is returned beyond that point, the problem is almost certainly at the location where responses first ceased. Troubleshoot that link and the routers servicing it.

Firewalls almost never answer ping or traceroute queries, so there is no response at that point (see Figure 11-37). After the firewall responses may resume.

Ping continuously for at least a minute. Verify that the number of requests is equal to the number of responses. If the problem appears to be intermittent, run the test for a prolonged period, or have the user run the test when the problem is next experienced. Discrepancies may indicate a marginal router or an intermediate link to the destination that is experiencing errors, and frames are being dropped. If fewer responses are received than the number of requests sent, try running a traceroute test several times to locate the remote router link that is experiencing problems. If traceroute results are good up to a certain point, and intermittent for hops beyond that point, the problem is probably at the location where responses first became intermittent. All results beyond that point are affected by dropped frames at that first location. Router configuration problems can also be revealed by a traceroute test (see Figure 11-38).

If a poorly performing server or service is located across a WAN connection, try logging in remotely and running a traceroute test from there back to your location. Compare the path reported from traceroute tests performed in both directions to see whether requests and responses are taking different paths. Asymmetric routing can easily cause TCP traffic to get out of order, which causes retransmissions and slow performance.

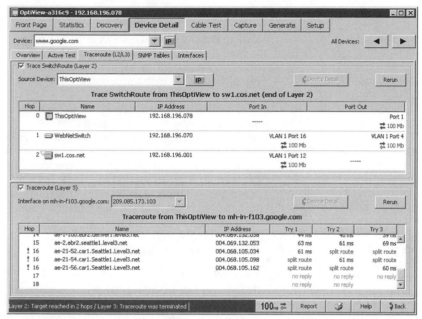

Figure 11-37. *OptiView Layer 3 traceroute test results show no response after a firewall*

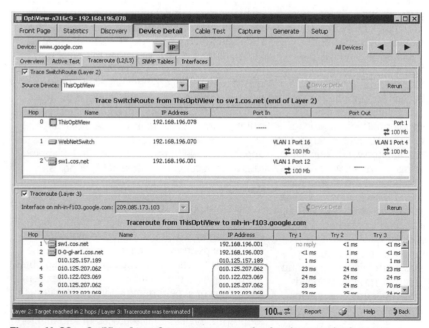

Figure 11-38. *OptiView Layer 3 traceroute test results showing a routing loop*

Watch also for changes in the path that indicate intermittent WAN links for which the routing protocols are trying to compensate.

Routing Problems

Assuming that both hosts are properly configured, a variety of routing problems can prevent connections from becoming established. The routers that make up the interconnected network path must share routing information. When there is a problem with this process, inconsistent information in the routing tables may prevent end-to-end connectivity.

Various routing protocols are used to communicate between routers. Routing protocols such as RIP use a method called distance-vector routing. Distance-vector routing assumes that the best path to a destination network is via the least number of hops. Due to this simplistic view of the network, protocols such as RIP sometimes make a poor decision and send traffic over a single slow WAN link instead of a series of two high-speed WAN links. The other major group of routing protocols are called link state protocols, which use complex algorithms, including the link speed, to pick the best path. Link state protocols typically make better routing decisions in complex networks.

The most common causes of inconsistent information in routing tables are physical link problems and incorrect router configuration information. When physical LAN or WAN links are going up and down, routers send routing updates to each other when a link status change is discovered. Until this new information can propagate throughout the network, various routers might not have the correct view of the network. Connection attempts made during this intermediate time period may fail because portions of the network are temporarily unreachable. These routing problems typically represent themselves as no response at all, or with "ICMP Destination Unreachable: Network Unreachable" messages.

Unless you are responsible for maintaining the router configurations, troubleshooting routing problems fall largely into four groups: dropped links, flapping links, capacity, and configuration.

Dropped Links

If a router detects that an attached link has failed, it announces the failure of that destination to all other routers in the same router domain. Link state protocols such as OSPF announce the failure to all routers affected at once, and they all pause to recalculate routes throughout the entire OSPF area, whereas distance-vector protocols such as RIP propagate the information more slowly from one router to the next.

If the link that failed is an uplink to the Internet or the only way out of one part of the network, traceroute shows results including this router. Following this router there is no response if the failed link was in the path to the destination. Of course if a parallel route exists, this failed link is avoided and traffic passes without interruption.

If the failed link was the only path, the router should return an ICMP Destination Unreachable: Network Unreachable message to any host attempting to use the failed path.

Flapping Links

If the failed link described earlier resumes operation, the routers once again pass this information among themselves. If the link is intermittent for some reason, this process of announcing the changing status of the link is repeated each time, resulting in the link flapping open and closed. Because it takes a small amount of time for the state change to propagate, there is an equal length of time where messages in transit may be left in limbo without a path to transit. This interim period, when some routers believe the path is open and others are passing information about its closure, is a well-known source of lost packets called a *black hole*. Traffic that cannot complete its passage because a route to the destination disappeared while in transit is discarded. Flapping routes are a common source of black holes.

Capacity

Routers are not often overwhelmed with the task of evaluating and forwarding traffic. Like everything else, you can purchase models with difference performance characteristics, and the higher-cost models perform correspondingly better. However, if the router is given complex configurations or is performing additional tasks such as firewall and SNMP activities, it is possible to reduce the available microprocessor and memory resources to handle the traffic to where problems become evident.

A more likely problem is that a lower-speed link becomes congested, and the buffer servicing that link is overrun with traffic, resulting in dropped frames. An indication of router or link congestion is ICMP Source Quench messages. The router may send these messages to a host, indicating that the host should slow down its transmission rate. Note that many TCP/IP implementations ignore these messages when they are received. ICMP echoes from a ping application are often useful to see whether traffic is being discarded due to congested links or routers because ICMP traffic is usually handled at a lower priority than data traffic.

Example 9: Theory Says That Won't Affect This

Another example of not trusting anything to behave as it should once you have begun troubleshooting is provided by a router with a serious flaw in the operating system that was easily corrected by downloading a newer version of the operating system. The small office network was lightly loaded, with less than 10 percent average traffic, even during peak periods right before and after lunch. However, connectivity to the Internet was erratic. It would work for a while, and then stop for a minute. Work and then stop. The problem was traced to when the buffer for the WAN connection became completely full with traffic waiting to be sent through the low-speed WAN connection. As soon as the outbound buffer filled to capacity the router reset itself, flushing all buffered traffic for all interfaces in the process. This would happen only when the outbound WAN buffer filled, which did not correlate with peak traffic periods on the LAN. The clue that provided the key to unraveling the mystery was that the SNMP variable for up time showed that the router had been running for less than one minute following one of the service interruptions. Instead of rebooting, the router should have simply dropped traffic that would have otherwise gone into the buffer for the WAN link. By rebooting and flushing all the buffers, the problem symptoms suggested more of a LAN problem than anything related to the WAN connection.

Configuration

Router configurations tend to be fairly complex. The most common configuration problems relate to simple typing errors in the configuration and commands that were not entered—usually because the person creating the configuration did not know the extra command was required. The results of configuration problems typically manifest themselves in four ways: the link does not pass traffic at all, the link is intermittent, the link passes traffic when it should not, or routing loops are created.

Describing all the possible configuration problems is the subject for an entire course of study, and in fact there are good courses available for configuring routers. Several of the many possible problems include the following:

- Improper configuration of routing protocol timers, such as the OSPF hello or dead timer. Setting these incorrectly can cause black holes and poor performance due to reconvergence.

- Static entries, such as manual ARP table entries and static routes. Configuring these variables as static entries can improve performance, but if the variable changes, the static entry becomes a troubleshooting liability that may be overlooked for a time.

- Incorrect mask, where requests from some hosts are forwarded and others are ignored. At the same time, it is important to understand that some router configurations rely on using an apparently incorrect mask.

  - Route aggregation or route summary, where a router closer to the Internet accepts all requests for a large group of subnets, and therefore uses a mask with more host bits than a router closer to the destination subnet.

  - Supernetting, where judging by the class code what appears to be multiple individual subnets are represented as a single larger subnet.

  - Artificial subnetting, where the stations within a subnet are given fewer host bits in the mask so that they cannot talk between groups, but the router has the proper subnet and routes any off-net requests properly. This and other related practices have been largely replaced with VLAN configurations on switches.

- Proxy ARP, where the router responds to ARP requests in cases where the router knows a route to the ARP destination IP address—even if that destination IP address is on the same local segment. Depending on the operating system or version, a router with proxy ARP enabled sometimes responds to all ARP requests—even if the router does not know a route to the destination. It either forwards requests to its default route (a default route is shown as an IP network of 0.0.0.0 in the router's routing tables) or it may discard them.

- Access list errors, where the list does not prevent traffic it was supposed to stop, and where too much traffic was blocked.

Nonrouters Sending Routing Protocols

UNIX and Linux workstations, as well as recent versions of Windows, most file server operating systems, and some other IP hosts, permit routing protocols to be enabled and look like routers to the local subnet. If the host is not provided with a suitable router configuration the result is often a black hole, where traffic is received by the host but never forwarded.

Either periodic surveys of the broadcast domains or constant attention to test results during routine network activities reveal the presence of nonrouters advertising routing protocols. In Figure 11-39, the Sun Microsystems MAC address reveals the probable presence of a Solaris server advertising routing protocols, if the system name is not already known to be a server.

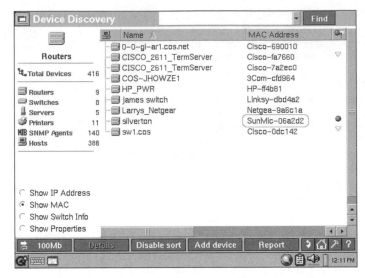

Figure 11-39. *EtherScope discovery results for routers*

If a second network adapter is placed into a Novell server, it automatically begins routing between the two attached networks, an action that can seriously impact its performance as both a server and a router. Although an inexpensive method of solving a short-term problem, this type of architecture design is poor, and true routers should be used where routing is appropriate.

Example 10: Helpful Features Are Not Always Helpful

One large distributed network using Novell NetWare servers had casually taken advantage of the routing capability of the server as part of the network architecture. All the users of a particular server were placed in a broadcast domain that was bounded by the server acting as a router. All the servers then connected to a broadcast domain that was serviced by a router that uplinked to the corporate network and on out to the Internet (see Figure 11-40).

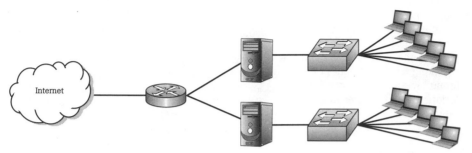

Figure 11-40. *Servers doubling as routers*

At first, all routine traffic was between clients and the server, with infrequent requests made of resources beyond the server each user was assigned to. Internet and nonlocal traffic increased over time without the network support staff noticing the gradual degradation of the server performance as it was required to spend ever greater amounts of its resources on routing traffic.

The design flaw, coupled with a WAN problem, was finally discovered after performance had degraded to the point where entire floors of the building would sometimes lose connectivity to the corporate network for minutes at a time.

Traceroute is a very effective tool for locating the nonrouters that cause these problems. Traceroute results show the address of the host that is black-holing traffic.

Duplicate IP Address

Another problem that can adversely affect routers is inaccurate data in the ARP tables. Each router builds a table showing which IP address is associated with which MAC address. If a host attempts to join a local segment with a duplicate IP address, it causes the table to replace the correct MAC address with the MAC address from the misconfigured host. Traffic that was destined for the original host is then sent to the second (misconfigured) host instead. To mitigate this problem temporarily (so you can get the network running until a proper correction is possible), have the router delete its existing ARP table and build a new one. If the ARP table continues to have prob-

lems, try shortening the ARP cache timeout. The ARP cache timeout parameter determines how long the router "trusts" information in the ARP table, and causes the router to discard entries that have been in the table for more than a configured period. For this temporary action to be effective, the duplicate IP address must be quickly located and corrected.

Firewalls and Security

Most dedicated routers have simple firewall capabilities. Implementing router firewall features is probably the first place to begin securing a network. It is important, however, that this simple protection is not used to replace formal firewalls, user account security, or application security. One of the most common mistakes in setting up access lists and filters is in not fully understanding the hierarchy of the filters and the rule syntax. Careful design and testing is required to avoid network service disruptions in the face of more sophisticated attacks, usually through Internet connections.

A typical firewall configuration permits almost anything to "originate from the inside" while denying almost everything originating from the outside (from the Internet). Problems are expected when a communications session is attempted from inside one firewalled network and must terminate inside another firewalled network. The likelihood of success is very low. Furthermore, the people responsible for maintaining the firewalls will be justifiably reluctant to open a path (called making a hole in the firewall) without a very good reason. Assume that this sort of connection will not work due to firewall rules, and contact the firewall administrators at both ends before troubleshooting.

Many firewalls appear to maintain state information for as little as five minutes of inactivity, and then lose important connections to systems beyond the firewall. Other firewalls maintain state information for so long (up to one hour or more) that latency through the firewall becomes high enough that performance suffers because the firewall is tracking too many connections.

NAT

In the late 1990s, there was much concern about running out of IPv4 address space. That concern appeared at around the same time as Internet denial of service and other attacks became commonplace. A quickly implemented preventative measure for attacks had the incidental effect of taking the pressure off the addressing problem. RFC 1918 allocated three address ranges for "private" use. These three ranges are just like any other address ranges; however, administrative restrictions applied by Internet service providers (ISPs) prevent traffic bearing those addresses from being forwarded to the Internet. The ranges are quite routable within an organization, and they were used in conjunction with firewalls and Network Address Translation (NAT) services to hide internal networks from the Internet. If traffic reaches your NAT or firewall but does not get beyond it, check the configuration of those two infrastructure devices. A vast array of problems relate to unsuitable configurations in those two services.

Having just said that those addresses will not be routed, be aware that it is entirely possible that the ISP itself may be using private address space within its network, and may be routing those address ranges internally. Performing a traceroute test from your location may reveal this "internal" use. If your ISP is not blocking those addresses from its client networks, it might be necessary for your organization to block them at the first Internet-facing router.

Private IP range use may also cause problems when using VPN or other remote access means to connect to another network. If both networks have route table entries for the same private IP subnets, those portions of the VPN host network are inaccessible through the VPN connection. This tends to be difficult to troubleshoot because it is unexpected.

Denial-of-Service Attacks

Denial-of-service attacks are a malicious attempt to prevent the target organization from being able to access the Internet or a particular service or server. The subject of a denial-of-service attack is often faced with the inability to communicate through their Internet connection due to the spurious traffic used to form the attack.

Although it is easily possible to determine the nature of the traffic and configure a filter in the firewall or router to prevent that traffic from entering the network, it does not prevent that traffic from consuming the capacity of the WAN link to the Internet. The only effective solution is to have your Internet service provider block the traffic before it reaches the relatively low bandwidth connection from your network to the Internet.

Trojan or Bot

A Trojan or Bot is a PC that has been compromised by an attack. During the attack, the subject PC is usually loaded with the software required to transmit a denial-of-service attack toward a selected target. Immediately or sometime later, the software loaded on the compromised PC (the Trojan or Bot) is instructed to begin the attack. To improve chances that the attack will not be traced back to the Trojan or Bot quickly, the IP source address of traffic involved in the attack is often loaded with something other than the true source address of the compromised PC.

This attack is then starting from the inside of your network going out, versus outside coming in. It also places your network in the awkward position of having some liability in causing the denial-of-service attack. Many network support staff are unaware of when a Trojan or Bot is at work. One good preventative protection is to set internal filters where your router or firewall permits only your legitimate subnet(s) as an outbound source address. Similarly, your mail server should be configured with some sort of e-mail authentication to stop outbound spoofing, phishing, and hoax messages from an infected PC.

SNMP Security

An unbelievable number of networks have made no effort to secure against compromise or attack. At a minimum, all the SNMP community strings should be changed to something other than the default settings. An extreme approach requires that only SNMP queries from a particular subnet, or even a single specific IP address, be the only authorized destination for responses.

Locking responses to a single IP address may be a good security measure; however, it would make troubleshooting difficult because field access to utilization and error information from switches would be denied.

Throughput Test

Performance bottlenecks are a fact of network life. In a healthy network, the primary bottlenecks are the throughput of the WAN links and the performance of the stations and servers. It is a common error to immediately assume that poor performance on a network is due to a slow network connection, and that increasing the speed of the local connection or installing a faster switch will solve the problem. Most switched networks operate with less than 1 percent average utilization on most ports.

There are two issues to consider when addressing performance: throughput and latency. Throughput is the measurement of bits flowing through a link. A 10Mbps Ethernet has more throughput than a 64kbps WAN link.

Latency is the delay of data through the entire system, including individual links and infrastructure devices. Dedicated resources, such as point-to-point WAN links, have a fairly constant latency. The router feeding such a link may introduce latency through variations in the amount of traffic buffered, but once in the link the latency is predictable. However, shared resources such as LANs, PCs, routers, and WAN services such as Frame Relay networks have a variable latency. When shared resources become loaded, the latency of data going through increases as traffic is buffered before being transmitted. Throughput may also decrease—depending on the WAN circuits involved. When congestion abates, the latency decreases and throughput might increase. For someone surfing the web, variations in latency have little effect other than a slight annoyance. For technologies such as videoconferencing and voice over IP, variations in latency can be extremely disruptive.

It is important to understand whether performance problems are throughput-related or latency-related before making changes (see Figure 11-41). At present, the primary architecture practice for applications that are sensitive to variations in latency is to over-engineer the network in such a way that these variations are unlikely to take place. When quality of service (QoS) configuration options become more mature, it will be safer to prioritize the delivery of these sensitive protocols instead of simply over-engineering to compensate for QoS shortfalls and interoperability issues.

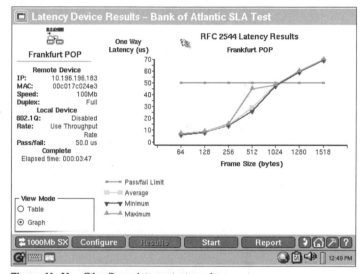

Figure 11-41. *EtherScope latency test results*

A crude throughput test is possible by using any traffic generator source to send traffic across the router or WAN connection and then monitor the distant LAN segment with another tool to ensure that the expected amount of traffic is arriving. If network management is available, use SNMP to gather statistics from infrastructure devices along the path while a known amount of extra traffic is being sent. Some problems are size related, so repeat the test using different frame sizes to ensure that there are no frame size–related problems.

Throughput testing is available in many forms and degrees of complexity and at many price levels. Some simpler throughput tests transmit configured or variable amounts of traffic between endpoints and report the measured throughput. More complex tests involve configuring endpoints to simulate multiple users, protocols, and/or applications simultaneously to check for how well routers and firewalls perform under proposed conditions prior to going live with a new application or protocol. Very complex tests involve gathering and analyzing actual traffic found in various parts of the network, and then modifying the traffic load and testing various scenarios across the current architecture. Again, this is used mostly to discover what the effect of a new application or protocol will be prior to using it, allowing the support staff time to adjust or improve the network infrastructure to accommodate the proposed new or changing load.

Going beyond throughput testing, various applications simulate your entire network. When the simulation is constructed in the software, you may try different infrastructure equipment and configurations or change link speeds until an optimum configuration is reached. Then the resulting network architecture and configurations may be implemented with some confidence that performance will be as designed for supporting your applications and user community.

Use throughput testing for these and other tasks:

- Perform a throughput test to see what bandwidth is available during idle and busy periods on your network—being careful not to deny network availability in the process.

- Use throughput testing to see whether the network is at fault, or the station, server, or software.

- Use throughput testing to check QoS configurations and other forms of priority queuing.

- Configure throughput testing to simulate your application to check a firewall configuration.

- Use a throughput test to check rate limiting on switches.

- Use throughput testing to learn what the actual uplink/downlink bandwidth is for ADSL links (see Figure 11–42).

- Perform a throughput test to discover whether your actual WAN performance matches what was contracted from your ISP.

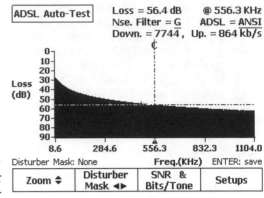

Figure 11–42. *990DSL Copper Pro test results for an ADSL Auto-Test. This is a test of a cable pair's capability to carry digital services, and requires a far-end terminating device. This test is normally conducted by the telco or ISP.*

Measuring latency variations across a WAN is somewhat awkward because it is hard to synchronize the sampling clock with very fine accuracy. Within a LAN, a dual port protocol analyzer can easily pick up traffic on both sides of various infrastructure devices and correlate latency down to tens of nanoseconds.

If precise latency is not required, it is possible to use two low-cost software protocol analyzers to make a simple round-trip latency measurement. Start gathering a trace file at both ends of the link. Send a ping from one end of the link, and stop the trace files at both ends when the response returns. Total round-trip time is calculated by measuring the time between departure of the ping request and return of the ping response at the sending end. Then from the second trace file measure the time difference between arrival and subsequent departure of the ping at the receiving end. You don't want to include the time the ping spent at the receiving end being received, processed, and responded to in the latency calculation. Subtract that time from the total round-trip time measured at the sending end to learn the approximate round-trip path latency (see Figure 11–43). Divide that by two to obtain the approximate one-way path latency. In this way you don't need a time sync because the two parts to the measurement are made independently using the separate clocks, and do not have to be correlated.

Although there may be asymmetry in actual one-way latency through the system, dividing the resulting round-trip latency in half gives an idea of what the one-way latency should be. Be sure to allow for delays in the system due to temporary congestion contributed by other traffic.

MTU

If the server or service in use is separated from the user connection by a bridge, router, or WAN connection, check the frame size in use locally and the maximum transmission unit (MTU) through the WAN connections. RFC 1191 and RFC 1981 describe how to discover the optimum MTU size for a given path.

The performance and efficiency of some links is affected almost as much by the number of frames as the size of the frame. A station sending many small frames consumes more bandwidth than larger frames because of the overhead added onto each frame. Furthermore, infrastructure devices are more affected by smaller frames because they spend approximately the same amount of microprocessor time evaluating small frames as large frames.

If the MTU of transmitted frames is too large, the infrastructure devices along the way must split the overly large frame into smaller frames using a process called fragmenting. Fragmenting is very inefficient and sometimes causes lost frames. If the IP header includes the don't fragment bit, the oversize frame is discarded along the way and an ICMP error is returned. Not all TCP/IP protocol stacks react correctly to the ICMP error and reduce the MTU, or are able to properly reassemble certain fragmented traffic. MTU has been a problem frequently enough that VPN applications often come with MTU adjustment utilities, such as shown in Figure 11-44.

VPN

Virtual Private Networks (VPNs) permit the logical creation of a secure link between the VPN client and the host network at the other end of the VPN link. All traffic crossing this logical link is encrypted above OSI Layer 3. Layer 3 is not encrypted because that would prevent end-to-end delivery across the Internet. VPN concentrators are typically placed either in parallel with firewalls or behind the firewall.

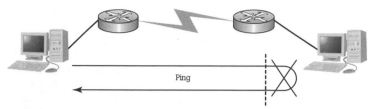

Figure 11-43. *Simple round-trip latency test*

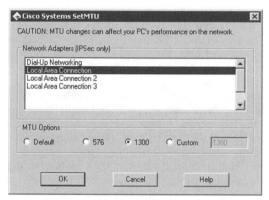

Figure 11-44. *MTU size adjustment utility from Cisco VPN client*

Recently, the MTU size has been the source of some VPN communication failures because the transmitting station is creating a packet that becomes too large after the extra header information is applied. This happens because VPNs are sensitive to many things, including fragmentation, and because the VPN traffic may be further fragmented if it is tunneled through another protocol such as PPPoE as it transits various ISP's internal LANs on the way to the destination. If you are having trouble transmitting after a link was established using a VPN, try reducing the MTU size by 50 or 100 octets at a time on the problem station. An Ethernet MTU of 1300 octets is a good place to start. MTU problems are likely if you can connect but cannot send much, if any, traffic.

If the VPN does not come up at all, it could be due to a firewall configuration. This is likely if the VPN has worked from other locations. Some applications do not support VPNs at all, so be sure to try more than one application when attempting to troubleshoot a VPN-related problem.

In either case, use of a protocol analyzer to gather a trace file of the attempted session should reveal clues about the nature of the failure.

In an attempt to reduce monthly fees for point-to-point links, such as connecting remote offices through dedicated Frame Relay circuits, some companies have been switching to VPN links. If routing protocols must also transit these virtual links, it might be necessary to set up a GRE tunnel to transport them. Other secure tunneling protocols such as IPSec are available, but they might not encrypt multicast routing protocols for transit through the tunnel.

Another observed source of VPN failure is the small office or home office router/firewall/NAT combination device. These infrastructure devices are typically connected to a DSL or cable modem connection and are very easy to install. Unfortunately, not all of them have proven capable of correctly NATing multiple VPN sessions to the same VPN concentrator. If one session is possible but multiple sessions are not, try a different model or brand, or contact the vendor for a software patch.

Server Problem

Although the infrastructure network is certainly subject to many problems, it is probably blamed for more that it is responsible for. There is arguably an equal or greater likelihood that the server or service is not adequately provisioned to support the set of tasks assigned to it, or that the user's PC or account is misconfigured. Server operating systems have been becoming progressively more stable over the years, and it is now unusual to have to restart the server from a cold-boot and watch to ensure that all required software driver files load without error. It may still be a useful thing to try during routine service downtime.

If network utilization is reasonable, check the servers or services to see whether they are experiencing high utilization (which is different from the network utilization).

Everything else being equal, servers with higher-speed CPUs, more memory, and faster disks can perform more work than slower systems. Do not forget that any slow point in a system creates a performance bottleneck for the entire system, and that there is always another bottleneck. At times, components such as faster network interface cards, separate drive controllers for each drive, or faster I/O subsystems may help more than a faster CPU. Insufficient memory, too small of a setting for the cache, fragmented hard drives, bottlenecks within the system such as one hard drive controller for multiple drives, a 16-bit network adapter, microprocessor-intensive transactions such as database recalculation, and too many services loaded all cause slow responses from the server.

It's important to keep in mind that not all applications are the same and may place different demands on systems and networks. For example, diskless workstations and centralized application software cause large transfers across the network at the same time they simplify application maintenance.

Many network operating systems permit the network administrator to lock out users when too many bad login attempts have been made. It's a good idea to set a low number for attempts, such as three, so you quickly discover when someone's account is being hacked.

Low Throughput WAN Links

Understanding the topology of the network and the path that traffic takes from one network to another is very useful in discerning performance-related problems. Many networks begin the process of interconnecting remote LANs using low-speed links. These slow links may be enough for the initial applications and for a small number of users. However, as more critical applications are deployed and as more users add traffic, WAN links are often the most obvious place to look for improved performance. These slow links not only add latency; they are often the primary source of congestion as more traffic is added.

Tools such as traceroute can help identify slow and congested links as the test displays the round-trip response time for each hop through the path. Comparing the traceroute path with link speeds can help identify routing problems that incorrectly make use of slow-speed links.

When the offered load is greater than the available bandwidth, the routers start to queue the data, and then transmits it as soon as they can. Traffic is discarded as the routers' buffers fill with queued data. Additionally, higher-level applications such as TCP time out following lost frames and attempt to retransmit the data, which, in some cases, makes the problem worse because even more data is sent. Advanced algorithms in some TCP implementations slow down retransmissions to prevent additional congestion.

If a slowdown in response time is noted over a WAN link, check what else is happening with that WAN connection during the slowdown. Use network management software or a diagnostic tool to check the utilization of the intervening links. Frame Relay links may discard excess traffic without generating any errors, so be wary of any WAN link operating near or at capacity. Errors or discarded traffic on a WAN link can easily explain dropped connections.

Installing web caching reduces off-net traffic for frequently used Internet resources. This option has two benefits: the WAN link is not used as heavily and users experience better performance.

Many popular streaming services are now available, such as radio stations streaming through the Internet. Users are unaware of the bandwidth impact on WAN connections that these services have. A less obvious problem that has appeared relatively recently is the inexpensive computer video camera that can be configured to stream the picture live onto the network. The novelty of making their image available to family and friends has caused some users to enable this feature, without realizing that their tiny camera is capable of producing such a large volume of traffic. Regular monitoring of uplinks and traffic across WAN connections reveals these problems.

The billing for WAN links varies from a flat rate to a fee based on octets transmitted. For the links where the billing is based on usage, it is fairly important to check what sort of traffic is routinely present on the link. Many network managers have been quite surprised to learn that a significant part of what they were paying for was simply routing or server broadcast updates. Taking care when selecting the routing protocol used over a WAN link, and in what traffic is routinely allowed over that link, can reduce the cost of a link considerably. Other WAN links can be configured to dial-on-demand. Again, router and server updates have been discovered to cause regular usage of links like this.

Summary

This chapter described troubleshooting of an installed network. Troubleshooting is approached in reference to the OSI Model because a lower-layer problem can easily cause misleading symptoms at higher layers.

- The available tool categories for testing, troubleshooting, and monitoring a network are described in detail. Special note is made of the capabilities and limitations of each tester category. Unlike media test tools, the functionality of many of the available network testing and monitoring tools implements a combination of several basic test categories and is therefore described herein as a hybrid of those basic test techniques. Knowledge of the capabilities and limitations of each tester used enhances your ability to successfully apply the tools to troubleshooting scenarios.

- Almost all user complaints can be summarized into three general groupings: can't connect, dropped connections, and poor performance. Although every network is different, an approach to isolating the cause of each grouping is provided, with suggestions listed in accordance with the OSI Model. Multiple tips and examples are provided to guide interpretation of test results and test failures, and to provide probable causes of a test failure.

- A listing of general or common troubleshooting considerations and scenarios is provided. Many of the Ethernet error conditions described in Chapter 4 are revisited from a field troubleshooting perspective. Several generalized monitoring suggestions are provided and are accompanied by a short description of the rational for each. Multiple tips and examples are provided to guide interpretation of test results and test failures, and to provide probable causes of a test failure.

- As with all other aspects of planning, installation, and maintenance of a network, the level of knowledge held is critical to the degree of speed or success experienced. This chapter is supported by additional information related to understanding how to apply the OSI Model to network troubleshooting provided in Appendix D, "Discovering Device Behavior," and Appendix E, "Techniques for Troubleshooting Switches."

The intent of this chapter is to provide sufficient troubleshooting information and guidance to allow most common problems to be approached in a manner that aids rapid problem isolation and resolution. It is not possible to provide a more exact approach because the number of ways in which networks are constructed with the same equipment is staggering. It is impossible to predict the architecture or implementation of any one network, and therefore a more generalized approach is both required and desired. It is likely that some parts of your network are significantly different from other parts. Full understanding of the information provided in this chapter permits a good technician to make the intuitive leap required for rapid and reliable problem isolation.

Chapter Review Questions

To aid in your comprehension of important concepts, the following questions are provided. Refer to this book's Introduction for a general legend that indicates the anticipated difficulty of each question. For answers to these review questions, see Appendix I, "Answers to Chapter Review Questions."

 1. Name four primary network tester categories, along with an identifying feature for each.

 2. What problems are protocol analyzers most effectively used to solve?

3. What is network management most effectively used to accomplish?

4. What are handheld network analyzers most effectively used for?

5. Why is discovering which layer or layers of the OSI Model a device operates at so important for troubleshooting? Be specific, and give an example to illustrate your position.

6. Is it appropriate to always start at the Physical Layer, or can testing be structured in such a way that testing can use the divide-and-conquer philosophy to eliminate OSI layers quickly? Give an example.

7. Into what three categories do virtually all user complaints fall?

8. If the users tell you that "nothing changed" that would affect the network, what sorts of things might they be overlooking that could affect their network performance or connectivity?

9. What might cause each of the following Ethernet errors?

- Collisions
- Late collisions
- Short frames
- Jabber
- FCS errors
- Ghosts

10. Why could it be a problem to have a client station connected to the same broadcast domain as a Microsoft NLB server cluster?

11. Why might it be said that the presence of link (the link LED is illuminated) is largely meaningless, but the absence of link (the link LED is not illuminated) suggests that you should troubleshoot?

12. List one significant reason why mapping a tiered application can be difficult.

13. What network problem is Spanning Tree there to prevent?

14. Under what conditions can a full-duplex connection be achieved? Is that always true?

15. Is a router function required to pass traffic between VLANs on the same switch? Explain your answer.

16. Is it possible for a switch to stop forwarding some types of traffic but to continue forwarding other types of traffic for no apparent reason?

17. What is perhaps the fastest, most effective method for stopping a broadcast storm? Explain your answer.

 18. What is the effect of a duplicate IP address?

 19. Is it possible for a host to communicate outside the local broadcast domain if the host is configured with an invalid IP address?

 20. Is there a simple way to discover what address the network is resolving a given DNS name to? If so, how?

 21. Are there other ways in which a host resolves a name to an address? If so, mention at least one.

 22. Ping and traceroute both validate the path to a distant network resource. How are they different?

APPENDIX A
Copper Test Failure Cause Tables

This appendix provides additional and more detailed lists of possible causes for certain cable test fault conditions to augment the short list presented in Chapter 10, "Troubleshooting Media."

Wiremap

Wiremap failures are most often found at cable termination points, either at the RJ45 (plug or jack) or at an intermediate cross-connect or patch panel. They involve opens, shorts, and various pairing faults. Table A-1 provides a detailed listing of the most common sources of wiremap failures.

Table A-1. *Common wiremap test failure fault sources*

Test Result	Possible Cause of Result
Open	Wires broken by stress at connections
	Cables routed to wrong connection
	Faulty or damaged connector
	Cuts or break in cable
	Wires connected to wrong pins at connector or punch block
	Application-specific cable (e.g., Ethernet using 1,2 and 3,6 only) *Check* Outlet Configuration *in setup.*
Short	Improper connector termination
	Damaged connector
	Conductive material stuck between pins at a connection
	Damage to cable
	Application-specific cable
Reversed Pair	Wires connected to wrong pins at connector or punch block
Crossed Pair	Wires connected to wrong pins at connector or punch block
	Mix of 568A and 568B wiring standards (1,2 and 3,6 crossed)
	Crossover cables used (1,2 and 3,6 crossed)
Split Pair	Wires connected to wrong pins at connector or punch block
"Bad patch cord" message appears	Poor quality patch cord used for channel
	Cable on permanent link interface adapter is badly distorted or damaged
	Wrong test standard selected

Note: *The "bad patch cord" message indicates excessive crosstalk over the first 2 meters of the cabling.*

Length

Both the TIA/EIA-568 and ISO 11801 standards specify a maximum twisted-pair cable length of 100 meters for LAN applications. Table A-2 provides a more detailed list of possible causes for length faults than the short list presented in Chapter 10.

Table A-2. *Common length failure fault sources*

Test Result	Possible Cause of Result
Length exceeds limits	Cable is too long
	NVP is set incorrectly
Length reported is shorter than known length	Intermediate break in the cable
One or more pairs significantly shorter	Damage to cable
	Bad connection

Standard practices dictate that length be defined by the length of the shortest pair. NVP varies per pair, meaning each pair could be reported with a different length. These two conditions can result in a cable with two of three pairs over the length limit, yet the link result is a Pass (e.g., a channel with 101, 99, 103, 102 meters for the four pairs). A Pass in this case is the correct interpretation.

Propagation Delay or Delay Skew

Propagation delay is the parameter used to determine how long the cable is, and delay skew is a measurement of the difference in arrival times between the fastest pair and the slowest pair in a link. Few causes result in failure of either parameter, and those are shown in Table A-3. The discussion for these two parameters found in Chapter 10 provides guidance in understanding these fault conditions.

Table A-3. *Common Propagation Delay or Delay Skew fault sources*

Test Result	Possible Cause of Result
Fail	Cable is too long (propagation delay)
	Cable uses different insulation materials on different pairs (delay skew)

Insertion Loss (Attenuation)

Insertion loss used to be called attenuation; however, at higher frequencies, some interaction with other conditions was observed and the parameter was renamed to include the effects of the other conditions. Insertion loss represents a decrease in signal. Table A-4 provides a more detailed listing of possible failure causes than found in Chapter 10.

Table A-4. *Common insertion loss test failure fault sources*

Test Result	Possible Cause of Result
Fail, *Fail, or *Pass	Cable is too long.
	Low twist rate or poor quality patch cables.
	Bad connection.
	High impedance connections. Use time domain techniques to troubleshoot.
	Inappropriate cable category (e.g., Category 3 cable used in a Category 5e application).
	Incorrect test parameters or test selection.

NEXT and PSNEXT

Near End Crosstalk (NEXT) represents a signal that leaks (or crosses over) from one cable pair to another. This causes the transmitting station to improperly hear some of its own transmissions. Power Sum NEXT (PSNEXT) is a measure of the combined crosstalk from all three adjacent cable pairs. Table A-5 provides a more detailed listing of possible failure causes than found in Chapter 10.

Table A-5. *Common NEXT and PSNEXT test failure fault sources*

Test Result	Possible Cause of Result
Fail, *Fail, or *Pass	Poor twisting at connection points.
	Poorly matched plug and jack (Category 6/Class E applications).
	Incorrect link adapter (Category 5 adapter for Category 6 links, or incompatible Category 6 adapter on Category 6 links).
	Poor quality patch cords.
	Bad connectors.
	Poor quality cable.
	Split pairs.
	Inappropriate use of couplers.
	Excessive compression caused by plastic cable ties.
	Wrong test standard selected (e.g., "Good" Category 5e cable tested to Category 6 limits).
	Excessive noise source adjacent to measurement. *Use the impulse noise test to check for noise.*
Unexpected Pass on good cable	Knots or kinks do not always cause NEXT failures, especially on good quality cable.
	Incorrect test standard selected (e.g., "Bad" Category 6 link tested to Category 5e limits).
	"Fails" at low frequency on NEXT graph but passes overall. When using the ISO/IEC standards, the 4dB rule states all NEXT results measured while insertion loss is less than 4dB cannot fail.

Return Loss

Return loss is a measure of reflections that bounce back to the transmission source. Return loss is a significant problem where the deployed technology requires that a cable pair be used simultaneously for transmit and receive, such as Gigabit Ethernet. The reflections cause problems in decoding the received traffic. Table A-6 provides a more detailed listing of possible failure causes than found in Chapter 10.

Table A-6. *Common return loss test failure fault sources*

Test Result	Possible Cause of Result
Fail, *Fail, or *Pass	Patch cord impedance not 100 ohms.
	Patch cord handling causing changes in impedance.
	Installation practices—excessive untwisting of pairs at connector (untwists or kinks of cable—the original twists should be maintained as much as possible for each wire pair).
	Excessive amount of cable jammed into the telecom outlet box.
	Bad connector.
	Cable impedance not uniform (poor quality cable).
	Cable impedance not 100 ohm.
	Impedance mismatch at junction between patch cable and horizontal cable (such as cable from different manufacturers).
	Poorly matched plug and jack (Category 6/Class E applications).
	Service loops in telecommunications closet.
	Inappropriate test parameters or test selection chosen.
	Water in cable jacket.
	Cable compression (tight cable ties, pinches, kinks, and so on).
	Defective link adapter.
Unexpected Pass	Knots or kinks do not always cause return loss failures, especially on good cable.
	Incorrect test parameters or test selection chosen (easier to pass return loss limits).
	"Fails" at low frequency on return loss graph but passes overall. Due to the 3dB rule, whereby all return loss results measured while insertion loss is less than 3dB cannot fail.

Table A-7. *Common ACRF and PSACRF test failure fault sources*

Test Result	Possible Cause of Result
Fail, *Fail, or *Pass	General rule: troubleshoot NEXT problems first. This normally corrects any ACRF problems. In addition to the NEXT and PSNEXT possible cause list, check for service loops with many tightly coiled windings

Resistance

The DC loop resistance test is not often included troubleshooting. Problems related to resistance manifest themselves as insertion loss problems. The quickest way to check to see whether there is a problem is to compare the resistance measurements for all four pairs in the cable. The results should be only slightly different. Troubleshoot the associated insertion loss problem if this test fails. Table A-8 provides a more detailed listing of possible failure causes than found in Chapter 10.

Table A-8. *Common resistance test failure fault sources*

Test Result	Possible Cause of Result
Fail, *Fail, or *Pass	Cable is too long
	Poor connection due to oxidized contacts
	Poor connection due to marginally attached conductors
	Thinner gauge cable
	Incorrect patch cord type

ACRF and PSACRF (ELF-EXT and PSELFEXT)

The Attenuation to Crosstalk ratio Far-end (ACRF) measurement is a calculated value based on measured test results for FEXT and insertion loss. The Power Sum form of this test represents the combined effects of all three adjacent pairs on the test pair. Troubleshoot the associated crosstalk or insertion loss problem if this test fails. Table A-7 provides a more detailed listing of possible failure causes than found in Chapter 10.

Characteristic Impedance

Characteristic impedance is not often included troubleshooting. Problems related to characteristic impedance manifest themselves as return loss. Troubleshoot the associated return loss problem if this test fails. Table A-9 provides a more detailed listing of possible failure causes than found in Chapter 10.

Table A-9. *Common characteristic impedance test failure fault sources*

Test Result	Possible Cause of Result
Exceeds limit or an anomaly is detected	Bad connection
	Cable compression (tight cable ties, pinches, kinks, and so on)
	Mismatch of cable types
	Water in cable jacket
	Incorrect terminator value (coaxial cable)
	Excessive loading at coaxial cable tap

Impulse Noise

Impulse noise represents voltage spikes that have the potential for disrupting a transmitted signal. The effect of this problem is often intermittent and might not appear during the time interval that a cable Autotest is running. A severe instance of this problem could prevent network equipment from linking. Cable testers offer specific long-duration tests to monitor for this problem. Table A-10 provides a more detailed listing of possible failure causes than found in Chapter 10.

Table A-10. *Common impulse noise test failure fault sources*

Test Result	Possible Cause of Result
Impulse noise is detected	Electrical devices near the cabling are generating noise pulses.
	There is an active link in the same bundle as the cabling under test.
	Verify that the tester and smart remote are operating correctly. Connect the units together and run an Autotest.

Alien Crosstalk Mitigation

When preparing for 10GBASE-T performance it is critical that all installed links first pass the in-channel tests. For any failing links, the following steps are suggested (in order of priority). Retest the link following each upgrade.

1. Replace the work area, patch, and/or equipment cords with Category 6A cords.

2. Reconfigure any cross-connect as an inter-connect.

3. Replace the interconnect with a Category 6A interconnect.

4. Replace any consolidation point connector with a Category 6A consolidation point connector.

5. Replace the work area outlet connector with a Category 6A work area outlet connector.

When alien crosstalk test results are available, locate the worst disturber and attempt to improve the quality of each successive worst disturber link until alien crosstalk passes on the victim link. Look for disturber links yielding the smallest worst-case margin numbers (or negative numbers) because these are the worst offenders (biggest contributors to PSANEXT). For each of the worst contributors, consider the mitigation actions listed below (in order of priority):

1. Reduce the alien crosstalk coupling by separating the equipment cords and the patch cords and unbundling the horizontal cabling.

2. An alternative to separating equipment cords is to utilize equipment cords sufficiently specified to mitigate the alien crosstalk coupling, such as Category 6 ScTP and Category 6A.

3. Reconfigure the cross-connect as an inter-connect.

4. Replace connectors with Category 6A.

5. Replace the horizontal cable with Category 6A.

After applying a mitigation attempt you should retest the interaction between the victim link and the modified disturber to see whether a noticeable improvement has been achieved in the worst-case margin of the offending test parameter.

APPENDIX B
Waveform Decoding Exercise

This appendix is a single, short, hour-long lab (if no supporting lecture is required), or it can be a series of lecture/lab modules. The lab has been shown to provide the greatest benefit if given very early in a basic networking program, such as the first day of a class that is completed in a week, or the first week of a longer course. The format of this appendix is that of lecture notes for the lab preparation.

Use of the lab early in a course is particularly effective because the process of manually working through the waveform and having to look up a new set of field definitions for each layer decoded makes the OSI Model and counting systems tangible and useful instead of apparently pointless abstract information that must be memorized. These short labs provide justification for much of the theoretical material, and the students will be much more interested in learning it. The immediate need for information to proceed with the lab offers an introduction for how to apply research techniques. Introducing protocol analysis early permits use of the protocol analyzer as a tool to support lecture content for each new topic. For example, if the lecture described the TCP three-way handshake, go capture one and examine it.

Whether in separate lecture/lab modules or as a single module, the first four waveform decoding exercise modules are intended to be performed together. Modules 5 and 6 are more advanced topics and may be skipped altogether, used later in the curriculum, or as extra credit at the instructor's discretion.

Module 1: Counting systems; encoding methods; and the OSI seven-layer model. (30–60 minute lecture)

Module 2: Decoding the waveform back into binary, reordering the binary, and identifying Ethernet field boundaries. (30–60 minute lab)

Module 3: Ethernet Length/Type field; how to locate, download, and read RFCs; and decoding Layer 3 of the waveform. Lecture on connection-oriented and connectionless protocols (TCP and UDP) for Layer 4, repeat RFC research and decoding of Layer 4. (30–60 minute lecture and lab)

Module 4: Protocol analyzer use. (30–60 minute lab)

Module 5: Lecture on Layers 5–7 protocols and on SNMP. Decoding Layers 5–7 of the waveform. (Lecture notes not provided.)

Module 6: Network security and methods of breaching security from within or from outside a firewall. The waveform includes a means for leaking data past a firewall—best seen from the protocol analyzer decode. (Lecture notes not provided.)

Modules 5 and 6 are recommended as optional because proceeding up the OSI Model into Layers 5–7 requires substantially more time and effort. The first four modules take comparatively little time for the very significant boost in understanding that they impart, and will make the student's progress through subsequent material easier and more meaningful.

The following information is provided as notes for delivering the suggested lectures and labs. It is by no means everything that could be covered in the course of the defined modules associated with this material. You are strongly encouraged to add to this outline.

Module 1: Counting Systems and Encoding Methods

This module introduces the concepts required for the next module. The counting systems used in relation to computers and networking are described, as well as several of the encoding systems used by Ethernet.

Counting Systems

Computers rely on the concept of *on* and *off* to perform any action. On and off is the equivalent of the binary counting system utilizing only the digits 1 and 0. Before describing how the binary counting system works, let's first review the decimal counting system that we use every day. The review will provide a reference for how the other counting systems are described here.

Decimal

The decimal counting system is based on the numbers 0 through 9. Decimal is depicted by writing the number 10 in subscript immediately after the number. For example, the number 22_{10} can be clearly expressed as representing decimal in this way.

A single decimal digit can represent any quantity between 0 and 9. If the current number were 9, adding 1 changes the number from a single digit to two digits. Thus, groupings are based on sets of 10. A complete set of 10 is shown by a change in columns, moving one column to the left.

A counting sequence:

0
1
2
3
4
5
6
7
8
9
10
11
12

Figure B-1 is a graphical representation of the placeholders represented by each digit in a given number. Because of size limitations, only the grouping increments of ones, tens, and hundreds are depicted. If it helps, look on the placeholder graphic as a method of counting beans. One bean per placeholder circle.

In Figure B-1, notice how there is a placeholder for nine sets in each column. Zero is represented by a lack of any populated placeholder in that column. Populating more than nine placeholders in any column is not possible because no placeholder is offered. To increase the number of used-placeholders, it is necessary to change columns. All the placeholders, plus the placeholder that forced the change in used columns, are moved to the next column to the left as a single entry. The second column, the 10s column, is populated by completed sets of the 1s column. The 100s column is likewise populated with completed sets of the 10s column, and so on.

Let's populate the placeholders with values using the decimal number 275 as an example. As indicated by the number itself, there are two populated placeholders in the 100s column, seven in the 10s column, and five in the 1s column. Although this appears obvious because of your familiarity with the decimal counting system, try calculating the number of placeholders required. Again, this is simple because the same counting system is used for the original number and the placeholders. This is intended to illustrate the concept that will be used shortly.

Base 10 Counting System

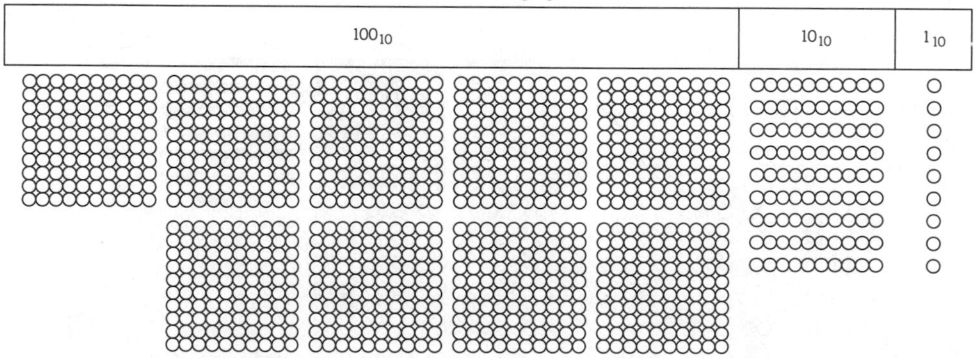

Figure B-1. *Set groupings in the decimal counting system*

The largest column required to hold the current number is the 100s column. Thus, subtract 100 from the number until it will no longer fit. This is possible twice, so two placeholders in the 100s column are populated. Subtract the next placeholder value from the number until that is no longer possible. This is possible seven times, so seven placeholders are populated. Repeating the process for the 1s column yields five populated placeholders.

Now that we have reviewed counting in decimal graphically, let's try the binary system using the same format.

Binary

The binary counting system is based on the numbers 0 and 1. Binary is depicted by writing the number 2 in subscript immediately after the number. For example, the number 1011_2 can be clearly expressed as representing binary in this way.

A single binary digit may represent 0 or 1. If the current number were 1, adding 1 changes the number from a single digit to two digits. Thus, groupings are based on sets of two. A complete set of two is shown by a change in columns, moving one column to the left.

A counting sequence:

0

1

10

11

100

Notice that the column changes for every other increase in the count. Based on this observation, the column values in the binary counting system can be calculated for the decimal equivalent by doubling the number repeatedly. The first column is 1, so the second column is 2, followed by 4, 8, 16, and so on. Writing these doubled numbers in a row and using subtraction and addition as appropriate to make the conversion can create a quick conversion manual calculator. Figure B-3 is a graphical representation of the placeholders represented by each digit in a given number. Because of size limitations, only the first eight grouping increments are depicted. The decimal equivalent of each column value is shown in the lower-left corner.

In Figure B-3, notice how there is a placeholder for only one set in each column. Zero is represented by the lack of a populated placeholder in that column, and the only other value permitted is 1. Populating more than one placeholder in any column is not possible because no placeholder is offered. To increase the number of used placeholders, it is necessary to change columns. All the placeholders, plus the extra placeholder that forced the change in columns, are moved to the next column to the left as a single entry. The second column, the 2s column, is populated by completed sets of the 1s column. The 4s column is likewise populated with completed sets of the 2s column, and so on.

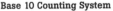

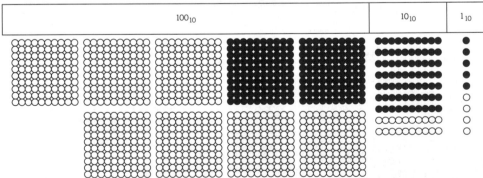

Figure B-2. *The required number of decimal counting system placeholders populated by the decimal number 275*

Base 2 Counting System

10000000_2 128_{10}	1000000_2 64_{10}	100000_2 32_{10}	10000_2 16_{10}	1000_2 8_{10}	100_2 4_{10}	10_2 2_{10}	1_2 1_{10}

Figure B-3. *Set groupings in the binary counting system*

Let's populate the placeholders with values using the decimal number 157 as the example. Deciding which columns should be populated is a little harder when you change numbering systems in the process. We will use the process outlined in the decimal counting system.

The largest column required to hold the current number is the 128s column. Thus, subtract 128 from the number until it will no longer fit. This is possible once, so the 128s column placeholder is populated. The remainder is 29, which is already smaller than the next column to the right and the column after that. Both of those columns then have unpopulated placeholders representing 0. Subtract the next placeholder value from the number until that is no longer possible. This is possible once, so the 16s column placeholder is populated. The remainder is now 13. Repeating the process for the remaining columns results in a placeholder populated in the 8s, 4s, and 1s columns (see Figure B-4).

Most people prefer the decimal counting system because we grew up working in that system. Computers will continue to operate on the binary counting system until quantum physics finds a way to cheaply build computers that can store more than *on* or *off* in a single location. Trying to count in binary or to write long strings of binary numbers would be tedious at best, so hexadecimal notation is used to reduce the number of digits required for many computer-related activities.

Hexadecimal

The hexadecimal counting system is based on the numbers 0 through 15. Unfortunately, the numeric representation of 15 in decimal requires numbers in two columns, and those values all represent values in only a single hexadecimal column. For numbers larger than 9, the alphabetic characters of A through F are used so that only a single "digit" is present as a placeholder. Hexadecimal is depicted by writing the number 16 in subscript immediately after the number. For example, the number $6D_{16}$ can be clearly expressed as representing hexadecimal in this way.

Note: *Because a lot of typed discussion occurs where simple ASCII text does not permit subscripting, hexadecimal is also often indicated with this format: 0x6D.*

Base 2 Counting System

10000000_2 128_{10}	1000000_2 64_{10}	100000_2 32_{10}	10000_2 16_{10}	1000_2 8_{10}	100_2 4_{10}	10_2 2_{10}	1_2 1_{10}

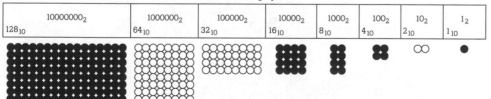

Figure B-4. *The required number of binary counting system placeholders populated by the decimal number 157. The binary equivalent of 157 is therefore 10011101.*

As indicated, a single decimal digit may represent any quantity between O and F. If the current number were F, adding one changes the number from a single digit to two digits. Thus, groupings are based on sets of 16. A complete set of 18 is shown by a change in columns, moving one column to the left.

A counting sequence:

0
1
2
3
4
5
6
7
8
9
A
B
C
D
E
F
10
11
12

Figure B-5 is a graphical representation of the placeholders represented by each digit in a given number. Because of size limitations, only the first three grouping increments are depicted.

The most obvious difference between hexadecimal and either binary or decimal is the quantity of placeholders represented in each column. Until it is represented graphically, the significance of a few extra placeholders per set is not appreciated.

In Figure B-5, notice how there is a placeholder for 15 sets in each column. Zero is represented by a lack of any populated placeholder in that column. Populating more than 15 (F_{16}) placeholders in any column is not possible because no additional placeholders are offered. To increase the number of used placeholders it is necessary to change columns. All the placeholders, plus the placeholder that forced the change in used

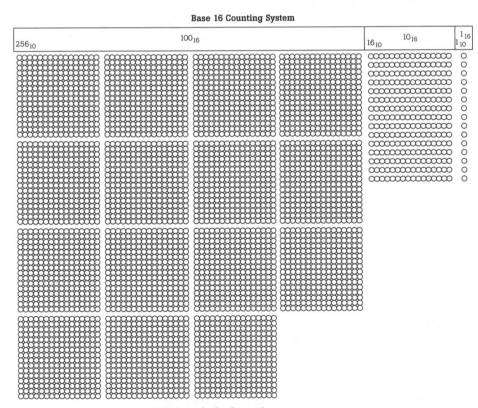

Base 16 Counting System

Figure B-5. *Set groupings in the hexadecimal counting system*

columns, are moved to the next column to the left as a single entry. The second column, the 16s column, is populated by completed sets of the 1s column. The 256s column is likewise populated with completed sets of the 16s column, and so on.

Let's populate the placeholders with values using the decimal number 157 as the example again. Deciding which columns should be populated is somewhat difficult because we are once more changing counting systems in the process. We will repeat the process outlined in the decimal counting system again.

The largest column required to hold the current number is the 16s column because the number is less than the number of placeholders in the 256s column. Thus, subtract 16 from the number until it will no longer fit. This is possible nine times, so nine placeholders are populated in the 16s column. The remainder is 13. The next column is the 1s column and the entire remainder is used to populate placeholders as shown in Figure B-6.

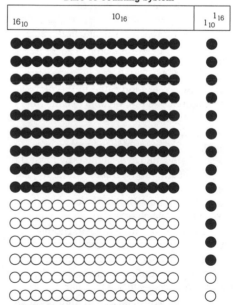

Base 16 Counting System

Figure B-6. *The required number of hexadecimal counting system placeholders populated by the decimal number 157. The binary equivalent of 157_{10} is 10011101_2 and is therefore $9D_{16}$ in hexadecimal.*

That is a fast tour through counting systems, so let's look at Table B-1 to help conversions. First, be aware that computer-related use of hexadecimal numbers is virtually always done to represent *octets*, or groups of eight binary digits. That means you will virtually never use the 256s column with hexadecimal conversions. Here is almost everything you will need in one table.

Table B-1. *Conversion among hexadecimal, decimal, and binary counting syst*

Hexadecimal	Decimal	Binary	4–Digit Binary
0	0	0	0000
1	1	1	0001
2	2	10	0010
3	3	11	0011
4	4	100	0100
5	5	101	0101
6	6	110	0110
7	7	111	0111
8	8	1000	1000
9	9	1001	1001
A	10	1010	1010
B	11	1011	1011
C	12	1100	1100
D	13	1101	1101
E	14	1110	1110
F	15	1111	1111

Also, compare at the calculation performed to obtain the binary conversion and the hexadecimal conversion in their respective sections earlier. Notice especially that the left four binary digits convert to a hexadecimal nine, and the right four binary digits convert to a hexadecimal D. This is always true: The left group of four binary digits converts to one hexadecimal number and the right to another. Thus, you have to memorize only how to convert the 1s column of hexadecimal. To simplify memorization, Table B-1 shows a fourth column that has leading zeros included for a total of four binary digits. That is how you usually see the binary when you are converting. After a surprisingly small number of calculations, converting between binary and hexadecimal becomes quite easy.

OSI Seven-Layer Model

Most things related to networking are best understood when aligned with or compared to the Open Systems Interconnection (OSI) model for network communications. The OSI seven-layer basic reference model was created by the International Organization for Standardization (ISO) as standard ISO/IEC 7498 (see Table B-2). At the time of its creation, the various networking protocols available were proprietary and offered little or no interoperability. The OSI seven-layer model has since become the most common reference point used when discussing network protocols, features, and hardware. For a complete description of each layer in the OSI seven-layer model, see ISO/IEC 7498-1 or ITU-T X.200.

Table B-2. *Simple OSI seven-layer model description*

Layer	Name	Purpose
7	Application	Provides interface with network users
6	Presentation	Performs format and code conversion
5	Session	Manages connections for application programs
4	Transport	Ensures error-free, end-to-end delivery
3	Network	Handles internetwork addressing and routing
2	Data Link	Performs local addressing and error detection
1	Physical	Includes physical signaling and interfaces

To aid in understanding various concepts and relationships, the following chart is offered (see Figure B-7). As much information as possible has been condensed into this chart to provide a visual reference. This basic information should become second nature to any networking professional for that person to be effective.

Each layer (except the Physical Layer) relies on the next lower layer to provide services as specified, but to perform these services in a manner transparent to the next higher layer. Imagine a higher layer opening a trap door and dropping a request in the form of a package with a note attached into a dark hole. The higher layer neither knows nor cares how the needed services are accomplished, only that if it waits at the trap door long enough a response usually appears.

As Figure B-8 shows, each layer adds a bit of header information as it handles the request from the next higher layer. The added information is intended for the corresponding layer in the receiving station, and is removed by that layer before the data payload is handed to the next higher layer over there. Almost everything received from, or handed to, the next higher layer is considered to be part of the data payload, and holds no special meaning to the current layer. As mentioned before, there is some interaction between adjacent layers, but most of the information is typically intended for the corresponding layer in the receiving station.

Even in the simplified conceptual depiction shown in Figure B-8, it should be evident that a small request from the user grows in size because each layer adds a little handling information to the request. Each layer adds the same amount of overhead to the message, whether it is large or small. The efficiency of a network is not very good for small frames but improves considerably as the message approaches the maximum size.

OSI Layers 5–7 tend to be interested in handling the request, whereas Layers 4 and below are more interested in delivering the request across the network. Not indicated in the graphic is the fact that each higher layer is usually able to work with a larger portion of a given request. The higher layer parcels out pieces of a request to the lower layer, and reassembles the pieces upon reception. The Data Link Layer is the only layer that places both a header and a trailer on the request, effectively framing it. The header includes addressing information for proper delivery, and the trailer holds error-checking information to ensure that the request arrived undamaged. Higher layers include error-checking information in the header. The Physical Layer takes the binary string that results from the framed request from the Data Link Layer and encodes it for transmission on the specified medium. The specified medium may be expecting light pulses, rising and falling electrical voltages, or radio waves.

OSI Layers

Gateway	7	Application		
	6	Presentation		
	5	Session		
	4	Transport		
Router	3	Network		
Bridge	2	Data Link	(a) LLC	
			(b) MAC	802.3 Ethernet / 802.11 Wireless / Other
Repeater	1	Physical	(c)	
		Medium	(d)	

(a) Logical Link Control Sublayer

(b) Media Access Control Sublayer

(c) Signal Encoding and Interface to Medium

(d) Medium (Cable and Connectors)

Figure B-7. *OSI seven-layer model compared to various interconnect device functions and media access protocols*

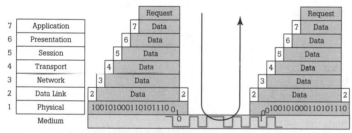

Figure B-8. *Conceptual view of the layering process associated with the OSI Model*

For the receiving station to decode the request it must be using the same encoding scheme and the same medium, which is obvious. Not so obvious is the fact that Ethernet uses signaling from one scheme to communicate link partner capabilities before potentially switching to another encoding scheme. The 10BASE-T link pulse has been adapted for use in Auto-Negotiation between link partners on twisted-pair cable. By transmitting coded groups of link pulses, the two link partners negotiate which is the fastest encoding scheme that both can support. Then they switch to that scheme and proceed.

After linking at the same speed and using the same encoding scheme, the two link partners are ready to service the user's requests. This is accomplished using the process described earlier and shown in Figure B-8.

To decode a received request, each header includes a code that lets the next higher layer know how to decode the request. For example, in the Ethernet header is a field called Length/Type. If the value in that field is at least 0600_{16}, the data payload is interpreted according to the indicated EtherType. An old partial list of EtherType codes is found in RFC 1700. A current complete list is found on the IANA web site (www.iana.org/protocols/). In the header for Layer 3 is another protocol code, and so on.

If someone were to hand-decode a single frame, they would need to manually repeat this process of identifying which code is in the header for each layer, and finding the instructions for how to decode the protocol indicated by that code. In a computer, the user installs software drivers for the particular software they are using. The driver software is customized with the encoding and decoding instructions for a limited set of protocols. If the received frame is not one of those known protocols, the frame is discarded by the first layer that cannot decode it.

Signaling and Encoding Methods

There are a considerable number of encoding and signaling schemes used for networking protocols. The intent of a signaling scheme is to convey information across a given medium at the highest possible density, with the lowest acceptable error rate and cost.

Because computers operate in binary, the signaling scheme will be representing binary information. Electrically, this can be described as *on* or *off* in the simplest terms. For an electrical signal to convey an alternating series of 1s and 0s, varying the voltage over time might produce the following signal.

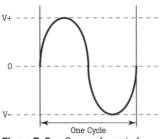

Figure B-9. *One cycle period. This timing interval is also used as the basis for one bit period with a number of networking protocols.*

Signals are often described by their frequency, or how many cycles per second they have. One cycle is shown in Figure B-9. In a complete cycle, the signal rises to the highest point, descends past the starting point to the lowest point, and returns to the starting point. This timing interval is described as one cycle period.

For most of the slower signaling schemes used in networking, one cycle also represents the time duration or interval for one bit period. For a few signaling schemes, the signal is held at a constant voltage for the duration of one period, and then changes to the next voltage between periods if necessary. In Figure B-10, the signal remains at the same voltage for however many cycle periods are required to transmit the binary values.

Figure B-10. *Simple signaling technique where zero volts equals a binary 0 and V+ equals a binary 1. This technique is known as NRZ (Non-Return to Zero).*

This form of signaling would be quite adequate for any networking need, except that electrical behavior and the laws of physics start interfering. A variety of problems are associated with transmitting signals. One obvious problem is that the interface components must be able to turn on and off or to transition fast enough to represent the signal. At lower speeds, this is not a problem. Another problem is that as the frequency of the signal (the number of cycles per second) increases, the maximum distance from the transmitter that they can be reliably recovered decreases. Yet a third problem is that if the signal were to represent a single binary value for a length of time, say a long string of 1s, the interface electronics in the receiver sometimes begins to lose track of what voltage it is seeing. This is called *baseline wander*. In fiber optic cables, the signals tend to spread out over distance due to the way they reflect down the fiber, so that high-frequency pulses start blurring together. A fourth problem is how to synchronize the clock at both ends of a link so that the signal is sampled at the right times to allow reliable recovery of the data.

This suggests that two issues need to be addressed at the same time. First, methods for reducing the frequency are very helpful in increasing the maximum transmission distance (and usually the amount of information contained in a single cycle at the same time). Second, transitions must occur regularly enough to establish and maintain clock synchronization (and avoid baseline wander).

In Figure B-10, the signaling is called *level sensitive*. As long as the signal remained at V+ it was sampled as a binary 1. When it was sampled at zero volts, it was a binary 0. Another way that signals are often sampled is on an edge. If the signal is rising or falling at the moment it is sampled, it is interpreted according to the edge direction or the mere presence of an edge. For example, a rising edge might indicate a binary 1. This system requires very good clocking and extremely small amounts of variation in the signal timing. If a transition takes place, but not at the exact moment when the signal is sampled, it will not produce the desired result. Variations in the timing, usually seen as oscillations between slightly too soon and slightly too late, are called *jitter* (see Figure B-11).

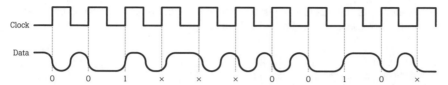

Figure B-11. *Illustration of how signal jitter causes inaccurate sampling of the data. X indicates a failure to properly sample the edge-sensitive signal.*

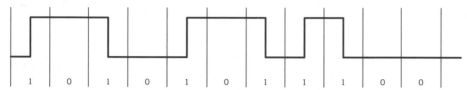

Figure B-12. *Encoding example where a transition in the center of the timing window represents a binary 1, and the absence of a transition indicates a binary 0. This technique is known as NRZI (Non-Return to Zero, Inverting on ones).*

As suggested, other systems rely on the presence or absence of an edge transition, instead of the direction the signal is headed during the transition (see Figure B-12).

The next example shows the signaling system used for Fast Ethernet, called Multi-Level Transmit–3 levels (MLT-3), which only transitions the signal for a binary 1 but uses +1, 0, and −1 volts for signaling. Each transition carries only the signal half of the peak-to-peak distance (see Figure B-13). This system allows for the highest information density so far for a single cycle. If four consecutive 1s were transmitted, it would occupy only a single cycle.

Many other and more complex signaling systems exist. However, this is adequate for a simple overview of the process and some of the reasons for encoding the signal differently.

Module 2: Decoding a Waveform into Ethernet

This module was created after capturing a single small Ethernet frame with a digital storage oscilloscope. The steps described in the module utilize knowledge of binary and hexadecimal, and the encoding used by 10 Mbps Ethernet (Manchester encoding) to convert the waveform into binary, and from there divide and convert the binary back into Ethernet fields that may be decoded.

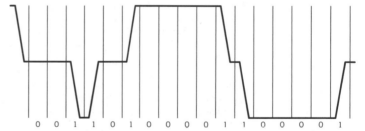

Figure B-13. *Encoding example where a transition in the center of the timing window represents a binary 1 and the absence of a transition indicates a binary 0. However, each transition travels only half the distance between the highest level and the lowest. This technique is known as MLT-3.*

10Mbps Transmission Process

First, a quick description of the process used by the 10Mbps versions of Ethernet to transmit a frame is provided. The fields present in a simple 802.3 Ethernet frame are shown in Figure B-14. The number below each field name represents the number of octets that are used by that field.

Preamble 8	Destination 6	Source 6	Type 2	Data	Pad 46 to 1500	FCS 4

Figure B-14. *Basic 802.3 Ethernet frame fields*

If sample data were shown for the first few fields in a frame, it might appear as follows. Each field is delineated above sample hexadecimal data for that field, and appears as it might be seen at the MAC Layer.

```
|        Preamble        |  SFD  |   Destination          |    Source     |  Length/Type | ...
55 55 55 55 55 55 55       D5     00 C0 17 A0 02 35 00 80 20 56 33 D4    08 06          ...
```

Using the hexadecimal to binary conversion process described in Module 1 of this exercise, the hexadecimal data for the first two fields in the Ethernet frame are converted to binary.

```
|                                           Preamble                           |    SFD    |
 01010101   01010101   01010101   01010101   01010101   01010101   01010101   11010101 ...
```

To transmit the frame, it must be passed from the MAC Layer to the Physical Layer. Ethernet encoding rules specify that each octet is transferred least-significant bit (LSB) first from the MAC Layer to the Physical Layer, so the bits are reordered on a per-octet basis (see Figure B-15). The FCS field is not reordered.

Before Reordering: MSB b_7 b_6 b_5 b_4 b_3 b_2 b_1 b_0 LSB

After Reordering: LSB b_0 b_1 b_2 b_3 b_4 b_5 b_6 b_7 MSB

Figure B-15. *Ethernet requires that each octet be transferred least-significant bit (LSB) first, so the order is reversed*

Conceptually, this is easiest to grasp as simply turning each octet over as shown in Figure B-16. The change is most identifiable in the Start of Frame Delimiter (SFD) octet.

Manchester encoding relies on the direction of the edge transition in the *middle* of the timing window to determine the binary value for that bit period.

In the encoding example in Figure B-17, there is one timing window highlighted vertically through all four waveform examples and labeled as *one bit period*. The top waveform has a falling edge in the center of the timing window, so it is interpreted as a binary 0.

Depending on how you view it, the second waveform is 180 degrees out of phase, or it is shifted half of one bit period to the side. It is otherwise identical. The result is that in the center

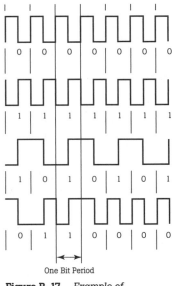

Figure B-17. *Example of Manchester encoding*

of the timing window for the second waveform there is a rising edge, which is interpreted as a binary 1. Thus, to discern the difference between a binary 0 and a binary 1, you must know where the timing window begins.

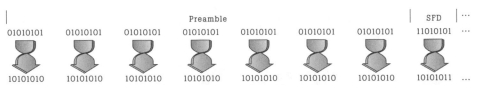

Figure B-16. *LSB-ordered octets received from the MAC Layer are serialized from left to right utilizing the Manchester encoding rules and transmitted on the appropriate medium*

Instead of a repeating sequence of the same binary value in the third waveform example, there is an alternating binary sequence. In the first two examples, the signal must transition back between each bit period so that it can make the same-direction transition each time in the center of the timing window. With alternating binary data, there is no need to return to the previous voltage level in preparation for the next edge in the center of the timing window. Thus, any time there is a long separation between one edge and the next, you can be certain that *both edges represent the middle of a timing window*. This will be a very useful tip later.

The fourth waveform example is random data that allows us to verify that whenever there is a wide separation between two transitions, both edges are in the center of a timing window and represent the binary value for that timing window.

After encoding the binary into Manchester, the Physical Layer transmits the resulting signal onto the attached medium (see Figure B-18).

Decoding the Waveform

Now that the basic process has been described, take out the lab sheet bearing the undecoded waveform. You will apply the knowledge about binary, hexadecimal, and Manchester encoding that has just been reviewed.

Step 1

Locate the boundaries of the timing windows. On your lab sheet there are light vertical timing marks placed appropriately. Compare the locations of those timing marks with the Manchester encoding examples shown in Figure B-17 and the section of decoded waveform in Figure B-18. Study the waveform and the examples until you feel that you could correctly annotate another sheet that did not have those timing marks. Remember the tip given earlier: Whenever there are widely spaced edges in the waveform, both edges (rising and falling) represent the center of a timing window. It is not possible to locate the timing boundaries in areas where the waveform has closely spaced edges without this tip or some other form of assistance. In those areas there is a consecutive pattern of the same binary value, but you will have to look forward or backward along the waveform to find a widely spaced edge to determine which it is.

Step 2

This step is possible only after you have found and marked some of the timing window boundaries. Using a pencil (almost everyone makes mistakes), mark the direction of the edge in the center of the timing window as shown in Figure B-19. After a short time, lean back and look at the spacing of the arrows you are using to mark the direction of the edge. Notice that despite how the waveform has narrow and widely spaced sections, your arrows are all evenly spaced.

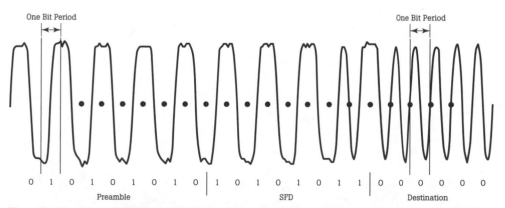

Figure B-18. *Actual 10BASE5 signal decoded. In two locations vertical lines were drawn to clearly delineate timing windows. In the center of both marked timing windows is an edge transition. Dots have been added at the boundaries of other timing windows to aid in decoding the binary data. The decoded binary is shown below the waveform along with the Ethernet field boundaries as appropriate.*

Step 3

Go back and write the binary value below each arrow as shown in Figure B-19, but only after you have marked some distance of waveform in that manner. Do not mark the binary values as you go because you will make mistakes if you are not watching the waveform closely.

Step 4

Look for the Start of Frame Delimiter (SFD), which appears at the end of the initial stretch of widely spaced waveform edges. There will be a change in the pattern, and you should have decoded a binary 11_2 right where the waveform pattern changed. Draw a vertical line through the waveform along the timing mark immediately to the right of the binary 11_2 pattern and before the next timing window. That line separates the end of the SFD from the beginning of the destination address. Count back to the left eight bits and draw another vertical line on the left clocking line for the eighth bit. That line marks the beginning of

the SFD (includes the binary 11_2) and the beginning of the previous Preamble field. Refer to Figure B-14 to obtain the number of octets required for each Ethernet field. For example, the SFD in Figure B-14 is shown with the number 1 below it. That indicates one octet, or eight binary bits. Count bits as indicated in Figure B-14, and mark off octet boundaries and Ethernet field boundaries until you have drawn small vertical lines between each octet and large vertical lines between each of the Ethernet fields leading up to the Data field.

Step 5

Convert the binary back to hexadecimal. Remember that the MAC Layer reordered the bits before handing them to the Physical Layer. You have to reverse that before converting back to binary. Most people perform the conversion incorrectly the first time. See Figure B-20 for a quick review of how the reordering occurs. Unlike the example in Figure B-20, you will not be converting the hexadecimal into ASCII.

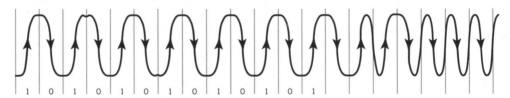

Figure B-19. *Appearance of the waveform after step 2 and during step 3*

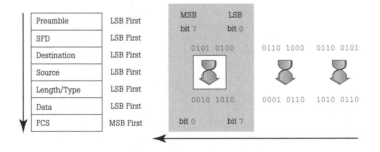

Figure B-20. *Reordering example (LSB first). In the example, the word "The" is converted from the appropriate ASCII hexadecimal codes into binary. The binary (shown above) is then LSB reordered before passing the binary from the Media Access Control Layer to the Physical Layer Ethernet implementation for transmission.*

Step 6

Identify the Layer 3 protocol contained in the Length/Type field. This step is performed after all the Ethernet header information has been marked into the correct fields and converted back into hexadecimal. If the conversion was not done correctly, the next operation will result in the wrong answer for Module 3.

- If the value in the Length/Type field is less than 0600_{16} (1536 in decimal), in most cases the contents of the Data field are decoded per the 802.2 protocol. If the value is less than 0600_{16}, the field indicates Length.

- If the value in the Length/Type field is equal to or greater than 0600_{16} (1536 in decimal), in most cases the contents of the Data field are decoded per the Ethernet II protocol. If the value is equal to or greater than 0600_{16}, the field indicates Type.

If your Length/Type field indicated a Type, you can look up the value in a table to learn which protocol is next in the Data field.

Module 3: Using Standards Documents and RFCs

In this module, knowledge from the 802.3 Ethernet standard is used to "read" the OSI Layer 2 data from the waveform. Using the value found in the Ethernet Length/Type field, the process for locating and reading RFCs must be mastered to decode and "read" Layer 3 of the waveform.

Standards and RFCs

There are two processes in use for determining the structure and specifications of various aspects of networking. One process is to go through the formal standards bodies, which has produced documents such as the 802.3 Ethernet specifications and the ISO/IEC 7498 OSI basic model. These standards and RFC issuing bodies include the Institute of Electrical and Electronics Engineers, Inc. (IEEE), the International Organization for Standardization (ISO), the Internet Engineering Task Force (IETF), and the American National Standards Institute (ANSI).

The IETF publishes the specification documents of the Internet Protocol suite as RFCs, but they can originate from anyone with a good idea. Read RFC 2223 for instructions on how to submit one. The Request for Comments (RFC) documents are now subject to nearly the same level of scrutiny as the other standards before they are published, but they used to be much more casual.

When the RFC process started in 1969, the idea was to put together a good proposal, post it on the fledgling Internet, and wait to see what your peers thought of the idea. After the idea had been vetted in this manner the proposal was either implemented by your peers or not. There was no standards organization behind the proposal to insist that it be done in the prescribed manner, universally across all platforms. That is perhaps the single greatest difference between what is published as a standard and what is published as an RFC. Everyone must comply with the standards, but there is no obligation (except pressure from your customers and your peers) for compliance with an RFC.

As the RFC process becomes more and more structured, and more customers come to rely on the information available through compliance with published RFCs, the difference between being required by the standard and being pressured by your customer is growing narrower. To learn more about the standards development process, read RFC 2026.

RFCs are available from many sites on the Internet. The best site discovered so far for obtaining published RFCs as well as work-in-progress, is probably the RFC Editor site. Start by going to the URL location www.rfc-editor.org.

Download the RFC Index and save it on your local drive. Be aware that it is updated regularly, so your downloaded copy should be replaced periodically.

In the index each entry has some valuable information. Here is a sample entry:

0760 **DoD standard Internet Protocol** J. Postel [Jan-01-1980] (TXT = 81507 bytes) (Obsoletes IEN 123) (Obsoleted by RFC0791) (Updated by RFC0777)

The most important information in the preceding entry is that RFC 760 is now obsolete and the replacement is RFC 791.

Step 7

To proceed with the waveform decoding exercise, search the RFC Index for the phrase *Assigned Numbers.* Make sure you find the RFC number for the latest version of that document, and then download it. There are more current protocol number sources, but for this exercise the RFC is satisfactory.

Step 8

Search through the RFC until you locate the section on *EtherTypes.* Once you have found that section, take the value that you decoded in step 6 of Module 2 and find it in the list.

Step 9

Go back to the RFC Index and search on the protocol name that you found. Be sure to use the full name and not an acronym because the RFC you want will be defining that protocol and usually does not mention the acronym in the title.

Step 10

Download the appropriate RFC for the protocol you have identified. Sometimes it is necessary to check several RFCs for the information you are seeking. If you downloaded the correct RFC, you will find a table or chart that begins with the following in Section 3:

These are the exact field listings for how to interpret the first part of the Data field. This document will guide you through decoding Layer 3 of your waveform. The format shown earlier is common to the RFC documents. The numbers across the top represent bits. 32 bits forms four octets, and you will often see fields aligning on the octet boundaries or 32-bit word boundaries, but not always.

In section 3 of the RFC, the text following the table or chart will provide a definition for how each field is specified and used.

Step 11

Take the information from step 10 and decode Layer 3 in your waveform. The portion of the preceding table corresponds to the 32 bits immediately following the end of the MAC Layer Length/Type field. The information is listed in the order you see it in your waveform. The Version field follows as the next four bits after the Length/Type field.

Step 12

Continue the process described in Module 2 to find and decode the protocol field from Layer 3. This value will be used to find the field definitions for Layer 4. Be careful when you look up the protocol in the Assigned Numbers RFC. Be sure to watch which counting system you are using.

Module 4: Using a Protocol Analyzer

Protocol analyzers are used to view the contents of individual frames taken from the medium, and offer functionality from Layer 2 up through Layer 7. They typically have a variety of built-in summary features that allow the user to see who is talking to whom, over which protocol, and how much.

Protocol analyzers come in two general configurations: software based and hardware based. The software protocol analyzer is usually unable to detect or report on MAC Layer errors effectively because it is relying on a standard network adapter. Software protocol analyzers tend to be somewhat limited in the amount of traffic that can be captured for the same reason. A typical network adapter is not well suited to capturing traffic at line rates because the typical workstation cannot process traffic at those rates. Dropped frames are not reported, and the user is not able to determine when a frame was missed. Hardware-based protocol analyzers usually have some level of integration to the front-end electronics and are able to see some of or all the errors on a link. The level of error detection is often related to the price. Hardware protocol analyzers are much more likely to be able to capture at line rates without dropping frames.

For both categories of protocol analyzer there are usually several software or hardware modules that can be added for a price. These range from support for multiple network access protocols (Ethernet, Frame Relay, Wireless, etc.), to an integrated *expert system* that compares the contents of a captured trace file against libraries of common symptoms related to specific faults or causes. Beyond the built-in or automated test summary functions, the ability to obtain useful information from a protocol analyzer is directly related to the user's knowledge about the inner workings of the protocol in question. Protocol analysis is usually the domain of the senior network support staff for that reason.

Using a protocol analyzer as part of the instructional process greatly enhances the clarity of the topic of discussion. It is one thing to sit back and listen about a particular protocol or process, but it is quite another to take that process apart bit-by-bit at the same time.

The software protocol analyzer used for the examples in this lab is OptiView Protocol Expert. The following is a quick way to begin exploring with a protocol analyzer, without having to learn what all the different functions are.

OptiView Protocol Expert in Five Buttons

This is a five–button quick-start for OptiView Protocol Expert.

The default logins for OptiView Protocol Expert are <acct:guest, pwd:public> and <acct:su, pwd:manager>.

1. Launch the application. Click the **Start** [▶] button, which you will find on the toolbar at the top of the Monitor View pane. One of the buttons looks like this, and causes Protocol Expert to automatically open the Detail View window to begin capturing everything on the NIC selected in the Resource Browser. If multiple network adapters are present, it might be necessary to select one of the available NICs from the Resource Browser first (see Figure B-21). You may also click the **Detail View** [▦] button in the toolbar at the top of the pane (see Figure B-22).

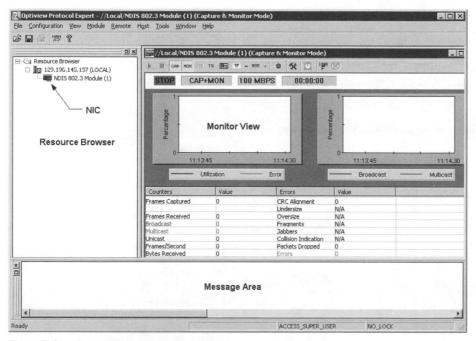

Figure B-21. *Protocol Expert start-up screen*

2. Click the **Stop** [■] button to halt the capture and automatically open the Capture View window. This allows you to see what sort of traffic you have captured so far. You may also click the **Capture View** [▦] button.

3. You are now looking at the four pane screen shown in Figure B-23. The long pane on the left shows the conversation represented by the selected frame on the top right. The top-right pane shows a summary of all the captured frames. The middle pane shows a field-by-field breakdown of the frame highlighted in the top window, and the bottom pane shows the raw, uninterpreted hexadecimal for the highlighted frame.

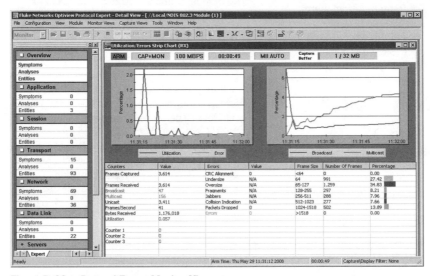

Figure B-22. *Protocol Expert Monitor View*

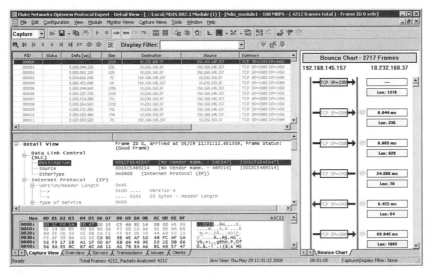

Figure B-23. *Protocol Expert Capture View*

This screen presents a lot of information to absorb on the first visit.

4. Click the **Expert View** button on the toolbar at the top of the screen to have the entire trace file examined for possible problems and warnings.

Congratulations. You have successfully used a protocol analyzer. For further exploration, here is a quick summary of what some of the other tool bar buttons do.

Figure B-24 shows the functionality of all the buttons on the toolbar for the first screen seen after launching the application.

Figure B-25 and Figure B-26 show the functionality of all the buttons on the second screen, which is available after the capture is stopped or the **Capture View** button has been clicked. Try clicking each of these buttons to learn how each of these built-in summary tests operate and how the contents of the capture file may be viewed in different ways.

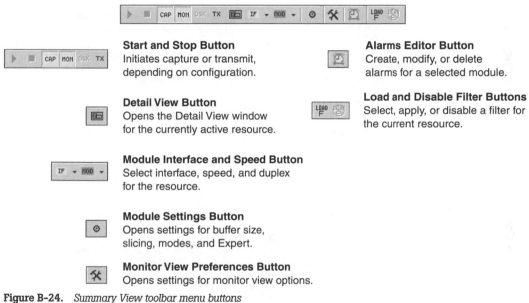

Start and Stop Button
Initiates capture or transmit, depending on configuration.

Detail View Button
Opens the Detail View window for the currently active resource.

Module Interface and Speed Button
Select interface, speed, and duplex for the resource.

Module Settings Button
Opens settings for buffer size, slicing, modes, and Expert.

Monitor View Preferences Button
Opens settings for monitor view options.

Alarms Editor Button
Create, modify, or delete alarms for a selected module.

Load and Disable Filter Buttons
Select, apply, or disable a filter for the current resource.

Figure B-24. *Summary View toolbar menu buttons*

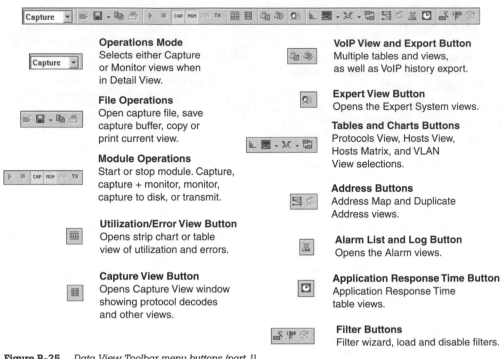

Operations Mode
Selects either Capture or Monitor views when in Detail View.

File Operations
Open capture file, save capture buffer, copy or print current view.

Module Operations
Start or stop module. Capture, capture + monitor, monitor, capture to disk, or transmit.

Utilization/Error View Button
Opens strip chart or table view of utilization and errors.

Capture View Button
Opens Capture View window showing protocol decodes and other views.

VoIP View and Export Button
Multiple tables and views, as well as VoIP history export.

Expert View Button
Opens the Expert System views.

Tables and Charts Buttons
Protocols View, Hosts View, Hosts Matrix, and VLAN View selections.

Address Buttons
Address Map and Duplicate Address views.

Alarm List and Log Button
Opens the Alarm views.

Application Response Time Button
Application Response Time table views.

Filter Buttons
Filter wizard, load and disable filters.

Figure B-25. *Data View Toolbar menu buttons (part 1)*

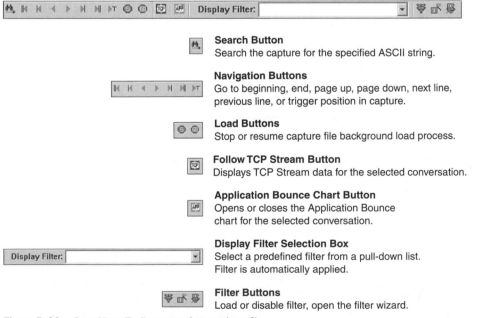

Search Button
Search the capture for the specified ASCII string.

Navigation Buttons
Go to beginning, end, page up, page down, next line, previous line, or trigger position in capture.

Load Buttons
Stop or resume capture file background load process.

Follow TCP Stream Button
Displays TCP Stream data for the selected conversation.

Application Bounce Chart Button
Opens or closes the Application Bounce chart for the selected conversation.

Display Filter Selection Box
Select a predefined filter from a pull-down list. Filter is automatically applied.

Filter Buttons
Load or disable filter, open the filter wizard.

Figure B-26. *Data View Toolbar menu buttons (part 2)*

Protocol Expert Lab

The frame used to create the waveform lab is available from the Fluke Networks web site (www.flukenetworks.com), and may be opened as part of this lab. You can also capture a similar frame from the classroom network.

Step 13

Open the Protocol Expert application. Either open the trace file containing the frame used to create the waveform lab or capture a new trace file.

Step 14

Click the **Capture View** 🖽 button to open the Detail View pane. If you capture a new trace file, look through the trace file for a frame of the same Layer 3 protocol as the Ethernet Length/ Type field indicated at the end of Module 2 and highlight it. Click the middle pane to freeze the top pane on the frame you are interested in. This also allows you to scroll the middle pane. Compare the decoded waveform with the information presented in the middle pane of the Detail View, field by field. Also compare the hexadecimal data from the bottom pane with the hexadecimal that you decoded from the waveform.

Step 15

Compare the information presented in the middle pane with the field descriptions in the RFC you used to decode Layer 3 of the waveform in Module 3. Having first hand-decoded this frame, you should be intimately familiar with the structure and contents of the frame. Comparing this new knowledge against what the protocol analyzer shows you about the same frame usually takes all the fear and mystery about a protocol analyzer.

Congratulations, you now have a very good understanding of what a protocol analyzer does! You should never have to hand-decode another frame—ever.

Please use the protocol analyzer to capture each type of frame discussed in any class or reference reading from this point forward. Compare the captured sample with the training material and the appropriate RFC for a much better understanding of what is presented. The experience you gain from examining the behavior of a protocol using a protocol analyzer places you several years ahead of your competition in the job market. Many networking professionals never master the protocol analyzer.

Note: *Although very infrequent, the center pane on a protocol analyzer (where the decode is presented) is sometimes inaccurate either due to an error or because something in the protocol has changed. Using the RFC or other protocol description document, it is possible to correctly reinterpret a frame or field by comparing the protocol description against the hexadecimal data from the bottom pane.*

APPENDIX C
Auto-Negotiation

This appendix provides a level of detail about the operation of Auto-Negotiation far beyond the concepts presented in Chapter 4, "Media Access Control Layer."

FLP Field Definitions

The following information about various FLP "page" information is very detailed and may be skipped by the casual reader. It is provided to allow the interested reader to learn more about what is actually negotiated, as a way of understanding more clearly what Auto-Negotiation is used for. References to an FLP burst indicate either a 16-bit or 48-bit Link Codeword exchange transmitted at the appropriate timing interval. The interval does not change when a 48-bit Link Codeword is exchanged instead of a 16-bit Link Codeword—instead, more of the interval is used for transmission.

Base Page

The Base Page is encoded with the fields shown in Figure C-1. The first five data bits represent the Selector field. The next seven data bits define the link partner's technology abilities, the next bit indicates whether the link partner supports the Extended Next Page function, and the last three bits are for signaling Remote Fault, acknowledging receipt of a page, and offering Next Page information.

D0	D1	D2	D3	D4	D5	D6	D7	D8	D9	D10	D11	D12	D13	D14	D15
S0	S1	S2	S3	S4	A0	A1	A2	A3	A4	A5	A6	XNP	RF	Ack	NP

Selector Field | Technology Ability Field

Figure C-1. *Base Page fields*

Selector Field

The Selector field for Ethernet is a fixed value of 00001 in binary. Note that the bit order is reversed in the FLP burst in accordance with the required LSB encoding for Ethernet (see Table C-1).

Table C-1. *Selector field coding options*

S4	S3	S2	S1	S0	Interpretation
0	0	0	0	0	Reserved
0	0	0	0	1	IEEE 802.3 Ethernet
0	0	0	1	0	IEEE 802.9 ISLAN-16T
0	0	0	1	1	IEEE 802.5 Token Ring
0	0	1	0	0	IEEE 1349
0	0	1	0	1	INCITS (FC-BASE-T)
1	1	1	1	1	Reserved

Technology Field

The Base Page Technology field encodes the link partner capabilities shown in Table C-2. Notice that the Base Page does not permit negotiating to 100BASE-T2 or speeds higher than 100Mbps. The link partners must exchange Next Page or Extended Next Page information to agree to operate at 1 Gigabit or 10 Gigabit speeds.

Table C-2. *Base Page Technology field definitions*

Bit	Interpretation
A0	10BASE-T half duplex
A1	10BASE-T full duplex
A2	100BASE-TX half duplex
A3	100BASE-TX full duplex
A4	100BASE-T4
A5	PAUSE operation for full-duplex links
A6	Asymmetric PAUSE operation for full-duplex links

The various Ethernet implementations listed in the Technology field are offered by setting the corresponding bit position to a binary 1.

Pause

The Pause function is available only for full-duplex configurations. A station operating in full duplex seeking to inhibit another station from sending it frames for a short period of time may transmit a Pause frame to its link partner. The Pause frame is a defined MAC Control frame addressed to MAC destination 01:80:C2:00:00:01 (or the link partner's true MAC address) and bearing a Length/Type field code of 8808 in hexadecimal. This frame is defined for use by the MAC Control Layer, and represents a multicast destination MAC address that has been reserved for use with Pause frames. Use of the Pause function is limited to the point-to-point full-duplex link on which it was transmitted.

Included in a Pause request is a time variable between 0 and 65,535 measured in 512 bit-time increments. The receiving link partner will suspend transmission until the time specified has passed.

If a link partner requested a long Pause period but becomes able to receive frames again sooner than specified, it may send a new Pause frame with a shorter or zero waiting period value. A timer value of zero indicates immediate resumption of transmissions. Any new Pause frame transmitted overrides previous Pause instructions in effect.

There may be a short delay before the Pause period is initiated. For Ethernet implementations of 100Mbps or less, the receiving station has approximately the same time increment as the requested Pause period before it must initiate the Pause period. A Gigabit receiving station has twice the requested time increment to begin the requested Pause period. At 10 Gigabit, the receiving station has 60 increments of the requested Pause period to initiate the pause. The Pause period also has a maximum interval, which is specified differently depending on the Ethernet speed implemented.

Asymmetric Pause

Pause is supported asymmetrically such that transmit and receive paths may be paused independently or symmetrically. Pause is supported only in full duplex.

Extended Next Page (XNP)

The Extended Next Page option was added at the same time as 10 Gigabit Ethernet. The duration of time required to negotiate the link parameters using multiple FLP exchanges didn't make sense when the signal encoding was so much faster.

If a link partner is willing and able to support Next Pages, it sets the XNP bit to binary 1. If both link partners indicate that they are XNP capable,

48-bit FLP Link Codewords will be exchanged after the Base Page. If both link partners indicate NP capability but only one link partner indicates the capability to use XNP, 16-bit FLP Link Codewords will follow. This ability is optional.

The XNP bit position (D12) in the Base Page is interpreted as an eighth technology ability bit if the Selector field decodes to 802.5 Token Ring.

Remote Fault (RF)

A station may signal detection of a fault condition by setting the remote fault bit to binary 1. It may also signal a local fault by first setting the remote fault bit to 1 and then restarting Auto-Negotiation. Further information about the detected fault may be communicated using Next Pages.

Acknowledge (Ack)

After a link partner has received at least three consecutive and consistent FLP bursts, that partner shall set the Acknowledge bit in its own FLP Burst to binary 1. The first link partner is not permitted to save a received Link Codeword until it sees the Acknowledge bit set in the received FLPs, indicating that the second link partner has properly received the first station's FLP bursts. This process is repeated with each successive optional Next Page. The last FLP burst that is acknowledged should be transmitted six to eight times before concluding the negotiation.

Next Page (NP)

If a link partner is willing and able to support Next Pages, it sets the Next Page bit to binary 1. Setting the Next Page bit to 0 notifies the link partner that no further link pages are available or that the Next Page capability is not supported. This capability is optional.

Next Page exchanges permit additional configuration parameters to be exchanged during Auto-Negotiation. Actually, the information communicated in a Next Page does not appear to be limited, and offers a very open platform for developers. If Next Pages are exchanged, the Ack2 bit is used to inform the second link partner that the first link partner is able to act on the information contained therein.

Message Pages

Message Pages contain 11 bits of predefined codes and two additional status bits (see Figure C-2). A Message Page precedes Unformatted Pages and indicates what sort of information they contain. This process is similar to how the Ethernet Length/Type field determines how the Data field should be interpreted.

| M0 | M1 | M2 | M3 | M4 | M5 | M6 | M7 | M8 | M9 | M10 | T | Ack 2 | MP | Ack | NP |

Message Code Field

Figure C-2. *16-bit link code word bit assignments for Message Pages*

The first 11 bits of the Message Page are encoded as shown in Table C-3. Only nine codes have been defined at this time, with a very large number being reserved for future expansion. Note that the bit order is reversed in the Message Page link code word.

Table C-3. *Message Page code*

Message Code	Binary	Interpretation
0	00000000000	Reserved.
1	00000000001	Null message.
2	00000000010	One Unformatted Page with Technology Ability field follows.
3	00000000011	Two Unformatted Pages with Technology Ability field follow.
4	00000000100	One Unformatted Page with binary coded Remote Fault follows.
5	00000000101	Organizationally Unique Identifier (OUI) tagged message.
6	00000000110	PHY identifier tag code.
7	00000000111	100BASE-T2 message code. One unformatted Next Page showing 100BASE-T2 ability follow.
8	00000001000	1000BASE-T message code. Two unformatted Next Pages showing 1000BASE-T ability follow.
9	00000001001	10GBASE-T/1000BASE-T message code. Extended Next Page showing 10GBASE-T/1000BASE-T ability follow.
10–2047	00000001001 to 11111111111	Reserved for future use.

MP 1—Null Message Code

Message Page code 1 is used by the first link partner as fill when it has no further Next Page information to exchange but the second link partner is still sending Next Page information.

MP2—Technology Ability Extension Code 1

Message Page code 2 is reserved for extensions to the Technology Ability field but has not been implemented yet. Use of this code informs the receiving link partner that one Unformatted Page follows.

MP3—Technology Ability Extension Code 2

Message Page code 3 is reserved for extensions to the Technology Ability field but has not been implemented yet. Use of this code informs the receiving link partner that two Unformatted Pages follow.

MP4—Remote Fault Number Code

Message Page code 4 is optionally used to provide specific information to the receiving link partner about what sort of fault was detected. If this Message Page is sent, one Unformatted Page follows with one of the following codes:

    0 = Remote Fault Test
    1 = Link Loss
    2 = Jabber
    3 = Parallel Detection Fault

MP5—Organizationally Unique Identifier (OUI) Tag Code

Message Page code 5 indicates that it is followed by four Unformatted Pages (see Table C-4). The first Unformatted Page contains the most significant 11 bits of the manufacturer's Organizationally Unique Identifier (OUI). The MSB of the OUI will be in bit position U10. The second Unformatted Page contains the next most significant bits of the OUI, and the remaining two bits will be in the most significant bits of the third Unformatted Page. Following the last OUI bits will be 8 bits of a user-defined code value specific to the OUI transmitted. The fourth Unformatted Page has 11 bits of user-defined code value.

Table C-4. *OUI tag code Unformatted Page code descriptions*

Unformatted Page 1		Unformatted Page 2		Unformatted Page 3		Unformatted Page 4	
MSB	**LSB**	**MSB**	**LSB**	**MSB**	**LSB**	**MSB**	**LSB**
OUI 23–13		OUI 12–2		OUI 1–0, User 8–0		User 10–0	
U10–0		U10–0		U 10–9, U 8–0		U 10–0	

Table C-5. *PHY identifier tag code Unformatted Page code descriptions*

Unformatted Page 1		Unformatted Page 2		Unformatted Page 3		Unformatted Page 4	
MSB	**LSB**	**MSB**	**LSB**	**MSB**	**LSB**	**MSB**	**LSB**
PHY 2.15–2.5		PHY 2.4–2.0 and 3.15–3.10		PHY 3.9–3.0 and User MSB bit		User 10–0	
U10–0		U10–0		U10–U1, U0		U10–0	

MP6—PHY Identifier Tag Code

Message Page code 6 indicates that it is followed by four Unformatted Pages (see Table C-5). The first Unformatted Page contains the most significant 11 bits of the PHY identifier, bits 2.15 to 2.5. The second Unformatted Page contains the next 11 bits of the PHY identifier, bits 2.4 to 2.0, and bits 3.15 to 3.10. The third Unformatted Page contains the remaining (least significant) bits of the PHY identifier, bits 3.9 to 3.0, and the most significant user code bit. The fourth Unformatted Page contains the remaining user code bits, bits 10 to 0.

MP7—100BASE-T2 Technology Message Code

Message Page code 7 indicates that two Unformatted Pages follow that define the link partner capabilities for the sending 100BASE-T2 station (see Table C-6).

MP8—1000BASE-T Technology Message Code

Message Page code 8 indicates that two Unformatted Pages follow that define the link partner abilities for the sending 1000BASE-T station (see Table C-7). Acknowledge bit 2 is unused with this message.

Table C-6. *100BASE-T2 Technology Ability codes*

Bit	Interpretation of Unformatted Page Bit Positions
Page 1, U0	100BASE-T2 half duplex
Page 1, U1	100BASE-T2 full duplex
Page 1, U2	100BASE-T2 Repeater/DTE (1 = Repeater, 0 = DTE)
Page 1, U3	100BASE-T2 Master/Slave Manual Configuration Enable (1 = Enabled)
Page 1, U4	100BASE-T2 Master/Slave Manual Configuration Value (1 = Master) Ignored if bit U3 = 0
Page 1, U5–U10	Master-Slave Seed bits (U5 = SB0, U10 = SB5)
Page 2, U0–U9	Master-Slave Seed bits (U0 = SB6, U9 = SB15) U10 is unused

Table C-7. *1000BASE-T Technology Ability codes*

Bit	Interpretation of Unformatted Page bit positions
Page 1, U0	1000BASE-T Master/Slave Manual Configuration Enable (1 = Enabled)
Page 1, U1	1000BASE-T Master/Slave Manual Configuration Value (1 = Master) Ignored if bit U3 = 0
Page 1, U2	1000BASE-T multiport/singleport device (1 = multiport)
Page 1, U3	1000BASE-T full duplex
Page 1, U4	1000BASE-T half duplex
Page 1, U5–U10	Reserved
Page 2, U0–U10	Master-Slave Seed bits (U0 = SB0, U10 = SB10)

Toggle Bit (T)

The Toggle bit is used to ensure that both link partners are in synchronization with reference to whether they are finished with the current link control word. After the Base Page, all further Next Pages have a Toggle bit, and the value placed in this field is alternated between 1 and 0 with each successive Next Page. The initial value is 1.

Acknowledge Bit

The Acknowledge bit is used in the same manner as was described for the Base Page.

Message Page Bit (MP)

The Message Page bit is used to distinguish between Message Pages and Unformatted Pages. A binary 1 in the Message Page bit indicates that the current Next Page should be interpreted as a Message Page, and a binary 0 indicates that it is an Unformatted Page.

Acknowledge 2 Bit

The Acknowledge bit is used to inform the link partner that the sending station can or cannot comply with the message. A binary 1 indicates the ability to comply; a binary 0 indicates that the station cannot comply.

Unformatted Pages

Unformatted Pages contain 11 bits of user-defined codes and the same five status bits as a Message Page (see Figure C–3).

The meaning of the 11 Unformatted Bits (U10–U0) is determined by the preceding Message Page code. The five control bits have the same use as described earlier for the corresponding bits in the Message Pages.

Extensions to Auto-Negotiation for 1000BASE-X

[See 803.3 Clause 37]

Auto-Negotiation using /C/ ordered sets instead of FLP bursts is defined by Clause 37. Because this definition is intended for synchronous protocols, usually over fiber optic implementations, there are a few peculiarities that make it distinct from the FLP Burst Auto-Negotiation.

The Base Page has several unassigned (reserved) bit locations, and these are always set to binary 0 (see Figure C–4). The general process is essentially the same for using /C/ ordered sets instead of FLP bursts. In fact, the Next Page definitions are the same (see Figure C–2 and Figure C–3).

Reserved Bits

Bit positions D0:D4 and D9:D11 are reserved at this time and should be set to zero.

FD and HD

If either (or both) of the FD and HD bits are set to binary 1, the sending station is offering the indicated technology capability. If a bit is set to binary 0, the technology capability is not offered. Full duplex has a higher priority.

D1	D2	D3	D4	D5	D6	D7	D8	D9	D10	D11	D12	D13	D14	D15	D16
U0	U1	U2	U3	U4	U5	U6	U7	U8	U9	U10	T	Ack 2	MP	Ack	NP

Unformatted Code Field

Figure C-3. *16-bit link code word bit assignments for Unformatted Pages*

D0	D1	D2	D3	D4	D5	D6	D7	D8	D9	D10	D11	D12	D13	D14	D15
					FD	HD	PS1	PS2				RF1	RF2	Ack	NP

Config_Reg Base Page Encoding

Figure C-4. *Auto-Negotiation Base Page when using /C/ ordered sets*

Pause (PS1 and PS2)

The two Pause bits are used together to indicate whether the sending station is able to support the Pause function, and whether Pause is supported asymmetrically such that transmit and receive paths may be paused independently or symmetrically (see Table C-8). Pause is supported only in full duplex.

Table C-8. *Pause ability coding options*

PS1	PS2	Interpretation
0	0	Pause is not supported
0	1	Asymmetric Pause toward link partner
1	0	Symmetric Pause
1	1	Both symmetric and asymmetric Pause supported

The standard offers a matrix to determine priority when multiple Pause configurations are offered.

Remote Fault (RF1 and RF2)

A station may signal detection of a fault condition by setting the remote fault bits as shown in Table C-9. It may also signal a local fault by first setting the remote fault bits and then restarting Auto-Negotiation. Further information about the detected fault may be communicated using Next Pages.

Table C-9. *Remote Fault coding options*

RF1	RF2	Interpretation
0	0	No Error
0	1	Station Offline
1	0	Link Failure
1	1	Auto-Negotiation Failure

A station might want to signal that it is going offline with the Remote Fault signal. If it does so, it is not necessary to complete a new Auto-Negotiation sequence. Link failure usually denotes loss of synchronization. Auto-Negotiation failure indicates that the link partner is unable to successfully complete the Auto-Negotiation sequence and cannot then link.

A station may optionally send Next Page information describing the fault more accurately.

Acknowledge and Next Page

Acknowledge and Next Page both are used the same as in a Base Page FLP.

Extensions to Auto-Negotiation for 10GBASE-T

[See 802.3 Clause 55.6.1]
Devices capable of 10GBASE-T are required to provide support for extended Next Pages. The format of the resulting extended Next Page Message Page is shown in Figure C-5.

Next Page Message Code (M0:M10)

The Message Code for 10GBASE-T is binary 00000001001. Refer to Table C-3 for a complete list of Message Code field values.

Flag Fields

The Flag fields are described earlier in this chapter under the Message Page section.

Master-Slave Seed Bits (U0:U10)

The seed bits are used as part of the Master-Slave resolution algorithm. If the other algorithm factors match, the link partner with the higher value for the seed bits becomes the Master. If the seed values are identical, this cycle of Auto-Negotiation fails and a new cycle will be initiated.

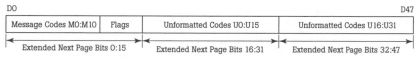

Figure C-5. *Extended Next Page format for a Message Page*

10GBASE-T Master-Slave Manual Config Enable (U11)

This bit is set to binary 1 if the Master–Slave configuration is to be set manually. The specific configuration of Master or Slave is then controlled by bit U12.

10GBASE-T Master-Slave Manual Config Value (U12)

This bit is ignored if bit U11 is set to 0. Master is configured by setting this bit to binary 1. Slave is configured by setting this bit to binary 0.

Port Type (U13)

The port type bit is used as part of the Master-Slave resolution algorithm. A multiport device has higher priority for being selected as Master than a single–port device. Port Type is configured for multiport by setting this bit to binary 1. Port Type is configured for single–port by setting this bit to binary 0.

1000BASE-T Full Duplex (U14)

If the link partner wants to offer the capability of configuring for 1000BASE-T full duplex, this bit is set to binary 1. If this bit is set to binary 0, this capability is not offered.

1000BASE-T Half Duplex (U15)

If the link partner wants to offer the capability of configuring for 1000BASE-T half duplex, this bit is set to binary 1. If this bit is set to binary 0, this capability is not offered.

10GBASE-T (U16)

If the link partner wants to advertise the capability of configuring for 10GBASE-T, this bit is set to binary 1. If this bit is set to binary 0, this capability is not offered.

LD Loop Timing (U17)

LD loop-timing capability is used as part of the Master–Slave resolution algorithm. If the link partner is capable of deriving clocking from the received signal for use in transmission instead of relying on an internal clock source, this bit is set to binary 1. If this bit is set to binary 0, this capability is not offered.

PHY Short Reach Mode (U18)

Short reach mode is used for cables that are no longer than 30 meters and comply with ISO Class F or Class E_A performance characteristics. The PHY is operating in short reach mode if this bit is set to binary 1. The PHY is operating in normal mode if this bit is set to binary zero.

Reserved (U19)

Bit U19 is reserved.

LD PMA Training Reset Request (U20)

The local device expects the link partner to re-set PMA retraining for each PMA training frame transmitted (every 16,384 symbol periods) if this bit is set to binary 1. The local device expects the link partner to reset PMA retraining continuously during every PMA retraining frame if this bit is set to binary 0.

Reserved (U21:31)

Bits U21:31 are reserved.

APPENDIX D
Discovering Device Behavior

Effective troubleshooting is difficult at best if your knowledge of the expected behavior of your network infrastructure devices is unknown. Knowing how to determine the operating behavior without access to the device console is therefore an important skill. Furthermore, it is a useful skill for verifying that the configuration has been implemented properly by the device. When the network is operating correctly this is rarely a concern, but when it is not operating correctly it is not safe to trust anything (such as theoretical expected behavior, behavior according to the configuration, and behavior reported by a device that might be marginal or failed). This appendix describes how to determine whether a device is operating at OSI Layer 1, 2, or 3.

At What Layer Does This Device Operate?

A popular advertising phrase from the mid-1990s was the collapsed backbone. Instead of constructing your network from a collection of discrete hubs, routers, gateways, and so on, you could collapse the functionality of all those products into one slotted chassis. The chassis backplane served as the network backbone, and allowed all the functionality formerly found in the network as discrete devices to be installed in separate card slots as single-function or multifunction cards or blades. It was somewhat difficult to tell from the front of the chassis what sorts of services were available from a given port for this generation of technology. With the integration of these services into the front-end silicon for each port that became common in the early 2000s, products are now available that offer LAN-to-WAN connectivity through a switch/router/firewall function in a package size comparable to an old four-port hub. Complex routing functions may occur between adjacent switch ports where the data is evaluated in the silicon servicing groups of four or eight ports, and never touches the backplane of the switch.

As a direct result of this integration of services into the silicon for each port, before you can effectively troubleshoot your network you will need to learn where each type of hub and switch found in your network fits in the OSI Model. This sounds absurd, but it is actually important. "Hubs" are available that act as full OSI Layer 2 bridges between each port, some switches perform OSI Layer 7 gateway services, and other switches are halfway to being an OSI Layer 1 repeater.

The wide range of services from infrastructure devices whose label suggests completely different behavior compels the troubleshooting staff to treat every device with caution. It is very annoying to be troubleshooting when

- A collision domain problem on a hub that uplinks to a switch port, only to discover that the presumed bridge was actually forwarding the errors onto the collision domain instead of isolating the collision domain.

- The "hub" you are using to connect a protocol analyzer inline between two devices is actually a bridge, and you are not capturing anything useful.

- The switch port you attached to in order to troubleshoot a broadcast domain problem is actually in a different broadcast domain because of VLAN configurations.

For troubleshooting purposes, always keep the following considerations in mind:

- Repeaters send everything, good and bad, to all ports other than the port it was received on.

- Bridges forward if the destination MAC is on another port, if the destination is unknown, or if the destination is a broadcast (in most cases multicast falls into this category). In this regard, a store-and-forward switch is effectively the same as a multiport bridge.

- Routers must accept the frame (MAC Layer broadcasts or MAC Layer unicast to the router MAC) before it will consider forwarding the frame. Once accepted by the MAC Layer interface on the router, there must be a Layer 3 destination known to the router (or default route enabled) before the frame will be forwarded.

- Switches forward according to bridge rules, but also use three basic techniques once the forwarding decision is made:

  — Cut-through forwards if the destination MAC address indicates it should be forwarded (see bridge rules), and forwards any error that occurs after the destination MAC address.

  — Modified cut-through (fragment free) forwards if the destination MAC address indicates it should be forwarded, but will not forward most errors. A corrupted frame must be larger than 64 octets to be forwarded. The "bad" part of the frame may appear anywhere because the switch will not validate the checksum and learn about the error until the entire frame has been received. If the frame is larger than 64 octets, the switch will have already begun to forward it before it has an opportunity to discover the error.

— Store-and-forward forwards only good frames where the destination MAC address indicates it should be forwarded. The checksum is always tested before forwarding.

• Switches with VLANs configured require a router or routing function to forward between VLANs (broadcast domains).

Test #1: Basic Functionality

Send a variety of traffic patterns through the test device to see how it responds. Use the configuration shown in Figure D-1 and the test frames shown in Table D-1. If the device is capable of different speeds (10/100/1000Mbps, for example), be sure to also try attaching the first tester at one speed and the second tester at a different speed while you rerun the basic functionality tests. Bridging is anticipated between different speeds.

Attach a tester capable of sending the various good and bad frames to the first port, and attach a tester capable of detecting and reporting those same good and bad frames on another port. The

second tester should monitor each port on the device in sequence for each test, and at each speed the port supports.

In Table D-1, boxes marked with a bullet (•) indicate that the traffic reached the monitored port. All except the last row uses MAC addressing and frame size or checksum to determine the device characteristics. The last row relies on having valid MAC and IP addressing for the networks found on both ports of the device being tested.

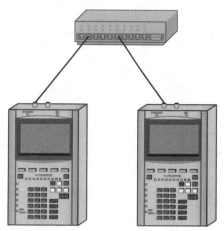

Figure D-1. *Test configuration for classifying an unknown infrastructure device*

Table D-1. *Simple matrix for testing an unknown infrastructure device to determine the most appropriate way to troubleshoot any problems associated with it*

Test Frame	Repeater	Cut-Through Switch	Modified Cut-Through Switch	Bridge	Router	Switch with VLANs
Good Frame to self	•					
Short Frame (< 64) to MAC broadcast	•	•				
Long Frame (> legal size) or FCS-errored frame to MAC broadcast	•	•	•			
Good Frame to MAC broadcast	•	•	•	•		
Good Frame to valid remote subnet destination	•	•	•	•	•	• (if a routed path is present)

Test #2: The Gray Area

Depending on the age of the hardware design, and on which forwarding technique the design was intended to offer, there could be two additional factors to test for:

- If the device being tested exhibits the characteristics of a bridge, check to see what cutoff point it is using for forwarding possibly illegally large frames. Transmit to the MAC broadcast destination address using frame sizes that include the following: 1519 octets, 1523 octets, and 2001 octets. These three sizes are one octet larger than the specified "legal" sizes in 802.3. The exact size that causes the bridge to stop forwarding may be learned by incrementing or decrementing the size by as little as one octet. Record the size where the frame stops passing through the bridging device.

Many newer bridging devices as identified earlier under the Bridge column in Table D-1 will forward at least 1522 octet frames. Oth-

ers forward even larger frames. This behavior allows 802.1Q VLAN-tagged frames to be forwarded even though this device is not participating in the VLAN.

- If the device being tested exhibits either of the two low-latency switch-forwarding techniques, try gradually increasing the quantity of short frames sent per second. If at some point the errors abruptly stop being forwarded, gradually decrease the error level again. They should resume forwarding again at a lower level. This test discovers the threshold setting for an adaptive or error sensing switch that changes to the store-and-forward technique.

Test #3: Find Any Configured VLANs

To discover whether VLANs are configured on devices that bridge, it will be necessary to move the second tester to all other ports while keeping the first tester on the same port. Have the first tester send good frames addressed to the MAC Layer broadcast address. If unreachable ports (probably a VLAN) are discovered, move the first tester to one of the ports that could not be reached, and retest all ports that were unreachable from the first connection. Continue moving the second tester into blocks of unreachable ports until all ports have been mapped.

Changes in diagnostic tool features have made VLAN management much easier. For example, using SNMP it is possible to quickly determine the presence and use of VLAN assignments on a local or remote switch, as shown in Figure D-2.

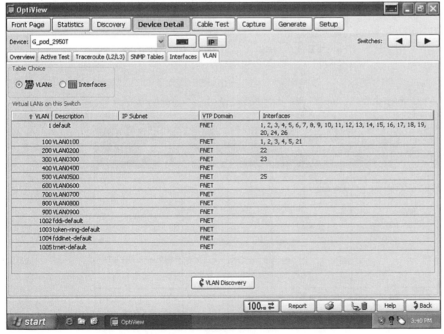

Figure D-2. *OptiView VLAN discovery test results*

How to Use the Test Results

This basic set of tests may be performed during normal operations in most cases. The resulting information is then used to direct any troubleshooting effort in the vicinity of that device as follows.

Collision Domain

For all devices that responded as a repeater, a cut-through switch, or a modified cut-through switch, troubleshoot problems as if all ports might be in the same collision domain.

In Figure D-3, the gray oval represents the collision domain and the clear oval represents the broadcast domain. There are actually four collision domains in this picture, one for each port on the switch.

If the device is capable of different speeds, you might find it necessary to troubleshoot each speed separately because even an inexpensive 10/100 hub is expected to bridge between speeds (see Figure D-4).

In Figure D-5, the potential collision domain is equal to the broadcast domain and both areas are represented by the gray oval. This change is due to the switch forwarding the frame before it is error checked.

Broadcast Domain

For all devices that responded as a bridge, troubleshoot any problems related to them as if each port on the device isolated collision domains but was part of the same broadcast domain. If the bridging device forwarded larger than 1518 octet frames, it will coexist with VLAN-tagged traffic. Many older bridges will not coexist with VLAN-tagged traffic unless they are participating in the VLAN, and you need to know which they are. The newest products will forward 2000 octet frames per the latest 802.3 updates and are compatible with envelope traffic where the forwarding switch is not configured to participate in the additions the envelope represents.

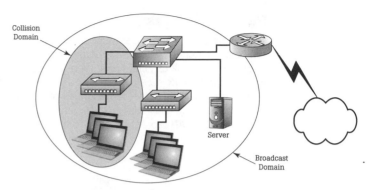

Figure D-3. *Diagram of a collision domain in a Store and Forward switched environment*

Figure D-4. *Logical diagram of a 10/100 hub. There is a collision domain at each speed, with a bridge between speeds. Auto–Negotiation or fixed configuration of the attaching device determines which collision domain it will join.*

10/100 Hub	
Port 1	10 Mbps Collision Domain
Port 2	
Port 3	Bridge
Port 4	
Port n	100 Mbps Collision Domain

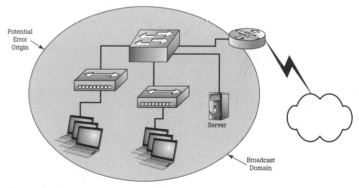

Figure D-5. *Diagram of the potential collision domain in a switched environment where low-latency forwarding is employed*

Different Network

Troubleshoot all devices that responded as a router or as though VLANs were configured as if each port (or block of VLAN ports) were in a different network—they are.

In Figure D-6, each oval represents a separate broadcast domain. For traffic to pass between VLANs, each VLAN would also have to include a router connection.

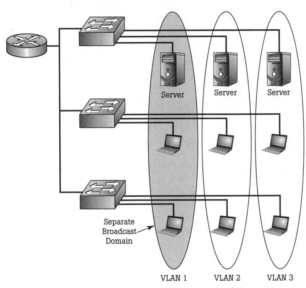

Figure D-6. *Separate broadcast domains created by VLAN configurations*

APPENDIX E
Techniques for Troubleshooting Switches

This appendix provides multiple options for troubleshooting network problems that involve switches. Because there are many different types of switches and many different ways to configure them, the various choices available for troubleshooting switches are accompanied with pros and cons to help determine whether the troubleshooting approach is suitable for the current problem symptoms.

What Problems Are Encountered in Switched Environments?

The problems found in a switched environment are generally the same as those experienced in a shared media environment. What happened, who did it, and how much? The primary difference is that answers need to relate back to a specific port.

Some of the issues that should be considered in a switched environment are

- How busy is each port?
- How do you identify and track the source of errors?
- What is the source of a broadcast storm?
- Are bridge forwarding tables operating correctly?
- Which stations are attached to this port?
- Is the switch rate–limiting any protocols or ports?
- Is this port in a VLAN, and if so, is it the same VLAN as the server or service?

How do you determine where to start looking for a reported problem in a switched network? Typically, it's not the switch that causes the problem but the inability to "see" inside it. This problem begins with the OSI Layer 2 bridging performed by a switch, and is exacerbated by enabling VLANs and other OSI Layer 3 and higher features and forwarding rules. Advanced switching features, such as OSI Layer 4 and higher forwarding and load balancing, require a strong knowledge of the switch configuration options in order to troubleshoot.

By installing a switch, you tend to create a collision domain on each port—that's simply the nature of a switch. If shared media hubs are attached to the port, the collision domain may grow to the maximum size allowed for that Ethernet implementation. Due to the dropping price of switching technology, most new networks have a single station per port, so the collision domain is only a single cable link.

The entire switch tends to be part of a single broadcast domain, including any number of other switches connected in series or in parallel. If OSI

Layer 3 features are enabled then multiple broadcast domains are created, equal to the number of VLANs. At the extreme, and if the switch features permit it, each port could be configured to be a separate broadcast domain. This configuration could reasonably be described as routed to the desktop. By creating a separate broadcast domain for each port, troubleshooting options are limited severely. A separate broadcast domain per port could also require a routing service in the switch to spend considerable CPU resources in forwarding traffic. The network situation where it is appropriate to require routing for every single request and reply is difficult to imagine, and this configuration should be avoided unless a good reason can be found.

A less obvious form of this configuration is common, and is found in networks where the servers are all located within one subnet or broadcast domain and all users are in some number of other subnets or broadcast domains. Virtually all requests must still be routed. With older routers the "cost" of forwarding was additional time, though recent routers do most of the forwarding in silicon instead of software, so the time penalty is greatly diminished. If maintenance activities must be limited to a single server room, consider placing servers in separate VLANs or configure the server interface as a VLAN trunk port. Then place the users that depend upon that server in the same VLAN. This configuration would allow the switch matrix to use OSI Layer 2 bridging for routine traffic, and only unusual or infrequent requests would be routed. If the server supports more than one user community, install additional network adapters in the server or configure VLAN trunking on the server NIC to maintain OSI Layer 2 connectivity to the users.

How Do You Find Which Port or Switch Has a Problem?

Short of monitoring the traffic passing through every port, almost the only effective method of troubleshooting a switched network is to ask the switch itself how the network is behaving. This is usually done with SNMP or by connecting to the console port of the switch. Obviously, directing queries through the console port is not desirable because you would have to physically touch every switch in the network. It is possible to minimize the impact of this alternative by setting up terminal servers that connect to the console ports. SNMP is a better choice most of the time because it allows you to make queries in-band from anywhere on the attached network, and it does that without any extra hardware. If you have implemented a network management system you may configure the switch to send an unsolicited response called an SNMP trap whenever utilization, errors, or some other parameter exceeds a specified threshold. Then use network management or a network monitoring tool to investigate what caused the threshold to be exceeded. There are some categories of problem that are satisfied by asking the switch, but many that are not.

Similarly, and more recently, you can configure the switches and routers to send flow protocols that report on forwarded traffic. This information may be used in much the same way as SNMP to provide trending and to provide alerting on deviations from normal.

The alternative is to wait for user complaints. In most networks this third option will be the more common solution. This method should not be discounted due to its simplicity—it is very effective. The user community has a very finely tuned subconscious sense of what the normal performance of the network is. Any perceived degradation of that sense of normal will result in a rapid complaint to the network support center. Once a user complains, you can start the troubleshooting process from his or her connection point. This method is entirely reactive.

Proactive efforts to prevent problems from affecting users include regularly interrogating each switch, and monitoring the quality of traffic on each switch port—just as any other segment would be monitored on a regular basis.

Once a problem has been reported or detected, there are many ways to approach diagnosis, and each has positive and negative aspects.

Techniques for Troubleshooting a Switch

There are more than 10 fundamental approaches used to gain visibility into a switch. Each technique offers a different view and has both positive and negative aspects. Like many other situations

related to networking, there is no single best answer. The most suitable solution will be determined primarily by the availability of resources (which tools are available and/or pre-installed), the skill level of the user, and the potential service interruption that will result from implementing that technique.

Even combined, these techniques are not able to monitor the attached network as well as when hubs—instead of switches—were common. It is extremely difficult to see all the traffic and errors that a switch is experiencing. Most troubleshooting assumes the traffic will pass between the station and an attached server or through the uplink. If two stations were passing information directly between themselves using peer-to-peer networking, the traffic would not pass through the uplink or to any other port on the switch. Unless you knew to look for it, it probably would not be detected. Errors tend to stop at the switch port, but could be forwarded depending on the nature of the error and the configuration of the switch. If forwarded, they are nearly always forwarded to only one other port.

For simplicity, the troubleshooting model will be a server attached to a switch as shown in Figure E-1. Some descriptions assume that the users in question are attached to the same switch; other descriptions assume that the users in question are accessing the server through the uplink leading to either another switch or to a router. The troubleshooting scenario is based on a user complaint that communications with the server are "slow." This problem description tells the support staff almost nothing. If, instead of troubleshooting, there is a security breach being investigated for possible forensic and legal uses, there are additional considerations regarding the infallibility of the technique.

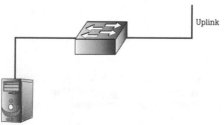

Uplink

Figure E-1. *Basic switch scenario*

Note: *Information related to multiple techniques will be described in association with the method where it fits best. Much of the information in this discussion applies to more methods than the one it is described for, and this information may account for trivial to fundamental differences in your results.*

Method 1: Access the Switch Console

The switch configuration is available via multiple means, including the following (see Figure E-2):

* Logging in through a TELNET session

* Logging in through an SSH session

* Logging in through a web session

* Logging in through the serial port of the switch

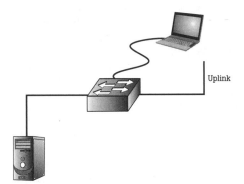

Figure E-2. *Console access*

A variety of runtime troubleshooting aides are available from some switches, though the feature set for these troubleshooting aides is quite different depending on the vendor and switch model. Advanced operating system commands permit more detailed examination of the forwarded traffic, but not in a user-friendly format. Considerable experience and theoretical knowledge is required to obtain benefit from several of these features.

Pros

Using console access is a great way to troubleshoot, as evidenced by the popularity and prevalence of this technique. A considerable variety of

network problems now revolve around switch configurations and actions taken by the switch in accordance with those configurations.

Gaining access to the switch console is nearly always possible via some method. The increasingly ubiquitous presence of wireless service and data services from cell phones has made it possible to manage a network from almost anywhere on the planet. If the network management system is configured to send problem notifications to mobile devices, the problems reported may be investigated immediately.

If the problem is related to the configuration, console access will permit problem resolution.

Cons

Senior network support staff or others with the password to the switch appear to rely on the configuration of the switch so heavily during the troubleshooting process that no other option is considered until this method has utterly failed to produce a resolution. Neglecting the other options may delay problem resolution and increase frustration. Not all problems will be revealed or solved via console access.

Routine console access commands reveal general utilization levels, but little or nothing about specific activity or root cause of a protocol failure. Furthermore, the information readily available via console access indicates what *should be* happening, but not always what *is* happening and might not reveal misbehavior on the part of the switch. Whether the operating system of the switch has bugs and whether the configuration is incomplete might not be evident from the configuration listing. In some cases, the configuration defaults are not revealed by dumping the configuration to the screen. Only the changes to the default configuration are shown, and it might be that a default setting is the source of network performance issue on your unique network.

Configuration data is useful in guiding troubleshooting efforts to see if the switch is operating as expected. However, configuration and performance validation requires one or more of the other switch troubleshooting methods.

For sensitive areas of the network, console access might not be permitted remotely, or might not be available from outside a configured group of allowed addresses. Frequently, the Help Desk and lower skilled support staff are not provided with the password, and thus are not allowed access to the console. Support staff with console access often are not involved in routine maintenance and troubleshooting activities. Consider how you would identify or solve many of your recent network performance issues if console access was completely denied to you.

Method 2: Connect to an Unused Port

The simplest approach to troubleshooting involves attaching a monitoring tool, such as a protocol analyzer, to any unused port on the switch (see Figure E-3). Connecting to an unused switch port then allows the monitoring tool access to the attached broadcast domain without disrupting service anywhere. The attached tool has the same access to the broadcast domain as any other station.

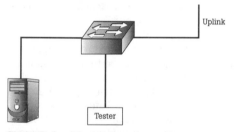

Figure E-3. *Monitor from any open port*

It is not possible to determine whether the unused port selected is in the same VLAN (broadcast domain) as the problem unless you have console access or network documentation that is atypically detailed and up to date. Also keep in mind that, even if your network documentation was current as of "now," the problem you are looking for may be a configuration or cabling error that invalidates the documentation on which you are relying.

Passive Monitoring

Passive monitoring requires no configuration or other effort.

Pros

If you are patient, through passive monitoring you will eventually see traffic from nearly all network devices attached to the broadcast domain. This is possible because of address table aging and basic bridge behavior. There are some devices that will transmit only on power up, or if queried directly, but eventually almost all devices eventually transmit.

Cons

Passive monitoring suggests that the monitoring device does not transmit. If no queries are sent, two situations exist simultaneously: the switch never learns the MAC address of the monitoring device, and no queries means no responses. You should expect to see very little traffic under most normal networking conditions, and the traffic seen will mostly consist of broadcast service announcements or broadcast-based protocols such as ARP.

Connecting such a tool to the network would be an excellent method of obtaining a starting point for a security breach of the network, and the randomly received unsolicited traffic may itself present a security breach. Secure networks should investigate instances of switch ports having active link, but no associated MAC address (or an unknown MAC address).

In Figure E-4, little traffic reaches the monitoring tool. The monitoring tool may see a few frames per second instead of the thousands per second that might be passing between the stations and the server.

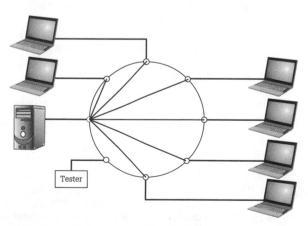

Figure E-4. *Switches forward traffic between the source and destination port*

Active Monitoring

Active monitoring suggests that the monitoring device has at least a minimal configuration suitable for the attached network.

Pros

Active monitoring, or more likely a mix of active and passive monitoring, is an excellent method of rapidly obtaining a list of stations on the broadcast domain as well as a good idea of what services may be available from those stations.

This method also helps identify many common networking problems, including duplicate IPs, misconfigured stations, and rogue DHCP servers or routers.

Cons

Actively soliciting traffic or interrogating the broadcast domain is useful for network discovery and for finding other classes of problem, but will not aid in resolving most slow connection problems.

Active discovery finds hosts but does not reveal what they are doing.

Background for Method 2

Satisfactory interpretation of results obtained using Method 2 depends on a good understanding of how bridges operate.

Bridge Behavior

As described in Chapter 1, "Using the OSI Model," the switch (which we are viewing as a multiport bridge) will only forward a very tiny amount of the traffic to the monitored port. This is appropriate behavior on the part of a bridging device because it is designed to prevent unnecessary traffic from reaching ports where it does not belong. There are several bridging techniques. While possible with some switches to enable and configure other techniques, the default for Ethernet is transparent bridging.

In a transparent bridge, it is up to the bridge to discover where the destination station is located. This is accomplished by flooding unknown destination frames to all ports except where the frame originated. As soon as the destination station responds to a query, all bridges involved will know which port subsequent traffic should be sent to,

and only that port. This is true for a single switch as well as each separate switch when attached in parallel or in a hierarchy of some sort.

The simplified method for this is for the switch to record the source MAC address for any traffic, and associate that address to a specific port. It does not matter if that port is servicing a single station, a hub, or an uplink to another switch. All traffic destined for that particular MAC address is forwarded to that port. Until the switch has observed a frame bearing a given MAC address in the source field it will not have a table entry to reference for traffic bearing that MAC address in the destination field, and all such destination traffic will be flooded.

Because there is no guarantee that the MAC address will remain associated with that port forever, there is an aging period for each entry in the bridging table. When an address is aged out of the table, the next frame sent to that discarded table entry MAC address will be flooded to all other ports again. The aging period value is affected by the switch vendor defaults, the switch configuration, static table entries, etc. Roaming wireless stations rely on aging and other techniques for rapid forwarding table reconvergence.

In review: Traffic forwarded to the monitored port in Figure E-4 will consist almost entirely of broadcast or multicast traffic, with a few frames resulting from unknown destinations appearing sporadically. These occasional frames are probably the result of aging of the bridge forwarding table or from broadcast-based protocols like ARP, and not often from truly unknown destinations. Many unwary technicians have seen the traffic distribution (nearly 100 percent broadcasts) but failed to noticed the exceptionally low utilization level. This results in the incorrect diagnosis of a broadcast storm, or that their network is experiencing unbelievably high broadcast rates as a part of normal operation.

Access Control

An increasingly popular form of access control is the 802.1X protocol, which supports various authentication methods for gaining access to the host network. Each station connecting to the switch must authenticate before it is joined to the broadcast domain. There are many ways this can be implemented, including: fully locking the station out, placing the station in a "holding" state on an isolated broadcast domain until the authentication challenge is satisfied, and placing the station on an unsecured broadcast domain with Internet access but no local access unless it is authenticated. Implementation of 802.1X will result in passive monitoring challenges that include, but are far from limited to

- No traffic at all. No traffic is forwarded to the port by the switch until the attached station issues an authentication request, and then only authentication traffic will be observed until the station satisfies the authentication requirements.

- Very little traffic. Only a limited subset of traffic may be observed until the station is authenticated. The specific types of traffic that may be seen falls into the "it depends" category and will be different for each network, and possibly for different connection points within the network. A very limited list of the many possibilities include

  - The switch may issue an authentication challenge but nothing else.
  - Spanning tree traffic may be seen.
  - Inter-switch communications may be seen (such as LLDP).
  - Flooded "unknown" destinations may be seen.
  - Broadcast and multicast traffic may be seen.
  - Traffic from within a quarantine broadcast domain may be seen.

However, despite any leakage the attaching station is not permitted to request any traffic from the protected network. The specific switch configuration may permit access to a quarantine network that permits visitors to access the Internet but blocks access to network resources within the protected network.

Duplex and Auto-Negotiation

The default state for virtually all new Ethernet interfaces today is for Auto-Negotiation to be enabled. This is good. Many vendors describe it as bad, primarily because the sales and support engineers don't have a solid understanding of how it works.

The likelihood of Auto-Negotiation actually failing to produce a viable link is very low. There are some implementations that do not operate correctly, but in almost all cases the vendor has learned about the problem and a new build of code is available to resolve the problem. If they are not aware of the problem they will be very interested in working with you to resolve it. Review IEEE 802.3 clause 28 for specific details; however, a very simplified description of Auto-Negotiation follows.

As described in Chapter 4, "Media Access Control Layer," a negotiating station sends a handshake signal called an FLP (Fast Link Pulse). This is composed of a burst of normal link pulses common to 10BASE-T. The FLP defines the capabilities of the negotiating station that sent them. If the link partner is also sending FLPs, they compare the offered capabilities and select the highest performance match in offered capabilities, change to that link technology, and begin communicating over it.

If the negotiating station did not detect FLPs from its link partner, it is *required* to choose half duplex for the connection. A negotiating station will not try to detect the link partner's duplex setting when FLPs are not received. This is the cause of most problems related to duplex problems. Far too many support engineers wrongly believe that the negotiating station will detect the duplex setting of the fixed-setting link partner.

Another misconception is that a duplex mismatch will cause a link failure. The link will experience errors if the duplex does not match, and the visible symptom will be slowness, but it will still pass traffic. If the duplex mismatch appears between two switches it is possible to review the reported interface errors and infer the duplex setting of each end of the link just from the nature of the reported errors.

From a monitoring and security perspective, the impact of a duplex mismatch is slight but still present. If the duplex mismatch is on the interface used by the passive monitoring tool, there probably won't be any perceived problem at all simply because it isn't transmitting. If the duplex mismatch is on a link where both link partners are actively transmitting, two factors come into play. The link will experience lost frames due to errors appearing late in the transmission, and are therefore not retransmitted by the MAC Layer. These lost frames will require higher layers to recover from any problem that might result. If enough frames are detected as normal collided frames and the MAC Layer attempts to retransmit them, the buffer eventually backs up and starts dropping frames intended for transmission on that interface. Lost frames could cause problems with problem analysis and forensic purposes, particularly because it is almost impossible to discover whether frames were dropped, how many frames were dropped, or when.

The default state for some switches is to disable any port involved in too many collisions, regardless of whether it negotiated to half duplex. This results in normal 802.3 medium arbitration collisions on a shared media collision domain, causing the switch to block or disable the affected port. As an example, Cisco permits this behavior to be changed with the parameter "errdisable."

Method 3: Configure a Mirror or Span Port

Most managed switches permit configuration of one or more monitoring ports. These features allow traffic from a selected port or ports to be copied to the monitoring port. This technique is usually referred to as port aliasing, mirroring, or spanning (see Figure E-5).

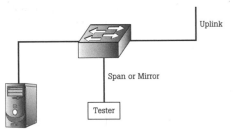

Figure E-5. *Configuring a mirror or span port for monitoring*

The ability to copy or mirror traffic to a fixed or selected output port on the switch is provided by most switch vendors. Older switches had a specific port that could be configured as this special monitoring port, but most newer switches may be configured to use any port as the output port for monitoring. Some permit multiple output ports while others support only one. A few models allow for the monitored traffic to be forwarded from another switch, such as Cisco's RSPAN feature, though there are capacity and performance issues related to this feature.

The features offered by the switch for this type of traffic monitoring vary by vendor and switch model, but the basic functionality is usually the same. Selected traffic is copied and sent to the monitoring port for analysis.

The mirror port is often a listen-only (egress) port, though a number of vendors permit configuring the port to be bidirectional (ingress/egress). Configuring a mirror port on the switch permits the monitoring tool to see a copy of the actual traffic between our reportedly slow user connection to the server (see Figure E-6). The traffic source for the mirrored port could be any other port on the switch, including an uplink port. The mirror source could also be a group of several other ports on the switch, or even one or more VLANs.

Pros

Port mirroring is one of the most common and effective methods of troubleshooting a switched network. This technique permits the monitoring tool to observe traffic between two or more stations that passes through the switch. The most common usage is in association with a protocol analyzer.

Cons

The implementation of this technique varies between vendors, but there are several common choices. Note that in almost all cases the forwarding technique employed by the switch will also be used to filter data sent to the monitor port. This means errors are usually filtered by the switch and do not appear on the monitor port. For troubleshooting purposes, port mirroring can sometimes be ineffective because an entire class of problems are concealed by the switch through some type of filtering.

Configuration of the mirror must be performed from a console session. This often involves bringing a PC along with the monitoring tool so that the switch can be reconfigured as required for troubleshooting. Lower level or third-party technicians are often not in possession of the password, and there is a real risk that improperly configuring the mirror will result in a network disruption.

It is easily possible to oversubscribe the capacity of the output port. This leads to inexplicable missing traffic in the output data stream, and an underreporting of the monitored link utilization. As more ports are included in the mirror, the chances increase that the capacity of the output port will be exceeded. An extreme instance of oversubscription is possible with switches that permit an entire VLAN to be mirrored. For data analysis and forensic purposes, it is important to know whether all traffic in the conversation was included for analysis, or that potential loss of some traffic has been accounted for. At the same time, it is important to understand the input capacity limits of the monitoring tool. For example, software protocol analyzers often cannot store anything close to line rate traffic.

Background for Method 3

Satisfactory interpretation of results obtained using Method 3 depends on a good understanding of how repeaters operate, and in the normal operation of an Ethernet collision domain.

Oversubscription

Output capacity on the monitor port is an important consideration. The output port has a TX and RX path. It was already noted that the TX path (ingress) from the monitoring device back to the switch may be blocked by the switch as part of the mirror configuration. Whether or not the TX path is blocked (whether the port is bidirectional or not), the RX path from the switch to the monitoring device is capacity limited. If you are mirroring a full-duplex port of the same speed as the mirror output port, the switch might easily drop traffic without notifying you. In this regard, it does not matter whether the monitoring device is connected at half or full duplex; the inherent limit to the output path is the same.

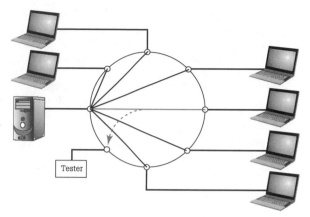

Figure E-6. *Logical effect of configuring a mirror or span*

Refer to Figure E-7, where the traffic associated with a server connected to a switch at 100Mbps in full duplex is mirrored to a monitor port. At full duplex, both the TX path and the RX path are able to support 100Mbps of traffic, for an aggregate throughput potential of 200Mbps. If you seek to mirror that traffic to another 100Mbps port, you can only use the TX path from the switch to the monitoring tool. The amount of mirrored traffic is therefore limited to a maximum of 100Mbps in this example. Despite a small amount of buffering provided by the switch to accommodate the inherently bursty nature of network traffic, traffic on the server's switch port that exceeds 50 percent of the combined capacity of the monitored full-duplex port will probably be dropped.

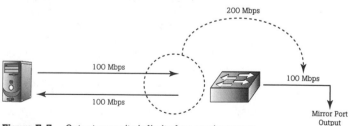

Figure E-7. *Output capacity is limited on a mirror port*

If multiple ports are mirrored to the monitoring port, the potential for this problem is correspondingly greater. Because most switches operate at far below their capacity, the problem might not be noticed right away.

The situation may be mitigated by connecting the monitoring device to a higher speed port, one that has the native output capacity to accept all the mirrored traffic. If the mirror output port in Figure E-7 were a Gigabit port instead of a 100Mbps port, the aggregate 200Mbps traffic potential would be easily accommodated

Port Clocking

One possible situation occurs when there is a burst of very high utilization, represented by the minimum interpacket gap being used. For example, each Gigabit Ethernet interface is engineered with a clock that matches the requirements of the Physical Layer encoding scheme (+/– 100 ppm). If one link partner's clock was +100 ppm and the other was –100 ppm, the input buffer can eventually overflow and some data will be lost. Most of the time there will be variations in the interpacket gap that will permit the slower receiver to catch back up and not drop anything, but it is possible to have an occasional FCS error due to clock variations and the resulting buffer problem. The expected reaction from the network is to shrink the interpacket gap slightly to avoid overrunning the buffer, but that will not always avoid the problem.

Switch Forwarding Techniques

Awareness of switch forwarding techniques and what will be forwarded once the decision is made seems to have fallen out of the pool of common knowledge. Assuming that you chose the correct port to span during a troubleshooting or forensic incident, it is unlikely that you will see any MAC Layer errors that might be present on the spanned port. Most switches sold today default to, or are only capable of, the store-and-forward technique. However, many of the legacy switches deployed may offer or default to low-latency forwarding

techniques. It is impossible to know which forwarding technique is employed without doing some research, and possibly some testing.

Three common forwarding techniques are employed, although other names have been used to describe them (see Chapter 1):

- Store-and-forward (traditional OSI Layer 2 bridge behavior)

- Cut-through (forward after the destination MAC address is known)

- Modified cut-through (forward after 64 bytes have been received—this is equal to the 10/100 Ethernet half-duplex timing concept of slot time, and represents the cutoff for when a legal collision may be detected)

The two low-latency forwarding techniques lost popularity after only a few years. This is probably due to the comparatively slight performance improvement coupled with the increase in troubleshooting difficulty associated with low-latency forwarding. At least one additional combination technique existed, which has sometimes been called error sensing or adaptive. This last technique uses one of the low-latency techniques until the error level exceeds a fixed or configurable threshold, then it changes to store-and-forward. The trick is discovering whether the error went away or whether the error is bad enough that the switch changed techniques. You might have paid extra for an intermittent error.

If one of the low-latency forwarding techniques is in use, any error observed might have come from the local collision domain, or could have come from anywhere within the attached broadcast domain—even several switches away.

If store-and-forward is used, you may safely assume that MAC Layer errors stop at the switch port (see Figure E-8). If a low-latency forwarding technique is employed, a detected error could have originated from anywhere inside the broadcast domain, not just "this side" of the switch port. This substantially alters troubleshooting considerations and assumptions.

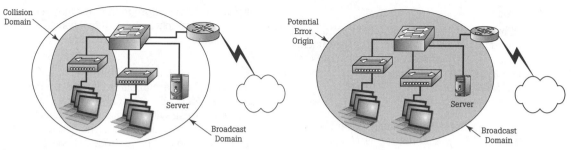

Figure E-8. *Potential error forwarding with store-and-forward (left) and low latency (right)*

At OSI Layer 2, a mirror output port will be subject to the same bridge forwarding technique as the rest of the switch. MAC Layer errors are almost never forwarded to a mirror output port.

The discussion so far has only considered OSI Layer 2 forwarding. The current marketplace offers a very broad and diverse feature set for switches, including forwarding at OSI Layer 3, Layer 4, and Layers 5–7; load balancing; rate limiting; content-based forwarding techniques; as well as proxy services and special buffering, filtering, and security options. Because these higher-layer features are vendor and model dependent, all are outside the scope of this basic description. Study the vendor documents to learn how the features operate to understand how to trouble-shoot them. In many cases, troubleshooting these features will require observing traffic before and after the switch simultaneously. Begin by using a protocol analyzer to examine traffic, and match the traffic to descriptions in the vendor documents. Once you can identify and explain correct behavior to someone else, you are ready to look for incorrect behavior.

Method 4: Connect to a Tagged or Trunk Port

The tester may be connected to a VLAN trunk port, or a port with one or more VLANs associated to it (see Figure E-9). This is similar to a span or mirror port, so all the pros and cons associated with that technique apply. Additionally, the tester must be capable of interpreting the VLAN tag or tags and/or organizing them by broadcast domain in order to create a useful view of the network.

On a trunk port, the tester might be required to participate in the trunk management traffic, such as Cisco's VTP.

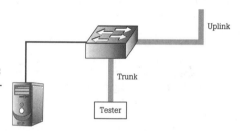

Figure E-9. *Connect to a VLAN tagged or VLAN trunk port*

Traffic observed on a tagged or trunk port will vary. Some possibilities include the following:

* The switch may present only VLAN tagged traffic to the port. Stations that are not participating in the VLAN will not be able to use the attached network resources.

* The switch may support both tagged and un-tagged traffic on the port, supporting both a VLAN trunk and local untagged stations. The native VLAN is often untagged on a trunk port.

* The switch may present traffic tagged for multiple VLANS to the port. In this configuration there is rarely any expectation that an end station will be attached, although servers may support multiple VLANs on a single connection.

Pros

Utilizing a VLAN trunk port would permit monitoring of a much larger portion of the attached network. Active discovery would benefit greatly by having broadcast domain access to multiple VLANs at once.

Cons

Few monitoring tools can take advantage of multiple VLANs simultaneously. Most are unable to do tagged discovery at all, relying instead on passive monitoring. Furthermore, the problem of oversubscription would be exacerbated by trying to monitor larger portions of the network. The switch should be applying normal forwarding rules to the trunk port, so only appropriate unicast destinations would be crossing the trunk, as well as unknown, aged, and broadcast traffic.

Method 5: Insert a Hub into the Link

This was perhaps the first switch troubleshooting method, and is still a common method of monitoring a problem related to a single switch port.

Using a shared media hub involves a strategic placement decision. The hub may be placed between switches or on a client link. In many networks, most traffic of interest will be received or transmitted by a shared resource such as a file server, as shown in Figure E-10.

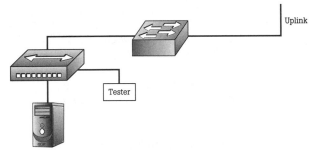

Figure E-10. *Inserting a hub inline between the attached station and the switch port*

For troubleshooting and forensic purposes, the monitoring tool may remain virtually invisible to the network as long as it does not transmit.

Note: *The use of aggregating taps may replace this method simply because it has become almost impossible to buy a shared media hub.*

Pros

Using SNMP to learn about traffic and errors is useful, but for good error analysis there is nothing like seeing them with the diagnostic tool directly. Placing a shared-media hub inline between a switch port and another interface allows a monitoring tool to be connected to the same collision domain. This technique enables the analyzer to see all traffic present. Access to all traffic greatly assists the network support staff in diagnosing a wide range of problems, including: user login failures, poor performance, and dropped connections.

This is one of the best troubleshooting situations for an issue related to a single station because almost nothing is hidden from the monitoring tool.

Cons

This approach is impractical in most situations, particularly where there are multiple servers to be monitored. Where do you locate the hub—on all server links? If you choose to move a hub around as needed, are you prepared to interrupt the network long enough to install it? Even if you are quick, this delay is usually long enough to cause dropped connections. Additionally, network resources such as servers may be connected via a technology or connection speed that your monitoring tool might not support.

Inserting a half-duplex hub between two full-duplex stations can significantly reduce the overall throughput of the link, introduce errors, and generally confuse the symptoms of the original problem or monitoring situation unless you are very aware of how your equipment works (switches, hubs, and testers).

Three common problems take place when a hub is inserted into the link:

- If the link was originally forced to full duplex, a new problem has been introduced into the link because the hub will be operating in half duplex.

- If the "hub" used was actually a partial or full bridge, you have not gained anything (see Appendix D, "Discovering Device Behavior").

- The link already had one or more hubs and the Ethernet architecture is now illegal, which causes late collisions (see Chapter 4 for architecture limits).

Even where adding a hub does not introduce new problems, the results will depend on the monitoring tool used. Virtually all software protocol analyzers have some level of blindness to activity on the attached collision domain. Many basic software protocol analyzers will only see traffic that is of a legal size because the NIC driver discards all traffic that are not legal and fully formed frames with no errors. Some software protocol analyzers take advantage of features in certain NICs that permit the software protocol analyzer to see some level of errored traffic. Seeing all errors on the collision domain almost always requires a hardware protocol analyzer or other tool with custom circuitry operating at the level of the Ethernet PHY (the part of the circuit that converts binary data to the correct signaling for the medium).

Background for Method 5

Satisfactory interpretation of results obtained using Method 5 depends on a good understanding of how repeaters operate, and in the normal operation of an Ethernet collision domain.

Hub Architecture Limits

Chapter 4 contains Ethernet error descriptions, architecture limits, and illustrations. Architecture limits are near the back of the chapter, at the end of each implementation description, ordered by link speed.

- **10Mbps Ethernet.** Up to four hubs may be used in series between any two distant PCs.
- **100Mbps Ethernet.** One or two hubs in series between any two distant PCs, depending on the operating characteristics of the hub.
  - Class I hubs might or might not be marked as such, but only one such hub may be used on a collision domain.
  - Class II hubs are usually marked, and there may be one or two used on a collision domain, but not more.
- **1000Mbps Ethernet.** Permits a single hub to be used on a collision domain, but they

are simply unavailable for purchase. There are no known shared media Gigabit Ethernet hubs manufactured at this time.

- **10,000Mbps Ethernet.** 10 Gigabit Ethernet does not permit half-duplex operation at all, so there are no hubs for 10 Gigabit Ethernet.

Switch Architecture Limits

There are no hard limits to the number of bridges (switches operating at OSI Layer 2) that can be placed in series or parallel. Your architecture design will impact network performance, though. The two most significant issues relate to broadcasts.

- If two bridges are operating in parallel, and both paths remain open, the first broadcast frame seen by one will cause an instant broadcast storm. Bridges are required to forward all broadcasts to all ports except the port on which it was received. The next bridge does the same, and the original broadcast returns to the first port via the parallel path. Some switch configurations offer a "trust me" setting, where you effectively promise the switch that you will not create a parallel path, and in return the switch will permit a new connection to access the network almost instantly (such as Cisco's "portfast").
- Even if Spanning Tree or some other mechanism is used to eliminate parallel paths, the greater the number of bridges participating in a single broadcast domain, the greater the amount of appropriate broadcast traffic will be seen. Broadcasts represent a useful and necessary function in the network, so they cannot be eliminated. Placing too many stations on a broadcast domain will raise the level of background broadcast traffic to the point where it becomes a noticeable cause of poor performance. Each station on the broadcast domain is required to process each broadcast frame, which interrupts whatever it was supposed to be doing for you.
- The Spanning Tree Max Age timer will limit Spanning Tree–enabled bridged networks to a maximum diameter.

Method 6: Place the Tester in Series

Inserting a monitoring tool in series in the link should avoid the problems related to inserting a hub in series, as the link could be operating in full duplex and not experience problems.

Pros

Unless there was a parallel path to the station being tested (the server in Figure E-11), such as wireless, there should be nothing the tester failed to see. Depending on the features of the monitoring tool, this technique could be very useful for any type of situation related to a single station or link. If the monitoring tool were inserted on a link going to the Internet it could be used for verifying firewall effectiveness or for gathering forensic information for an investigation.

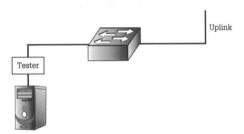

Figure E-11. *Inserting a monitoring tool in series*

Even passively, the monitoring tool can track which link partner is the source of any MAC Layer errors, and can monitor requests made by the attached station to ensure that responses from the network returned. Most problems related to an inability to connect to a server or service should be easily identified.

Cons

The technique has two significant potential problems:

- If encryption is used on the link, even being in series will not allow viewing of higher-layer data.

- Ethernet does not permit shared use of a single cable other than 10Mbps coax. If the inline monitoring tool did not have an additional management port, the monitoring

tool would either have to perform bridging in order to transmit, or it would have to be passive.

In-line monitoring tools are generally expensive, and are not widely deployed as a result.

Method 7: Place a Tap Inline on a Link

The terms *tap* and *splitter* are often used interchangeably, though splitter usually applies to fiber optic links. Taps take data received on each interface and copy it to the monitor output. Because a link has data traveling in two directions (TX and RX) there will be two data streams to duplicate (see Figure E-12 and Figure E-13).

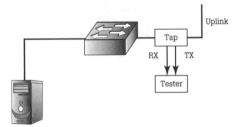

Figure E-12. *Inserting a tap inline*

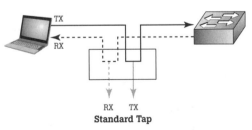

Figure E-13. *A standard tap presents data from one direction on each output port*

On a fiber optic link, the splitter is rated by how much light is taken from the primary path and redirected to the monitoring path. Typical splitter ratings include ratios of 80:20, 70:30, or even 50:50. Using the first example, 80 percent of the light continues through the splitter to its original destination, and 20 percent of the light is redirected to the monitor output. It is important to match the tap to the cable type. For example, a multimode capable tap cannot be used on a singlemode link. You should not use a multimode 50nm tap on a 62.5nm link. Most non–aggregating fiber taps are unpowered.

For copper cable links, depending on the complexity of the encoding process, a tap may be required to interpret the data much like the original destination receiver. Then, the tap would retransmit the received data to the tap output. For this reason, it is important to match the tapped path to the capabilities of a copper tap. Many older copper taps are able to tap a 10/100 Ethernet link but not a Gigabit Ethernet link. Some newer taps can only tap a Gigabit Ethernet link. Still other (newer) taps can tap all three speeds (10/100/1000). Copper taps are almost always powered, and will normally maintain the tapped link by closing relays if power is lost. When power returns, there might be a brief service interruption as the tap resets the link via relays.

There are two significantly different types of tap available: the traditional or standard tap, and the new aggregating tap.

Standard Tap

Using standard taps means that the monitoring tool either sees the request or the response, but not both. To see both the request and the response the monitoring tool needs two analysis input ports, one for the TX path and one for the RX path.

Aggregating Tap

Aggregating taps provide both the request and response in a single output stream (see Figure E-14). Aggregating taps often also provide configurable ingress capability (the monitoring tool can send and receive through the tap output port). Aggregating taps may also offer more than one output port, so that two or more test tools can receive the same output traffic.

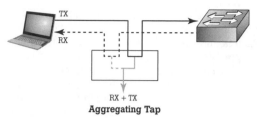

Figure E-14. *An aggregating tap combines data from both directions onto one or more output ports*

Pros

Tap use presents many advantages over configuring span or mirror ports, and avoids the problems related to inserting a hub in series. Due to their comparatively low cost they may be placed inline on critical links and simply left unused until the need arises.

For a junior support person and for forensic purposes it is a good method because it is not necessary to have the password for the switch. The tap can be inserted in series quickly with a very short loss of link state on the affected link. Once installed, a tap also permits monitoring tools to be installed and removed at any time with no risk of network disruption, and are therefore good choices for both troubleshooting and forensic purposes.

Most taps are output (egress) only, and an attached monitoring tool will be invisible to the network. Many of the new aggregating taps may be configured to support input (ingress) as well as output, which thereby permit the monitoring tool to interrogate the network or respond to management queries by injecting traffic into the network through the monitored link. Both configurations can be viewed as having positive aspects, depending on the goal.

A standard tap provides a copy of all traffic on the link, including any errors that might be present. A standard tap does not experience oversubscription because it has a separate output for each direction (TX and RX). This permits the monitoring tool access on par with a hub in series without the drawback of forcing the link to half duplex or creating a duplex mismatch. A standard tap is always output (egress) only.

Aggregating taps have a growing feature set, including the ability to filter specific traffic from the link and send only selected traffic to the monitor port. For high-speed links, this can be very useful because it reduces the amount of traffic that must be examined by the monitoring tool or technician. Aggregating taps are fairly new on the market, and are expected to undergo considerable feature evolution in the short term.

Most aggregating tap product lines offer single or multiple output ports, depending on the model. Additional output ports permit a variety of tools to view the same monitored data in parallel, usually for different purposes.

In a switched environment, an aggregating tap is overall the fastest and easiest method of gaining access to the data passing through a selected link. Aggregating taps are the new "hub" for troubleshooting.

Cons

One of the more significant issues related to using taps is the signal loss (attenuation) inherent with applying any inline tap; copper or fiber. This loss of power clearly implies that if a link is already suffering from cable faults or excessive distance, the tap could easily cause the link to fail by taking too much signal from the primary transmit path. A splitter can easily cause a 3 dB loss in power on the tapped link. Some transmitters are more robust than others, so even if installation of a splitter at one end causes the link to fail, it may still be possible to install the splitter at the other end of the link without causing it to fail.

Copper taps cause similar signal loss problems because some of the signal is needed by the tap to read the passing traffic. For copper, this is also the equivalent of additional attenuation, and also may cause the tapped link to fail during the installation process if the link being tapped is very long or is already experiencing cable problems. Copper taps require power, as the signal is recovered and retransmitted to the monitor port. A high-quality copper tap will not disconnect the tapped link if power is lost to the tap. Instead, there might be a brief interruption as relays reset the monitor state to a pass-through mode, or there might be a brief interruption as the relays reset the monitor state when power returns.Direc-

tion counts, and problems and/or delays will be encountered if the fiber tap (and the occasional copper tap) is installed "backward," resulting in a lack of output to the monitor port(s). The challenge is that a link requiring a tap is often highly utilized, and if the improper installation is not detected immediately it could be weeks before the next maintenance window is available to reverse the connections.

The latest generation of aggregating tap uses a bridging function to combine the data streams from the RX and TX data paths. As a modified bridge link:

- Aggregating taps are subject to the oversubscription problem described in Method 3 (refer to Figure E-7).

- Bursty traffic, which is common to networking, may or may not exceed the buffer inside the aggregating tap. The presence of the buffer may obscure some data loss, and would be a very significant concern for forensic analysis. Most reactive troubleshooting would not be affected by data loss through oversubscription or by having a burst exceed the buffer, because the cause of a reactive troubleshooting problem is usually related to the majority of the traffic present.

- Filtering applied by the aggregating tap might be discarding the traffic of interest. A filter applied for a prior event might still be active, which would affect both troubleshooting and forensic activities. And the act of filtering may cause the aggregating tap to drop additional frames due to CPU overhead in the tap.

- MAC Layer errors are dropped because bridges don't forward errors. Everything else is flooded to the monitor port. This is perceived as a significant drawback by the industry because standard taps forward errors, and aggregating tap vendors are expected to correct this limitation.

- Aggregating taps often have very limited bridging capabilities, and might not forward frames larger than a maximum sized VLAN tagged Ethernet frame (1522 octets). This means that 802.3as compliant frames that may be as large as 2000 octets might not be forwarded, and so-called jumbo frames might not be forwarded.

So far only aggregation taps that support "injection" (ingress traffic from the monitoring tool) have support for Power over Ethernet (PoE), so inserting a standard tap will often turn off a PoE-powered station. This is most noticeable when troubleshooting VoIP phones and wireless access points, which are likely to rely on PoE.

Because copper taps are usually active, it is possible for a link to fail on the network but the connection to the router remains up. That is, the link on the network side of the tap is down but the tap is holding the link to the router up. This will cause the router to believe that the failed link is still up, and it will forward traffic into the disconnected link. The problem will persist until someone arrives to troubleshoot the loss of connectivity, or forces the router interface into an administratively "down" state where a redundant backup link takes over. Fiber optic taps are typically passive, so this is not a problem.

Method 8: Use SNMP-Based Network Management

SNMP was created to learn what was going on within distant areas of the network without having to monitor constantly or to be in each physical location. SNMP permits long-term trend analysis as well as short-term detail analysis. SNMP is mostly based around a query/response model, which implies that a management station must be constantly querying the network to discover problems (see Figure E-15). To permit the network to inform the management station of a problem without waiting for the correct query to reveal the problem, SNMP defines the capability to send an unsolicited response, called a trap. The trap function permits a managed device—the SNMP agent—to notify the management station that predefined conditions have been met or exceeded, and attention is warranted. Receipt of some or all traps may cause the network management station to invoke user notification routines, such as email and pager alerting.

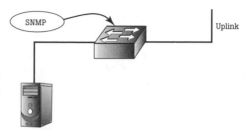

Figure E-15. *Using SNMP to query network infrastructure devices remotely*

SNMP is probably the most common method of monitoring a switched network today. The SNMP console does not have to be anywhere near the monitored device as long as there is a routed path to the target and security configurations permit the console to communicate with the agent in the switch.

Because switches do not routinely forward errors, using SNMP is perhaps the best method of locating ports experiencing errors. The switch might not forward an error, but it is certainly aware of the presence of errors. There are a variety of MIBs available from most switches that support SNMP. A MIB (management information base) is a dictionary of available queries accompanied by possible responses and the meaning of each response. Each MIB supported offers the management console a different or more detailed view of network conditions in or around the monitored device. In addition to private MIBs, which typically have customized support for each switch and level of operating code, the Standards or RFC-based MIBs can be used very effectively to monitor a switched network. In increasing order of detail, the following MIBs are useful for troubleshooting, though many others are useful, too:

- RFC 1213—MIB II
- RFC 1643—Ethernet-Like Interface MIB
- RFC 2819—RMON Ethernet
- RFC 2021—RMON 2

RFCs may be updated or enhanced following their introduction, so always check the latest RFC index for updates. For example, RFC 1213 is updated or enhanced by at least five newer RFCs (2011, 2012, 2013, 2358 and 2665). In addition to the MIBs defined by these RFCs, which contain excellent information on utilization and errors, the bridge MIB (RFC 1493, 1525, and 2674) is very useful for troubleshooting. Security is a concern when using SNMP to monitor a network. If SNMP agents are unrestricted, potentially anyone anywhere could be monitoring activity on your network or modifying your switch configurations. SNMP is often enabled by default with a very common default password when the switch or any other SNMP agent is sold. SNMP passwords are called community strings, and are both case and punctuation sensitive. Community strings are transmitted in clear text, which in itself creates a security risk. SNMP version 3 offers authentication and encrypted communication to address this exposure.

At a minimum, the default community string should be changed immediately. SNMP agents may be configured to respond to different community strings for different levels of access, to queries from a specific subnet and no other, to queries from a specific IP address and no other, and many other configurations. The routers and firewalls that provide a path to those SNMP agents may impose restrictions on SNMP, or may block SNMP entirely. If you are able to reach the agent using SNMP, the agent still has to support the MIB you are querying. Most vendors support the standard MIBs adequately, but some vendors do not. In some cases it is necessary to upgrade the operating system on the switch before it is capable of supporting a desired public or private MIB.

There are many reasons why your switch might not respond to a specific SNMP query. Once the proper MIB is available and any access problems are resolved, SNMP is a very useful tool for monitoring and trending.

Pros

Using network management systems to automate network monitoring is an excellent method for learning about changes in traffic patterns over time, as well as investigating network activity during troubleshooting or forensic events. Using SNMP, it is possible to obtain almost any information about your network, providing that a properly situated agent supports the MIB.

For best effect, the network management system should be adjusted over time so that normal behavior is counted as such, and any abnormal behavior (excessive or missing traffic) is flagged for operator attention.

The specific resources available for detailed investigation will depend on capabilities built in to the network infrastructure or deployed specifically for monitoring and diagnosing key network links or resources.

If the right resources are in place, a protocol analyzer capture file may be started automatically as a result of observed network behavior. Intrusion detection systems may be configured to monitor for symptoms which suggest that the network is under attack from external or internal agents.

Cons

With SNMP, you can get almost anything, including a packet capture file if the agent supports it. However, most don't. Therefore, you are usually limited to knowing who used which protocol with whom. If there is a protocol problem, or a problem with timing, that cannot be diagnosed unless a capture is available. Most devices reported as supporting RMON actually only support four of the nine groups. This limited subset is referenced by several names, including RMON Lite.

SNMP is a lower priority activity than forwarding traffic. If the agent becomes busy it may suspend gathering of SNMP statistics during some or all of the high-traffic event. This is the statistical equivalent of dropping frames. In many newer routers, the front-end ASICs are handling the routine traffic, and only unusual situations reach the CPU of the router. Using an SNMP console to query a router may easily elevate the CPU utilization periodically to between 10 percent and 100 percent. This can be very alarming to the support staff. Multiple SNMP consoles querying a single device at the same moment have the ability to cause it to crash entirely, depending on how the device was engineered.

Despite being a traditional mainstay for discovering what normal is, or for locating abnormal behavior, many network management systems are so complex that they are never properly and completely configured, or require enough daily attention that the network support staff cannot adequately maintain them without people whose sole function is to operate the network management system. In many businesses this quickly leads to a situation where the network management resource is abandoned, or only used for specific short-term situations. On an annual basis, the cost of keeping the network management resource current can approach or exceed the purchase cost.

Most networks use the common data paths for SNMP monitoring and don't have alternative means of reaching distant network segments. If a key infrastructure path goes down, SNMP can only agree that the distant segment is unreachable, and cannot help troubleshoot unless an alternative path exists.

Background for Method 8

Satisfactory interpretation of results obtained using Method 5 depends on a good understanding of what is available from various SNMP MIBs, and how that information might be applied or interpreted in the context of a particular type of network problem or situation. See Appendix F for more information about SNMP.

Intrusion Detection Examples Using SNMP

Intrusion detection systems may be configured to monitor for symptoms which suggest that the network is under attack from external or internal agents, looking for such thing as

- **ipReasmFails (1.3.6.1.2.1.4.16).** The number of failures detected by the IP reassembly algorithm. Monitored at hosts to determine possible attacks as well as network delivery problems.

- **tcpAttemptFails (1.3.6.1.2.1.6.7).** The number of times TCP connections have made a direct transition to the CLOSED state from either the SYN-SENT state or the SYN-RCVD state, plus the number of times TCP connections have made a direct transition to the LISTEN state from the SYN-RCVD state. This can be an indication of incoming attacks.

- **udpNoPorts (1.3.6.1.2.1.7.2).** The total number of received UDP datagrams for which there was no application at the destination port. This counter can be indicative of reconnaissance against your network.

Knowing Which SNMP MIB You Are Using

SNMP utilizes a great many MIBs—some of which are RFC based and others that are vendor and model specific. Failing to understand exactly what was asked may lead to misunderstandings. For example, in Figure E-16, a server is queried using three different MIBs. In each case the query is analogous to "how busy are you?"

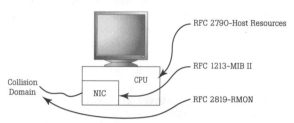

Figure E-16. *Various queries related to current utilization*

The first query asks how busy the CPU is in that server. This is entirely dependent on what applications are running on the server at that moment, and has little or nothing to do with network activity.

```
RFC 2790 [Host Resources]: hrProcessorLoad
(1.3.6.1.2.1.25.3.3.1.2)
```

The average, over the last minute, of the percentage of time that this processor was not idle.

The second query asks how much traffic passed through the NIC in that server. This is entirely dependent on traffic addressed to the server (including broadcasts), and may or may not have any relation to how busy the attached network is. For example, the attached network could be experiencing 35 percent traffic load but the server is only accepting 7 percent of that traffic. The SNMP response would be 7 percent. Note that this query ignores the outbound traffic, which is another MIB OID.

```
RFC 1213 [MIB II]: ifInOctets
(1.3.6.1.2.1.2.2.1.10)
```

The total number of octets received on the interface, including framing characters.

The third query asks how busy the network segment is where that NIC is attached. This is entirely focused on network activity, of which some of that traffic may or may not be destined for that server. Using the same example, the attached network could be experiencing 35 percent traffic load but the server is only accepting 7 percent of that traffic. The SNMP response would be 35 percent. If the server is using a standard NDIS driver, it might be seeing only the "good" traffic, and might not be capable of seeing the errors even though the query is for a MIB that would report the errors. A large number of RMON probes rely on what amounts to a clone PC with a standard NIC operating with a standard NDIS driver. Many can see few if any errors.

```
RFC 2819 [RMON]: etherStatsOctets
(1.3.6.1.2.1.16.1.1.1.4)
```

> The total number of octets of data (including those in bad packets) received on the network (excluding framing bits but including FCS octets).

If the user is not aware of the exact meaning of each metric it is easy to be led to the wrong conclusion. This is particularly true considering the user interface for a network management system, which often uses red, yellow, and green to indicate status. Color does little to discriminate between different types of "busy"; you must already know the possible sources of the warning to interpret the warning properly.

MIB Accuracy

Sometimes an SNMP agent's implementation of a specific MIB is not accurate, and responses to queries are simply wrong. Less frequently, the SNMP manager software doesn't correctly interpret a response, or there is a mismatch between the MIB versions in the agent and manager. It doesn't happen that often, but programming errors occasionally result in inaccurate responses. You might have the proper response but be using different versions of the MIB on the monitored device and the management station. A new version of the MIB may change the meaning of the response.

Example: You purchase a used network toaster. After taking it home you download the latest MIB from the manufacturer's web site. When you put the first slice of bread in to be toasted and query the toaster with your SNMP management station,

the toaster responds to your query for the cooking setting with a value of 3. The MIB in the old toaster had only three responses:

1 = Warmed slightly

2 = Browned

3 = Reduced to charcoal

Your new MIB, intended for the latest model of network toaster, has seven responses ranging from 1 = warmed slightly to 7 = reduced to charcoal. Due to the mismatch in MIBs, you believe that a setting of 3 means that your toast will be browned instead of burned.

Method 9: Have the Switch Send Flow Technology Summaries

Flow technologies are one of the answers to the problem of troubleshooting a switched network. It is very likely that flow technology use will join the other three core skills expected of someone involved in the IT industry (cable test, protocol analysis, and SNMP-based network management). Using this technique the router becomes your inline diagnostic or management probe.

Flow technologies keep track of who has been talking with whom, using what protocol, how many bytes and packets were sent by each, and so on, and then a summary report of this is sent to the flow receiver (see Figure E-17). The amount of data gathered is reduced enormously over a protocol analyzer capture file. Only the summary reports cross the network to the flow receiver where statistics are compiled.

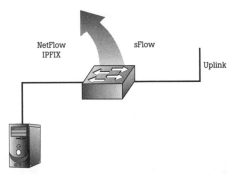

Figure E-17. *Switches may be configured to export flow summaries to a monitoring station for trending and analysis*

There are many different flow technologies in use today. Some choices include NetFlow, IPFIX, J-Flow, cflowd, and sFlow.

Pros

Compared to SNMP, flow technologies offer some good trade-offs. The switch is not required to store reports about observed behavior for long periods of time (comparatively speaking). Flow reports typically time-out and are exported in 30 minutes or less, where SNMP studies may easily be keeping data for well over a day.

Hardware or software probes are not required. Flow data comes from the network infrastructure itself. In most cases your existing infrastructure can already output flow summaries. Perhaps not the low-end switches near the user connections, but almost certainly in the network core and on the WAN edges where you are often most interested. A few extra configuration lines and it is running.

The flow receiver could be anywhere in your enterprise network, though some WAN links may be expensive enough that flow receivers located in geographically strategic locations would be preferred. Sizing of the flow reports sent to the flow receiver may be estimated at between 3–5 percent of the monitored traffic rate. Depending on the nature of the traffic, it could be less than 1 percent or over 10 percent.

Flow data is sent constantly to the flow receiver. SNMP requires that the monitoring station poll the SNMP agent on a regular basis to obtain the data.

Cons

The most widely available flow technology at the time of this writing is NetFlow, created by Cisco. Alternatives are available if you don't have a Cisco infrastructure. RFC 3917 standardized a version of NetFlow as IPFIX, so this should become more available soon.

sFlow is a sampled flow technology defined in RFC 3176. It provides similar statistics on the amount of traffic and who participated in the conversation. sFlow may be configured to sample every nth packet, or randomly. Because the traffic is always sampled, this technique is useful for growth planning, general trend analysis, and go/ no-go troubleshooting. Packet sampling makes it virtually impossible to report on sequences of packets from an individual transaction. Because of the sampling, this technique might not be suited to some security-related activities. Some infrastructure devices also support NetFlow or IPFIX sampling, though the same reduction in effectiveness applies.

Unlike NetFlow and IPFIX, sFlow operates at OSI Layer 2 and will report statistics on non-IP traffic, though this advantage is slight as IP has become by far the dominant protocol.

Depending on when the flow ends or the time-out period takes effect, the flow summary is usually not sent for anywhere between 1 and 30 minutes. It is not quite a real-time monitoring situation, though the constant nature of its reporting leads one to treat it that way.

Flow summaries are almost always sent unencrypted, so it is possible to spoof them.

When compared with SNMP, the flow summaries are likely to report slightly less traffic. For example, NetFlow summaries will report IP traffic but not other Layer 3 or lower-layer traffic. Assuming that the correct MIB is queried, SNMP will report all traffic on the interface.

Method 10: Set Up a Syslog Server

Most infrastructure devices support sending syslog information to a syslog server for collection (see Figure E-18). Syslog is most often used for application and server management and security auditing.

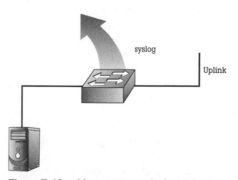

Figure E-18. *Most servers and other infrastructure devices may be configured to export syslog messages*

The level of detail reported is controlled by adjusting the setting for verbosity, which is usually set to somewhere between catastrophic only to everything down to trivial (see RFC 3164, where messages types are defined). Messages sent include, but are not limited to, errors and events (login, login failure, process start and stop, etc.) and repetitive routine operations.

Pros

Syslog will report errors and events and routine operations with no further administrative effort beyond a basic configuration in the switch that includes a destination IP address for the syslog server.

Because syslog is sent continuously (as needed) after it is configured, there is an on-going record of activity that is available for immediate or historical review and investigation.

Syslog is arguably one of the best tools for troubleshooting some types of authentication problems.

Cons

Syslog can generate vast amounts of useless data. Trying to sift through the logged messages looking for the source of a problem, or proactively searching for potential problems or security breaches, can be particularly daunting. The mind-numbing quantity of unimportant messages that must be examined and judged while looking for the information of interest has spawned the creation of syslog mining utilities and purchased applications that are able to catalog and group messages and provide flexible search features.

Syslog is prone to generating significant volumes of useless information in a short period of time if the logging level is too broad, or not reporting events that would be of interest if the logging level is too restricted.

Method 11: Use the Server (Host) Resources

Virtually all computers and network adapters come with some sort of diagnostics. Vendor-supplied diagnostics typically report most of the things that would affect day-to-day use and operation.

Computer Diagnostics

Computer manufacturers typically have some level of hardware diagnostic application that either ships with the computer or is downloadable from the vendor web site. For the most part, these diagnostics are related exclusively to the operation of the standalone hardware, but hardware failures may be directly related to network problems.

Also, the NIC manufacturer often has downloadable diagnostic utilities to assist with NIC configuration and troubleshooting. Use these utilities to check for speed and duplex, as well as any reported errors. The NIC driver software installed on the computer does not make it easy to find this information, if it is available from the NIC driver at all.

Operating System Diagnostics

Operating systems, such as Microsoft Windows and UNIX or Linux, have various diagnostic capabilities.

Perhaps the two simplest Windows diagnostics are the msconfig utility and the NIC statistics window. Msconfig permits you to review the system configuration, including NIC driver information, and the NIC statistics show how much traffic the system has accepted from the network and how much it thinks it sent to the network. These numbers usually relate directly to results from the MIB II query from Method 8. There could be much more traffic presented to the NIC than is being accepted, which would be revealed with RMON queries as shown in Figure E-16.

It is difficult to choose a best example of a simple UNIX or Linux diagnostic because this is an Open Source operating system, and there are so many to choose from. The diagnostics available from this type of operating system range from simple to highly capable and complex tools that have features very similar to the third-party category later in this chapter.

Third-Party Diagnostics

Use third-party diagnostics (such as a software protocol analyzer) on the station to isolate protocol-related problems. There are simple protocol analysis products available from the Internet, as well as comprehensive purchased products that include many built-in report tools and libraries of common fault symptoms (usually called *experts*).

Many other types of diagnostics are available, including SNMP-based network management and specialized tools for a variety of network-related diagnostics, investigation, and trending uses.

Method 12: Use a Combination of Methods

Some networking problems are satisfactorily addressed with a single troubleshooting method. Others require the combined results from two or more methods to properly quantify or isolate the situation.

One example of this might be to use a hardware protocol analyzer to monitor the input and output data paths from an infrastructure device—such as a switch—and then use another method to stimulate the link with some sort of traffic. The results of this test would determine whether the switch or other device had modified the traffic during transit, whether the traffic was being filtered by some security mechanism, by what priority the traffic was being forwarded (important for some types of application, such as VoIP), and what the switch latency is.

Troubleshooting Methods: Conclusion

A commonly used troubleshooting method is to wait for user complaints. This method should not be discounted due to its simplicity—it is very effective. The user community has a very finely tuned subconscious sense of what the normal performance of the network is. Any perceived degradation of that sense of normal will result in a rapid complaint to the network support center. Once a user complains, you can start the troubleshooting process from his or her connection point. The problem with this method is that it is entirely reactive.

Ideally, the approach used by network support staff should be proactive. Proactive efforts to prevent problems from affecting users may include regularly interrogating each switch and monitoring the quality of traffic on each switch port—just

as any other segment would be monitored on a regular basis. Implementing tactics such as monitoring and trending switch port statistics and using tools that allow you to see inside switches will help move some ways from a reactive troubleshooting mode to a proactive trouble prevention mode. It is probably impossible to be completely proactive.

Regular training for all staff involved in network support or forensic activities is critical. There has been a disturbing trend over the last few years where theory, network design, and problem investigation and resolution for anything below the Network Layer has been overlooked or ignored because of the move from shared media to single-user-per-switch-port network designs. Because problems only affect a single user, it has been convenient to ascribe the problem to coincidence or to the hardware involved being outdated. Outdated in this case is often anything more than two or three years old. Many apparently inconsistent symptoms or test results are ignored, where additional training would have allowed these symptoms and test results to suggest specific fault conditions or behavior. The lack of understanding of the underlying technology below the Network Layer has blinded a whole generation to these situations. The relatively recent transition of wireless technologies going from a bleeding-edge curiosity to a fully deployed and ubiquitous presence is forcing many to rediscover the impact of shared media and perhaps raises questions about what might be happening on the wired network. When faced with network support or forensic situations it is impossible to have too much training about how each element within the network behaves normally, so that abnormal behavior is recognized and unexpected symptoms can be explained and compensated for.

APPENDIX F
Simple Network Management Protocol

This appendix provides a very basic description of the SNMP protocol. The description includes details about the three versions of SNMP. An example of how an SNMP packet appears on a network, and several examples of how SNMP data may be viewed in different network management applications are shown.

SNMP Operation

Simple Network Management Protocol (SNMP) is based on two entities: the manager and the agent. The manager software is typically implemented as a graphical user interface with large databases of saved responses. The agent is typically software residing on infrastructure networking equipment or something attached to the network, such as a file server. The most common use is to have the manager software make periodic queries (GET) for the current status of agents running in routers, switches, servers, and so on. The manager may also send configuration changes (SET) to the agent. SNMP is typically sent over UDP Ports 161 (to agent) and 162 (to manager).

This query/response model requires the manager software to initiate all communications, which might not allow for timely discovery of a situation that needs attention. To accommodate rapid problem discovery, SNMP permits the agent to be configured to send an unsolicited response (TRAP) if configured conditions are met, such as utilization or error levels exceeding a particular threshold.

The query itself is formed from a library of possible queries called a Management Information Base (MIB). The manager must ask questions from the set offered by a specific MIB, and the agent must be using the same MIB to properly respond. There are two types of MIB: public MIBs that generally come from RFCs; and private MIBs that are created by equipment manufacturers to support specific models of equipment, and even specific versions of software and feature sets within a model line.

An example MIB query is for the manager to send a string of numbers to the agent. The numbers identify a hierarchically organized tree structure leading to the single element of information sought (see Figure F-1). To ask for how long the agent has been running since it was either turned on or rebooted, the manager might ask for the MIB II variable of 1.3.6.1.2.1.1.3. The variable being queried, referred to as an Object Identifier (OID), is decoded in the following format: iso.org.dod.internet.mgmt.mib2.system.sysUpTime. The agent's response lists the same OID, plus the value found for that variable.

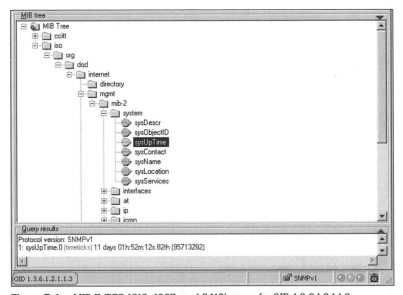

Figure F-1. *MIB II (RFC 1213, 1907, and 3418) query for OID 1.3.6.1.2.1.1.3 representing system up time (sysUpTime). In this MIB browser application the bottom line of the screen (circled) reveals the OID for any highlighted MIB variable.*

It is unusual, but easily possible, for a private MIB query and a public MIB query for the same information to reveal a different response. This is usually due to a MIB version mismatch or a coding error in the agent, which returned an incorrect response. Protocol analysis is used to validate that the manager software is not interpreting the response incorrectly, and that the response was as displayed.

Each SNMP query is accompanied by information to aid both the manager and agent in interpreting the query. Listing F-1 is an excerpt from a protocol analyzer, shown in two parts. The top part is the decoded SNMP part of the response.

The top part has been interpreted by the protocol analyzer to make reading the contents easier. The bottom part is the actual hexadecimal (and ASCII representation) of the entire Ethernet frame containing the query. In the bottom part of Listing F-1, a portion of the frame is highlighted in bold. This bold portion corresponds to the OSI Layer 5–7 part of the frame, starting with the Class statement at the beginning of the top part and continuing down to include the Object Length value of 214 (D6). Following that is the data represented by the response for OID 1.3.6.1.2.1.1.1—the system description (sysDescr).

Listing F-1   *Protocol analyzer decode of a sample SNMP GetResponse frame*

```
---- Simple Network Management Protocol ( SNMP ) ----
Class:                    0 (00...... Universal)
Encoding:                 1 (...1..... Constructed)
Tag Number:               16 (Sequence)
Sequence Length :         257
Version Class:            0 (00...... Universal)
Version Encoding:         0 (..0..... Primitive)
Version Tag Number:       2 (Integer)
Version Length :          1
Version Value:            0 (Snmp Version 1)
Community Class:          0 (00...... Universal)
Community Encoding:       0 (..0..... Primitive)
Community Tag Number:     4 (OctetString)
Community Length :        6
Community Value:          public
PDU Class:                2 (10...... Context-Specific)
PDU Encoding:             1 (...1..... Constructed)
PDU Tag Number:           2 (Get Response)
PDU Length :              243
Request ID Class:         0 (00...... Universal)
Request ID Encoding:      0 (..0..... Primitive)
Request ID Tag Number:    2 (Integer)
Request ID Length :       2
Request ID Value :        271
Error Status Class:       0 (00...... Universal)
Error Status Encoding:    0 (..0..... Primitive)
Error Status Tag Number:  2 (Integer)
Error Status Length :     1
Error Status Value :      0( No Error )
Error Index Class:        0 (00...... Universal)
Error Index Encoding:     0 (..0..... Primitive)
Error Index Tag Number:   2 (Integer)
Error Index Length :      1
Error Index Value :       0
Class:                    0 (00...... Universal)
Encoding:                 1 (...1..... Constructed)
Tag Number:               16 (Sequence)
```

Listing F-1 *Protocol analyzer decode of a sample SNMP GetResponse frame (Continued)*

```
Sequence Length :       230
Class:                  0 (00......  Universal)
Encoding:               1 (..1.....  Constructed)
Tag Number:             16 (Sequence)
Sequence Length :       227
Object Class:           0 (00......  Universal)
Object Encoding:        0 (..0.....  Primitive)
Object Tag Number:      6 (Object Identifier)
Object Length :         8
Object ID:              {1.3.6.1.2.1.1.1.0} (sysDescr.0)
Object Class:           0 (00......  Universal)
Object Encoding:        0 (..0.....  Primitive)
Object Tag Number:      4 (OctetString)
Object Length :         214
Object Value:           Cisco Internetwork Operating System Software
                        IOS (tm) 2500 Software (C2500-DS-L), Version 11.3(11a), RELEASE
                        SOFTWARE (fc1) Copyright (c) 1986-1999 by cisco Systems, Inc.
                        Compiled Mon 20-Sep-99 07:43 by jjgreen
```

```
0000:  00 C0 17 A0  02 17 00 00  0C 7E E1 84  08 00 45 00   .À. .....~á...E.
0010:  01 21 D5 E4  00 00 FF 11  AC F3 C0 A8  9A 01 C0 A8   .!Õä....óÀ¨..À¨
0020:  9A 69 00 A1  04 17 01 0D  DC FD 30 82  01 01 02 01   .i.¡....Üý0.....
0030:  00 04 06 70  75 62 6C 69  63 A2 81 F3  02 02 01 0F   ...public¢.ó....
0040:  02 01 00 02  01 00 30 81  E6 30 81 E3  06 08 2B 06   ......0.æ0.ã..+.
0050:  01 02 01 01  01 00 04 81  D6 43 69 73  63 6F 20 49   ........ÖCisco I
0060:  6E 74 65 72  6E 65 74 77  6F 72 6B 20  4F 70 65 72   nternetwork Oper
0070:  61 74 69 6E  67 20 53 79  73 74 65 6D  20 53 6F 66   ating System Sof
0080:  74 77 61 72  65 20 0D 0A  49 4F 53 20  28 74 6D 29   tware ..IOS (tm)
0090:  20 32 35 30  30 20 53 6F  66 74 77 61  72 65 20 28    2500 Software (
00A0:  43 32 35 30  30 2D 44 53  2D 4C 29 2C  20 56 65 72   C2500-DS-L), Ver
00B0:  73 69 6F 6E  20 31 31 2E  33 28 31 31  61 29 2C 20   sion 11.3(11a),
00C0:  52 45 4C 45  41 53 45 20  53 4F 46 54  57 41 52 45   RELEASE SOFTWARE
00D0:  20 28 66 63  31 29 0D 0A  43 6F 70 79  72 69 67 68    (fc1)..Copyrigh
00E0:  74 20 28 63  29 20 31 39  38 36 2D 31  39 39 39 20   t (c) 1986-1999
00F0:  62 79 20 63  69 73 63 6F  20 53 79 73  74 65 6D 73   by cisco Systems
0100:  2C 20 49 6E  63 2E 0D 0A  43 6F 6D 70  69 6C 65 64   , Inc...Compiled
0110:  20 4D 6F 6E  20 32 30 2D  53 65 70 2D  39 39 20 30    Mon 20-Sep-99 0
0120:  37 3A 34 33  20 62 79 20  6A 6A 67 72  65 65 6E 10   7:43 by jjgreen.
0130:  A9 82 AA                                             ©.ª
```

SNMPv1

There are many resources available for researching SNMP, although perhaps the first full description of the protocol was in RFC 1067 and updated in RFC 1157 (see RFCs 1065 through 1067, and 1155 through 1157). That version has become known as SNMPv1.

In SNMPv1, there were five fundamental message types (protocol data units [PDUs]):

- **GetRequest.** A request or query sent by the network management asking for the value represented by a specified OID.

- **GetNextRequest.** A request for the next value in a sequence or table, such as the next interface number in the ifIndex table. An entire MIB tree may be learned using Get-NextRequest.

- **GetResponse.** The answer sent by the agent in response to the query. The response includes the requested OID followed by the value that OID represents.

- **SetRequest.** A configuration change request, akin to modifying the configuration of some device through the command line or user interface.

- **Trap.** An unsolicited response usually based upon an event such as a configured threshold violation; for example; more than n percent utilization.

SNMPv2

SNMP was updated to version 2 by RFC 1448 (see RFCs 1441 through 1452). In this update, several new message descriptions (PDUs) and some security features were added. SNMPv2 also added the concept of manager-to-manager communications.

In SNMPv2, the defined PDUs became

- **GetRequest.** A request or query sent by the network management asking for the value represented by a specified OID.

- **GetNextRequest.** A request for the next value in a sequence or table, such as the next interface number in the ifIndex table. An entire MIB tree may be learned using Get-NextRequest.

- **GetBulkRequest.** A request for an entire sequence or table, such as the entire ifIndex table. This command was introduced to improve data transfer efficiency.

- **Response.** The answer sent by the agent in response to the query. The response includes the requested OID followed by the value that OID represents.

- **SetRequest.** A configuration change request, akin to modifying the configuration of some device through the command line or user interface.

- **SNMPv2-Trap.** An unsolicited response usually based on an event such as a configured threshold violation; for example, more than n percent utilization. Traps are sent by the agent.

- **InformRequest.** Sent from one manager to another manager, somewhat like a trap sent from an agent. By the time SNMPv3 was official, the "manager-to-manager" part was changed to be any SNMP device to another.

The security features in SNMPv2 were not popular, and what became known as SNMPv2c was eventually used in place of the security features (see RFC 1901 through 1908). SNMPv2c uses the community-based security scheme from SNMPv1. This still left SNMP exposed and eventually listed as one of the top 10 security vulnerabilities in a network because the password (community string) was sent unencrypted.

An additional security scheme was defined in RFCs 1909 and 1910, which was generally known as SNMPv2u. This scheme and another were used as the basis for SNMPv3 to address the security vulnerabilities of SNMP.

SNMPv3

Encryption and authentication were two of the important features defined by SNMPv3 (see RFC 3411 through 3418). Although RFC 3584 describes how the three versions of SNMP may coexist, versions 1 and 2 are actually superseded by version 3. The single step of using encryption went a considerable way toward returning SNMP to being a desirable way to monitor a network. SNMPv3 also included some remote configuration.

In RFC 3416, the defined SNMPv3 PDUs became

- **GetRequest.** A request or query sent by the network management asking for the value represented by a specified OID.

- **GetNextRequest.** A request for the next value in a sequence or table, such as the next interface number in the ifIndex table. An entire MIB tree may be learned using the GetNextRequest.

- **GetBulkRequest.** A request for an entire sequence or table, such as the entire ifIndex table. This command was introduced to improve data transfer efficiency.

- **Response.** The answer sent by the agent in response to the query. The response includes the requested OID followed by the value that OID represents.

- **SetRequest.** A configuration change request, akin to modifying the configuration of some device through the command line or user interface.

- **SNMPv2-Trap.** An unsolicited response usually based on an event such as a configured threshold violation; for example, more than *n* percent utilization. Traps are sent by the agent.

- **InformRequest.** Sent to provide notification of an event or condition, somewhat like a trap sent from an agent.

- **Report.** This PDU first appeared in RFC 1905 and was described as an aspect of error reporting between SNMPv2 entities in RFC 1909.

Configuring the security for SNMPv1 and v2 is as simple as typing the password (community string), but configuring SNMPv3 access requires more time and effort at both ends of the conversation (see Figure F–2).

SNMP Use

SNMP was one of the three cornerstones of network maintenance, and was the primary network monitoring solution until flow protocols were introduced. It is still very widely deployed, and continues to serve a key need for maintenance and monitoring. The SNMP protocol is used by a variety of applications to solicit information about network behavior and status, and then evaluate the information for reporting or alerting purposes.

A typical network management application represents either individual network entities such as a router with a simplified icon, or a grouping

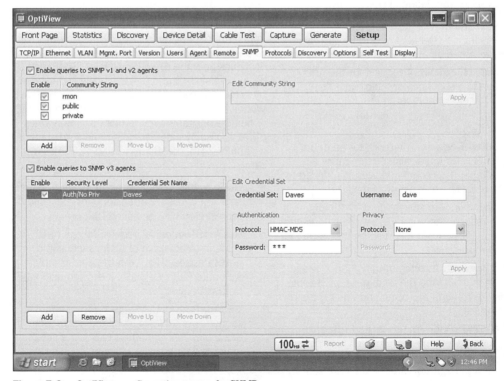

Figure F-2. *OptiView configuration screen for SNMP*

of entities or a portion of the network by a different simplified icon. At the top-level display are usually a small number of interlinked icons showing red, yellow, or green status colors (see Figure F-3). Clicking on an icon zooms the display in on the portion of the network represented by the top-level icon, and the display is replaced with a new and more specific subportion of the network—again represented by further icons (see Figure F-4). This drill-down process continues until an individual network resource is selected. By following the yellow or red icons during drill-down, it is possible to quickly learn which network resource needs attention. Having selected an individual network resource, the display changes to provide information as appropriate for that device.

Other approaches to displaying information using SNMP sources include correlating related data and presenting a display customized to troubleshooting rather than ongoing network monitoring (see Figure F-5 and Figure F-6).

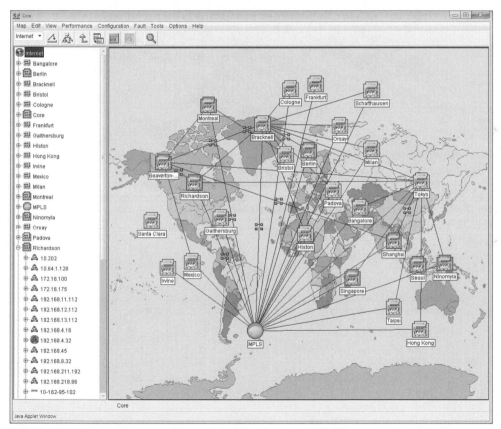

Figure F-3. *Sample top-level icon display for a typical icon-based network management platform. Icon color indicates relative health for the portion of the network represented by the icon.*

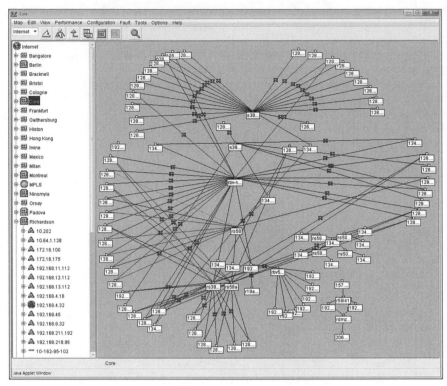

Figure F-4. *Sample first drill-down display for a typical icon-based network management platform. The top-level icon carries the "worst" color of all subordinate portions of the network. Observing icon color as you drill deeper allows rapid problem source discovery.*

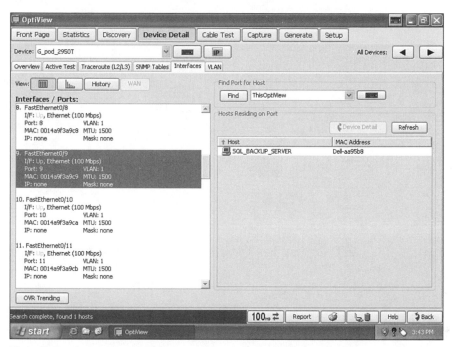

Figure F-5. *Sample troubleshooting presentation of the SNMP interface data. OptiView performs multiple queries and organizes the resulting information for best use during troubleshooting.*

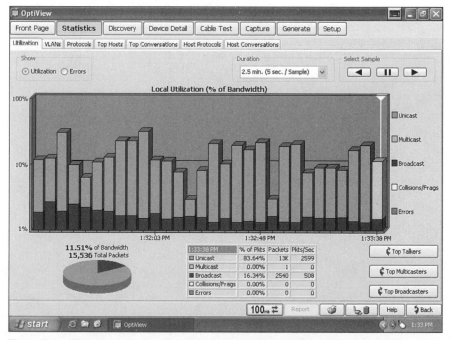

Figure F-6. *Sample troubleshooting presentation of SNMP RMON utilization. OptiView performs queries to the local or remote RMON history study and then presents graphical utilization and error results.*

APPENDIX G
Troubleshooting with a Protocol Analyzer

Using a protocol analyzer for troubleshooting can be accomplished in three general ways:

- Use the built-in or automated test suites to allow the analyzer to sift and sort the traffic into graphs and charts for you to review. Based on your knowledge of the network and the protocol behaviors, you can identify abnormal trends or activity.

- Use the optional built-in expert system to analyze the capture file, comparing the traffic against libraries of known problem symptoms and reporting any problem matches.

- Use knowledge of the protocol behavior and the application to read through the traffic captured in the trace file and follow the steps required for normal protocol behavior, and noting any discrepancies between observed activity and expected activity.

The third method for using a protocol analyzer requires knowledge of the protocols and normal network behavior to be successful. This requirement for protocol knowledge will be immediately evident as the protocol trace file in this appendix is explored. Also keep in mind that this trace file was cleaned and all superfluous traffic removed so that there were no distractions. It can be a significant challenge to find the right set of frames for analysis, particularly if the problem is intermittent or if the traffic of interest is a small part of a high-bandwidth, high-utilization link.

Amazingly, some technicians and network engineers are so knowledgeable about protocols and typical network behavior that simply providing a trace file containing the problem with no explanation is enough to allow them to report what was wrong. The rest of us use protocol analysis as more of a last resort. If we have not been able to find the problem using other means, we may reluctantly pull out a protocol analyzer and look to see what is actually happening on the wire. The reluctance comes from certain knowledge that infrequent use of a protocol analyzer usually means that it can take a long time to understand what is happening during the time represented by the trace file. If the application was written in-house, it may be that only the programmer knows what happened.

The amount of knowledge required to be successful with protocol analyzers is not actually as great as what is implied, but it must be at a minimum level for many protocols. Often you must also know something about the network or the problem symptom for the problem to be isolated. The required knowledge situation has improved considerably since Ethernet and TCP/IP "won" the race for network dominance. For those protocols, the information in this book can get you started, but further study will still be necessary.

Explaining how to use protocol analysis to read a trace file translates into explaining what the protocol is doing and noticing when it did not behave as expected. Following is an example of reading and explaining a very simple trace file where one client PC successfully connected to an Internet web site.

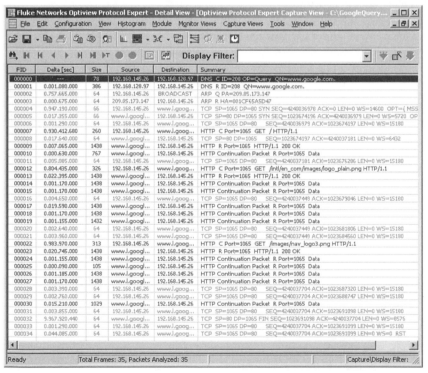

Understanding a Web Page Connection

The beginning of the capture file shown in Figure G–1 records a PC web browser being directed to www.google.com. After the page loaded, the web browser window was left idle.

- The first two frames captured show the PC (192.168.145.26) making a DNS query to discover an IP address for the web page www.google.com.

Figure G–1. *Protocol decode summary for a PC opening a web page as seen in OptiView Protocol Expert*

- After obtaining IP address 209.85.173.147 for the www.google.com query, in frames 2 and 3 the PC uses the ARP process to learn the MAC address, which may be used as a local destination for that IP address.

- In frames 4 through 6, the PC opens a TCP connection with the server responding to IP address 209.85.173.147. These three frames represent the TCP three-way handshake.

- Frames 7 through 31 show the home page of the web site opening.

- Frames 32 through 34 show the end of the connection.

This summary is graphically represented in Figure G-2, where pertinent details are extracted from the protocol capture file.

In Figure G-2, the first thing to notice is that the PC takes a comparatively long time to do anything (except for TCP ACKs, which are handled very low in the protocol stack—the operating system is scarcely involved). The infrastructure resources all respond very quickly. This is obvious without even taking time to study what the protocols are doing.

DNS Query

Very few Internet users know the IP address of a desired web server. Instead, they know, guess, or cross-link to the web page for that site. For the PC to fulfill the request to open a web page, it absolutely must know the MAC and IP address used to reach the

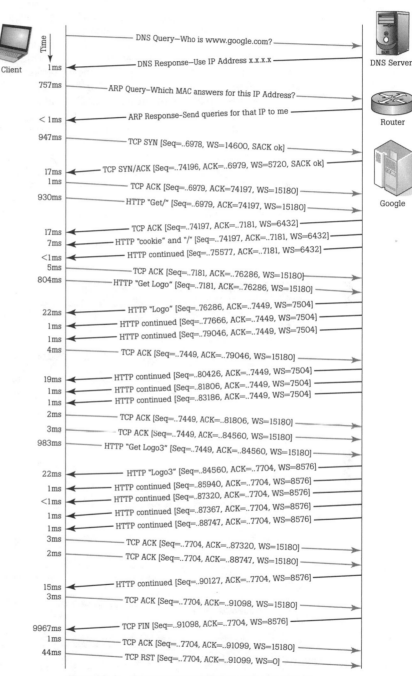

Figure G-2. *Graphic representation of the exchange shown in Figure G-1*

destination web page. To begin the process, the PC performs a DNS query to convert the name of the web page to an IP address (see Figure G-3).

The query for www.google.com is answered in Figure G-4, but the DNS name for the response IP address is different (www.l.google.com). Furthermore, the DNS server responded with four IP address choices for where to direct the query. It is common for a DNS name to have more than one responding server for geographically distributed load sharing and other similar purposes. Modifying the DNS record also allows the destination IP address to be changed quickly. Because the most common way of contacting a network resource is by name, use of DNS records to change which server is responding gives the support staff an easy way to redirect users if the network resource

is down for maintenance or is simply moved to a new hosting site. The user never knows that the destination IP address has changed.

DNS records may be shared between DNS servers in a zone transfer, or the tables may be replicated or maintained manually. If a change is made to one DNS server and the change is not propagated to all others who respond for that query, it is easily possible for some queries to work and others to fail after the server's IP address changes. To learn the IP address of the first (or only) IP address in a DNS response, try a command prompt ping to the DNS name (see Figure G-5). The nslookup command is also used more specifically for name resolution.

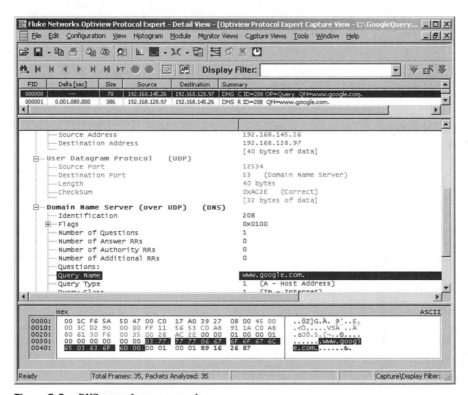

Figure G-3. *DNS query for www.google.com*

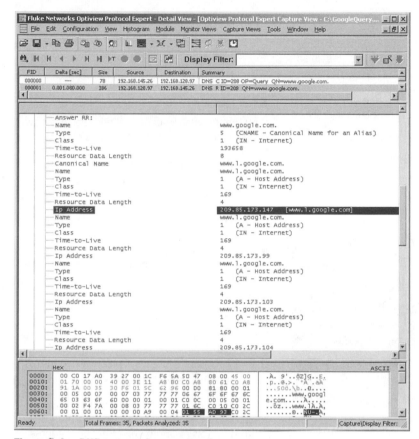

Figure G-4. *DNS response for www.google.com*

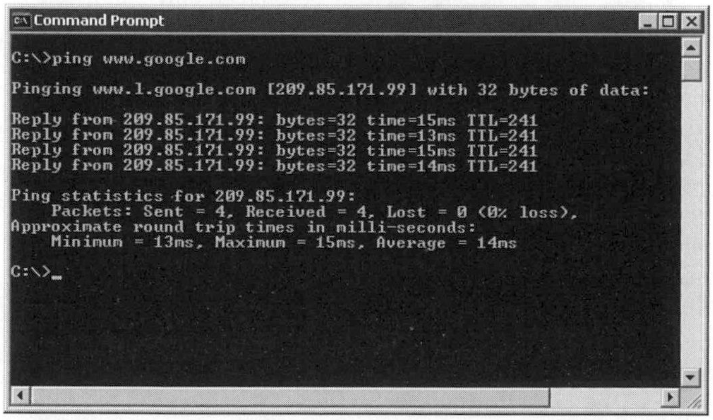

Figure G-5. *Ping utility used to resolve DNS name and simultaneously verify connectivity*

The ping utility must first translate the ping request from DNS name to IP address. The ping utility shows which the first IP address resolved for the name. The nslookup utility shows all addresses found in the response. When troubleshooting, compare the IP address resolved from a problem PC to that resolved at a working PC to see whether there are DNS problems (see Figure G-6). Try loading the web page using the IP address obtained from the working PC instead of the DNS name. If the problem PC failed to resolve an IP address at all, verify that a DNS server is included in the PC's IP configuration.

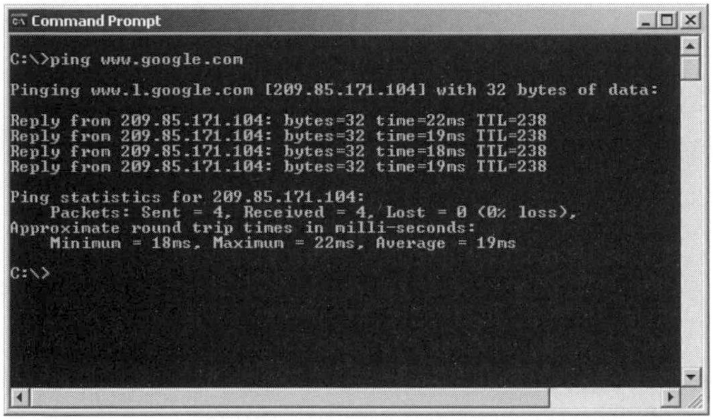

Figure G-6. *Ping resolution of the same DNS name from a different site*

If a protocol analyzer or some other suitable utility (such as nslookup) is handy, check to see whether there are additional IP addresses provided in the DNS response and whether one of the additional IP addresses work while the first does not. If a different IP address works, troubleshoot DNS. Start by discovering which DNS server provided an incorrect IP address. Of course, one web server might be down just then, or there could be Internet access problems to that server, too. The web page query in this example should work equally well (today) using any of these choices:

- http://www.google.com
- http://www.1.google.com
- http://209.85.173.147

- http://209.85.173.99
- http://209.85.173.103
- http://209.85.173.104

ARP Query

Now that the station has an IP address for www.google.com, it needs to know which MAC address to use to reach that IP address. Frames 3 and 4 reflect the ARP process, where the PC creates a temporary association between a local MAC address and the IP address for www.google.com. Figure G-7 shows the PC sending a broadcast looking for any station that responds for the specified IP address. The PC does not care if the responding MAC address is the destination or if it is a router leading to the destination. From the PC's perspective, it provides the same end result either way.

Notice that in Figure G-7, the PC has left the destination (Target) Ethernet address set to zeros. The protocol analyzer interprets the six-digit prefix for that address as coming from a Xerox NIC. This is because the all-zeros prefix was originally registered by Xerox. In fact, the zeros MAC address is effectively blank in this query.

In Figure G-8, the first router in the path toward www.google.com responds to the ARP request. In this example, the MAC Layer addressing information matches the ARP field for Sender Ethernet Address, but that is not always true. Sometimes there is a mismatch between these two fields, and that has the potential to cause connectivity problems.

TCP Connection

To proceed further in opening the requested web page, the PC must now establish a connection to the web server. Frames 4 to 6, shown in Figure G-1 and Figure G-2, show the TCP three-way handshake. The summary information for these three frames is shown in italics and is explained in this section.

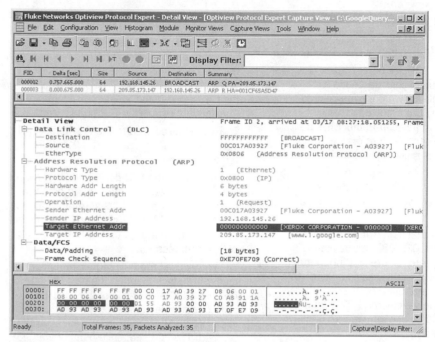

Figure G-7. *ARP query where the PC is attempting to find a MAC address to temporarily associate to the web server's IP address*

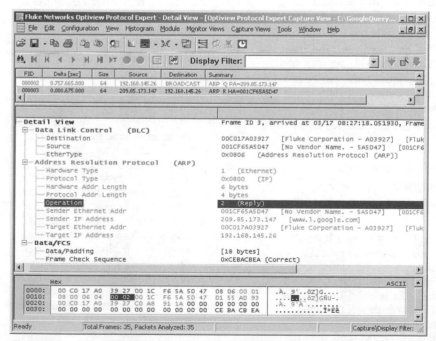

Figure G-8. *ARP response that provides a MAC address for the PC to use in reaching the specified IP address*

Frame 4 Summary

TCP SP=1065 DP=80 SYN SEQ=4240036978
ACK=0 LEN=0 WS=14600 OPT={ MSS SACKperm }

- The PC used a TCP source port of 1065. This is above the group of ports described as *well-known* (well-known ports are defined up to 1023). The PC is expected to select an *ephemeral port* (the port number has no significance other than as a reference for this connection) and is randomly selected from the port numbers above the well-known port range.

- The PC sent the SYN segment to the destination TCP port of 80, which is a well-known port for HTTP.

- The PC declared that its starting sequence number was 4240036978. This sequence number is interpreted as the starting number (representing zero) for this session. Each TCP data field octet transmitted by the PC causes this number to be incremented. This number is also incremented by one for certain TCP flags, such as the SYN flag.

- The PC used a zero value for the ACK sequence number (this will be provided by the server). The ACK flag is not set in this first frame.

- The segment length is zero, indicating that no payload data is being sent in the TCP data field in this frame.

- The window size declared by the PC is 14,600 octets, indicating how much buffer has been set aside for holding received TCP data until it can be processed.

- The PC is offering to use the Selective ACK option.

Frame 5 Summary

TCP SP=80 DP=1065 SYN SEQ=1023674196
ACK=4240036979 LEN=0 WS=5720 OPT={ MSS SACKperm }

- The server is using the well-known TCP port of 80 as the TCP source port. This indicates that the server has a process running which responds to TCP port 80. Web servers respond to TCP 80, or some other selected TCP port that the server administrator feels will be harder to guess (and therefore hack into), such as TCP 8080. If TCP port 80 is not used, the user community must know and specify the correct TCP port. For example, if TCP port 8080 were used instead of the default web page TCP port of 80, the following would be typed into the web browser as the destination: *http://www.google.com:8080*. A colon separates the DNS name from the TCP port number if a nonstandard or specific TCP port is used.

- The server responded to the destination TCP port of 1065 in response to the PC's SYN request.

- The server set the SYN flag as a formal request to the PC to open a connection. In doing so, the server declared that its starting sequence number was 1023674196. Again, this is interpreted as the starting number (representing zero) for this session.

- The server used the PC's sequence number for the ACK, incrementing the value by one because a SYN flag is one of the flags that causes sequence numbers to be incremented to ensure that important events are explicitly counted. The PC's sequence number was 4240036978, and this acknowledgment is incremented to 4240036979. Because the server sent the frame, the ACK sequence number acts as a formal acknowledgment to the PC that all TCP data octets up to that number have been received successfully from the server. In this case, the server formally acknowledged receipt of just the SYN request from the PC.

- The segment length is zero, indicating that there is no payload data being sent in the TCP data field in this frame.

- The window size declared by the server is 5,720 octets, indicating how much buffer has been set aside for holding received TCP data until it can be processed. It is normal for a server to reserve less buffer space than a client PC because it must allocate memory resources for every client that connects. If it allocated a large buffer for each PC, it would quickly run out of available memory and be able to service only a small number of client PC connections. (A TCP SYN attack is a denial-of-service attack that exploits this, and causes the target server to allocate all available memory to fake connection requests and thereby denies access by legitimate clients.)

- The server is offering to use the *Selective ACK* option.

Frame 6 Summary

TCP SP=1065 DP=80 SEQ=4240036979
ACK=1023674197 LEN=0 WS=15180

- The PC is using the ephemeral TCP source port of 1065, and continues to do so throughout this connection.

- The PC is continuing to send to the server's well-known TCP destination port of 80, and does so throughout this connection.

- The PC used the server's sequence number in the acknowledgment, including an increment of one for the SYN request that the server made. The acknowledged sequence number is now 1023674197. This ACK completes the three-way handshake, and a connection is now open between the server and the PC.

- The PC used sequence number 4240036979 for itself, which matches what the server acknowledged in frame 00005.

- The segment length is zero, indicating that no payload data is being sent in the TCP data field in this frame.

- The PC's window size is now 15,180. Although window size changes dynamically during a conversation, it usually decreases and then returns to the original value. This was a somewhat unexpected increase because the initial window size is usually not increased like this during the three-way handshake. The change indicates that the PC has more buffer available for received and unprocessed TCP data from the server than it had before.

Further information is available from the detailed frame decoding presented in the second pane of the protocol analyzer. From that detail, several additional TCP operational details will be highlighted.

Frame 4 Decode Details

In Figure G-9, the following additional TCP operational details are found:

- The only TCP flag that is set is the SYN flag. The PC is requesting a connection by setting the SYN flag. The sequence number sent is the random value that represents the starting point for counting TCP data sent from the PC (4240036978).

Figure G-9. *TCP protocol decode detail for the PC's SYN request (frame 4)*

- The PC is announcing that it is expecting a maximum segment size (MSS) of 1460 octets.

- There is a TCP option present (Selective ACK), so the TCP header length is indicating a header size of 28 octets (header length = 28 bytes). Options must end on 32-bit boundaries, so there are two octets of header padding occupied by the *no operation* code, for a total of 8 octets of options.

Frame 5 Decode Details

In Figure G-10, the following additional TCP operational details are found:

- Both the TCP flags for SYN and ACK are set. The server is acknowledging the PC's connection request with the ACK flag, and it is at the same time requesting a connection by setting the SYN flag. The ACK sequence number is what the PC sent plus 1 to formally acknowledge receipt of the SYN (4240036979). The sequence number sent is the random value that represents the starting point for counting TCP data sent from the server (1023674196).

- The server is announcing that it will use a maximum segment size (MSS) of 1380 octets. This means that the server believes that the network can transmit a segment containing 1380 octets of TCP data to clients without having to fragment the frame into two frames along the way. It is likely that someone has adjusted the MSS lower on the server to accommodate overhead from tunneled connections such as Virtual Private Networks (VPNs) without causing frame fragmentation.

- There is a TCP option present (Selective ACK), so the TCP header length is indicating a header size of 28 octets (header length = 28 bytes). Options must end on 32-bit boundaries, so there are two octets of header padding occupied by the *no operation* code, for a total of 8 octets of options.

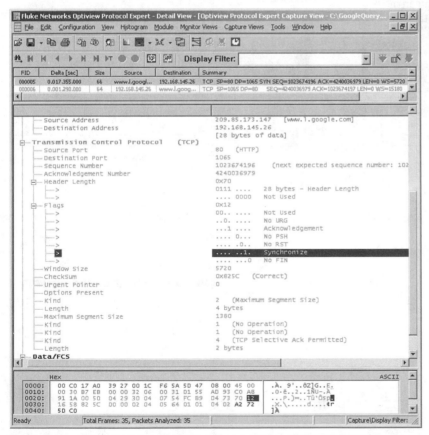

Figure G-10. *TCP protocol decode detail for the web server's ACK and SYN request (frame 5)*

Frame 6 Decode Details

In Figure G-11, the following additional TCP operational details are found:

- The only TCP flag, which is set is the ACK flag. The PC has acknowledged receipt of the server's SYN request and has increased the sequence number sent by the server by 1 accordingly (1023674197).

- The TCP header does not include any options, so the header size is the minimum size of 20 octets (header length = 20 bytes).

- The PC has increased the size of its temporary receive buffer to 15,180 octets.

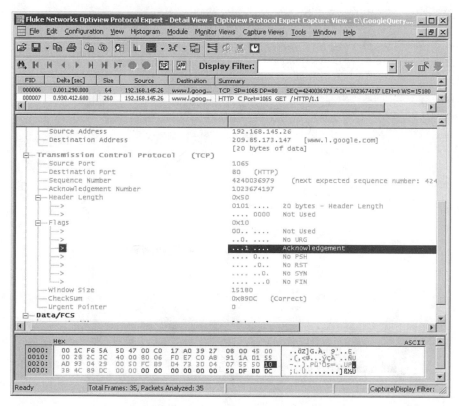

Figure G-11. *TCP protocol decode detail for the PC's ACK of the server's SYN request (frame 6)*

Data Transfer

The three-way handshake was completed with frame 6, and a connection is now open between the PC and the web server. The PC now asks for the home page at www.google.com (indicated by the slash (/) in the Get statement (see Figure G-12). This is about the simplest possible web query.

The remaining frames from frame 8 to frame 31 show the server fulfilling the first Get request, acknowledgments for data sent, a second Get request, and the data and acknowledgments for that as well. Data transfer similar to this is described in detail in Chapter 7, "Transport Layer," so it will not be repeated.

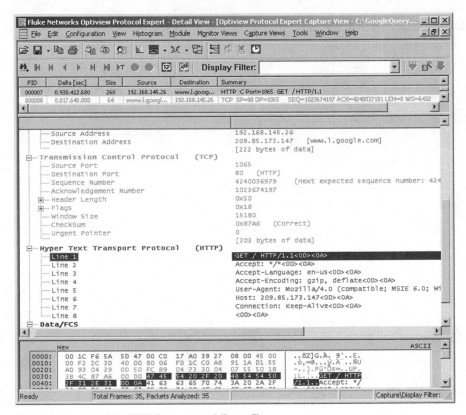

Figure G-12. *The PC's HTTP Get command (frame 7)*

Closing the Connection

The next transaction of note occurs after nearly 10 seconds of inactivity. The web server decides that this idle time suggests that nothing further is likely, so it closes the session to free up resources for another user. This is accomplished by sending a FIN request to the PC, asking to close the connection (see Figure G-13).

In frame 33, the PC acknowledges the FIN request. Strangely, in frame 34, the PC then issues a connection RST (reset) command. This is an abrupt termination of the session that the server was already closing (see Figure G-14).

DNS Failure

As a comparison, an additional protocol trace file was captured. This time, a command prompt window was opened and a ping was issued to the www.google.com web site, but the "o" characters were improperly replaced with Os. This caused the DNS lookup performed by the ping utility to fail (see Figure G-15).

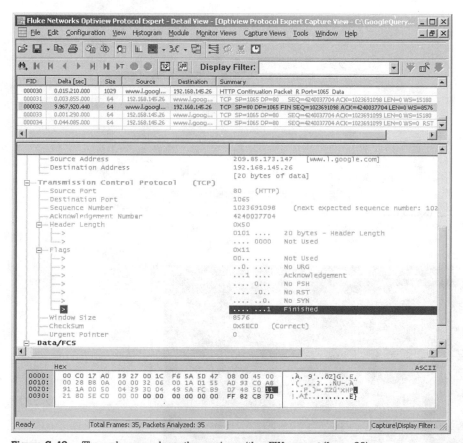

Figure G-13. *The web server closes the session with a FIN request (frame 32)*

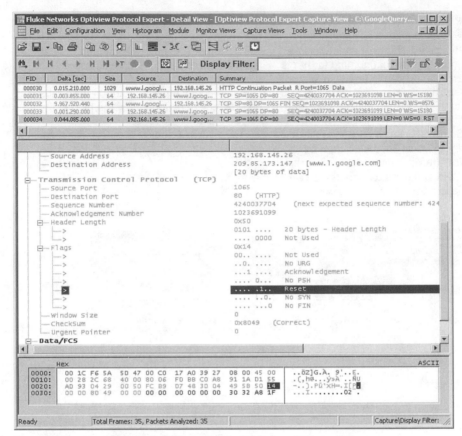

Figure G-14. *The PC resets the TCP session, closing it abruptly (frame 34)*

Figure G-15. *Ping utility failed to resolve mistyped www.g00gle.com*

The protocol trace file for this failed ping op- eration reveals two frames: the outbound query and an empty response, indicating the DNS server could find no such name in its own tables or in any more authoritative DNS server tables. DNS servers are typically configured with the address of other DNS servers closer to the Internet core. These interlinked DNS servers share information as appropriate, or make references to other DNS servers believed to hold authority over specific fully qualified DNS names.

Note that in Figure G-16, the highlighted field in the decode pane is the last thing appearing in the lower hexadecimal viewing pane before the 4-octet checksum (FCS) field. The server had nothing to report in response to the query, but it did answer.

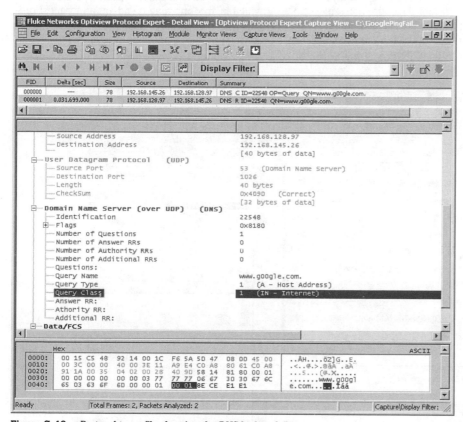

Figure G-16. *Protocol trace file showing the DNS lookup failure*

Protocol Analyzers and Protocol Knowledge

The preceding information is part of what can be learned by just a short protocol capture file or two. The limitation on what can be learned is the user's knowledge of normal protocol operation for each protocol in use. Other features of protocol analyzers may be utilized without going as deeply into the protocol activities. For example, rather than the drawing showing the series of transactions in Figure G-2, most protocol analyzers present a bounce chart for the entire conversation that includes the currently highlighted frame.

By clicking the Application Bounce Chart button a new pane appears in the display. By

dragging the side of the pane, you may expose more or less of the decode summary in the center (over the arrow). In Figure G-17, frame 7 is highlighted in the decode summary, which is then shown in yellow on the bounce chart. Double-clicking a frame in the bounce chart will likewise move the highlight in the decode summary. Also in Figure G-17, the mouse (not shown) is hovering over frame 10, which causes an informational pop-up to appear, describing certain information about the frame being hovered over.

Multiple built-in simple analysis features are available, too, and may be adequate for most protocol analyzer uses. For example, for a breakdown of which protocols appear in the active trace file, click the Protocol Distribution View button and see Figure G-18.

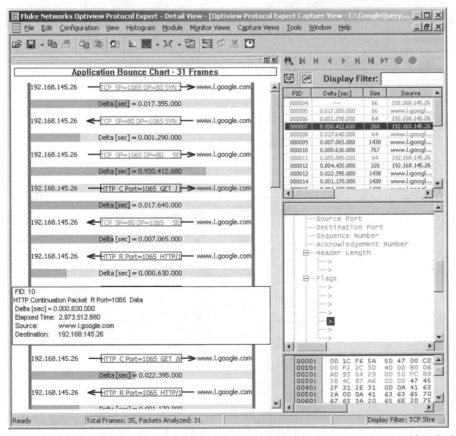

Figure G-17. *Bounce chart for this TCP conversation. The cursor is hovering over frame 10 in the bounce chart but is not shown in the screen capture. This caused the detail pop-up to be shown for frame 10.*

Another popular built-in feature for many protocol analyzers is the library of known problem signatures that is compared against the contents of the active protocol trace file to see whether suspected problems exist. Libraries such as this are referred to as *experts* or *expert systems* 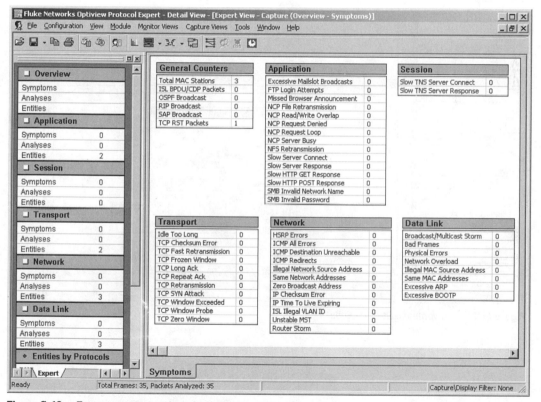.

Because the only odd situation in the protocol trace file has been the single use of Reset (RST) by the PC when closing the session, there is little to report in Figure G-19.

Protocol Name	Total Frames	Rel % Frames	Total Bytes	Rel % Bytes
ARP	2	5.71	128	0.63
ETHERNET II	35	100.00	20104	100.00
UDP	2	5.71	464	2.30
IP	33	94.28	19976	99.36
DNS	2	5.71	464	2.30
TCP	31	88.57	19512	97.05
HTTP	31	88.57	19512	97.05

Figure G-18. *Distribution of protocols for the active protocol trace file example*

Figure G-19. *Expert symptom analysis for the active protocol trace file*

Many of the selections are also hyperlinks. In Figure G-20, the Network Entities cell was clicked, and the main viewing pane was changed to show statistics about all the entities found in the active protocol trace file. If instead the First Frame cell was clicked beside one of the IP addresses shown, the main viewing pane would revert to the three-pane protocol decode view, and that frame would be highlighted.

Each button at the top of the display represents some useful feature. A large percentage of all protocol analyzer users do not often stray away from simple button use to delve into the protocol details.

See the last part of Appendix B, "Waveform Decoding Exercise," for a summary listing of what each of the buttons or button groups offers in this protocol analyzer.

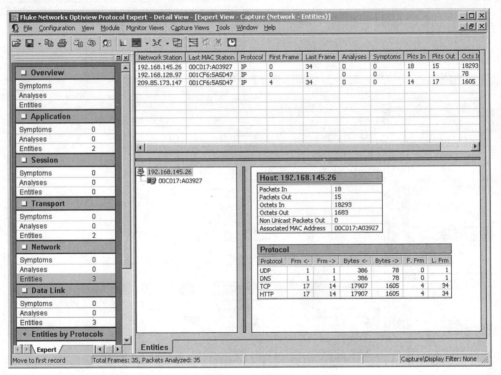

Figure G-20. *Navigating built-in hyperlinks*

APPENDIX H
Network Diagnostic Products Used in This Book

Most Fluke Networks tools used for examples and screen captures in this book are briefly described in this appendix. For more information, visit the Fluke Networks web site (www.flukenetworks.com/). The information here only illustrates examples for the types of tools available for maintaining networks. Many other fine products are available from Fluke Networks and other vendors.

The tool best suited for a particular person will depend on many factors, but most importantly the following:

- Skill and knowledge level of the user
- Job the user is performing
- Level of access to infrastructure devices (do they have the password?)

Technology also plays a part in deciding which tools apply best to your situation. The adage "each network is unique" is painfully true.

Before buying tools to help maintain your network, try to arrange for a product evaluation so that you can try the prospective product on your network and obtain feedback from each of the proposed user groups. Verify that it does the job and provides clear information, and that the proposed user is comfortable with it. Some tools are too complex; others are too simplistic for certain jobs or users.

Almost all networks have migrated from largely shared media networks to almost completely switched networks, although shared media is again increasing in the form of wireless. Trouble-shooting a switched network presents serious difficulties in isolating and identifying the source of problems.

What Tool to Start With?

The network support staff for a large organization should consider tools that fit the organizational structure. A proposed structure of network operations, network engineering, network technicians, and Help Desk is offered as an example.

Network Operations

The network operations center (NOC) is usually associated with SNMP-based network management solutions. Recently this has been expanded to include the new fourth mainstay of network support: flow protocols. Flow protocols provide a similar level trend analysis to what SNMP has long provided, except that it shows the data by protocol and user through a specific port or throughout the organization, not by utilization from a specific port. These solutions obtain input from some or all of the network infrastructure devices, and based on that input report anomalies and problems as they are detected. Daily activities for the NOC staff involve remote access and monitoring. This team may also be partially responsible for maintaining the core router configurations and network security activities, and may be the liaison between the organization and the ISP(s) used by the organization. In some organizations this position is also involved in datacenter activities such as system backups and server maintenance.

Basic skill set required for network operations:

- Strong syslog, SNMP, and flow protocol skills
- LAN/WAN monitoring and troubleshooting
- Strong knowledge of routing protocols
- Firewall/security management and intrusion investigation
- Applications monitoring is becoming more common

Support Tool Requirements

Data summarization, thresholds, alarming, and other similar features are important because this category of user is typically responsible for large geographies. Top-level information should be simple and direct, with drill-down for details conveniently available.

Specific network operations support tool features include

- Historical trend analysis for utilization, protocols, conversations, and errors
- Real-time analysis for utilization, protocols, conversations, and errors

Network Engineering

A network engineering staff typically has good protocol analysis skills, holds the password to all the routers, and has found it necessary to learn the "personality" of many network applications to keep them running. This staff is usually responsible for the bulk of the security and expansion planning and deployment, while still monitoring day-to-day operations. The network engineer typically has the highest skill and knowledge level in the department.

The following is the basic skill set required for network engineering:

- Network discovery, mapping, and documentation
- Traffic monitoring to determine which protocols are on the network
- SNMP polling, syslog analysis, and flow protocol use
- Host management utility use for infrastructure and server maintenance and monitoring
- LAN/WAN design, installation, and maintenance
- Intimate knowledge of routing protocols
- Design and implementation of network operations monitoring solutions, Help Desk application maintenance
- Wire-speed hardware–based packet capture and protocol analysis to measure before/after network/application response times
- Firewall/security management and intrusion investigation
- Ability to locate cable faults and add and certify new cable runs (copper or fiber)

Support Tool Requirements

As long as the data is presented well, and the level of detail can be drilled-into or otherwise managed, it is difficult to provide too much detail.

Specific network engineer support tool features include

- Historical trend analysis for utilization, protocols, conversations, and errors
- Real-time analysis for utilization, protocols, conversations, and errors
- Protocol analysis
  - Line rate capture capability for LAN/WAN technologies
  - Latency and jitter measurement capability with < 100ns accuracy

- Advanced feature analysis tools for VoIP, MPLS, and so on
- Expert analysis library

Network Technicians

Network technicians are typically more knowledgeable about network issues than Help Desk staff, but less knowledgeable than a network engineer. They may or may not be competent with a protocol analyzer, and they may have limited access to the network infrastructure passwords. A technician's daily activities require much more detailed information and flexibility from diagnostic tools than the Help Desk. The most effective network support departments permit network technicians to earn enough responsibility and authority to solve problems, not just identify and isolate them. For this purpose, they might not have password access to the routers, but usually have password access to the switches.

The following is the basic skill set required for network technicians:

- End-user software and hardware troubleshooting and support for both PCs and networking issues
- Help Desk software installation, use, and maintenance
- May provide end-user training
- Network discovery, mapping, and documentation
- SNMP polling to baseline switch and router performance, possibly using a preconfigured network management application
- Traffic monitoring to determine which protocols are on the network
- Wire speed, hardware packet capture, and protocol analysis to measure before/after network/application response times
- Host management utilities (telnet/ssh) to view and change infrastructure device configurations
- Ability to locate simple cable faults, or the ability to add and certify a few new cable runs (usually copper)

Support Tool Requirements

A moderate level of detail is acceptable and necessary for this category of user, but it is still possible to provide so much detail that the tools are avoided. Specific network technician support tool features include

- Real-time analysis for utilization, protocols, conversations, and errors

- Simple SNMP capabilities for checking things such as up/down status on interfaces, interface errors, interface utilization, and so on

Network/PC Support Help Desk

The Help Desk staff typically has operating system and applications usage knowledge but little networking knowledge. The best tool for this level of user is one that is mostly automated and reports very simple results. The testing should validate basic connectivity on the network. From these results the Help Desk should be able to communicate to the network technician what is and is not working. This gives the network technician a clear starting point, and little if any troubleshooting should require a duplication of the initial troubleshooting efforts performed by the Help Desk.

The following is the basic skill set required for network/PC support Help Desk:

- Customer interaction skills more important than PC or networking skills, but evidence of those skills are required as minimum entry-level job skills (various certifications accepted)

- Help Desk software user, primarily focused on maintaining good documentation, timely responses, user updates, and responsibility for an issue until problem resolution

- Provide desk-side support when problems cannot be resolved remotely

- Troubleshoot far enough to fully document the problem and escalate as necessary

- Monitoring the activities of escalation technicians forms a large part of on-the-job training necessary to move to next higher job level

Support Tool Requirements

Fast, simple handheld tools with simplified messages. If tools provide too much detail, this category of user may avoid using them. Specific network/PC support Help Desk tool features include

- Cable fault detection

- Link and error detection

- Basic networking service discovery and problem detection

- In-line monitoring and problem detection

- Ping and traceroute

- Preconfigurable service or server validation (TCP port-based connection verification)

Media Test

Fluke Networks participates closely in the ongoing development of cable testing standards and applies the research conducted for standards development to improve our suite of cable test products.

DTX 1800 Cable Analyzer

The DTX Cable Analyzer Series offers comprehensive cable testing and fault analysis for both copper and fiber optic cable installations. This series of cable analyzer is among the most accurate and fastest on the market today, with features that are in the forefront of cable testing technology (see Figure H-1).

The most common users of a cable analysis and certification tool are found in the following table.

Note: *In the tables,* ● *indicates that the level of user really needs the described capability on a daily basis.* ◗ *indicates that something is useful to that level of user but not critical, either because it is a peripheral requirement or because it is only occasionally required.*

	NOC	Engineer	Technician	Help Desk	Installer
DTX 1800		◗	●		●

The DTX series cable analyzer offers full support for copper cabling, with optional patch cord testing, alien crosstalk testing, fiber test support, and an OTDR. If a link should fail testing, the DTX Series provides quick, easy-to-understand directions to identify the point of failure (distance from the tester) and the possible reason(s) for the failure. These directions not only tell you the problem, but also identify corrective actions your test technicians can take to solve the problem quickly. Instead of spending time executing trial-and-error corrections—and retesting to find out whether the problem has been resolved—the installer knows exactly where to look and what to do to fix the failing link. All test results may be saved and managed within the companion LinkWare PC software.

The optional DTX Compact OTDR module identifies breaks in the fiber link, as well as connections or splices with excessive loss. The fiber loss/length modules as well as the Compact OTDR module offer an integrated visual fault locator (VFL). The VFL helps you locate many near-end fiber faults and can be used to verify continuity and polarity.

OptiFiber Certifying OTDR

OptiFiber integrates power/loss, fiber length measurement, OTDR analysis, and fiber connector end-face imaging to provide a higher tier of fiber certification and diagnostics (see Figure H-2). The companion LinkWare PC software documents, reports, and manages all test data. OptiFiber enables network owners of all experience levels to certify fiber to customer specifications and new industry standards, troubleshoot connection-rich links, and thoroughly document results.

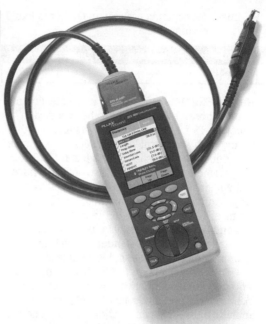

Figure H-1. *DTX-1800 Cable Analyzer main unit with permanent link adapter (remote unit not shown)*

Figure H-2. *OptiFiber OTDR tester for singlemode and multimode fiber optic cable*

The most common users of an OTDR are found in the following table.

	NOC	Engineer	Technician	Help Desk	Installer
OptiFiber		●	▶		●

The TIA TSB-140 includes two tiers of testing that can be chosen by a designer to be specified in a project. Tier 1 accommodates loss and length testing with an optical loss test set (OLTS), coupled with end-face inspection. Tier 2 testing includes the parameters of Tier 1 and also an OTDR trace of the installed cable plant. By incorporating the proposed two-tier testing method, installers have the most complete picture of the fiber installation and network owners have proof of a quality installation. Recent IEC standards also include the recommendation of a second level of testing.

OptiFiber delivers on Tier 2 certification by integrating bidirectional two-fiber dual-wavelength insertion loss and automated OTDR pass/fail link analysis a one-two combination you will find only with OptiFiber. But OptiFiber doesn't stop there. It also offers fiber end-face grading. OptiFiber allows you to certify every link with one tool by

- Measuring loss and length
- Analyzing the OTDR trace
- Grading the connector end-face

OptiFiber integrates the features that matter most when troubleshooting enterprise networks. These networks are characterized by relatively short lengths of fiber within data centers or between buildings. Fibers are terminated with connectors and segments connected with short patch cables. No other OTDR lets you see both ends of short patch cables, allowing you to see the condition of your connectors so you can quickly and efficiently diagnose and fix the problem.

- Event characterization analysis
- Advanced multimode modules with event dead zone of 0.5 meter at 850nm
- Advanced singlemode modules with event dead zones of 1 meter at 1310/1550nm
- A unique map of the channel that illustrates the location of all connectors

- Automated OTDR trace and event test limits
- 250x and 400x high magnification video end-face inspection

OptiFiber simplifies OTDR analysis by automating certification and troubleshooting. In Auto OTDR mode OptiFiber automatically

- Optimizes launch conditions for the best resolution
- Makes dual wavelength OTDR measurements—850/1300nm or 1310/1550nm
- Identifies and characterizes the fiber link and its events
- Compares the results to user-defined limits for immediate Pass/Fail link and event certification
- Saves time spent setting and moving cursors

For advanced troubleshooting, you can view a trace at two wavelengths, automatically step from one event to the next and zoom in on those of interest, and measure event loss. Events are also summarized in a table.

More than 85 percent of all fiber failures encountered are due to contaminated fiber end-faces. Such contamination is easily seen with OptiFiber's video inspection system. View end-faces under 250x or 400x magnification.

You can inspect fibers installed in patch panels and devices without disassembly with OptiFiber's video probes. The probe is inserted through bulkhead adapters letting you test 10 times faster than traditional scopes. And it's safer for your eyes because there is no direct optical path to you.

With FiberInspector, you can see the condition of the fiber end-face. You can assign a pass or fail grade to the fiber and append a comment. You can apply a scale to help determine the fiber type, and you can save the image for use in certification reports and other documents.

Troubleshooting starts with a simple link diagram that technicians can easily read and interpret. OptiFiber's ChannelMap presents the OTDR data in a simple diagram, or map, showing the number and location of connectors (see Figure H-3). No interpretation necessary. OptiFiber is the only OTDR solution available with this unique technician-friendly feature.

With ChannelMap, you can

- Quickly verify the composition of the link
- Identify patch cables as short as 1 meter in length

You might need a direct measurement of optical power to aid in source and link performance verification. With OptiFiber's optional power meter module, you have 850nm, 1300nm, 1310nm, and 1550nm optical power measurement capability. A single module integrates both power meter and OTDR capabilities, minimizing the number of tools you need to carry with you into the field. All loss/ length modules are also capable of making power measurements.

Then use the companion LinkWare cable test management software to present this test data in a single certification report that can be archived or submitted as proof of a properly installed and terminated installation (see Figure H-4).

AnalyzeAir Wi-Fi Spectrum Analyzer

AnalyzeAir is a Wi-Fi spectrum analyzer comprising a custom PCMCIA card and software that lets you identify, monitor, analyze, and manage all RF sources and wireless devices that influence your 802.11 network's performance and security—even providing visibility of unauthorized or transient devices.

AnalyzeAir takes the cost and complexity out of spectrum analysis. Unlike single-function RF analyzers or expensive tools that provide RF information without device identification and location, AnalyzeAir provides an easy-to-understand, fast-start solution, allowing you to quickly resolve RF problems that prevent WLAN connectivity and impact performance.

AnalyzeAir software includes the following features:

- RF spectrum analysis for troubleshooting and optimizing 802.11a/b/g/n WLANs operating in the 2.4GHz and 5GHz frequency bands
- Real-time device detection and identification
- Device Finder that pinpoints the location of interfering devices

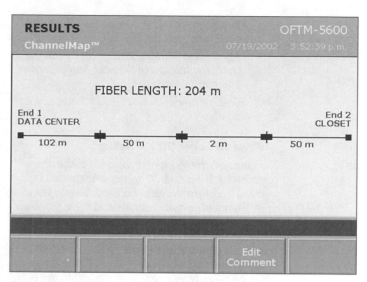

Figure H-3. *OptiFiber ChannelMap example*

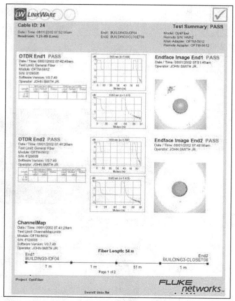

Figure H-4. *LinkWare test results page for a saved OptiFiber test*

- Designed for IT network professionals who need answers, not just data
- Affordable, portable solution for use on the OptiView Integrated Network Analyzer or on a laptop/tablet PC
- Real-time spectrum analysis wherever you need it

Physical Layer (RF) Visibility

AnalyzeAir provides clear visibility of the unlicensed 2.4GHz and 5GHz frequencies used by 802.11 a/b/g/n WLANs. You don't have to be an RF engineer to quickly locate and solve problems on your wireless network. AnalyzeAir software wraps the tools RF experts use in an easy-to use interface, putting the power of automated RF analysis into your hands.

With AnalyzeAir you have the ability to determine what could be causing connectivity problems on the network by identifying them by type and location. It helps you solve plaguing performance problems caused by interference by looking at the RF spectrum in real time. When the interference occurs, you can quickly identify the offending devices and determine their physical locations.

Device Listing

AnalyzeAir software interprets the RF energy in the spectrum or channel and lists the devices that are transmitting—associating real devices on the energy pulses. With AnalyzeAir software, you know what the problem is immediately and can quickly identify it. To find out more information about a device, simply click on it. AnalyzeAir software's user-friendly interface puts valuable information at your fingertips, so you can troubleshoot your network quickly. AnalyzeAir automatically identifies Bluetooth devices, cordless phones, microwave ovens, analog video cameras, and RF jammers (see Figure H-6).

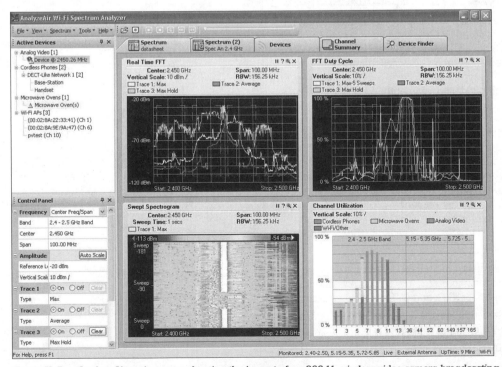

Figure H-5. *AnalyzeAir main screen showing the impact of an 802.11 wireless video camera broadcasting at a frequency between channels 6 and 11, and interfering with both*

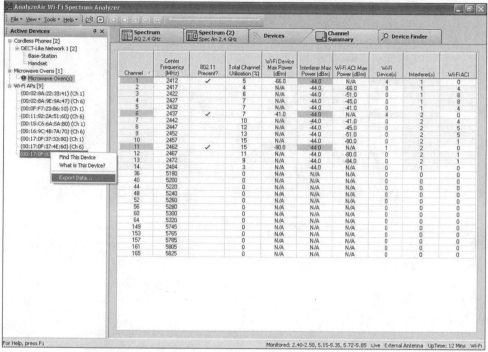

Figure H-6. *AnalyzeAir channel summary screen showing a table of channels monitored during this test, detected devices, and statistics about 802.11 performance for each channel reported*

Device Finder

Device Finder makes it easy to locate troublesome or unauthorized devices. Just click on the offending device and Device Finder will tell you its signal strength. As you move closer or farther away from the device, Device Finder's signal strength will change. Using this dynamically changing signal, you can quickly narrow in on the offending device and determine its exact location (see Figure H-7).

Save Spectrum Information for Later Analysis

Record and save time-correlated spectrum information for later analysis, similar to protocol analyzers. Technicians can record events in the field, save them to a file, and take the results back to the central network operations center. Need to track your spectrum behavior? Use AnalyzeAir software to create a baseline and periodically log new events to track changes across your network.

Device Impact Statistics

AnalyzeAir lists the devices using your RF spectrum and shows the impact of each device or interference source on your network whether it is expected, unauthorized, or transient. How much is a microwave oven affecting your network? Which channels is it degrading? AnalyzeAir will show you.

Device and Security Alerts

AnalyzeAir provides color-coded flags to identify interfering devices that are impacting your network or possible security risks. Easily customize AnalyzeAir's alerts and their levels to fit your needs.

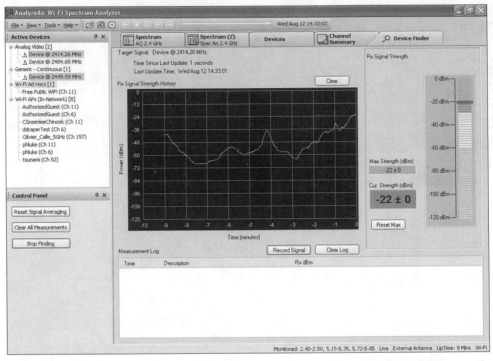

Figure H-7. *AnalyzeAir Device Finder screen showing signal strength changes as the analyzer approaches a selected interference source using a directional antenna*

View Multiple Charts and Plots

You can create custom diagnostic view configurations, choosing from 10 available plots and charts. Each plot or chart can be customized to display only the specific data you require.

Available graphs include the following plots and charts:

Plots:

* Real-time FFT
* FFT Duty Cycle
* Swept Spectrogram
* Power vs. Freq
* Power vs. Time

Charts:

* Active Devices
* Devices vs. Channel

* Devices vs. Time
* Channel Utilization
* Channel Utilization vs. Time
* Interference Power
* Signal-to-noise Ratio

Network Analysis: Hybrid Handhelds

The hybrid handheld testers discussed in this section incorporate SNMP, various local and remote discovery techniques, traffic analysis, network services testing, protocol analysis, and media test capabilities.

OptiView

The OptiView series of network analyzers has both LAN and WAN models, plus optional wireless support (see Figure H-8).

The most common users of a high-level portable network diagnostic and troubleshooting tool are found in the following table.

	NOC	Engineer	Technician	Help Desk	Installer
OptiView Network Analyzers	●	●	◗		

OptiView Integrated Network Analyzer

The Integrated Network Analyzer model of the OptiView series is designed as a tactical "first-in" diagnostic tool. As such, it will perform a lengthy list of discovery and diagnostic tests immediately and automatically upon being connected to a live Ethernet connection. During this process it creates an inventory of all discovered devices on the local broadcast domain. The other models in the series are intended for more strategic, permanent, or semi-permanent installation, and although they also perform discovery first the subsequent monitoring is optimized for long-term statistical monitoring rather than short-term aggressive discovery.

The OptiView Integrated Network Analyzer is a portable enterprisewide tool that combines protocol analysis, active discovery, SNMP device analysis, and RMON2 traffic analysis into a mobile solution. In addition to the instrument display, the web-enabled user interface allows up to seven remote users to access a single unit simultaneously, each operating an independent and separate analysis instance. Some of the available features are as follows:

- 10/100/1000 wired and 802.11 b/g/a/n WLAN plus spectrum analysis possible from one solution
- Wireless, VoIP, and Application Troubleshooting Expert options available
- 802.1X authentication
- Gigabit line rate capture, traffic generation and throughput testing

Figure H-8. *OptiView Integrated Network Analyzer (INA) model*

- Free string match filtering and triggers with the ability to control capture and provide detailed event analysis
- VLAN trunk analysis
- Infrastructure device analysis includes support for SNMPv3
- Application Troubleshooting Expert option validates network services and provides detailed application flow analysis
- Management port for out-of-band remote control

As soon as the analyzer is connected to the network, it automatically begins to discover devices on the network, with no interaction required, by monitoring traffic and actively querying hosts. Support staff can immediately see what is on the network and where it is connected, by switch, slot, and port number. They can investigate and quickly locate "suspect" devices and with minimum effort identify problems associated with device misconfigurations. Quickly and easily identify top talkers, multicasters, and broadcasters or select top conversations to determine which hosts may be overutilizing resource bandwidth. Determine who is using server bandwidth by viewing top conversations to a single host. (See Figure H-9.)

The analyzer categorizes devices into interconnect devices (routers, switches, SNMP hubs and access points), servers, printers, SNMP agents, and other hosts. Additionally, networks are classified by IP subnets, VLANs, NetBIOS domains, and IPX networks, together with host membership within each classification. Network devices that may be experiencing problems are also discovered. Examples of problems detected include duplicate IP addresses, incorrect subnet masks, default router not responding, and many more.

The analyzer can also be configured to perform a discovery on an off-broadcast domain subnet to provide visibility of devices at remote sites. It can generate HTML format inventory reports of devices on the attached network and on networks at remote sites if so configured (see Figure H-10).

When connected to a switch trunk port, the analyzer detects all VLANs available on that trunk, measures the traffic distribution across all the VLANs, and provides the user with the capability to select a specific VLAN. If an individual VLAN is selected, device discovery, traffic statistics, and packet capture data will be displayed for only that VLAN.

The OptiView Analyzer offers switch statistics, including the following:

- A tabular view of all switch port configurations, including the identity of each host and where it is connected to the switch for both Layers 2 and 3.

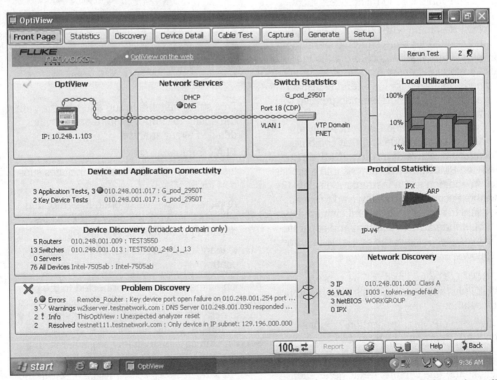

Figure H-9. *OptiView main screen. The analyzer will automatically gather the information shown, immediately following connection to a live Ethernet link.*

FLUKE *networks*™

Integrated Network Analyzer III	6/29/2009 4:30:01PM

010.250.000.100
OptiView-a31ac5
(255.255.254.000)

IP Inventory

Subnet/Name		MAC Address	IP Address	Subnet Mask	SNMP	DNS	WINS	DHCP
						IP Services		
Subnet: 010.000.000.000				255.255.254.000				
ET000400C5CDC6		Lexmrk-c5cdc6	010.250.000.060					
fw-cos-1a-office		Junipr-b9ea06	010.250.000.062					
010.250.000.066		Radsys-44906e	010.250.000.066					
na-cos-1-bmc		Fluke-a315f1	010.250.000.085					
ThisOptiView		Fluke-a31ac5	010.250.000.100		V1			
NPI32AE5D		HP-32ae5d	010.250.000.159					
IP Services:	IPX Printer							
Oakland		HP-faa180 a31ac5	010.250.000.179		V2			
IP Services:	SNMP Switch, Transparent Switch							
Power PETE		Netgea-f57212	010.250.002.105					
IP Services:	SNMP Switch, Transparent Switch							
AP350-IOS-1		Cisco-55ff20	010.250.008.100		V2			
IP Services:	SNMP Switch, Transparent Switch, WAP							
SV-PV		Dell-ef5db8	010.250.008.101					
sr-cos-1		Cisco-0dc145	010.250.008.129			•		
IP Services:	Proxy Arp Router							
sw-cos-3		Cisco-3d6341	110.250.008.143	255.255.255.000				
TC-750		Dell-09dcb8	110.250.008.189					•
XTEAM		Dell-9a66e7	129.196.197.171					
Subnet: 172.016.000.000				255.255.000.000				
172.016.002.010		Dell-bdcc60	172.016.002.010					
172.016.008.010		Acist-cfb31d	172.016.008.010			•	•	•
Subnet: 192.168.021.000				255.255.255.000				
192.168.021.010		IBM-669914	192.168.021.010					

Figure H-10. *Example of OptiView Reporter inventory report detail*

- A graphical view of utilization and error rates on each switch port to see oversubscribed or errored ports at a glance. Detect over-utilization, excessive errors, and locate inactive switch ports to determine whether performance problems are related to link speed or duplex misconfigurations or are related to the number of hosts on a port.

The Trace SwitchRoute feature enables you to see the exact path two devices use to communicate through your switch fabric. Trace SwitchRoute begins its discovery from the specified source device and traces the path to the specified target device. For each switch in the path, the displayed results include the DNS name and IP address, the interswitch connections by port number, together with link speed and VLAN information. Highlighting any device in the Trace SwitchRoute name column and selecting Host Detail allows you to view that device's network configuration information. Figure H-11 shows an example.

To speed deployment of IEEE 802.1X, the OptiView Series III is capable of performing a full 802.1X transaction with an authentication server to ensure correct credentials are being deployed. The analyzer supports 802.1X authentication through most common EAP (Extensible Authentication Protocol) types, 15 in total, allows import of software certificates, and can store multiple authentication profiles to allow connectivity to different broadcast domains or networks with multiple authentication servers for deployment, validation, and troubleshooting. A connection log for detailed 802.1X protocol exchange analysis is also generated.

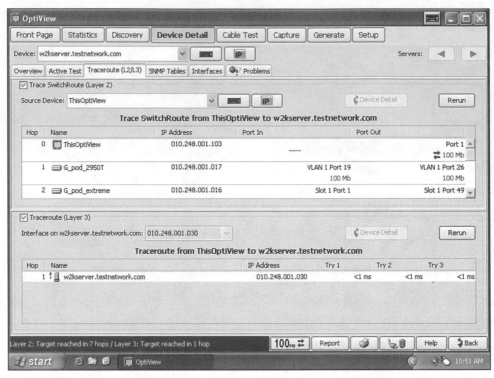

Figure H-11. *OptiView Trace SwitchRoute example*

It offers Gigabit line rate packet capture and filtering to troubleshoot problems where packet-level analysis is required and perform advanced troubleshooting when deploying new applications. Sophisticated capture filters allow collection of more relevant data and limit the amount of traffic to analyze by filtering on individual addresses or conversation, address range for IPV4, IP subnet, and protocols. Match any set of words or phrases when detected (regardless of the position in the packet—payload or header) in real time to trigger the analyzer to start or stop capturing and/or filter traffic. Use free string match to capture traffic around any application error message, detect traffic containing certain words or phrases in non-encrypted emails, web pages, file transfers, or documents to identify illicit use of the network or detect downloading of restricted documents based on content or filenames (.doc, .xls, .pdf). Additionally, use free string match to identify and

track applications that are not allowed on the network, such as streaming media that may consume valuable bandwidth or P2P traffic that may pose a security risk. A total of eight sets of triggers or filters can be defined to trigger a capture unattended for later analysis, allowing analysis when you have time, not when the event occurred.

Through the user accounts screen, you can add and modify analyzer security information for each individual analyzer user, which prevents unauthorized use of certain analyzer features for easier compliance with regulatory requirements. Features that can be disabled include packet capture and decode, traffic generation, remote user interface, and analyzer configuration.

Help is contextually linked to each screen in the analyzer. While that help screen is displayed, you may select other information from the table of contents, choose an index entry, or perform a full text search on any help topic or term.

Network information discovered can be stored on the optional removable hard drive, which allows the analyzer to be moved from classified environments of different levels and between classified and unclassified systems by simply replacing the hard drive.

OptiView also comes in rack-mountable models suitable for a distributed analysis monitoring solution. There are different models with features customized for the Physical Layer interface. All models offer similar packet capture capabilities and similar upper-layer features, including presentation of the discovered host by IP address and best name (DNS, NetBIOS, or SNMP), with differentiation between various types of host devices such as routers, servers, SNMP agents, and user workstations. All models also offer a dedicated 10/100Mbps Ethernet RJ45 management port that allows it to be controlled remotely from any point on the network using the OptiView Analyzer Remote Software (included with the analyzer). Up to eight users can access any single analyzer and perform different analysis concurrently.

OptiView Workgroup Analyzer

The OptiView Workgroup Analyzer (WGA) provides almost the same basic 10/100/1000 Ethernet monitoring and analysis features as the Integrated Network Analyzer model in a rack mount appliance form-factor (see Figure H-12).

EtherScope

The EtherScope Analyzer provides an instant view of the state of the network with its information-rich Autotest Results main screen and tri-color LEDs (see Figure H-13). Multiples tests run concurrently, speeding problem discovery. The EtherScope connects directly to 10/100/1000 Ethernet network links. The information provided by the EtherScope is similar to that provided by the OptiView, but with a more summarized or simplified data presentation.

Figure H-12. *OptiView Workgroup Analyzer (WGA) model*

Figure H-13. *EtherScope Network Assistant*

The most common users of a midlevel portable network diagnostic and troubleshooting tool are found in the following table.

	NOC	Engineer	Technician	Help Desk	Installer
EtherScope		◗	●	●	
MetroScope		◗	●		◗

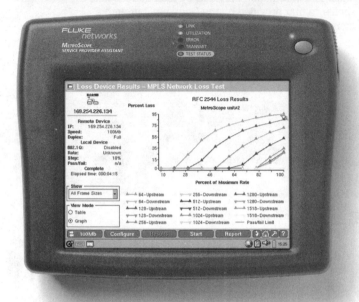

Figure H-14. *MetroScope Service Provider Assistant*

The EtherScope has a second model line called MetroScope, which is optimized for metropolitan Ethernet and service provider use (see Figure H-14). One key feature of the MetroScope model is the RFC 2544 automated test suite. Complete support is included for throughput, latency, loss, and back-to-back modes at up to line-rate Gigabit speeds. The test suite can be performed using a variety of peer, reflector, and loopback schemes. All performance tests can be run with RFC sizes or user-selected sizes, including jumbo frames and with complete control of VLAN ID and Class of Service. Delay-sensitive applications such as VoIP and IP-TV require low packet jitter for acceptable operation. Although RFC 2544 testing does not include jitter, MetroScope Service offers jitter testing with microsecond accuracy.

Another MetroScope feature is the server response tool for determining the TCP application port responsiveness of advanced or managed services such as email, DNS, file, and web, and TCP application port testing operates just like a client, removing many of the PING obstacles such as firewalling and low priority ICMP provisioning.

EtherScope is designed as a tactical "first-in" diagnostic tool. As such, it performs a lengthy list of discovery and diagnostic tests immediately and automatically upon being connected to a live Ethernet connection. During this process it creates an inventory of all discovered devices on the local broadcast domain. Figure H-15 shows a sample

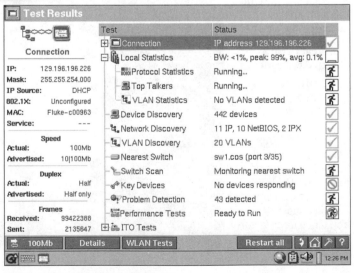

Figure H-15. *EtherScope main screen*

of the information available shortly after simply attaching EtherScope to a network connection. Each category may be drilled-into for more detail.

There are detailed test results for each of the main screen categories, which can be viewed by selecting the category or by using the pull-down menu (see the pull-down menu from the top-left corner). Various utility options are available from the tool menu on the bottom right. Both menus are shown in Figure H-16.

If you are using a separate management VLAN. the switch management entity is often not visible to the discovery process. To support this network configuration you may add switch management addresses as user-defined devices. EtherScope automatically queries the switches to determine the nearest switch, interface, and VLAN for each discovered device. EtherScope identifies VLANs configured on discovered switch interfaces and allows you to drill-in to see interface status, connected host details, and trend interface data (see Figure H-17).

The EtherScope series is also able to monitor 802.11 b/g/a/n wireless networks (see Figure H-18 and Figure H-19).

The feature set found in the EtherScope testers (EtherScope and MetroScope) were designed after extensive analysis of the day-to-day activities of the job category defined as *network technician*. The level of detail presented is consistent with the detail required by this job function. For more detail and extended capabilities see the OptiView series testers. For less detail and simpler operation see the NetTool and LinkRunner series testers.

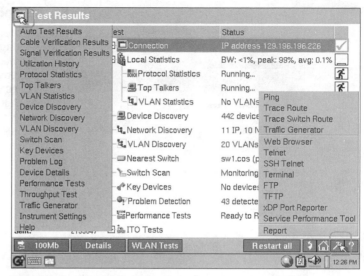

Figure H-16. *EtherScope menu options*

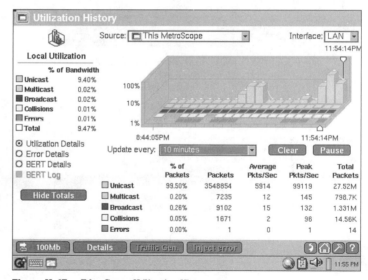

Figure H-17. *EtherScope Utilization History screen*

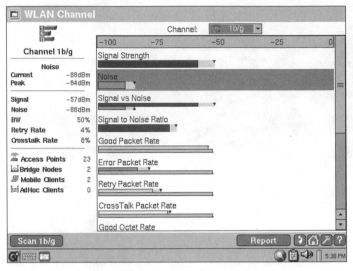

Figure H-18. *EtherScope wireless channel analysis screen*

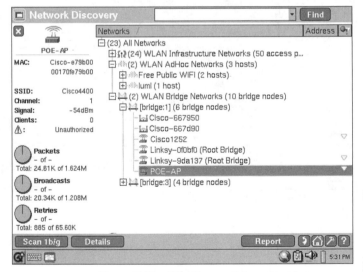

Figure H-19. *EtherScope wireless network access point discovery summary*

NetTool

NetTool Series II is the only handheld troubleshooting tool with inline vision into 10/100/1000 Ethernet links to see the actual traffic between the network and end devices like PCs, VoIP phones, access points, and security cameras (see Figure H-20). By analyzing network device conversations, you can view detailed configuration information to troubleshoot compatibility and connectivity issues.

Figure H-20 *NetTool Series II*

The most common users of a low-level portable network diagnostic and troubleshooting tool are found in the following table.

	NOC	Engineer	Technician	Help Desk	Installer
NetTool		◗	●	●	

Several popular features of the NetTool Series II include the following:

- **NetProve diagnostics.** Isolate device and application connectivity issues in seconds

- **Inline Gigabit vision.** Quickly troubleshoot network problems with powerful inline vision into 10/100/Gig traffic between switches, PCs, IP phones, and other devices

- **NetSecure monitoring and authentication.** Identify spyware, malware, and viruses with port monitoring; troubleshoot authentication issues with 802.1x log

- **VoIP troubleshooting.** Connect inline for visibility into VoIP calls to quickly diagnose IP phone boot-up and call control problems and to measure key call quality metrics

- **PoE Measurements.** Verify readiness of PoE systems and troubleshoot PoE device problems

- **Spot available network resources.** See MAC and IP addresses, subnet and services offered by active servers, routers, and printers

- **IntelliTone digital signaling.** Quickly and safely locate cables on active networks

Connect either directly to the network or end device for traditional single-ended testing, or connect inline between an end device (in this example, a PC) and the network to monitor the interactions between the two (see Figure H-21). The test begins when Autotest is selected.

Figure H-21 *NetTool inline summary screen*

The test continues until stopped. Test results may be viewed as detected. For example, the link configuration including advertised and actual speed and duplex settings may be seen almost immediately (see Figure H-22).

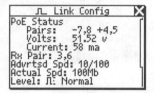

Figure H-22 *NetTool link configuration screen*

The segment information including IP networks, switch name, port, and IP address and native VLAN is available as soon as adequate traffic has been observed (see Figure H-23).

Figure H-23 *NetTool segment identification screen*

If problems are detected, NetTool will present the fault information in simple descriptions (see Figure H-24).

Figure H-24 *NetTool problem log screen*

The optional inline VoIP test puts the power of inline testing in the hands of frontline technicians, giving you the ability to monitor VoIP service at the edge (see Figure H-25).

Figure H-25 *NetTool inline test setup*

The Boot Log displays key boot events, such as DHCP address acquisition, DNS lookup of call servers and gateways, downloading of operating files, and call server registration (see Figure H-26). NetTool VoIP supports complete troubleshooting of the IP phone boot process including Physical Layer tests of structured wiring, patch cables, switch port configuration, VLANs, and PoE voltage.

```
 ┌──────── Log VoIP ────────[X]┐
 │ >TFTP FILE REQUEST          │
 │ CTLSEP00120101031C.tlv      │
 │ srv: 192.168.159.005        │
 │ >TFTP FILE REQUEST          │
 │ SEP00120101031C.cnf.xml     │
 │ srv: 192.168.159.005        │
 │ >TFTP FILE REQUEST          │
 │ P00308000500.loads          │
 └─────────────────────────────┘
```

Figure H-26 *NetTool inline Boot Log screen*

The VoIP Log displays call control events, QoS configuration, and call quality metrics. The log records call setup, configuration, and tear down of a call in progress. As the call proceeds, the RTP configuration is displayed, including IP addresses and ports used, VLAN priority or Diff Serv, and codec. When the call is competed, the log displays the RTP quality metrics, such as jitter and dropped packets.

The NetProve feature runs connectivity and service availability diagnostics. NetProve allows for up to 10 catalogs representing various segments of your network—organize by servers, devices, applications, workgroups, and/or sites.

NetTool Pro and VoIP models offer reporting capabilities that allow you to download and share test results—from identifying network resources to PC configuration—with your entire team.

LinkRunner

LinkRunner Pro was designed after observing the daily routine of network technicians and Help Desk staff. A significant amount of time was devoted to "moves, adds, and changes" related to relocating users and network connections. This small, fast, and simple handheld tool is optimized to make this task as quick and painless as possible (see Figure H-27). It is also very useful in locating or ruling out the most common causes of network difficulties before a problem is escalated to more senior staff.

The most common users of this low-level portable network diagnostic and troubleshooting tool are found in the following table.

	NOC	Engineer	Technician	Help Desk	Installer
LinkRunner		▷	●	●	▷

An important part of resolving connectivity issues is finding which switch port a user is connecting to (see Figure H-28). LinkRunner Pro supports IEEE Link Layer Discovery Protocol (LLDP) in addition to the Cisco and Extreme Discovery Protocols (CDP and EDP). That allows technicians to speed problem resolution by quickly and precisely locating the nearest switch port. LinkRunner Pro will display the announced device information address, slot, and port of the nearest LLDP device. The new LLDP standard has been adopted by Cisco, Avaya, Extreme, Nortel, Mitel, and many other equipment vendors.

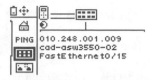

Figure H-28 *LinkRunner nearest switch port identification*

Although today's cabling plants are much more stable than in the past, cabling faults still account for the vast majority of basic continuity problems. LinkRunner Pro will detect all basic cabling faults including miswires, crossovers, reversals, breaks, shorts, and splits. It also speeds cable troubleshooting with built-in TDR (Time Domain Reflectometry) to measure the distance to breaks and shorts.

LinkRunner Pro gives technicians two ways to optimize locating and ID-tagging cables. IntelliTone digital toning and the hub-blink feature can be used to

*   Locate cables on active networks
*   Isolate cables within bundles
*   Zero in on ports at a patch panel
*   Visibly locate a port on the nearest switch

When no test documentation is available, closing trouble tickets can be a frustrating and time-consuming process. Finger pointing among groups and redundant testing are just a couple of the wastes that occur. LinkRunner Pro significantly reduces this waste by generating objective, professional test reports that can be printed or routed electronically. With the included LinkRunner Connect Software, all the following connectivity status indicators can be saved, uploaded, and printed:

*   Link status, including device capabilities and actual link speed/duplex

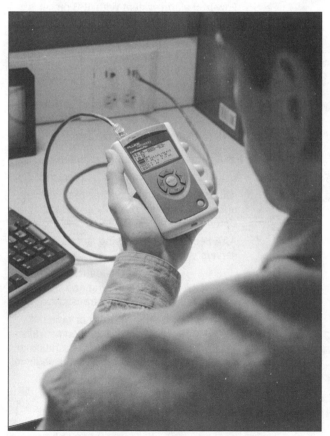

Figure H-27 *LinkRunner Pro*

- 802.1X security settings, including EAP type and username
- DNS, DHCP, and default router information, including IP, subnet, and MAC address
- Ping results for each device, including min, max, and average response times
- PoE service availability, including voltage level and pairs
- Nearest switch name, slot, and port information (LLDP/CDP/EDP)
- Cable test results, including length, wiremap, and faults

Protocol Analysis

OptiView Protocol Expert is available as software only or with hardware capable of line-rate capture and monitoring at speeds up to 10 Gigabit (see Figure H-29). The analyzer provides seven-layer packet decodes and real-time network health statistics.

The most common users of protocol analyzer are found in the following table.

	NOC	Engineer	Technician	Help Desk	Installer
OptiView Protocol Expert	●	●	◗		

Here is a partial list of OptiView Protocol Expert's standard features:

- Complete seven-layer packet capture and decodes
- Real-time application monitoring and response time analysis
- Application bounce charts for visualization of application performance
- Protocol analysis integration with any OptiView analyzers
- Automated Expert problem discovery
- Cisco ISL and 802.1Q VLAN traffic analysis
- Powerful alarm system with 150 preset alarms that trigger notifications via email, paging, and SNMP trap
- Advanced multistage filtering enables triggering or capturing of specific events
- Single-click instant display filters
- Scheduled captures for off-hour packet captures
- DNS resolution of IP addresses

Here is a partial list of its optional features:

- Remote viewing and control of other software analyzers as well as the hardware analyzers: OptiView Link Analyzer and OptiView XGig
- AAA Security support using standard TACAC servers
- Customized packet editing and creation for retransmission
- Replay of captured packet file and traffic pattern generation to load network segment
- Centralized configuration and updates of remote link analyzers within an enterprise environment

Figure H-29 *OptiView Protocol Expert XLink hardware protocol analyzer platform*

Here is a partial list of its hardware features:

- Full line rate capture and analysis of up to 10 Gigabit links
- Time synchronize packet analysis across multiple 10G ports and/or 1G ports for redundant and asymmetric route analysis
- Daisy-chain up to three four-slot chassis for synchronization of up to 48 1-Gigabit or 24 10-Gigabit Ethernet ports
- Flexible chassis blade architecture
- Chassis can be populated with any combination of blades, including
  - Two-port 10 Gigabit Ethernet blade
  - Four-port 1 Gigabit Ethernet blade
- 4GB of RAM per blade for capture buffer storage
  - 2GB of RAM per 10 Gigabit port
  - 1GB of RAM per 1 Gigabit port
- Utilize inline taps or run traffic directly through analysis ports on XLink blades
- Capture frame sizes up to 16,384 bytes
- Clock resolution down to 5 nanoseconds
- Configurable packet slicing from 4 bytes or greater
- Supports up to 32 simultaneous users
- Capability to capture idle frames and flags

The list of built-in tests is important because it is rare that protocol analyzers are used to immediately examine protocol decode details. Instead, the built-in features are used to review the captured traffic by various statistical groupings, such as conversation matrices and protocol distribution charts. It is customary to sort the captured file using the built-in statistical test suites, or to filter the captured file down to a manageable size or used to isolate just one station or protocol before examining the protocol decode details. Many problems can be isolated by using these statistics to identify usage patterns that might be out of the norm. When statistical analysis doesn't immediately lead to a solution, advanced capture or display filters may be generated from the statistics to help isolate capture studies. For very specific issues complex filter statements may be written

for up to seven levels of filter conditions, down to the bit level.

Although some form of protocol analysis is available from the hybrid products, having a dedicated protocol analyzer is almost a requirement for medium to large sites.

Capture

If you normally use files captured by another means and stay away from high-speed core links, a software protocol analyzer is likely sufficient for your needs. Misdiagnosing a problem due to incomplete information and dropped packets, or spending considerable time arriving at the conclusion that not all the traffic was captured, is particularly frustrating. The problem becomes worse as the line speed increases. A hardware solution is usually required to ensure that all the traffic has been captured or analyzed.

Hardware analyzers may also be used to simultaneously capture from both the transmit and receive paths from a single link using a tap, or to synchronize a capture across an entire 802.1AX link aggregation where multiple Ethernet ports are used to create a single logical link.

Built-in Features

The list of built-in features is particularly important, and should be examined carefully. Most use of protocol analyzers employs these features, so the variety and ease of use is paramount. Most particularly, you don't have to be a protocol expert to use the built-in features and still be successful.

Alarms and Triggers

OptiView Protocol Expert offers 150 predefined alarm conditions to effectively alert you to network degradation or excessive traffic. Alarm conditions trap abnormal or intermittent problems at the time they occur, ensuring you will have the data to study during intermittent brownouts. Custom alarm conditions are easily created using capture filters and OptiView Protocol Expert's powerful custom counter feature.

For each alarm, multiple actions can be defined and triggered based on severity, including

- Saving alarm messages into a log file
- Stopping and saving a capture session
- Sending email or pager notification
- Sending an SNMP trap
- Launching an application or custom script program

Triggers may be configured as simply or as complex as desired (see Figure H-30). Not all faults happen while you are watching, so it is often necessary to define conditions that lead up to an event, or symptoms indicating that an event has just occurred to initiate an unattended capture.

The Expert System will identify symptoms, per OSI layer, including

- **Application Layer.** Excessive ARP, excessive BOOTP, NFS retransmission, HTTP Get response, HTTP Post response, slow server connect, slow server response
- **Transport Layer.** Nonresponsive station, TCP/IP checksum error, TCP/IP fast retransmission, TCP/IP retransmission, TCP/IP frozen window, TCP/IP long ACK, and TCP/IP SYN attack
- **Network Layer.** ICMP errors and unstable Multiple Spanning Tree
- **Data Link Layer.** Illegal MAC source address, broadcast/multicast storms and physical errors

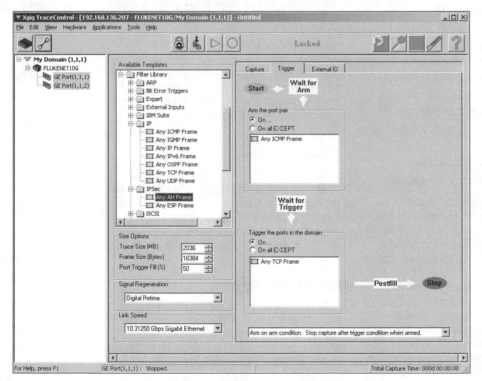

Figure H-30 *Menu-driven capture trigger configuration*

Data Storage and Reporting

All traffic analysis in OptiView Protocol Expert may be exported to comma-separated variable (.csv) files. These files can be used in conjunction with spreadsheets to create quick graphical reports and custom analysis of the statistics. Additional data logging stores key traffic utilization and error statistics for data sampling at user-defined intervals over a long period of time.

Flow Protocols Analysis

Either as a standalone flow analyzer, or as an element of an integrated suite of tools presented via a portal application, flow protocol monitoring is the latest "must-have" feature in the arsenal of tools for network support.

Visual Performance Manager

Visual Performance Manager is an integrated portal application and database that presently has extensive integration into three subordinate data-gathering application engines: NetFlow Tracker, Application Performance Monitor, and Visual UpTime Select. The portal may also be configured to open a page into virtually any other web-enabled solution. The flow protocol subordinate data source (NetFlow Tracker) may also be installed and operated separately, without the portal integration.

The most common users of flow protocols and other console-based monitoring solutions are found in the following table.

The portal aspect of Visual Performance Manager has been used to place integrated monitoring data from one or more of the three highly integrated subordinate data sources onto the same page as a web camera image of the data center at a remote site, the web interface for the router servicing that remote site, and the web interface to a key application hosted out of the remote site.

Visual Performance Manager is often used as a common portal to launch into many of the other user interfaces, including

- **PfR Manager.** PfR Manager is Fluke Networks' complete graphical user interface for Cisco's Optimized Edge Routing (OER) and Performance Routing (PfR) technologies. PfR is the latest WAN route optimization from Cisco Systems that utilizes customer's existing Cisco equipment. This technology optimizes traffic across two or more WAN connections to both save bandwidth costs and improve network performance. PfR is an evolution of a prior Cisco technology call

Optimized Edge Routing (OER), but with a much broader scope. PfR Manager takes this powerful PfR networking technology and simplifies it into an intuitive, browser-based format. Instead of reading and typing on the command-line interface, PfR users instead can point and click their mouse making installation, configuration, monitoring, and reporting easy. Furthermore, the software provides executive, historical, and filtered reports.

- **EtherScope or OptiView.** The web-based remote control user interface into EtherScope or the graphic user interface for OptiView is easily accommodated as an additional choice.

- Any other HTTP based user interface or web page.

Some of the features available through Visual Performance Manager include

- Auto-discovery of applications and servers—both IP and legacy
- Detailed VoIP analysis and troubleshooting, including predeployment assessments and individual call troubleshooting
- Verify service provider SLA performance
- Complete Layer 1 and 2 visibility
- Packet capture and protocol decode at each location
- Up to 1-second granularity
- Reporting and baselining
- Real-time monitoring and troubleshooting
- Scalability to meet the needs of small and large deployments
- Integration with existing or new solutions

	NOC	Engineer	Technician	Help Desk	Installer
Visual Performance Manager	●	●	❭	❭	
Visual UpTime Select	●	●	❭	❭	
NetFlow Tracker	●	●	❭	❭	
Application Performance Monitor	●	●	❭	❭	

Application Performance

Analyzing the performance of critical applications is becoming simpler. Newer monitoring solutions permit tier-by-tier examination of critical *n*-tier applications, troubleshooting of end-user performance problems associated with *n*-tier applications, isolation of problem sources and domain, and intelligent alarming for performance related to *n*-tier applications. Specific features related to analyzing application performance include

- Monitor critical multi-tier application response time from the server farm to the end user. Corroborate end-user performance complaints to quickly pinpoint the problem domain to application, server, or network

- Transaction forensics allow you to drill down into specific HTTP, SQL, and Citrix session to understand exactly which transaction is causing the performance degradation

- Correlate end-user activity with the application back end to quickly segment performance issues between LAN, WAN, and data center

- Back-in-time troubleshooting capabilities allow even the most elusive issue to be identified and corrected even after the anomaly has occurred, eliminating the need to deploy packet-capture solutions and wait for the problem to occur again

- Alarm lifecycle provides visibility into degrading performance over time, allowing you to identify significant changes intelligently and not just based on static thresholds and having to sort through dozens of meaningless alarms

- Support for both TCP and UDP applications provides comprehensive applications visibility and control

Network Performance

Networks contain vast amounts of data about themselves. The trick is to gain access to that data and present it in a format useful for support activities. At a minimum, the data presentation should offer insight into how traffic usage is affecting network performance.

- In-depth visibility into the LAN, WAN, and data center allows you to better deploy, manage, solve, and optimize your entire distributed infrastructure to ensure quality of experience

- WAN performance and carrier SLA monitoring help an organization understand the true performance and validate whether expensive WAN build-out is truly needed to improve performance or if other optimization techniques could be used, potentially saving organizations a significant expenditure

- See how traffic usage is affecting overall network performance to understand where optimization, load balancing, and so on should be made

- Granular visibility of correlated data across the entire infrastructure helps to isolate root cause and problem domain isolation even across distributed network environments, helping organizations maintain SLA

- Provides critical visibility for MPLS-based/ private IP VPN networks, including monitoring IP subnet-to-IP subnet connectivity and CoS settings by applications and threshold

VoIP Performance

As telephone service changes from a dedicated system to another form of traffic on the network, it is important to ensure that voice quality does not diminish in the transition. A network monitoring system must aid in the deployment of VoIP, providing an assessment of VoIP readiness and in optimizing VoIP performance (see Figure H-31 and Figure H-32).

- Assess predeployment network readiness and provide network baseline metrics of infrastructure capacity for converged applications

- Enable post-deployment VoIP performance trending and management measuring the stability of this critical application against established baselines to ensure end-user quality of experience

- Isolate, identify, and troubleshoot poor VoIP performance for individual calls, including per-call metrics such as MOS, jitter, latency, and packet loss, which assists with faster problem identification and reduced MTTR

- Understand the impact of voice and data applications on a converged network to optimize prioritization to ensure acceptable end-user quality of experience

Visual UpTime Select

Visual UpTime Select is based on a modular architecture that enables enterprises to leverage software modules depending on their individual needs for 1 to 4,000 sites. Each module focuses on different characteristics for application and network performance management:

- **VoIP.** Monitors individual voice calls with MOS metrics and degradation factors including packet loss, delay and jitter. Manages VoIP lifecycle of assess, monitor, manage, and optimize performance

- **AppSummary.** Auto-discovers application running across your

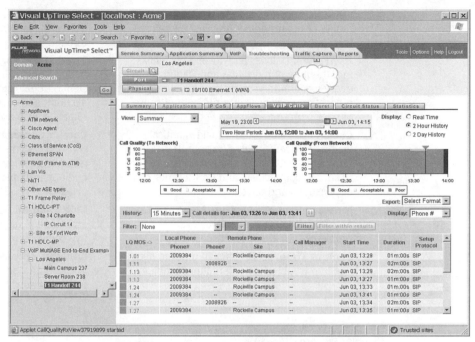

Figure H-31 *Visual UpTime Select summary for VoIP calls related to a selected site*

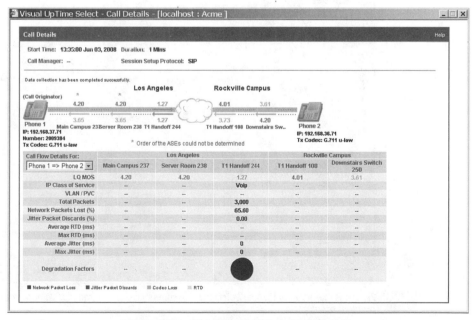

Figure H-32 *Visual UpTime Select detail for VoIP a specific call over a specific path*

network, allowing you to easily identify new, rogue, or unauthorized applications before they impact the enterprise

- **AppFlows.** Delivers end-to-end visibility into the flow of individual applications from every location in your enterprise, helping you quickly and easily determine the root cause of poor performance

- **Class of Service (CoS).** Provides critical visibility for MPLS-based/private IP VPN networks, including monitoring IP subnet-to-IP subnet connectivity and CoS settings by applications and threshold

- **Network Troubleshooting.** Managing Layer 1–3 performance in a real-time setting to problems that are currently occurring

- **Back in Time.** Looks "back in time" to manage and troubleshoot intermittent problems

over the past two-weeks in an integrated, graphical view looking across Layers 1 through 7

- **Traffic Capture.** Provides a full-function protocol analyzer at every site, enabling IT staff to troubleshoot issues at remotes sites via point and click of a mouse even when remote staff is not local

- **Service Summary.** Highlights a single, consolidated view of network health to effectively manage and troubleshoot network- and application-related performance issues (see Figure H-33).

- **VoIP Planner.** Determines VoIP readiness and manage ongoing deployments with active call testing

- **LAN Visibility.** Segment and monitor traffic within a LAN or individual LAN segments to pinpoint issues that may not impact the WAN

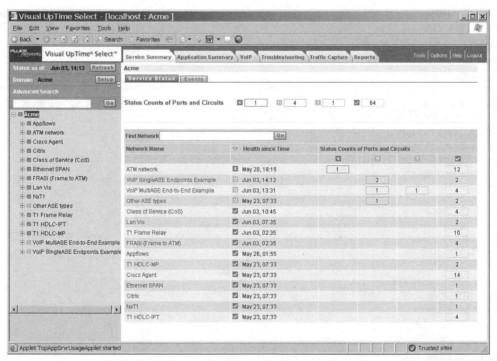

Figure H-33 *Visual UpTime Select service summary screen example. Color coding permits rapid identification of problem areas.*

- **IP SLA Router Polling.** Delivers IP SLA metrics from Cisco SAA-enabled routers without a hardware device

NetFlow Tracker

NetFlow Tracker utilizes flow data from the network to provide insight into how traffic usage is impacting network performance (see Figure H–34). With it, you can

- See into the LAN, WAN, and data center
- Manage network convergence
- Optimize MPLS performance

Managing Network Convergence

The complexity of managing IP networks handling data, voice, and video requires tools that provide the insight needed to make informed decisions about capacity management, quality-of-service provisioning, and forward capacity planning (see Figure H–35). Extensive drill-down is available into interfaces, protocols, and conversations from nearly every screen throughout the user interface.

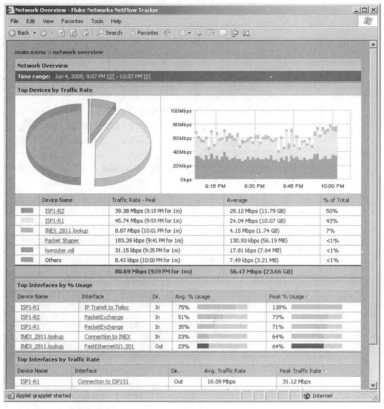

Figure H-34 *NetFlow Tracker provides in-depth application views for TCP and UDP, including critical n-tier applications*

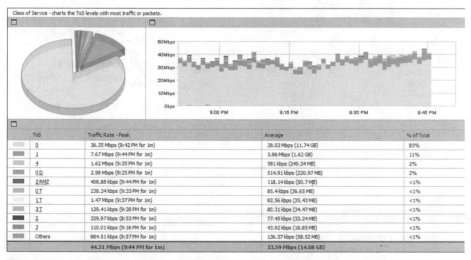

Figure H-35 *NetFlow Manager report showing the relative volume of priority traffic*

Optimize MPLS Performance

To effectively monitor and manage MPLS networks, there is a need to monitor traffic flows to and from all network segments. Any-to-any site connectivity introduces complexity requiring complete visibility of network performance between sites, and network managers must be able to ensure proper class of service configuration while validating carrier SLAs. Security concerns include P2P, hacking, virus, and multicast applications (see Figure H-36).

When managing the performance of an MPLS network, a true picture of application and traffic flows is necessary to ensure an informed investment and better understand whether infrastructure build-out is needed or if network optimization will solve performance problems. Features include

- **Customizable home page.** In conjunction with executive summaries, each user may be assigned a default start page with meaningful specific data relevant to that person or team.

- **Archiving.** Expired real-time data may be archived to another storage system and may be remounted for reporting purposes.

- **Full coverage.** Every flow record, per minute, up to the last two minutes is captured.

- **Safe integration** with any third-party management product, using secured URLs.

- **Layered long-term historical reports** in multiple time frames and time slices.

- **Powerful filters** for any combination of flow record contents from the long-term or real-time databases.

- **Report relevance to multiple audiences.** For example, real-time operations compared to capacity planning or application manager.

- **Multicast egress support**

- **MPLS VPN/VRF aware.** Saving considerable administration time for creating reports on dynamic MPLS-based network infrastructures.

- **Bidirectional reporting** showing complete picture of traffic flows in both directions across the network.

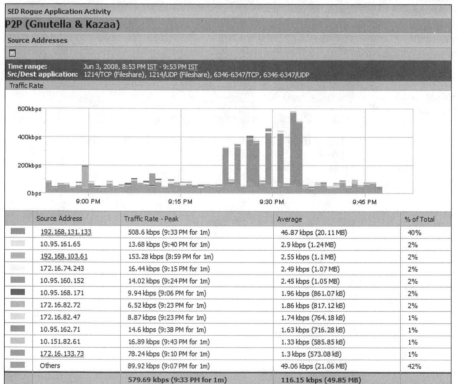

	Source Address	Traffic Rate - Peak	Average	% of Total
	192.168.131.133	508.6 kbps (9:33 PM for 1m)	46.87 kbps (20.11 MB)	40%
	10.95.161.65	13.68 kbps (9:40 PM for 1m)	2.9 kbps (1.24 MB)	2%
	192.168.103.61	153.28 kbps (8:59 PM for 1m)	2.55 kbps (1.1 MB)	2%
	172.16.74.243	16.44 kbps (9:15 PM for 1m)	2.49 kbps (1.07 MB)	2%
	10.95.160.152	14.02 kbps (9:24 PM for 1m)	2.45 kbps (1.05 MB)	2%
	10.95.168.171	9.94 kbps (9:06 PM for 1m)	1.96 kbps (861.07 kB)	2%
	172.16.82.72	6.52 kbps (9:23 PM for 1m)	1.86 kbps (817.12 kB)	2%
	172.16.82.47	8.87 kbps (9:23 PM for 1m)	1.74 kbps (764.18 kB)	1%
	10.95.162.71	14.6 kbps (9:38 PM for 1m)	1.63 kbps (716.28 kB)	1%
	10.151.82.61	16.89 kbps (9:43 PM for 1m)	1.33 kbps (585.85 kB)	1%
	172.16.133.73	78.24 kbps (9:10 PM for 1m)	1.3 kbps (573.08 kB)	1%
	Others	89.92 kbps (9:07 PM for 1m)	49.06 kbps (21.06 MB)	42%
		579.69 kbps (9:33 PM for 1m)	116.15 kbps (49.85 MB)	

Figure H-36 *NetFlow Manager detailed reporting example showing the source and volume for rogue traffic*

Application Performance

Visual Performance Manager provides the ability to view individual interaction between client and server for any application through the Application Performance Monitor (see Figure H-37). Key features include

- Complete response time analysis for streaming and nonstreaming TCP and UDP (streaming and nonstreaming) applications

- Monitor VoIP, video convergence, and other multimedia applications that use UDP for transport

- Watch DNS and DHCP server performance and correlate to other applications that are dependent

- Aggregate statistics are kept for both TCP and UDP such as volume, data rate, data transfer time, and application response time

- Performance statistics and transactions for custom TCP and UDP applications

- Deep analysis features for business-critical applications such as Citrix, Oracle, MySQL, Microsoft SQL Server, and HTTP

Verifying that the user experience (total response time) is a starting point, the next troubleshooting step is to isolate where a delay is only affecting a single user from one site, the whole site, or multiple sites (see Figure H-38).

- Corroborate end-user performance complaints to quantify the business impact

- Compare an individual end-user's experience to that of the other users at that site

- Quickly determine whether a problem is isolated to one user or is affecting many users

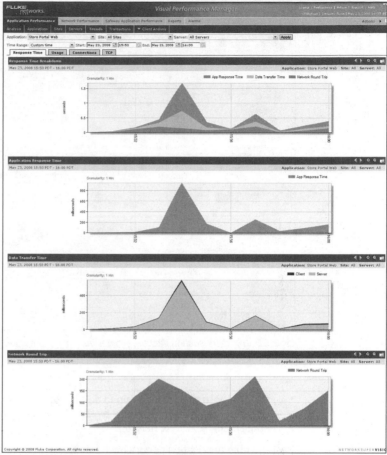

Figure H-37 *Application performance monitoring may be narrowed to very narrow selection criteria for problem investigation and reporting*

Once a site, server, or application is isolated, drill-down into the problem is required to determine further troubleshooting information, or to provide trend analysis to plan for specific or general upgrades (see Figure H-39).

- Corroborate end-user performance complaints to quickly identify the problem domain.

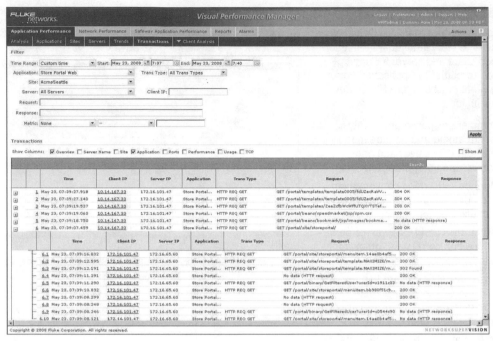

Figure H-38 *Transaction Viewer provides visibility into requests and response detail, response time breakdown, TCP metrics, bytes, and packets*

- Use response time breakdown to determine whether the problem is caused by the application, server, or network.

Back-in-time application performance troubleshooting features permit you to select just the view of the data you need to solve a specific issue by using the flexible filters, such as

- Period of time
- Specific application
- User groups, sites, subnets, and servers
- Transaction type

This allows you to cut the mean time to resolution dramatically over traditional troubleshooting approaches.

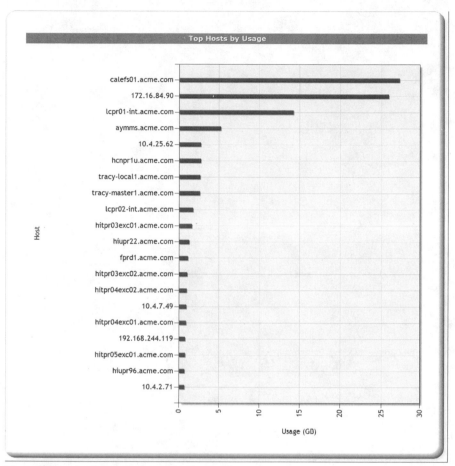

Figure H-39 *Application Performance Top Hosts reporting excerpt. This report shows IP hosts with the highest usage on the domain for a selected period.*

APPENDIX I
Answers to Chapter Review Questions

This appendix provides answers to the Chapter Review questions found throughout the book. In some cases the answers provided are more extensive than might be expected from the reader.

Chapter 1

1. ISO/IEC 7498 or ISO/IEC 7498-1, and ITU-T X.200

2. It provided a framework by which other protocols could be referenced.

3. A patch cable would align with the lowest part of the diagram, below Layer 1 in the OSI Model. A patch cable is not defined by the OSI Model, but is instead defined by the media standards such as TIA/EIA-568 and ISO 11801.

4. The Application Layer provides an interface to network users.

5. The Presentation Layer provides format and code conversion services as necessary between dissimilar operating systems.

6. The Session Layer manages connection services for higher layers as needed.

7. The Transport Layer ensures error-free, end-to-end delivery of data.

8. The Network Layer handles internetwork addressing and routing.

9. The Data Link Layer performs local addressing and error checking.

10. The Physical Layer includes physical signaling and encoding for the media access protocol and medium.

11. A repeater always forwards a signal.

12. A repeater forwards everything it detects, good or bad. It even attempts to forward noise, although it interprets the noise into the closest approximation of the corresponding properly formed Ethernet binary. The repeater creates additional output if the detected input event does not last long enough to meet the requirements for a jam signal.

13. A bridge forwards a signal unless there is a reason not to.

14. A bridge, or a switch operating as a bridge, forwards all properly formed Ethernet frames (no errors) if

    - The destination is unknown.
    - The unicast destination is known to be on another port.
    - The destination is a form of broadcast.

A bridge does not forward a frame when both the source and destination reside on the same port. Bridges do not forward errors.

15. A router forwards only if conditions require it.

16. A router forwards frames for destinations where a route is known or where a default route is configured, as long as other configurations do not deny forwarding (such as an access list). A router may forward a frame from the source to the destination on the same port if the network and router configuration warrant it. Routers do not forward errors.

17. Although a switch is generally thought of as a multiport bridge between any two given ports (depending on features and configuration), it may operate at any OSI layer. Thus, using the terms defined so far, it may operate as a repeater, bridge, router, or gateway.

18. **Cut-Through.** The frame is forwarded immediately after the destination address is received.

    Modified Cut-Through (or Fragment Free). The frame is forwarded after 64 bytes are received.

    Store-and-Forward. The frame is forwarded after receipt and error checking are complete.

    Adaptive (or Error-Sensing). Cut-through is used until the detected error level exceeds a threshold, and then store-and-forward is used until the error level again drops below the threshold.

19. It depends. If the switch is using store-and-forward, it is acting as an OSI Layer 2 bridge and does not forward errors. The collision domain is isolated. If the switch is using one of the other forwarding techniques, frames with Ethernet errors may be forwarded and troubleshooting is adversely affected.

20. Cut-through, with latency equal to the preamble, SFD, destination address, outbound port queuing, and any processing time in the switch required to make the forwarding decision.

21. Store-and-forward, with latency equal to the entire frame size, outbound port queuing, and any processing time in the switch required to verify the checksum and make the forwarding decision.

22. The user has access to the network cables (media), Layer 3 by way of host addressing, and Layer 7 by way of user application configurations. At these three layers in the OSI Model, the user is able to disrupt the network. At Layers 1, 2, 4, 5, and 6 there is no easy access to anything that would disrupt the network.

23. Network management is described as a strategic tool used continuously for trend analysis.

24. Protocol analyzers are used to view the contents of individual frames taken from the medium, and offer functionality from Layer 2 up through Layer 7. Additional features include libraries of common symptoms are often available as "experts," which make interpretation easier for novices.

25. Software protocol analyzer: Might not see errors, probably does not capture at line rate, may drop frames without any indication that they were dropped. Less expensive.

    Hardware protocol analyzer: Sees errors, captures at line rate without dropping. Much more expensive.

26. Handheld network testers were created to bridge the gap between the senior network support staff and the Help Desk staff. They generally include the most commonly used features from the other three categories. The primary focus is to validate or troubleshoot end-to-end connectivity up through Layer 3.

27. Cable testers are used for two general use models: to certify the cable plant, and to locate simple faults to restore network service. For the first use, cable testers offer very high-performance product with a very simple Pass/Fail test result and the capability to store multiple test results. For the second use, cable testers offer much reduced functionality suitable for solving problems such as opens, shorts, and miswires.

28. The nature of bridge/switch operation is to limit data flow to just the correct destination interface. This prevents network monitoring tools from seeing what is happening inside the switch. Flow protocols report on traffic forwarded by the switch, and thereby take the place of traditional passive monitoring tools in some regards. Without flow protocols, it is very difficult to know what happened inside the switch.

29. No. Knowledge of networking theory and network behavior permits a technician to rule out some layers, depending on the results of tests performed. However, the thought process behind troubleshooting should always begin at the level of the medium.

Chapter 2

1. ISO: Classes A, B, C, D, E, E_A, F, and F_A. TIA: Categories 3, 5e, 6 and 6A.

2. TIA/EIA-568-B TSB-155

3. Increased heat in the cable plant, and the associated risk of fire.

4. At a minimum, the wiremap test evaluates for
   - End-to-end continuity
   - Shorts between any two or more conductors
   - Reversed pairs
   - Split pairs
   - Transposed pairs

5. A reversed pair affects the end-to-end continuity within a wire pair. A transposed pair affects the end-to-end continuity between wire pairs.

6. The former (TIA/EIA-568-B) is a cable standard; the latter (T568B) is the pin color code assignment specification for an RJ45 connection as designated within the former.

7. Both are pin color code assignment specifications for RJ45 connections. In T568A, the green wires appear first on pins 1 and 2, forming a pair. The orange wires are used on pins 3 and 6. In T568B the green and orange wires trade places, and orange appears first on pins 1 and 2.

8. The most common method of inferring the presence of a split pair using a cable tester is a gross failure of the NEXT test on two pairs of the same cable. Failure of this test for two pairs suggests that each wire pair is not twisted around itself; instead, each pair is comprised of one wire from each of two pairs.

   Two other tests techniques infer the presence of a split pair: gross failures of impedance and of capacitance.

9. Ethernet recognizes a *crossover cable* when wire pairs 1,2 and 3,6 are transposed, as would happen if T568A and T568B are used on opposite ends of the same cable.

10. For rough calculations, the value of 20cm (eight inches) per nanosecond is used to determine how far a signal travels on a typical Ethernet cable (with a nominal NVP of 69). Thus, the signal travels about 200cm or 80 inches in 10 nanoseconds.

11. To make a TDR measurement, the tester applies a pulse of energy to the wire pair and then measures the amount of time required for a reflection of the pulse to return to the tester on the same wire pair.

12. Delay skew is the difference between the electronic length measurement for the shortest and longest pairs within one cable. The TDR per-pair test results are typically used for this measurement. Delay skew may not exceed 50ns over 100 meters.

13. The attenuation test measures how much of the transmitted signal arrives at the receiver end. The test results report how much signal is lost. Attenuation (loss) increases as the frequency of the transmitted signal rises.

14. Insertion loss is generally linear until around 100MHz. After that, the effects of other cable influences start causing noticeable deviations from a linear result (the test results are visibly irregular).

15. Impedance mismatches are the most common cause of return loss, and connectors along the link are the most predominate location of impedance changes.

16. Crosstalk may be reduced by increasing the twist rate on a wire pair so that the influence of a signal external to the pair is distributed evenly over both wires, and only causes the DC voltage level to change. Note: Twisted-pair signals are measured as a voltage difference between one wire and the other within a pair (differential signal), so simultaneous changes to both wires do not affect the differential signal. As frequencies increase, it becomes more important to vary the twist rate of pairs within the cable as well, so that adjacent pairs do not align and permit pair-to-pair crosstalk within the cable jacket. The different twist rates per-pair cause the physical lengths per-pair to be different, and that difference is measured by delay skew—so there is a maximum limit to how different the varied twist rate may be.

17. ACR assumes that external noise is insignificant and does not include it. SNR includes external noise in the crosstalk part of the measurement.

18. NEXT is measured closest to the signal source, whereas FEXT is measured at the distant end of the cable-under-test—away from the signal source.

19. ACRF includes FEXT results, which are made at the end of the cable away from the signal source. FEXT is most affected by the connecting hardware, so the problem is most likely found at the far end termination (away from the signal source).

20. NEXT results represent the test measurement results for one adjacent wire pair. PSNEXT results represent the computed loss for NEXT measurements to the other three pairs in the cable, not just a single adjacent pair.

21. Ethernet implementations where multiple pairs are used simultaneously in parallel are susceptible to problems revealed by power sum tests.

22. Alien crosstalk represents crosstalk influences from outside the cable-under-test, whereas NEXT and FEXT measurements represent crosstalk influences from adjacent wire pairs within the cable-under-test. The greatest source of alien crosstalk is usually adjacent cables in a cable tray or wire-tied together for some distance.

23. Impedance changes cause signal reflections back toward the signal source. Because impedance changes typically occur at connections, there is often an increase in crosstalk at the same location.

24. Impulse noise is usually measured by counting the number of voltage spikes that exceed a fixed or configured voltage threshold in the tester.

25. A cable fault related to DC resistance would cause a corresponding change in the attenuation of the cable; therefore, attenuation or insertion loss test results would reveal the DC resistance fault.

26. The channel link includes the patch cords used at both ends of the horizontal cable (the 90 meters of cable often installed "in the wall" represents the permanent link). Note that the actual user patch cables are required for the channel test, not a single set of patch cables that are moved from test location to test location. Changing patch cables after the channel test is complete invalidates the test results.

27. A current measurement of less than 20mA is unlikely to disrupt data. Note that higher measurements usually suggest electrical system problems and could constitute a safety or fire hazard in addition to potentially disrupting the network.

Chapter 3

1. None of the wavelengths fall within the range "seen" by the human eye; all can be harmful.

2. Fiber shards are glass, which is transparent when wet. If the shard pierces flesh, it takes on the coloration of the flesh or blood and is detectable almost only by touch. It is very difficult to find and remove if it is not still protruding from the point of entry.

3. Orange, aqua, and yellow, respectively.

4. The terms describe the number of paths light may travel down while traversing the cable. That is, in singlemode the fiber core is so narrow that the wavelengths of light used are not able to bounce around (one mode). In multimode the light bounces off the walls within the core and takes multiple paths (modes) as it traverses the cable.

5. Dispersion is caused by light from a single pulse arriving at the far end of a cable at varied times. The difference in time is attributed to the path length that the photons took down the fiber. Photons that traveled relatively straight down the center of the fiber core arrive first; photons that took a longer path because of the angle at which they bounced down the core arrived later. Dispersion grows worse with additional distance traveled.

6. As distance increases, dispersion causes the edges of a light pulse to round off and may blend into the previous or following pulse. This makes it difficult or impossible to decode the binary from the light pulse.

7. Modal bandwidth.

8. The bend radius must be less than that which would cause light to exceed the critical angle. Light passing through the cable must not exceed the critical angle when bouncing off the interior of the core, or light escapes the core and is lost as attenuation.

9. Step index fiber is made entirely from the same type of glass, whereas graded index is made with a gradual change in the glass index as you move farther away from the center of the core.

10. Vertical cavity surface emitting laser (VCSEL), Fabry-Perot (FP), and distributive feedback (DFB) lasers.

11. An overfilled fiber launch is when the light source illuminates the entire exposed end of the fiber core. This technique is used with less powerful light sources and is intended to transfer as much light into the cable as possible.

12. Short cable runs often have enough light bouncing at angles that would soon cause those light rays to leave the core that power readings are unrealistically high. Using a mandrel removes the light that would not normally reach the end of a longer cable run by forcing it out of the core right away. This results in more reliable and repeatable power measurements.

13. When a preform is created by layering new glass from the outside toward the center of the core, collapsing the preform sometimes leaves a small residual of imperfect glass at the center. Use of a special launch cable permits laser light sources to transfer light power more completely into an older multimode cable by bypassing this imperfect material at the center of the core via an off-center launch point.

14. These two terms represent a tiny amount of light that is reflected back to the launch point by the basic crystalline structure of the glass itself and minor variations in the density of the glass throughout the entire cable. This scatter is what an OTDR measures along the length of good segments of cable.

15. UPC has a (flat) perpendicular surface, whereas APC is terminated at an 8° angle off perpendicular.

16. 1 = C and D; 2 = A.; 3 =B.

17. Light sources take a short time to stabilize the power output. If the light source has not been turned on long enough before the power reference measurement is set, the light source might not have stabilized yet. This measurement is also significantly affected by temperature. If the tester was stored in a vehicle outside in the winter, it should be allowed to warm to room temperature prior to making a set reference power measurement. Similarly, a hot instrument coming inside during the summer should be allowed to cool to room temperature before use.

18. The connection from the light source to the first patch cable must never be disturbed after the reference is set or the reference measurement must be retaken. The fiber alignment with the light source changes each time the connection is disturbed, and this materially affects the accuracy of the reference measurement result. Also, the light source must be on long enough to stabilize the light power output. Turning the light source off would change the light output and require another reference measurement.

19. Flashlights, laser pointers, LED "keychain" lights, and so on.

20. An optical loss test set is able to measure total optical power differences only between cable ends; an OTDR permits you to view faults and other events along the length of the cable.

21. A connection is dirty.

22. Tier 2 testing includes OTDR capabilities.

Chapter 4

1. The IEEE published standards may be purchased as early as the beginning stages of development via its web page and other sources, and are available 12 months after release as a free download for private use (no business use—they must purchase) for as long as the pilot program is funded.

   802: Overview & Architecture

   802.1: Bridging & Management

802.2: Logical Link Control

802.3: CSMA/CD Access Method

802.4: Token-Passing Bus Access Method

802.5: Token Ring Access Method

802.6: DQDB Access Method

802.7: Broadband LAN

802.10: Security

802.11: Wireless

802.12: Demand Priority Access

802.15: Wireless Personal Area Networks

802.16: Broadband Wireless Metropolitan Area Networks

And so on.

2. The most common is contention, in which stations transmit whenever the medium appears to be idle. If two or more stations attempt to utilize the medium simultaneously, an arbitration scheme recovers and reschedules transmissions.

The second method is token passing. An electronic "token" is circulated according to some ordering scheme, permitting each station an equal opportunity to transmit according to the ordering process.

3. A patch cable would align with part of the 802.3 Ethernet standard, and its performance characteristics are included as part of required link definitions for Ethernet. A patch cable would not be described by OSI Layer 1.

4. Never.

5. A repeater does its best to interpret binary 1s and 0s from any signal detected on a port, and forwards the resulting binary to all other ports.

6. If the two stations are separated by a repeater, they are said to be in the same collision domain. Any network infrastructure device that does not propagate a collision separates collision domains: such as an OSI Layer 2 bridge or an OSI Layer 3 router.

7. True. Note that, for the purists, there is a slight difference in the size of the interframe gap when compensating for 10GBASEW implementations, and an extra field is appended in half duplex for shorter frames in 1000BASE-T.

8. False. Each speed, and almost each implementation at that speed, is handled differently when converting the binary to encoded signal for transmission on the medium.

9. LSB means "least significant bit first," where the binary digit with the smallest value within an octet is transmitted first. For Ethernet, the MAC Layer uses octets in MSB order, but the Physical Layer reverses them for transmission. LSB is sometimes referred to as "little end-ian," meaning the bit with the least binary value is seen first.

MSB means "most significant bit first," where the binary digit with the greatest value within an octet is transmitted first. Token Ring is an example of a protocol in which MSB is the transmission order.

10. The order is as follows:

7 octets—Preamble

1 octet—Start Frame Delimiter (SFD)

6 octets—Destination Address

6 octets—Source Address

2 octets—Length/Type Field

(varies)—Data (46–1500 octets)

4 octets—Frame Check Sequence (FCS)

11. DIX Ethernet combined the definitions for the 802.3 Ethernet Preamble and SFD into a Preamble field. The DIX Preamble is the same length and has the same binary description as the two 802.3 Ethernet fields.

Also, the DIX Type field was called the 802.3 Length field. Originally its use was different: DIX used the field to specify which protocol was encapsulated in the Data field and the 802.3 specified the number of octets appearing in the Data field.

A later change to 802.3 grandfathered in the DIX Type definition by calling the 802.3 field Length/Type.

12. DIX Ethernet is also known by the names Ethernet II and Ethernet Version 2.

13. If the value in the field is up to 05DC hexadecimal, it is considered a Length field. If the value is equal to or greater than 0600, it is considered a Type field. However, some historical Type definitions appear in the hexadecimal numbers below 0600.

14. Several common protocols were in use when DIX and 802.3 defined this field; one was Novell IPX. In that protocol, the 802.3 Length is specified and the receiving station must examine the first octets of the Data field to see whether the value FFFF appears first—indicating IPX.

    The other protocol is a variation of 802.2 LLC called SNAP (Sub Network Access Protocol). It is discovered by checking the first octets of the Data field. For SNAP, the first two octets are AAAA.

    If those two patterns are not found, the frame is assumed to be 802.2 LLC.

15. When transmitting in half duplex on 1000BASE-T, an extension field is appended to the end of the transmission whenever the frame being transmitted is less than 512 octets. This addition is made to meet the timing requirements for collision detection. The field is not present when operating at the same speed in full duplex.

16. When an Ethernet frame is tagged, the two-octet 802.1 Tag Type and the two-octet Tag Control fields are inserted just after the Source address, and just before the Length/Type field.

17. An end-station or an older infrastructure device may discard the frame for being longer than the maximum untagged frame size of 1518 octets. More recent hardware and software are tolerant of frames up to 1522 octets in length owing to the addition of VLANs in recent versions of 802.3. An end-station may still discard the frame if it is not participating in the VLAN.

18. Both of the following two frame definitions are vendor dependent, and are not supported by 802.3.

    Jumbo frames may meet all 802.3 Ethernet requirements with the exception of the Data field size. Although industry has asked for jumbo frames to be added to the Ethernet specification, the IEEE 802.3 standards body declined the proposal. Thus far all vendors have agreed that the nonstandard jumbo should never appear on links below 1 Gigabit in speed.

    Cisco produced and supported a vendor proprietary VLAN protocol called ISL before the 802.3 adopted 802.1Q VLAN tagging. The Cisco solution placed a vendor-defined 26-octet header before the original (standard) Ethernet frame, and an additional 4-octet FCS afterward. This effectively took the original frame and encapsulated it unchanged in the proprietary VLAN tag format.

19. There are actually three maximum sizes. For an ordinary station, the maximum size would be 1518 octets. For a station participating in special configurations, or a bridge, the maximum size would be 1522 octets for a VLAN-tagged frame or 2000 octets for an Envelope frame.

20. The standard permits up to 1024 stations per collision domain. Due to increased amounts of data transmitted by contemporary applications, that number should probably be less than 20. A station frequently consuming large amounts of bandwidth should be placed on a separate collision domain entirely (a separate switch port).

21. Because Ethernet is a shared medium and all stations are supposed to receive all transmissions, any error symptom should appear equally to all stations on the collision domain. This suggests that troubleshooting will be difficult.

22. In half duplex, each station is affected by the transmissions of all other stations on the collision domain. In full duplex the station may transmit whenever it wants, without regard to any other station's transmission activities.

    In full duplex, there are no collisions.

    A full-duplex architecture may be longer than would otherwise be permitted because round-trip timing limits are not imposed.

23. In 10Mbps Ethernet versions, the Preamble is used for clock synchronization in the receiver because this is an asynchronous system.

    100Mbps and faster versions of Ethernet are synchronous in nature, so the Preamble's only use is to maintain compatibility with legacy speeds of Ethernet, and it is not required for anything.

24. There are two answers. The official minimum size is 64 octets, but that excludes the required timing information. If the required timing information fields are counted, the minimum size is 72 octets. The timing information is discarded before the message is passed up the protocol stack, so the MAC Layer only "cares" about 64 octets—the *official* minimum frame size.

25. The device forwards the frame, either because it tolerates VLAN tagging or because it is configured to participate in thc VLAN.

    The device discards the frame because it is larger than the maximum untagged frame size of 1518 octets. This implies that the device is not capable of or configured to participate in a VLAN.

26. SlotTime is the mechanism used to determine round-trip timing within a collision domain. Architecture and framing rules are specified such that a legal frame sent from one of two most widely separated stations within the collision domain can reach the other station, collide, and the collision fragments return to the transmitting station before slotTime expires. A collision occurring after slotTime is illegal and results in an error.

27. In Gigabit Ethernet, an extension field was added to make the frame long enough that the transmitting station would still be sending when any collision fragments had time to return (in half duplex). Without this extension, repeaters would not be possible because an entire minimum sized frame (64 octets) could have been transmitted by the sending station before the beginning of the frame reached any other station.

28. The transmitting MAC Layer removes one octet of interframe gap for each 104 octets of frame transmitted, and restores them at the receiving end.

29. Using the formula $0 \le r < 2^k$ the maximum waiting interval would be 2^7, or 128. $128 \times 51.2\text{ms} = 6,553.6\text{ms}$ (~6.5 seconds).

30. No. Collisions are the method by which Ethernet arbitrates access to the medium. They are a normal part of Ethernet operation.

31. No. Due to the distributed nature of the architecture, and in fact due to signal propagation characteristics, many small differences exist between what one station and another detect. All stations within a collision domain see only the same properly formed frames.

32. A collision fragment is less than 64 octets in length and has an invalid checksum.

33. The primary difference between a local and remote collision is that the NIC detects either an overvoltage condition (on coax) or simultaneous activity on the TX and RX circuits during a local collision. Remote collisions do not exhibit the overvoltage or simultaneous TX/RX activity.

34. A late collision is the same as a local collision, only the size of the frame is larger than slotTime.

35. No. A late remote collision cannot be explicitly detected. However, in some cases it is possible to infer the presence of a late remote collision by examining FCS-errored frames for the characteristic jam pattern appearing where the FCS field should be.

36. The 802.3 definition for jabber relates to how a repeater should handle stations that transmit continuously and are disrupting the collision domain. This is not the commonly accepted definition. The common definition of anything in excess of 1518 octets is taken from the RMON MIB definition.

37. By the RMON definition, yes. By the 802.3 standard, anything up to 1522 octets should be tolerated—just in case the frame is tagged, although the maximum transmission unit (MTU) is still 1500 octets. This may result in some disagreement between reporting tools.

38. A long frame has a valid FCS, although it is longer than 802.3 permits. Again, this definition comes from the RMON standard.

39. It would be a long frame because the FCS is valid.

40. A runt is about the same as a collision fragment, resulting from a local or remote collision. It could also be a short frame. The standard gives a specific size range of 74 bit times but less than a minimum frame size, and specifically excludes collisions.

41. Just one bit different, anywhere between the beginning of the destination address and the end of the FCS field.

42. Alignment errors have too many bits, but not enough extra bits to form an additional octet.

43. A range error represents a discrepancy between what legal value the length field claimed and how many octets were actually counted.

44. For the LANMeter product, which pioneered the measurement, FNET defined a ghost as an event longer than 72 octets but lacking an SFD.

45. Generally speaking, it is a means for two Ethernet stations to negotiate the best speed and duplex settings.

46. The pulse is the same, although FLPs contain many normal link pulses (NLPs). Also, the appearance of FLP bursts is at the same timing intervals as NSPs.

47. The two interfaces would agree to operate at 100BASE-T2 according to the ranked priority list.

48. Because an AutoNegotiating device is required to assume half duplex when the link partner does not negotiate, the switch links at 100BASE-TX but in half duplex. This results in a duplex mismatch and the server performance is very poor.

49. You can either force both link partners to full duplex or permit both to offer and negotiate to full duplex. Any other configuration results in a duplex mismatch. (You could also have 10 Gig interfaces, which do not support half duplex at all.)

50. The minimum size of a frame, including the preamble, is 72 octets. SlotTime for Gigabit Ethernet is 512 octets. Subtracting 72 from 512 results in 440 octets. The 440 octets of extension bits represent about 86 percent of the transmission event. Viewed another way, the cable was effectively idle during the extension period and represents lost bandwidth for most of the transmission event.

51. Because it is already operating in full duplex due to the synchronous nature of the protocol, using it in half duplex is similar to discarding half of the bandwidth.

52. Because it takes so long to find out whether someone else is trying to use the medium too, sending additional frames as part of the same transmission event makes up for some of the inefficiencies of half duplex.

53. Manchester encoding. Binary 1 is determined by a rising edge in the center of the timing window. Binary 0 is determined by a falling edge in the center of the timing window.

54. For coaxial implementations, the cable can be idle for days as long as the station has nothing to transmit. For 10BASE-T, the cable exhibits link pulses about eight times per second when the station has nothing to transmit, but may otherwise be idle for days. This is possible because 10Mbps versions of Ethernet are asynchronous and include timing synchronization in the form of the preamble.

55. 10Mbps implementations of Ethernet allow for a maximum of four repeaters to be present in series between any two distant stations. This also means there can be five cable segments attaching the two stations to the repeaters. The "3" rule applies to coaxial implementations, and states that two of the five segments must be link segments. Each 10BASE-T segment is a point-to-point link, and therefore qualifies as a link segment, so the "3" rule does not apply.

56. Refer to Figures 4–39 and 4–40. Five 500 meter coaxial cable segments, plus 10 AUI cables used to attach the stations and the repeaters, provides a maximum distance of 3000 meters.

57. No. 10BASE2 permits 30 connections per segment. If the center segment were populated with repeater connections, there would be 30 segments that may be populated with stations. 30 segments times 30 stations per segment is only 900 stations.

58. Hubs count as repeaters, so the four-repeater rule applies. You may connect four hubs between any two distant stations.

59. Whenever the backplane in two or more hubs is joined by either stacking or as part of a chassis, the result counts as a single repeater.

60. Yes. Architectures with UTP cables in excess of 150 meters have been observed to work satisfactorily. The engineering for 10Mbps Ethernet was very conservative.

61. Barely. Per the timing limits for each element of the link there is only 0.04 bit times of slack in the standard, however virtually all the 100Mbps Ethernet components on the market today outperform the minimum requirements. Architectures with UTP cables up to about 115 meters have maintained link, although at that length the performance was beginning to suffer.

62. Two encoding systems are used in Fast Ethernet. 100BASE-FX uses NRZI encoding, where a high-to-low transition in the middle of the timing window represents a binary 0 and a low-to-high transition represents a binary 1. 100BASE-TX uses MLT-3 encoding, where a voltage level transition in the middle of the timing window represents a binary 1 and no transition represents a binary 0. The actual signal on the wire is scrambled after encoding, so learning the correct value requires descrambling and decoding first.

63. You do not. The architecture rules are quite different.

64. Class I repeaters may introduce up to 140 bit times of latency, whereas Class II repeaters may introduce only up to 92 bit times of latency. If the repeater does not indicate its class designation, it is probably a Class I repeater. Repeaters adapting between FX and TX are also presumed to be Class I.

65. There are two answers. If Class I repeaters are used, the two stations may be 200 meters apart. If Class II repeaters are used, the two stations may be 205 meters apart.

66. 1000BASE-SX and 1000BASE-LX use NRZ encoding. Unlike the NRZI encoding used in 100BASE-FX, this encoding is level sensitive. A high level is equal to a binary 1, and a low level is equal to a binary 0.

    1000BASE-T uses 4D-PAM5 encoding. This scheme is so complicated that it cannot be easily explained. You must descramble and decode a four-part symbol to learn the value of an entire octet at once.

67. You cannot apply the rule at all. Gigabit Ethernet only permits a single repeater when operating in half duplex, but for all practical purposes there are no Gigabit Ethernet repeaters.

68. 10GBASE-LX4, 10GBASE-R, and 10GBASE-W all use NRZ encoding, which is level sensitive. A high level is equal to a binary 1 and a low level is equal to a binary 0.

69. Neither. This is normal and expected Ethernet arbitration for the medium.

70. None at all from Station 2. Software protocol analyzers typically reject bad frames, so nothing would be passed from the NIC to the protocol analyzer application. Also, the only part of Station 2's transmission that went on the wire was timing information (Preamble), which is discarded anyway and would be discarded by all but a few hardware protocol analyzers. Besides, when it arrived at Station 1 it would be causing a collision and would be discarded.

71. Again, none at all from Station 1. The arriving portion of the frame is instantly part of a collision and discarded. No portion of the frame would be expected to arrive intact.

72. No. The arriving data is always part of a collision, and collided data is completely unreliable. You would never know whether the bits received were accurately received or the results of the collision. In both cases, the transmitting station was already transmitting when the colliding signal arrived; otherwise, it would not have begun transmitting. Thus, the Preamble is all that would be present when the collision began.

73. No. The arriving data is still part of a collision, and collided data is completely unreliable. You would never know whether the bits received were accurately received or the results of the collision. You could never trust the addressing.

74. You have no way of knowing. Within a collision domain, all stations are supposed to receive all transmissions or the arbitration rules for Ethernet do not work correctly. The odds of the collided frame being destined for any one station could be calculated by knowing how many stations existed in the collision domain.

Chapter 5

1. The bridge. The frame carrying the unknown MAC destination is flooded to all ports except the port on which it was received. If a reply is observed (actually, any frame bearing the unknown MAC destination as a source address), the bridge records that information in the bridge forwarding table and acts on that information according to the bridge forwarding rules. This process occurs in each bridge in the broadcast domain.

2. The station. Each source-route bridge appends its identity into the RIF field in the broadcast frame as it is forwarded to all ports except the port on which it was received. The receiving station reads the RIF field to learn the path to the original sending station, and inserts that path information into traffic sent to the original sending station. Acting on the assumption that the first frame to arrive took the shortest parallel path, if multiple copies of the initial query are received, only the information in the first RIF field is retained.

3. The source MAC address only. For an OSI Layer 2 bridge, that is all that is important. It cannot make use of the destination MAC address because it cannot be certain where that host is, or even that it is turned on. Bridges are OSI Layer 2 devices, so the IP address is irrelevant.

4. The first two choices relate to OSI Layer 3, which a bridge or switch acting as a bridge does not care about. The bridge floods the unknown destination frame to all ports except the port on which it was received.

5. Because bridges separate collision domains, the bridge assumes that if it (the bridge) heard the frame, the destination host has also already heard the frame. It does nothing.

6. The destination MAC address must be that of another station within the broadcast domain that has transmitted recently enough that it has not aged out of the bridge forwarding table. The source MAC address is not important for the forwarding of this frame and could be anything, and the higher-layer addressing is not considered at all.

7. The destination MAC address could be either of two possibilities:
   - The same as the source MAC address.
   - The destination MAC address could be for another host, on "this side" of the

bridged (switched) connection, which has transmitted within the aging period of the bridge forwarding table.

The source MAC address could be anything (presumably the address of the transmitting station), and the higher-layer addressing is not considered at all.

8. There are two ways to accomplish this:

   • One method would be to use a form of broadcast address.

   • The other method would be to transmit the frame to an unknown MAC address (one that is not in the bridge forwarding table because it has never transmitted, has aged out of the table, or does not exist on the broadcast domain).

   In both cases the frame should be flooded to all other ports in the broadcast domain by the bridge/switch.

9. Spanning Tree prevents bridge loops.

10. Spanning Tree is often used to dynamically manage parallel paths for redundancy purposes.

11. The bridge with the lowest Bridge Identifier number is elected to be the root bridge. If there is a tie, the MAC address breaks the tie.

12. The number of broadcast domains equals the number of VLANs. Each VLAN is a separate broadcast domain.

13. The *pause* operation is the only option presently defined for the MAC Control.

14. All traffic for the single conversation would pass through only one interface involved in the link aggregation. There would be 40 percent utilization on one interface, and no utilization from this FTP transfer on the other three.

15. No, the link aggregation would redistribute traffic over the remaining three interfaces.

16. According to the standard, the aggregation should form itself if the bridge detects that more than one interface is directly connected to another bridge where link aggregation is enabled and the critical parameters match.

17. The loopback command does what its name implies. It causes all subsequent traffic to be returned to the sender (until another OAM command restores normal operation). This is very useful for troubleshooting certain classes of network problems.

18. The LLC protocol is limited to 127 possible protocols. The SNAP extension to the LLC protocol was created to permit more than 127 protocols to be defined. By registering an organizationally unique identifier (OUI), companies can create and define large numbers of their own subprotocols within SNAP.

19. The encapsulation choices are 802.3, 802.2 LLC, 802.2 SNAP, and Novell Raw (which predated the appropriate standard). These four encapsulations were easily configurable in older versions of the Novell operating system, and are actually separate protocols and not strictly encapsulation choices.

Chapter 6

1. There is no fixed association between MAC Layer and Network Layer addressing. Due to this, the Address Resolution Protocol (ARP) creates a temporary association.

2. A subnet is a distinct logical network separated by routers. Broadcast domains are also separated by routers. However, multiple subnets may exist on a single broadcast domain. For a host in one subnet to communicate with a host in another subnet on the same broadcast domain, a router is still used to pass the traffic from one subnet to the other.

3. One of the better sources for RFCs is www.rfc-editor.org, which was created by the person who was the first editor for RFCs. Many other sources exist.

4. The rfc-index.txt document lists all RFCs, indicating whether each has been superceded as part of each entry. If an RFC was superceded, the new RFC number is listed. Be sure to update your copy of this document regularly because new RFCs are being introduced regularly.

5. Yes. The MAC Layer addressing is changed to reflect the address of the router port that forwards the frame onto the next link. The Network Layer addressing is not typically changed when a router forwards.

6. 91 percent of a minimum-sized Ethernet frame carrying IP and TCP is overhead, and only 9 percent is data.

7. False. The three reserved ranges begin with an address taken from each space (Class A, B, and C). However, except for the Class A block, which is a single Class A subnet range (/8), the address reservations contain multiple Class B and C subnets. Note the CIDR notation where the 172.x.x.x block is /12 instead of /16, and the 192.x.x.x block is /16 instead of /24.

8. A sample workstation address is 192.168.145.249. If that address is converted to hexadecimal, the 32-bit hexadecimal address is C0A891F9. Because decimal numbers are much easier for people to work with than hexadecimal, the practice of converting each octet (two hexadecimal digits) to decimal and separating converted octets with a decimal point was initiated.

   Dotted-decimal address: 192 168 145 249

   Hexadecimal equivalent: C0 A8 91 F9

   In the preceding example, only the last octet changes as you move from PC to PC around my part of the network. This is much easier to remember than the hexadecimal.

9. Subnetting permits an assigned address block to be divided into subblocks or subnetworks, each representing a different logical network. This is a means of more efficiently utilizing the available pool of IPv4 addresses. Many other facts might be mentioned here.

10. This is typically done in the context of public address space that has been issued to a specific company or individual by the official issuing organization. In subnetting, you divide a given address range into smaller pieces. In supernetting, you take several given address ranges and combine them into a single larger space. To supernet, the address spaces must be contiguous and must fall on appropriate binary boundaries.

11. There are three common definitions.

    - The portion of the actual address indicated by the address class (such as the leftmost 16 bits in a Class B address—123.123.x.x).

    - The issued network address plus the portion of the host address space that was consumed by subnetting the original address block (such as the leftmost 16 bits in a Class B address plus eight more bits taken from the host address to form multiple smaller logical networks—123.123.123.x).

    - The portion of the host address space that was consumed by subnetting the original address block, but not including the original issued address; for example, x.x.123.x.

    After one of the three processes mentioned determines the address, the subnet is the logical network, and all other bits to the right in the address represent host address.

12. The address represents a rare unicast to a host on only the attached subnet. The subnet mask is not contiguous, and therefore probably is not supported by most software. The subnet addresses available for this configuration are

    x.x.xxxxxx0x.0–x.x.xxxxxx0x.11111111

    x.x.xxxxxx1x.0–x.x.xxxxxx1x.11111111

    This might be written as x.x.x.0–x.x.x.255 and x.x.2.0–x.x.2.255. This dotted-decimal representation is deceptive, however, because the noncontiguous bit (least significant bit) in the third octet may skew the answer depending on the network address.

13. The first octet shows this to be a Class C address. By definition, that would mean that the leftmost three octets are fixed, yet the subnet mask shows that the host identifier field extends into the "fixed" part of a Class C address.

The subnet mask is not contiguous. One of the binary bit positions was accidentally skipped over in deciding which bits were network identifier and which were host identifier bits.

The range of host addresses possible with this set of data is 197.78.165.0 through 197.78.165.255, and 197.78.167.0 through 197.78.167.255—although you probably have to convert all to binary to see this.

14. The minimum configuration would include four elements:
  - Source IP address
  - Subnet mask
  - Default router
  - DNS server

15. Octet position 17 shows the value 11, which is in the location of the IP Protocol field. Because this field is transmitted in hexadecimal but used as a decimal equivalent, we look up the value 17 (decimal) in RFC 1700 and learn that it is UDP.

16. ICMP Port Unreachable indicates that the message reached the destination PC but there was no service running for the requested port. This often results from entering the wrong station in a query (such as typing an IP address for a station that does not act as a web server into a web browser), or when the service on the destination server has been shut down or has locked up.

17. IPv4 = 4,294,967,296 (~4 billion)

  IPv6 = 340,282,366,920,938,463,463,374,607,431,768,221,456 (~3 undecillion).

18. Zero substitution (elimination) may be made with double colons, which may appear only once in an address.

  Removed leading zeros:

  0000:0000:0000:0000:0000:0000:123.234.12.34

  becomes ::123.234.12.34

  Removed zeros within an address:

  1080:0:0:0:8:800:200C:417A

  becomes 1080::8:800:200C:417A.

19. My MAC address is 00-0B-DB-DB-9E-46.

  In EUI-64 format, my IPv6 address would be FE80::020B:DBFF:FEDB:9E46/64.

20. Anycasting is new in IPv6. An Anycast looks the same as a normal unicast address but represents multiple recipient interfaces. To be an Anycast, the host must be configured to recognize the address as an Anycast. This is similar to multicasting, except that it does not rely upon a predefined address or address range.

21. IPv6 does not support broadcasting, and it replaced that service with a more flexible multicast service.

22. Unlike IPv4, an IPv6 header is fixed in size and is always 40 octets.

23. The working maximum size is limited by the MTU of the path, which would be 1280 on an Ethernet network. The maximum size is 65,535 octets unless the Payload Length is set to all zeros, in which case the payload could be as large as 4,294,967,295 octets (called a jumbogram).

24. Extension headers appear as the first part of the data payload. They are considered part of the data for framing purposes.

25. The Next Header field would have the value of 0x58h.

Chapter 7

1. A system of cumulative acknowledgments, where each octet sent causes a counter (sequence number) to increment accordingly. By tracking the sequence numbers and comparing them with the sequence numbers included in new segments, the receiving host is able to ensure error-free reception of all data, in order, and with no duplicates.

2. The two parameters are completely different. Maximum segment size (MSS) refers to the maximum number of octets that may appear in each transmission. The window size indicates how much temporary buffer the receiving host has set aside for received data that has not been processed yet.

3. Two things: First, the ports up to 1023 are called *well-known* ports and represent published services common to networks, such as FTP and Telnet. Second, a client PC should never use a port below 1024 for the ephemeral port number when establishing a new TCP connection.

4. A TCP socket consists of an IP address and the TCP port that host is using for this connection. A sample socket might be 192.168.123.21:80. That socket represents a given host IP address and the TCP port used by a web server for HTTP.

5. The steps required for a three-way handshake are as follows:

   1. The first segment is a connection request (SYN) segment carrying the socket of the requesting host. Included is the initial sequence number for that host.

   2. The second segment is an acknowledgment (ACK) for the first host's SYN request. Included is the second host's connection request (SYN), plus the second host's own initial sequence number.

   3. The third segment is the first host's acknowledgment (ACK) for the second host's SYN request.

6. A graceful close is initiated by the FIN flag. A reset (RST) may be issued to abruptly terminate a session.

7. The PC's initial sequence number would be incremented by one for the SYN connection request control flag, and by one more for the FIN connection close request control flag. Thus, the final sequence number would be 352, as no other data was sent.

8. You would ensure that the window size was as large as possible on the receiving host (the server if you were copying the file to the server, and the PC if you were copying it from the server).

9. None at all. Slow start is effective only on large data transfers.

10. TCP is connection oriented, whereas UDP is connectionless. This means that TCP tracks all data sent, requiring acknowledgment for each octet. UDP does not use acknowledgments at all, and is usually used for protocols where a few lost datagrams do not matter.

11. The network infrastructure usually discards excess UDP traffic to control congestion.

Chapter 8

1. The seven strategic concepts are
   - Management involvement in network decision making
   - Preparation and planning
   - Problem prevention
   - Early problem detection
   - Quick problem isolation and resolution
   - Investing more in tools and training rather than additional staff to accommodate growth
   - Quality improvement approach to network management and maintenance

2. If you can reconstruct or troubleshoot any part of the network with no prior knowledge of the network, just this documentation, it is complete and accurate enough.

3. With a good functional diagram, the source of many troubleshooting problems is obvious and the problem may be very quickly isolated. Without a functional diagram, it can be particularly difficult to troubleshoot many problems.

4. A baseline determines normal behavior. After normal is known, a judgment can be made about whether normal is also acceptable and any appropriate remedial action can be planned.

5. A trend baseline should observe a minimum of one entire week, 24 hours each day, to discover and document normal business trends as well as late-night maintenance, scheduled backups, and other similar periodic events.

6. A few types of information that can be learned from response time testing are to verify LAN and WAN connection paths, learn average response times, isolate intermittent paths and interconnect devices, and so on.

7. A few types of information that can be learned from application monitoring are to isolate which server or application within a tiered application server farm is the source of a slowdown, reveal load-balancing problems, exonerate servers when a client or network path is the problem, and so on.

Chapter 9

1. The technician must know what "normal" is for the network. The technician must have a working knowledge of how the network operates day to day, and what typical traffic loads are likely. The technician must also know what minor misbehavior and errors are considered "normal," although they might not be acceptable.

2. Study, listen to others, take good notes, try to formulate a hypothesis for what might be wrong, and propose tests to validate or invalidate the hypothesis. Above all, document what you did. Do not go to one extreme or another in your troubleshooting process. Always consider other options and seek faster permanent solutions—get the network running, and then troubleshoot the removed or altered thing in the lab later. This question has many possible answers because it asks for an opinion.

3. The eight steps are as follows:

    1. **Identify the exact issue.** Get a good problem description and have the user show you the problem if possible.

    2. **Re-create the problem.** Make certain that you have a good grasp of the problem, and try to duplicate it. Repeatable problems are much easier to solve.

    3. **Localize and isolate the cause.** Use whatever means are available to confirm or eliminate as many possibilities

as possible. When you are done, you should have identified the boundaries of the problem as well as you are able. "Divide and conquer" is an excellent approach here.

    4. When you believe that you have a firm grasp of the problem, **formulate a plan** that solves the problem exactly.

    5. **Implement the plan.** Based on your understanding of the problem, implement a plan that solves the problem. If the problem changes in nature following your implemented solution, return to step 3.

    6. **Test to verify that the problem has been resolved.** You and the user should both attempt to complete the original task that was failing, as well as several other related and unrelated tasks, to ensure that the problem is solved and that new problems were not introduced.

    7. **Document the problem.** Now that the problem is solved, make excellent notes on which symptoms were most important, and how better to test for those symptoms or situations next time. Also list the steps required to resolve the problem.

    8. **Provide feedback to the user.** If you want the user's assistance in the future, and you want to avoid anything that might cause a similar problem, you must educate the user on proper network use and which reported symptoms provided you the most benefit.

4. Open a remote session into the switch or router and have the command typed to make the desired change. Then open a second remote session and type the command to reverse the change and restore operation as it was before your attempt to make the change. When both are ready, make the change. If all you have to do to back out a bad change or command is to press Enter, you are far less likely to disrupt the network while troubleshooting during the workday.

A second possible answer would be to back up the configuration before starting so that the entire configuration may be restored in the event of a problem. This takes a lot longer, however.

5. If the user does not agree that the problem has been taken to its conclusion (whether or not the problem was fixed), the relationship between the support staff and the user community deteriorates, and it is more difficult to solve problems later. Also, providing feedback on the cause of the problem may help avoid similar problems in the future.

6. Follow the OSI Model up from the cable. Study media issues, issues between the NIC and the first hub or switch, issues between the NIC and the first router, and so on. After mastering the fundamentals, understanding how later topics relate will be easier.

Chapter 10

1. Three copper cable tester categories are

   Continuity testing/toning. The ability to verify end-to-end wire continuity and to locate an unlabeled cable from among many.

   Pair tester. The ability to detect cable faults, including a split pair.

   Cable analyzer. The ability to perform frequency-based testing in addition to locating cable faults

2. An asterisk indicates that the measured result was so close to the accuracy uncertainty limits of the tester that it *could* indicate a false pass or a false fail result.

3. Yes. A prior grade of cable may pass a higher-quality cable test if the materials and workmanship for the original installation were good.

4. Yes. If the cable was not well installed, was located near a noise source, was installed with inferior connecting hardware, and so on. Furthermore, some early versions of Category 6 cable and connecting hardware might not certify if mixed with another brand of cable and connecting hardware.

5. The three reasons are
   - If cable ties are too tightly cinched, they alter the properties of the cable and introduce faults. If they are particularly tight, they can permanently damage the cable and replacement would be necessary to recover from the problem.
   - Aligning the cables too carefully in parallel in the wiring closet and along cable raceways introduces or worsens alien crosstalk.
   - Locating a suspect cable during a troubleshooting incident can be particularly difficult, or may require removal of the cable fastenings altogether if the cable system is fastened with permanent ties, with many ties close together, or with too many cables per bundle or pathway.

6. RJ45 plugs are not all the same because
   - The pins inside the RJ45 connector are manufactured differently for use with solid and stranded wire.
   - The frequency rating of the RJ45 connector must match or exceed the frequency rating of the cable installation. Most higher-quality RJ45 plugs have markings indicating the rating of the plug, such as Category 5e.

7. RJ45 plugs and RJ45 jacks can be damaged by poor handling in these ways:
   - The crimp tool used for attaching RJ45 plugs to the wire may flex and incompletely crimp the pins down into the connector. This would cause intermittent or open pins, and might also cause damage to the RJ45 jack.
   - RJ45 plugs may be subject to abuse that bends the plastic separators between pins in such a way that a good connection with the wires in an RJ45 jack is not possible.
   - Pins inside the RJ45 jack may be bent flat by poorly crimped RJ45 plugs.
   - Pins inside the RJ45 jack may be knocked from their track and shorted against adjacent pins by mishandling.

8. Three possible causes are
   - Pair 4 was cut about 15 feet from the cable end.
   - Pair 4 is open at an intermediate connection point (patch panel or wall jack?) about 15 feet from the cable end.
   - The cable insulation is different on Pair 4, resulting in a different NVP value and longer latency down Pair 4 than the others.

9. Two possible causes for insertion loss to fail are
   - The cable is too long.
   - There is a very poor connection somewhere, such as dirty or oxidized contacts or a loose connection.

10. Poor workmanship at the connector. NEXT fails most often because the twisting was not maintained properly right to the connection.

11. Return loss faults can most easily be located with a TDR test.

12. Time-domain reflectometry (TDR) and time-domain crosstalk (TDX) testing reveal the location of most cable faults.

13. Four fiber optic cable tester categories are

    Continuity testing. The ability to verify end-to-end fiber continuity; also useful for determining cable pair polarity.

    Optical Loss Test Set (OLTS). May also be known as an attenuation, loss, or power tester—the ability to measure the amount of power (light) lost over the entire cable path.

    OTDR. The ability to perform loss testing in addition to locating cable faults.

    End-face inspection. The ability to view the termination/polish quality, looking for imperfections or contamination (dirt).

14. Testing for polarity, length, and attenuation.

15. The cable jacket is typically marked with length at the time of manufacture. Note the length marking at both ends, and subtract the shorter from the longer to determine the difference—which is the length of this cable.

16. Each media access implementation specifies the modal bandwidth requirements for cables used. An old cable type that worked fine for a different technology or implementation over a long distance could be specified for a distance as short as 26 meters if used with a new high-speed implementation or technology.

17. False. Microbends can be disruptive, although the effect is more pronounced with higher wavelengths. A microbend at 850nm may be scarcely noticeable, but the same microbend at 1550nm may be a significant problem.

18. The following represent several possible answers for each type of fault:
    - **Large Reflective Event.** Dirty, scratched, cracked, misaligned, or unseated connector, sharp bend or crack, or a connection between mismatched fibers.
    - **Small reflective event with high loss.** A very sharp bend, a crack, or a mechanical splice with high loss.
    - **Large reflective event with gain.** A connection between mismatched fibers.
    - **Small gain event.** A splice between mismatched fibers.
    - **Small loss event.** Bad fusion splices, a splice between mismatched fibers, or a bend.
    - **Ghost after the cable end.** Duplicate reflections caused by light bouncing back and forth between connectors.
    - **Ghosts in the middle of the cable.** A highly reflective connector or a connector that is not seated properly.
    - **Hidden event.** The event is within the dead zone of the previous event.

19. Some troubleshooting options are listed, although none should be left in place following the test, and the pencil lead is not recommended at all.

    • Pencil lead rubbed over the patch cable tip to attenuate the signal

    • The patch cable loosened in the connector and taped down, using an air gap to attenuate the signal

    • A meter or more of fiber patch cable rolled into a tight circle (approximating a mandrel) to attenuate the signal

    • A multimode patch cable inserted as the last cable in a singlemode run to attenuate the signal

    Although none of these are recommended, when judiciously applied they appear to have temporarily solved the problem and permitted the link to come up. All have potential problems associated with them. The pencil lead may be transferred into the connector, creating a cleaning problem. Taping a cable into a slight air-gap situation can leave tape residue where you don't want it. Creating a mandrel effect carelessly can cause you to break the fiber accidentally. If the multimode cable is inserted at the launch point, the multimode-to-singlemode connection may transfer so little power that there is now insufficient light to allow a link—be sure to try this only on the receive fiber. In all cases, a proper attenuator should be installed if the test is effective, and none of these temporary solutions should remain in place following the troubleshooting validation test.

Chapter 11

1. Four primary network test categories are

    Cable Testers. The ability to detect and locate various cable faults.

    Protocol Analyzer. The ability to display the exact fields found in each network frame, to correlate observed traffic by time, to provide simple summaries for observed traffic (such as top talkers and frame size distribution), and sometimes to offer libraries of known

fault conditions that can be compared against observed traffic to attempt to flag any suspected problems.

Network Management. The ability to develop trend analysis based on requested reports of network activity, the ability to compare trends against thresholds to provide alerting of existing or impending problems, and to permit the user to view or modify configuration settings of various network infrastructure equipment remotely.

Flow Protocols. The ability to develop trend analysis based on continuously reported network activity at a more granular level than SNMP typically reveals, and the ability to compare trends against thresholds to provide alerting of existing or impending problems.

Two hybrid categories are

Handheld Network Testers. The hybrid category of *handheld network tester* is not a primary category, but rather a blending of primary category features designed for rapid in-the-field use.

Advanced Analysis Products. The advanced analysis category is also a hybrid or specialized version of the primary categories and most often utilizes protocol analysis, network management, flow protocols, or a combination of these abilities to do deep or detailed analysis of certain applications, protocols, or aspects of networking.

2. Protocol analyzers are most effectively used to solve protocol problems. Secondary functionality is available in the form of baseline reporting, utilizing all the report-printing functionality. This includes simple trend-graphing capability.

3. Network Management is used most effectively to monitor long-term changes in traffic trends, as well as providing early notification about impending or sudden network outages.

4. Handheld network analyzers are best used as first-in diagnostic tools when problems are first reported. They permit rapid triage of network problems by lower-skilled technical staff, and are able to confirm or eliminate the most common network fault conditions quickly.

5. It is very important to understand the parts of the network that might be affected by a particular error or symptom. The boundaries imposed by changing OSI Layers can clearly limit the propagation of some errors, and have no effect at all on others.

   If you do not know what layer your hardware operates at, it makes troubleshooting particularly difficult. For example, if you are troubleshooting a switched network and you are seeing FCS errors, not knowing what layer the switch is operating at would lead you to conclude that FCS errors could only affect the link between the tester and the switch because a bridge (the switch) does not forward Ethernet errors. In fact, it is possible for the switch to forward Ethernet errors if it is using a low-latency forwarding technique. Forwarding an error would mean that the error could have come from any other port on the switch, including an uplink port from another switch.

6. When the person troubleshooting understands the basic technology, tests may be selected that almost immediately validate several OSI layers at once. For example, a successful ping largely validates everything up through Layer 3 in one test for a connectivity-related fault. There are still faults that may exist even though ping succeeded, but they are usually related to slowness.

7. Virtually all user complaints fall into these three categories:

   - Can't connect
   - Dropped connections
   - Slow or poor performance

8. Countless things directly or indirectly affect network performance or connectivity. The simple and obvious ones are changes to any software or hardware on the PC, connecting or disconnecting cables, cable damage by office furniture, use of high current draw appliances (copiers, heaters, coffee pots, etc.), electrically noisy appliances (vacuums, fans, etc.), and so on.

9. **Collisions.** Almost anything can cause a collision to be detected. The simple answer is that two or more stations attempted to transmit at or near the same time. A more complex situation might involve external noise, duplex configuration problems, architecture problems (too many repeaters), cable faults, and so on. Usually collisions are not errors, but are instead the simple media arbitration mechanism for Ethernet.

   Late Collisions. Almost always caused by architecture problems or duplex configuration problems. Occasionally they are caused by cable faults where the transmitting PC "hears" its own transmission, or external noise disrupts the transmission.

   Short Frames. Almost without exception this is a software driver flaw.

   Jabber. Often caused by noise intruding on the cables or by a marginal or failed NIC. On rare occasions it is caused by a feedback loop created by a parallel path in the repeater architecture (two crossover cables instead of one).

   FCS Errors. Usually caused by external noise, cable faults, or duplex configuration problems. On rare occasions it is caused by software driver problems or marginal or failed NICs.

   Ghosts. Always caused by Physical Layer faults. Sometimes due to cable workmanship or cable defects, sometimes caused by improper cable configurations (such as stubs on coax), sometimes caused by noise intruding on the cable system and being propagated by the repeaters.

10. The client station would receive a copy of all server requests, which occupies significant bandwidth on the local link, and delay any client request accordingly. Any broadcast traffic shared between servers also causes the client to evaluate each received broadcast frame to see if that station should care about it, and occupies client CPU time, and slows the responsiveness of the client station accordingly.

11. The link LED is controlled by software in recent infrastructure equipment. It is not unusual to disconnect the cable from a switch port during a troubleshooting incident and observe that the link light remains on. On the other hand, if the link light does not come on when a station is connected during a troubleshooting incident, it is reasonably safe to suspect a problem.

12. Perhaps the biggest reason is that none of the parties involved in the application (network support, server support, application support, etc.) are usually aware of all the interactions. It is also difficult because even if a protocol analyzer is used to map and define conversation pairs and protocols, it is difficult to translate that information into a label for what the application is using that conversation and protocol to accomplish.

13. Spanning Tree is there to prevent bridging loops, which result in broadcast storms.

14. Full duplex can be achieved if both link partners participate in Auto-Negotiation (and can link at FDX), or if both link partners are hard configured for full duplex. No, not all Auto-Negotiation or fixed duplex configurations are robust enough to work correctly every time. Some multivendor equipment combinations simply do not link with one configuration or the other.

15. Yes. A VLAN is an arbitrarily defined broadcast domain, which is an OSI Layer 2 network. For traffic to leave or enter a VLAN, it must pass through an OSI Layer 3 router. Sometimes the router function is part of the switch; other times it is another infrastructure device connected to the same VLAN somewhere but not necessarily connected to this switch.

16. Yes, of course. Operating system corruption, marginal or failed components, and an unknown number of other causes can result in exotic behavior on the part of any infrastructure device. The most recent example of this seen by the author was that a DHCP address could be obtained through a specific switch, and the usual broadcast and unknown destination traffic was observed, but no outbound traffic went anywhere—including a ping

attempt to the DHCP server. Rebooting the switch solved the problem temporarily.

17. Disconnect uplink cables until all the utilization LEDs abruptly stop showing red. You have just disconnected one of the two parallel connections and the network is again operational. Reconnect any uplink that does not appear to affect the problem. Now find the other uplink that was operating in parallel with the link just disconnected.

18. Two hosts with the same IP address cause either intermittent connection problems for both hosts or severe problems for one host. If the duplicate involves network infrastructure gear, intermittent service is given to all hosts until the duplicate is resolved.

19. Yes. If a local router has Proxy ARP enabled, it does its best to forward traffic for that host despite the incorrect addressing. In some cases, another subnet on the routed network actually owns the address space to which the incorrectly configured host's IP address belongs. In such a case, the requests may leave the broadcast domain but the responses are likely to be sent to the actual subnet and not back to this host.

20. Yes. Ping is often used to test the availability of a host with a given IP address, but it can just as easily be used with a DNS name. The ping utility first performs a DNS lookup, and then it sends the ICMP Echo to that resolved address. Nslookup is a more direct and complete way to discover what DNS is returning.

21. Yes, and they are all possible sources of communication failures. One of the most generally accessible to users is the hosts file. If the user modifies the hosts file to provide faster and more reliable connections to a commonly used network resource, access utterly fails if that resource changes its IP address later. Some virus or other network compromise attacks involve adding entries to the host file to direct common user queries to an exploit site. Some anti-virus applications preload the host file with entries to block known exploits.

22. Ping provides a total round-trip response time. Traceroute provides a hop-by-hop path as well as a round-trip response time to each.

INDEX

Symbols

A

E

F

J–K–L

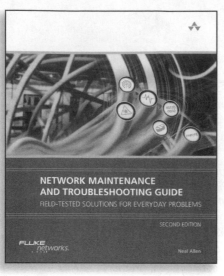

FREE Online Edition

Your purchase of **Network Maintenance and Troubleshooting Guide** includes access to a free online edition for 45 days through the Safari Books Online subscription service. Nearly every Addison-Wesley Professional book is available online through Safari Books Online, along with more than 5,000 other technical books and videos from publishers such as, Cisco Press, Exam Cram, IBM Press, O'Reilly, Prentice Hall, Que, and Sams.

SAFARI BOOKS ONLINE allows you to search for a specific answer, cut and paste code, download chapters, and stay current with emerging technologies.

Activate your FREE Online Edition at
www.informit.com/safarifree

> **STEP 1:**   Enter the coupon code: IZTFTZG.

> **STEP 2:**   New Safari users, complete the brief registration form.
>   Safari subscribers, just log in.

If you have difficulty registering on Safari or accessing the online edition, please e-mail customer-service@safaribooksonline.com